Marriage and Family

Individuals and Life Cycles

Hamilton McCubbin
University of Minnesota

Barbara Blum Dahl
University of Minnesota

MACMILLAN PUBLISHING COMPANY
New York

COLLIER MACMILLAN PUBLISHERS
London

Marriage and Family

Individuals and Life Cycles

Cover Photo—Everett C. Johnson/Leo de Wys
Cover and Text Designer—Madelyn W. Lesure
Photo Researcher—Teri Leigh Stratford
Photo Editor—Stella Kupferberg
Production Supervisor—Jan M. Lavin
Copy Editor—Susan Ginger

Macmillan Publishing Company
866 Third Avenue, New York, New York 10022
Collier Macmillan Canada, Inc.

Library of Congress Cataloging in Publication Data:

McCubbin, Hamilton I.
    Marriage and family life cycles.

    Bibliography: p.
    Includes index.
    1. Family life education—United States.   I. Dahl,
Barbara B.   II. Title.
HQ10.M39   1985   306.8′0973   84-11810
ISBN 0-02-379000-8

Printed in the United States of America

Printing   4 5 6 7   Year 6 7 8 9 0

ISBN 0-02-379000-8

*To our special families who grew with us, supported
us, and who made the difference in our life cycles.*

My parents, Betsy Chisayo McCubbin and Jonathan McCubbin
My wife, Marilyn
My son, Todd
My daughters, Wendy and Laurie

H.M.

My parents, Reba May Blum and Robert D. Blum, Jr.
My husband, William Dahl
My children, Julia Elizabeth and Susan Melissa

B.D.

PREFACE

We wrote this book to shed light on the dynamic nature of relationships and families and to encourage students to reflect on their life experiences and relationships. Using a life cycle perspective, we focus on how individuals enter into meaningful relationships, and how the depth and intensity of these relationships change over time. In addition to many new topics, we cover most of the traditional topics covered in marriage and family texts, but have made a concerted effort to highlight these topics where they have the greatest meaning or importance, that is, in those stages of individual or family development where they are most likely to be issues and may even shape the course of individual or family adjustment.

We emphasize the notion of choice in our book and identify the choices that individuals are faced with in relationships, since these choices have a powerful impact on the family unit, its transitions, and how well the unit adapts to change over time. We believe that students taking a course in marriage and the family are also facing choices in relationships and will continue to do so throughout their lives. This book is intended to be a thought-provoking guide to relationships, marriage, and family life. Furthermore, it encourages students to begin to place themselves in the various phases of family transitions. Once there, students can personalize the learning experience by examining the past and anticipating the future.

Several important people have contributed to this book through their research, practice, and theory building. First, we thank Regents Professor Reuben Hill who spent a few special moments with us in California at the Naval Health Research Center and encouraged us to write about families. We also appreciate the efforts of Catherine Davidson, former editor of the Family Stress and Coping Project, and Bob Lamm, writer, who contributed to the development of each chapter and who made a special effort to make ideas, feelings, thoughts, and concepts come alive in this text. Special gratitude goes to Maryann Syers-McNairy who gave of herself and her expertise to keep the book on schedule, worked in the development of the instructor's manual, and helped us to bridge the geographic distance between the two authors. We would also like to thank Doctors Joan Patterson, David Olson, Brent Miller, and James Maddock who offered their expertise and scholarship in the development of select chapters. We thank our research assistants, Todd McCubbin, Kay Lapour, Alida Malcus, and Deanna Strese, who put enormous time and energy in researching, computerizing, and verifying information. We give special thanks to Susan Rains-Johnson, our principle secretary, and Sharon Crowder, our supportive secretary in California, who saw to it that the manuscripts were typed, revised, retyped, and revised many times over, with the unwavering belief that this book would ultimately reach print.

This book would not have been possible without the outstanding organizational and personal support we received at the University of Minnesota. Therefore, we thank Deputy Vice President Richard J. Sauer and Dean Keith McFarland, who granted us the opportunity, encouraged us to pursue this effort, and provided us the resources. We also thank our associate administrator Emma Haugan, senior secretary Dorothea Berggren, secretary Gloria Swanson, and accountant Patricia Bender.

Finally, we thank our editors Carol Luitjens and Butch Cooper at Wiley who shared a vision with us, created this special opportunity, and who nurtured this book to completion. These relationships, which moved through transition, were very special. We want to thank the editorial staff at Wiley—particularly Susan Giniger, Maddy Lesure, Stella Kupferberg and Jan M. Lavin—who saw to it that the book was given that special artistic touch. We also thank the many people who reviewed the earlier drafts of the chapters, offered us specific guidance and suggestions, and who took the time to bring our ideas closer to the needs of students interested in relationships, marriage, and the family.

Hamilton McCubbin
Barbara Blum Dahl

CONTENTS

Introduction: Marriage and Family Relationships in the 1980s

KEY TOPICS

—the major trends in marriage and family life in the United States—
—why we need to understand family relationships—
—basic functions of the family within society—
—the search for personal fulfillment through marriage and family relationships—

American presidents have traditionally spoken of the family with great reverence. In the 1960s, Lyndon Johnson called it "the cornerstone of our society"; in the 1970s, Jimmy Carter suggested that "the family was the first government." More recently, in 1982 Ronald Reagan wrote that "a hallmark of our democratic way of life has always been the importance we place on our families. Families are the best source of love, acceptance, and guidance a child can have" (National Council on Family Relations, 1982: 5; Steiner, 1981: 4–5, 16). Behind these comments, there is often an assumption that the family is a static, unchanging human institution. The assumption is false: families and family structures have changed throughout history in response to wars, revolutions, depressions, industrialization, and other social and economic conditions.

In recent decades, there have been marked changes in the family patterns of the United States. These changes are best understood by examining data from the U.S. Bureau of the Census. Every ten years since 1790, the federal government has attempted to count all persons and households in the nation. The information gathered through the census provides researchers with a reasonably reliable demographic portrait of the American people. It is important to note that census data are collected by households, not by families. One family may be spread over several households, as is true of many separated and divorced families. At the same time, several families may share the same household, as is common among many lower income or refugee families. A household may also consist of individuals who do not consider themselves to be a family, such as three college roommates who share an apartment. While households are not exactly the same as families, information about households is extremely valuable in assessing patterns of family life.

Two trends in American family patterns are particularly noteworthy. First, the average size of households is shrinking. As Table 1–1 illustrates, in 1980 more than half of all American households consisted of one or two persons. As a result, the average household size reached its lowest level in the nation's history (Masnick and Bane, 1980).

There are a number of reasons for this development. The children of the "baby boom," born between 1946 and 1958, were setting up households for themselves by the 1970s and the early 1980s. As adults in their twenties and thirties, they have tended to remain single longer than their parents did, and they have generally chosen not to continue living at home. Therefore, many of these younger adults now live alone or with a roommate, while their parents are left without children in one- or two-person "empty nest" households. In addition, married couples are delaying having children longer than earlier generations did and are having smaller families. Finally, fewer Americans are living in extended family situations with grandparents, aunts, or uncles than was true in the past.

The second significant trend in American family life is the declining proportion of households headed by a husband and a wife. Table 1–2 indicates that throughout the pe-

Table 1–1 Household sizes, 1950–1980

Year	Number of households (1,000)	Distribution of household sizes (Percentages) Number of Persons					Mean size
		1	2	3	4	5 +	
1950	43,468	10.9	28.8	22.6	17.8	20.0	3.37
1960	52,610	13.1	27.8	18.9	17.6	22.6	3.33
1970	62,874	17.0	28.8	17.3	15.8	21.1	3.14
1975	71,120	19.6	30.6	17.4	15.6	16.8	2.94
1980	79,108	22.5	31.3	17.5	15.8	13.0	2.75

Sources: Current Population Reports, "Households and Families by Type: March, 1978," Series P-20, No. 340 (1979), Table B; Current Population Reports, "Population Characteristics," Series P-20, No. 366, "Household and Family Characteristics," March, 1980; U.S. Bureau of the Census, "Historical Statistics of the United States, Colonial Times to 1970," Part I (1975), pp. 41–42.

Table 1–2   Components of household increase, 1950–1979

Years	Total net increase in households (1,000)	Percentage of total increase		
		Husband/ wife	Other families	Unrelated individuals
1950–1955	4,320	50.4	6.2	43.2
1955–1960	4,925	61.0	3.4	35.6
1960–1965	4,637	52.5	10.8	37.6
1965–1970	5,965	50.9	9.9	39.3
1970–1975	7,719	28.8	24.4	46.8
1975–1979	6,210	11.5	19.7	68.8

Source: Current Population Reports, "Households and Families by Type: March, 1979 (Advance Report)," Series P-20, No. 345 (1979), Table 3.

The 1980 U.S. Census provided information which helped us in understanding current trends in American family life.

riod 1950 to 1970 more than half of all new households were formed by married couples. By contrast, in the period 1975 to 1979, only 11.5 percent of new households included both a husband and a wife.

The trends discussed above are interrelated. More and more Americans are choosing to live alone. Since the divorce rate is rising, there is an increase in the number of households headed by divorced or separated adults. Many households are headed by single mothers; some have divorced while others never married. In addition, more unmarried Americans are living together as couples than was true in earlier decades. While these patterns are evident among all groups of Americans, they are more pronounced in black families than in white families (Cherlin, 1981; Masnick and Bane, 1980).

Given the sharp decline in husband-wife households, it seems clear that the traditional ideal of "marriage and family" has become somewhat less central to the American social structure. Public opinion polls reveal that there has been a major shift in attitudes and expectations about family life. As one consequence, remaining single no longer has the social stigma that it once held.

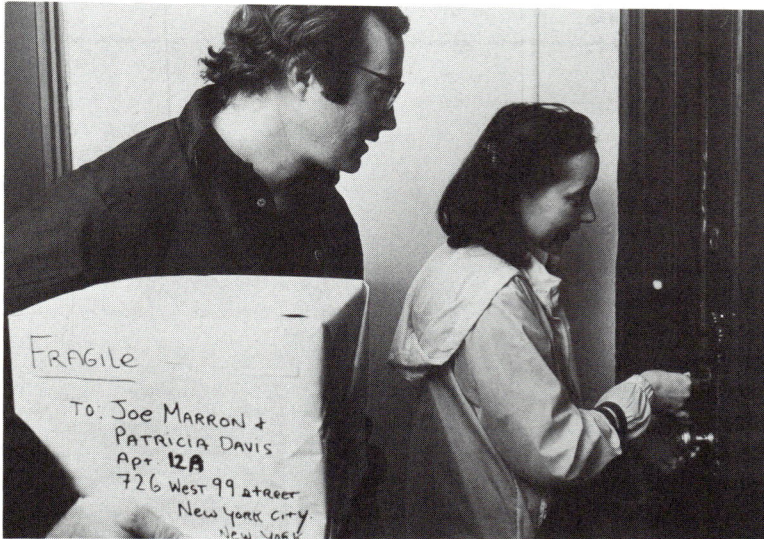

In the 1980s an increasing number of American couples are choosing to live together without being married.

According to survey data in the late 1950s, 80 percent of Americans believed that people who had never married were ''deviant'' or ''immoral.'' However, by the late 1970s, 75 percent of respondents accepted singlehood as a normal lifestyle.

An overwhelming majority of Americans (96 percent) continue to believe that two people sharing a life and home together is ideal. Nevertheless, marriage is no longer viewed as essential for a healthy and satisfying life—or even for the raising of children. In a recent poll, more than half of the respondents approved of couples living together without marrying, while over 70 percent found it morally acceptable for a single woman to bear and raise children. Americans have become much more tolerant of divorce than they were 25 years ago, and there is greater approval of homosexual relationships between consenting adults (Yankelovich, 1981).

The impact of these trends in living patterns and of changing public attitudes echoes across all phases of the family life cycle. This will be clear throughout the textbook as we examine such topics as divorce and remarriage, single parenthood, and two-career families. In this chapter, however, we will focus on the nature of family relationships.

The Importance of Family Relationships

While each society has held different notions of what constitutes a family, the family has functioned throughout history as the most significant institution shaping human interactions. Will and Ariel Durant called it ''the nucleus of civilization.'' Not only is our sense of self inextricably tied to our sense of family, but most of our deepest and most intimate emotions result from family ties.

As Americans have become increasingly anxious about the ''state of the family,'' scholars have taken greater interest in the same issues. Marvin Sussman (1978) has suggested that future historians may view the 1970s as the decade of ''The Great Family Debate.'' Growing concern over changes in family patterns has led to the emergence of a new field of history, known as family history, which focuses on the study of family life throughout the ages.

Transmitting Norms and Values

From earliest childhood, we learn the "right" and "wrong" ways to act and even feel in social situations. We learn that food is generally eaten with utensils, that valuable objects will break if we drop them, that it hurts to be called names by other children, and so forth. The complex process of preparing an individual to become a functioning and contributing member of society is known as **socialization**.

Without question, the family is the primary agent of socialization in the United States and other societies. The young child's lengthy period of dependency underscores the overriding influence of the family. Although the school, the peer group, and the mass media also serve as important agents of socialization for the young child, the family plays a critical role in shaping the child's be-

Early in life children begin internalizing the values and behaviors observed in their families.

liefs and values. Researchers have consistently found that young children of all social classes have few, if any, sources of learning comparable to the family. Children are especially likely to adopt the key values of their parents if their families encourage open communication and provide emotional support (Aldous, 1978; Bossard and Boll, 1966; Havighurst, 1962; Ritchie and Koller, 1964).

As one aspect of its socializing function, the family exerts a strong formative influence on the political values of its offspring. This is not simple "generational determinism"; children do not faithfully adopt the viewpoints of their parents. Nevertheless, because of the impact of the family, political beliefs tend to persist across generations—even in the face of massive social changes (Dalton, 1980).

Legitimizing Inheritance

Throughout history, the family has played a crucial role in the transfer of land, wealth, and material possessions. Before the American Revolution, laws of inheritance were based on the principle of **primogeniture**. Wealth could only be inherited by and from males: the firstborn son usually received the bulk of his father's estate. Today, however, it is a principle of American law that an individual may select almost any person or institution to inherit his or her estate. This right is known as **testamentary freedom**. Generally, people name close family members as beneficiaries of their estates.

What if someone dies **intestate**, that is, without a will? In such cases, the laws of each state govern the distribution of wealth and property. Again, family ties weigh heavily; a person's spouse and children usually share in the entire estate. In most states, children receive at least 50 percent of the estate of a deceased parent (Sussman, Cates, and Smith, 1974).

Legitimizing Sexual Activity and the Position of Children

While certain societies have approved sexual activity outside the context of marriage, children resulting from such sexual liaisons have often been regarded as undesirable and labeled as "illegitimate." According to Bronislaw Malinowski (1974), the "principle of legitimacy"—the belief that no child should be brought into the world without a father—is universal and has helped to perpetuate the family. The father, like the mother, is viewed as indispensable for the full sociological status of the child.

Although the "principle of legitimacy" may be universal, the form that it takes in any particular society will vary depending on a number of factors. These include the value that the society places on virginity, its acceptance of or hostility to premarital intercourse, and its likelihood of viewing offspring as a burden rather than an asset. In societies that consider premarital intercourse to be immoral or illegitimate, marriage serves as a means of legitimizing sexual activity. Yet, even in societies that accept premarital sex, marriage is often essential for a child to receive full acceptance within the larger group.

Rose Laub Coser and Lewis A. Coser (1974) have analyzed the relationship between social revolution and the "principle of legitimacy." They point out that during periods of social revolution such nations as France and the Soviet Union attempted to change the status order by destroying the "principle of legitimacy." However, new status orders arose after these revolutionary periods, the stability of the family was restored, and social stigmas against illegitimacy were reinstated.

During the 1960s and early 1970s, the United States experienced a period of serious political conflict and social unrest. Americans became more accepting of many forms of behavior that had previously been viewed harshly, including the bearing of children outside of marriage. While the 1980s have been widely portrayed as a more conservative era, it remains to be seen if there will be a swing back toward the "principle of legitimacy."

The Family's Contribution to Human Development

Historically, the family has served the obvious function of producing and caring for children, thereby providing new generations that will allow human societies to continue. In the past, the family held primary responsibility for the protection, socialization, vocational and intellectual education, and emotional support of its members. More recently, the educational functions of the family have become obsolete as a result of the phenomenon of **differentiation**—the specialization of institutional functions that characterizes our complex urban society. At the same time, the family's responsibilities for early socialization and emotional support of children have become even more important (Manuchin, 1974).

The family makes many other contributions to children's development. By observing interactions between family members, a young child obtains important information regarding role interaction and sex-role identification. The key role of the family in the formation of identity, self-image, and self-esteem is widely recognized. Finally, in the midst of the complex demands and stresses of contemporary life, the family provides a refuge, a source of emotional gratification, and a sense of purpose for its members (Anthony and Chiland, 1978; Stolte-Heiskanen, 1974).

The Search for Personal Fulfillment

As the women's liberation movement grew in focus and sophistication during the 1970s, it challenged many individuals—both male and female—to reexamine their goals and priorities. One result has been an increasing inclination to evaluate activities and relationships on the basis of whether they provide joy and fulfillment.

Under this approach, life within a family should be a satisfying experience rather than a series of dreary duties. If the traditional family ideal proves to be alienating or restrictive, changes will be made. Some men give up responsible, prestigious positions in order to find a trade or occupation that may be more personally satisfying. At the same time, many women declare that being wife and mother is not enough and seek meaning in careers outside the home. No longer is it sufficient to "make the best of things"; there is greater willingness to risk and experiment in the hope of achieving a life that is emotionally rich.

Mark and Abby, a married couple in their early thirties, are examples of those who strongly value self-fulfillment. He is a public interest lawyer who hopes to "humanize the system" from within; she is the assistant editor of a corporate magazine.

Seeking personal fulfillment beyond being a wife and mother, many women have established themselves in satisfying and demanding careers outside the home.

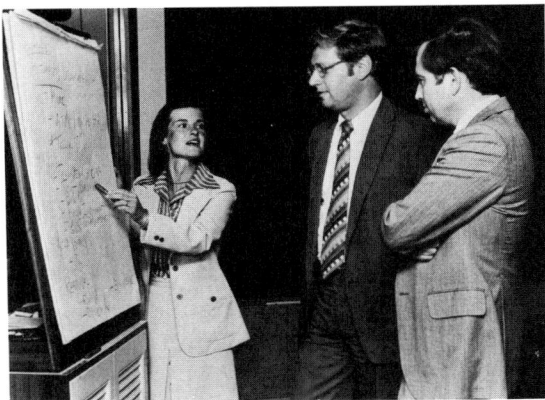

Married for six years, they originally decided to postpone having children until they were more firmly established in their respective careers. But Abby is now unsure about the difficulties of balancing motherhood and work outside the home.

Both husband and wife speak with exhilaration about the relative freedom of contemporary life. Yet they worry about the long-range consequences of their day-to-day pursuit of fulfillment. Abby reveals that "sometimes I'm afraid of ending up with nothing because I crave so much out of life. I know you can't have everything. But I'm not sure what to give up and what to hang on to." Mark admits that "I value my freedom and independence more than almost anything I can think of. . . . If I had to calculate the odds, . . . there is about the same chance I'll end up empty-handed as there is that I'll get what I want out of life" (Yankelovich, 1981: 49–54).

A 1979 study of almost 3,000 working Americans suggested that younger, better educated professionals are especially likely to place high value on self-fulfillment (Yankelovich, 1981). However, Lillian Breslow Rubin (1976: 120) has stressed that working-class women are increasingly concerned about nonmaterial fulfillment goals such as intimacy, companionship, and sharing. Of course, like more affluent Americans such as Abby and Mark, working-class women have learned that the road to personal fulfillment can be long and difficult. One woman, speaking with obvious frustration, told Rubin:

I'm not sure what I want. I keep talking to him about communication, and he says, "Okay, so we're talking; now what do you want?" And I don't know what to say then, but I know it's not what I mean.

The quest for fulfillment has contributed to the shrinking size of American households (singlehood and marriage without children become more acceptable), to the declining proportion of households headed by a husband and a wife (as people leave unsatisfying marriages), and to other changes in the nation's family patterns. As we will discuss more fully in Chapter 2, there has been a dramatic rise in such alternative family forms as the single-parent family and **cohabitation** (''living together'' without marriage).

Even within the traditional **nuclear family** with a husband, a wife, and children living together under the same roof, there have been noticeable changes stemming in part from the search for fulfillment. One of the most striking developments has been the emergence of what Diana Baumrind (1980) calls ''sexual symmetry'' in child care. As more women work outside the home and men become more involved in childrearing, their roles as parents become somewhat more similar. Thus, Michael Lamb (1977) found that children between one and two years of age were showing an increased desire to spend time with their fathers. Fathers were also showing increased interest in their children—especially if the children were male.

As greater numbers of women join the labor force, fathers become increasingly involved in tasks which in the past would have been performed only by mothers.

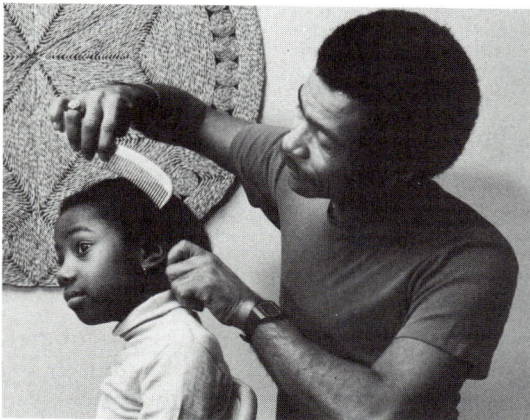

Clearly, many American families still adhere to the traditional model under which childrearing is viewed as ''women's work.'' But some families have gone as far as to reverse that pattern: the wife becomes the main breadwinner while the husband assumes principal responsibility for child care. This is but one reflection of the major changes in thinking about the appropriate roles of women and men within the family (Rapoport and Rapoport, 1975).

Summary

In recent decades, there have been marked changes in the marital and family patterns of the United States. Two trends are particularly noteworthy: the average size of households is shrinking, and a declining proportion of households are headed by a husband and a wife. Americans no longer view marriage as essential for a healthy and satisfying life—or even for the raising of children.

The family has functioned throughout history as the most significant institution shaping human interactions. Without question, it is the primary agent of socialization in the United States and other societies. The family also legitimizes the transfer of land, wealth, and material possessions, and legitimizes sexual activity and the position of children.

Americans have become increasingly inclined to evaluate activities and relationships on the basis of whether they provide joy and fulfillment. There is greater willingness to risk and experiment in the hope of achieving a life that is emotionally rich. One study suggested that younger, better educated professionals are especially likely to place high value on self-fulfillment. But working-class women have also become more concerned about fulfillment goals such as intimacy, companionship, and sharing.

Discussion Questions

1. According to the text, most Americans no longer believe that marriage is a prerequisite to a satisfying life or for raising children. How do you feel about this? What do you feel you need to achieve to attain a happy and satisfying life?

2. In recent years Americans have become increasingly concerned with evaluating activities and relationships on the basis of whether they are personally self-fulfilling. What do you think has contributed to this trend and what are the consequences for the family?

3. The text described briefly new family patterns. What type of family structure would you ideally like to develop? How would roles and responsibilities be divided?

Key Words

Cohabitation	**Nuclear Family**	**Testamentary Freedom**
Differentiation	**Primogeniture**	
Intestate	**Socialization**	

Suggested Readings

Masnick, George, and Bane, Mary J. *The Nation's Families, 1960–1990*. Boston: Auburn House, 1980. A readable description of trends and social changes in household composition, family structure, and women's working patterns.

Steiner, Gilbert. *The Futility of Family Policy*. Washington, D.C.: Brookings, 1981. A critical review of the problems in defining a single ''American policy.''

Yankelovich, Daniel. *New Rules: Searching for Self-fulfillment in a World Turned Upside Down*. New York: Random House, 1981. An exploration of the effects on Americans of new societal attitudes and the problems and promises of the trend for self-fulfillment.

CHAPTER TWO

Relationships: Studying the Family

KEY TOPICS

—the various family forms in the United States—
—the increase in single-parent and remarried families—
—whether the extended family is actually declining in importance—
—the role of family social scientists in the study of family relationships—
—how family social scientists apply the scientific method—
—theoretical frameworks used in the study of family relationships—
—the advantages of applying a family life cycle approach—

One of the most successful television programs of the 1950s and early 1960s was the series, ''Father Knows Best.'' First telecast in 1954, ''Father Knows Best'' has been described as ''the classic wholesome family situation comedy.'' The Andersons, a white, middle-class, Midwestern family with three children, lived a rather comfortable and peaceful existence. Jim Anderson (played by Robert Young) worked as an insurance agent, while his wife Margaret (played by Jane Wyatt) was a full-time homemaker. Their children's anxieties and jealousies were always easily resolved after a few calming words from Father. ''The Andersons were truly an idealized family, the sort that

viewers could . . . wish to emulate'' (Brooks and Marsh, 1979: 196).

''Father Knows Best'' was a far cry from ''Dallas,'' ''Dynasty,'' ''Three's Company,'' and other popular television shows of the 1980s. In the tranquil world of the Andersons, there was no divorce, no abortion, no incest, no homosexuality. The problems of the Anderson children rarely became more serious than needing a date for the big dance. Disagreements arose, but the Andersons were certain to pull together quickly into a cohesive and supportive family unit.

Even as an idealized family, the Andersons would hardly appear believable on American television today. Like the larger society, the American family is in an era of significant turmoil and transition. Some argue that the family is disintegrating as a result of more liberal attitudes toward premarital sex, extramarital sex, and divorce. Others are more optimistic and suggest that the family is merely adapting to profound social and economic changes. Certainly, all observers would agree that the traditional nuclear family (in which father knows best) is no longer the sole and unquestioned model of ideal family life (Dyer, 1979; Manuchin, 1974).

Family Forms in Contemporary America

In the 1970s, social scientists such as Amitai Etzioni (1977) and Urie Bronfenbrenner (1977) argued that the institution of the family was becoming increasingly obsolete. Bronfenbrenner suggested it was "clear that the American family is disintegrating" and worried about the rise of a new "uncaring society." Whether or not these dire predic-

tions are accurate, many Americans obviously feel that their personal needs are not being successfully met within the confines of traditional nuclear family arrangements. Consequently, some individuals have turned to alternate or "variant" family forms (Cogswell and Sussman, 1972; Steiner, 1981; Sussman, 1978).

A *nuclear family*, like that of the idealized Andersons, is defined as "a household of husband, wife, and children living apart from both sets of parents with husbands as breadwinners and wives as homemakers" (Sussman, 1971). As Table 2-1 indicates, only 16 percent of American families correspond to this traditional model, long regarded as "normal." Therefore, "variation, either by chance or choice, is now the norm" (Rapoport, Rapoport, and Strelitz, 1980: 109).

In his article, "Can the Family Survive Alternate Lifestyles?" Bert Adams (1973) identifies three broad categories of alternatives to conventional marriage and family lifestyles: (1) alternatives that are parallel to marriage and family, for example, an unmarried heterosexual couple living together;

Table 2-1   American family forms, 1982

Family type	Percentage distribution
Husband and wife (with children)	
Husband working	16
Dual working (both husband and wife employed)	22
Husband and wife (without children)	
Husband working	10
Dual working	16
Single parent	11
Cohabiting unmarried couples (with and without children)	3
Other (unemployed couples with and without children, extended kin families, childless couples with only wife employed, etc.)	22

Source: Current Population Reports, Series T, Nos. 380, 381.

(2) alternatives that can be incorporated into a family's structure, for example, an older relative coming to live with the family; and (3) alternatives that would replace traditional patterns, such as a commune. In this chapter, we will examine six major alternatives to the traditional nuclear family: the single-parent family, the stepfamily, the dual-worker family, living together, communal family and group marriage, and the extended family.

Single-Parent Family

Ellen Wilkins lives in a small brownstone apartment with her five-year-old son, Daniel. Her life, like that of most single parents, is almost impossibly busy. Each morning, she cooks breakfast for Daniel, takes him to nursery school, and then rushes to her part-time job as a word processor for a publishing company. She leaves in the late afternoon to pick up her son and bring him home for dinner. Ellen spends two nights a week taking evening classes in counseling. Other nights are devoted to doing the required readings and writing papers—but Ellen doesn't begin her schoolwork until after Daniel has gone to sleep.

Ellen is vocal about the strains of her life. "It's rough, it's really rough. My ex-husband is no help at all. He's tight with child support money and almost never babysits. He'll come over on a Sunday, play ball with Daniel for an hour, and think he's made a big sacrifice of his valuable time. What about my time? I never have a moment to myself. I can't remember the last time I saw a movie or a concert with a friend. My son is a real joy, but when things get frantic I start resenting him, and it isn't his fault."

The single-parent family is currently the fastest growing family type in the United States. In 1982, almost 22 percent of all American families with children had a single

Presently, the fastest growing family type in America is the single-parent family.

parent as compared with 8.5 percent in 1960. Of these, about 20 percent were mother-child families, while about 2 percent were father-child families (*U.S. News and World Report*, November, 1983). In certain cases, the single-parent situation may continue throughout the childrearing period. However, like Ellen Wilkens, a substantial number of "parents without partners" probably hope that their situation will be only a temporary alternative to married family life.

What accounts for the dramatic rise in single-parent families? There are many contributing factors: the increased economic independence of women, greater societal acceptance of divorce, the liberalizing of adoption laws, and scientific advances in artificial insemination. While many single-parent families emerge after the breakup of a marriage, others reflect childbearing by unmarried women. In fact, according to the Census Bureau, the number of families headed by never-married mothers rose from 234,000 in 1970 to 1,092,000 in 1982—an increase of 314 percent (*The New York Times*, August, 1983).

Contemporary rhetoric about the disintegration of the nuclear family often ignores the fact that single-parent families have always been part of American life. It is a myth that nearly all children in colonial America grew up in homes with two parents. Some parents had to travel away from their families in order to find work; others were victims of the high death rates of preindustrial times (Sussman, 1978). Indeed, fearful speculations about the rise of single-parent families ignore another important truth: there is no solid empirical research proving that two parents are better than one. Most authorities now believe that one good parent is sufficient for a child's healthy development and may in fact be more of an asset than two parents in severe conflict (Burgess, 1970; LeMasters, 1970; Parsons, 1965).

Stepfamily

It has been estimated that one child in five under the age of 18 in the United States is presently living with a stepparent (Pollock, 1981). Thus, in the context of rising divorce and remarriage, the stepfamily, that is the family formed when a husband or wife remarries and one or both adults in the remarriage brings children to the newly established relationship, has become an important form of American family life. Although current literature on stepparenting is quite limited, most researchers agree that both adults and children face difficult role adjustments. Michael Norman (1980: 46) notes that "the stepfamily is an instant family, created at the moment the marriage vows are spoken. The ties are impromptu, the relationships without guidelines."

Children may view the natural parent as a traitor for having chosen a new spouse, and may feel that the stepparent is an intruder interfering where he or she does not belong. The stepparent may feel guilty, insecure, or

As the numbers of divorces and re-marriages rise, the "instant family," created at the moment the marriage vows are taken, has become an important form of American family life.

resentful about the responsibilities of caring for stepchildren. Moreover, the relationship between the newly married couple and the absent parent can be a source of strain—especially when there are disputes about visiting rights, custody, or child support. The three problem areas most frequently mentioned by parents in a remarriage are disciplining children, adjusting to children's personalities and habits, and winning their acceptance (Kompara, 1980; Maddox, 1975; Messinger, 1976; Schlesinger, 1975).

Of course, while the difficulties of stepfamily relationships are evident, there are certain benefits for children after a remarriage. Sociologist Frank F. Furstenberg points out that stepfamily relationships offer the child a large pool of relatives—including a new set of stepgrandparents, aunts, uncles, and cousins. One seven-year-old proudly listed his assets by stating: "Hey, did you know that I have two mommys and two daddys and two houses and a brother and two sisters and six dogs and a cat?" (Norman, 1980: 54).

Dual-Worker Family

No longer is the typical American wife a full-time homemaker. Instead, there has been a striking rise in "dual-worker families" in which women work outside the home. When both partners work, women are no longer totally dependent on their husbands for financial support. The ability to earn a living affects a working wife's self-concept and reshapes her relationships with other family members. Since power and decision-making are often associated with the role of family breadwinner, dual-worker families tend to be more egalitarian than traditional nuclear families (see Box 2–1).

A key difficulty in the dual-worker family is simply finding the time to fulfill child-care and domestic responsibilities. As Leslie and Leslie (1977: 284) observe: "One of the most striking things about dual-career couples is how incredibly busy they are." Free time is clearly at a premium as the two parents juggle their schedules in order to perform household duties. Nevertheless, family life may prove to be happier and less stressful because of the economic advantage of living on two incomes (Rapoport and Rapoport, 1978).

Living Together

Russell: I had been married before, for ten years, divorced, and my son was living with me. I was married from the time I was nineteen and was a father from the time I was twenty. . . . I was not interested in getting into a legal relationship that was going to have a long-term, negative effect. I didn't want to be in a relationship where the woman needed my signature. I am talking about when we go into a restaurant and Mara pays for dinner, and the waiter puts the charge in front of me. Or where she is called "Mrs. Hurley." That has a debilitating effect in the long run. It is like water over a rock.

Mara: I had never lived with anyone. . . . To me, the fact that I was living with a man implied a great deal of commitment. . . . Really, I never felt that I had to be married. . . . I had no feeling that I had to be married in order to prove that I was acceptable. I think that women are feeling this less and less, depending on the environments they live in. By the time I did meet Russell, I had a resistance to changing my identity or my status. . . . I was also aware, from past relationships I had had with men, of the dangers and of the tendency of a woman to gain much of her identity through a man. Even though emotionally I felt I was beyond that point,

BOX 2-1

Tom and Nancy, A Dual-Career Couple

Tom, age 44, and Nancy, age 37, have been married for 13 years. They are the parents of Carolyn, age 11, and Ben, age 3. Tom works as a research scientist for an aerospace company and Nancy is an occupational therapist in a large metropolitan hospital. They have lived for 10 years in a pleasant suburban neighborhood where they are both fairly active in community and school affairs. Their marriage, after some initial rough spots, has acquired a comfortableness which seems to be based, in part, on a sense of sustaining commitment. . . .

At the time of their meeting, Tom was 30 years old and Nancy was 23. . . . The couple married after a year of courtship. Nancy had made it clear that she found a good deal of satisfaction in her career and that she expected to work, at least half time, even when the couple had young children. Tom supported Nancy's career ambitions and admired her dedication.

At the end of the second year of marriage (when Carolyn was approximately four months old), Tom left the small company where he had been working to take a laboratory research position with his present, larger company. The position offered him greater time flexibility and more of a chance to "do my own thing." The company had a flex-time system that permitted Tom to begin work later in the morning and continue past the usual quitting time. This meant he could stay home in the morning for a while with Carolyn (and, later, with Ben) while Nancy went to

work. She would then pick up the children at their regular sitter's house and be with them in the late afternoon. . . .

Having established himself professionally, and having a relatively undemanding job, Tom felt greater freedom to spend time with Nancy and his children. Like Nancy, he had taken care of his younger siblings on occasion while he was growing up. This seemed instrumental in freeing him from hangups about a man taking care of small children and sharing domestic responsibilities. Tom and Nancy operate on an informal domestic and child-care task schedule, but there is a lot of "doing whatever needs to be done by whoever is around when it needs doing." There is a sense of cooperation between the partners in this regard. . . .

In summary, Tom and Nancy are representative of many (perhaps most) dual-career couples, who find this marital lifestyle generally satisfying. Neither partner feels he or she must make disproportionate sacrifices in order to have a career and a family. They have maintained a flexibility in dealing with the demands placed on their lives and show a relative freedom from gender-role stereotyped notions of what is and is not "proper" spouse behavior. . . . Although not free of problems, they are motivated to work on rough spots and attempt to keep channels of communication open.

Source: Rice, 1979: 144–150.

I still didn't like to be defined by society as someone's wife, Mrs. Someone. (Fullerton, 1977: 618–621)

Mara and Russell rejected marriage in favor of the most common alternative to the traditional nuclear family: *cohabitation*. This term is used to refer to an unmarried heterosexual couple who live together. The Census

Bureau has estimated that the number of couples who cohabit skyrocketed from 523,000 in 1970 to 1.9 million in 1982 (*U.S. News and World Report*, June 20, 1983).

Cohabitation has become much more common among American college students. One researcher, James M. Henslin (1980), has suggested that as many as one-third of all students live as a couple during their college years. He adds that, while sex is certainly a major aspect of students' cohabiting relationships, their primary reason for living together is a desire to experience mutual respect and affection.

In most cases, cohabitation among adults is a premarital living experiment that, if successful, may lead to marriage. However, with the rising frequency of divorce, cohabitation is viewed by many as an alternative to remarriage—even if one or both partners have children. Since the nation's tax laws make it financially advantageous to remain unmarried, there can be an economic incentive for living together rather than marrying. Certainly this is true for a growing number of elderly couples relying on social security benefits or pension income who find that they cannot afford to get married and must instead be content with living together.

Communal Family and Group Marriage

Margaret Mead once said that "no matter how many communes anybody invents, the family always creeps back." Still, despite the skepticism of Mead and other critics, Americans continue to turn to communes in search of common goals such as meaningful human interaction, personal growth, spiritual rebirth, "getting back to nature," or radical political change.

At present, there are perhaps 1000 to 1500 communes in the United States. Most members are in their twenties or thirties and typically come from middle-class or upper-class homes. Many communes are characterized by a quest for togetherness, intimacy, and an extended family atmosphere. Interestingly, in an effort to minimize the physical, emotional, and financial burdens of raising children alone, some single parents have banded together into communal living arrangements (Berger, et al., 1971; David, 1978; Kempler, 1976).

Communal living has a long history in the United States and Western Europe. Ramey (1972) has broken down communes into three types: religious communes such as those of the Amish; utopian communities such as the Walden Two experiments; and evolutionary societies such as the kibbutz movement in Israel. Communes may be urban or rural; there are vast differences among them in attitudes toward division of labor, sexuality and sex roles, childrearing practices, and relations with the larger society (Kanter, Jaffe, and Weisberg, 1975; Rapoport, Rapoport, and Strelitz, 1980).

Group marriage, by definition, consists of three or more individuals who consider themselves married to each other. They live together communally and share home, money, children, and sexual intimacy (Kilgo, 1972). Although popular publications such as Robert Rimmer's *The Harrad Experiment* (1966) generated interest in group marriage, most researchers agree that there are probably fewer than 100 such marriages currently in existence in the United States. One of the few studies of this form of family life found that most participants were well-educated, legally married couples from middle-class backgrounds (Constantine and Constantine, 1972, 1973).

In general, the alternative family forms discussed thus far tend to reject constraints and to emphasize opportunities for their individual members. Noting that these alternatives minimize family obligations, Betty Cogswell (1975) has questioned whether such relationships can persist over a significant time period. Yet there has been a recent increase in the use of personal contracts by those engaged in cohabitation or group living arrangements (see Box 2–2). Such contracts often place restraints on each member in order to ensure equal opportunity for development. Apparently, the concept of mutual obligation remains important to many

BOX 2-2

Excerpts from a Cohabitation Contract

WHEREAS: Consort I and Consort II love each other; and

WHEREAS: the parties desire to share joint rents and to share the same dwelling; and

WHEREAS: the parties are having sexual relations and have decided to live openly together.

NOW, THEREFORE, in consideration of the following covenants, it is agreed as follows:

1. The parties agree to be emotionally committed to each other and to love, honor, and respect each other until the first to occur of the following:
    A. until death they do part;
    B. until this agreement is substituted by lawful marriage between the parties;
    C. until either party decides to move out of the joint residence.

4. The parties each agree to use their own names and in all respects to identify themselves as single people.

5. Neither party shall use the credit of the other.

6. Neither party shall claim alimony or rights in community property against the other.

11. The following items will be payable promptly using the ''equal obligation system'':
    A. Entertainment of both consorts together (such as theatre tickets, dinner out, etc.).
    B. Gifts for mutual friends.
    C. Vacations taken jointly.

12. The parties shall maintain a cookie jar for the purpose of depositing all receipts, bills, cash register tapes, and evidence of payment of joint funds. The parties shall go through this jar monthly for the purpose of divvying up expenses and making appropriate compensation.

13. The parties shall each be responsible for the maintenance and cleanliness of the joint residence equally or as nearly equally as possible (and especially scrubbing the bathroom), except that the following day-to-day tasks are assigned as follows:
    Consort I: laundry.
    Consort II: cleaning kitchen floor, taking out garbage.

28. The parties agree to use birth control measures and their best efforts to avoid conception unless or until they jointly decide to have offspring.

30. In the event the parties agree to have a child, then all expenses directly related to pregnancy and delivery shall be divided equally.

Source: Adapted from Hirsch, 1976: 96–111.

Americans who seek alternative forms of family life (Sussman, 1975).

Social Change and Family Relationships

Compare the tranquil television world of ''Father Knows Best'' with family life in a hit series of the 1980s, ''Dynasty.'' Virtually every married character commits adultery at one time or another. Alexis (Joan Collins) sabotages her daughter's relationship with a man out of jealousy. Daughter-in-law Sammy Jo attempts to sell her son back to his grandfather, tycoon Blake Carrington (John Forsythe). And does father know best? Hardly. When Blake finds his bisexual son Steven saying a tender goodbye to a former male lover, Blake lashes out in rage and kills his son's lover.

The reality of American family life, along with its representation in the media, has changed dramatically since the 1950s. Thus, alternatives to the traditional nuclear family have arisen in a period of far-reaching social and economic transformation (Reiss, 1976). For example, as singlehood and cohabitation have become more acceptable, the average size of the American household has reached an all-time low—just under three persons per household (see Chapter 1). There has also been an unprecedented increase in the number of dual-worker households.

Paul Glick (1975), a leading scholar in the study of family change, notes that the basic shift in American attitudes toward marriage and family life has led to profound demographic changes. In the period 1960 to 1980, the average age of marriage rose from 20.3 to 21.3 for women and from 22.8 to 23.8 for men (Bureau of the Census, 1980). Wider availability of higher education has contributed to the delay in marrying, but so has the growing belief that a young woman or man has the right to pursue alternate lifestyles.

The rising divorce rate of the United States has also been a factor in the emergence of new family forms. According to 1980 projections, half of all recent marriages will end in divorce and 40 percent of children born to recently married couples will experience divorce. Divorce has been socially accepted in most communities and has become easier to obtain than ever before because of changes in the legal system. In addition, the general level of affluence in the United States has increased during the twentieth century. Researchers have found a positive relationship between economic prosperity and the incidence of divorce (Stinnett and Birdsong, 1978).

There is little doubt that, like divorce, other departures from traditional nuclear family life are more likely in a period of relative affluence. Deferred gratification is no longer essential; individuals feel free to pursue greater fulfillment by experimenting with new lifestyles. Not surprisingly, it is primarily persons from middle-class backgrounds who experiment with variant family forms (Cogswell, 1975; Marciano, 1975).

The emergence of the women's liberation movement in the late 1960s and early 1970s has had profound repercussions on American family life. Feminism has provided psychological support for women who wish to work outside the home and establish identities apart from their husbands and children. As these women have moved forward in their careers, some have come to view childrearing as a less important source of self-esteem. Many have turned to day care in order to function both as mothers and as members of the paid labor force.

While the women's movement has made some headway in eliminating sex-role stereotyping in the occupational world, less progress has been made in restructuring new roles for women and men in the home. Men are becoming somewhat more involved in childrearing and household maintenance (see Box 2–1), yet these duties remain unequally shared. In some families, less rigid role definitions have led to confusion, insecurity, and ultimately conflict between wives and husbands. As such conflict becomes more prevalent, nontraditional lifestyles may seem more desirable (Rapoport and Rapoport, 1975; Stinnett and Birdsong, 1978).

Decline of the Extended Family: Myth or Reality?

When thinking of the *extended family* of the past, most of us imagine a large, early American home with three or more generations living under one roof. It is assumed that family members of all ages shared work and play, and were ready at a moment's notice to assist in manual tasks or offer emotional support. Yet recent historical research has challenged these nostalgic images of the extended family. According to Peter Laslett (1972: xi), ''the nuclear family household constituted the ordinary, expected, normal framework of domestic existence.'' Most American houses were small; few families were able to live together as an extended unit and work land jointly. In fact, while the extended family has remained a cherished ideal in both traditional and modern societies, it has been feasible mainly for members of higher socioeconomic groups (Dore, 1958; Goode, 1964: Seward, 1973).

Several studies have documented the continuing importance of the extended family in contemporary American life (Litwak, 1960; Sussman and Burchinal, 1962; Rapoport, Rapoport, and Strelitz, 1980). For certain ethnic groups, such as Native Americans and Mexican Americans, assistance from an extended family is characteristic. Such kin relationships may be very meaningful even if family members do not share the same home.

A study by Ethel Shanas (1973) revealed that the majority of older persons in American cities—as well as cities in England, Denmark, Israel, Poland, and Yugoslavia—live either in the same household or within ten minutes of a son or daughter. More than 70 percent of the elderly persons questioned had had personal contact with at least one of their children within the previous week. Surveys in the United States indicate that ''visiting with relatives'' is the most frequently cited leisure-time occupation (Hughes, 1971).

Of course, people are especially likely to try to ''reach out and touch someone'' from an extended family during a time of need. During periods of stress, many individuals reevaluate their kin relationships and realize how helpful relatives can be (Drabeck, et al.,

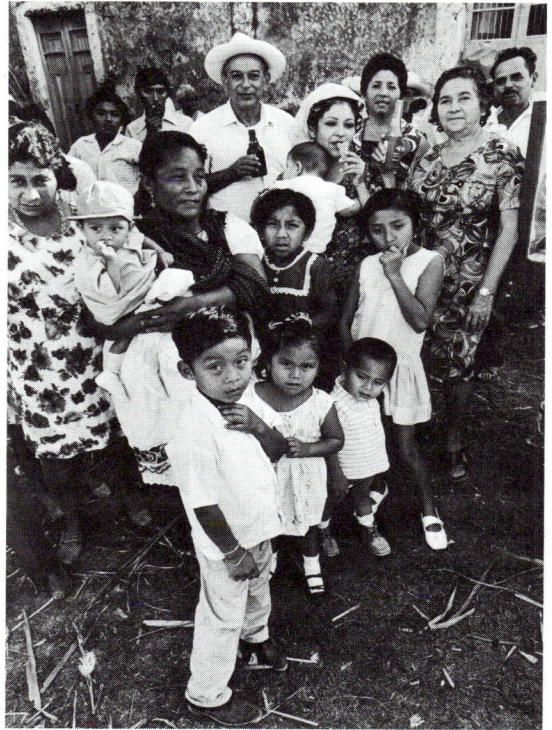

The role of the extended family is particularly important within contemporary Mexican-American culture.

1975). Thus, Litwak and Szelenyi (1969) found that respondents in both the United States and Hungary were most likely to cite relatives as the group that would provide substantial assistance with long-term difficulties (e.g., help during a lengthy illness). This was true even of respondents who stated that they had ''no relatives in town.''

Given the economic stresses of the 1980s—inflation, unemployment, the high cost of financing a home purchase, the difficulty of living on social security and pension income—there may be an increase in the number of households composed of several generations. Moreover, as the rise in single parenthood continues, the emotional support of an extended family network may seem welcome.

As an example, a single mother like Ellen Wilkens may decide that it would be best to live with her parents for a few years while she finishes her night courses in counseling. Her living expenses would be reduced, her babysitting problems would be solved, and both mother and son might benefit from the company and concern of two older relatives.

Some Americans may choose to join in an **affiliated family**—a family in which one or more older persons recognized as part of a kin network and called by a kin term shares in the family's responsibilities and emotional life (Clavan and Vatter, 1972). If Ellen and her son Daniel began sharing an apartment with Ellen's aunt Frieda, they would be forming an affiliated family.

The Work of Family Social Scientists

All of us function from time to time as "people watchers." We think about our friends and family, or even about strangers we see in public places, and wonder about their personal lives. Family social scientists have a similar curiosity, but they use the tools and theories of contemporary social science in order to study people's relationships. Included under the general label of "family social scientists" are scholars from a wide range of disciplines, including sociology, psychology, social work, and medicine.

Family social scientists have focused on seven basic questions: (1) How do people's relationships come into being? (2) How do relationships become intimate relationships? (3) How do relationships develop into marriages and family units? (4) How do family units change during the life cycle? (5) How do families respond to stress and to social and psychological difficulties? (6) How and

why do family units come to an end? and (7) What brings about the formation of new relationships and family units?

The Scientific Method

Social scientists use the **scientific method** to study human relationships. Specifically, they rely on concepts, variables, theories, and standard research procedures. The basic building block for social scientists is a **concept**, a general idea of or notion about human relationships. For example, conflict and supportive communication are two important concepts used in the study of relationships and family life.

Once key concepts are identified and defined, social scientists attempt to measure them through use of specific **variables**. A researcher studying conflict within families may count the number of "nasty" or "hurtful" words that each member uses in discussions at home. The total of such statements made would be the variable; it could range from zero to infinity, depending on how long family interactions were recorded by researchers. Similarly, a researcher studying supportive communication within families may count the number of hugs or encouraging remarks.

The scientific method focuses on the relationship between two or more variables. Social scientists use statistical measures to test the strength and direction of the association between variables. Thus, if we observed that the greater the number of supportive communications the higher the self-esteem of family members, we would conclude that there is a positive relationship between supportive communication and self-esteem. The greater the support, the higher the self-esteem. By contrast, if we observed that the greater the number of nasty and hurtful comments the lower the self-esteem among family members, we would conclude that there is an inverse relationship between conflict and self-esteem. The greater the conflict, the lower the self-esteem.

In applying the scientific method, researchers are guided by *theories* about the phenomena under study (such as family relationships). A theory links key concepts and helps to predict behavior. In the case of family social science, theories are used to advance scholarly understanding of why families behave and interact as they do. They help to explain the complex process involved in building, developing, and changing family relationships.

Family Social Science Theories

At present, there is no one theory that fully explains relationships and the dynamics of family life. Since it is virtually impossible to develop a single comprehensive theory that will answer all the seven basic family research questions outlined earlier, social scientists have emphasized the study of specific aspects of family life, such as the transition to parenthood, families in retirement, or changing sex roles. As a result, a more limited set of concepts and variables has been introduced and linked into theoretical frameworks. Such partial theories help researchers, policymakers, and counselors to better understand family life.

Generally speaking, family social scientists have focused on four broad theoretical areas. They are interested in (1) how the ecological environment shapes the nature of family relationships and human development; (2) the changing nature of family relationships in the context of historical time; (3) the day-to-day interactions among family members; and (4) how the family unit develops and changes over the course of the life cycle. The theoretical frameworks that follow are attempts to better understand these four areas.

The Family Ecological Framework

Urie Bronfenbrenner (1979), an internationally renowned psychologist, has proposed that we examine the family as part of the "ecological environment"—that is, as part of the larger network of social institutions. According to this theory, the family can be pictured within a set of nested structures, each inside the next. The individual family member is at the center of this environment and is "nested" within an immediate setting which includes the family. This setting is known as a **microsystem**.

Bronfenbrenner stresses that the individual and family are also influenced by a mesosystem, an exosystem, and a macrosystem. The **mesosystem** includes those settings in which a developing person actually participates, such as a workplace, a school environment, and a neighborhood. The **exosystem** consists of social settings that affect what happens within the individual's immediate environment—even if he or she does not directly enter such settings. For example, the nation's economy is part of an exosystem that has direct impact on individual and family units. Finally, the **macrosystem** is a social setting that includes a community's ideology and its organization of social institutions. Each of us, and each of our families, is influenced by the overall American culture and by the country's capitalist ideology.

The Historical Framework

Sociologist Glen Elder, Jr. (1975) has emphasized the need to understand human relationships as embedded within a "life course." He views relationships as being involved in three basic time dimensions: **individual time** (a person's own life span from birth to death); **social time** (a person's timetable as characterized by important social events and transitions, such as marriage and retirement); and **historical time** (the social era in which a person is born and lives).

As an example of how these time dimensions diverge, let us briefly look at the early British feminist, Mary Wollstonecraft. Wollstonecraft's individual time was her life span from birth in 1759 to death in 1797. Her social time included the death of her mother in 1782; the publication of her most famous book, *A Vindication of the Rights of Woman*, in 1792; the birth of her daughter Fanny Imlay in 1794; and her marriage to philosopher William Godwin in 1797. Wollstonecraft's historical time, the late eighteenth century, was particularly marked by the American and French Revolutions.

Glen Elder argues that the study of the historical time dimension is important because individuals and families are embedded in the social context (or **cohort**) of a particular era. Thus, people married during the same period of time, such as the Depression of the 1930s, can be referred to as a marriage cohort or a Depression cohort. Families of American soldiers killed during the Vietnam War of the 1960s and 1970s can be studied as a Vietnam family cohort.

Sociologists are especially interested in birth cohorts, which consist of persons born in a particular year or period of time, such as all individuals born in the years following World War II. Through cohort studies, sociologists can compare the life course of certain individuals and families with another group born at a different time. Such family-oriented research offers valuable insights about the impact of social change on family relationships.

In a national survey of 1000 married couples, David Olson (1983) and his colleagues examined the sharing of decision-making and domestic responsibilities. The researchers found that, while young couples without children emphasized sharing of

What will family social scientists learn from comparing the "Class of 1985" cohort with another group of individuals born at a different time?

household duties, this was not the case for most respondents. Married couples in their later years were much less likely to favor egalitarian roles, particularly after their children had left home.

Does this mean that people's commitment to egalitarian roles diminishes as they progress through the family life cycle? Not necessarily. If we use Elder's historical-cohort framework to examine Olson's findings, we can conclude that there are important differences in the marital cohorts being questioned. In contrast to older couples studied, young married couples of the 1980s grew up during an era of serious dissatisfaction with traditional sex-role arrangements (see Chapter 3). When members of this younger cohort reach their fifties and sixties, they may continue to feel that decision-making should be shared by wives and husbands.

The Structure-Function Framework

The structure-function approach, perhaps the dominant theoretical framework of American sociology, is associated with such influential social scientists as Talcott Parsons and George Murdock. Yet this approach actually has its basis in anthropology. The family is viewed as a social system and as a unit performing certain essential functions for the larger society of which it is a part. These include reproduction, caring for children, and socialization into the basic norms and values of society (Parsons, 1953).

Thus, the relationship between the family and society is a functional one. A family's success is measured by how well it meets the critical needs of society. Kando (1978: 191) notes that "the family is not viewed as active in social change, but rather as a defensive, survival-oriented, and adjustive entity." Similarly, Hill and Hansen (1960: 303) suggest that the individual family member is seen mainly as "a reactive bundle of statuses and roles."

As is clear from these comments, the structure-function framework is primarily concerned with the maintenance of social institutions. Family-related issues are examined in terms of how society is held together. For example, in analyzing the increase in teenage pregnancies, functionalists might emphasize the low number of births in American society. Teenage parents can then be seen as contributing to society by producing needed offspring.

The Interactional Framework

Based primarily on the work of George Herbert Mead (1934), the interactional approach views the family as a "unity of interacting persons" (Hill and Hansen, 1960: 302–303). Proponents of this theoretical view, derived from both sociology and social psychology, believe that human beings are individual actors whose behavior is a function of social settings.

Interactionists emphasize that the concept of **role** is of central importance in understanding human behavior. Each individual occupies certain positions within the family; each position carries with it specific social roles (the "good provider," the responsible older sister, and so forth). Since the interactional approach focuses on interpersonal behavior rather than on cultural or institutional aspects of family life, it is especially valuable in studying family communication, decision-making, and problem-solving.

The Exchange Framework

George Simmel (1950) argued that we can best understand human relationships by examining the exchanges that occur between family members—what they give to each other, receive from each other, and take from each other. This framework, commonly known as exchange theory, underscores the importance of "rewards" and "costs" within family interactions.

For example, it is possible to view divorce as resulting from an imbalance of costs and rewards. When both men and women attach increasing value to independent and personal growth, the traditional marital relationship often experiences greater stress. The wife may feel the need to work outside the home in order to achieve greater satisfaction; the husband may resent losing the satisfactions he obtained from her work as a full-time homemaker. Her search for new rewards will necessitate adjustments in family relationships. If tension and conflict escalate, each spouse may come to feel that the benefits of remaining married no longer outweigh the emotional frustrations and costs.

The Developmental Framework

The developmental approach views families as changing over time. The family is seen as a unit of interacting individuals who influence one another and also influence (and are influenced by) the larger culture. Critical periods of individual and family development are highlighted. The developmental approach combines ideas from several disciplines, borrowing the notion of family life cycle from rural sociology, awareness of developmental tasks from the study of human development, concepts of social class and social change from sociology, and learning theory from psychology (Duvall, 1977; Hill and Hansen, 1960).

Beginning as a simple husband-wife pair, a family is studied throughout its history. The focus on expected change within the family, which differentiates the family developmental approach from other frameworks, also creates a need for new concepts that introduce the idea of social roles and explicitly point to social change. Therefore, theorists working with this approach have coined such terms as position, role sequence, and role cluster.

Position consists of a certain location in social groups which brings with it particular rights and duties, for example, being a father or a sister (Bates, 1956). A family position is composed of various roles; thus, the wife-mother position may include the roles of breadwinner, companion, and teacher. The term **role sequence** includes the behavioral changes in a role over time. A parent's role as a disciplinarian will certainly shift as his or her children move into adolescence. The responsibilities remain, but the specific disciplinary tasks are quite different. Finally, the term **role clusters** refers to the total array of roles (e.g., affection giver, disciplinarian) that any one position (e.g., husband-father) may contain at any one time (Deutscher, 1959).

The Family Development and Life Cycle Perspective

The images of nature's seasons are often used in describing stages of the human life cycle—from the blossoming spring of adolescence to the cold winter of death. In "September Song," the hero sings of the contrast between youth and middle age: "It's a long, long while from May to December/And the days grow short when you reach September" (Levinson, et al., 1978: 7).

The term "life cycle" suggests that, like the changing of seasons, the journey from birth to death has a distinctive character and follows a basic pattern. While no two families are identical, there are similarities in the experiences that each goes through within a lifetime. For this reason, the **family life cycle** approach is a useful framework for studying certain aspects of family life, and we have, thus, chosen it to guide the presentation of our text.

This perspective focuses on process and change, particularly changes in the internal structure, organization, and interactions of the family. The family life cycle approach allows researchers to take a long-range view of family life, as well as to understand and identify specific problems and strengths characteristic of each phase of family development. The family life cycle may be divided into several stages or may be considered in relation to two periods: the expanding family period or the contracting family period (Duvall, 1971; Hoover and Hoover, 1979; Nock, 1979; Stolte-Heiskanen, 1974).

Stages of Family Development

Joan Aldous (1978: 80) defines a **stage** as "a division within the lifetime of a family that is distinctive enough from those that precede and follow it to constitute a separate period." This concept allows theorists and researchers to gain insight into the particular vulnerabilities of families during each stage of the family life cycle. In fact, as Aldous points out, social scientists offer predictions about family behavior based solely on the stage a family has reached in its life cycle. Such predictions may involve a family's income level, degree of marital satisfaction, or extent of parent-child conflict.

Reuben Hill and Roy Rodgers (1964) view stages of family development as conve-

niences that permit the study of "properties" of the family at various points in its development. Although there is widespread agreement that family life can be effectively divided into stages, there are differences of opinion as to what differentiates one stage from another, what sequence is followed, and what causes a family to leave one stage and move into another. Nevertheless, models with stages of the life cycle allow families to compare their experiences with a "normal" pattern of development (Hill and Joy, 1980).

In preparing a report for the 1948 White House Conference on the Family, Evelyn Duvall and Reuben Hill developed what has become the most frequently used system for categorizing family life into stages. They suggested three key criteria for defining stages: (1) changes in the number of family members; (2) developmental stages of the oldest child; and (3) the retirement status of the husband-father. Using these criteria, Duvall and Hill (1948) divided the family life cycle into eight stages (see Table 2–2).

The Duvall and Hill system of categorization rests on the assumption that interdependence among family members is common. Thus, each time someone is added to or leaves a family, there will be substantial changes in family interactions. The same will be true whenever the oldest child

Table 2–2   Family life cycle stages based on the Duvall and Hill criteria

Stage I	Establishment stage
Stage II	Families with infants
Stage III	Families with preschool children
Stage IV	Families with schoolchildren
Stage V	Families with adolescents
Stage VI	Families with young adults
Stage VII	Families in the middle years (post-parental)
Stage VIII	Aging families

Source: Duvall, 1971: 144.

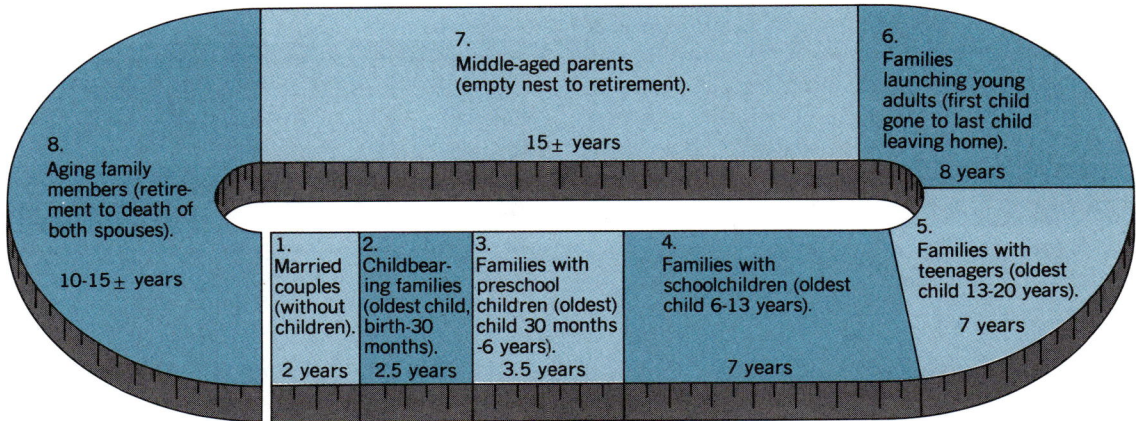

Figure 2-1 The family life cycle by length of time in each of eight stages. (*Source*: Duvall, 1977, p. 148.)

reaches a new developmental stage. As family members adapt to new circumstances and important roles shift, a new stage of development begins. Duvall (1977) has gone as far as to use census data to plot the time usually taken by an American family in each stage of the life cycle (see Figure 2-1).

Other researchers, using different criteria, have offered alternative models of the family life cycle. For example, Rodgers (1973) focused on the developmental tasks of both the oldest and youngest children within a family, and devised a 24-stage system. More recently, Nock (1979) and Aldous (1978), noting that other classification schemes focus on intact, two-parent nuclear

families, have emphasized the need for models that will be relevant for nontraditional family forms.

Aldous has devised a six-stage classification system for single-mother families that have experienced divorce. She uses three criteria: women's careers outside the home, their marital status, and the school careers of their children (see Table 2-3). The stage criteria for nuclear families would be applicable prior to the divorce. If a woman were already working outside the home at the time of her divorce, Stage II would be replaced by Stage III. This stage might be labeled "Women with Schoolchildren" if divorce occurred shortly after childbearing.

Table 2-3   Stages for single-parent families of divorced women

Stage I	Establishment of the single-parent family
Stage II	Women institute or reinstitute their work-life careers
Stage III	Women with adolescents
Stage IV	Women with young adults
Stage V	Women in the middle years
Stage VI	Retirement of women from work-life careers or from responsibilities as parents

Source: Aldous, 1978: 93.

Some families experience painful transition periods as they move from one stage to another; others seems to progress almost effortlessly from stage to stage. To account for such variations, Burr (1972) created the concept of "ease of transition." Rapoport (1963) identified four critical transitions, to which Hill (1971) added a fifth:

1. The crisis of marrying.
2. The crisis of first parenthood.
3. The crisis of deparentalization (added by Hill).
4. The crisis of launching or leavetaking.
5. The crisis of retirement and disengagement from leadership.

There are parallels between Rapoport's list of transitions and the Duvall-Hill model of the family life cycle. However, Rapoport's formulation has a unique advantage since it enables social scientists to give greater attention to the difficult transition between certain stages (Hill and Joy, 1980).

Many stages of the family life cycle persist over significant time spans. Even if one stage blends easily into another, each has distinctive qualities and challenges. Families in the same stage—whether nuclear families or alternate family forms—must face problems unlike those encountered in past stages of the family life cycle (Aldous, 1978).

Application of the Family Developmental and Life Cycle Perspective

The family development and life cycle perspective has numerous practical uses. A young couple planning for the future can anticipate specific demands and stresses that they are likely to experience during later stages. For example, in planning for the birth of their first child, they can discuss how they will deal with increased strain on their finances, their time alone, their relations with in-laws and friends, and so forth. Such conversations will in no way solve later problems, but they can effectively prepare a couple for difficulties that often arise.

Family counselors can also make use of the development and life cycle perspective. Louise and Sam Brooks, both in their early forties, decided to seek assistance because of frequent conflicts with their two teenage children. Counselor Diane Rodriguez helped all four family members to see that each was individually at a difficult developmental transition. Sam had just been promoted to a supervisory position in his factory and was uneasy about relationships with former peers. Louise had decided to leave her career as a dental assistant and apply to business school. Their elder daughter Sarah was in her senior year of high school and anxious about her college applications, while younger daughter Carol had transferred from a small private junior high school to a much larger public school. Through counseling, the Brooks family came to see that their tensions were heightened because they were simultaneously experiencing significant changes—most of which were associated with movement toward new stages of the family life cycle.

Without question, families differ in their ability to anticipate problems that will occur later in the life cycle. Nevertheless, family life education has become an increasingly popular and effective means of helping families to prepare for later transitions and crises. In many cases, it is comforting simply to realize that all families must eventually confront many of the same challenges as they move through the family life cycle.

Summary

The American family is currently in a period of significant change and transition. Many Americans feel that their personal needs are not being successfully met within the confines of traditional family arrangements. Consequently, some individuals have turned to alternate or "variant" family forms— among them the single-parent family, the stepfamily, the dual-worker family, cohabitation, and communal families. The single-parent family is currently the fastest growing family type in the United States. There has also been a striking rise in "dual-worker families" in which women work outside the home. In general, alternative family forms tend to reject constraints and to emphasize opportunities for their individual members.

Alternatives to the nuclear family have arisen in the midst of far-reaching social and economic changes in American society. These include the rising divorce rate, the relative affluence of recent decades, and the emergence of the women's liberation movement. Several studies have documented the continuing importance of the extended family in contemporary American life. Such relationships are especially important in a time of need.

Family social scientists use the tools and theories of contemporary social science in order to study people's relationships. In their use of the scientific method, they rely on concepts, variables, theories, and standard procedures of research. At present, there is no one theory that fully explains the relationships and dynamics of family life. Among the most influential theoretical frameworks used to study specific aspects of family behavior are the family ecological framework, the historical framework, the structure-function framework, the interactional framework, the exchange framework, and the developmental framework.

The family life cycle approach focuses on changes in the internal structure, organization, and interactions of the family. The concept of stage allows theorists and researchers to gain insight into the particular vulnerabilities of families during each stage of the life cycle.

Evelyn Duvall and Reuben Hill have developed the most frequently used system for categorizing family life into stages. Their eight-stage system rests on the assumption that interdependence among family members is common. Other researchers, using different criteria from those identified by Duvall and Hill, have offered alternative models of the family life cycle. Joan Aldous devised a six-stage classification system for single-mother families that have experienced divorce.

Discussion Questions

1. In your view, what is the most important function of the family? Why is this function more important than others?

2. American courts are becoming increasingly involved in what were formerly considered "family matters." For example, a wife in Oregon brought suit against her husband for rape; a 24-year-old son sued his parents for malpractice in parenting. Does it seem desirable to bring such matters into court? Should they be viewed instead as private family business?

3. What are the advantages and disadvantages of single-parent families, stepparent families, and dual-worker families? In answering, draw on your own personal experiences as a parent or child if you have lived in such family situations.

4. From the cocktail party to the college lecture hall, the ''state of the American family'' is a frequent topic of discussion. Some argue that the family is a dying institution, while others believe it will persist because it is the best way of coping with rapid social change. How do you feel about the future of the family? Why?

5. Have you ever lived in an extended family situation? What do you see as the benefits and drawbacks of this form of family life?

6. Researchers have found that families are more content during certain periods of the life cycle and more pressured during others. Which periods would you expect to be characterized by contentment? Which would you expect to be most pressured? Why? What has been your personal experience?

7. At what stage of the family life cycle are you? What are some of the unique satisfactions and stresses of this stage for you and for other family members?

Key Words

Affiliated Family	**Individual Time**	**Role Cluster**
Cohort	**Macrosystem**	**Role Sequence**
Concept	**Mesosystem**	**Scientific Method**
Exosystem	**Microsystem**	**Social Time**
Family Life Cycle	**Position**	**Stage**
Group Marriage	**Role**	**Variable**
Historical Time		

Suggested Readings

Bane, Mary Jo. *Here to Stay: American Families in the Twentieth Century*. New York: Basic Books, 1976. Provides helpful data on the stability of the family as an institution.

Bell, Robert R. *Worlds of Friendship*. Beverly Hills, Calif.: Sage Publications,* 1981. Explores gender-related variations in friendship patterns and variations in friendship during stages of the family life cycle.

*Here and elsewhere in this text we suggest readings published by Sage Publications, Inc. These may be obtained by writing to Sage at P.O. Box 5024, Beverly Hills, Calif., 90210.

Hill, Reuben. *Family Development in Three Generations*. Cambridge, Mass.: Schenkman, 1970. A classic study of Midwestern families which relies on interview data.

Seward, Rudy Ray. *The American Family: A Demographic History*. Beverly Hills, Calif.: Sage Library of Social Research, 1978. Traces the history of the American family from colonial times to the present, and offers some surprising and original conclusions.

Sex Roles: Challenge in Relationships

KEY TOPICS

—the meaning of sex roles—
—the influence of biological differences between the sexes—
—sex roles in other cultures—
—socialization into traditional sex roles—
—feminist critiques of socialization theories—
—how social class and racial background affect learned sex roles—
—traditional and egalitarian roles in family relationships—
—gender identity and the family life cycle—

Man for the field and woman for the hearth:
Man for the sword and the needle she:
Man with the head and woman with the heart:
Man to command and woman to obey:
All else confusion.

—Alfred, Lord Tennyson

Many, if not at all, of the personality traits
  which we have called masculine or feminine
are as lightly linked to sex as are the
clothing, the manners, and the form of
headdress that a society at any given period
assigns to either sex.

—Margaret Mead

How is it that this world has always belonged
  to the men?

—Simone de Beauvoir

A fourteen-year-old away at summer camp sent the following letter home:

Mom and Dad,

I played the game of my LIFE! All the guys were older than me. I was playing second base, batting first. Nothing went by me in the field. I caught flies, dove for grounders and caught bullet throws to the bag. . . .

I was up at bat four times. Once I hit a smash out to center which they caught, twice I walloped solid singles and once I got an R.B.I. which tied up the score. . . . I was playing my *best*! I wasn't nervous at all and I stopped feeling like I needed to prove myself.

The author of the letter was Abigail Pogrebin, the only girl in the game and the daughter of MS. Magazine founder and editor Letty Cottin Pogrebin (1980: 361).

Many Americans adhere to traditional notions that certain behavior is "masculine" (such as playing second base) and should be restricted to males, while other behavior is "feminine" and should be restricted to females. However, in the last two decades, feminists in the United States and other countries have been increasingly successful in challenging these traditional assumptions. Consequently, there has been not only a boom in women's sports (vividly symbolized by the first-ever running of a Women's Marathon in the 1984 Olympics), but also a growing tendency for both females and males to engage in behavior previously seen as inappropriate for their sex.

In this chapter, we will analyze the assumptions about sex-typed behavior that have governed expectations about men and women. We will describe the possible impact of biological differences on people's behavior, but will also emphasize that our feelings about "appropriate" behavior are learned in our families and from society. We will also provide a brief overview of the impact of sex roles on family relationships throughout the life cycle.

Sex Roles and Gender Identity

A role in a play is a part for an actor; it includes certain scripted actions, ways of walking, talking, expressing feelings, and so forth. A **sex role** is a part that an individual plays as a social actor—the patterns of feeling and behavior deemed appropriate or inappropriate because of her or his gender. The "script" comes from social expectations about masculine and feminine nature: men should be brave, strong, ambitious, and aggressive, while keeping their feelings under control; women should be gentle, nurturant, passive, dependent, and expressive of their feelings.

Sex roles are based on social **norms**—the agreed-upon standards of acceptable behavior within a society. These norms—such as the norms that men should keep their feelings under control and women should be passive—influence our judgments not only of others but also of ourselves. Thus, if you are male and prone to tears during highly emotional moments or female and likely to dominate classroom discussions and arguments, you may judge yourself harshly be-

Today many men and women refuse to accept traditional notions of sex roles.

B O X   3 - 1

Research Brief:
Do Women's Relationships with Their Fathers and Mothers Influence
Their Feelings About Traditional Marital Roles?

William H. McBroom, a sociologist from the University of Montana, Missoula, was interested in examining the impact of a woman's relationships with her parents and her social class background on her attitude toward traditional sex roles. He selected a sample of 148 single women students at the University of Montana whose median age was 20.4 years. Each respondent filled out a questionnaire concerning her childhood relationships with her mother and father, her socioeconomic status, and her feelings about stereotyped expectations concerning men and women.

- Researchers found no systematic relationship between the women's sex-role attitudes and their social class backgrounds.
- If a woman has not had a good relationship with her father, she is likely to reject the traditional sex-role orientation. If she has had a good relationship with him, she is as likely to accept traditional sex-role elements as she is to reject them.

- In contrast to relationships with fathers, women's relationships with their mothers seem to have little impact on their sex-role orientation.
- The only pronounced effect of social class is seen among women who had good childhood relationships with their fathers. For such women, the lower their socioeconomic background, the more traditional are their sex-role attitudes.

McBroom concludes that the childhood relationship between women and their fathers appears to be the central factor in their later sex-role orientation. "While not serving as role models in the narrow sense, fathers are an important source of role influence for their daughters, particularly where there are good personal relationships between father and daughter" (p. 1032).

Source: William H. McBroom, "Parental Relationships, Socioeconomic Status, and Sex-Role Expectations," *Sex Roles*, 1981, 7 (10).

cause you have internalized traditional sex-role assumptions. Sex roles, then, are part of our concept of ourselves, our **gender identity** (Feldman, 1980).

Sex roles are of great interest to psychologists, sociologists, and other social scientists. Psychologists focus primarily on "inner" personality traits and stereotypes associated with femininity and masculinity, while sociologists emphasize patterns of "outer" behavior or interaction in society. For example, a sociologist studying the paid labor force of the United States would note that most truck drivers are male while most nurses are female. Family sociologists have

studied the inclination of judges in child custody cases to assume that mothers are innately better at parenting than fathers. Box 3-1 details a recent study of parental relationships, socioeconomic status, and sex-role expectations.

The Cause of Sex Roles: Biology or Culture?

How do gender differences come about? Do sex roles result from biological differences between the sexes? Or do women and men

What is the probability that this young girl and her classmates will grow up scoring less well on mathematics achievement tests than their male counterparts?

learn to behave differently because of the effects of culture and society?

We know that women as a group score consistently lower than men as a group on mathematics and science achievement tests. (Notice that we said ''as a group''; some women score extremely high, while some men score extremely low. But women's average scores are consistently somewhat lower than men's average scores.)

Does this mean that women's brains function differently than men's, that they are not as equipped to do math problems? Does it mean that the male power structure—which for so long prohibited women from receiving any type of formal education—is still inhibiting women in the traditionally male preserves of math and science? Or is it that women lose interest in these subjects because

they fear that achievement in math and science will make them less attractive to men?

In short, are traditional sex roles the result of ''nature'' (biological differences), ''nurture'' (culture and socialization), or some combination of both?

Genetics: The Biological Evidence

No one disputes that there are biological differences between the sexes. The controversy arises, however, when we try to establish links between these biological differences and the behavior of men and women. Specifically, does biology limit the potential achievements of one or both sexes?

Men and women differ in their genetic structure. Women have two ''X'' **chromosomes**; men have one ''X'' and one ''Y'' chromosome. The complex links between genes and behavior are now being researched; it is impossible to say at this time how differences in chromosome structure may affect women's and men's behavior. We do know that genetic structure determines physical development. The average male is taller, heavier, and more muscular than the average female. Women develop breasts and can bear and nurse children; men cannot.

It is not unreasonable to assume that men did the hunting and heavier physical labor in earlier societies because they were better suited to do so, while women raised the children because they could breast-feed them and food was scarce. Perhaps these differing behavioral patterns for women and men in such societies were the result of **adaptation**; that is, the traits helped them to survive and reproduce at a time when subsistence was a full-time job. But should these differences matter in an industrialized era in which most heavy labor is done by machines and even the fighting of wars relies on sophisticated technology?

Researchers have speculated that certain

behavioral differences are due to male and female **hormones**. Both men and women produce the male hormone, androgen, and the female hormone, estrogen, but in differing quantities. The male embryo's "Y" chromosome gives a "command" to release androgen at specific stages of **prenatal** development. The hormone signals the embryo to develop as a male, with male body shape and male sexual organs. Later on, hormones influence bodily changes during puberty; for example, androgen gives signals to the male's body for the growth of facial and body hair and for the deepening of the voice.

Thus, hormones clearly play a role in human physical development. But what effect do they have on emotional development and actual behavior? Again, this question is still being debated and studied. Some research shows that the male hormone testosterone appears to stimulate aggressive behavior in female animals. At the same time, a female hormone, prolactin, seems to stimulate nurturing, motherly activity in male animals (Rose, et al., 1972).

John Money and his colleagues have conducted studies on those rare individuals known as **hermaphrodites** who are a mixture of male and female biology. The researchers have looked, for example, at girls who received more androgen at birth than is normal for females. While genetically they were girls with XX chromosomes, they behaved more like our society expects boys to act. That is, they enjoyed rough games, were physically active, and preferred toy trucks to dolls. Money speculates that early exposure to the male hormone influenced the behavior of these girls (Money and Ehrhardt, 1972).

Hormones may also have an impact on certain differences in brain functions. Jerre Levy of the University of Chicago has found differences in the way male and female brains are organized. In Levy's view, men's brains work in such a way as to give them superior visual-spatial skills, while women's brains may give them an advantage in verbal skills (Durden-Smith, 1980). Men are therefore better at dealing with abstract concepts; women are more effective in picking up information from the surrounding environment about people, sounds, and so forth. These brain differences may result from the release of certain hormones at critical periods of prenatal development.

From the point of view of human evolution, such differences make sense. Men were the hunters and needed good visual skills. In addition, they had to be extremely goal-oriented to succeed in their work. Women lived in groups and took care of children and the sick; thus, sensitivity to others was a crucial skill. As noted earlier, the development of these patterns had an adaptive value in terms of survival and reproduction (Durden-Smith, 1980).

Still, we must emphasize that the research on hormonal effects remains at an early and primitive stage. The biological differences between the sexes which exist serve only as loose boundaries within which culturally learned differences appear. For example, while prenatal exposure to androgen may have predisposed the girls in Money's study toward more aggressive, "boyish" behavior, they also needed a social environment that would encourage (or at least allow) such behavior.

Estelle Ramey (1973) points out that while men and women vary as groups in their respective levels of male and female hormones, there can also be striking hormonal differences between one man and another or one woman and another. Ramey stresses that these individual differences in levels of testosterone, estrogen, and other hormones are much more significant than any generalized differences between the sexes.

Thus, while the biological basis for sex-related distinctions is important, the role that society and culture play is probably more significant. Our biological nature may be like a rough piece of stone from which society, like a sculptor, chisels, sharpens, and defines the shapes of male and female behavior. Research in the next decade should begin to clarify the complex interrelationship of genetic and hormonal differences, environmental influences, and the behavior of women and men.

Culture: The Anthropological Evidence

How, then, does society shape differences between men and women? Cross-cultural studies, generally conducted by anthropologists, have shown that the typical behavior of males and females in other cultures is quite different from traditional ''masculine'' and ''feminine'' behavior in the United States.

Margaret Mead, in her pioneering anthropological study, *Sex and Temperament in Three Primitive Societies* (1933), observed three distinct tribes in New Guinea. She found that one of them, the Arapesh, expected both women and men to be warm, cooperative, and nurturing, and generally to exhibit traits that we have traditionally described as ''feminine.'' By contrast, among the Mundugumor tribe, both sexes exhibit traits seen as ''masculine'' in American society: they were aggressive, competitive, and prone to fighting and controversy. Finally, in the Tchambuli tribe, the character traits seemed the reverse of those expected under our traditional norms. Women were dominant, controlling, and hardworking, while men were emotionally dependent, irresponsible, and extremely concerned about personal appearance. Mead's famous study is often cited by those who argue against the view that biology is the cause of sex differences. If biological distinctions dictate our behavior, they argue, then how can one explain the vast differences in the lives of the Arapesh,

the Mundugumor, and the Tchambuli—not to mention the difference between these three cultures and our own?

Anthropologists have also noted that a power dynamic is often attached to sex-role distinctions. In early societies, men's role as hunters and warriors gave them more prestige than women. With that prestige came power: men could distribute food for the entire community and determine its social structure. By contrast, women's influence was limited mainly to the domestic sphere. They were not really participants in the public sphere and gained few rights (Rosaldo and Lamphere, 1974).

In societies where women control their economic well-being, they develop more power. Anthropologist Peggy Sanday (1973) has illustrated this pattern through her study of the Afikpo Ibo women of Nigeria. Ibo men had traditionally controlled money and tribal social life because they grew the yam crop—a main source of food with important religious significance. When the tribe increased its contact with European cultures, the cassava plant (used for tapioca) was introduced to them.

The Ibo men disdained the new plant, preferring to continue growing the religiously valued yam. However, they permitted women to cultivate the cassava and to keep any profits from its sale. Subsequently, the cassava proved to be extremely lucrative, and the Ibo women became financially independent. With financial independence, the women became less subservient to their husbands and a more powerful force within tribal culture.

Society: Learning Evidence

How do we learn society's standards about appropriate behavior for each sex? Socialization is the general term used to describe the process of learning social roles. Most differences between females and males are learned through family interactions, socialization in schools, and the mass media.

Social learning theory holds that children are rewarded for conforming to their parents' expectations and are punished for behavior that meets with disapproval. Thus, Johnny's parents beam with pride when he shows prowess on the basketball court, but gasp with horror if he displays an interest in becoming a dancer. Johnny learns to act "like a boy" in order to please his parents.

In 1983, Sally Ride became a role model for many young American girls when she became the United States' first female astronaut in space.

The process of differential treatment of girls and boys begins the minute children are born. Adults describe infant girls as "delicate," "sweet," or "dainty" and hold them more carefully. By contrast, boys are perceived as more active and are described as "bouncing," "sturdy," or "handsome" (Papalia and Olds, 1979). As toddlers and preschoolers, children learn that baseball and trucks are for boys while dolls and "dressing up" are for girls.

A study by Judith G. Tudiver (1980) demonstrated the differential socialization of preschool-age children. Both mothers and fathers tended to be permissive and supportive with daughters, but did not feel that daughters needed to achieve or perform. However, parents of sons stressed the importance of achievement and independence. Fathers, in particular, were extremely concerned about socializing sons into a rather rigid definition of the masculine role. Tudiver (1980: 44) concludes that "a great deal of pressure" is associated with the socialization of sons, which "probably reflects the high value associated with being male in our society."

Children and adolescents are influenced by the role models available in a society. If they see that most doctors, police officers, and U.S. Senators are male, while most nurses, secretaries, and early childhood teachers are female, they will begin to draw conclusions about which jobs are for them and which are not. "Real-life" role models affect children's thinking; so, too, do the role models presented in literature (including comics and children's books), film, and television.

In a 1979 report, the U.S. Commission on Civil Rights was highly critical of television stereotyping of women and minorities. The report (1979: 61) concluded:

Female characters are far more likely than male characters to be portrayed as having no identifiable occupation. When they are shown in an occupation, it is most frequently as a secretary, nurse, homemaker, household worker, or student.

The commission also noted that women were frequently seen less than fully clothed in sexually exploitive roles. Actress Kathleen Nolan, former president of the Screen Actors Guild, has stated: "Women . . . are desperately disheartened to be faced . . . with the disgraceful trash . . . being transmitted in the guise that this is the American woman" (*Broadcasting*, June 5, 1978: 55).

Feminist Critique: Sex Roles and Social Control

Jessie Bernard, a feminist sociologist, has suggested that theories about sex roles which emphasize the role of socialization tend to let the power structure off the hook too easily. In Bernard's view, power and control are the real motives behind the division of sex roles. Since the male sex role has higher status, men attain power over women and gain control of many of society's valued rewards.

Bernard (1975: 17) argues that socialization theorists make this male-dominated power structure seem respectable and reasonable, and are too complacent about the denial of equal opportunities to women. She believes that these theorists are saying, in effect, to women:

Sorry, girls, too bad you haven't got what it takes. . . . I know it isn't your fault, I know it's just the way you were socialized as a child. You'd be just as superior as I am if you had played with trucks instead of dolls. But what can I do about it after all?

Bernard and other feminists are critical of socialization research because it fails to challenge the power structure that keeps women and men in unequal and prescribed roles.

Barbara Bovee Polk (1974: 418–419) has offered a useful summary of the feminist "power analysis" of sex roles and cultural differences between men and women:

1. Men have power and privilege by virtue of their sex.
2. It is in men's interest to maintain that power and privilege.
3. Men occupy and actively exclude women from positions of economic and political power in society.
4. Although most males are also oppressed by the system under which we live, they are not oppressed, as females are, *because* of their sex.
5. Feminine roles and cultural values are the product of oppression. Idealization of them is dysfunctional to change (see Box 3–2).

Feminists believe that traditional sex roles are used to keep women in their (disadvantaged) place. In the view of Letty Cottin Pogrebin (1980: 40), the messages of sex role stereotypes can be condensed into two simple propositions: boys are better, and girls are meant to be mothers.

Social Class, Race, and Socialization

The social status and racial or ethnic background of a family will have significant impact on the ways in which children are socialized into sex roles. Lillian Breslow Rubin (1976: 126) has described the vivid contrast between the socialization of boys in middle-class and working-class homes:

Not once in a professional middle-class home did I see a young boy shake his father's hand in a well-taught "manly" gesture as he bid him good night. Not once did I hear a middle-class parent scornfully—or even sympathetically—call a crying boy a sissy or in any way reprimand him for his tears. Yet, these were not uncommon observations in the working-class homes I visited. In-

B O X   3 - 2

Working-Class Women's Antifeminism

In her book, *Worlds of Pain*, Lillian Breslow Rubin (1976: 131–132) documented a difficult yet memorable conversation with a working-class woman about the feminist movement. The conversation began with Rubin asking her what she knew about the movement, and the woman replying: ''I don't know anything about it, and I don't care to know either.''

''You sound angry at the women's movement.''

''That's right, I am. I don't like women who want to be men. Those libbers, they want men and women to be just alike, and I don't want that to happen. I think men should be men and women should be women. They're crazy not to appreciate what men do for women. I like my husband to open the car door for me and to light my cigarettes. It makes me feel like a lady.''

Rubin interjects that many women used the same words in interviews: ''I like a man to open the car door and light my cigarettes.'' Admittedly perplexed by the repeated emphasis on these two behaviors, Rubin asked this woman: ''When was the last time your husband opened a car door for you or lit your cigarette?''

At first, the woman was startled by the question and her face became filled with color. But she quickly threw her head back, began laughing, and replied: ''I've gotta admit, I don't know why I said that. I don't even smoke.''

Rubin observes: ''Of course she doesn't know why. To know would mean she'd have to face her fears and anxieties more squarely, to recognize that in some important ways the movement speaks to the issues that plague and pain her in her marriage. If, instead, she can reach for the stereotypes, she need not deal with the reality that . . . her own discontent is an example of what so many women out there are talking about.''

deed, . . . even as young as six or seven, the working-class boys seemed more emotionally controlled—more like miniature men—than those in the middle-class families.

What accounts for this difference? John Scanzoni (1975), a sociologist who specializes in the study of sex roles, suggests that working-class parents enjoy limited employment opportunities and generally are restricted to jobs that demand conformity. By contrast, more affluent parents have benefited from greater educational opportunities and have developed a wider sense of human potentials. They are more likely to emphasize reasoning and discussion in interactions with their children, and to encourage both sons and daughters to express their feelings and achieve in school.

For members of minority groups, such as blacks or Native Americans, there are often ''double binds'' in sex-role socialization. For example, like white children, black children learn that men are expected to be the achievers in society. But they also learn that achievement is denied to black men regardless of their abilities or aspirations. An all-pervasive racism has forced black men into low-paying, low-status jobs and has constantly reinforced their powerlessness. Thus, the double bind: if you are ''really a man,'' you will be strong and successful, but if you are black it will not be possible to realize these goals (Cazenave, 1979).

Interestingly, black families are accustomed to the dual-worker pattern and tend to be much more flexible in terms of sex-role divisions than whites are. Black women have always had to work outside the home—first through the demands of slaveowners and later in the cities in order to support their families. In certain situations, black women were viewed as less threatening than black men and were more successful in finding work. Consequently, in defiance of sex-role stereotypes, black women have often displayed such characteristics as strength, initiative, and independence.

Clearly, the meaning and impact of sex roles are defined by the overall social structure of a society. While general stereotypes about females and males will influence the socialization of all children, there will nevertheless be differences in socialization based on one's social class and racial or ethnic background.

Sex Roles and Family Relationships

Sex roles have an impact not only on individual development, but also on the interactions between husbands, wives, and children. The sex-role orientation of various family members may be a major source of strain—especially if some adhere to traditional norms about sex roles while others prefer more egalitarian arrangements. It should be noted that social scientific research on the impact of sex roles is just beginning; the results to date are far from conclusive.

Traditional Sex Roles and Family Relationships

Larry Feldman (1980) of the Center for Family Studies at the Family Institute of Chicago has carefully reviewed current research on sex roles and family relationships. Feldman concludes that sex-role learning has a negative influence on intimate relationships because it inhibits the full range of emotional expression and interaction.

For example, men who accept the traditional masculine role have difficulty expressing feelings of love, joy, and sadness. They also find it hard to seek and receive emotional, physical, and financial assistance from their wives and children. Acceptance of help will be seen as an admission of weakness and therefore "unmasculine." Women with a traditional sex-role orientation have difficulty asserting themselves to get what they want and need. They may react to problems in an emotional manner and fail to develop useful problem-solving skills.

It is easy to see how these patterns could affect marital relationships. Ruesch and his colleagues (1974) studied the interactions between wives and husbands during arguments and found that each sex made roughly the same number of "rejecting" statements ("My mother always said that you'd never amount to anything"). However, the researchers also learned that husbands made three times as many reconciling or resolving statements, such as apologies or suggestions for compromise. Inhibited by traditional sex roles, the wives reacted emotionally—which sometimes limited productive communication and problem-solving.

Feldman suggests that members of a couple can reinforce or encourage each other in their sex-typed behavior. A husband may fail to share his feelings of love or frustration, and his wife will then complain about how "he never talks to me." He, in turn, comes to view her as a "nag" and becomes even less communicative. As the cycle of conflict deepens, each spouse clings more fiercely to the traditional sex roles they learned during childhood.

Confining sex-role expectations can restrict a couple's sexual relationship. One evening Anna felt like making love with her husband Joe and considered trying to take the initiative. But then she worried: "Am I turning into an unfeminine, aggressive woman? Women aren't supposed to take the lead in sex. Will he think I'm terrible?'' So she sat back and watched television instead.

What if Anna had given in to her impulses? How would Joe have reacted? He might have been threatened by her behavior, thinking that ''it's my job to get sex started between us. Doesn't she think I'm man enough anymore?'' Joe might act cool or even rejecting, which would discourage Anna from taking the lead again. His reaction would reinforce her fears about being ''unfeminine''; her subsequent lack of initiative would substantiate his view that ''it's better when the man is in control.'' As we can see, Anna's and Joe's beliefs about appropriate sex roles set limits on their sexual interactions.

Rigid sex roles not only reduce the positive potential of human interactions; they sometimes lead to real emotional or physical harm. Women may engage in manipulative behavior because they do not feel able to openly assert themselves in more honest and positive ways. If Joe insists that he and he alone will make all decisions about whether he and Anna will go to the movies—and about which film they will see—Anna's only option may be to convince Joe that her preferences are actually his.

Some men, in applying the male sex role of strength and dominance, use violence to assert their control over women and children (Coleman, 1980). One husband, reflecting on how he felt before a violent fight with his wife, explained: ''I wanted her to come and sit by me when I watched the football game on TV. . . . I just wanted her there, and she wouldn't stay. I thought, 'She's my wife, and she has to be here when I say so.' '' Psychologists label such behavior ''dysfunctional'' because it causes harm and disturbs the functioning of the marriage and family.

The parent-child relationship can also be restricted by traditional sex roles. For example, studies have revealed that while mothers hold their infant children as often as fathers, they have different reasons for doing so. Mothers hold children to feed them, cuddle them, or nurture them in some way; fathers mainly hold children to play with them. Mothers committed to a nurturing role may later find it difficult to discipline children, whereas fathers may feel comfortable roughhousing with children but be unable to offer warmth and affection. Again, confining sex roles limit parents' relationships with their children (Lamb, 1977[ab]; Nye, 1976).

Changing Sex Roles and Family Relationships

The changes in the status of American women over the past 25 years have had an enormous impact on family relationships. In 1980, 70 percent of all Americans stated that they would vote for a qualified woman for President of the United States (Gallup, 1980). Today, the majority of women with children work outside the home; they are found in all types of occupations. As Figure 3-1 demonstrates, there has been a dramatic increase in the proportion of women found in such male-dominated jobs as bartending, pharmacy, law, and engineering. Women now expect to join the nation's paid labor force. While they work because of economic rewards, they also want the lift for their self-esteem that such employment provides (General Mills American Family Report, 1981; Prial, 1982).

Sociologist John Scanzoni (Scanzoni and Fox, 1980) has noted that women in the paid labor force have adopted a new attitude toward family life. Traditionally, women have been expected to put the family before their own personal achievements and say, ''When the family does well, I do well.'' However, as women move into the labor force—and especially into demanding careers—they have adopted the traditional male attitude of ''If I do well, the family does well.''

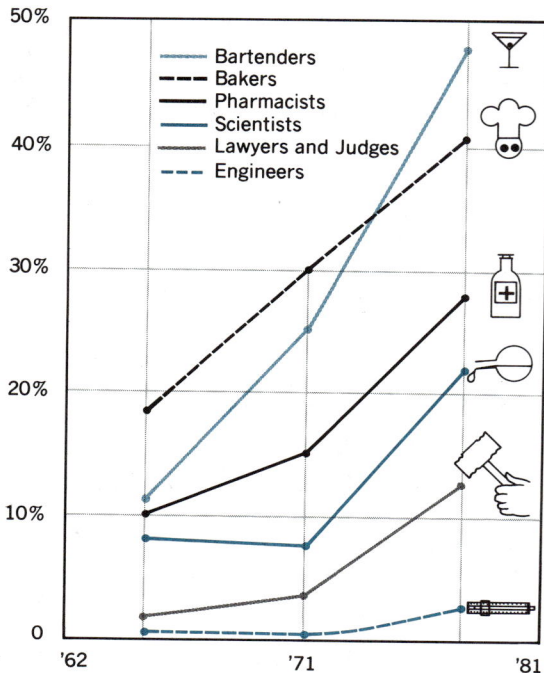

Figure 3-1 Women in traditionally male jobs. The figure shows women as a percentage of the total employed in each group. (*Source: The New York Times*, November 15, 1982.)

Unfortunately but predictably, this shift in attitudes has brought increased conflict to American families. As women's roles have changed, lines of authority and responsibility are no longer clear. It is no longer automatic, for example, for men to pay bills or women to do the laundry. Even when a family is inclined to reallocate roles in a more egalitarian way, there is no fixed model of an egalitarian family that people can follow. The resulting uncertainty adds to the conflict, confusion, and stress of family life (McCubbin, 1979).

Reuben Hill (1978: 62) points out that male scientists, scholars, and other high-level professionals are committed to an inflexible belief system that mandates 60 or more hours of work per week and leaves lit-

tle room for family responsibilities. Hill quotes from the diary of a Boston University colleague who found it difficult to share family duties with his physician-wife:

I resented that degree of involvement; it seemed to interfere terribly with the work I wanted to achieve. I found such duties a drain of my time, which could be devoted to other more rewarding things.

Given the persistence of such attitudes, it is not surprising that when wives enter the paid labor force, husbands do not significantly increase the amount of time they devote to child-care and household tasks.

Family counselors report that many clients are finding it hard to overcome childhood socialization and adapt to changing sex roles. Let us examine the example of John and Marie Williams. Marie has recently gone back to her career as a travel agent after raising three children, the youngest of whom is in first grade. But two of the children are having trouble in school, and conflicts between Marie and John have become more frequent and bitter.

Marie feels guilty about "neglecting" her children, but at the same time is thrilled to be back doing work that she finds rewarding. Nevertheless, John wants Marie to quit her job and blames the children's difficulties on her. He insists that the family doesn't need her income—even though their debts have increased and the car needs major repairs. Perhaps more significantly, John feels jealous of Marie's dealings with other men at her job.

The counselor has helped this couple to reexamine their views about proper family roles. John now admits that he feels threatened by Marie's career: "Sometimes I think I'm less of a man because my wife is earning good money as a travel agent. I worry that I'm losing my authority in the family." Marie, recalling an argument that occurred one night as John was cooking dinner, ad-

Sex role decisions, such as who comforts a hurt child, may require daily review and debate as lines of authority and responsibility are no longer clear-cut.

mits that she, too, feels scared about change: "I guess I still feel guilty about going to work. When I saw him cooking, I wanted him to mess the whole thing up. I wanted the kids to see that only I could make us a good meal."

Psychologist Sandra Bem (1975) describes the adjustment Marie and John are making as learning "androgynous" role orientations. The term **androgynous** means both male and female. It comes from the Greek words *andros* (meaning male) and *gyne* (meaning female). Androgynously oriented males can express their feelings well and are more nurturant than traditionally masculine men. Androgynously-oriented women are more likely to be assertive, skilled at problem-solving, and self-reliant than women with a traditional sex-role orientation. A sociological perspective on androgyny emphasizes the sharing of both work and family responsibilities by husband and wives (Feldman, 1980; Orlofsky and Windle, 1978).

Why do certain parents accept the androgynous model? John DeFrain (1979) interviewed 122 androgynous parents in Lancaster County, Nebraska; all participated in marriages in which neither spouse was responsible for more than 60 percent of all family child-care time. Parents reported that they shared child-care duties because:

- They believed children would benefit if both parents were equally involved in child-care.
- Wives were working outside the home for financial reasons and wished to continue.
- Wives were dissatisfied with the full-time role of homemaker and wanted careers outside the home.
- Husbands believed that their wives were more interesting when they worked outside the home.
- Husbands loved their wives and wished to relieve them of the burden of full-time child-care.

Significantly, 57 percent of the androgynous parents described themselves as professionals such as attorneys, bankers, professors, and accountants. In terms of political views, the vast majority described themselves as liberals (30 percent) or moderates (47 percent).

As American attitudes toward traditional sex roles have changed, there has been a corresponding change in government policy on family-related issues. In response to women's growing economic independence, new legislation has been passed to prohibit the

B O X   3 – 3

Research Brief:
Does How a Woman Defines Her Sex Role Influence Her Level of Stress and Coping?

Joan Patterson and Hamilton McCubbin of the University of Minnesota were interested in examining the relationship between a woman's sex role orientation, how she coped with a major source of stress, and the level of stress she experienced. Eighty-two wives of Navy aviators who were on an eight-month deployment were interviewed three times: before, during, and after the separation. The researchers were interested in looking at differences between wives with higher than average masculine traits *and* higher than average feminine traits (androgynous women) compared to women who scored low on either or both masculinity and femininity.

- There was no difference between androgynous and nonandrogynous women in the amount of stress they experienced as a result of the separation.

- However, androgynous wives used a wider variety of coping behaviors to manage the stressful situation. The use of this more balanced coping repertoire was associated with wives experiencing lower levels of stress.

- The coping strategies that worked best to lower the level of stress resulting from separation were "developing self-reliance and self-esteem" and "being optimistic and accepting the military lifestyle."

The authors concluded that an androgynous sex-role orientation has an indirect effect on lowering stress. Women who are high in both femininity and masculinity seem better able to employ a wide range of coping behaviors.

Source: Patterson and McCubbin, 1984.

---

denial of credit on the basis of sex. Sex discrimination has been outlawed in many types of jobs, and some employers have responded to government pressure by adopting "equal opportunity" and "affirmative action" programs aimed at increasing employment of women and minorities. Even laws already on the books—such as regulations governing social security and employer-sponsored retirement plans—are being reexamined to see if they discriminate against women.

Sex Roles and the Family Life Cycle

Changes in traditional roles have reshaped family life during every stage of the life cycle. Our concept of our gender identity influences the type of partner we choose, our career and family goals, and our behavior within intimate relationships. If we are committed to androgynous and egalitarian values, it will certainly affect our decisions and priorities. Even our ability to cope with stress may be enhanced or limited to some degree, depending on our sex-role orientation (see Box 3–3).

Table 3–1 highlights the sex-role issues that are evident throughout major transitions in the family life cycle. Some of these issues must be faced again and again as families encounter new developmental challenges. For example, a traditionally minded couple may decide that the wife will do all the cooking and cleaning, but may be forced to reevaluate this agreement if she later becomes unhappy and overburdened. A more

Table 3–1 Sex-role issues and the family life cycle

Transition 1: Choosing relationship	Transition 2: Marriage	Transition 3: Having children	Transition 4: Middle and later years
How will relationship affect personal options?	*Dividing responsibilities* for earning income and household tasks—who does what?		
What kind of partnership—traditional or egalitarian?	*Power*—who makes decisions?		
	Learning to be expressive of feelings and autonomous		
	Deciding when and if to have children		
	Conflict—whose job and time are more important?	*Dividing responsibilities* for child care	
		Teaching children gender roles	
			Learning to express feelings to children, *learning to discipline*
			Adjusting to new social roles: retirement and empty nest

androgynous couple may switch to rather traditional arrangements after the birth of its first child. Sex-role decisions are rarely final; the question of who does the dishes may require daily review and debate.

We will develop many of these sex-role issues throughout subsequent chapters of this textbook. For the moment, it is important to identify sex-role division as a key concept in understanding how and why families change during the family life cycle. Most of us may have been given blue or pink blankets as babies, depending on our sex. But times have changed, and gender-based distinctions are being questioned as never before.

Summary

Sex roles are those patterns of behavior and ways of feeling deemed appropriate for men and for women. They are based on social norms or expectations, agreed-upon standards of behavior. Sex roles have a sociological aspect, focusing on patterns of "outer" behavior or interaction in a society, and a psychological aspect, focusing on "inner" personality traits and stereotypes.

Sex roles develop primarily through learning. There are genetic and hormonal differences between men and women, but the precise impact of these differences on human behavior is still being studied. Cross-cultural studies reveal that sex roles differ widely in different societies. Social learning theory emphasizes that children learn sex roles by being rewarded for "appropriate" behavior and punished for behavior that violates traditional norms. Feminist scholars have criticized socialization research because it fails to challenge the male-dominated power structure.

Sex-role learning varies depending on one's social class and racial or ethnic background. Traditional sex-role orientations can have a negative impact on family relationships because they limit acceptable emotional expression and behavior for each sex. However, the changing roles of women and men have created uncertainty and even conflict as families redivide responsibility for household tasks, child-care, and earning a living. Many individuals are striving for an androgynous role orientation that allows people to go beyond traditional notions of masculinity and femininity.

Developmental Task   A Personal Profile: *Sex Roles and You*

For each of the ten characteristics listed below, decide how well it describes you. Circle 1 for TRUE if it describes you well. Circle 0 for FALSE if it does not describe you.

	TRUE	FALSE
1. I am very independent	1	0
2. I can express my emotions easily	1	0
3. I seldom give up easily	1	0
4. I am very sensitive and responsive to the feelings of others	1	0
5. I feel challenged to master difficult tasks	1	0
6. It is important to me to be kind and gentle to others	1	0
7. I am very helpful to others	1	0
8. I stand up well under pressure	1	0
9. I feel confident about my ability to get things done	1	0
10. I am able to devote myself completely to others	1	0

Add up the numbers you circled to get your score.

SCORE = 8–10   You have a nontraditional sex role orientation since you score high on both masculine and feminine attributes. This is often called an ANDROGYNOUS sex-role orientation.

SCORE = 0-7   You have a more traditional FEMININE sex-role orientation if you scored TRUE for items 2, 4, 6, 7, 10.

You have a more traditional MASCULINE sex-role orientation if you scored TRUE for items 1, 3, 5, 8, 9.

Discussion Questions

1. How do you feel about the "nature versus nurture" controversy? Would you side with those who stress the primary importance of biological influences? With those who believe that environmental influences are dominant? Or would you reject the "either-or" quality that this debate sometimes shows?

2. Many American mothers and fathers are currently taking on social roles that were formerly the exclusive domain of the opposite sex. How do you think this will influence the development and sex-role orientations of their children? How do you feel about this trend?

3. What conflicts do you see as likely to occur as women and men move toward "androgynous" role orientations?

4. As a woman or man, how have changing sex roles affected your personal and family relationships? Do you consider these changes positive or negative?

5. One often hears the expression, "Viva la différence," used in comparing men and women. Do you think this expression is appropriate in such discussions? Why?

Key Words

Adaptation	**Hermaphrodite**	**Sex Roles**
Androgynous	**Hormones**	**Social Learning**
Chromosome	**Norms**	**Theory of Sexual**
Gender Identity	**Prenatal**	**Identity**

Suggested Readings

Johnson, Marian F., and Stockard, Jean. *Sex Inequality and Sex Role Development*. Englewood Cliffs, N.J.: Prentice-Hall, 1980. Uses theories and data from several disciplines to explain sex roles and sexual inequality in the United States and around the world.

Kacerquis, Mary Ann, and Adams, Gerald R. "Implications of sex-typed childrearing practices, toys and mass media materials in restricting occupational choices of women." *The Family Coordinator*, 1979, *28*, 369–375. Reviews gender stereotyping and agrees that female aspirations and occupational choices are limited by stereotypic practices.

Kitano, Harry H.L., and Kikumiera, Akermi. "The Japanese-American family." In Endo, Russali, et al. (ed.), *Asian-Americans: Social and Psychological Perspectives. Volume II*. Palo Alto, Calif.: Science and Behavior Books, Inc., 1980. Shows how American immigrant families adapt traditional sex roles in new surroundings.

Mirante, A. "A reinterpretation of role dominance in the Chicano family." *The Family Coordinator*, 1979, *28* (4), 473–479. Uses research data to challenge the stereotypic view of sex roles among Chicanos.

Schaffer, Kay F. *Sex Roles and Human Behavior.* Cambridge, Mass.: Winthrop, 1981. Uses historical and theoretical perspectives and looks at the development of gender roles; discusses the benefits and disadvantages of traditional and alternative roles.

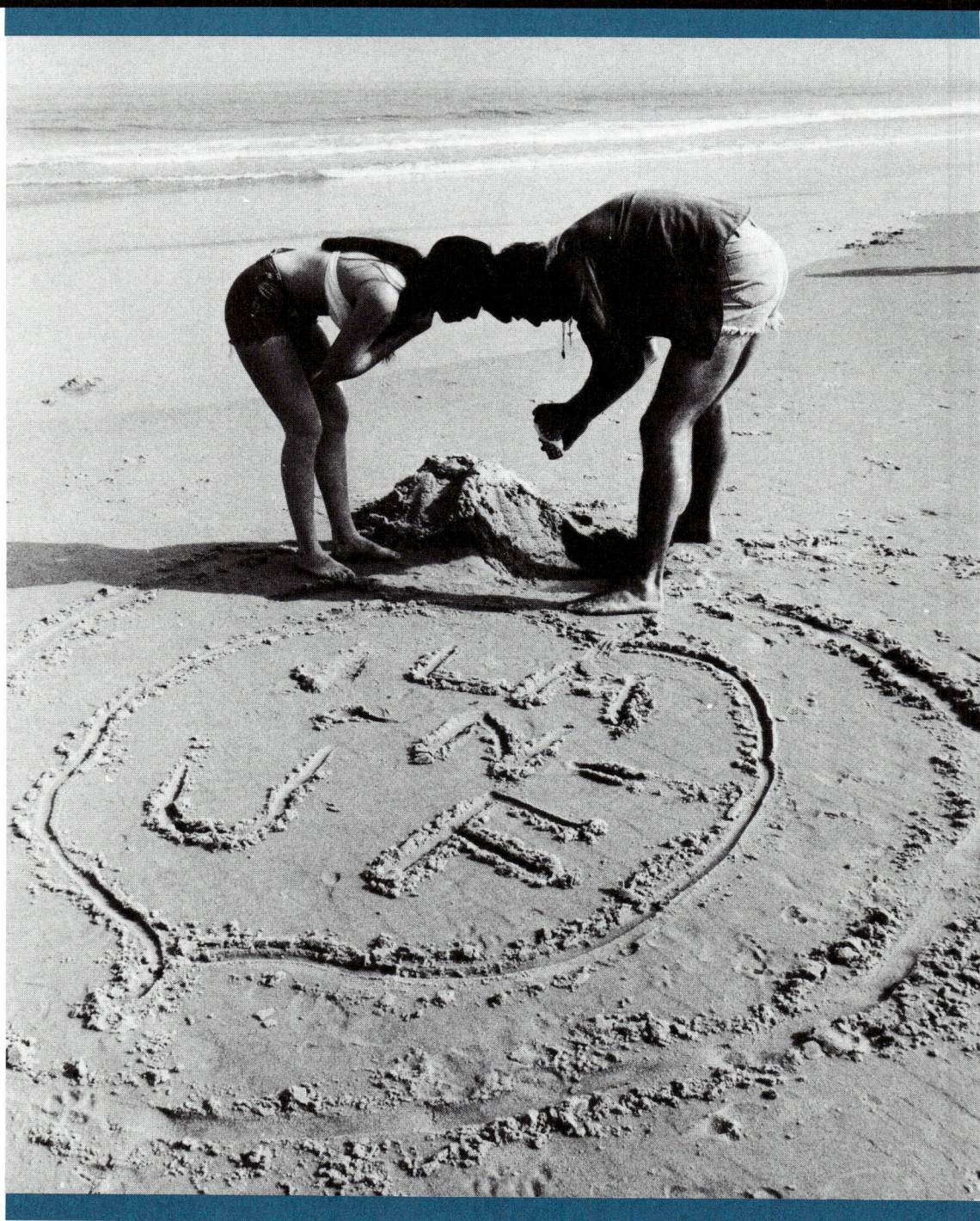

Loving Relationships: The Search for Intimacy

KEY TOPICS

—why we seek loving relationships—
—the nature of intimacy and support—
—how love is learned—
—what it means to ''fall in love''—
—different styles of loving—
—how men and women love—
—the role of self-esteem in relationships—

Gwen, a 24-year-old accountant, has been married two months. ''I'm afraid I made a terrible mistake in marrying Phil,'' she confesses, tears welling up in her eyes. ''He's so possessive. He doesn't want me to spend a minute alone or with my friends. But, when we're together, he hardly pays attention to me. I really love him, but I'm getting more and more frustrated.''

Andrew, a 26-year-old actor, grins from ear to ear when he talks about Sarah. ''She's terrific! I feel we really click. I mean, I've never felt this way before. Sometimes, when I see her, I'm so happy I want to burst. I must be in love.''

For Gwen, love is a source of misery; for Andrew, it is pure delight. This one emotion is a tangle of contrasts, conflicts, and contradictions. It brings us the highest, soaring pleasures and the sharpest pain. It is the greediest of feelings, demanding more and more of the loved person, yet it is also the essence of giving. While most of us—like Gwen and Andrew—speak of love as a response to another person, the way we love reveals a great deal about how we feel about ourselves.

In this chapter, we will focus on the love between women and men—sometimes called romantic love, erotic love, or conjugal love—that is at the core of relationships, marriages, and families. We will explore how love is learned from our families, our friends, and the media. We will look at the meaning of intimacy and at what couples gain from intimate relationships. Finally, we will analyze the vital role of self-esteem in the expression of love.

Relationships

Human relationships are the key to family life in the United States. We structure our lives around relationships with others. We seek close friends, we commit ourselves to others, we live in families—all because of the rewards, satisfactions, and pleasures that relationships can offer.

What do we mean by a **relationship** between two people? Obviously, there must be some close association or connection between them that lasts over a period of time. Some use the term "relationship" to describe only very intimate or close liaisons, such as those between lovers or between parents and children. Some restrict use of the term to individuals who are sexually involved with each other. Still others define a "relationship" as occurring whenever two people have ongoing expectations of each other—as do close friends.

It is generally agreed that both partners must be receiving some satisfaction—though not necessarily the same type or level of satisfaction—from a relationship. For example, Ellie finds Paul an exciting sexual partner.

Paul, however, enjoys the prestige he gains from dating Ellie, who works for a well-known law firm. These lovers gain different benefits from their relationship. By contrast, Tom and Kate find each other good company and share the same basic purpose: the desire for companionship in a relationship.

In recent years, "relationship" has become the dominant term in our society for describing all types of coupling. It has replaced "dating," "affair," "engagement," and even "marriage" in marking the status of a couple. All the older terms describe more fixed arrangements with clearer responsibilities and less flexible roles. Increasing use of the hard-to-define term "relationship" mirrors a real shift toward more flexible types of involvements.

Why We Seek Relationships

An intimate relationship with another person is a means of overcoming isolation. Psychiatrist Erich Fromm (1956), who has written extensively about love and relationships, suggests that every human being has a strong need to overcome isolation and become close to others. This deeply felt desire, he adds, is the reason for many types of behavior; for example, it pushes some Americans to join religious cults that promise to erase the boundaries of the self through union with the divine.

As is true of cult members, many lonely individuals find social groups and engage in conforming behavior. In one social circle, everyone wears a certain brand of running shoes and spends hours listening to jazz; in another, everyone wears three-piece suits and reads the *Wall Street Journal*. By identifying with a larger group, people overcome isolation and open up among others. However, in Fromm's view, cults and conformity are, at best, temporary methods for overcoming isolation. At worst, they are empty, hopeless efforts that bring "pseudo-unity."

The only fully satisfying way to escape isolation is through a loving, intimate relationship.

Social scientists have found support for Fromm's ideas. Both animals and human beings appear to need intimate contact with others in order to develop and live healthy lives. Experiments on laboratory monkeys who were isolated at birth from all contact with their mothers or other monkeys showed that the animal subjects failed to develop normally (Harlow and Harlow, 1962). Similarly, many human babies who are hospitalized and institutionalized for long periods of time following birth—and thus deprived of the loving attention of a parent—give up on life altogether.

A true story about the thirteenth century ruler Frederick II tragically illustrates this point. He wanted to discover which was the first language, and he thought he might discover what babies spoke instinctively by isolating a group of newborns in a room where

Individuals seek contact with others through loving, intimate relationships.

no one ever spoke with them. The experiment was a disaster; all the infants died from a lack of loving attention before uttering a sound! Like babies, adults receive physical and emotional benefits from being with loved ones. Close involvement with a loved person seems to have a soothing effect, and has been correlated with a long life and low rate of heart disease (Lynch, 1977).

Family and Peer Influences on Relationships

While the desire to overcome isolation is a basic element of human nature, each of us seeks relationships in a distinctive, highly personal way. Our cultural backgrounds, family lives, friendships, and life experiences all shape our expectations about relationships and behavior in intimate involvements.

Family Influences

Psychoanalyst Erik Erikson, a widely respected observer of how humans develop and change over time, has proposed an eight-stage model of human growth throughout the life cycle to which we will often refer in this textbook (see Table 4–1). To one degree or another, these stages all revolve around solving problems concerning our relationships with others—first with our parents, later with our peers.

For example, the first stage of a baby's life, according to Erikson, is a time for resolving feelings of "trust versus mistrust" in the baby's relationship to the parents. The baby must learn that she can count on her parents to feed her when she is hungry, hold her when she is frightened or angry, change her diapers, and keep her clothed. She must learn that when her parents leave the room, they will come back.

Erikson believes that if the baby learns to trust her parents, she can build on this trust and move on to the next developmental

Table 4-1   Crises of human development

Stage	Conflict	Resolution
Infancy	Trust vs. mistrust	HOPE
Early childhood	Autonomy vs. shame, doubt	WILL
Play age	Initiative vs. guilt	PURPOSE
School age	Industry vs. inferiority	COMPETENCE
Adolescence	Identity vs. identity confusion	FIDELITY
Young adulthood	Intimacy vs. isolation	LOVE
Maturity	Generativity vs. self-absorption	CARE
Old age	Integrity vs. despair, disgust	WISDOM

Source: McCubbin and Figley, 1983, p. xxii.

stage. Her early positive experience will enable her to more easily trust others later in life. However, if the baby is not cared for well—if she is abused or neglected—she may learn that parents cannot be trusted. A residue of this early mistrust may linger in close relationships during adolescence and adulthood.

In their first months, then, babies learn to experience love from their families. According to Erich Fromm, children are not loved for *what* they are—because they are smart or beautiful or happy—but *because* they are. Their very existence brings pleasure to parents. Love in the initial stages of life is closely tied to fulfillment of children's needs. By being loved, children learn to see themselves as both lovable and able to love. By being stroked, and caressed, and carried, and cuddled, and cooed to, by being loved, the child learns to stroke, and caress, and cuddle, and coo to, and love others (Montagu, 1971).

Thus, receiving parental love is crucial to learning how to love. But parents also teach loving (and unloving) behavior through the ways they interact with one another. Children watch what parents do and learn to imitate them. Do they kiss and hug one another? Do they sit silently and avoid one another's gaze? Or do they turn to violence during moments of tension and conflict?

Children who grow up in violent homes— where they or a parent is subject to violence—are much more likely to become violent in their later adult relationships. This "cycle of violence" means that family abuse is passed on from one generation to the next (see Chapter 8). Of course, other patterns of interaction can be learned at home as well: children can imitate respectful, affectionate behavior that they see in their parents' relationships.

A family's racial or ethnic background can influence the ways in which love is expressed. Leo Buscaglia (1982: 116), a lecturer on love, recalls the physical expressiveness in his large Italian family:

Everybody hugs everybody all the time. On holidays, everyone gets together, and it takes 45 minutes just to say hello, and 45 minutes to say goodbye. Babies, parents, dogs—everybody's got to be loved!

Other ethnic groups express love in a different manner (see Box 4-1). Scandinavian families generally feel more comfortable with handshakes than with bearhugs. But this does not mean that Italians love more deeply than Scandinavians—only that each group has its own style of expressing love.

Some psychologists have observed that certain families are "love-poor." These families act as if love were unimportant; they

B O X 4 – 1

Matchmaking in China

"Male, 27, worker, loyal and sincere, father employed, younger brother and sister at university, 5 feet 1 inch tall, spine slightly crooked, seeks to marry employed woman comrade."

Personal advertisements to find a mate—once derided as a decadent custom of the bourgeois West—have begun to appear in certain Chinese newspapers. This is but one aspect of a new attitude toward dating, love, and marriage in the world's largest Communist nation. In Peking alone, the government has opened four official matchmaking centers. The Ritan Park office matched up 600 couples within a three-month period in 1980; of these, apparently 200 fell in love.

Traditionally, China has held to rigid moral codes and has offered little in the way of night life. Since the revolution, Chinese men and women have been expected to concentrate on work and politics rather than on love. However, the government has become worried about the problems of its lovelorn citizens. "These young people are agonizing over their failure to wed," one Chinese newspaper explained. "Their enthusiasm for work and study is dampened."

Another response to the problem has been the publication of manuals on "The Art of Dating." One manual advises young males to carry a badminton racket and a book on the first date "to give the girl the impression you are studious and healthy." It also offers women helpful advice about undesirable males: "The unscrupulous type rounds corners full speed on his bicycle."

Source: John Brecher with Melinda Liu, "Comrade Lonelyhearts," *Newsweek*, December 29, 1980: 27.

may substitute lavish gifts, trips, or other material items for close emotional interactions. Therapists Marcia and Thomas Lasswell (1982: 102) note that adults who grew up in love-poor families often "try to avoid situations and relationships in which love might be found. Many do not seem to know *how* to love." Clearly, the first critical lessons in learning love take place in our families: as we were loved as children, so we learn to love others.

Peer Influences

As children become older, they begin to learn about love from their friends and their peer "reference group"—the group they wish to be part of or identify with. They come to know other children and establish relationships outside the family. Between the ages of 6 and 12, children are learning important information about societal sex roles—how men and women are expected to behave (see Chapter 3). They often develop "crushes" on friends and schoolmates.

Among the rituals of early adolescence are kissing games, passing of love-notes in school, and whispering of gossip about who likes whom. Carlfred Broderick (1966), a family researcher, has studied this early "puppy love" and found it to be a very common phenomenon. While a child may mean something different than an adult does when speaking of love, there is nevertheless a definite emotional attachment underneath the child's "crush."

During adolescence and young adulthood, the struggle to establish relationships outside the family becomes a focus of activity. Such relationships are one means of strengthening a growing sense of individual identity. Erik Erikson suggests that the young person must struggle with the conflict of "intimacy versus isolation" in these years. He or she either learns to risk emotional involvement with another or, fearing such closeness, chooses to remain isolated and alone. The failure to establish relationships in this developmental stage can have lasting impact on one's future. Erikson (1968: 135–136) points out that "where a youth does not accomplish such intimate relationships with others—and, I would add, with his own inner resources—he may settle for highly stereotyped interpersonal relationships and come to retain a deep sense of isolation."

It is during these years that we learn what makes us feel loved or unloved. We may be influenced by idealized images of love presented in the media: the ideal love described in the lyrics of a rock song or the way a beautiful film star looks at her leading man. At this stage of growth, we are especially vulnerable to internalizing these media fantasies of love, sex, and romance. If we take them too seriously, we may search in vain for real-life experiences that match the media enchantment.

Intimacy

Intimacy and love are closely related. Like love, intimacy can take many forms, but it does imply closeness—usually the special closeness that lovers feel. Intimacy means knowing the inside of someone, seeing what may be hidden from the world. Saying that people are "intimate" is a sometimes roundabout way of noting that they have a sexual relationship. However, one can be intimate friends with someone without becoming sexually involved.

Types of Intimacy

David Olson (1977), a researcher who has studied marriage and relationships, has identified at least seven types of intimacy:

1. Emotional—loving and supporting one another.
2. Sexual—enjoying a mutually satisfying sex life.
3. Social—sharing the same friends; joining the same groups, such as a church or political party.
4. Intellectual—talking about ideas, values, or theories; exchanging impressions of literature; debating political beliefs.
5. Recreational—enjoying a sport or a hobby.
6. Aesthetic—sharing the same taste or ideas of what is beautiful, such as a love of impressionist art or the ocean.
7. Religious—holding similar religious beliefs, or a shared sense of life's purpose and meaning.

Intimacy means shared experience, shared in a way that both partners choose and enjoy. One partner cannot force intimacy on another. Olson defines an intimate relationship as one in which a couple has more than one basis for intimacy. It cannot be only sexual, or only intellectual, or only recreational if the couple is to be truly intimate.

What do couples receive from such sharing? Perhaps most important, we learn that someone else cares for us and will "be there" in difficult moments. Social science researchers have used the term **social support** to describe the assistance that people receive in intimate relationships. Physician Sidney Cobb (1982) has distinguished three types of social support: emotional support, esteem support, and network support. Emotional support—whether in the form of hugs, kind words, or birthday gifts—gives us the feeling that we are cared for and loved. Esteem support, such as a sincere compliment about our work achievements or personal strengths, leads us to believe that we are respected and valued. Network support, as when friends help us in jobhunting or in painting a new apartment, lets us know that we are part of a network of communication, caring, and mutual obligation.

While love is not identical to social support, the two concepts certainly overlap. When one genuinely loves another person, there will be an exchange of affection, esteem, information, and assistance. Both concepts suggest an emotional commitment to the welfare of the other. Cobb believes that social support is essential if we are to maintain good physical and emotional health throughout the life cycle. It is especially important in managing change and stress (see Chapter 17).

"States" of Intimate Relationships

We may be tempted to fantasize that a couple in a supportive intimate relationship shares every interest, spends every possible moment together, and never experiences bitter conflict. But this idealized image is far from accurate. Some researchers (Miller, Nunally, and Wackman, 1975) who have studied communication among couples have described four distinct relationship "states":

1. Togetherness: Both partners focus their involvement and energies on the same thing. For example, a couple takes a backpacking trip together on which they are alone and totally dependent on one another.

2. Leading/supporting state: One partner takes the lead, focusing his or her energies on an outside interest or activity, while the other follows, offering encouragement and support.

3. The push/resisting state: One partner pushes the other into focusing energy in a certain direction. For example, a wife in-

A couple can be truly intimate only through shared experiences that both partners choose and enjoy.

sists that her husband take a greater role in household duties and child care; he responds with excuses and resentment.

4. Apartness: The couple focuses its energy on different interests. A man takes a vacation alone each February so that he can visit baseball spring training in Florida. His wife has a regular golf game every Saturday with women friends.

Realistically, intimacy involves an interplay between time spent together and time spent alone, between giving and taking. Individual interests and time apart need not be a threat to a couple's intimacy; they can give a relationship time to breathe. As Herbert Zerof (1978; 178) writes in his book, *Finding Intimacy*, intimacy means being able to move apart without fear of losing one another. "Clamoring for closeness only kills it," adds Zerof. "Trying to hold on to intimacy can make it stale and formal."

Love

If real-life intimate, loving relationships are not quite the same as glorious movie romances, how are they different? To borrow a phrase from a popular song, "What is this thing called love?"

> He's not much on looks,
> He's no hero out of books,
> But I love him.
>
> Two or three girls has he,
> That he likes as well as me,
> But I love him.
>
> I don't know why I should
> He isn't true . . .
> He beats me too . . .
> What can I do—
>
> —"My Man," sung by Billie Holiday

Love is . . . the child of Resource and Need. He is not delicate and lovely, as most of us believe, but harsh and arid, barefoot and homeless, sleep-

ing on the naked earth, in doorways, or in the very streets. . . . He is gallant, impetuous, energetic, a mighty hunter and a master of tricks and devices and artifice . . . sorcery, enchantment, seduction.

> —Plato

> And in the end,
> The love you take
> is equal to the love you make.

> —John Lennon and
> Paul McCartney

The subject of love has been discussed and lamented since human communication began. Whether it is the words of Plato, the teachings of Christ, or the current "top 40" songs, our understanding of love comes from many sources. Like blues singer Billie Holiday, some feel overpowered by a strong but irrational love. Others, such as Plato, see love as both selfish and generous; hungry for the beloved, but full of energy and trickery. Still others agree with the Beatles, who proclaimed: "All you need is love."

What is Love?

Love is an emotional response between two people. It is based on a recognition of attractive qualities in the other person: his good looks, her wit, his kindness, her charm. "I noticed his eyes right away," recalls one woman. "She's tough, strong, knows what she wants," says a young man about his girlfriend. People in love feel delight and pleasure in each other's company and look forward to being together. They also care about the well-being of their partner; lovers want one another to be happy and make efforts to bring that about.

The concept of love has changed over time. In ancient days, love was thought to be an arrow shot by the mischievous boy Cupid into the hearts of men and women. When hit by an arrow, people were deprived of all good judgment and ability to reason. Another view of love was as a form of deception. The Roman poet Ovid, in his book *The Art of Love*, described flirtation and seduction in terms of "putting one over" on the partner. He offered hints on how to hide one's less attractive qualities and trick the other person into love.

During medieval times, the ideal of **courtly love** was depicted in stories of heroes performing gallant and courageous acts to win the attention of some distant, aloof maiden. Current romance novels, in the tradition of courtly love, build up love as the supreme rapture, the highest form of pleasure humans can experience. Usually, a poor young woman excites the passions of a handsome stranger, who turns out to be a rich member of a European royal family. A passage might go something like:

. . . he laid her down and began to adore her while she knew even in pure bliss that it was happening in surroundings devoid of anything connected with her own past, making the new beginning for which she had yearned. The sun and the flower scented air and the sound of the cascade combined to create a harmonious whole with every shared kiss and movement and loving murmur (Laker, 1982: 222).

Undoubtedly, they lived happily ever after, as do any respectable fairy-tale lovers.

Falling In and Out of Love

If someone is single and unattached, does that mean that he or she is automatically ready to fall in love? A newly divorced man may be so bitter about his èx-wife that he swears he will never trust a woman again. A young woman committed to career advancement may feel that it isn't the right time for a serious romance. Sexuality researchers William Masters, Virginia Johnson, and Robert Kolodny (1982) have suggested that there may be a state of **love readiness** in which one is particularly receptive to and interested in finding love.

If you are actively looking for a partner, if

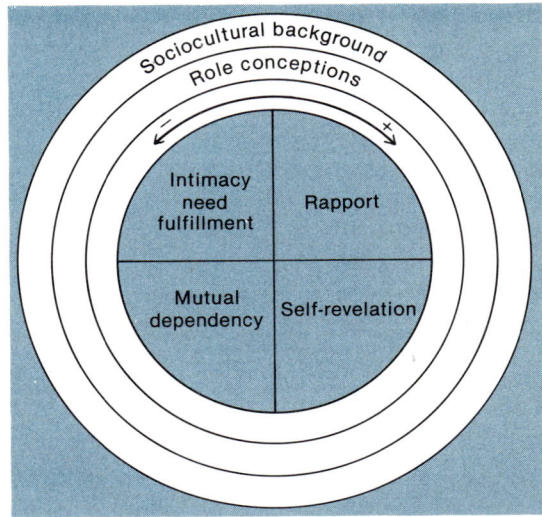

Figure 4–1 Graphic presentation of the wheel theory of the development of love. (*Source*: Reiss, 1980, p. 129.)

you feel lonely and believe that a new love affair would be the cure, if you feel bored with casual, impersonal sexual encounters, you may be in a state of love readiness. But this concept is neither foolproof nor proven; you may insist you're ready but have no luck. The researchers merely argue that there are times in the life cycle in which one is more (or less) receptive to falling in love.

Sociologist Ira Reiss has developed a "wheel theory of love" which describes what happens when people "fall in love." Reiss (1976) believes that couples go through four stages (see Figure 4-1), a kind of pattern that, like a wheel, seems to gain momentum as it turns. The wheel begins to turn when two people feel rapport with one another—an ease, an understanding, an attraction. "Whoever loved who loved not at first sight?" asked William Shakespeare in "As You Like It." This "love at first sight" is, perhaps, an intense feeling of rapport.

Let us use the example of Kevin and Rita to describe the wheel theory. Kevin and Rita attended the same college and met at a dorm party. They began talking, and later, when a group of students left to go out for pizza, they trailed along. However, when everyone reached the pizza parlor, Kevin and Rita sat somewhat apart from the group. Kevin mentioned that he was working part-time as part of a film crew for a documentary; Rita talked excitedly about her film history course. They established a rapport and felt attracted to each other.

At the second stage, Kevin and Rita began the difficult process of self-revelation, which includes sharing of interests, ideas, fears, ambitions, and personal history. Kevin asked Rita for another date, and they went to a French film on campus. After the movie, Kevin told Rita of his ambition to become a director; Rita revealed that she hoped to become a film critic for a major newspaper. Each was supportive of the other's goal. They shared stories about their family backgrounds, their experiences during high school, and their romantic ups-and-downs. Later that evening, they returned to Rita's room and made love—another element of self-revelation.

The third turn of the wheel involves the development of mutual dependencies; each person comes to rely on the other for various individual needs. Kevin and Rita began seeing each other regularly, both during the week and on weekends. He lent her money when she had to buy an expensive textbook; she advised him on a special project for a film class. In many, day-to-day ways, their lives were becoming interdependent. Each had come to assume that the other's help and support was available.

The fourth and final turn of the wheel involves the fulfillment of personality needs. Kevin was insecure about his abilities and relied on constant encouragement; Rita enjoyed feeling that she could take care of someone. Thus, their needs blended well together; their personalities seemed to meet

the other's needs. As they shared more experiences—a film festival in Colorado, a camping trip in Canada, the wedding of a friend—they became even closer. The wheel had come full circle, spinning them from their initial rapport to a mutually fulfilling and intimate love relationship.

The sociocultural background and role conceptions of the individuals provide the context for the interpersonal processes described in Reiss's wheel theory. Role conceptions influence all four of the processes, as they define what one should do or expect in a love relationship. Likewise, the specific types of role conceptions that exist in a

Falling in love involves self-revelation, a process which includes sharing fears, ambitions, interests and ideas.

group are shaped by the socio-cultural background; e.g., education and religion (Reiss, 1980).

Unfortunately, as Reiss points out, the wheel can ''spin'' couples out of love as well. For example, Sarah and Roger, who lived together, had a longstanding battle over money. After one especially serious argument, they did not speak for several days. During that time, they began to grow apart and confided in friends that they thought the relationship might end. (Reiss would describe this as having their personality needs met elsewhere.) Their rapport diminished, and there was no self-revelation—just a bitter silence.

A few days later, Sarah and Roger ''made up,'' but their truce proved to be brief. They were soon arguing again, and each found excuses to stay out of the apartment whenever possible. They became less dependent on each other and finally decided that living apart would be best. Reiss believes that just as falling in love has a momentum, so, too, does falling out of love—only in reverse gear.

When love relationships end, there is usually a feeling of bitterness, pain, and anger. Only about 15 percent of couples who end relationships do so with the consent of both partners. In the other 85 percent of cases, one partner wants out while the other tries to hang on. Men appear to be more persistent in wanting to keep a dying affair going; women are more often the ones who want it to end (Hill, Rubin, and Peplau, 1976; Walster and Walster, 1978).

Styles of Loving

While most Americans believe that love can last a lifetime, many also report that they have fallen in love more than once. Some people seem prone to falling in love often, while a small number claim that they fall in love continually. One person who answered a *Psychology Today* survey happily reported having fallen in love 131 times! And that was at the ripe old age of 28. At the other end of the spectrum are those who have fallen in love only once and stay in love.

When we compare the expectations of the ''love-prone'' with those of ''long-time'' lovers, we find major differences. The first group strongly believes that love is based on some mysterious but powerful ''chemistry''—a physical attraction or sexuality that stirs two people. They feel, however, that this chemistry has a short life. Most expect that their love affairs will be brief, and perhaps stormy and unhappy, experiences. By contrast, the long-time lovers see love as based on trust—a trust that deepens over time. Each group has sharply varying ideas about what love is really about; not surprisingly, the way they actually act in loving relationships is also quite different (Rubenstein, 1983).

John Allen Lee (1973), a Canadian researcher, interviewed people about their definitions and expectations of love. He identified at least six types of lovers, each with particular ideas and styles of loving:

1. Erotic lovers. Sexual love obsesses them. They have an intense desire for physical intimacy and are inclined to view sex as the essence of a loving relationship.

2. Playful lovers. For them, love is a game or amusement. They are ''no-strings'' lovers who do not take relationships too seriously, do not become close to their lovers or dependent on them, and do not expect love to last a long time.

3. Companions. These lovers value peaceful, caring exchanges of affection more than deep and intense passion. Their love tends to be long-lasting.

4. Manic lovers. Their emotions are on a continual roller coaster, bouncing up and down almost daily. They are inclined to be possessive, jealous, and totally focused

on the objects of their love, who occupy their thoughts 24 hours a day. Manic lovers have an endless need for attention and affection.

5. Pragmatic lovers. These are practical individuals who carefully seek compatible partners whose personality, background, and interests match their own. A pragmatic lover who wants children, for example, will be sure that a prospective partner also does before becoming deeply involved.

6. Selfless lovers. This is the ''brotherly love'' of religious teaching. Selfless lovers give without demanding anything in return. They are patient and respectful of others.

Most persons are not any one of these pure types, but instead have traits and qualities of two or three of them. Lee suggests that mutually satisfying love relationships are more likely between people who primarily fall into the same category and therefore share similar expectations. For example, a companion lover might be worn out by the sexual demands of an erotic lover. A playful lover would certainly resist the emotional intensity and obsession of a manic lover. To a large extent, people's expectations of what love is all about determine the style of loving they adopt.

Women and Men in Love: Some Differences

The French film director François Truffaut has stated that ''in love women are professionals but men are amateurs'' (Rubenstein, 1983: 49). He means that women feel they have more at stake in love; therefore, they take these relationships more seriously.

Social science research reveals that women are more wary of love than men. Once committed, women express their feelings more intensely. Men are more willing to take risks in the name of love: they are more likely to fall in love sooner (and ''harder'') than women. One study of college-age couples found that by the fourth date, 27 percent of the males but only 15 percent of the females reported that they were in love (Kanin, Davidson, and Scheck, 1970; Mursheim, 1980).

Men tend to be more idealistic about love than women; they feel that a sincere love can conquer all practical difficulties. As noted earlier, they are more likely to try to hold on to a dying relationship, and they find it more difficult to be ''just friends'' with former lovers. Men are three times more likely to commit suicide after a breakup than women are; men are also more likely to respond to rejection with murder. For all that, however, men tend to be happier in love than women.

Women are careful at the early stages of relationships, perhaps because they have been socialized to see lovers as potential husbands. They tend to be more critical and more demanding of their partners. One divorced man recalled that his wife ''seemed to think there really was a man who could sweep her off her feet, bring her salvation, change her life completely. She was always looking for that kind of lover, and was never timid about letting me know I wasn't him.''

Marriage and Love

''I married a good-time Charlie,'' says Cindy sadly. ''I knew he liked to take a drink, but I thought that was his way of relaxing, of unwinding. Besides, he was so much fun after he'd had a few, always the life of the party. . . . Six months after the wedding, I woke up and realized I had married a hopeless alcoholic.''

''I met Ellen when I changed a tire for her one rainy night on the freeway,'' recalls Art, now 40. ''She seemed so fragile, like she needed someone—me!—to take care of her.

While we were dating, I was the knight in shining armor. I guess I got off on it for a while. But, after ten years of marriage, . . . well, she's so darned helpless she can't balance a checkbook. She can't lift a bag of groceries, and she still can't change a tire!''

Romance depends on idealizing the beloved person. At the initial stages of love, the loved one seems so wonderful that it is hard for the lover to see her or his inevitable human weaknesses. Erich Fromm (1956) writes that lovers experience a kind of joint egoism, centered totally on themselves, absorbed only in their little world. But it is a wonderful feeling, a heightened state of consciousness full of exhilaration and excitement. Philosopher Bertrand Russell once said that romantic love is the source of the most intense delights that life has to offer. With this in mind—and in marked contrast to cultures that mandate arranged marriages—most Americans feel strongly that romantic love should precede marriage or other long-term commitments.

Most of the great stories of romance and love are about couples who love from afar, who are separated by obstacles and social barriers, but who nevertheless love intensely and passionately. Romeo and Juliet were kept apart because their families hated each other; Tristan and Isolde had to love in secret because she was married. When the boy from the wrong side of the tracks and the banker's daughter fall madly in love, class differences stand in their way. The difficulties these storybook couples have in coming together seem only to heighten their love and fan the flames of passion.

Not surprisingly, the illusions and idealizations of romance wither over time as a couple experiences the day-to-day pressures of married life. Many would not go as far as the twelfth-century noblewoman Marie, Countess of Champagne, who argued that ''love cannot exert its powers between two people who are married to each other'' (Ru-

benstein, 1983: 46). Still, it is hard to maintain total romantic bliss when your spouse snores beside you every night or walks around the house in curlers and a mud pack.

If love is blind, it has been written, marriage quickly restores the sight. Like Art and Cindy, whom we quoted above, many Americans find that the very traits that seemed so attractive during courtship are increasingly annoying after marriage. Perhaps if things had worked out differently for the world's most famous ''star-crossed lovers,'' Juliet would have found Romeo's impetuous nature a bit trying after a few years, and Romeo might have complained that her endless talking was driving him crazy!

Evelyn Duvall and Reuben Hill (1960: 340) have observed that the illusions of romance often seem like a cruel hoax after a few months of marriage. In their view, the romance that brought the couple together will ideally flower into an abiding and more firmly rooted **conjugal love**:

Conjugal love grows as the marriage progresses, thrives on companionship, common experiences, and the . . . happy episodes which are scattered throughout a rich marriage. Conjugal love builds on the familiar, the momentos, the souvenirs, and waxes stronger with each additional year of marriage. . . . it grows from continuous association.

Conjugal love is a more quiet, tranquil feeling that replaces the soaring intensity of romance. Harvey, a 45-year-old teacher, admits, ''It wasn't until we'd been married for years that I truly began to appreciate Marion. She is always there, even at times when it would be more pleasant to get rid of me. She's really special.'' Recent research, however, has found that couples married more than 20 years seem to have a more romantic conception of love than those at earlier stages of marriage. Perhaps romance is present in marriage as an undercurrent, surfacing strongly in certain periods and receding in others (Knox, 1970).

B O X 4 – 2

The Lover and the Beloved

In one recent survey, almost half of the couples questioned appeared to have an inequality of affection. That is, they felt that one partner loved more than the other (Rubenstein, 1983). Distinguished novelist and playwright Carson McCullers (1977: 26–27) addressed this delicate issue in her memorable novella, *The Ballad of the Sad Cafe*:

> First of all, love is a joint experience between two persons—but the fact that it is a joint experience does not mean that it is a similar experience to the two people involved. There are the lover and the beloved, but these two come from different countries. Often the beloved is only a stimulus for all the stored-up love which has lain quiet within the lover for a long time hitherto. And somehow every lover knows this. He feels in his soul that his love is a solitary thing. He comes to know a new, strange loneliness and it is this knowledge which makes him suffer. So there is only one thing for the lover to do. He must house for himself a whole new inward world—a world intense and strange and complete in himself. . . .

> A most mediocre person can be the object of a love which is wild, extravagant, and beautiful as the poison lilies of the swamp. A good man may be the stimulus for a love both violent and debased, or a jabbering madman may bring about in the soul of someone a tender and simple idyll. Therefore, the value and quality of any love is determined solely by the lover himself.

> It is for this reason that most of us would rather love than be loved. Almost everyone wants to be the lover. And the curt truth is that, in a deep secret way, the state of being loved is intolerable to many. The beloved fears and hates the lover, and with the best of reasons. For the lover is forever trying to strip bare his beloved. The lover craves any possible relation with the beloved, even if this experience can only cause him pain.

Love . . . or Addiction?

Alice: I'm slowly going crazy with Burt. He's so cut off from his feelings and so unresponsive to me that I feel I'm with a robot. In the beginning, he was kind of romantic, but now there's nothing coming from him but silence and disinterest. When I complain he says that's the way he is. Even though I'm frustrated and miserable, I can't get myself to leave him. In fact, I get very frightened when I think about it seriously.

Jason: Dee is irresponsible and selfish much of the time. She'll put me down in front of other people and sometimes flirt with other men right in front of me. If I get annoyed, she accuses me of trying to suffo-

cate her. . . . At this point, I can't see anything she gives me, yet whatever it is that's binding me to her seems stronger than I am.

(Halpern, 1982: 2–3)

Alice and Jason are in an all-too-common predicament. They find themselves in relationships that are unsatisfying, unfulfilling, and even self-destructive. They are both miserable, yet they feel powerless to leave their partners. Some therapists compare such individuals to drug addicts or alcoholics; their addiction is not to a substance but to another person. In all cases, the addict cannot "kick the habit," may receive a few intense "highs," and yet is certain to suffer through years of pain, guilt, and self-hatred (see Box 4–2).

Psychologist Howard Halpern (1982) believes that such love addicts are bound to destructive relationships because they believe they will otherwise be incomplete, empty, and lost. Alice may be telling herself, "If I leave Burt, I'll never find another lover, and my life may as well be over." Jason may also feel terrified by the prospect of being alone. Love addicts are imprisoned in their addiction, Halpern argues, by inner compulsion and fear. They will only recover when they pay more attention to their own (badly damaged) self-esteem.

Mature Love

We have seen that, at its worst, love can be addictive, compulsive, agonizing. This leads naturally to the question: how can we avoid such disastrous "love"? How can we achieve healthy, mature relationships?

Self-esteem

If we were writing a prescription for a fulfilling and satisfying relationship, the first ingredient would be a healthy dose of self-esteem. As Howard Halpern (1982) points out, mature love is not an addiction. It is not driven by inner compulsion or fear, and can only exist in freedom. Mature love depends more on the way that a lover feels about herself or himself than on the intensity of feeling between the partners. It is an active process of giving of oneself, rather than a greedy taking from someone to fill the emptiness one feels inside. To be a loving person, one must feel that one's love and its expression are important, meaningful, and valuable to the loved person.

But, you may wonder, isn't it illogical to put so much emphasis on the self? Isn't love really about the other? Don't we fall in love because of what someone else is like: his irresistible smile, her musical laugh? Isn't it true that a selfish person is so self-impressed and self-absorbed that he or she would make a poor, ungiving lover?

Not entirely. Selfish people do not make very good lovers; however, their selfishness reflects low (not high) self-esteem. Such individuals think only of "me-first" and are incapable of attending to anyone's else's needs or interests unless they happen to coincide with their own. This is because selfish people feel empty and insecure inside. Often they fear they are unworthy of anyone else's caring and concern.

By contrast, individuals with high self-esteem are not as preoccupied with themselves. They make friends more easily than those with low self-esteem, have less difficulty in speaking their minds, and are less sensitive to criticism (Coopersmith, 1967). In short, liking oneself is an essential precondition for caring about others and giving to them. Erich Fromm (1956: 58–59) writes:

If I am attached to another person because I cannot stand on my own two feet, he or she may be a lifesaver, but the relationship is not one of love. The idea expressed in the Biblical "Love thy neighbor as thyself" implies that respect for one's own self cannot be separated from respect and love and understanding for another individual.

Self-esteem begins with self-acceptance; we must feel at ease with our strengths and shortcomings. We must appreciate our own splendid gifts and passions—a fine singing voice, a flair for baking, great legs, or an enthusiasm for cycling—before we can genuinely appreciate the equally splendid aspects of someone else. Leo Buscaglia (1982: 264) describes such self-acceptance as "not trying to be a banana when you're really a peach":

There are people who may want me to be a banana. . . . Isn't it all right to say to them, "I'm sorry, I cannot be a banana. I would love to be a banana if I could for you, but I'm a peach.'' And you know what? If you wait long enough, you'll find a peach lover. And then you can live your life as a peach, and you don't have to live your life as a banana. All the lost energy it takes to be a banana when you're a peach!

How can one bolster sagging self-esteem? Here are some suggestions based on observations of people with high self-esteem (Hamachek, 1971):

- Work from strength. Do things that excite you and that you are good at. Don't do things just because someone else thinks you should do them. Deriving satisfaction from work or hobbies can be vital for appreciating yourself.
- Accentuate the positive. Compliment yourself when you do well; forgive your-self when things go badly. Focus on your achievements; don't dwell on your failures. You may not look like Robert Redford, you may not sing like Linda Ronstadt, but so what? Look instead to your own gifts and improvement.

- Don't get carried away with fantasies. It's easy to paint a rosy picture of what life would be like ''if only.'' ''If only I were thinner,'' ''if only I had married Mark instead of Bob,'' and so forth. Daydreams and fantasies can sometimes take the place of genuine satisfaction, and can make real life seem dull and disappointing by comparison. But life isn't a fairy tale in which people live happily ever after in eternal bliss, without financial problems, emotional conflicts, or illness. Stick to reality; if it isn't satisfying, try to change it.

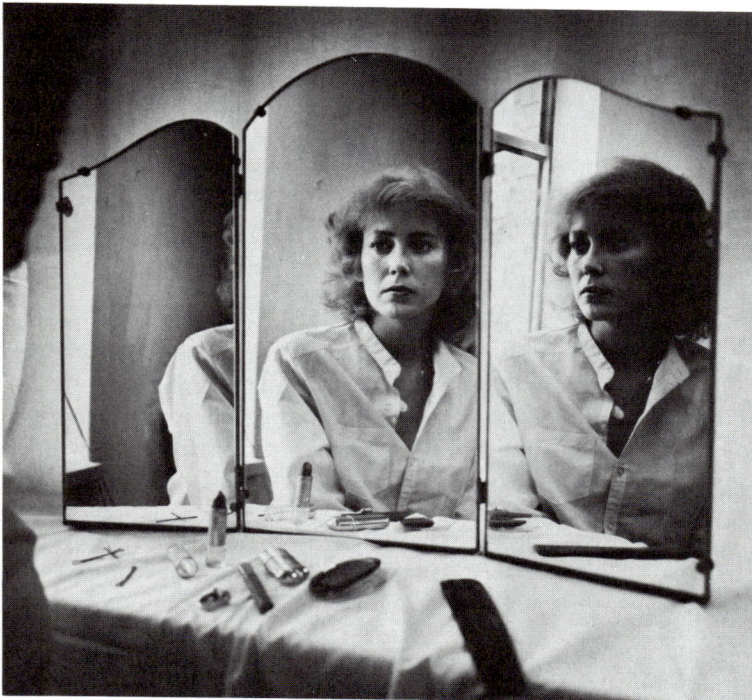

Mature love is dependent upon how individuals feel about themselves. It is a giving process rather than a taking from someone to fill the void of loneliness.

- Relax! The worries and uncertainties you feel are common to everyone. It's only human to feel down on yourself at times. Don't let it overwhelm you.

Giving: The Active Verb of Love

Erich Fromm has identified four key aspects of giving. First, it means caring for another, "an active concern for the life and growth of that which we love." If a woman proclaims that she "loves" plants but never waters them, her love is not genuine. It is a sentimental love, a love without action. Caring means taking action and even risks out of concern for the other person.

Second, a giving love involves taking responsibility for another, taking on the loved one's needs and concerns. A mother cares deeply about what happens to her baby and acts to ensure that her child will grow and succeed. But responsibility can lead to possessiveness and domination without the third key element of giving: respect. Respect means feeling happy when the loved one is achieving happiness on his or her own. It has been said that the most difficult aspect of being a parent is "letting go" and allowing the child to become more independent. This is also an issue for members of a romantic couple; jealousy and possessiveness can destroy love.

The final aspect of giving is seeking knowledge about the loved one. This means learning about the partner, seeing him or her without distortion, faults and all. It also means developing an appreciation for the unique qualities of the loved one. In Buscaglia's terms, one must value the partner as a peach, rather than insisting that he or she become a banana. This process of learning about another person—infused and made meaningful with care, responsibility, and respect—is the means to a continuing, satisfying, mature love.

Summary

A relationship is an ongoing, purposeful association with another person. The main motivation for seeking relationships is the desire to overcome personal isolation. We learn about relationships and love from our families and from peers. The experience of being loved as an infant is crucial to the ability to give love in later life.

Intimacy and love are closely related. An intimate relationship is based on shared interests, beliefs, or activities. Intimacy provides social support (emotional support, esteem support, and network support) necessary for maintaining health and managing stress.

Love is an emotional response to attractive qualities in another person. It takes the form of a heightened interest and concern for the loved one, and a pleasure in being with him or her. Falling in love can be described as a wheel with four turning points: establishing rapport, self-revelation, growing mutual dependency, and fulfillment of personality needs. When couples fall out of love, this process turns in reverse until the initial rapport fades away.

Styles of loving change with changing expectations. Erotic lovers, playful lovers, companions, manic lovers, pragmatic lovers, and selfless lovers all have different ideals of what love should be like. Consequently, their styles of behavior as lovers are different. Men tend to fall in love more easily than women and hold more romantic ideas about love. Women tend to see love in more practical terms.

Conjugal love is the love that grows over time in a long-lasting relationship. Unlike romantic love, which is based on idealization of the partner, conjugal love is based on shared experiences, memories, and mutual interests.

Unlike addictive love—which is based on

loneliness, a feeling of personal inadequacy, and low self-esteem—mature love is freely given and based on high self-esteem. It is active, not passive. The basis for mature love is care, responsibility, respect, and knowledge of the loved person.

Discussion Questions

1. Think of a song lyric, a story, or a movie dealing with romantic love. What does this example suggest about the nature of love? How much influence do you think these media images have on your expectations about real-life relationships? How much influence do you think they have on other people's relationships?

2. "Love is impossible in a society that values money and possessions as much as American society does today." Do you agree or disagree? What is the relationship between love and money? Between love and other social values and ideals?

3. The authors describe "love-poor" families. What characteristics do you think a "love-rich" family might have?

4. Magazines aimed at young women have regular articles on problems in relationships—how to handle jealousy, to improve communication, and so forth. But men's magazines rarely run that kind of article. Why do you think this is the case?

5. In your view, what constitutes an intimate relationship? How do intimate relationships fulfill the personality needs of partners? Give some specific examples.

Key Words

Conjugal Love **Love Readiness** **Social Support**

Courtly Love **Relationship**

Suggested Readings

Braithwaite, Ronald L. "Interpersonal relations between black males and black females." In Gary, Lawrence E. (ed.), *Black Men*. Beverly Hills, Calif.: Sage Publications, 1981. Discusses issues affecting intimacy in black couples.

Montagu, Ashley. *Touching: The Human Significance of the Skin*. New York: Harper and Row, 1971. Explores the physical and emotional role of touching in intimacy and human growth.

Pope, Kenneth S. *On Love and Loving*. San Francisco, Calif.: Jossey-Bass, 1980. A comprehensive overview of current knowledge about love, which evaluates recent literature and reports new findings.

Schwartz, Gary, and Marten, Don. *Love and Commitment*. Beverly Hills, Calif.: Sage Publications, 1980. The story of one woman's experiences from her first teenage romance to her marriage. Based on weekly interviews over a span of six years.

Walster, Elaine, and Walster, William G. *A New Look at Love*. Reading, Mass.: Addison-Wesley, 1978. A readable discussion of compassionate and passionate love.

CHAPTER FIVE

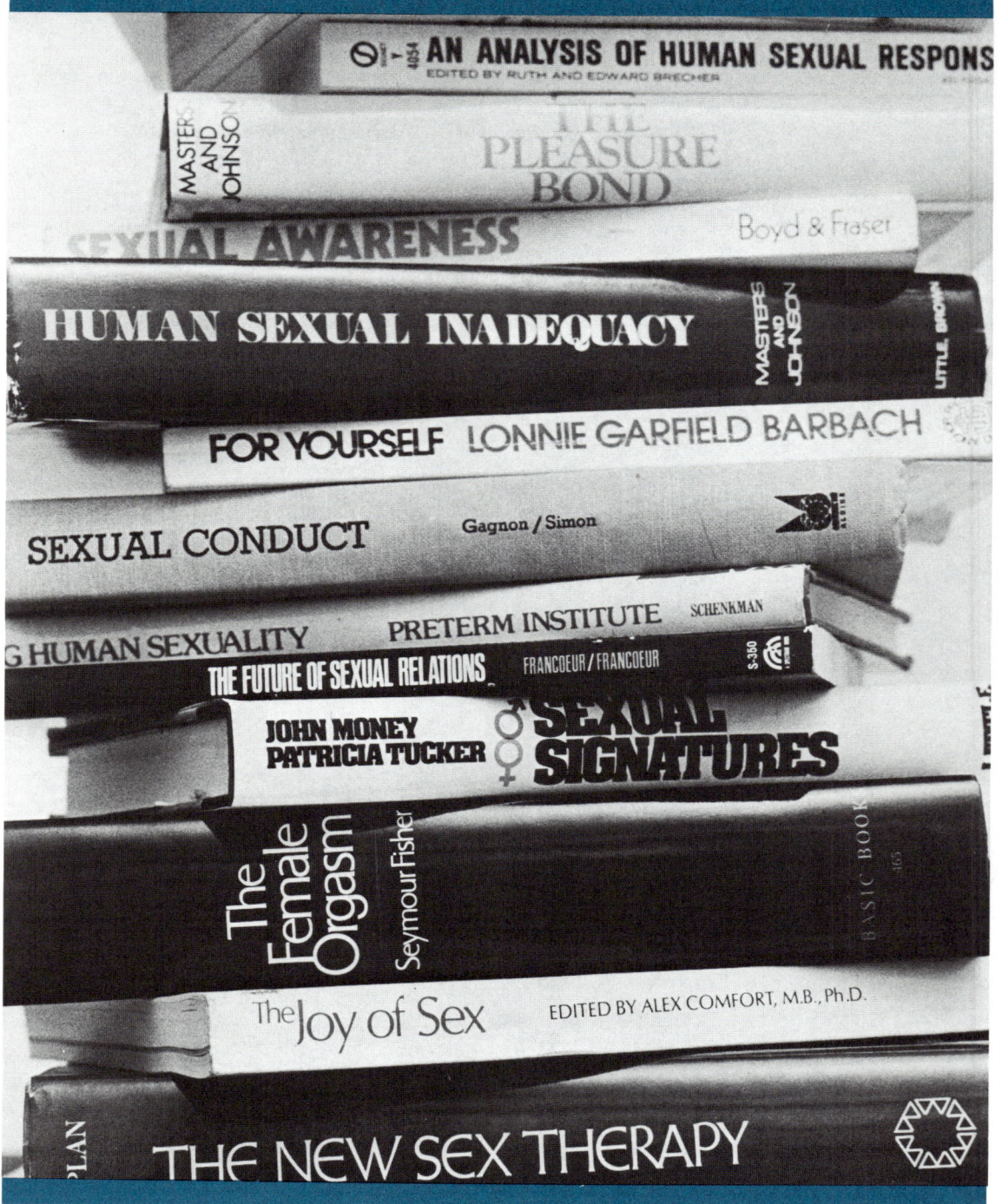

Sexuality

KEY TOPICS

—the changing American sexuality—
—the physiology of sex and reproduction—
—forms of sexual expression—
—the double standard—
—sex, love, and self-awareness—
—birth control methods—
—abortion—
—sexual violence—
—sexually transmitted diseases—

In earlier periods of American history—even as recently as a few decades ago—it was considered neither polite nor healthy to talk about ''sex.'' There were virtually no courses on sexuality taught at schools and universities. Movies and television programs avoided such subjects as teen pregnancy, vasectomy, and homosexuality. Since sex was widely viewed as ''dirty,'' children were punished for masturbation and other forms of sex play. But in the 1980s, things are quite different. It is easier than ever before to obtain reliable information about sex. ''How to'' manuals detailing sexual techniques and experiences abound. Articles and surveys about human sexuality are common not only in *Playboy* but also in popular family magazines found in supermarkets and beauty salons. Television and film have become increasingly open about showing intimate behavior and dealing with sexually related themes. Bumper stickers praising the sexual prowess of divers who ''do it deeper'' or cowboys who ''stay on longer'' symbolize the nation's candid (and sometimes obsessive) discussion of sexual matters.

Changing Sexual Attitudes and Behavior

Although sex before marriage is hardly a new phenomenon, the last 25 years have seen a growing acceptance of such behavior. Many more Americans are engaging in premarital sex; the increase is most striking

B O X 5 – 1

Research Brief:
Sex Among College Students

Ira Robinson and Davor Jedlicka (1982) of the University of Georgia conducted a replication study of earlier surveys of premarital sexual behavior and attitudes among college students. A "replication study" involves repeating an earlier study by asking the same or similar research questions and using similar methods and procedures with a new sample in order to see if similar results will be obtained.

Robinson and his colleagues have surveyed college students every five years since 1965 about their premarital sexual behavior and attitudes. The results of their 1980 survey, which involved 169 males and 230 females, provide interesting contrasts with earlier findings.

Table 5–1 Percentage of college students having premarital intercourse in 1965, 1970, 1975, and 1980

Year	Males	Females
1965	65.1	28.7
1970	65.0	37.3
1975	73.9	57.1
1980	77.4	63.5

Source: I. E. Robinson, and D. Jedlicka "Change in Sexual Attitudes and Behavior of College Students from 1965 to 1980" *Journal of Marriage and the Family*, February 1982, 237–240.

What Did the Authors Find

- There was a steady increase in premarital intercourse from 1965 to 1980. The increase was most dramatic for females—34.8 percent over this period (see Table 5–1).

- In the period 1965 to 1975, there was a dramatic decrease in the percentage of both women and men who believed that premarital sex was immoral. However, in 1980 a greater proportion of students viewed premarital sex as immoral than was true in 1975.

- The authors have used the term "sexual contradiction" to describe the basic discrepancy in their findings: while there has been an increase in the number of students who believe that premarital sex is immoral, there has nevertheless been an actual increase in sexual behavior for both males and females.

- Attitudes regarding sexual behavior are stricter for the opposite sex than for one's own sex, suggesting a new "double standard."

among females. A 1980 study found that 78 percent of 19-year-old unmarried males and 69 percent of females were no longer virgins (Zelnik and Kantner, 1980).

Clearly, many young men and women have decided that marriage is no longer an essential requirement for a sexual relationship (see Box 5–1). Premarital sex is viewed as acceptable if there is stability, affection, and emotional commitment—what Reiss (1960) calls "permissiveness with affection." Whereas the old pattern used to be

love then marriage then sex, the new pattern is love then sex and perhaps marriage later on. Henry Bowman and Graham Spanier (1978) suggest that sexual attitudes depend less on parental views of sexual morality and more on the influence of peers.

The sexual revolution has changed marital sex as well. Both men and women have more sexual experience by the time they are married than was true in the past. Both expect to give and receive sexual satisfaction, and are less inhibited from exploring new sexual techniques because of guilt or embarrassment. Extramarital affairs have also become more common. According to a 1983 study, one-third of husbands and wives surveyed had at least one extramarital affair. By the time they reach their forties, half of all married persons have had an affair (Rubenstein, 1983).

It is difficult to explain why there has been such a major change in American sexual attitudes and behavior. The influence of Sigmund Freud and other psychologists has led to concern about the effects of sexual repression on people's emotional lives. Widely published sex studies, such as those of William Masters and Virginia Johnson in the 1960s and 1970s, have assisted people in learning more about sexuality. The invention of more reliable birth control methods has freed couples from the fear of pregnancy and allowed them to become bolder about sexual expression. Finally, the change in women's roles described in Chapter 3 has affected the mood of the times. In part because of the women's movement (see Box 5–2), women have become more aware of their own sexuality and more insistent about their own sexual satisfaction.

There has been a certain degree of backtracking toward traditional sexual standards in recent years. In part, the new sexual conservatism has been inspired by fear of sexually transmitted diseases such as herpes and AIDS, which will be discussed in detail later in this chapter. Yet fear is not the only cause for this shift in behavior; there has also been somewhat of an attitudinal change.

We noted in Box 5–1 that today's college students are more likely to believe that premarital sex is immoral than students were in 1975. The same may well be true of the general public. In a 1969 survey conducted by *Psychology Today*, 17 percent of males and 29 percent of females stated that sex without love was either unenjoyable or unacceptable. When *Psychology Today* asked the same ques-

tion in 1983, it learned that 29 percent of males and 44 percent of females felt this way (Rubenstein, 1983).

Still, no one expects a full return to the sexual mores of earlier periods of American history. The sexual revolution is very much with us, and its effects have unquestionably reshaped the nature of marriage and family life in the United States. In this chapter, we will examine the changing American sexuality, beginning with a biological brief on human sexuality and reproduction. Various forms of heterosexual and homosexual expression will be discussed, and particular attention will be given to the traditional "double standard" of sexual behavior and how it has affected women.

In the second half of Chapter 5, we will address the connections between sex, love, and self-awareness. Information about birth control methods will be presented, as will the related and disturbing issue of teenage pregnancy. We will examine the controversy over legalized abortion, which continues to bitterly divide Americans. The ugly reality of sexual violence, expressed in the forms of rape and incest, will be discussed. Finally, we will study sexually transmitted diseases, including gonorrhea, syphilis, herpes, and AIDS.

Human Sexuality: A Biological Brief

Many of you may be well informed about the structure and functions of the human sexual anatomy. However, it may surprise you to learn that many American adults have little knowledge of their bodies. Therefore, we will begin with some fundamentals about human sexuality.

The Female

The external sexual organs of the female consist of the clitoris, the mons pubis, the in-

B O X   5 - 2

The Hite Report

One of the most hailed and condemned studies of sexuality in the 1970s was *The Hite Report*, first published in 1976. Feminist author Shere Hite (1976) developed a questionnaire that was eventually answered by more than 3,000 American women, ranging in age from 14 to 78. Respondents were asked intimate questions about masturbation, orgasm, intercourse, clitoral stimulation, lesbianism, and the sexual revolution. Hite's work—although attacked by some social scientists for failing to use random sampling techniques—was unprecedented in that, using rather open-ended questions, Hite simply asked women to discuss and describe their sexual feelings and experiences.

The Hite Report had a powerful impact on many American women in opening up discussions about women's sexuality. As one respondent wrote on her questionnaire:

I cried when I first read through this. There is so much I've lied about for so long; I'd already come to understand that, but wanted to fill out the questionnaire to make myself write it down. Undoubtedly, you will have helped many women in just this way, and publication of the results will reach many more who as I did, will read the truth they couldn't tell themselves (Hite, 1976: 47).

Among Hite's provocative conclusions was the "the right to orgasm has become a political question for women" (p. 137). Hite suggested that women were often servicing men in bed, helping them to have orgasms while the men failed to reciprocate for women. Traditionally, some experts on sexuality had suggested that orgasms were more important for men than for women. But, as one of Hite's respondents wrote, "Whoever said orgasm wasn't important for a woman was undoubtedly a man" (p. 129).

Hite also found that only 30 percent of her subjects were able to achieve orgasm regularly through intercourse. This led her to another controversial conclusion, that the reproductive model of sex exploits women:

The sequence of "foreplay," "penetration," and "intercourse" (defined as thrusting), followed by male orgasm as the climax and end of the sequence, gives very little chance for female orgasm, is almost always under the control of the man, frequently teases the woman inhumanely, and in short, has institutionalized out any expression of women's sexual feelings except for those that support male sexual needs (p. 384).

While there were challenges to both the methodology and the conclusions of *The Hite Report*, few could deny that it had a major role in provoking greater discussion of women's sexual dissatisfaction. Many female readers reacted vividly to the moving testimony of Hite's respondents, and initiated new conversations about women's sexuality both in the mass media and in their own bedrooms.

---

ner lips, the outer lips, and the vaginal opening. Collectively, these parts are known as the **vulva** (see Figure 5–1).

The **clitoris** is the most erotic and sexually sensitive part of a woman's body, and thus is extremely important in female sexual response. It is similar to the male penis in that both develop from the same embryonic tissue. In addition, both have a similar structure: a shaft and a glans. Like the penis, the clitoris varies in size from one woman to another. It swells when a woman is sexually aroused, and it is erectile. The clitoris is the only part of the female anatomy with no known reproductive function; all other organs serve dual sexual-reproductive functions. In various cultures, and in various periods throughout history, the clitoris has been subjected to mutilation. Clitoridectomy (the surgical removal of the clitoris) was occasionally practiced in the United States during the Victorian era as a "cure" for "compulsive masturbators." It has also been performed in the Middle East, Africa, and Latin America, and is still practiced today in Kenya and some parts of Egypt (Daly, 1979; Slob; 1982).

The **mons pubis** is the fatty pads of tissue covered with pubic hair which lie below the skin over the pubic bone. It is the most visible part of the female sexual organs and contains nerve endings that can produce sexual excitement. The **labia majora** (outer lips) are two folds of skin covered with pubic hair lying along both sides of the vaginal opening. The **labia minor** (inner lips) are two hairless folds of skin located between the labia majora and along the edge of the vaginal opening. These folds protect the inner genitalia and function as minor **erogenous zones** (parts of the body that are especially sensitive to sexual stimulation).

In addition to the clitoris, mons pubis, and labia majora and minora, a pair of glands called the Bartholin's glands is located just outside the vaginal opening. The purpose of these glands is to secrete fluid to lubricate the vaginal opening and facilitate penetration.

The internal sexual organs of the female consist of a pair of ovaries, a pair of fallopian tubes, the uterus, the cervix, and the vagina (see Figure 5–1). The **ovaries** are the primary sex organs of the female. About the size of an unshelled almond, they lie on either side of the uterus in the lower abdominal cavity. The ovaries have two important functions: to produce eggs (ova) and to se-

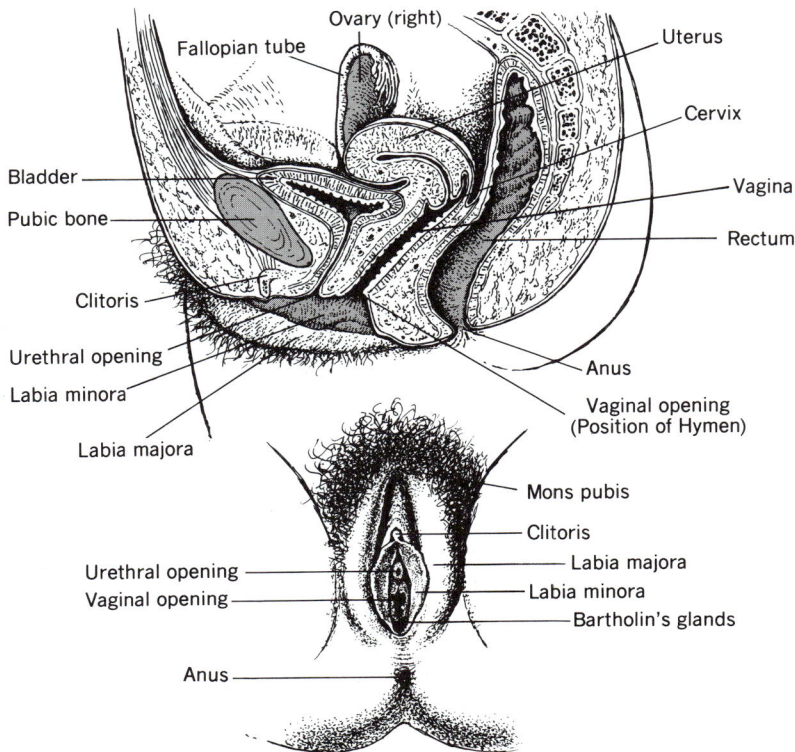

Figure 5–1 Female sexual anatomy. Shown are the important sexual and reproductive organs of the body (top) and the external genitals (bottom). (*Source*: Hoult, Henze, and Hudson, 1978, p. 172.)

crete the female hormones estrogen and progesterone. A female child is born with approximately 400,000 immature eggs. By the time she reaches puberty, only 10,000 will remain. Nevertheless, this is far more than the number needed to produce the roughly 400 eggs that will ripen during a woman's fertile years of childbearing. Beginning at puberty, usually one egg ripens each month and is released. This process is called **ovulation**.

The **uterus** (womb) of a woman who has never been pregnant is about 2½ inches in length, is about the size of a fist, and is shaped somewhat like an upside-down pear. The narrow, lower third is called the cervix and opens into the vagina. The top is called the fundus and the main portion is the body. The entrance to the uterus through the cervix is very narrow and usually contains a mucous plug to prevent foreign substances in the vagina from passing into the uterus. The uterus serves as the site of fetal development. It has three layers: the endometrium or inner layer, which is sloughed off at menstruation and creates most of the menstrual discharge; the myometrium or middle layer, which is made up of the strong, elastic muscles that accommodate a fetus; and an outer layer or perimetrium.

The **vagina** is a tube-like organ about 3 or 4 inches long. It extends from the cervix to the vaginal opening or introitus. The vagina serves as the passageway through which menstrual flow is discharged, and it is also the organ into which the penis is inserted during intercourse. The vaginal walls, made up of three layers, are extremely elastic and capable of expanding to the extent necessary during intercourse or childbirth. With age, the walls become somewhat thinner and less flexible. While the lower third of the vagina near the introitus is sensitive to erotic stimulation, the upper two-thirds contain almost no nerve endings. Being highly sensitive and surrounded by muscles, the introitus may

reflect a woman's psychological response to sex. If she is fearful or anxious, the muscles may tighten, making it difficult for the penis to penetrate.

The **fallopian tubes**, which are extremely narrow and lined with hair-like projections called cilia, are connected to the uterus. They serve as the pathway through which the egg leaves the ovaries and the sperm reaches the egg. Fertilization typically takes place in the upper end of the fallopian tubes (or infundibulum). The fertilized egg travels through the fallopian tubes into the uterus and attaches itself to the uterine wall.

Although women's breasts are not actually sex organs, they have psychological, erotic, and reproductive significance. The breasts consist of about 20 clusters of mammary glands and a fatty, fibrous tissue that surrounds these clusters. The nipple, out of which the milk flows, is at the tip of the breast. Its many nerve endings make it important in erotic stimulation. The area surrounding the nipple is called the areola. Although breast sizes and shapes vary, size does not affect a woman's ability to nurse. Since small breasts have the same number of nerve endings as large breasts, changing the size and shape of her breasts may make a woman feel more feminine and sensual, but it does not affect her sexual response from a strictly biological standpoint.

The Male

Male sexual anatomy consists of the external genitals, the penis and the scrotum, and the internal genitals: the testicles, epididymis, vas deferens, prostate gland, Cowper's glands, and seminal vesicles (see Figure 5–2).

The **penis** serves important functions in sexual pleasure, reproduction, and elimination of urine. It is a tubular organ with three major parts: the part attached to the body (the root), the main part (the body), and the

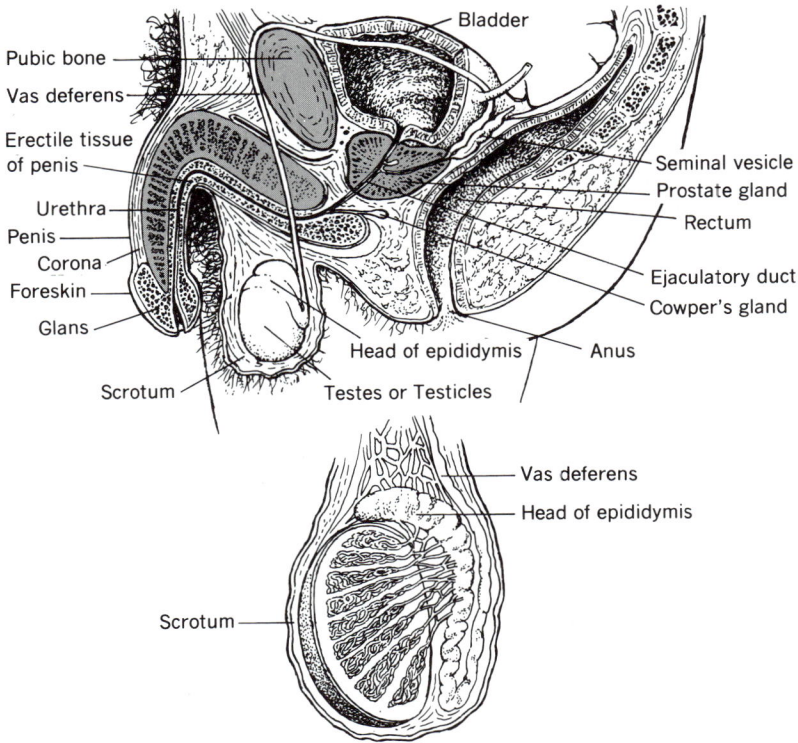

Figure 5–2 Male sexual anatomy. Shown are the external and internal organs of the body. (*Source*: Hoult, Henze, and Hudson, 1978, p. 167.)

tip (known as the glans). The raised ridge separating the glans from the body of the penis is called the corona. The glans and the corona are most sensitive to sexual stimulation. Three long cylinders of spongy tissue filled with blood vessels and nerves make up the internal structure of the penis. In the unaroused state, they contain little blood. However, during erection they become filled with blood (engorged) and expand, making the penis stiff. The skin of the penis is hairless and arranged in loose folds, thereby allowing for enlargement during erection. The foreskin of the penis is an additional layer of skin that forms a sheath-like covering over the glans. It may be present in the adult male, or it may be absent if removed by surgery (a process called **circumcision**). Usually, circumcision is done either for hygienic purposes, as in the United States, or for ritu-

alistic reasons. For example, circumcision has been a religious custom among Jews for thousands of years.

The penis has been the focus of a great deal of attention throughout history; indeed, in some cultures the male genitals have become the object of religious worship (phallic worship). In contemporary society, the penis is both sexually and psychologically significant to the male. Besides being the part of a man's anatomy that is most sexually responsive, it is often the part about which he is most emotionally sensitive. Concern over the size of one's penis has become common since it is erroneously related to masculinity and the ability to be a good lover. While men vary considerably in the size of the organ—generally from about 2½ to 4½ inches in length—there appears to be a tendency for the small penis to grow proportionately more than the large penis during erection. The average erect penis is about six inches long. Penis size is hereditary but is unrelated to a man's height or weight.

The **scrotum** is a loose pouch of skin located at the base of the penis which holds the testes. The **testes** are two, oval-shaped organs that serve as reproductive glands. Like the ovaries, they have two major functions: to produce sperm and to produce the male sex hormone, testosterone, which stimulates growth of facial hair, thickens the vocal cords, and causes other developments we associate with the onset of puberty. Both testes are about the same size, although the left one usually hangs lower than the right. Within each testicle, there are a number of chambers containing several hundred tightly coiled, thread-like tubes known as seminiferous tubules. These carry out the important function of sperm production, that is, spermatogenesis. One of the interesting phenomena of the male anatomy is the fact that the scrotum and testes can move up and close to the body or down and away from the body. While emotional factors may cause this to happen, temperature changes are usually responsible. Hot temperatures will cause the scrotum to move down and away from the body, whereas cold temperatures will cause the scrotum to shrivel and move close to the body. This mechanism is extremely important to the production of sperm since spermatogenesis requires a consistency of temperature, generally about one degree below normal body temperature.

Unlike the female, who has all her eggs present at birth, the male does not begin producing his fertilizing agent, the sperm, until the onset of puberty. After puberty, the adult male continually produces approximately 200 to 300 million sperm per day. A mature sperm is very tiny—in fact, it is the smallest human cell. It consists of a head, a neck, a midpiece, and a tail. Sperm pass out of the testes into a long single tube, the epi-

didymis, which is coiled into a small crescent-shaped region on the top and side of each testicle. Here the sperm may be stored until mature, usually for a period of up to six weeks. The sperm then pass into another tube, the vas deferens, a U-shaped tube about 18 inches long that runs up the body cavity behind the bladder, then descends and attaches to the top of the prostate gland. As the tube passes through the prostate, it narrows and is called the ejaculatory duct, which opens into the urethra.

The urethra has the dual function of conveying sperm and urine; sperm move through the urethra out into the penis. The prostate lies below the bladder. About the size and shape of a chestnut, it is composed of muscle and glandular tissue. The prostate secretes an alkaline fluid that composes the major portion of the semen or ejaculate. While the average ejaculation contains about five million sperm, the presence or absence of sperm does not change the appearance of the ejaculate—although its composition varies with individuals and from time to time. The volume of the average ejaculate is roughly one teaspoonful; it may be thick and viscous or thin and watery. When an ejaculation takes place, semen is propelled through the urethra by a spasm or contraction of the gland. The prostate is small at birth, enlarges during puberty, and usually shrinks in old age.

The Cowper's glands are located just below the prostate. During sexual arousal, they secrete a small amount of clear alkaline fluid that appears as a droplet on top of the penis before ejaculation occurs. It is thought that this secretion neutralizes the acidic urethra. The secreted substance, sometimes called precoital fluid, may contain some sperm, consequently, a woman may become pregnant even though the man has not ejaculated. On each side of the prostate gland are small sac-like glands known as seminal vesicles. While their function is unclear, it is believed that they (along with the prostate) secrete fluid that makes up semen and that they specifically secrete a fluid that activates the sperm.

Sexual Pleasure and Sexual Response

Based on learning, past experiences, values, attitudes, and beliefs, each individual comes to personal decisions about her or his sexual life. The individual defines which sexual acts are pleasurable and which are not, when sexual activity is enjoyable and when it is not, and with whom it is desirable and with whom it is not. A great deal of variation can occur; clearly, what is sexually exciting for one person may be distasteful or unenjoyable to another.

Sexual responses are controlled by more than simple spinal reflexes. They can be brought under voluntary control and may be initiated by fantasies and other psychological conditions. Thus, the idea that sex is "all in our heads" may not be far from the truth; the brain has critical influence in producing sexual responses.

Recent research suggests that sexual response may be as unique as a fingerprint. In their work with 382 women and 312 men, Masters and Johnson (1966) suggest that, while the range of sexual response is impressive, it can nevertheless be described for both men and women in terms of four overlapping stages: excitement, plateau, orgasm, and resolution. The two basic physiological processes that occur during these stages are **vasocongestion** (when large amounts of blood flow into the blood vessels of a region) and **myotonia** (when muscles contract throughout the body).

The excitement phase is the beginning of erotic arousal. It may last from a few minutes to several hours, depending on the individual and the circumstances. Vasocongestion takes place at this stage; it leads to arousal and erection in the male and lubrica-

tion of the vagina for the female. During the excitement stage, both men and women experience increases in pulse rate, blood pressure, respiration, and saliva production. In addition, a "sex flush"—a reddening of the skin somewhat like the measles—appears on the chest, abdomen, and thighs of about 75 percent of women and 50 percent of men. As the excitement phase continues, men's testicles are drawn up to the base of the body and the scrotum thickens. In women, the glans (or tip of the clitoris) swells, the breasts become engorged with blood, and the nipples become erect from contractions of the muscle fibers surrounding the nipple. The labia majora and minora thicken and begin to dilate, the upper two-thirds of the vagina expands in what is termed a "ballooning" response, and the cervix and uterus pull up (see Figures 5–3 and 5–4).

During the plateau phase, the bodily changes that began during the excitement phase intensify. Vasocongestion reaches its peak; pulse rates, blood pressure, and respiration become more rapid for both men and women. In women, the formation of the orgasmic platform occurs. There is a thickening of the tissues around the outer third of the vagina which causes the vaginal entrance to become smaller. The clitoris draws up into the body, the breasts become more engorged, and the uterus enlarges. The color of the labia minora changes from pink to dark red in women who have had no children, and from red to a purple color among women who have given birth. In men, the penis is fully erect during the plateau phase. The testes become so engorged that they may become twice as large as they were before arousal. They are also more firmly drawn up to the base of the body. The secretion from the Cowper's glands may appear on the head of the penis.

The **orgasm** phase is short, being only three to ten seconds in duration. The process of orgasm is similar in both females and

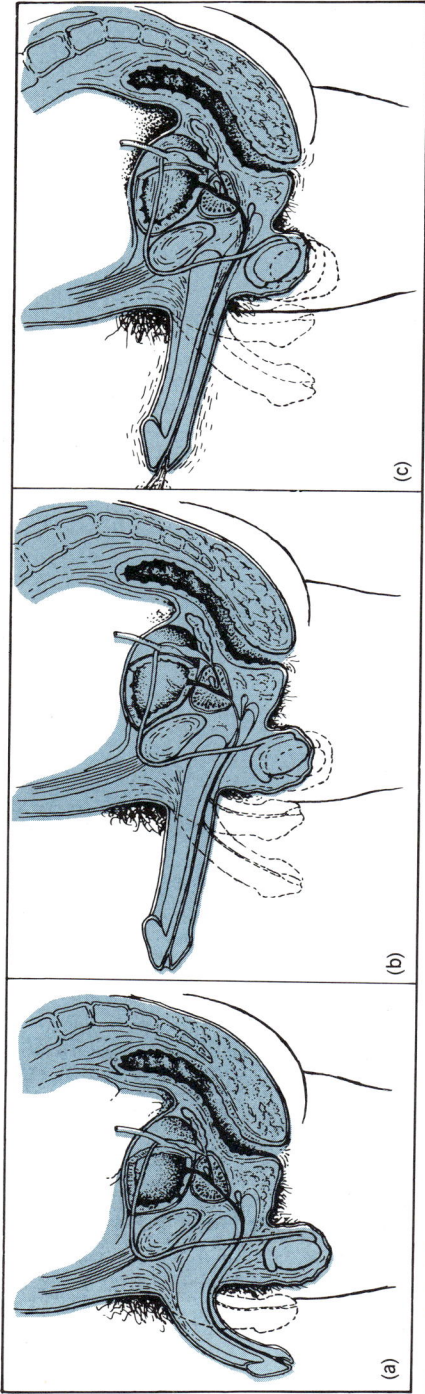

Figure 5-3 The sexual response of the male genitals. Shown are the male genitals (*a*) in the unaroused state, (*b*) in a highly aroused state, and (*c*) during orgasm. Note the contractions of the sexual organs. (*Source:* Hyde, 1979, p. 163.)

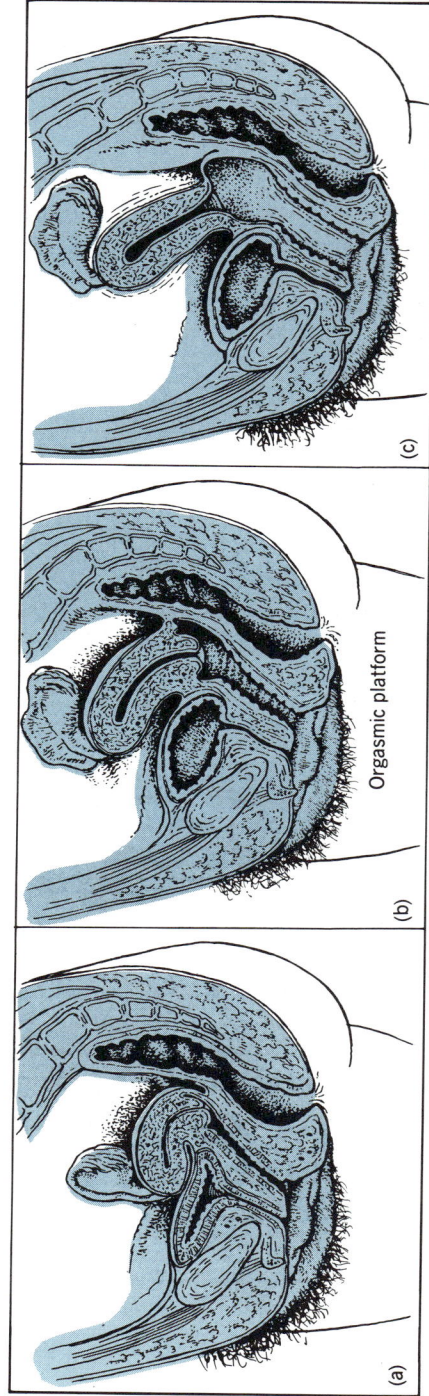

Orgasmic platform

Figure 5-4 The sexual response of the female genitals. Shown are the female genitals (*a*) in the unaroused state, (*b*) in the aroused state plateau, and (*c*) during orgasm. Note the contractions in the muscles surrounding the vagina. (*Source:* Hyde, 1979, p. 165.)

males: a series of rhythmic muscular contractions that occur at intervals of about 0.8 seconds. In the male, the contractions or spasms are associated with ejaculation caused by contraction of the prostate gland and other organs. In the female, the orgasmic contractions usually begin at the top of the uterus and move downward toward the vagina. Both sexes experience increases in blood pressure, respiration, and pulse rates during orgasm. Muscular contractions occur throughout the body—in the arms, hands, legs, buttocks, face, and back.

Unlike men, who experience only one orgasm at a time, some women may have many orgasms during a single sexual encounter—although this is less common than was once believed. The number and intensity of orgasms may not, however, be the sole factors determining women's sexual fulfillment. Sexual satisfaction may also be a function of her emotional state, changes in her menstrual cycle, and the quality of her relationship with her sexual partner.

Male orgasm consists of two stages. In the first, what Masters and Johnson have called the stage of "ejaculatory inevitability," the ejaculate is forced into a bulb at the base of the urethra. In the second state, both the urethral bulb and penis rhythmically contract, forcing out the semen. Unlike male orgasm, which leaves obvious proof that it has occurred, female orgasm is not so readily apparent and there is greater opportunity for "faking" it.

The final phase of sexual response is resolution; during this stage, the individual's body generally returns to the unaroused state. The longer the excitement and plateau phases have been, the longer it will take to achieve resolution. During this stage, men typically enter a "refractory period" and are unable to be sexually aroused. The length of this period varies considerably depending on the individual. Women do not usually experience a refractory period; thus, they may go through the four stages of sexual response again and again, experiencing successive orgasms.

Reproduction

We all know that conception occurs when the male sperm meets the female's egg. Specifically, on about the fourteenth day of a woman's menstrual cycle, she ovulates (i.e., an egg is released from the ovary into the body cavity). During intercourse, the sperm enter the fallopian tubes and are propelled by the cilia lining down toward the egg. They sometimes arrive 60 to 90 minutes after ejaculation.

While the great majority of the sperm never get close to the egg, one sperm is sufficient for conception. The exact mechanism that allows one and only one sperm to enter the egg is unknown. However, it is believed that a swarm of sperm gather around the egg and secrete the enzyme hyluronidase. This dissolves the thin, gelatinous layer called zona pellucida which surrounds the egg, and allows one sperm to penetrate.

Contrary to the commonly held belief that conception occurs in the uterus, it actually takes place in the outer third of the fallopian tubes. After conception, the fertilized egg or **zygote** continues its journey down the fallopian tube. After about 36 hours, the process of cell division begins; it will ultimately see this single cell develop into a fetus. Within five to seven days after conception, the mass of cells attaches to the lining of the woman's uterus where it will receive nourishment and continue to grow. (For more information on pregnancy and childbirth, see Chapter 10.)

Forms of Sexual Expression

Unlike many tribal societies—where adolescents are given explicit instruction in how to provide sexual pleasure—our society assumes that most sexual skills will be learned by "doing what comes naturally." As the profusion of best-selling sex manuals of the last 20 years makes clear, however, many Americans feel they need to become better informed about sexual interactions.

Sexual Self-stimulation

Masturbation and fantasy are forms of one-person sexuality or **autoeroticism**. The term **masturbation** refers to some form of direct physical stimulation of oneself, such as stroking, fondling or rubbing genitals, breasts, or other body parts. Masturbation was often viewed negatively in earlier societies; some religions consider it a sin. One aspect of the recent sexual revolution has been to attack the stigma about masturbation and to view this practice as simply one more way of achieving sexual satisfaction.

Sexual fantasies are common, especially during masturbation and sexual intercourse. They are more frequently reported by men than women, but this difference may be decreasing (Masters, Johnson, and Kolodny, 1982). While the nature of such fantasies varies dramatically from person to person, certain themes are widespread. Many Americans fantasize about switching partners: a married man may imagine having sex with a neighbor's wife, while a 17-year-old female may dream of making love to a male rock star. Conquest fantasies—where one dreams of being a king, a general, a movie star, or some other powerful figure who can easily seduce others—are frequently reported in studies of sexual fantasy. Some men and women fantasize about being conquered and forced to have sex with someone else (Delora and Warren, 1977; Friday, 1973, 1979).

Having a specific fantasy does not mean that the individual actually wants that experience to happen. In fact, those who try out their fantasies in "real life" often find that their experiences are not as exciting as they had hoped. In part, this is predictable since the individual totally controls the script in a fantasy. There are no complications resulting from someone else's wrong moves, or headaches, or reluctance—or insistence on acting out their own fantasy! Sexual fantasizing is appealing because it is not only enjoyable but also safe. One can fantasize any type of sexual encounter without any fear of being hurt or hurting another.

Fantasies can also help people to rehearse sexual scripts or overcome fears. One man explained: "I've always been embarrassed about the size of my penis, which seems very small. In my fantasies, the woman I'm with always remarks on how big my penis is, and seems in awe of its power. I found that if I used this fantasy when I was with someone, I was much less nervous. It sounds silly, but I really felt better about myself" (Masters, Johnson, and Kolodny, 1982: 251).

Sex with a Partner

There are many ways to interact sexually with another person. These include kissing and touching, foreplay and intercourse, and oral and anal sex.

Kissing and Touching

While both kissing and touching may be viewed as preliminary to sexual intercourse, they are also experienced as pleasurable activities in themselves. **Petting** is the term generally used to describe intimate caressing and fondling that stops short of intercourse. While kissing and touching are common forms of sexual expression in American culture, techniques and preferences vary considerably. Some individuals prefer being kissed on the mouth; others enjoy kissing or touching other erogenous zones such as the earlobes, neck, or breasts.

Although both kissing and touching may be viewed as preliminary to sexual intercourse, they are pleasurable activities in themselves.

Foreplay and Intercourse

Foreplay is the term given to sexual activity that precedes and leads into intercourse. It includes kissing, touching, holding, and caressing one's partner in order to arouse one another. Morton Hunt (1974), in a survey of couples, found that foreplay lasts an average of 15 minutes. However, this period of intimacy can be much longer or shorter, depending on the situation.

Intercourse or **coitus** is the penetration of the penis into the vagina. Styles and positions of intercourse vary; past experience, personal preferences, and moods will affect what the individual enjoys on a given day. Recent research on sexual techniques shows that couples are doing more experimenta-

tion, perhaps to maximize the pleasure for both partners. Some prefer the traditional "missionary" position, face-to-face with the man on top. Others prefer that the woman be on top, that both partners lie on their sides, or that the man enter the woman from the rear. While experimentation may be valuable, some couples become obsessed with finding the "right" technique which will provide the perfect experience.

Oral and Anal Sex

Until fairly recently, oral and anal sex were regarded as unusual sexual behavior and were avoided by most heterosexual couples. However, according to a survey by researcher Carol Tavris, oral sex is now practiced to some extent by most American couples (Tavris and Sadd, 1977). **Cunnilingus** (stimulating a woman's genitals with the tongue) was used often or occasionally by 87 percent of respondents. **Fellatio** (stimulating the penis or scrotum with the tongue or mouth) was reported by 85 percent of the couples questioned.

According to this study, anal sex is not as popular. Only 43 percent of the women surveyed by Tavris reported that they had tried anal sex, and most said they did not enjoy it as much as other sexual activities. Both oral and anal sex can be part of precoital foreplay or can be practiced instead of intercourse. However, for reasons of health, it is important not to introduce material from the anal area into the vagina.

Homosexuality

American society has traditionally held a negative view of male homosexuals and lesbians. Homosexual behavior has been viewed as being "obscene and vulgar" (Institute for Sex Research, 1970) and has been outlawed in most states. However, in the last 15 years, there has been a dramatic change in attitudes and public policy, due in good part to the rise of an active gay rights movement. In 1974, the American Psychiatric Association removed homosexuality from its list of "mental disorders." As of 1982, more than 35 communities (including some of the nation's largest cities) and four states had passed legislation or taken executive action to prohibit discrimination against lesbians and gay males in employment, housing, and other areas. In Hyde's (1979) terms, gays have become "the new minority" challenging prejudice and mistreatment.

Actually, very few individuals are 100 percent heterosexual or 100 percent homosexual. Sexual orientation is more accurately seen along a continuum of response. Alfred Kinsey, the noted sex researcher, devised a seven-point scale to illustrate this continuum (see Figure 5–5). He took into account the person's psychological responses, inner experience of himself or herself, and overt sexual activities. Based on Kinsey's data, it is clear that a significant proportion of Americans have engaged in at least incidental homosexual behavior (scale category #1).

The lifestyles of gay men and lesbians will be described in greater detail in Chapter 6. In terms of sexuality, homosexuals experience the four phases of the sexual response cycle in the same sequence as heterosexuals. Homosexuals also engage in many of the same forms of expression practiced by heterosexuals, including masturbation, kissing and touching, and oral and anal sex. Both gay males and lesbians tend to spend a good deal of time caressing their partner's bodies before approaching genital areas (Rathus, 1983).

Many Americans have accepted the traditional stereotype that all male homosexuals are effeminate while all lesbians are masculine. In actuality, this stereotype is far from accurate. Joseph Harry (1983: 217), in a review of academic studies of homosexuality, concludes that intimate gay and lesbian relationships rarely approximate the "butch/ femme" model. He adds that "gay relationships are more likely to be patterned after a 'best friends/roommates' model than after a heterosexual sex role model."

Sex and Communication

As we have seen, many forms of sexual expression are open to American males and females. However, any type of sexual interaction with a partner—whether heterosexual or homosexual—is strongly influenced by the couple's ability to communicate with each other.

"I love Tom," explains Janet, "but I have to admit that our sex life isn't great, at least for me. I've never had an orgasm dur-

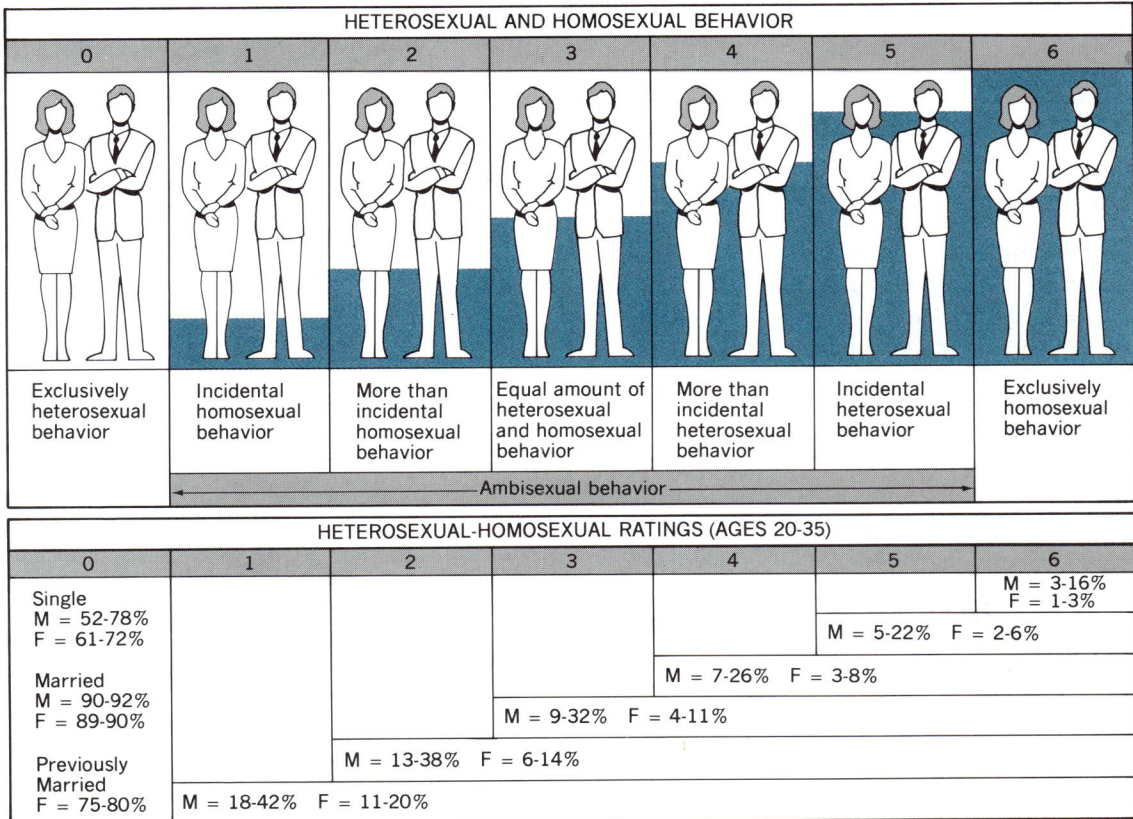

Figure 5-5 Heterosexual-homosexual rating scale. Scale and figures adapted from Kinsey's data for males (M) and females (F) published in 1953. The ranges of percentages result from different ratios in various subgroups within the seven categories. These categories themselves are somewhat arbitrary, and the whole scale should therefore be read as a continuum. (*Source*: Kinsey, et al., 1953, p. 488.)

ing intercourse. He always seems to come so fast . . . five minutes at the most. I'm just getting excited and he's already finished, so I just fake orgasm.

"When he asks me if I enjoyed it, I have to say, 'It was fantastic!' It would hurt him too much to say anything else. Also, what if he thinks there's something wrong with me, that I'm frigid? How can I tell him the truth?"

Janet's situation is not all that uncommon. Many Americans find it difficult to speak honestly about their sexual feelings, pleasures, and frustrations—even with a long-term lover or spouse. Sexual technique is often regarded as something that we all naturally understand. We are supposed to instinctively know how to please our sexual partners. Consequently, it may seem frightening to admit that we are *not* so all-knowing—and perhaps even more intimidating to inform a lover that he or she may not be either.

If one is dissatisfied sexually, how can this

be communicated most effectively? It is not necessary to offer a lecture on anatomy or develop a detailed play-by-play blueprint. The best alternative may be to communicate during intimate moments by talking or guiding the partner's hands and body movements. Thus, Janet could gently ask Tom to slow down a bit during foreplay and intercourse, or could attempt to send him the same message with nonverbal cues. If he became a bit more open to communicating about their sexual relationship, she might suggest buying a sex manual and reading and discussing it together.

As one example of poor communication about sex, Masters and Johnson (1979) have reported that relatively few heterosexual men and women have told or shown their partners how they like to have their genitals touched. Figure 5–6 shows the relationship between effective communication and sexual satisfaction within marriage. The findings directly contradict the view that great sexual companions never need to talk about sex.

The message seems clear: good communication is a key element of rewarding sex.

The alternatives—storing up frustrations and resentments, lying, faking orgasms—can be destructive to a couple's sexual and emotional closeness.

The Double Standard: Male and Female Roles

One of the major changes in American sexual behavior during recent decades has been the growing challenge to the traditional "**double standard**" regarding male and female sexuality. In the past, it was widely believed that men wanted sex more than women. They were expected to take the lead in all sexual encounters; women were supposed to lie back passively and endure an essentially unpleasant experience. "Good" women were obligated to "submit" to sex purely to satisfy their husbands. Only women of dubious moral standards were expected to really enjoy sex.

The pioneering research on sexual behavior conducted in the 1940s and 1950s by Dr.

Figure 5–6 Communication in marriage and satisfaction with sex. (*Source*: Blumstein and Schwartz, 1983, p. 222 & 223, *American Couples: Money, Work, Sex*, New York: William Morrow and Company, Inc.

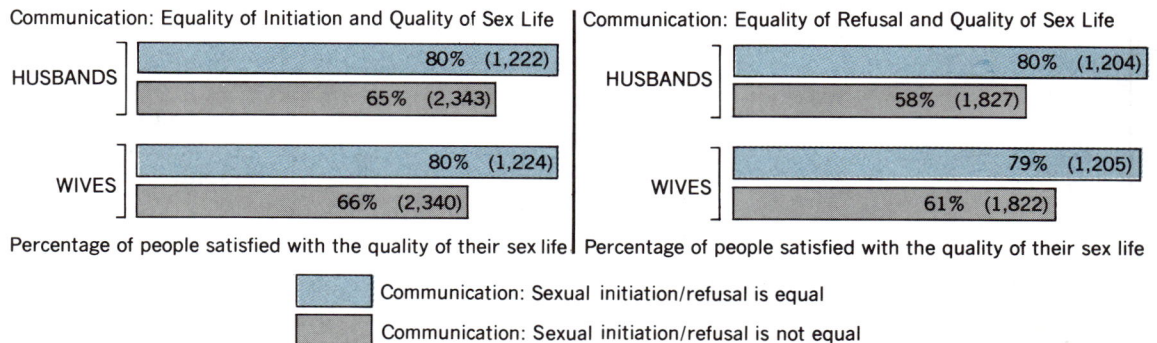

Communication: Equality of Initiation and Quality of Sex Life	Communication: Equality of Refusal and Quality of Sex Life
HUSBANDS — 80% (1,222) / 65% (2,343)	HUSBANDS — 80% (1,204) / 58% (1,827)
WIVES — 80% (1,224) / 66% (2,340)	WIVES — 79% (1,205) / 61% (1,822)
Percentage of people satisfied with the quality of their sex life	Percentage of people satisfied with the quality of their sex life

Communication: Sexual initiation/refusal is equal

Communication: Sexual initiation/refusal is not equal

(Number in parentheses are the number of people on which the percentages are based)

Couples who can communicate openly about their sexual relationship — who can initiate and refuse sex on an equal basis are more satisfied with their sex life.

Alfred Kinsey and his colleagues confirmed these traditional notions to at least some extent. Men seemed to be more sexually active than women and were more likely to report that they enjoyed sex. Men were more frequently involved in both premarital and extramarital sexual experiences (Kinsey, et al., 1948, 1953; Terman, 1951). Of course, given the social pressures of the 1940s and 1950s, men were certainly freer to admit to such feelings and experiences than were women. Nevertheless, the Kinsey data do suggest that a double standard regarding sexual pleasure and activity genuinely influenced behavior.

By the 1970s, however, these differences in male and female sexuality were beginning to narrow. In particular, there was a significant increase in the number of women who reported having orgasms. In the 1950s, Kinsey found that 30 percent of the women he interviewed rarely or never reached orgasm during intercourse. However, in 1974, Morton Hunt's survey of American sexuality found that only 10 to 15 percent of women rarely or never had an orgasm.

A key reason for this change was the greater awareness about sex: both women and men are more informed about their bodies and their sexual responses. Few couples still believe that women are incapable of sexual pleasure; many have changed their patterns of intimacy and intercourse so that women can achieve orgasm more often. Partly as a result, women now seem to enjoy sex more than they did in the 1940s and 1950s. In a study conducted by Carol Tavris for *Redbook* magazine, one-third of women questioned said they wished they had sex more frequently (Tavris and Sadd, 1977).

Women are concentrating on reaching orgasm more than they did in the past, whereas men are attempting to delay their own orgasms. Consequently, the pace of sex has slowed for many couples; intimate encounters are lasting longer. In the 1950s,

Kinsey found that three-quarters of married men ejaculated within two minutes after entering the vagina. But, in the 1970s, Hunt found that intercourse lasted an average of ten minutes. The greater acceptability of techniques that involve direct stimulation of the clitoris, such as manual stimulation and cunnilingus, also contributes to the apparent increase in the frequency of women's orgasms.

As another aspect of the changes in American sexuality, women are taking a more active role in intercourse. In the past, men initiated most sexual encounters, determined the tempo or pace, and decided when the interaction would end—generally after ejaculation. Now, as Masters and Johnson report, women are assuming a greater role in coital sex. For example, it is often more satisfying for them to let their partners know when they are ready for intercourse. They may take the lead and insert the penis into the vagina rather than having the men do so, possibly before women are ready.

Women are also communicating more with their partners about the desirable tempo of sex. Men may immediately begin intercourse with deep, hard penile thrusting, but most women become more stimulated initially by slower, shallower thrusts. In general, there is more sexual experimentation by couples than was true in the past. People are using a wider variety of positions during intercourse, perhaps because women have told men that the "missionary position" is not always the most enjoyable for them. By actively participating in sex, women have improved their own enjoyment and have relieved men of the burden of having to be sex experts (Hite, 1976; Masters and Johnson, 1970; Masters, Johnson, and Kolodny, 1982).

Gender differences in masturbation are decreasing as well. Kinsey's interviews in the early 1950s showed that 82 percent of 15-year-old boys had masturbated to orgasm, but only 20 percent of 15-year-old girls had done so. By the late 1970s, however, one study found that three-quarters of 18-to 30-year-old women reported they had masturbated during adolescence (Kolodny, 1980).

In many ways, then, the differences in male and female sexual behavior—so evident a generation ago—are rapidly disappearing. Yet the double standard is far from extinct. For example, it is still more acceptable for men to have casual sex; women are more likely to take an ''it's OK if I love him'' attitude. In the view of a woman quoted in *The Hite Report*: ''I think the sexual revolution is very male-oriented and anti-woman. . . . A man who has many lovers is 'sowing his oats'; a woman who has many lovers is a 'prostitute' or 'nymphomaniac' '' (Hite, 1976: 468).

Kaplan and Sager (1971) suggest that there is a basic difference between male and female sexual and emotional patterns. Men begin by emphasizing genital sexuality and only later come to appreciate the more sensuous and emotional aspects of sex. By contrast, women begin with an emphasis on sensuality and emotions, and only later develop their capacity for an intense genital response.

Sex and Love

Most of us, at some point in our lives, are forced to confront basic questions about the relationship between sex and love. Is it wrong to have sex with someone you don't love? With someone you know you'll *never* love? Is sex necessarily better with a partner you love? How important is sex in a romantic relationship?

To begin our examination of sex and love, we will begin, perhaps surprisingly, by focusing on self-love. As we noted in our discussion of love in Chapter 4, it is difficult to genuinely love others if you feel negatively about yourself. The consequences of this dilemma are quite evident in people's sexual and romantic relationships.

Sex and Self-esteem

Barbara, an intelligent, 19-year-old college student, thought of herself as ugly and unattractive. She was sure she would never have a boyfriend, marry, or have a family. One night at a party, she met a 32-year-old man, Don, whom she found boring and stuffy. Nevertheless, because he was interested in her, she went back to his apartment and began a sexual relationship with him. Barbara felt guilty because she didn't care for Don, but continued their relationship for most of a year because she felt he was the best she could get. Sex between them was unsatisfying for Barbara; it was almost a form of revenge against herself.

Sexual choices are largely an individual matter. They are deeply influenced by our attitudes toward ourselves, as was certainly the case for Barbara. If we see ourselves as unattractive, as unexciting, as sexually incompetent, as unlovable, it can have unfortunate effects on our relationships. We may end up alone and lonely; it is difficult for someone else to love us if we are filled with self-hatred. Or we may select partners who share some of our negative feelings about ourselves.

Our sexual feelings and self-images are certainly shaped by socialization within the family (Zuengler and Neubeck, 1983). All of us, to some extent, absorb our parents' attitudes toward sexuality. Parents who punish a child for masturbating or for playing sex games with other children communicate an ambivalence about sex—or a more forceful view that sex is evil and dirty—which may contribute to the child's sexual difficulties later in life (Masters and Johnson, 1970; Money, 1980). Moreover, the example of our parents' relationship can be a positive or negative role model. If they seem at ease with their bodies, at ease with touching and affection, at ease with each other, it will assist us in learning that sexual intimacy is a normal and healthy part of life.

Researchers have established that sexuality is a part of ourselves all the way from infancy to old age. There is evidence that male fetuses have erections in the womb and infant females have vaginal lubrication (Masters, Johnson, and Kolodny, 1982). A nationwide survey of sex among the elderly by Bernard Starr and Marcella Weiner (1981) indicated that even very old people report a continuing and strong interest in sex. Table 5–2 summarizes the most important sexual issues that arise throughout the life cycle. Most of these changes will be discussed in greater detail in later chapters.

Sex and Loving Others

There are many different ways of expressing love; sex is merely one important way. Obviously, many types of love do not normally involve sexual relations, such as love between parents and children, brothers and sisters, or close friends. The term **platonic relationship** is used to describe a close friendship that does not include sexual expression; it generally refers to a nonsexual friendship between a man and a woman.

As noted earlier in the chapter, there has been a substantial increase in premarital sex in the United States. Nevertheless, some couples choose to abstain from premarital sex because of religious or moral beliefs. Others, including married couples, may love each other and yet have little desire for sex. Some couples who care deeply for each other may end their sexual relationships yet remain close and enjoy each other as companions.

Angela, a member of a conservative evangelical church in the Midwest, believes that sex outside of marriage violates God's laws and is disrespectful of herself. She did sleep with a man just before graduating from high school "because I was curious, and was afraid I'd be left behind forever if I didn't." For her, it was the wrong choice because it violated a deeply felt belief.

Megan, 27, has no moral or religious qualms about premarital sex, yet finds sex without love an empty experience: "It's boring. If I don't know the guy, and don't really care about him, the whole thing seems absurd to me. Half the time, I feel like I'm not really there. By the next day, it's as if nothing had happened."

By contrast, some individuals find that loveless sex can fulfill other personal needs. Masters, Johnson, and Kolodny (1982: 308) quote a 31-year-old woman:

I'd been married for 10 years and had always been faithful, but I kept wondering what it would be like to have sex with someone else. One night I was out with some friends and we met a few guys who bought us drinks. . . . One of them was real good looking, and flirted with me, and I sort of flirted back. We went off to a motel for three or four hours, and it was beautiful sex, fantastic sex, just like in a novel. But that was the end of it, and it just felt good to know that I'd had the experience.

For Paul, premarital sex was a valuable learning experience. His first sexual encounter with a girl occurred when he was 14 and helped him to feel less scared about sex. At age 28, he married a woman he had been living with for two years. "I wanted the experience of sex with many women before I was married," he explains. "I think it has made me a better lover. I never felt guilty. It was no big deal to me."

As these examples illustrate, it is difficult to generalize about the relationship between sex and love. Masters and Johnson point out that there is really no reason why sex with a loved partner should provide greater physical satisfaction than sex without love. They

Table 5–2   Sexuality throughout the life cycle

Stage	Sexual expression
Prenatal	Sexual reflexes in the fetus
Infancy	Parent-child bonding through eye contact, cuddling and other forms of physical contact that teach the child about intimacy
	Genital play a possible source of pleasure for the infant
Early childhood	Awareness of genital differences between the sexes
	Curiosity about birth and where babies come from
	Observation of physical interactions between parents
	Awareness of sensual feelings aroused in genital play
Schoolage	Games involving sexual experimentation with same-sex or opposite-sex children
	Genital play a deliberate activity
	Parental reactions to sex play have a great influence on the child's later attitudes toward sex
	Homosexual activities common
Adolescence	Many rapid physical changes experienced
	Masturbation more frequent, often accompanied by fantasies
	Increasing heterosexual activity that may or may not include physical sexual encounters
	Peer pressure a factor in sexual activity
Early adulthood	Internal need manifested to become sexually knowledgeable
	Sexual needs fulfilled through marriage and/or other forms of sexual activities such as dating and open marriage
	Sexual pleasure balanced with other sources of satisfaction such as career or parenthood
Middle adulthood	Evidence of vulnerability to midlife crisis, particularly for males, leading to questioning of sexual capabilities
	For many women a burst of energy as a result of freedom from responsibilities from children and housework
	For divorced or single adults difficulties of dating because of feelings about their physical appearance or feelings that time is running out
Late adulthood	Decreased coital frequency
	Sexual capacities of older adults denied by false cultural stereotypes

also suggest that people should take an active role in making sexual choices, rather than being passively dictated by social pressures or guilt feelings. Each of us has to come to personal decisions about when and with whom to share the intimate experience of sex. Discussing our feelings with friends, family members, or a counselor can be helpful in developing our personal values and facing sensitive decisions.

Reproductive Issues: Birth Control and Abortion

The issues of birth control and abortion have been extremely controversial in the United States and other societies. In terms of public policy, each issue has raised questions about the respective roles of the individual and government in controlling reproductive decisions.

Birth Control

Strictly speaking, birth control refers to one's ability to prevent a birth from occurring. The practice of contraception dates back as far as ancient Egypt, Greece, and Rome (Katchadourian and Lunde, 1972). Today, we take for granted the availability of such birth control methods as the pill, the IUD, the diaphragm, and the condom. Yet this was not always the case.

In 1873, after pressure from such groups as the New York Society for the Suppression of Vice, the federal government passed the Comstock Law. This statute prohibited sending birth control information through the mail on the grounds that such material was ''obscene and indecent.'' Many states adopted even more restrictive legislation which prohibited passing birth control information from one person to another.

It was only through the dedicated efforts of Margaret Sanger, Emma Goldman, and other activists that it became legal to distribute birth control information and contraceptives. Sanger, for example, was arrested in 1916 for establishing a birth control clinic in Brooklyn, New York. Even with the educational campaigns and legal challenges mounted by such reformers, statutes prohibiting the sale of contraceptives remained in effect in some states until 1965. In that year, the Supreme Court overthrew such a law in the landmark case of *Griswold* v. *Connecticut* (Rathus, 1983).

While premarital sex is now generally accepted in our society—particularly among individuals under the age of 30—pregnancy resulting from such encounters is generally viewed as undesirable since the couple is rarely ready for marriage. Nevertheless, many young people who are sexually active make no attempt to prevent pregnancy. In a nationwide study conducted in 1975, 80 percent of sexually active, never-married females aged 15 to 19 indicated that they had engaged in sexual intercourse at some time without using contraceptives (Shah, Zelnik, and Kanter, 1975). Moreover, in a study of 393 sexually active college females, Crist (1971) found that 65 percent either used one of the least effective contraceptive methods (i.e., rhythm, douching, or withdrawal) or no contraceptive at all.

What accounts for this pattern? Hoult, et al. (1978) points out that some young people lack information about contraceptive information, while others fail to take precautions because they believe that love must be spontaneous. More remarkably, it appears that many adolescent girls believe they cannot become pregnant despite having intercourse—simply because they haven't made a conscious choice to become pregnant (Babikian and Goldman, 1971; Shouse, 1975)!

The consequences of such misinformation have become increasingly serious: teenage pregnancy is a major social and medical problem in the United States. The nation's adolescent childbearing rate is among the world's highest and exceeds the rates of many developing countries. According to one survey, about 10 percent of American adolescents become pregnant, and 6 percent give birth each year (McKenry, et al., 1979). Clearly, many of these teen mothers are both emotionally and financially unprepared for the demands of parenting. We will examine the issue of teen pregnancy in greater detail in Chapters 6 and 12.

Ideally, birth control should be effective,

relatively easy to use, readily available, acceptable to both partners, relatively safe, and capable of permitting satisfactory intercourse (Bowman and Spanier, 1978). Available methods of contraception do not necessarily meet all these criteria. However, as Calderone (1964) points out, any method is better than no method. The most effective type of birth control is the one that will be acceptable to the couple—acceptable enough that they will use it consistently.

Sterilization

Sterilization, the only permanent form of birth control, is the most widely used method of birth control in the United States (Kash, 1984). The two major methods of sterilization for women are **tubal ligation** (major surgery in which the fallopian tubes are cut) and **laparoscopy**. The latter method, popularly called "band-aid surgery," involves making a small incision in the abdomen and cauterizing (burning) the fallopian tubes with a small instrument. Both procedures make it impossible for the egg to move down the fallopian tube and therefore prevent sperm from reaching the egg. Even after sterilization, the ovaries continue to release an egg each month, menstrual periods continue, and the woman's ability to achieve orgasm is unimpaired.

Male sterilization can usually be accomplished by a minor, 15- to 20-minute operation known as a **vasectomy**. Usually performed in a doctor's office or clinic with a local anesthetic, a vasectomy involves making a small incision in the scrotum through which the physician cuts, ties, and coagu-

No contraceptive method is effective unless a couple finds it acceptable enough to use consistently.

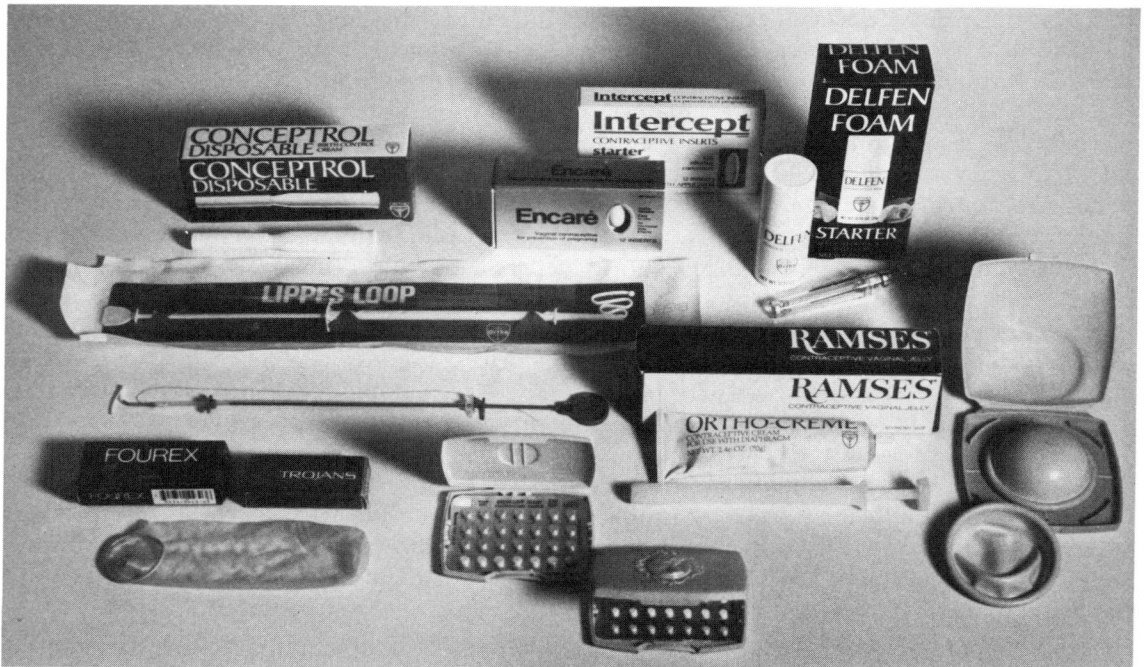

lates the vas deferens. Subsequently, the man continues to produce both semen and seminal fluid, but the sperm are prevented from entering the penis. If performed on a healthy, well-adjusted male, vasectomy will not affect his ability to achieve erection or orgasm.

The Pill

Ten million users make the "Pill" the second most widely used contraceptive method in the United States (Kash, 1984). Oral contraceptive pills regulate a woman's hormonal balance so that ovulation does not occur. They are extremely effective since conception cannot take place without ovulation.

The most widely used type of pill—the "**combination**" **birth control pill**—contains a mixture of synthetic estrogen and synthetic progesterone (progestin). Until 1975, a second type of oral contraceptive, the sequential pill, was available. However, its effectiveness was not as great as the combination pill. Complications resulting from use led to the demise of the sequential pill. Two rather recent innovations are the mini pill (which contains progestin only) and the "morning after" pill (which was approved for emergency uses, such as after rape, by the Federal Drug Administration in 1973).

The main advantage of the "combination" pill is that, if properly used, it is essentially 100 percent effective. The pill is also favored by some women because it does not interfere with intercourse, it is not messy, and it reduces menstrual flow and premenstrual tension and cramps. However, there are disadvantages, such as a higher possibility of developing blood clots or high blood pressure and a greater susceptibility to vaginitis. Some women experience nausea, weight gain, and increased depression and irritability when they use oral contraceptives.

As is well known, there has been intense public and scientific debate about the safety of the birth control pill and about its side effects. By 1975, contraception had been blamed for 472 deaths in the United States, of which 452 were due to the impact of the pill on the cardiovascular system (*Science Digest*, 1983). The highest category of risk involves women on the pill who smoke. One study found that women who both smoke heavily and use the pill have a 39 times higher risk of heart attack than women who neither smoke nor use the pill. In terms of cancer, though much research remains to be done, there is presently no conclusive evidence that the pill causes cancer of the ovaries, uterus, or breast (Ory, et al., 1980; Rathus, 1983; Shapiro, et al., 1979).

Periodic Abstinence

Periodic abstinence (natural family planning or rhythm) is the only form of "natural" birth control. It requires the systematic avoidance of sexual intercourse during a woman's fertile period (around ovulation).

This method is based on the assumption that ovulation takes place at about the same time in each menstrual cycle, approximately 14 days, plus or minus two days, prior to the onset of menstruation. Important related assumptions are that the ovum survives for 24 hours and that the sperm remains viable for up to two days. Thus, if a woman is to avoid pregnancy, she must abstain from intercourse for eight days during each 28-day cycle. However, since many women do not consistently have 28-day cycles, they must calculate their "safe" periods by one of three methods: the calendar method (a woman records and calculates her own cycle), the basal body temperature method (a woman takes her body temperature to record when she is ovulating), or the cervical mucous method (changes in cervical mucous are used to determine safe days).

The advantages of this method of contraception are that it is cheap, it has no side effects, and it helps a woman become more aware of her bodily functions. The disadvantages include a high rate of failure and the requirement of sexual abstinence for at least eight days per month (and often two or three weeks). Moreover, about six months is required to collect the data on one's bodily functions to make the method work. It is best to learn the techniques involved in periodic abstinence from someone qualified to explain how to interpret bodily changes during the menstrual cycle.

The IUD

The **intrauterine device** or IUD is a small, flexible piece of sterile plastic material with nylon strings used for birth control. The strings are attached to facilitate removal and to insure that the device is still in place. Some IUDs also contain metal. The device is anatomically engineered to conform to the shape and size of the uterine cavity. It must be inserted by a doctor or nurse practitioner, and it then remains in place until a woman wishes it to be removed.

Many different types of IUDs are available; some, like the popular Lippes loop, are named for their inventors. Medical experts are not certain of exactly how the IUD prevents conception. The most popular theory is that the presence of the device irritates the walls of the uterus, with the result that the fertilized egg cannot be implanted. The chemical composition of the device may also affect conception. For example, the small amount of copper added to some IUDs is thought to have an additional contraceptive impact.

The advantages of the IUD include its effectiveness (second only to the pill) and its simplicity. Once the device has been inserted, a woman merely must check periodically to see that the strings are in place. The IUD does not interrupt or have any effect on intercourse. Disadvantages include possible side effects such as cramping, abdominal pain, irregular bleeding, and urine and tubal infections. Most seriously, the IUD leads to perforation of the uterus, which can be fatal, in about one in 10,000 women.

The Diaphragm

The **diaphragm** is a shallow, cup-like device made of soft rubber with a springy outer edge. It fits tightly between the pelvic bone and the wall of the vagina and covers the cervix. The primary action of the diaphragm is mechanical; it simply blocks the entrance to the uterus so that sperm cannot swim up into it.

The diaphragm can be obtained with a doctor's prescription and must be used in conjunction with a spermicidal jelly or cream in order to be effective. It may be inserted up to six hours before intercourse and must be left in place for at least six hours afterwards. If accurately fitted and cared for properly, the diaphragm is an effective method of contraception. Users should, however, have yearly examinations in which they are measured to insure that the diaphragm is still fitting properly—especially if the user gains or loses ten pounds, or becomes pregnant.

Diaphragms were in widespread use before the advent of oral contraceptives and acceptance of the IUD. Their popularity subsequently declined sharply, but diaphragms are still preferred by some women who refuse to use the pill. The advantages of the diaphragm include its effectiveness (if used properly, it is 95 percent effective) and the absence of side effects. However, many people dislike this method of birth control because they feel it ruins the spontaneity of intercourse; the woman must remember to insert the diaphragm before penetration begins. Some women also dislike it because they are required to touch their genitals and handle messy creams and jellies. For certain couples, use of a diaphragm is more acceptable if the man inserts it as one part of sexual foreplay.

The Condom

The **condom** or "rubber" is a latex rubber sheath, or tissue from the intestine of a lamb, that covers the penis and thereby prevents entry of sperm into the vagina. To be effective, the condom must be placed over the erect penis shortly before intercourse—not just before ejaculation since fluid containing sperm may already have been produced. The condom should always be worn so that a little space is left at the end for the seminal fluid to accumulate following ejaculation.

Condoms are the most common form of contraception across the world. In the United States, they are widely available for purchase without a prescription. If used properly and conscientiously, the condom is an effective method of birth control—actually more effective than most people think. Failures are largely due to tearing of the sheath or to condoms slipping off after ejaculation.

Other than sterilization and withdrawal, the condom is the only form of birth control presently available to men. It is cheap and readily available, and has the additional benefit of offering protection against the transmission of venereal disease. However, many men feel that use of a condom lessens their physical pleasure during intercourse. Both men and women have complained that it interferes with the spontaneity of lovemaking.

The Cervical Cap

The **cervical cap** is somewhat like a large rubber thimble. It fits tightly over the cervix and, like the diaphragm, blocks the entrance to the uterus. Spermicidal jelly is put inside the cap before it is inserted; the cap is held in place by suction. Some women prefer to leave it in place for days or weeks, and put in jelly before each intercourse.

The cervical cap is about as effective as the diaphragm. The main advantage is that it can be left in place for days or weeks, although some women find that they develop a bad-smelling discharge if they do so. An important disadvantage of this method is that the cap can sometimes become dislodged during intercourse. While widely used in Great Britain, cervical caps have not yet been approved for use in the United States. They are currently being tested by doctors and clinics.

Spermicides

Vaginal foams, creams, jellies, and similar chemical contraceptives are widely available in American drugstores and do not require a prescription. They are inserted through use of an applicator into the vagina—much as a tampon is. **Spermicides** work in two ways: by killing sperm on contact and by blocking the entrance to the cervix so that sperm cannot swim into it. In order to be effective, they must be inserted shortly before intercourse.

Spermicides are preferred by some women because they are easily available and have no side effects. The major disadvantage is that if used alone—without a condom or diaphragm—they are not particularly effective in preventing conception. Spermicides have also been criticized for being messy, for tending to leak out after intercourse, and for interfering with spontaneity during lovemaking.

Douching and Withdrawal

Two of the oldest methods of birth control are douching and withdrawal. Vaginal **douching**—flushing out the vagina after coitus, generally with a spermicidal solution—is a completely ineffective method of birth control. It merely washes out the vagina. No matter how quickly after intercourse a woman douches, hundreds of sperm will already have entered the uterus.

Withdrawal (also known as coitus interruptus) means that the man withdraws his penis from the vagina just before orgasm in order to ejaculate outside the vagina. This, too, is a highly ineffective birth control technique. Long before ejaculation, the man has excreted sperm-filled fluid that can cause pregnancy.

Abortion

One possible consequence of the failure or nonuse of a contraceptive method is abortion. **Abortion** is usually defined as the expulsion or removal of the fetus from a woman's body before it is viable (that is, before it can survive on its own outside her body). Whereas miscarriage or **spontaneous abortion** occurs without deliberate interference, the term ''abortion'' is generally used to refer to direct intervention by surgical, chemical, or other means to terminate an undesired pregnancy. In the past, medical considerations were the chief reason for abortion. However, since the 1973 Supreme Court decision of *Roe* v. *Wade*, which gave women in all fifty states the constitutional right to an abortion during at least the first six months of pregnancy, the situation has changed. Abortions are now more commonly performed for psychiatric, humanitarian (e.g., cases of rape), or eugenic (e.g., fetal abnormalities) reasons.

The method used for abortion depends on the length of pregnancy. If the pregnancy is of less than 12 weeks' duration, abortion may be carried out by **dilation and curettage** (D and C). This is a routine operative procedure in which the cervix is dilated and a spoon-like instrument called a curette is inserted through the cervix to scrape the lining of the uterus and remove embryonic material.

Vacuum aspiration, also used through the twelfth week, has virtually replaced the D and C as the most common procedure for abortion in the United States. A simple, safe procedure with little discomfort, vacuum aspiration involves dilating the cervix and introducing into it a small tube, which removes the contents of the uterus through vacuum pressure. To induce abortion between the thirteenth and twentieth weeks, a saline solution or the hormone oxytocin can be injected into the amniotic sac to produce labor contractions. Another alternative is a **hysterotomy**. This surgical procedure, comparable to a Caesarean birth, involves removing the fetus through the abdomen.

Some people continue to believe that abortion can be produced by ingesting substances such as lead, acids, castor oil, and quinine. Such remedies have been passed on from generation to generation. Yet no such oral treatment will accomplish abortion without doing harm to the mother (Ellis and Abarbanel, 1961). Mechanical methods such as hot douches, hot baths, and hitting the abdomen are equally ineffective.

From an international perspective, the practice of abortion is affected by an endless variety of traditions, customs, and restrictions. Nevertheless, there is a noticeable trend toward liberalized abortion laws. A study by Tietze (1981) indicates that 9 percent of the world's population lives in countries that allow abortion on request at least during the first three months of pregnancy. Other nations allow abortion subject to various conditions. Figure 5–7 presents global comparisons of abortion rates.

Abortion has been one of the most controversial issues in American politics during the last 15 years. On one side are those who call themselves ''pro-life,'' including many political conservatives and religious fundamentalists. These Americans see the fetus as a human life rather than as a potential baby; therefore, in their view, abortion is essentially murder of an unborn person. ''Pro-life'' groups cite data that, since the 1973 decision in *Roe* v. *Wade*, the annual number of abortions performed in the United States has risen from 744,000 to 1.5 million. In 1980,

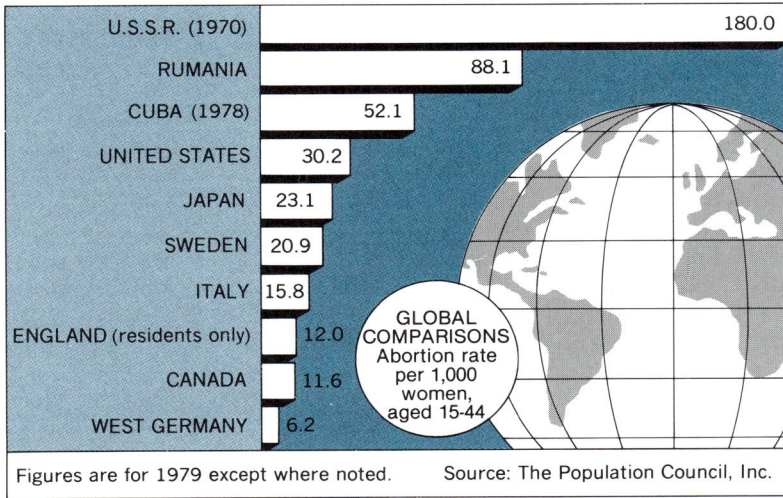

U.S.S.R. (1970)	180.0
RUMANIA	88.1
CUBA (1978)	52.1
UNITED STATES	30.2
JAPAN	23.1
SWEDEN	20.9
ITALY	15.8
ENGLAND (residents only)	12.0
CANADA	11.6
WEST GERMANY	6.2

GLOBAL COMPARISONS Abortion rate per 1,000 women, aged 15-44

Figures are for 1979 except where noted.   Source: The Population Council, Inc.

Figure 5–7 Global comparisons of abortion rates. (*Source*: *Time* Magazine, April 6, 1981, p. 27.)

abortions terminated about one-third of all pregnancies in the nation (*Time*, April 6, 1981). For advocates of the "right-to-life" philosophy, such figures are morally intolerable.

On the other side of the issue are those who call themselves "pro-choice," among them many feminists and civil libertarians. These Americans believe that women, not legislators or judges, should have the right to decide whether and under what circumstances they will bear children. "Pro-choice" advocates note that legalized abortion is especially important for the 17 percent of rape victims and 25 percent of incest victims who become pregnant (Pasnau, 1972). For feminists, the "bottom line" is that no law will ever *prevent* women from having abortions. They recall with sadness and anger that, prior to the 1973 Supreme Court decision, many American women died at the hands of "backroom" abortionists and in desperate attempts to self-abort (see Box 5–3).

"Right-to-life" groups won a key Congressional victory in 1976 with passage of the Hyde Amendment, which prohibited use of federal Medicaid funds to pay for abortions except when the mother's life was in danger or when she was the victim of rape or incest. For poor women, this meant that while they retained the right to legal abortions, they were often unable to pay for them. In 1977, Rosaura Jimenez of Texas became the first woman known to die of complications following an illegal abortion after implementation of the Hyde Amendment.

The ultimate goal of anti-abortionists is to prohibit all abortions. Under the proposed human life amendment, introduced by Senator Jesse Helms of North Carolina, "The paramount right to life is vested in each human being from the moment of fertilization without regard to age, health, or condition of dependency." Critics have charged that if this amendment is added to the Constitution, the fertilized egg could be granted more legal rights than an adult female citizen. In the view of attorney Rhonda Copelon (1981: 46), the human life amendment would criminalize abortion as murder, thereby "subordinating women's bodies, health, work and even lives to fetal survival."

In June, 1983, "pro-choice" groups won two critical victories. The Supreme Court,

B O X   5 – 3

Gloria Steinhem Recalls Her Own Abortion

I remember the fear. Just out of school, working as a waitress in a London coffee shop, I searched naively and secretly through magazines and library shelves for a way to get my life, my self, my future back. With all my heart, I did not want to be pregnant. The years ahead seemed blocked by a brick wall.

Those three desperate winter months have always stayed fresh in some cell of my mind. I remember chemists who sold me bitter powders that did not work. I remember that, to my surprise (and uniquely in my life), I thought there

was no way out. Yes, I finally found a kindly doctor who was willing to sign the complicated legal permission still necessary in England then. He sent me to a woman gynecologist who took most of my scholarship money for the next year—but who set me free. Even so, I told no one for years; not until the end of the sixties when women began supporting each other by breaking our silence.

Source: Steinem, 1981: 43.

---

by a vote of six to three, reaffirmed its controversial decision in *Roe* v. *Wade* and struck down an Akron, Ohio ordinance intended as a model for local anti-abortion legislation. Subsequently, the Senate defeated the human life federalism amendment proposed by Senator Orrin Hatch of Utah. This amendment, if passed, would have allowed each state to restrict or prohibit abortion within its own jurisdiction. The vote—the first ever on a constitutional amendment to restrict abortions—was 49 in favor and 50 against, far short of the 67 votes needed for passage (Greenhouse, 1983; Shribman, 1983).

Of course, court decisions and legislative votes can never resolve the debate over when life begins. At the time of *Roe* v. *Wade* in 1973, the Supreme Court gave women the right to have abortions up to the moment of viability, which at that time was placed at 24 to 28 weeks. However, since that time, there have been advances in neonatal care and a growing interest in the field of fetology. The age of viability accepted by medical experts has dropped; doctors are now able to keep alive fetuses as young as 20 weeks old. Some people even believe that the day will come

when all fetuses can be kept alive—in a test tube if not in a nursery incubator.

Sexual Violence

We generally think of sexual interactions between two persons as involving love, affection, or at least mutual desire. However, certain interactions—sometimes thought of as sexual—are better characterized in terms of dominance, conquest, and violence. The most dramatic examples are forcible rape and incest.

Susan Brownmiller (1975: 376), author of the pioneering study, *Against Our Will: Men, Women, and Rape,* defines **rape** as follows:

A sexual invasion of the body by force, an incursion into the private, personal inner space without consent—in short, an internal attack from one of several avenues and by one of several methods—constitutes a deliberate violation of emotional, physical, and rational integrity and is a hostile, degrading act of violence that deserves the name of rape.

Women often experience rape at gun- or

B O X   5 – 4

Date Rapes

"It's hard to make women understand that if they do get raped while they're in college, it's more likely to be on a date than in a dark alley," says Amy Levine, director of the Rape Prevention Program at the University of California at San Francisco.

Date rape—also known as acquaintance rape—is one of the least reported, and potentially one of the most emotionally damaging, forms of sexual assault. Ellen Doherty, coordinator of a Rape Intervention Program at a New York City hospital, notes: "It is the hardest for women to talk about, even to their close friends, much less to the police. . . . Not only has her body been vi-

olated, but her trust in another human being has been betrayed, and her faith in her own judgment has been shaken."

Psychologist Mary Koss of Kent State University has conducted one of the few studies that measures the incidence of nonstranger rape. She found than more than half of the women students questioned had experienced verbal or physical sexual aggression at some point in their lives. One in eight had been raped, although many described their experiences without labeling them as rape.

Source: Barrett, 1982: 48–51, 130.

---

knife-point. Many rapes are "gang rapes," committed by two or more assailants. Stereotypes about this crime suggest it is typically committed by persons unknown to the victim, but in fact a substantial proportion of rapes are committed by friends, co-workers, neighbors, dates, and family members (see Box 5–4).

In 1980, according to the Federal Bureau of Investigation, there were 82,000 forcible rapes in the United States. However, the FBI and other sources believe that an estimated 165,000 to 700,000 rapes go unreported each year. Based on one estimate, a rape occurs in this country every six minutes. The chances of a woman being raped at some point in her life are now one in ten (*Good Housekeeping*, 1982).

Traditionally, rape was blamed on the victim, reflecting the sexist biases of many societies. If a man committed rape, it was somehow the woman's fault for provoking him. This unfortunate view contributed to the massive underreporting of rape; victims feared disapproval from family and friends.

However, the feminist movement of recent decades has vigorously challenged mistreatment of rape victims by the police, the courts, hospital personnel, the media, and the society as a whole.

Women's anti-rape groups have been established across the nation to reeducate people about this violent crime and to counsel rape victims and persons close to them. To a significant degree, feminists have been successful in reshaping public awareness of rape and relevant legislation. As one example, some states have adopted statutes that make it a crime to rape one's spouse. Nevertheless, despite changing attitudes and public policy, the FBI still views rape as the fastest growing crime in the United States (*Women's Almanac*, 1977).

Incest, like rape, is a form of coerced sexual intimacy based on a desire for dominance and conquest. The main distinction, of course, is that incest involves family members—typically fathers and daughters or brothers and sisters. More than 90 percent of incest victims are female, whether children or adults, while most abusers are male. An incestuous relationship can continue over a long period of time; however, the average age of the victim when incest begins is between six and eleven years (Janeway, 1981; Watkins, 1983).

There are approximately 5,000 reported cases of incest per year in the United States, but all experts agree that underreporting is massive. As is true of rape, victims of incest frequently are not believed or are blamed. In the view of the Child Abuse Unit of Santa Clara County, California, a figure of 100,000 cases per year would be a "very conservative estimate." A 1981 report in *Newsweek* asserted that incest in the United States had reached "epidemic" proportions (*New York Post*, 1981; *New York Times*, 1979; Sawyer, 1980: 43).

According to David Finkelhor, author of *Sexually Victimized Children* (1979), incest is found in a wide variety of families, including poor urban families, isolated rural families, and middle-class and affluent families. Finkelhor praises the feminist movement and the child protection movement for increasing public concern about incest: "The women's movement made sexual abuse an important focus. . . . When social workers began to battle physical child abuse, they saw that sexual abuse was equally critical" (Sawyer, 1980: 43). Incest and other forms of child abuse will be discussed further in Chapter 11.

Sexually Transmitted Diseases

When people engage in sexual intercourse, oral sex, or anal sex, there is a possibility of contracting an infection. When such an infection is transmitted, primarily through sexual contact, it is called a **sexually transmitted disease** (STD). While a number of common infections can be transmitted through sexual intimacy—including pubic lice or "crabs" and venereal warts—the most serious types of STD are gonorrhea, syphilis, genital herpes, and AIDS.

As is the case with unwanted pregnancies, most people feel that "it can't happen to me." However, statistics prove otherwise. With the exception of syphilis, rates of sexually transmitted diseases in the United States have reached epidemic proportions. Most cases occur in the 15- to 29-year-old age group; it is currently estimated that 50 percent of American young people will contract a STD by the time they are 25!

The present increases in STDs appear to be related to the growing sexual permissiveness of recent decades and the shift away from the condom (which decreases the probability of infection) to the pill (which actually increases susceptibility). If you suspect that you have contracted a STD, it is important to seek medical attention. Most states have laws protecting the confidentiality of patients, even if they are minors living with their parents.

Gonorrhea

The World Health Organization has ranked **gonorrhea** as second in prevalence among communicable diseases, behind only the common cold. For women, the symptoms of this disease are often difficult to detect. There may only be a mild irritation or discharge, which many women tend to ignore. Unfortunately, if gonorrhea is not treated, sterility is likely to follow within a few months.

In males, by contrast, painful symptoms are generally evident three to five days after infection. They include a burning sensation upon urination, some pus or blood in the urine, and a yellowish, pus-like discharge from the urethral opening at the tip of the penis. Since these symptoms are obvious, most men seek immediate treatment. They are usually given a large dose of penicillin, administered in the buttocks, and are cured in a short time.

Syphilis

Syphilis has several stages. The incubation period ranges from eight days to ten weeks, with an average of 21 days. In the first stage, a round, ulcer-like, painless sore called a chancre appears. If left untreated, the sore will disappear in about two weeks. However, the disease then enters a secondary stage which includes a generalized body rash that does not itch or hurt. Hair loss, sore throat, fever, and headache may also occur (Goldstein, 1976).

If the secondary rash is left untreated, it will disappear in two to six weeks. The latent stage of syphilis, which may last many years, will then result. This stage has no visible symptoms; about half of those who enter it will remain in it permanently with no further complications. However, the other half move into the extremely dangerous tertiary stage of syphilis. These persons can experience severe damage, ranging from heart disease to blindness and insanity.

The treatment for syphilis, like gonorrhea, is penicillin. The large doses needed to treat gonorrhea are not required in curing syphilis. If an individual is allergic to penicillin, tetracycline can be used effectively for both diseases.

Herpes

The anecdote goes: ''What's the difference between true love and herpes? Herpes lasts forever!'' But no one is laughing. **Genital herpes** is a highly contagious venereal disease that has been contracted by an estimated 10 million to 20 million Americans. At least 300,000 new cases are occurring each year (*U.S. News and World Report*, August, 1982).

Herpes is spread by sexual contact with an infected person. Similar to cold sores on the lips, which are caused by another type of herpes virus, the symptoms of genital herpes are small, painful blisters that form in men on the penis or in the urethra and in women on the cervix or the vaginal walls. After a few days, the blisters turn into sores and eventually heal. The virus then becomes dormant for an indefinite period—days, weeks, or months—but can be reactivated at any time for reasons that remain unclear. Some people have reported that their herpes blisters return when they are under stress.

The most serious consequences of herpes are the effects on infants born to infected women. Severe brain damage to the child, sometimes fatal, is an all-too-common result. Herpes is taken very seriously not only because it is so widespread (as many as one adult in seven may have it), but also because at present there is no known cure. Doctors advise persons who have herpes blisters or sores not to have sex until ten days after the sores are healed; otherwise, they may infect their partners.

Fear of contracting herpes has unquestionably reshaped the behavior of many sexually active Americans. The one-night stand with a stranger met in a singles' bar is no longer approached so casually; moreover, a trip to see a prostitute may be a high-stakes gamble. Perhaps symbolically, *Playboy* employees now jokingly refer to the swimming facilities at Hugh Hefner's Los Angeles mansion as ''the herpes pool.''

Counseling professionals have reported a ''leper effect'' associated with herpes; patients with the disease may come to feel that they are ugly, dangerous, and ''damaged goods.'' One California man explained that he did not date for two years after learning that he had herpes: ''I thought anyone in their right mind would stay away from me. You don't take the phone number; you don't want to go through the rejection'' (Leo, 1982: 64).

In response to this growing problem, groups like the Herpes Resource Center of Palo Alto, California have been established. The Center has 30,000 members in 45 chapters across the nation. It attempts to reassure sufferers that they are not alone and can learn to live normal lives. In line with this approach, one Seattle physician notes that he treats many herpes patients who are successfully coping: ''They have to live with having the disease, but it doesn't consume them'' (Leo, 1982: 66).

AIDS

In July, 1983, Secretary of Health and Human Services Margaret Heckler stated that the federal government's number one priority was the deadly disease AIDS. **Acquired immune deficiency syndrome**, commonly known as AIDS, is a fatal disease that attacks victims by wiping out their immune systems. This leaves them defenseless against many common infections, as well as the serious skin cancer known as Kaposi's sarcoma. It is believed that AIDS is communicated either through intimate sexual contact, use of infected needles, or transfusions of contaminated blood. But medical researchers remain unsure of exactly how AIDS is caused, how it spreads, and how it can be cured (Isaacson, 1983).

What is known is that the incubation period for AIDS can range from six months to three years. Most seriously, close to 100 percent of AIDS patients diagnosed two or more years ago have died. As of December, 1983, there were 2,803 reported victims of AIDS, 1,146 of whom had died. Four high-risk groups accounted for the overwhelming majority of AIDS cases: sexually active male homosexuals (72 percent), intravenous drug users (17 percent), immigrants from Haiti (5 percent), and hemophiliacs (1 percent) (Dowd, 1983).

One consequence of AIDS has been public hysteria about contagion. Thus far, there is no evidence that the disease can be transmitted by casual contact with victims, food, or air. Nevertheless, horror stories about mistreatment of AIDS victims abound. Some have been shunned by hospitals, airlines, and ultimately even undertakers. A Minneapolis man with AIDS reports that he is no longer welcome at a gay bar where he once won a pageant ''because they're afraid I'd contaminate the place.'' His parents have not visited him in the hospital because

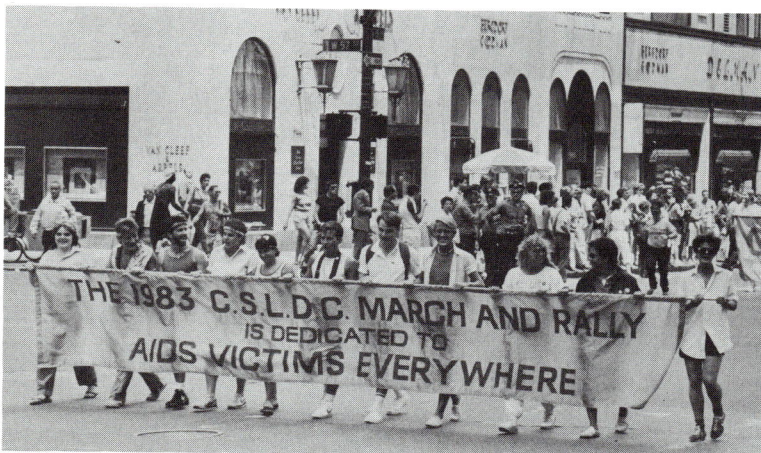

Finding a cure for AIDS, a disease which can be communicated through intimate sexual contact, has become a top priority for American health authorities.

"they feel I'm being punished for my lifestyle" (Banaszynski, 1983: 1A, 4A).

There is little doubt that AIDS has contributed to a backlash against homosexuals and gay rights. In a 1983 "op. ed." article in the *New York Times*, William Beauchamp (1983: E21), an openly homosexual faculty member at Southern Methodist University, argued that a "second AIDS epidemic" of fear and intolerance of gays is becoming evident in the United States. Just as the herpes scare has been associated with more cautious sexual behavior among many heterosexuals, fear of AIDS is apparently having the same effect on many homosexuals. For both straights and gays, the days of a carefree sexual revolution may be over.

Summary

Americans have become increasingly more accepting of premarital sex and diversity of sexual expression. The effects of the sexual revolution have unquestionably reshaped the nature of marriage and family life in the United States. One major change has been the growing challenge to the traditional "double standard" regarding male and female roles.

There are many forms of sexual expression, including sexual self-stimulation (masturbation and fantasy), kissing and touching, foreplay and intercourse, and oral and anal sex. Good communication between partners is a key element of rewarding sex.

It is difficult to genuinely love others if you feel negatively about yourself. Sexual choices are an individual matter influenced by one's family upbringing and personal values. While some Americans equate sex and love, others feel that sex without love is an acceptable option.

Historically, the issues of birth control and abortion have been extremely controversial. Available birth control methods include the pill, periodic abstinence, the IUD, the diaphragm, the condom, the cervical cap, spermicides, douching and withdrawal (both highly ineffective), and sterilization. A key 1973 Supreme Court decision, *Roe* v. *Wade*, gave women in all 50 states the constitutional right to an abortion during at least the first six months of pregnancy.

The most serious types of sexually transmitted diseases are gonorrhea, syphilis, genital herpes, and AIDS. With the exception of syphilis, rates of these diseases in the United States have reached epidemic proportions. Herpes and AIDS have had a chilling effect on people's interests in casual sexual encounters.

Discussion Questions

1. How has the invention of the birth control pill affected American sexual behavior? What other social changes have reshaped patterns of sexuality?

2. "The brain is the most important sexual organ." Do you agree or disagree? Why?

3. In your view, do men and women differ in their motives and desire for sexual relationships? If so, how and why do they differ?

4. Is sex without love morally acceptable? Discuss.

5. Some Americans feel that no form of sexual expression should be rejected as ''deviant'' if it involves two consenting adults who enjoy the interaction. Do you agree?

6. What changes in sexual attitudes and behavior do you foresee in the next 15 years?

Key Words

Abortion	**Foreplay**	**Platonic Relationship**
Acquired Immune Deficiency Syndrome (AIDS)	**Genital Herpes**	**Rape**
	Gonorrhea	**Scrotum**
Autoeroticism	**Hysterotomy**	**Sexually Transmitted Disease (STD)**
Cervical cap	**Incest**	
Circumcision	**Intercourse**	**Spermicides**
Clitoris	**Intrauterine Device (IUD)**	**Spontaneous abortion**
Coitus	**Labia majora**	**Syphilis**
Combination Birth Control Pill	**Labia minora**	**Testes**
	Laparoscopy	**Tubal ligation**
Condom	**Masturbation**	**Uterus or ''Womb''**
Cunnilingus	**Mons Pubis**	**Vacuum aspiration**
Diaphragm	**Myotonia**	**Vagina**
Dilation and Curettage (D and C)	**Orgasm**	**Vasectomy**
Double Standard	**Ovaries**	**Vasocongestion**
Douching	**Ovulation**	**Vulva**
Erogenous Zones	**Penis**	**Withdrawal**
Fallopian Tubes	**Periodic abstinence**	**Zygote**
Fellatio	**Petting**	

Suggested Readings

Boston Women's Health Collective. *Our Bodies, Ourselves.* New York: Simon and Schuster, 1976. Discusses the emotional and health aspects of being a woman.

Brownmiller, Susan. *Against Our Will: Men, Women, and Rape.* New York: Simon and Schuster, 1975. Discusses rape and its damaging impact on women.

Comfort, Alex. *The Joy of Sex.* New York: Simon and Schuster, 1972. Offers a light-hearted description of sexual techniques.

Diagram Group. *Man's Body: An Owner's Manual*. New York: Paddington Press, 1976. Discusses the sexual and health aspects of being male.

Diagram Group. *Woman's Body: An Owner's Manual*. New York: Paddington Press, 1976. Discusses the sexual and health aspects of being female.

Haeberle, Erwin, J. *The Sex Atlas*. New York: Continuum, 1982. A complete, in-depth atlas of the physiological, psychological, and sociological aspects of sex.

CHAPTER SIX

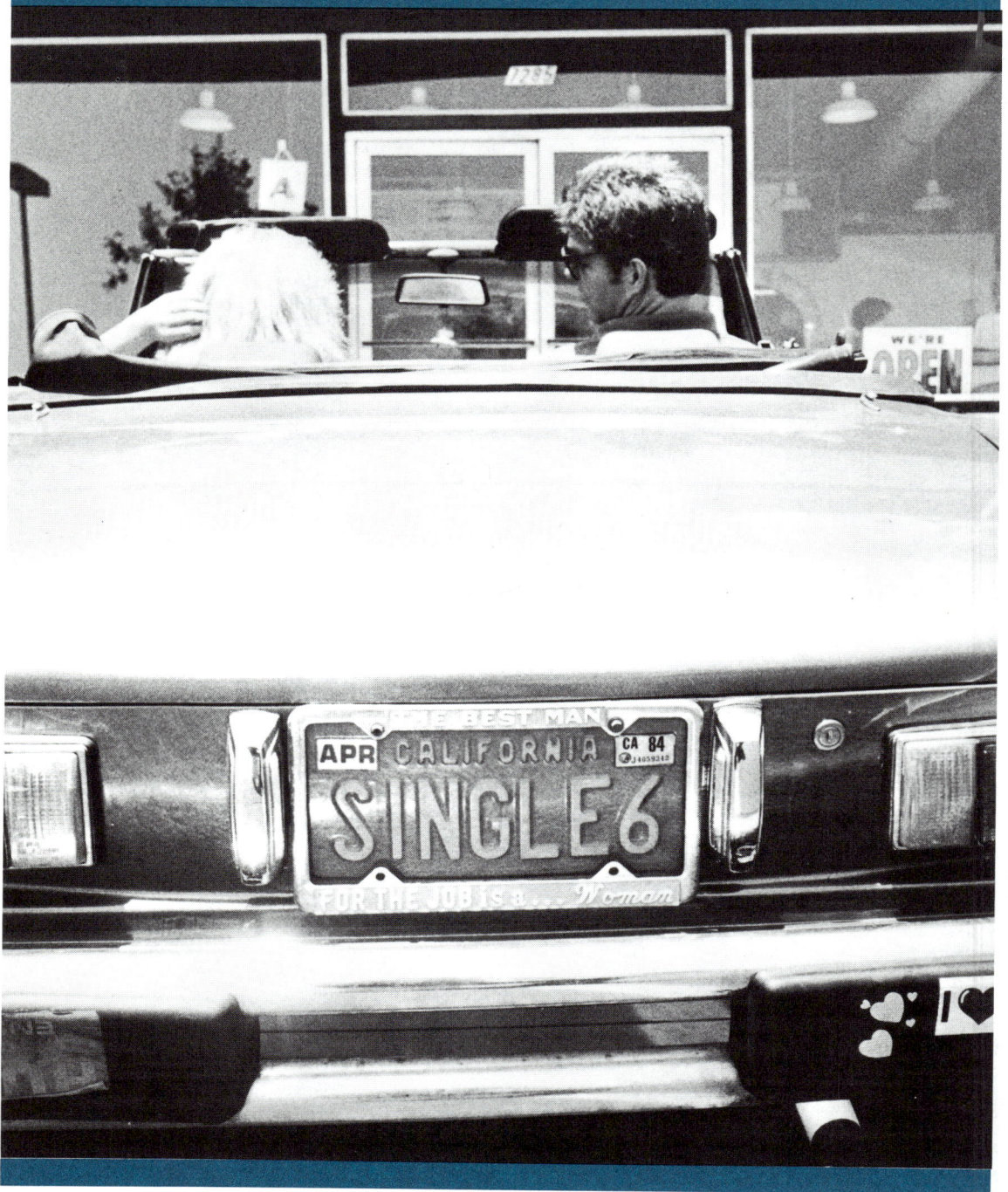

Choosing Relationships: Singlehood and Cohabitation

KEY TOPICS

—the rise in the number of single Americans—
—reasons for singlehood—
—pushes and pulls of singlehood and marriage—
—reasons for cohabitation—
—trial or common law marriage—
—homosexual relationships and lifestyles—

This chapter is about making choices— choices about relationships. While between 90 and 95 percent of American men and women will marry at least once during their lifetimes (Bane, 1976), they can at least consider other possibilities. It is true that marriage remains the preferred type of intimate relationship in our society; despite the rise of divorce, there is no sign that the institution of marriage will become obsolete (Cherlin, 1981). Nevertheless, as was discussed in Chapter 2, an increasing number of individuals are turning to patterns of living that fall outside of the traditional life cycle concept but are often preliminary to, rather than alternatives to, marriage and family: **singlehood** and cohabitation (living together).

Ruth, a 37-year-old federal employee, was divorced five years ago. She has become an enthusiastic advocate of singlehood and lives in a Washington, D.C., suburb with a dog and two cats. ''I can do what I want, when I want, as I want,'' she states. ''The only constraints are those I impose on myself'' (Sanoff, 1983: 54).

Stan and Margot, both in their late twenties, have lived together in a Denver apartment complex for three years. They have no plans to marry. "Why should we? We're happy as we are," says Stan. "It isn't important whether we go through some big public ceremony," adds Margot. "What matters is how we feel about each other. My father won't accept my living with Stan, but I'm 27 years old. I can't live my life to please him."

In this chapter, we will more closely examine the lives of Americans like Ruth who are single and of those, such as Stan and Margot, who are living together. It is important to remember that while most adults who live alone or with a lover are heterosexual, some are not. Consequently, we will also discuss the relationships and lifestyles of lesbians and gay men.

Going It Alone: Singlehood

One of the main explanations for the shrinking size of American households (see Chapter 1) is the dramatic rise in the number of single men and women. Between 1970 and 1980, there was a 60 percent increase in the number of persons living alone. Currently, about 33 percent of all males over the age of 18 and 40 percent of all females are single (Stein, 1981). One-third of all singles have never been married; others have been divorced or widowed and find themselves single again (see Figure 6–1).

Advertisers have been quick to aim new products at single professionals with large incomes and no family expenditures. For example, a condominium complex being constructed for singles in Coconut Grove, Florida, has units for $90,000 to $135,000. Its marketing director explains that the complex is for those who "want to go out the front door and jog, play tennis, run by the marina and eat in the restaurants." While this

young, affluent group receives enormous media attention, it is nevertheless true that the majority of single Americans earn less than $10,000 per year (Cargan and Melko, 1982; Sanoff, 1983: 55).

Reasons for Singlehood

How has singlehood become a more respectable and viable option for American men and women? A number of general factors have contributed to this important social change:

• *More people are marrying later.* The average age of first marriage in 1962 was 22.9 years for men and 19.9 for women. By 1982, however, the averages had risen to 25.2 for men and 22.5 for women. In addition, more Americans are choosing not to marry at all. Among those presently in their twenties, the number of individuals who will never marry is expected to be twice as great (8 to 9 percent) as in the previous generation (Stein, 1981).

• *The "marriage squeeze" has reduced the field of eligible partners.* As we will discuss further in Chapter 7, women tend to marry men who are two to three years older than themselves. When the "baby boom" generation (those born between 1946 and 1957) came along, women born at the beginning of the boom found a shortage of available men two to three years older. Demographers called this the **"marriage squeeze."** Males born between 1954 and 1957 encountered the squeeze in a different way; there were not enough women for them to marry because of the rapid drop in the birth rate after the "baby boom" ended.

At present, there is a bulge in the proportion of single people since the "baby boom" generation is growing up. Some observers predict that the proportion of singles will decline as this generation gets older and more of them marry (Cargan and Melko, 1982).

• *There is increased acceptance of sex outside of*

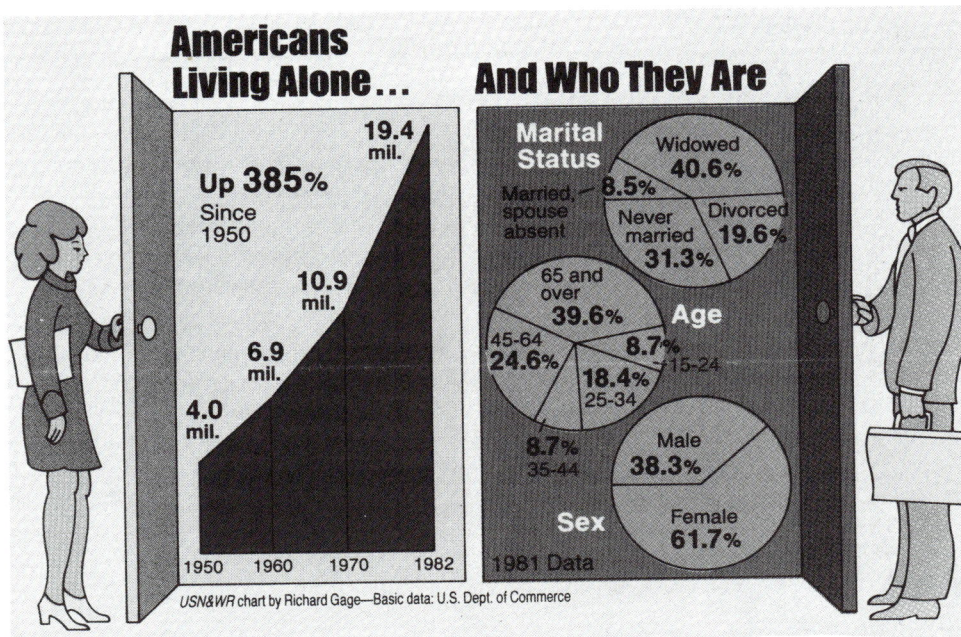

Americans Living Alone...

Up **385%** Since 1950

19.4 mil.

10.9 mil.

6.9 mil.

4.0 mil.

1950 1960 1970 1982

USN&WR chart by Richard Gage—Basic data: U.S. Dept. of Commerce

And Who They Are

Marital Status

Widowed 40.6%

Married, spouse absent 8.5%

Never married 31.3%

Divorced 19.6%

Age

65 and over 39.6%

45-64 24.6%

8.7% 15-24

18.4% 25-34

8.7% 35-44

Sex

Male 38.3%

Female 61.7%

1981 Data

Figure 6–1 Number of Americans living alone. (*Source: U.S. News and World Report,* February 21, 1983, p. 54.)

marriage. Improved and more available birth control methods, the possibility of obtaining legal abortions, and greater social tolerance of nonmarital sexuality have made singlehood a more attractive option.

• *The women's movement has increased opportunities for women and reshaped women's attitudes.* More women than ever before are going to graduate or professional schools and are seeking fulfilling work outside the home. The feminist critique of marriage emphasizes women's unequal and subservient role, and has led many women to question whether marriage is for them.

• *There have been growing doubts about the institution of marriage.* Feminist questioning about marriage has been merely one aspect of a general challenge to the institution. The rising divorce rate has made both men and women wonder whether marriage can work for them. Some feel that marriage constricts

personal or career growth; others are bitter in the aftermath of divorce.

Typology of Singlehood

The stereotypes about single persons range from the wealthy young man who likes driving fast cars, taking expensive vacations, and dating lots of women to the eccentric elderly woman with 108 cats. Like all stereotypes, there is enough half-truth in these images to make them popular. In reality, American "singles" are a highly diverse group in terms of their ages, income levels, and motivations for being single.

Peter Stein, a researcher who has studied singlehood, has proposed a typology of singlehood as one way of clarifying this diversity (see Table 6–1). For example, Janice is in her mid-twenties and has one year to go in her M.B.A. program. "I don't want to be

Table 6–1   Typology of singlehood

	Voluntary	Involuntary
Temporary	Never-married and formerly married who are postponing marriage by not currently seeking mates, but who are not opposed to the idea of marriage.	Those who have been actively seeking mates for shorter or longer periods of time, but have not yet found them. Those who were not interested in marriage or remarriage for some period of time but are now actively seeking mates.
Stable	Those choosing to be single (never-marrieds and formerly married). Those who oppose the idea of marriage for various reasons. Those who will not marry because of their religious positions and vows.	Never-marrieds and formerly marrieds who wanted to marry or remarry, have not found a mate, and have more or less accepted being single as a probable life state.

Source: Stein, July/August, 1978: 1–11.

married while I'm in graduate school!'' she exclaims. ''I don't have the time now. But, when I finish, sure, I hope I'll find the right person and marry.'' By contrast, Leo is a Roman Catholic priest who plans to remain unmarried in accord with his religious vows.

Janice and Leo differ on the stable-temporary dimension shown in Table 6–1. While both currently wish to be single, Janice hopes to change her status in the future while Leo does not. In the future, they may also be at opposite ends of Stein's voluntary-involuntary dimension. Both are presently choosing voluntarily to be single; ten years from now, if Janice remains unmarried, it may not be a satisfying and voluntary choice.

Never-Married Parents

As noted in Chapter 2, the single-parent family is currently the fastest-growing family type in the United States. Most single parents have been married, but the number of never-married mothers tripled in the 1970s. For the first time in the United States,

never-married parents exceeded widowed parents in number (Hogan, 1983). By 1980, 18.4 percent of all births were to women who had never been married.

In some instances, women choose to have children without being married because they do not believe in marriage. They prefer the independence associated with singlehood, yet still wish to bear and raise children. In other cases, women unintentionally become pregnant, then decide to keep the children rather than choose adoption or abortion. There has been a major change in American attitudes toward children born out of wedlock. In contrast to the harsh and judgmental view of illegitimacy characteristic of earlier times, pollster Daniel Yankelovich (1981) found that about half of those surveyed now feel it is acceptable for a woman to have a child without being married.

Community attitudes may play a role in the significant differences in unmarried pregnancies among black and white women. In the 1970s, two out of three black women who gave birth were unmarried, compared with one out of eight white women. Apparently, for many blacks, having a child is not tied to marriage (Cherlin, 1981).

The special challenges of single parenthood will be discussed more fully in Chapter 14. For most single mothers—whether divorced or never-married—the overwhelming reality of daily life is poverty. Struggling to meet expenses and raise a family on one income—and a woman's income at that—can be a significant problem. However, many still find the experience of single parenthood to be rewarding. While the vast majority of never-married parents are women, more men have recently shown interest in raising their children and have been awarded legal custody (Smart, 1983).

Racial Differences

As a group, fewer blacks than whites are married (see Figure 6–2). Whites tend to marry sooner than blacks; white marriages tend to last longer. As noted earlier, more black women than white women have children outside of marriage. Partly as a result, 41 percent of all black families with children are headed by women, compared with 12 percent of white families (Cherlin, 1981).

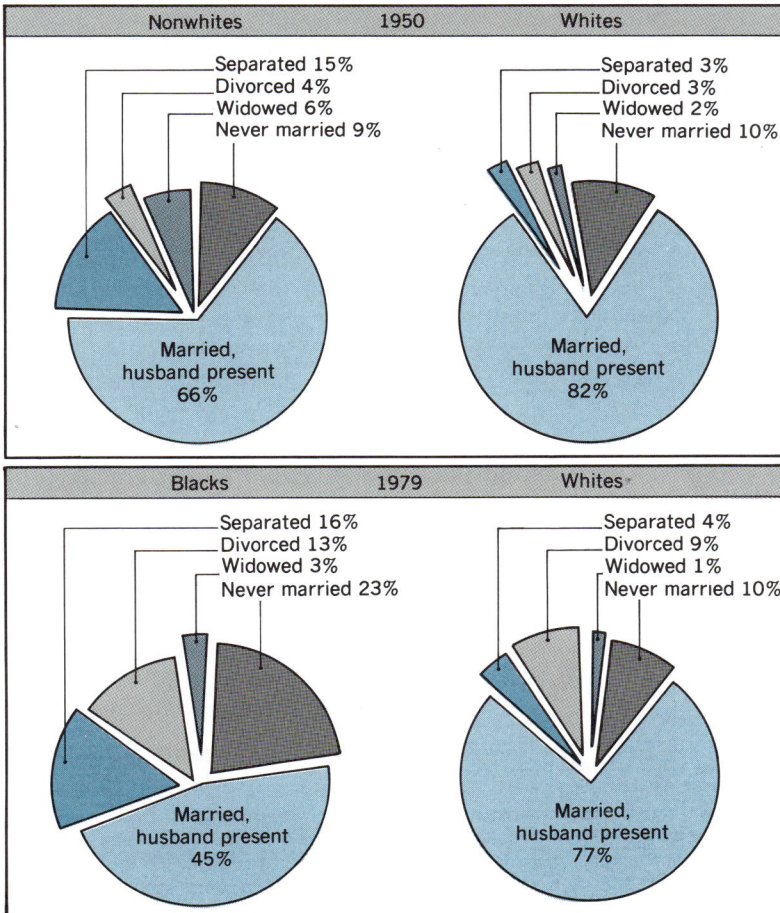

Figure 6–2 Current marital status of women aged 25 to 44, by race or color, 1950 and 1979. (*Source*: Cherlin, 1981, p. 98.)

BOX 6-1

A Single Black Woman Speaks Out

In a 1982 article in Ms. Magazine entitled "Working at Single Bliss," professor and author Mary Helen Washington (1982: 55–59) spoke openly of her life as a single black woman and the pressures she faced:

"'You're so lucky, footloose, and fancy-free, with no responsibilities,' a friend with two children once said to me. Ostensibly that's a compliment, or at least, it's supposed to be. But underneath it's really a critique of single people, implying that their lives do not have the moral stature of a life 'with responsibilities.' . . .

"If anything, a single person may be more aware of the responsibility to discover and create meaning in her life, to find community, to honor her creativity, to live out her values, than the person whose life is circumferenced by an immediate and intimate family life. . . .

"The message I got from the black community about single life was . . . forceful. So many black girls heard these words, they might have been programmed tapes: 'Girl, get yourself an education, you can't count on a man to take care of you.' . . . 'Any fool can get married but not everyone can go to school.' . . .

"They thought the worst thing a woman could do was to get into financial dependency with a man—and it was not that they hated or distrusted men so much as they distrusted any situation that made an already vulnerable woman more powerless."

What accounts for these differences? Some historians and sociologists (Frazier, 1939) have traditionally viewed this as a legacy of slavery, during which many black families were forcibly separated and sold to different slaveowners. However, historian Herbert Gutman (1976) has shown that most black families remained two-parent families both during and long after slavery.

Current research indicates that the decline of marriage among blacks has accelerated since the 1940s. Andrew Cherlin (1981) and others have demonstrated that the poorest, least educated blacks are the least likely to be married. Sociologists have observed that never-married, single-parent households are more common among the poor as a rational response to contemporary urban conditions and pervasive racism. They reject the view that black families are "sick" or in need of cure. The problem is simply money; the high unemployment rate for poor urban blacks leads to financial troubles and consequently to greater family conflict.

By contrast, other kin relationships and extended family ties among blacks may be more stable and enduring. Anthropologist Carol Stack (1974), in her study of black kin networks, has shown how the exchange of child care, loans, or housing among extended family members and friends creates a stable family environment for poor families. For them, the extended family may actually be more practical than the nuclear family. Financial pressures and caretaking responsibilities can be shared among a greater number of people.

In Box 6–1, a single black professional woman offers personal testimony about the messages she received from her community about marriage and single life.

Pushes and Pulls of Singlehood

People may enter and reenter singlehood and marriage at various points in their lives. For example, Joe remained single until age 26, then married after great pressure from his parents and a remark or two from his boss about "settling down." But the marriage did not last and, at 29, Joe found himself single again. At this point, Joe had a new appreciation for the personal freedom that singlehood allows. But he was often lonely and felt ''left out'' at holiday times when his friends went to see their families.

Like Joe, many single men and women feel both the advantages and the strains of single life. Peter Stein has generated a table of the ''pushes and pulls'' of singlehood and marriage—the influences that shape our decisions to remain single, to marry, and to stay married (see Table 6–2). Some of these factors are social, some economic, some emotional. In general, both singlehood and marriage have distinctive advantages; the relative importance of these advantages varies throughout the life cycle.

On the positive side, many Americans enjoy the flexibility and freedom that come with being single. For example, remaining single has often been the choice for men and women who prefer to dedicate themselves to their work. This has especially been true for

Table 6–2   Pushes and pulls of marriage and singlehood

Marriage	
Pushes (negatives in present situations)	Pulls (attractions in potential situations)
Socialization	Approval of parents
Pressure from parents	Desire for children and own family
Desire to leave home	Example of peers
Fear of independence	Romanticization of marriage
Loneliness	Physical attraction
No knowledge or perception of alternatives	Love, emotional attachment
Job availability, wage structure, and promotions	Security, social status, social prestige
Social policies favoring the married and the responses of social institutions	Legitimation of sexual experiences

Singlehood	
Pushes (to leave permanent relationship)	Pulls (to remain single or return to singlehood)
Lack of friends, isolation, loneliness	Career opportunities and development
Restricted availability of new experiences	Availability of sexual experiences
Suffocating one-to-one relationship, feeling trapped	Exciting lifestyle, variety of experiences, freedom to change
Obstacles to self-development	Psychological and social autonomy, self-sufficiency
Boredom, unhappiness, and anger	
Role playing and conformity to expectations	Support structures: sustaining friendships, women's and men's groups, political groups, therapeutic groups, collegial groups
Poor communication with mate	
Sexual frustration	

Source: Stein, July/August, 1978: 1–11.

women, at least until recently. The rigid sex roles and social proprieties of a nineteenth-century middle-class marriage would have left Emily Dickinson with little opportunity to write or publish her poetry. Today, members of both sexes may decide to make work a priority. Single persons apparently spend longer hours at work than married people; many feel strong emotional ties to their careers and co-workers (Stein, 1978).

Many individuals enjoy the freedom and flexibility that come with being single.

Being single provides the personal freedom that many Americans value highly (Duberman, 1977; Glick, 1979; Yankelovich, 1981). Singles can more easily experiment with their own sexuality. Their sexual relationships can be casual and varied, or they can be restricted to one special person. Unlike those who are married, a single individual can make decisions about her or his life, such as returning to school or accepting a career move, without considering how someone else would be affected. Many singles cite privacy as another valued aspect of the single life (Bradley, et al., 1977).

Yet single life can be far from glamorous. The tradeoff for personal freedom and privacy is often loneliness. ''It's very hard to come home after a tough day and have no one to complain to or unwind with,'' said one 34-year-old divorced man. Another single male, well known at work for his 15-hour workdays, confessed that one reason he stayed at the office so long was to avoid his empty apartment. Persistent and severe loneliness can lead to health problems such as heart disease, alcoholism, and depression (Bernikow, 1982).

Indeed, single people in general are less healthy than their married peers and do not live as long. Among singles, the divorced and separated show the poorest health status, perhaps reflecting the painful transitions they have faced. Never-married men seem particularly vulnerable to poor physical and mental health (Bernard, 1972). As a group, singles (but especially the divorced and separated) are more likely to have feelings of depression, worthlessness, and sexual apathy. Suicide rates are also higher among single Americans.

Some experts have suggested that the problem may not be being single (as opposed to married), but rather the absence of a strong network of social support (Cargan and Melko, 1982; Stein, 1981). If one is sick and troubled about something, are there

The single life is not always swinging; the trade-off for personal freedom and privacy can be loneliness.

close friends or family members to turn to? Or is there no one available to offer support? Many singles report that friends are a critical source of emotional comfort (Bradley, et al., 1977). The important role of social support will be discussed further in Chapter 17. Interestingly, individuals who remain single throughout their lives are not especially lonely during old age because they are accustomed to being alone—which may be a major and painful adjustment for the widowed (Gubrium, 1975). Indeed, older unmarried women have the best physical and mental health of any group in their age category.

There are certain economic disadvantages to singlehood. Women are less likely than men to hold high-paying jobs, so single women, without access to a second male income, will likely have a lower standard of living than married men or women. This disparity is particularly acute for single mothers. Many elderly singles are extremely poor and depend on small social security checks for their sole income.

There may also be job discrimination against single persons. In a recent survey, fewer than 2 percent of all senior managers of major corporations were single. Corporate personnel managers tend to feel that unmarried persons are "less stable" or "more given to snap decisions" than those with spouses; this may be a factor in certain promotions (Jacoby, 1974). Yet, as Stein (1981) points out, such discrimination can be difficult to pinpoint: "Is a woman not promoted because she is divorced or because she is a woman? Is a man kept back because his boss suspects he is gay, or because he has never married?"

Making a Connection: Living Together

Pete moved into Karen's apartment six months after they began dating. "After a while, it became ridiculous," he laughs. "I was there every night anyway. My roommates never saw me; my parents kept bugging me about how they could never get me on the phone." They have now been living together for seven years. "We both like things as they are," says Karen. "We've considered marriage, but neither of us really wants to. I'm definitely not comfortable with words like, 'Till death do us part.' I can imagine living with Pete for a long, long time. It seems like I already have. But *promising* that I will, well, I have trouble with that.'' ''It's the same for me,'' adds Pete. ''I've been the best man at weddings for both my brother and my old roommate. Neither stayed married for more than two years. They used to look down on my relationship with Karen. Never quite said it, but there was always this feeling that we couldn't be really serious about each other. If we were, we'd be rushing to the altar. Funny thing is, my brother's still the same way,'' concludes Pete. ''Still has a real smug attitude about Karen and me. He's always talking about finding a new wife. I'll bet anything that he'll be married and divorced a second time. Meanwhile Karen and I will still be together, unmarried, and happy.''

As we discussed in Chapter 2, an increasing number of American couples are choosing to live together without marrying. In 1980, about 2.3 percent of all couple households were cohabiting. While this proportion may seem small, it is nearly double the 1970 figure. Among those under 25, the likelihood of cohabitation increased at least 800 percent during the 1970s (Glick and Spanier, 1981). Although many people still do not approve of this arrangement, most have come to accept it. A sign of how this lifestyle is accepted is the willingness of the courts to hear cases defining unmarried partners' rights and obligations. These **palimony** cases occur when one cohabiting partner sues the other for financial support after the relationship ends.

Pointing to the increasing acceptance and the fact that many cohabiting couples eventually marry, Cherlin (1981) argues that living together is becoming accepted as the first stage of marriage. This practice is becoming more popular not only among younger Americans, but also among the elderly (Yorburg, 1978). Cohabitation is primarily an urban phenomenon; proportionately, more blacks than whites live together without marriage.

Reasons for Cohabitation

The factors contributing to the rise of cohabitation are similar to those that account for the increase in singlehood. Nonmarital sex is more acceptable than ever before, while there is unprecedented uncertainty about marriage. The young, like Karen and Pete, may desire serious, intimate relationships but fear long-term commitments. Financial considerations are also important; the skyrocketing costs of housing encourage many couples to opt for one rent rather than two (Henslin, 1980).

Studies of young people living together show that such couples feel their relationships are emotionally rewarding and help them to gain self-confidence. Most believe the experience will improve their chances of creating a good marriage because they gain a better understanding of what marriage might be like. In fact, in her study of Cornell students who were living together, Eleanor Macklin (1972, 1974) found that three-fourths stated they would never marry without living with their partner first. There is no evidence, however, to show that those who cohabit before marriage have better or longer marriages than those who do not (Clatworthy and Schied, 1977).

Most couples who live together do not regard their situation as permanent; such relationships generally end within two years (Glick and Spanier, 1981). Robert and Margaret Blood (1978) point out that most cohabiting college couples have been emotionally and sexually involved for several months. Although they may not wish to marry, moving in together often seems like a natural ''next step'' in the evolving relationship. Couples do not tend to view cohabitation as a "trial marriage," but instead seek to enjoy the experience for its own sake (Macklin, 1972). One study found that 90 percent of individuals engaged in cohabitation planned to marry eventually—but not necessarily to the person they were presently living with (Yorburg, 1978).

Older Americans often choose cohabitation as a means of overcoming financial hardships. Until recently, social security regulations discouraged remarriage of widowed participants; living together became a practical, even necessary option. As is true of younger couples, the elderly may also find cohabitation to be an effective way of avoiding loneliness.

For example, Margaret, 67, has been

Cohabitation often seems like the natural "next step" in a developing relationship.

married two times and has no interest in doing so again. After retirement from her job as a legal secretary, she lived in a downtown apartment complex instead of her old suburban neighborhood and began feeling lonely. "All my friends died, or I just lost touch with them," she recalls. Subsequently, Margaret met Arnie through a program that matches elderly persons as housemates. Both of them were hesitant at first, but now they are delighted with the arrangement. Margaret sometimes cooks for Arnie or makes his bed, but she likes the feeling that she doesn't have to report to him. "I enjoy our intimacy and companionship. I can't imagine living any other way," she says emphatically.

Sex Roles in Cohabitation

We know that those who cohabit tend to feel strongly about the need for personal growth and the importance of maintaining individuality. Consequently, one might expect that such couples would respect and practice sex-role equality (see Chapter 3). However, this is not necessarily the case.

A 1978 study did find that, when asked to write contracts for their relationships, cohabiting partners were more likely than married couples to view their relationships in egalitarian terms. Many emphasized that mutual acceptance of the other's individuality was the key to the relationship. Some respondents were willing to make contracts mandating joint responsibility for cooking and cleaning and separate financial arrangements (Weitzmann, et al., 1978).

Yet several researchers have noted that women who live with male lovers seem to do most of the cooking and housework, just as in traditional marriages (Cole, 1977; Yllo, 1978). It seems likely that sex roles within cohabiting relationships are subject to the same pressures that affect sex roles within marriages. Childhood socialization, the examples of one's parents, and personal values and expectations all shape one's sex-role behavior (Stafford, et al., 1977).

James M. Henslin (1980: 112), after a review of the literature on this issue, observes that "females tend to do 'female' things while males tend to do 'male' things." Henslin pointedly concludes:

. . . there is no reason to assume that because people violate conventional sexual norms and enter a cohabiting relationship, they are therefore "liberated" and are striving for sex-role "equality." . . . In fact, there is nothing about cohabitation that in and of itself leads to sex-role equality. Just as in marriage the reality of sex roles must be worked out by those living together, so it is with cohabitation.

Trial or Common Law Marriage

Trial marriage is a form of cohabitation in which a couple is explicitly interested in establishing a permanent relationship. While not legally married, the couple nevertheless feels a long-term commitment to the relationship. The decision to experiment with a trial marriage may seem reassuring to individuals who are fearful of marriage, and especially to those whose parents divorced or have themselves been divorced.

The idea of trial marriage was suggested as far back as 1926, when Ben Lindsey wrote a book entitled *The Companionate Marriage.* Although his ideas were not received warmly at that time, the concept was later revived by Margaret Mead (1966). Mead suggested a two-step marriage based on Lindsey's model. Step one involved a marriage with a simple ceremony, limited economic responsibilities, no children, and easily accessible divorce. If the couple moved successfully through step one, they could then undertake step two: the parental marriage. Mead's proposal was innovative in that it separated two critical commitments often linked together in marriage: the commitment to marry someone and undertake a long-term

relationship, and the commitment to bear and raise children together. Nevertheless, her ideas and other trial marriage proposals have been criticized because, by its very nature, a trial marriage deemphasizes commitment. Therefore, it is suggested, trial marriage cannot serve as a valid test of whether a "real" marriage would or would not work (Berger, 1971).

Like trial marriage, **common law marriage** is a type of cohabitation entered into by mutual consent of both parties. How does this actually work? In the 15 states that recognize common law marriages (or in the District of Columbia), a couple simple declares their intent to live as husband and wife. They are then considered legally married. Their marriage can only be dissolved through divorce, annulment, or death; their children are considered legitimate. While common law marriage has a long and practical history among lower class communities, it is becoming more common on all social levels. In most cases, if individuals enter a common law marriage in one of the states that recognizes such arrangements, it will then be respected as well in other states.

Homosexual Relationships and Lifestyles

Gene, 55, is a free-lance illustrator; Henry, 56, is an executive in a department store. Originally best friends in a small town in Illinois, these men have lived together for 38 years. Henry and Gene began their sexual closeness during high school, but did not label their behavior as homosexual. "I think we loved each other without knowing it," Henry recalls. "Without putting it into words, either." Each served on separate battle fronts during World War II. They corresponded frequently and with increasing in-

B O X   6 - 2

Gay Parents

Many gay men and lesbians are parents. Joseph Harry (1983) has estimated that about one-third of lesbians and one-fifth of gay men have been heterosexually married. Perhaps half of these marriages resulted in children; in fact, many homosexual parents report that they remained married longer than they otherwise would have because of their love for their children.

"My children to me are the miracle of all time," claims British writer and broadcaster Hallam Tennyson, greatgrandson of the famed poet Alfred Lord Tennyson. Now divorced and openly homosexual, Hallam Tennyson speaks of his son and daughter with great feeling:

> Ros and Jenny are straight, but perhaps because I'm gay, they have a natural identification with the handicapped of society. I loved bringing them up. My nostalgia was not for my own childhood, but for theirs: It was one of the happiest times of my life (Maddox, 1982: 66).

Of course, like heterosexual parents, gay parents find that childbearing can be demanding.

Marnie and Janet, both lesbian feminists, have lived together for seven years. They are jointly raising Janet's two children and Marnie's child. Leisure time is at a premium in their relationship. In Marnie's words:

> Time without kids? But the kids are *always* there. Virtually. For a period we would keep every Thursday and we'd get a sitter and we'd go out . . . alone together. But we both got so busy that it wasn't practical. From time to time we just go out with other adults. We're really only alone after nine when they go to bed (Blumstein and Schwartz, 1983: 496).

Contrary to popular prejudices, there is no evidence that children of lesbian mothers or gay fathers are any more confused or disturbed than children of divorced parents in general. Nor is there any evidence that the offspring of gay parents are any more likely to become homosexual themselves (Maddox, 1982). Nevertheless, American courts have remained reluctant to grant child custody or even visiting rights to homosexual parents (Harry, 1983).

tensity. When they returned home, they soon acknowledged their love for each other. Henry's family strongly disapproved of the relationship; consequently, they left their home town and moved to Chicago to be together. They have survived as a couple for nearly four decades despite Gene's occasional nonmonogamy. The main bone of contention between them does not involve sex, love, or money, but instead travel. Gene remarks, "I hate taking trips. I'm totally against traveling—I mean, I'm a person who likes to stay at home." Henry laments, "I can't get Gene to take a vacation with me. I've begged and pleaded. . . . Last year I went to California and had such a good time. And all the while I'm there, I just wish Gene was with me."

Researchers Phillip Blumstein and Pepper Schwartz (1983: 502–508), who used Henry and Gene as one of the case studies in their recent book, *American Couples*, concluded that "Henry and Gene have spent their lives together and nothing is going to break them up. . . . Their emotional life is secure and well-protected. . . . This is a childhood romance that flowered into adult commitment."

Like Henry and Gene, between 5 and 10 percent of Americans are homosexual, although far fewer are openly so. Some gay men and lesbians live alone, some with roommates, and others with long-term lovers. A substantial minority, formerly involved in heterosexual marriages, are parents (see Box 6–2).

Paul, 24, is, in a sense, a homosexual "single." He is not involved in one primary relationship, but instead enjoys a number of sexual and emotional attachments. Because of his work as a salesperson for an investment firm, Paul travels regularly. He values the opportunity to become spontaneously involved with other men; he also has lovers whom he has seen on and off for two years. "I have no interest in a serious relationship right now," he says. "I like to meet people, have a good time . . . just casually. No promises, no commitments."

As the examples above illustrate, homo-

The Gay Rights movement has given many homosexual couples the social support needed to openly reveal their identities and choices in personal relationships.

sexual relationships do not follow any one set pattern. Not surprisingly, they present as much variation as heterosexual relationships. Researchers have identified three key types of relationships: (1) the partners live together monogamously; (2) the partners maintain a steady, long-term relationship but are free to seek other sexual encounters; and (3) people come together for a short time (often a few hours) primarily for sex (Bell and Weinberg, 1978; Silverstein, 1979).

Research has shown that lesbian couples are more likely to live together than gay male couples and are also more likely to be sexually exclusive. Peplau (1981) found that 87 percent of lesbian couples studied had been sexually exclusive during the last six months, compared to 46 percent of gay male couples. Silverstein (1981: 113–140) has divided gay men into "home builders" (such as Henry and Gene) and "excitement seekers" (such as Paul). He suggests that the "monogamy battle" is a critical conflict faced by gay couples.

As discussed in Chapter 5, relationships between homosexual couples are likely to be patterned after a "best friends/roommates" model. Most homosexual or lesbian couples, and especially those influenced by the feminist and gay liberation movements, explicitly reject the role divisions found in traditional heterosexual couples and marriages.

Joseph Harry (1983) points out that two important factors contribute to a general egalitarianism in gay relationships. Most couples are dual-worker couples in which neither partner economically supports the other. Few gay relationships have one partner serving as a full-time homemaker. Moreover, there is a further basis for economic equality since both partners are of the same sex and therefore (in the case of two women) face the same degree of sex discrimination in jobs and income. By contrast, working women in heterosexual couples and marriages earn significantly less than their male partners. Based on such considerations, Harry (1983: 219) concludes that gay relationships "often may be more egalitarian than heterosexual ones."

There can be great pressure on intimate homosexual relationships as a result of the opposition of families, religious authorities, psychologists, and the general society. "The social isolation is so killing," one woman told a researcher (Tanner, 1978: 114). A gay man added: "I just couldn't bring Jack home to my parents' house; they would have had hysterics. Holidays were always very sad times."

This fearful attitude—characteristic of homosexuals who remain "in the closet" hiding their identities and closest relationships—has become less characteristic in the last 15 years. Through the rise of the gay rights movement, lesbians and gay men have become much more open and vocal in demanding equality and an end to persecution. Indeed, the word "**gay**" was adopted as an identifying term to imply an acceptance of one's own sexuality and a lack of shame about one's lifestyle.

Summary

Singlehood has become a more respectable and viable option for Americans because more people are marrying later, the "marriage squeeze" has reduced the field of eligible partners, there is increased acceptance of sex outside of marriage, the women's movement has increased opportunities for women and reshaped women's attitudes, and there have been growing doubts about the institution of marriage.

The single-parent family is the fastest growing family type in the United States. Most single parents have been married, but the number of never-married mothers tripled in the 1970s. About half of those surveyed now feel it is acceptable for a woman to have a child without being married. For most single mothers—whether divorced or never-married—the overwhelming reality of daily life is poverty.

Many Americans enjoy the flexibility and freedom that come with being single. Privacy is another valued aspect of the single life. Yet the tradeoff for such advantages is often loneliness. In general, single people are less healthy than their married peers and do not live as long. There are also economic disadvantages to singlehood.

An increasing number of American couples are choosing to live together without marrying, thus engaging in cohabitation. The factors contributing to the rise of cohabitation are similar to those that account for the increase in singlehood. Many young persons who live together believe that the experience will improve their chances of creating a good marriage because they gain a better understanding of what marriage might be like. However, most couples living together do not regard their situation as permanent; such relationships generally end within two years. Sex roles within cohabiting relationships are subject to the same pressures that affect sex roles within marriage. The decision to experiment with a trial marriage may seem reassuring to individuals who are fearful of marriage.

Some gay men and lesbians live alone, some with roommates, and others with longterm lovers. A substantial minority, formerly involved in heterosexual marriages, are parents. There is as much variation in gay relationships as there is among heterosexual couples. However, most gay couples explicitly reject the role divisions found in traditional heterosexual couples and marriages.

Developmental Task A Personal Profile:
Is Singlehood for You?

Circle the number in the TRUE column if the statement is true for you

or

Circle the number in the FALSE column if the statement is false for you

	TRUE	FALSE
I want the security of someone being there for me	0	1
I would like to have someone to invest in	0	1
I like sharing things and feelings with someone close to me	0	1
I want to have child(ren)	0	1
I really want the freedom to pursue my own career goals in my own way at my own pace	1	0
If an opportunity (travel, new job, etc.) comes along, I want to be able to take advantage of it	1	0
I don't like to be tied down with too many responsibilities	1	0
I prefer to have my own way about things	1	0

Add up the numbers you circled and mark your score on the line below.

8   7   6   5   4   3   2   1   0

Singlehood	Singlehood	Singlehood
Good Idea	Perhaps	Think Again

Discussion Questions

1. What specific advantages do you see for yourself in being or becoming single?

2. What advantages and disadvantages do you see in cohabiting relationships?

3. How do you feel about Margaret Mead's proposal for a two-step, trial marriage?

4. Should ex-partners in cohabitation relationships have the right to take each other to court and demand the equivalent of alimony?

5. Should gays and lesbians be allowed to legally marry?

Key Words

Common Law Marriage

Gay

Marriage Squeeze

Palimony

Singlehood

Trial Marriage

Suggested Readings

Blumstein, Phillip and Schwartz, Pepper *American Couples*. New York: William Morrow, 1983. An in-depth exploration of different types of couples' relationships including cohabiting, married, and lesbian and gay relationships.

Cargan, Leonard, and Melko, Matthew. *Singles: Myths and Realities*. Beverly Hills, Calif.: Sage Publications, 1982. An in-depth study that dispels many stereotypes about singles.

Clark, Don. *Loving Someone Gay*. New York: Signet, 1978. A popularized guide to help gay men and their families and friends to develop strong and supportive relationships.

Macklin, Eleanor D. "Nonmarital heterosexual cohabitation: an overview." In Macklin, Eleanor D. (ed.), *Contemporary Families and Alternative Lifestyles*. Beverly Hills, Calif.: Sage Publications, 1983. A brief review of the prevalence and trends in nonmarital heterosexual cohabitation and recent literature addressing this lifestyle.

Staples, Robert. *The World of Black Singles: Changing Patterns of Male/Female Relations*. Westport, Conn.: Greenwood Press, 1981. Data from in-depth interviews shed light on the largest group among American blacks: nonmarried men and women.

CHAPTER SEVEN

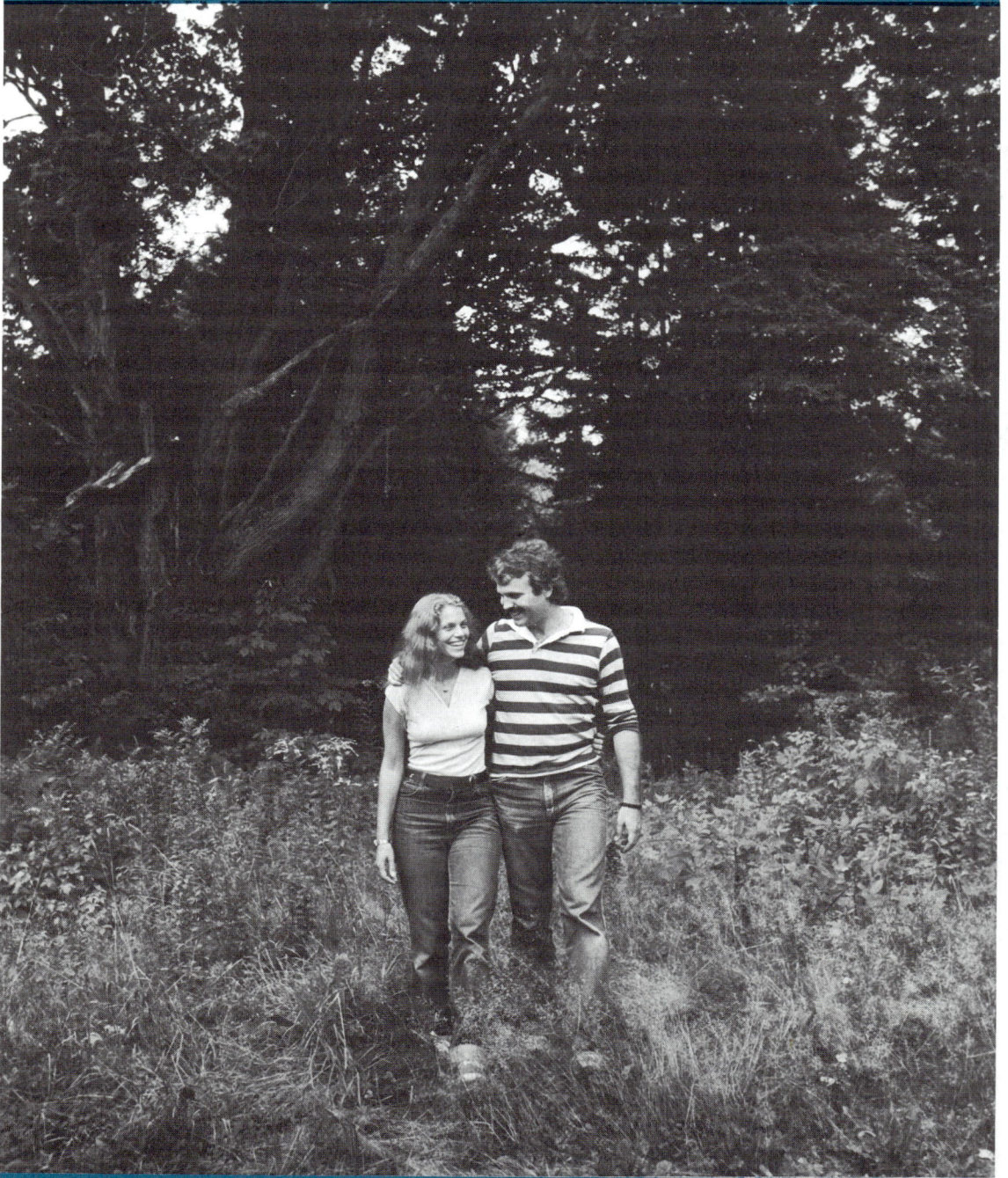

Transition to Marriage

KEY TOPICS

—*changes in dating behavior*—
—*male and female differences regarding dating*—
—*individualistic and sociocultural theories of mate selection*—
—*intermarriage*—
—*emotional and financial readiness for marriage*—
—*premarital counseling*—
—*marriage and the law*—
—*predicting marital success*—

According to the *Encyclopedia Britannica's* section on animal courtship, the male bowerbird constructs an impressive architectural structure solely for purposes of courtship. The Hepialus butterfly emits a type of perfume to captivate the female, while the tree cricket Oecanthus signals interest through a sweet liquor produced by his own body. In comparing human courtship to that of animals, Elaine Hoffman Baruch (1980: 57) notes that "we lack many of the built-in advantages of animals, having to supply them at the liquor, drug, and clothing stores."

In earlier periods of American history, courtship was centered in ice cream parlors and dancing pavilions. Walking someone home from school could be a major step in the courtship process. If a couple became close, they could reach the magical stage of "going together," as described in Louise Dutton's (1923: 20–21) novel, written in 1923:

There was a thing called going together. That was what Sally Belle wanted. You went with a boy. He was your fellow then, and you were his girl. When you were old enough you got engaged and married. Engaged girls marked towels and napkins and had to be kissed. They never had any fun. Being engaged was stupid, but going together was beautiful. . . . You were not an odd girl. You were not left out. . . . You could belong to a crowd. You had somebody to walk home with you, pay for your ticket at shows, send you valentines, . . . You were—well—going together.

In this chapter, we will examine courtship, "going together," and other aspects of the transition from singlehood to marriage. We will discuss the process of dating and the differing ways it is experienced by males and females. Individualistic and sociocultural theories of mate selection will be analyzed. We will also focus on people's preparation for marriage, marriage as a legal institution, and factors associated with marital success.

Dating

Jack drives over to Susan's house to pick her up and take her to a movie. When he arrives, he spends ten minutes in the living room making uneasy conversation with Susan's parents. Jack has worn his new sweater, of which he is very proud, but Susan's father grumbles that "in my day, a young man would come for a date wearing a jacket and tie." Then Susan comes downstairs, obviously nervous, and gets into an argument with her mother about her failure to do the dishes.

After what seems like an eternity, Jack and Susan finally leave for the movie. They strain to make conversation on the way to the theater. Jack, in an attempt to appear sophisticated, talks about all the European cities he visited during a trip the previous summer. Unfortunately, instead of impressing Susan as he had hoped, Jack merely succeeds in intimidating her. Susan has never been more than 200 miles from her home town, and becomes more and more quiet as Jack goes on about his travels.

They go out for coffee after the movie, but things don't get any better. Susan loved the film; Jack found it boring and pretentious. There is an uncomfortable silence as each wonders how the other could feel that way. Then Susan begins talking about her interest

In the early stages of dating, each individual puts on "masks" by attempting to project an image that will attract the other.

in becoming a surgeon and the prejudices against female doctors. Jack is unsympathetic and makes a crack about "women's libbers." By the end of the evening, it is clear that Jack and Susan will not be seeing each other again.

A "first date" can be a difficult, anxiety-provoking situation. Sociologist Robert Winch has referred to dating as "window-shopping" and to courtship as a "bargaining process." In the early stages of dating, each partner puts on "masks" by attempting to project personalities that will please and attract the other. Over time, of course, these masks are stripped away, and each person's true qualities—both positive and negative—emerge (Barnard and Fain, 1980).

Changes in Dating Behavior

Dating is no longer what it used to be. While Americans still go out on rather formal dates, as was true of Jack and Susan, many pair off in a less defined manner. Bernard Murstein (1971), a researcher on mate selection, has found that college students typically associate within a large group of male and female classmates. Members of the group may begin dating or even form couples while still retaining their ties to the larger group. Similarly, in a survey of 334 college students, David Knox and Kenneth Wilson (1981) found that the largest proportion, about one-third, met their current partners through a friend. In Box 7–1, we see that the widespread use of home computers may change dating behavior in the future.

People validate their expectations about love, dating, and relationships through peer group interactions and through movies, television shows, love songs, and romance novels. They learn what they are likely to feel, how to act, and even when to break up (Schwartz and Merten, 1980). The changing mores of our society have clearly reshaped traditional notions of dating. For example, in the survey cited above, over half of the college students stated that they drank alcohol on their last date, and more than 20 percent revealed that they smoked marijuana. Almost half of males and about one-fourth of females felt that intercourse was appropriate by the fifth date (Knox and Wilson, 1981).

Davis (1973) has identified six tasks that are critical in initiating a dating contact:

1. Determining whether the other person has the necessary qualifiers. Is he attracted to her? Does she feel comfortable being with him?

2. Determining whether the other person is available. Most people will not pursue someone who is already involved.

3. Finding an opener that gets the other person's attention. "Didn't I hear you say you're taking a class from Professor Smith? I took one of his classes last year. They say he's been using the same lecture notes since he started teaching!"

4. Discovering an integrating topic for conversation. It will certainly help if both persons are passionate lovers of classical music, baseball, or foreign films.

5. Projecting a "come-on self." At this point, one person must make clear what type of relationship he or she has in mind. Traditionally, a man asks for a woman's phone number in a suggestive tone of voice.

6. Calling to arrange a second meeting. At this point, the dating process formally begins.

Because of conventional sex-role norms, men have been expected to take the initiative in the process described above. However, these patterns have changed to at least some extent; women are freer to openly show their interest in men than was true in the past.

B O X   7 – 1

Research Brief:
Mate Selection of Tomorrow

What implications will the wide availability of home computers have on the way mates select each other? At present, computer dating agencies administer questionnaires that ask applicants for information about their appearance, race, religious preference, age, marital history, occupation, income, hobbies, and so forth. Responses are transferred onto computer cards for eventual matching.

As Davor Jedlicka (1981) suggests, changes in computer technology will soon make it possible for more interactive computer applications designed to aid dating and mate selection. People would be free to pass along personal advertisements ("Age 29, blond hair, green eyes, executive with marketing firms, seeks serious relationship . . ."), to send messages, and even to carry on conversations on their home computers.

Jedlicka argues that interactive computer technology will offer distinctive benefits for those seeking partners and mates. These include:

- A broader, more efficient search of potential mates than is possible through face-to-face interactions.
- Less stigmatization of those with unconventional lifestyles and preferences. People could anonymously disclose such information on the computer, knowing that those with hostile reactions would not respond.
- Greater emphasis on the exchange of ideas, feelings, thoughts, interests, and beliefs—as opposed to superficial initial judgments about how people look. Jedlicka notes that many Americans, particularly aging women, withdraw prematurely from the mate selection process because of the heavy emphasis on appearance.
- The possibility of sharing important personal matters early in the relationship without fear of face-to-face rejection.

Jedlicka (1981: 376) concludes that "computers can enhance open and honest communication. . . . Far from dehumanizing and depersonalizing society, computers could lead to suitable face-to-face relations with fewer misunderstandings and disappointments than can be experienced in the search for love, sex and affection."

Source: Jedlicka, 1981: 373–376.

Male and Female Differences

Louis: "I hate having to spend tons of money on a date just to impress a girl. Why should she think I care about her more just because I spend a fortune? What does money have to do with it?"

Alice: "I'm not for sale! It's nice if someone takes me out to an expensive restaurant. But whether he does or doesn't, I don't owe him anything. I resent being expected to sleep with someone because he bought me a dinner and took me to a movie."

Despite the impact of the women's movement, dating relationships—and especially first dates—are still based on an "exchange system" rather than egalitarian standards. Men feel pressure to "put out" financially by spending money on an expensive dinner and entertainment; women feel pressure to "put out" sexually by going to bed with men in return for their expenses. As the quotes above dramatically illustrate, members of each sex bitterly resent this "buying and selling" atmosphere (Milano and Hall, 1978).

There is a continuing difference in the sexual standards of men and women (see Chapter 5). For women, much more so than for men, sex before marriage is likely to occur only with a partner for whom they deeply care. Collins (1974) reports that males approach dating from a "psycho-biological orientation" and focus mainly on satisfying their sexual needs. By contrast, the orientation of females is "psycho-affectional"; they primarily seek affection, rapport, intimacy, and love.

There is little trust shared in the early stages of dating. Both sexes fall back on traditional norms (e.g., gentlemanly and lady-like behavior) in the midst of an awkward, uncertain situation. They develop certain strategies and techniques—in effect, "games"—to deal with the difficult demands of dating. Although these games may disappear as a relationship becomes more serious, Milano and Hall (1978: 106) stress that "males and females initially relate to one another as if in a marketplace."

Many observers have suggested that traditional sex roles still dominate in dating relationships. "I may be a 'take-charge' type at work," says one female executive at a New York bank, "but I still want *him* to do the asking out!" Caroline Bird Franck, writing in the *New York Times* in 1977, argued that strong and independent women are attracted to strong and independent men, men who are sophisticated and accomplished. However, in Franck's view, such men prefer to be with compliant, submissive women who do not threaten their dominance.

Data on the amount of violence between dating partners reinforces the persistence of traditional roles. One survey of college students found that 22 percent had experienced some form of violence—pushing, hitting, shoving, or biting—in a dating relationship. Other estimates have ranged as high as 60 percent (Cale, et al., 1982; *Time*, September, 1981).

A violent partner attempts to work out feelings of anger or jealousy through physical attack. For example, after dating for three months, Steve slapped Valerie because he thought she was flirting with another man. After they began living together, he increasingly flew into violent rages because he falsely believed she was unfaithful. On some occasions, he threw Valerie to the floor, dragged her around by her hair, and, in her words, "literally beat the hell out of my face" (*Time*, September, 1981: 66). Eventually, Valerie left Steve. Nevertheless, in many instances, such patterns of violence during dating may set the stages for traditional marriages in which men dominate through the threat or actual use of violence.

McDaniel (1969) found that female college students are more assertive in the earliest stages of the courtship process. They enter dating relationships feeling equal to males in terms of rights, power, and authority. At the stage of "going steady," however, a growing "receptivity" (or passivity) gradually replaces their assertiveness. Finally, by the time they are engaged and ready to be married, such women have become even more passive. Remembering the "nature-nurture" debate discussed in Chapter 3, McDaniel's study seems to suggest that women's submission to male dominance is a socially learned, rather than a biologically dictated, behavior.

Selecting a Marriage Partner

In the United States and most contemporary Western societies, dating is one important aspect of the overall process of mate selection. Our culture rejects the practice of "arranged marriage," under which parents or other family elders select appropriate partners for their marriageable children. In an arranged marriage, important criteria for selection include the health of the prospective spouse, how well he or she can contribute to the family income or household, and economic benefits for the family if the marriage takes place. When people select their own mates as Americans do, attraction, affection, and compatibility are more central in decision-making (Coppinger and Rosenblatt, 1968; Rosenblatt and Cozby, 1972; Stephens, 1963).

Personal Factors Influencing Choice

When people make their own decisions about marriage partners, love can be a critical factor in determining their choices. A 1974 Roper poll showed that 83 percent of American women and 77 percent of men cited love as their main reason for getting married. Similarly, in a more recent survey, love was again the most common rationale for marriage (Pietropinto and Simenauer, 1979).

The Pietropinto survey revealed interesting differences between generations, ethnic groups, and socioeconomic classes. For example, blacks gave companionship rather than love as their primary reason for marrying. Hispanics were more interested in love than blacks, but not as interested as whites. Blue-collar workers were less motivated by love than white-collar workers and were more likely to marry in order to gain regular sex. Finally, couples currently over 50 years old reported that they had married primarily to establish home lives, while students showed much less interest in a married home life.

We noted in Chapter 4 that positive self-esteem can be essential for a healthy love relationship. According to therapist Virginia Satir (1967), the way we feel about ourselves has a great deal to do with our choice of mates. We choose those who act toward us as we feel toward ourselves; therefore, if we think of ourselves as worthless, we may choose someone who treats us poorly. On the other hand, a person may attempt to compensate for his or her deficiencies by selecting someone who treats him or her well.

Compatibility—the extent to which a couple's characteristics fit together—is certainly important in selecting a marriage partner. Robert and Margaret Blood (1978) have identified three types of compatibility: compatibility of temperaments, needs, and values. One partner may almost always be active, nervous, and excitable, while the other is totally calm and even-tempered. While such differences are not always negative, they can create conflicts. Even the fact that you are a "morning person" (in your energy peak early in the day), while your spouse is a "night person" (most active and productive late in the evening) can lead to serious problems.

Compatibility of needs is especially advantageous in a marriage since each partner's needs can be satisfied simultaneously. Marilyn is an aspiring novelist whose family never took seriously her interest in writing. She is talented but insecure, and is productive only when she enjoys a great deal of encouragement. Phil, her husband, was the oldest of five children and spent a great deal of his adolescence caring for his two youngest sisters. He takes great pride in his ability to be a supportive friend, older brother, and husband. Their needs complement each other well; Phil needs to nurture others while Marilyn needs extensive nurturance.

Among those needs considered as **complementary needs** are dominance and submission, nurturance and succorance (being taken care of), and recognition and deference. People also feel other types of needs, known as **parallel needs**, which are not gratified by their partners. Among these are the needs for achievement and affiliation (being close to other people). The variety of needs felt by each individual greatly complicates mate selection. A desired partner may satisfy many of our multiple and even conflicting needs; yet he or she may fail to satisfy others that seem important.

Sharing similar value orientations and beliefs makes relationships much more enjoyable—beginning on the first date. After a computer-arranged dance at Iowa State University, couples who agreed on the importance (or lack of importance) of dancing ability, campus popularity, fraternity membership, stylish clothing, and good looks were most satisfied with each other and found it easier to converse (Coombs, 1966). Moreover, during their first 18 months of dating, Duke University students moved closer to marriage if they shared the same standard of family success: husband/wife companionship, healthy and happy children, economic security, or a respected place in the community (Kerckhoff and Davis, 1962). According to Burgess and Wallin (1943), the perception that another person shares our values facilitates his or her attractiveness in our eyes.

It must be noted, however, that marital interactions can be substantially different from premarital interactions. Two people who seem highly compatible while dating may prove to be totally incompatible after marriage. Wesley Burr (1976) suggests that the marital relationship of your partner's parents will provide valuable clues about your ultimate compatibility with that person. The more similar your prospective spouse's parents' marriage is to your own "ideal" marriage, the greater the likelihood of postmarital compatibility.

Sociocultural Factors Influencing Choice

Even though Americans are not restricted by arranged marriages, our choices in mate selection are limited to a relatively small field of eligible candidates. Two cultural forces have notable influence on our mate selection: **exogamy**, or the pressure to marry outside a specified group, such as one's immediate family; and **endogamy**, or the pressure to marry within a certain group, such as one's own religion or social class.

It is not surprising that we tend to meet, become attracted to, and marry persons similar to ourselves in age, educational level, social class background, race, and religion. **Homogamy**, the term given to this tendency, means "marrying among the same." Whether consciously or unconsciously, we are drawn to those who share important social, economic, and cultural characteristics with us. This is partially because we generally meet people similar to us in school, at work, in our communities, and at social functions. Sociologists use the term **propinquity** (or nearness) to describe this phenomenon; we tend to marry those with whom we come into close or regular contact.

Family influences on mate selection can be extremely important. On the most obvious level, this involves pressuring children to marry someone of "their own kind" (Eckland, 1980). However, on a more subtle level, families influence mate selection by deciding where to live. The neighborhood in which a family lives is usually an important indicator of their social class background, and residential propinquity is a significant factor in whom we meet. Think of all the marriages to the boy or girl next door, or between high school sweethearts.

Some researchers have suggested that upper class families take an active role in preventing close associations between their children and children from lower classes. The wealth of these families allows them to live in upper class neighborhoods and to send their children to private schools. This restricts the children's friends, neighbors, and schoolmates to a narrow range of backgrounds (Rosen and Bell, 1966).

Homogamy can be beneficial to marital success (Burr, 1976). Both Susanna and Walter come from middle-class families who valued literature, music, and art more than material possessions. Each absorbed their parents' values and has the same goals for their children. Consequently, although neither parent makes a great deal of money, they are a happy couple. "We don't mind having a small apartment and used furniture," says Susanna. "We have enough money to buy books, to go to the opera now and then, to take our kids to painting and dance classes. That's what's important to us."

Theories of Mate Selection

The freedom to choose our own mates has led theorists to the question: Why do we choose one possible mate over another? The many theories that have been offered in response to this question can be divided into two general types. **Individualistic theories** of mate selection, such as the notions that "likes attract" or "opposites attract," stress the importance of our emotional experiences and our subconscious needs and drives. By contrast, **sociocultural theories** emphasize that a variety of controls (such as race, religion, social class, and lack of physical proximity) reduces the availability of certain individuals as potential mates.

While individualistic theories such as "likes attract" are quite popular, it is difficult to test them empirically to determine if they are actually valid. Researchers have found significant correlations between husbands and wives on a number of personality traits (Cattell and Nesselroade, 1967). However, it has not been possible to conclude whether the shared qualities brought these couples together or whether the similarities resulted from being married for a period of time. The view that "opposites attract" has been formulated into a definitive theory, known as the theory of complementary needs (Winch, 1958). The example cited earlier of Marilyn and Phil would be offered as an illustration of this theoretical view. Unfortunately, researchers have generally been unable to identify patterns of complementary differences among married couples.

In addition, they have learned that people's perceptions of their spouses' personalities are often an inaccurate representation of the spouses' actual qualities (Udry, 1966).

Other individualistic theories are based on the radical notion that mate selection is guided by instinct (usually that of the male). For example, Carl Jung argued that every man carries within his genes an "archetypal form" of a specific female image. When the "right" woman (who fits the archetype) comes along, the man becomes instantly aware that he has found his mate (Evans, 1964). The "parent image" theory, also an individualistic approach, suggests that each of us chooses a mate who in temperament and physical appearance resembles our parent of the opposite sex. Although it seems logical to expect that a father or mother image might influence mate selection, there is as yet no evidence available to support this theory.

Sociocultural theories of mate selection stress the impact of such factors as race, religion, social class, and propinquity in determining why we choose one individual over another. One commonly cited sociocultural approach is exchange theory (see Chapter 2), which views marriage as an exchange of the assets and liabilities of each partner. For example, a male doctor may "exchange" his social status and income for the exciting opportunities and connections offered by his wife, a noted stage actress. Each may consider the marriage to be a fair exchange of desirable assets.

Another sociocultural approach to mate selection is SVR theory, or stimulus-value-role theory. Developed by Bernard Murstein (1971), SVR theory sees mate selection as a three-stage process in a society where "free choice" is the rule. For example, Joe was interested in meeting Helen after he saw some of her photographs in a student art exhibition. Even before he met her, he was excited by her artistic talent. As an aspiring writer,

Joe placed great value on creativity. When he met Helen at a departmental party a few weeks later, they "hit it off" immediately. Helen was attracted to Joe physically and was thrilled by his interest in and praise for her work. Thus, the initial stimulus—even before they actually met—was encouraging to both partners. In the second stage described by Murstein, Joe and Helen began to compare values. At the party, they talked about college, about artists they admired, about poets and novelists whose work had moved them. During the next few weeks, they met regularly for lunch and dinner and went together to films, art exhibitions, and concerts. They compared attitudes toward religion, politics, sex and love, food, friends, and everything else. While they did not agree across the board, their basic values seemed similar. Even when they disagreed, they were able to discuss their differences amicably and showed respect for the other's point of view. During Murstein's final stage of mate selection, the role stage, Joe and Helen increasingly confided in one another about their family backgrounds, their romantic theories, and their fears and insecurities. Well aware by this time that their relationship was quite serious, each partner shared their hopes and conflicts about intimate relationships. They spoke at length about how well they worked together as a couple, about the roles each played in the relationship, and about their sexual attitudes and needs.

Joe and Helen agreed that they ultimately wanted to marry and raise children together. Yet each felt that they were too young, that they needed to get started in their respective careers before beginning family life. Consequently, they decided to live together until they were ready to marry. Joe and Helen felt that their love would survive because they shared similar values, hopes, and expectations. Each believed that the other would continue to meet their most important needs

in an intimate relationship. Note how similar SVR theory is to the wheel theory proposed by Ira Reiss (see Chapter 4), which moves from deepening rapport to fulfillment of a variety of emotional needs. In fact, SVR theory has been shown to be useful in studies of friendships as well as romantic relationships.

Intermarriage

Jean, a 35-year-old black radiologist, has been married for ten years to Arthur, a 39-year-old white laboratory technician. They met at the university hospital where they both work. The couple has little to say about the subject of racial intermarriage; each feels that too much attention is given to race in

Increasing numbers of Americans are intermarrying across ethnic, racial, and religious lines.

American society. "We're human beings trying to make a marriage work, not representatives of our races," says Jean with some frustration. "When I think of Arthur, I don't think of Arthur-Who-Is-White. I think of an individual, of a warm, sincere man who loves practical jokes, who plays a mean jazz saxophone, who's a total workaholic in the hospital." Arthur adds that he, too, sees his spouse in a color-blind way. "Jean isn't like anyone else I've ever known. She's not like white people, she's not like black people, she's totally different even from the rest of her family. She's Jean, that's all, and I love her for who she is."

Roger, a 45-year-old Jewish architect, has been married for 15 years to Maria, a 39-year-old Greek Orthodox lawyer from Athens. Unlike Jean and Arthur, they are extremely conscious of their differences in religion and nationality. "We've raised our children to be Jewish and Greek Orthodox, to be American and Greek, all at once," says Roger. "It couldn't be any other way. Each of us is proud of our heritage. We want our kids to have the best of all of it." Maria notes that a few family members on each side have condemned their approach to intermarriage, but most have ultimately been won over. "In the end, they have to see what a rich family life we have. I think my kids are lucky, being part of two great traditions."

As the examples above illustrate, not all married couples follow the principle of homogamy, or "marrying among the same." Despite strong endogamous pressures to marry within certain groups, there is an increasing incidence of **intermarriage** among Americans across lines of race, religion, and ethnicity. Ethnic intermarriage is rising most rapidly, followed by religious intermarriage. About 40 percent of all American marriages now involve partners of differing religious backgrounds; Jews have the highest rate of interreligious marriage. While the

rate of racial intermarriage remains low, the 1979 figure (3 percent) was more than double that of 1963 (1.4 percent) (Cretser and Leon, 1979; Maretzki, 1977; Yorburg, 1978).

A sex bias is common among American mixed marriages: the husband is usually the member of the minority group and the wife the member of the majority group. While it was once believed that interracial marriage was restricted to the lower classes, Monahan (1976) has found that professional and white-collar groups are well represented in interracial marriages. Rosenthal (1970) found a pronounced tendency for divorced persons to remarry someone of a different religion.

There are numerous motivations for an interracial or interreligious marriage, among them the reasons frequently cited for marriages by those of similar backgrounds. As is true of Jean and Arthur, as well as Roger and Maria, most intermarried couples report that love was the key force behind their decision to marry. Often their love had to be strong enough to overcome severe familial and social pressures against intermarriage.

Researchers have found that propinquity—residential, occupational, and educational—is the key factor influencing intermarriage in contemporary society (Downs, 1971; Heer, 1966). For example, an American soldier stationed in Okinawa may marry a Japanese woman; if he had been stationed in Omaha, Nebraska, he might have married a Nebraskan instead. Jean and Arthur, as noted earlier, met in the hospital where they both worked; Roger and Maria were graduate students at the University of Michigan during the late 1960s and met at a Student Senate meeting.

There are other reasons for intermarriage. Some may enter such marriages to be "different" or to rebel against their parents. Others may claim they are motivated by high ideals; such persons may wish to "prove" their lack of bias by marrying someone from a minority group. For certain individuals, there may be a desire to improve their economic or social status by intermarriage. Although people generally deny it, concepts of superiority and inferiority can influence their mate selection (Char, 1977).

At present, about 50 percent of marriages in Hawaii are intercultural. Over 60 percent of third-generation Japanese-Americans in that state are intermarrying. However, while intermarriage appears to be an accepted practice in Hawaii, it remains suspect in the eyes of many Americans across the nation. Resistance to a couple's decision to intermarry is common; in some instances, family members and friends threaten to permanently sever relations with the intermarried couple. Such threats may result from fear, prejudice, or pressure to conform to the patterns of the majority.

On the basis of certain studies, it is easy to argue that mixed marriages face handicaps right from the start. Downs (1971), in a survey of interracial marriages, found that two-thirds of respondents saw a mixed marriage as less likely to succeed than a marriage between two persons of the same race. The reasons for this pessimism ranged from "lack of social acceptance" to "marriage has enough problems, mixed marriage just adds one more." More than 70 percent of those questioned were convinced that children from mixed marriages "face a life of prejudice and harassment."

On the other hand, some studies have come to just the opposite conclusions. For example, Monahan (1971) found that marriages between blacks and whites in Kansas did not show any special likelihood of divorce. Indeed, such intermarriages were somewhat more stable than marriages between blacks. Monahan concludes that whether or not a certain type of racial inter-marriage will endure depends on the particular races intermarrying, the social circumstances surrounding the couple at the time, and the nature of the marital partners themselves. This formulation may be valid for intermarriages in general.

Mate Selection and Remarriage

As Bruce Eckland (1980) points out, most theories of mate selection—whether individualistic or sociocultural—focus on engaged or married couples. Almost no attention is given to other kinds of couples, including those having illicit or adulterous affairs. In addition, Eckland cautions that this emphasis on courtship and marriage has virtually obscured the fact that individuals separate, divorce, and remarry. Thus, for some Americans, mate selection is a more or less continuous process.

Current data suggest that about one-fourth of all men and women will marry more than once during their lives. After divorce, three-quarters of all women and five-sixths of all men will remarry (Furstenberg, 1980a). There is more likely to be a significant age difference between the partners in a remarriage than in a first marriage.

The majority of second marriages (56 percent) are successful—that is, at least in the sense that they do not end in divorce (Glick, 1980). This may mean that people learn how to make a marriage work after their initial failure. It may also mean that they become more careful (and less self-destructive) in their mate selection. We will examine divorce and remarriage in greater detail in Chapter 14.

Preparation for Marriage

There are many things to consider before undertaking a marriage. Ideally, a couple should be both emotionally and financially ready for married life. Legal requirements, which vary from state to state, must be satisfied. The transition into marriage can be quite difficult; some couples find it useful to take the "preventive medicine" of premarital counseling.

Personal Readiness

While a couple may seem compatible and feel they are deeply in love forever, this does not necessarily mean that they are ready for marriage. A marital relationship, even without children, involves long-term responsibilities. Many couples, while capable of intense romance and passion, are not able to handle the strains of day-to-day married life.

Studies have revealed that the younger a couple's ages at marriage, the higher the likelihood of divorce (Shoen, 1975). As noted in Chapter 6, in 1979 the average age of marriage in the United States had risen to 25.2 for men and 22.5 for women. Nevertheless, age is at best a crude index of emotional and social maturity, which does not necessarily accompany emotional maturity. According to Blood and Blood (1978), an emotionally mature person has the ability to establish and maintain personal relationships, to give and receive, and to assume responsibility for meeting the needs of others. This may or may not be true of those who marry in their twenties—or, for that matter, of those who marry in their forties or sixties.

Rapoport (1963) has identified three critical tasks that must be accomplished as part of one's preparation for marriage:

1. Making oneself ready to take over the role of husband or wife.
2. Disengaging from especially close relationships that interfere with commitment to the new marital relationship.
3. Accommodating one's premarital lifestyle, and patterns of gratification, to the new marital relationship.

If these tasks are successfully completed, the individual probably has the emotional maturity needed for marriage. Yet there is another steep hurdle, social maturity, which does not necessarily accompany emotional maturity. The socially mature spouse has dated enough, and been "free and independent" enough, to know that faraway pastures are not always greener. In short, he or she will accept the compromises and imperfections of living with and loving someone without assuming that every attractive stranger would be a better mate or without glorifying the lives of unmarried friends.

Financial Adequacy

It is simply a myth that "two can live as cheaply as one." Consequently, it is best for a couple to be prepared for the financial burdens of marriage, especially if they plan to have children. There is no set answer as to how much money will be needed; to some extent, the amount will depend on the couple's values. In most cases, the higher their joint income, the more likely they are to feel they can afford to marry.

Many American families, especially among the middle class, are willing and eager to offer financial assistance to children who are marrying. Marvin Sussman (1953) found that more than 75 percent of the New Haven families he studied gave regular financial help to their married children. While some younger couples willingly accept such aid, others would not think of taking money from in-laws. The latter value their hardwon independence from their parents, and they fear that monetary gifts or loans might lead to emotional obligations and demands.

What happens when college students in their late teens or early twenties marry? Typically, parents continue to pay tuition since college savings are thought of as belonging to the children—whether or not they are married. However, the newly married couple is often expected to be fully responsible for their other expenses.

Engagement

In Western societies, the **engagement** is an important period of transition during which couples prepare for marriage. In part because of the dramatic rise in cohabitation (see Chapter 6), a formal engagement period is much less common in the United States than was true in earlier decades. Many couples live together for months or even years and then decide to marry.

Ideally, the engagement allows time for a couple to better understand each other's values, behavior, and future role expectations. Unfortunately, many engagements do not prepare couples adequately for marriage because they are too short. An engagement of a few days or weeks hardly provides an opportunity for prospective marriage partners to make careful decisions about money management, living arrangements, in-law relations, and so forth. Nor does it offer a transition period in which each partner can gain the respect and approval of his or her own family and of future in-laws.

While most engagements result in marriage, it is no longer considered a disgrace to break an engagement. Friends and family usually conclude that "it's better they found out now rather than after the wedding." The traditional view of engagement as a marriage forecast was supported by the research of Burgess and Wallin (1953). This classic, decade-long study of engagement focused on 1000 engaged couples. Burgess and Wallin found that those couples who got along well during their engagement would generally do the same during marriage. They also found that the longer the engagement, the more successful the later relationship; similarly, the more time engaged people actually spent together, the better the later relationship. The researchers listed five

major causes of broken engagements: minimal emotional involvement, extended geographical separation, parental opposition, cultural differences, and special personality problems of one or both members of the couple.

For most engaged couples, this period is a time of pleasurable anticipation. No longer involved in the competitive "dating game," they can relax and enjoy the fact that they have found *the* person for them. Since marriage is a mark of high status in our society, the engagement signals a major achievement for both the man and woman.

Easing the Transition into Marriage

According to Wesley Burr (1976: 275), the transition into marriage is one of the most complex changes people ever attempt: "It is probably not as large a transition as . . . becoming a parent, but it is still . . . a challenge for all of us and an awesome ordeal for some of us." In his book, *Successful Marriage: A Principles Approach*, Burr identifies four key principles that can help to ease this transition (see Figure 7–1).

Burr's first principle is the "learning

Figure 7–1 Principles affecting the transition into marriage. (*Source*: Burr, 1976, p. 289.)

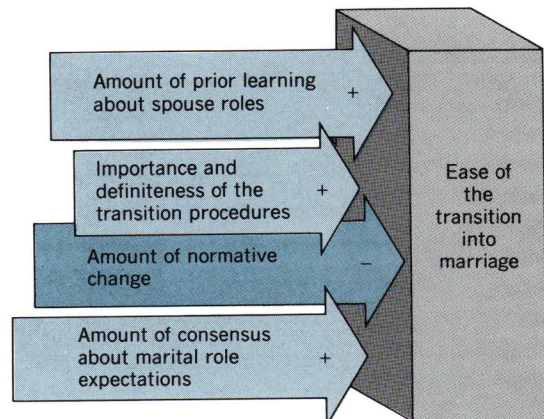

about the spouse role principle." Simply stated, the more one learns about what marriage is actually like, the easier the transition will be. Such learning can come from observing one's own parents, from observing newlyweds, from talking with friends who are married, from reading about marriage, or from courses on marriage and family life. Burr stresses that, if such learning is to ease the transition, it must be accurate and realistic. The romanticized and sensationalized distortions of married life often put forth in the media are far from helpful.

Second is the "transition procedures principle." By this, Burr means that the more definite and important the transition procedures are, the easier the transition will be. In most societies, the procedure for moving from singlehood to marriage involves elaborate and longstanding rites of passage. As an example, a traditional American wedding typically involves lavish preparations and is a highly visible occasion.

Burr's third principle, the "normative change with marriage principle," states that the greater the amount of change in a person's routine life as he or she takes on the role of spouse, the more difficult the transition. Thus, if a wedding occurs at about the same time as other stressful changes, such as leaving one's parents' home, graduating from college, and looking for one's first job, it will make the transition into marriage much more demanding.

Sex and money are two key areas that are particularly relevant here. Couples who have lived together before marriage, or who have had a long-term sexual relationship, may experience only minor changes in their sexual life after the wedding. By contrast, those who abstained from premarital sex will find that they must adjust to becoming lovers, living together, and being husband and wife simultaneously. This can complicate the transition period. Money is also a key consideration because conflicts about finances are the number one problem in many American marriages (Landis and Landis, 1968). Burr suggests that it may be helpful to make certain systematic changes, such as combining financial resources, before the wedding rather than just after it.

The final principle in Burr's model is the "consensus about marital expectations principle." Here he suggests that the more the couple agrees on how they ought to act as marital partners, the easier the transition will be. Obviously, if Jane thinks it important to maintain individual interests and friendships after marriage while her husband Bill believes they should do everything together, they will soon encounter serious problems.

David Olson (1972), a researcher and therapist who has worked extensively with couples preparing to marry, offers the following guidelines and recommendations designed to make marriage more meaningful and rewarding:

1. Individuals should not be encouraged to marry at an early age. Instead, they should wait until they have matured emotionally and become established in their chosen professions.

2. Individuals should not be encouraged or pressured into marriage. Singlehood should be viewed as a respectable lifestyle.

3. Individuals and couples should be encouraged to experiment with a variety of lifestyles in order to better select the option most appropriate for them.

4. Couples should be encouraged to relate openly and honestly rather than play the traditional "dating-mating game."

5. Couples should not marry until they have established a meaningful relationship and resolved major difficulties between them. Marriage does not solve problems; it is more likely to intensify them.

6. Parenthood should be a joint decision of marriage partners. This decision should follow rather than precede marriage.

7. Couples should not have children until they have established strong and viable relationships.

Premarital Counseling

Skyrocketing divorce statistics have led to widespread preventive programs to protect marriages. Schools have introduced family life and sex education courses beginning as early as junior high school. Churches have established programs for engaged couples to assist them in planning for marriage. In addition, social service agencies have begun to offer premarital counseling for young couples. In 1970, California became the first state to provide that minors (those under the age of 18) applying for a marriage license may be required to participate in premarital counseling (Shonick, 1975).

Alina and Richard, a young, engaged Californian couple, received premarital counseling through a Los Angeles community health agency. During their first session, they met jointly with their counselor, a social worker named Margaret. Her initial goal was to have each describe their backgrounds, career goals, and reasons for marrying. Margaret also hoped to see how Alina and Richard interacted and what expectations they had about marriage.

On the whole, the session went well. Alina talked about her job as an executive secretary and how she was saving money to go to business school. Richard, a salesman for an electronics firm, noted that there were excellent prospects for advancement in his field. Margaret was impressed with the careful financial planning of the couple, but worried about the fact that Richard dominated the conversation and often answered questions directed at Alina.

During their second visit to the agency, Margaret spoke alone with Alina, then with Richard, then finally with the two together. Her talk with Alina quickly turned to the couple's communication problems. "I know he loves me, but he doesn't listen to me enough," complained Alina. "He's so quick to say, 'We feel this way', or even, 'She feels this way,' without asking how I actually feel. If I criticize him about it, he gets super-defensive."

When Margaret spoke with Richard, she asked him if he felt he and Alina had communication problems. "Yes, we do," he responded. "I know I'm overbearing sometimes. Still, it's not really that bad." "But do you know how it makes her feel?" asked Margaret. This led them into a more candid discussion of the issue. In the joint session, Richard brought up the subject of his verbal dominance; he and Alina had a heated but useful exchange and left with a much better understanding of each other's feelings.

During their final session, Alina and Richard, along with their parents, met with Margaret. The session focused on the young couple's future living arrangements. Alina's parents had been pressuring them to move into an apartment in their building after the wedding. After discussion guided by the social worker, all finally agreed that this would be unwise. Alina's parents understood that the couple needed a bit more distance from both sets of in-laws and that this was not intended as a rejection.

At the end of the program, Margaret sent a letter to Alina and Richard, certifying that they had completed the required sessions. She also included a brief evaluation of their strengths and weaknesses as a couple. Both Alina and Richard were grateful for the counseling experience. "Three sessions didn't solve all our problems," observed Alina, "but it helped. We're a little more open about a few rough areas than we were before." Richard adds, "I hated the idea of going—until I actually did. It wasn't fun, but I know I learned a lot.''

Generally, the aim of premarital counseling is to help couples assess their readiness and resources for marriage (see Table 7-1). Counselors cannot offer serious treatment for emotional problems in a few short sessions. Therefore, they explore instead such important areas of daily life as financial management, family planning, career and educational goals, and use of recreational time. Above all, counselors stress the value of effective communication between marital partners. Premarital counseling basically serves as a preventive measure to help couples prepare for the initial transitions and problems of married life (Shonick, 1975).

The Wedding

Although marriage is celebrated in every society, the rites that mark it vary from simple rituals to elaborate ceremonies. Many contemporary wedding customs can be traced to magical beliefs and pagan rites; however, they have lost their original meaning and have taken on new significance. For example, while the wedding ring was once thought to be symbolic of bondage—the rope tied around a woman when wives were captured—it now symbolizes the eternity of wedding ties. Rice was once seen as an offering to appease evil spirits; today, some see it as a symbol of fertility and throw rice to express the wish that the couple will have many children.

As in the past, the majority of American weddings are traditional religious ceremonies. In 1970, 75 percent of all marrying couples preferred a religious ceremony; in 1972, 80 percent of all first marriages were solemnized formally (Seligson, 1973). However, since the late 1960s, an increasing number of couples have become actively involved in planning the ceremony. Some write their own vows and include favorite

Table 7-1 Goals of a three-phase premarital program

Premarital inventory	Couple's discussions in small groups	Communication skill training in couple's groups
1. Increase couple's awareness of relationship strengths and potential problem areas.	1. Increase couple's ability and willingness to share with other couples.	1. Build communication skills like sympathy, empathy, and self-disclosure.
2. Facilitate a couple's discussion about their relationship.	2. Develop other couples as friends.	2. Build skills for resolving conflict and problem-solving.
3. Establish relationship with clergy, counselor, or married couple.	3. Learn how other couples relate and deal with issues.	
4. Prime for postmarital enrichment or counseling.		
5. Referral to intensive counseling if problems too serious arise.		

Source: Olson, 1983: 72.

In focusing on the meaning that the couple attaches to their relationship, wedding ceremonies serve both a social and personal function.

passages from the Bible or treasured poems. Traditional wedding music may be discarded in favor of popular songs or classical pieces. Perhaps most significantly, many women are no longer promising to "love, honor, and obey" their husbands. The words "love and honor" are still heard, but "obey" is increasingly falling out of favor.

Some cynics view formal weddings as desirable only in order to obtain "lots of loot." This ignores the fact that weddings are important social and psychological events. Socially, they create new family units; psychologically, they require fundamental role changes for the couple and their families (Blumberg and Paul, 1975). As Bowman and Spanier (1978: 178) conclude:

The wedding creates status, rights, and opportunity. It has a social function in that it helps focus the meaning of a couple's relationship and has a personal function in that it is a major vehicle for the couple's expression of mutual commitment.

Marriage and the Law

In the United States, each of the 50 states controls its own laws in marriage and domestic relations; therefore, the law varies from state to state. In general, the legal requirements for marriage have to do with age (teenagers may need parental consent), mental competence (prohibitions against marriages involving those judged insane or mentally deficient), family relationships (outlawing incestuous marriages), and waiting periods (the time span between applying for a marriage license and permission to marry). Although each state has its own standards, a marriage that is legal in one state will be recognized as valid in all others.

In the United States and most other societies, women continue to lose legal rights by marrying. Arlene Skolnick (1978: 242) notes that "the married woman's loss of legal rights can be traced to the feudal doctrine of **coverture**, the notion that the husband and wife are a unity." In practice, this has traditionally meant that by marrying, these two individuals become one legal person: the husband. Until this doctrine was revised in the late nineteenth century as a result of pressure from women's rights advocates, married women had virtually no legal rights whatsoever.

Even today, although domestic relations laws vary from state to state, the unwritten marriage contract of American society generally carries with it four basic assumptions: the husband is the head of the household; the husband is responsible for financial support of the family; the wife is responsible for domestic services; and the wife is responsible for child care (Weitzman, 1975). Typically, when a woman marries, she assumes her husband's name, his place of residence, and his social and economic status. If she chooses to retain her maiden name, she may encounter difficulties in obtaining a driver's license or charge accounts. If she is attending a state university as a state resident but marries an out-of-state student, she may be forced to pay higher out-of-state fees. In addition, in certain states married women lose some of their rights to control property and cannot enter into contracts on the same basis as a single woman or man.

Not surprisingly, because of the rise of the feminist movement and the growing interest in egalitarian marriages, there has been increasing challenge to such institutionalized sexism. Many states have begun to revise their domestic relations laws so as to promote financial and role equality between husbands and wives. This has influenced court decisions regarding division of property, alimony, and child custody. Moreover, as noted in Chapter 5, certain states have made marital rape a crime, thereby eliminating the previous legal backing for a husband's violent sexual assault of his wife.

While **premarital contracts** have long been a custom among such peoples as the Druse of Lebanon (see Box 7–2), for many years use of such contracts in the United States was mainly restricted to wealthy older persons marrying for a second time. Such

FEIFFER

B O X 7 – 2

Research Brief:
Marriage Contracts Among the Druse Sect of Lebanon

While marriage contracts in Western countries have become more popular as part of the movement toward sexual equality, such contracts have long been a custom of many traditional societies. In an effort to examine the meaning and ramifications of such agreements, Paul D. Starr and Nura S. Alamuddin (1981) studied 3398 marriage contracts negotiated in the period 1931 to 1974 by members of the minority Druse sect of Lebanon.

The Druse, also found in substantial numbers in Israel and Syria, cherish many traditional values of the Mideast but are monogamous in their marriage practices. Their marriage contracts provide legal and religious sanction for a couple's union, and reflect long and detailed negotiations by elders representing the bride and groom. The standard contract form specifies, among other things, the physical status of the bride and whether she is a virgin, a widow, or a divorcee.

Most negotiations focus on the *mahr*, a payment made by the husband or his family to the bride or her kin. The *mahr* may include money, clothing, jewelry, furniture, or appliances useful in establishing a household. It may be paid before, during, or after the signing ceremony, or it may be deferred to serve as a kind of insurance in case the husband dies before the wife or divorces her.

In studying the use of the *mahr* among the Druse sect, the researchers found that:

- Virgins were seen as worthy of a much higher *mahr* than either widows or divorcees.

- The great majority of Druse marry within their social class.

- If a lower class Druse wishes to marry a woman from a higher class, he will generally have to pay a high *mahr*. However, if a high-status groom wishes to marry a lower class bride, his status will be considered a great reward and the *mahr* need not be high.

- A large *mahr* will be sought if the bride is to move far from her family after marriage. In part, this is a form of protection since her family will be less able to assist her.

- An undesirable male suitor may be discouraged diplomatically through insistence on an exceptionally high *mahr*.

Starr and Alamuddin conclude that the use of marriage contracts in the Mideast is a "long-established safeguard for women," who occupy a subordinate position within society.

Source: Starr and Alamuddin, 1981: 8–10.

individuals wished to insure that their wealth would be properly distributed at the time of their deaths. More recently, however, newly married couples are choosing to write premarital contracts that deal with such issues as responsibility for financial support and household duties, management and control of money, and planning for children.

Critics of premarital contracts point out that they are not legally binding and reflect a rather pessimistic attitude toward married life. For some, these contracts are a crass and unwarranted formalizing of an intimate relationship. However, one financial counselor argues that, in a nation in which half of marriages end in divorce, it is better to be crass than sorry (Train, 1980). A New York matrimonial lawyer adds: "Entering marriage without a premarital contract is like going into a business venture under someone else's rules" (Belkin and Goodman, 1980: 30). Special legal steps can be taken to draw up a contract providing for property settlements and child custody arrangements if the marriage ends.

Marriage contracts have also become more common in ongoing marriages, where they may be used to redefine the partners' roles and responsibilities after such changes as the arrival of children or the return of the wife to a career. Many marriage counselors and instructors in marital relations advocate the use of such contracts as a way of dealing with the conflicts of day-to-day married life (Sager, 1976). Similar contracts may be especially valuable for those living in alternate family forms such as cohabitation, homosexual couples, and communes (see Chapters 2 and 6).

Predicting Marital Success

As noted earlier, length of courtship is a key factor in predicting marital success. The longer the relationship, the greater the probability that the marriage will be happy and satisfying; the briefer the relationship, the higher the probability the marriage will be unhappy and end in divorce (Burgess and Cottrell, 1939; Locke, 1951). Although studies do not explain why length of courtship has this effect, the important causal factor is probably how well the couple gets to know each other before the wedding (Burr, 1976). It may be easier for a man and a woman to fantasize about everlasting happiness if they spend time at the beach or at romantic dinners than if they must paint a small apartment or balance a checkbook. Given time to discover incompatibility, those without hope of resolving problems may decide not to marry (Blood and Blood, 1978). In a study of working-class British couples, Slater and Woodside (1951) found that, while only 50 percent of those who married less than a year after meeting were happy, the proportion went up to 59 percent for those who waited at least a year before marriage and 63 percent for those who waited two to three years.

It is also true that the older individuals are at the time of marriage, the greater their chances for marital success (Burgess and Cottrell, 1939; Burgess and Wallin, 1953; Landis and Landis, 1968). Teen marriages, of course, are especially prone to failure. After the mid-twenties, however, age has little impact on marital success (Burr, 1976). While some researchers suggest that the key factor is not age itself but rather other qualities associated with age, such as emotional maturity, others argue that age truly is the key.

A number of studies have shown that the more education a person has experienced, the greater the likelihood that he or she will have a successful marriage (Burgess and Wallin, 1953; Goode, 1956; Kephart, 1954). Unfortunately, none of these studies has clarified which maritally relevant skills are obtained through higher education. It may be that, as with age, education has a clear relationship to marital satisfaction because it enhances people's maturity.

All of the major marriage prediction studies (Burgess and Cottrell, 1939; Burgess and Wallin, 1953; DeBurger, 1961; Locke, 1951) have indicated that the more your parents and friends approve of your prospective mate, the more likely your marriage will succeed. In addition, research has suggested that the more conventional a couple is, the greater their chances for a successful marriage (Burgess, et al., 1963; Burr, 1976; Udry, 1974). The greater the desire for children of a couple contemplating marriage, the more likely that their marriage will succeed (Burgess and Cottrell, 1939; Locke, 1951). It must be noted, however, that it remains to be seen whether these older findings will continue to be relevant in the 1980s.

Wesley Burr (1976) suggests that the

"similarity principle" is a good predictor of marital success. The more alike the couple is in any area of life—whether it be social class, race, religion, role expectations, values, or interests—the better their chance of success. Burr singles out one area in which dissimilarity is particularly difficult to handle: when the husband has lower status or prestige than the wife.

A number of researchers have indicated that the greater the consensus about role expectations, the greater the likelihood of marital success (Luckey, 1960; Sarbin and Allen, 1968; Stryker, 1964). Unfortunately, as Burr (1976) observes, it is virtually impossible to identify all of our role expectations before marriage. Many are not yet formed and will not become clear until we actually experience the demands of married life and parenthood.

Summary

Sociologist Robert Winch has referred to dating as "window-shopping" and to courtship as a "bargaining process." While many Americans still go out on rather formal dates, others pair off in a less defined manner. Women are now freer to take initiatives in the dating process than was true in the past.

Personal factors influencing mate selection include love, self-esteem, and compatibility of temperaments, needs, and values. Individualistic theories of mate selection stress the importance of our emotional experiences and our subconscious needs and drives. By contrast, sociocultural theories emphasize that a variety of controls (such as race, religion, social class, and lack of physical proximity) reduce the availability of certain individuals as potential mates.

Two cultural forces have notable influence on our mate selection: exogamy, or the pressure to marry outside a specific group, and endogamy, or the pressure to marry within a certain group. Many Americans practice homogamy by "marrying among the same" in terms of age, educational level, social class background, race, and religion. However, an increasing number are opting for intermarriage.

Ideally, a couple should be both emotionally and financially ready for marriage. Both emotional and social maturity may be essential if a marriage is to succeed. The period of engagement allows time for a couple to better understand each other's values, behavior, and future role expectations. Studies have shown that couples who get along well during engagement will generally do the same during marriage.

The transition to marriage is one of the most complex changes people ever attempt. Some couples have found it helpful to receive premarital counseling from members of the clergy or professional counselors. In general, the aim of premarital counseling is to help couples assess their readiness and resources for marriage.

As in the past, the majority of American weddings are traditional religious ceremonies. Each of the 50 states has its own legal requirements for marriage. In the United States and most other societies, women continue to lose legal rights by marrying. Both premarital contracts and contracts in ongoing marriages have become more common in recent years as a means of specifying partners' roles and responsibilities.

Length of courtship is a key factor in marital success. The older individuals are at the time of marriage, the greater their chances for marital success. Education also appears to have a positive impact on marital relationships. Wesley Burr suggests that the more similar a couple is in any area of life—whether it be social class, race, religion, role expectations, values, or interests—the better their chance of marital success.

Developmental Task   Matching to Match

Matching to Match is designed to be completed by both partners together in a relationship. Decide whether each statement is a weak, moderately weak, moderately strong, or strong point in your relationship and circle the number corresponding.

BUILDING BLOCKS FOR A LASTING RELATIONSHIP	weak	mod. weak	mod. strong	strong
1. Realistic expectations: We are realistic about the demands and difficulties of marriage.	1	2	3	4
2. Egualitarian role: We agree on how to share decision-making and responsibilities.	1	2	3	4
3. Communication: We feel that we are understood by each other and are able to share our feelings.	1	2	3	4
4. Conflict resolution: We feel that we are able to discuss and resolve our differences.	1	2	3	4
5. Financial management: We both have a realistic budget, and we agree on money matters.	1	2	3	4
6. Leisure activities: We share interests and enjoy time together and apart.	1	2	3	4
7. Sexual relationship: We feel comfortable discussing sexual issues and preferences with each other.	1	2	3	4
8. Children and marriage: We agree about having/not having children and about childrearing responsibilities.	1	2	3	4
9. Family and friends: We have a good relationship with parents, in-laws, and friends.	1	2	3	4
10. Religious orientation: We agree on religious values and beliefs.	1	2	3	4

ADD UP THE NUMBERS YOU CIRCLED.

WHAT YOUR SCORE MEANS: If your score is between 35 and 40 points it suggests that your relationship is strong; between 25 and 34, moderately strong; between 16 and 24, moderately weak; and between 10 and 15, weak.

Source: Adapted from D. H. Olson, ''Couple Feedback Sheet,'' St. Paul, Minn.: University of Minnesota, 1981.

Discussion Questions

1. Reflecting on your own experiences in dating and (if relevant) mate selection, which of the following factors have been most important in your choices: age, education, race, religion, social class, attractiveness, propinquity (residential, educational, or occupational)? Which factors have influenced you least?

2. How influential has your family been in your decisions about dating and mate selection? Do they usually concur with or object to your choices? What did you do, or what would you do, if they vehemently objected to your choice of a mate?

3. Which of the following is most important to you: love, home life, or companionship? Why?

4. In terms of compatibility with a potential partner, which of the following do you see as most important: compatibility of needs, values, or of temperament? Why?

5. If you are presently married or have been in the past, how long was your courtship? Do you think this period of time was adequate? If you are not married, were you ever in a relationship that almost led to marriage? If so, what kept you from marrying that person?

Key Words

Compatibility

Complementary Needs

Coverture

Endogamy

Engagement

Exogamy

Homogamy

Individualistic Theories

Intermarriage

Parallel Needs

Premarital Contracts

Propinquity

Sociocultural Theories

Suggested Readings

Chapman, Jane Roberts, and Gates, Margaret. *Women into Wives: The Legal and Economic Impact of Marriage*. Beverly Hills, Calif.: Sage Publications, 1977. A well-documented examination suitable for students and for the general public.

Chesser, Barbara Jo. ''Analysis of wedding rituals: an attempt to make weddings more meaningful.'' *Family Relations*, 1980 (April), *29* (2), 204–209. Gives information on the meaning of aspects of the wedding ceremony and encourages couples to plan a mutually satisfying ceremony.

Jedlicka, Davor. ''Automated go-betweens: mate selection of tomorrow?'' *Family Relations*, 1981, *30*, 373–376. Examines computer dating techniques and the advantages they offer in finding possible mates.

McGinniss, Alan. *The Romance Factor*. San Francisco: Harper and Row, 1982. Offers practical advice on how to achieve and maintain loving relationships.

Yankelovich, Daniel. *New Rules: Searching for Self-Fulfillment in a World Turned Upside Down*. New York: Random House, 1981. Uses survey research data and in-depth interviews to discuss commitment to and sacrifice for marriage versus the emphasis on self-fulfillment and individual growth.

CHAPTER EIGHT

The Marital Relationship

KEY TOPICS

—developmental tasks of marriage partners as individuals and as a couple—
—how changing sex roles have affected the exchange between husbands and wives—
—the balance of power within marriages—
—spouse abuse—
—marital sexuality—
—marital strengths—

The modern individual family is founded on the open or concealed domestic slavery of the wife.
—Friedrich Engels

All right, Edith, you go right ahead and do your thing. But just remember that your thing is eggs over easy and crisp bacon.
—Archie Bunker,
in ''All in the Family''

I never really thought I'd get married. To me, marriage looked like a skinny little negative space into which I would never be able to squeeze myself and all my aspirations.
—Marlo Thomas

Most marriages don't add two people together. They subtract one from the other.
—James Bond

A 1983 article in *U.S. News and World Report* concluded that ''marriage is back in style after two decades during which men and women dabbled at alternative lifestyles.'' In 1982, a record 2.5 million couples entered into the state of holy matrimony. Many Americans—even those marrying for a second time—are choosing to have large, old-fashioned wedding ceremonies. Noting the high rates of divorce and remarriage, sociologist Jerry Talley of Stanford University observed: ''People may be disappointed in a marriage partner, but they are not disappointed in marriage in general'' (Sanoff, 1983: 44).

Marriage has been described as the

"axis" around which family life revolves (Satir, 1964). Two persons publicly commit themselves to one another, each bringing labor and love in exchange for economic and personal rewards. In this chapter, we will examine the dynamics of marital interaction, focusing on the husband-wife relationship. The developmental tasks of marital partners, sex roles within marriage, marital violence, and marital sexuality will be analyzed. In later chapters, we will show how the marital relationship changes when the couple undertakes parenthood.

Challenges and Responsibilities: Developmental Tasks in Marriage

Marriage launches people into a new and often unfamiliar way of day-to-day life. Despite what many wish to believe, it does not magically complete the maturing process. Instead, marriage brings new developmental tasks and challenges for the couple and for each partner as an individual. These include acquiring the self-image of husband or wife; realigning loyalties so that the spouse comes first; participating in establishing a new home; assuming one's share of marital responsibilities; becoming a more satisfying and satisfied sexual partner; and relating to parents and in-laws as married daughter or son. Duvall (1977: 192) concludes that "being married involves coming to terms with what is expected—by one's culture, by one's mate, by one's self and as a couple."

Individual Tasks

Erik Erikson (1963) believed that marriage was an important step in individual development because it represented the overcoming of isolation and the reaching outside of oneself to establish intimacy. The separation from one's parents that began so tentatively at the end of childhood is completed by joining in a marital relationship. Thus, marriage is one sign of personal growth, of preparing for a mature and productive adult life.

Traditionally, marriage was seen as a very significant part of women's identity. While men's identity was derived from work or other achievements, women's status and ambition was closely tied to that of their husbands. For some women, then, the search for individual identity came after the establishment of intimacy within marriage (Sanguilano, 1978). It must be noted, however, that this pattern has changed to a significant extent in recent decades. The contemporary feminist movement has encouraged women to seek meaning and identity through career achievements as well as through marriage and parenthood.

Couple and Community Tasks

Marriage is a continual process of learning to accept and respect differences. Some partners begin by blindly idealizing a spouse, but it quickly becomes apparent that the spouse has weaknesses and limitations. Two persons must develop closeness and harmony despite the fact that each has distinct preferences, interests, values, and expectations. Inevitably, this requires that they reshape their behaviors and expectations to a certain degree. Developing a sense of loyalty and trust in your partner and in the marriage is critical in getting through the "rough spots" of marriage.

Not only is marriage a relationship between two persons; it is also a formal arrangement between the couple and the larger social world. One young woman remarks, "My husband and I got married after living together for two years. Things between us didn't change too much; what was different was the way that other people treated us." The married couple is frequently viewed as a unit by their families, friends, and the community. Marriage is a sign of coming-of-age, of "settling down" and accepting responsibilities. Acceptance of the new couple by others helps them define and adjust to their new status.

Sex Roles in Marriage

Jessie Bernard (1972), a prominent sociologist, has suggested that within a marital relationship there are actually two marriages: his and hers. In other words, husbands and wives often experience marriage very differently. Bernard points out that married women have higher rates of depression and illness than single women, while married men experience fewer depressions and illnesses than single men. These differences stem at least partly from the traditional sex roles we learn (see Chapter 3); wives are socialized to meet the emotional needs of their husbands rather than focusing on their own needs.

Researchers use the term **marital roles** to refer to the different tasks performed by husbands and wives. We can list at least seven:

1. The provider role—earning money to support the family.
2. The housekeeper role—cooking, cleaning, and looking after the home.
3. The child-care role—looking after the child's material needs.
4. The child-socialization role—teaching children socially responsible behavior.
5. The recreational role—sharing interests and activities with one's partner.
6. The sexual role—being a responsive sexual partner.
7. The therapeutic role—being a good listener, a sounding board for problems; offering support and encouragement.

The more that marital partners reward each other in these seven roles, the better the relationship (Nye and McLaughlin, 1976).

The allocation of marital rewards differs from marriage to marriage and may depend on whether a couple favors traditional or egalitarian values. Traditional couples are more likely to assign certain roles (such as provider and housekeeper) to one spouse or the other. Egalitarian couples often favor sharing of all important roles.

Traditional or Egalitarian

Paula and Allen have been married for 29 years. When they married in the early 1950s, Paula quit her job as a teacher because "married women didn't work." Allen felt strongly that, as a man, he should be the sole provider for his family. Paula had two daughters and became a full-time homemaker.

By the mid-1960s, Allen had a thriving furniture store that demanded a great deal of his time. He was making a substantial income, but was largely unable to take vacations or even quiet weekends with his family. With the children now in school, Paula had an increasing amount of free time and began to feel bored. She thought about teaching again, but Allen insisted that she stay home: "People will think my store isn't doing well if you get a job. Besides, you've got everything you want."

Over the next few years, Paula became even more dissatisfied and frustrated. She began to watch television programs that emphasized women's "sacrifices" in marriage and read a number of magazine articles about women's liberation. One morning, the school superintendent, with whom she had worked many years before, asked her to substitute for a teacher who was suddenly hospitalized. Without consulting Allen, Paula accepted the job and subsequently resumed full-time teaching.

"I had to take the job; I was going crazy," remembers Paula. "I decided that Allen would simply have to go along with it." Allen still doesn't like the fact that Paula is working. "And I won't help with the housework," he adds adamantly. "One battle at a time," replies Paula.

At the time that Paula and Allen married in the 1950s, women were expected to stay home and raise children while men were expected to be the sole breadwinners for their families. Any other arrangements were considered unusual, peculiar, not really "right." As the women's movement garnered public attention in the 1970s and more women moved into the workforce, the **traditional marriage** became much less common. By 1981, 54 percent of married women with children worked outside the home; moreover, nearly 45 percent of all women thought the ideal lifestyle included both marriage and career (Gallup, 1982).

Paula's oldest daughter, Susan, was married in 1979. Susan, a successful art dealer, is active in the feminist movement. She and her husband Brian have an **egalitarian marriage**. Both work outside the home; they share expenses and housework equally. Susan has retained her maiden name and has bank accounts and credit cards in her own name. "We are two separate individuals," says Susan, "and we have equal rights and responsibilities in our marriage. How can it be a real sharing any other way?"

Of course, many couples would argue with Susan; they do not share her "egalitarian" ideals. Some women who have full-time jobs outside the home nevertheless feel that their first duty is to be wife and mother. But Susan's and Brian's style of marriage, while not the norm, has unquestionably become more prevalent in the last 20 years.

While most Americans see these changes as a departure from established traditions, black families have long accepted a more flexible role structure. Because black family incomes have been much lower than white family incomes, more black wives have always worked (Scanzoni, 1975). Consequently, patterns of family roles and responsibilities have been much less rigidly defined. Of necessity, black husbands participated in the work of caring for the home and children. It was only when white middle-class families began to adopt the egalitarian model that scholars and magazine writers took notice of such marital patterns.

Since the demands of marital partners change during the stages of the life cycle, it is not surprising that traditional and egalitarian roles change as well. A national survey of 1140 couples revealed that, while young couples in their late twenties emphasized shared roles, those in later stages of the life cycle favored more traditional roles. In good part, this may be explained by a generational effect. Older couples are maintaining the traditional roles established decades ago; younger couples have been influenced by the current trend toward egalitarian values (Olson, et al., 1983).

While supporters of egalitarianism have sometimes argued for total equality within marriage, Rhona and Robert Rapoport (1975: 421) have put forward a concept of **equity**: "The presence of equal opportunity plus the feeling of fairness if there is an inequality of conditions." Equity allows for the possibility of variation in roles and responsibilities rather than rigid adherence to equality in all respects. Thus, in a marriage based on equity, one spouse might handle all cooking duties while the other is responsible for cleaning up after meals and food shopping. It would not be necessary to divide all food-related tasks in an absolutely equal way as long as each partner felt that the division of labor was fair and satisfying.

Sex Roles and Marital Satisfaction

Definitions of sex roles affect people's satisfaction within marriage. For example, when Paula and Allen were first married, they happily settled into traditional roles that each viewed as appropriate. Later, however, Paula's desires changed while Allen's did not. She wanted to work outside the home; Allen preferred to maintain the status quo. At this point, conflict developed and each partner became somewhat less satisfied with the marriage. Marital satisfaction means that each partner is living as he or she wishes; this enhances feelings of well-being (Peterson and Gove, 1980; Scanzoni and Fox, 1980).

As was clear in Paula's and Allen's relationship, traditional sex roles can become confining to one or both partners. Nevertheless, the widespread questioning of long-accepted norms has also resulted in problems. The 1980s are a time of confusion in terms of sex-role divisions and responsibilities. Many men, especially working-class men, thought that they would satisfy their wives by being good providers. Yet, like Allen, they have found that their wives suddenly want something quite different. Not only do women like Paula want careers outside the home; they are also demanding greater communication, sharing of feelings, companionship, and intimacy within marital relationships (see Chapter 9).

Men are not the only ones suffering from confusion. For women who prefer traditional roles, there is an issue of self-respect since they feel that the value of homemaking and motherhood is being downgraded. As one woman said, "It seems that no one has much use for an aspiring housewife these days" (Stein, 1981: 29). For women who are

"Can I call you back? Jim and I are struggling with our roles."

Drawing by Koren; © 1983 The New Yorker Magazine, Inc.

Today, women who prefer the traditional role of homemaking may have problems with self-esteem since being "just a housewife" is often downgraded.

working outside the home, there is pressure to be a "superwoman" and simultaneously excel at the roles of career woman, wife, and mother (see Chapter 15). In either situation, the result can be increased stress and marital difficulty.

Of course, changing sex roles can also have a positive effect on marital satisfaction. Susan and Brian, the egalitarian couple described earlier, view their sharing of roles and responsibilities as critical to their success as a couple. "We'd never make it otherwise," says Brian. "I know; I tried to dominate the relationship with my previous girlfriend. I felt the man should control everything. Well, I couldn't stop her from leaving me."

"I had trouble with Susan's feminism at first," he continues. "I sure didn't want to do housework. And it scared me that she was so strong and decisive. But, over time, I

learned, I realized, that what she was saying was true. If I gave up trying to dominate—if I gave her a little more space to be herself—I could relax a lot more. So I don't control everything? So I admit I'm needy, too? It feels wonderful to have a real partner, to really share everything: the financial pressures, the crummy jobs around the house, our fears, *everything*."

The Changing "Exchange" of Marriage

What impact have changing sex roles had on the emotional side of marriage? We can summarize the effect this way: as sex roles change and partners become less dependent on each other for economic necessities, personal fulfillment and emotional satisfaction become much more important in marriage (see Chapter 1).

In the past, marriage was, in an important sense, a basic economic "exchange." Men needed wives to do the tedious work of food preparation, to make clothing, and to take care of the household; women needed husbands as primary wage earners. Each spouse brought certain skills to the marriage and expected something in return. Married couples also expected to be loved and esteemed, but the economic exchange shaped the marital relationship and the division of roles.

Today, women who hold full-time jobs do not need to be married for financial reasons. Their standard of living would generally be lower without their husbands' contribution, but they would still be able to support themselves. Consequently, both singlehood and divorce have become more feasible for American women. Cherlin (1981: 53) notes that "widening opportunities for women allow couples to separate who are unhappy with their marriages for other reasons."

Married couples still rely on each other to earn money and contribute to the joint family income. Most families who bought a home in the late 1970s or early 1980s, for example, needed two incomes to make the costly mortgage payments. Nevertheless, the importance of economic partnership as a basis for marriage has diminished; partners are now primarily seeking emotional support, sexual satisfaction, and companionship.

For example, when Anne began working after six years of marriage, she became much less dependent on her husband Bob. She made many friends at her job, most of whom Bob "couldn't stand." At work, Anne felt people regarded her with great respect and listened to her opinions; at home, Bob never seemed interested. Soon she found she was no longer sharing her ambitions or problems with him.

"I find myself much more involved in my work than my marriage," says Anne sadly. "It's just more satisfying. I want to stay married, I want things to get better with

Bob, but I'm not sure it's worth the struggle and sacrifice." For Anne, the economic security of her marriage is important, but ultimately not as important as the emotional costs. "I know I can make it on my own. I'm not getting paid a fortune, but I can get by on my salary. I don't want to leave Bob, but if things get any worse, I will."

In certain instances, changing sex roles can lead to an "opposition of interests" in a marriage rather than complementary ones (Waller and Hill, 1951). On the other hand, the added income from a wife's working can reduce the financial stress on a family. This may be emotionally beneficial for both partners, as is true for Jack and Vera, a young black couple who hope to have two or three children. "We both grew up in working-class families," says Vera. "We want our kids to have economic advantages that we never did. Jack used to worry all the time that he wasn't making enough at his job. Now that we're both working, we put away money every month, and we're more relaxed. We know that we'll be able to provide well for our children."

Power in Marriage

The balance of power within marriages has been of particular interest to researchers since the publication of Blood and Wolfe's (1960) study of decision-making in Detroit marriages. They proposed the "resource theory" of marital power, which suggests that decision-making power primarily reflects the resources available to each individual in meeting the needs of a spouse.

By "resources," Blood and Wolfe mean roles and achievements outside the marriage in formal organizations (such as the workplace) or voluntary associations (such as religious and communal organizations). Participation in such groups increases the power of the spouse because it maximizes his or her status in the community and increases "ex-

B O X   8 – 1

Types of Power within Marriage

Sociologist Constantina Safilios-Rothschild (1976) has identified eight basic types of power that can be exercised within a marriage:

1. Authority or legitimate power. The power entrusted to one spouse by prevailing cultural or social norms (such as by traditional notions of male superiority and female inferiority).

2. Dominance power. The power that a domineering spouse claims or forces the other to yield through coercion, threats, or violence.

3. Resource power. The power with which a spouse is vested because he or she offers desirable and necessary resources, such as money and social prestige.

4. Expert power. Power granted on the basis of special knowledge, skill, expertise, or experience, such as cooking or driving a car.

5. Influence power. The degree to which one

spouse can successfully exert pressure on the other (for example, by advising the partner to ask for a raise or seek a new job).

6. Affective power. Manipulation of one spouse by bestowing or withdrawing of affection, warmth, and sex. An example is found in the Greek story of *Lysistrata*: Athenian women refused sexual relations with their husbands as an antiwar protest.

7. Tension management power. Control that one spouse achieves by managing existing tensions and disagreements, perhaps by using tears, pouting, or endless debating to get the other to "give in."

8. Moral power. The power that a spouse may claim through recourse to religious, moral, or legal norms which indicate the fairness of his or her claim for power.

pert knowledge" and decision-making skills. Thus, the prestige of being a bank president or star athlete spills over into one's marriage. Respect in the community is transferred into greater authority within the home.

Researchers agree that the spouse who is the more active participant in such social networks gains greater marital power (Burr, et al., 1979; Farber, 1966; Komarovsky, 1967). This is true among all social classes, but specific networks will vary among classes. For the middle class, the most viable social network is the voluntary association. By contrast, lower and working class Americans are much less likely to join organizations. For men of these classes, the neighborhood male peer group is often employed as a power resource; for their wives, the kinship network is most relevant. Participation in

such informal groups increases **marital power** because it reduces one's dependence on a husband or wife for satisfying emotional and companionship needs.

David Olson and Ronald Cromwell (1975) have questioned whether decision-making is the most useful and valid way of measuring family power. Constantina Safilios-Rothschild (1976), a sociologist who has studied sex roles and power, has identified several different types of power exercised in a marital relationship (see Box 8–1). She also notes that the power structure in a family is by no means rigid and permanent. It tends, on the contrary, to be fluid and to change during the various stages of family life (Blood and Wolfe, 1960; Michel, 1967; Safilios-Rothschild, 1967). For example, Alice became more powerful in her marriage when her husband lost his job. Suddenly, she was the sole breadwinner and no longer depended on his higher salary.

A recent study by Phillip Blumstein and Pepper Schwartz (1983) suggests that money plays a central role in determining marital power. The researchers found that, for men, money represents identity and power; for women, it represents security and autonomy. Money establishes the balance of power not only in marriages, but also for heterosexual couples living together and gay male couples. In terms of marriage, women who work outside the home hold greater marital power than full-time homemakers. Not only does this work enhance women's

Women who work outside the home enjoy greater marital power than full-time homemakers.

self-esteem; it also boosts their power because men respect people who work at paying jobs (Doudna, 1983).

Marital Violence

One way of enforcing or establishing a power relationship in a marriage is through violence. Although recent media coverage of marital violence might lead one to believe that it is a recent phenomenon, violence has long been a part of married life. Estimates of incidence vary, but it is quite evident that marital violence is widespread, affecting perhaps 25 to 30 percent of all marriages to some extent (see Box 8–2).

Spouse abuse is found in every social class and ethnic group. Research has revealed that upper-class, well-educated men with professional and executive positions are guilty of wife beating (Langley and Levy, 1977; Pagelow, 1976). Jacobson (1977: 3) reports that "proportionally, there are just as many family violence calls to the police in well-to-do Fairfax County, Virginia, as there are in middle class Norwalk, Connecticut, or the 30th precinct of West Harlem."

Violence between marital partners can take the form of hitting, shoving, grabbing, and hair-pulling, as well as use of weapons to threaten and harass. Women may throw objects or use weapons in order to equalize their disadvantage in terms of lesser physical strength (Gelles, 1974). In many instances, at least one of the partners has been drinking heavily before violence occurs. Researchers and therapists agree, however, that, while drinking may accompany domestic violence, it is not the basic cause of violent behavior.

Murder, the most extreme form of violence, is also a part of certain family interactions. Based on FBI reports, domestic quarrels accounted for more than 8 percent of the

BOX 8-2

Research Brief:
Factors Contributing to Spouse Abuse

Through telephone interviews with 1553 women who were married or living with a male partner, Hornung, McCullough, and Sugimoto (1981) collected data on the incidence of three types of spouse abuse: psychological abuse, physical aggression, and life-threatening violence. In addition, researchers looked at the patterns of occupation and educational level of the couples as possible factors associated with increased levels of abuse.

Among the researchers' findings were the following:

- 68 percent of the couples studied had experienced at least one act of domestic violence during the last year.
- Among couples who did experience some form of abuse, an incident occurred on the average of once every two weeks.
- Women who work outside the home are more likely than full-time housewives to be in a marital relationship that involves violence.
- The incidence of psychological abuse increases as the educational level of both men and women increases.
- There is increased risk of all three types of

abuse when the occupational levels of partners are incompatible—that is, where one partner's job has a higher status than the other's job.

- There is a much lower risk of abuse, especially life-threatening violence, when the man is an occupational overachiever—that is, when he has less education than most others in his occupation. The opposite, however, is true for women; their occupational achievement increases their risk of abuse.

The authors suggest that spouse abuse is a more common problem than is generally recognized. Although the incidence of physical aggression and life-threatening violence is considerably lower than psychological abuse, they argue that the latter may have serious implications for mental health and may contribute to stress-related illnesses such as chronic depression and cardiovascular disease.

Source: C. A. Hornung, B. C. McCullough, and T. Sugimoto, "Status Relationships in Marriage: Risk Factors in Spouse Abuse," *Journal of Marriage and the Family*, August 1981, 675–692. This article won the 1982 Reuben Hill Award for the National Council on Family Relations.

homicides committed nationwide in 1982. In 3.4 percent of the cases, the husbands were victims, while in 4.8 percent of cases the wives were killed. (These figures, however, are down substantially from corresponding 1975 statistics which indicated that more than 15 percent of homicides were committed by spouses.)

Although members of both sexes commit acts of spouse abuse, by far the greatest amount of violence is done by men against their wives (Steinmetz, 1978; Straus, 1974). For this reason, some feminist researchers and activists have criticized use of terms

such as "spouse abuse" and "domestic violence," arguing that these sex-neutral terms obscure the disproportionate nature of male violence. Men's wife-beating is often an expression of power, frustration, and desire for control. "First he hit me because I wasn't watching TV with him; half an hour later, he hit me because I *was* watching TV with him," said one battered woman. Cultural ideals of "tough" masculine heroism, expressed continually in the mass media, can reinforce the idea that violence is an acceptable form of expression.

Violence is also a learned response to

stress or challenge. For example, it is not unusual for violence to begin in a marriage when the wife becomes pregnant for the first time (Prescott and Letko, 1977). Although one might expect this to be a joyful time for the prospective parents, the husband may feel worried about increased financial responsibilities or may fear that his wife will shift all of her attention and affection to the baby.

As is true of rape (see Chapter 5), female victims of spouse abuse are often unfairly blamed for the behavior of their violent husbands. It is somehow argued that they "provoked" the assaults and, in extreme cases, even that they enjoy such attacks. When battered women remain living with their attackers, it is sometimes seen as an indication that they don't really object to the assaults.

Again, as is true in terms of rape, the feminist movement of recent decades has insisted that society not "blame the victim"— in this case, battered women. Laurie Woods and John Corwin (1977: 4), two attorneys who have actively worked to protect the rights of battered wives, argue:

Women do not enjoy being beaten. They stay with their husbands because they have nowhere else to go. They cannot support themselves and their children as single parents. Welfare . . . is hardly an attractive alternative.

Police, courts, social agencies, even the families of battered women all pressure them to stay with the man and "work things out." The woman is told that it is her social obligation to keep the family together, at any price. The carrot is coupled with the stick: the man threatens to kill her if she dares to leave him.

The result is an overwhelming psychological effect which cripples women and leaves them prisoners of their marriages. And then the women are blamed for tolerating the abuse and told that they must obviously be enjoying it. Catch 22. The wonder is not that so many women stay, but that any surmount the obstacles in their paths to leave.

As one consequence of the new public awareness of wife-beating, shelters for battered women and their children have been opened across the United States and in many other nations. About one-third of the women in shelters in this country never return to their partners; another third return only after the men agree to major changes in the relationship (Minnesota Department of Corrections, 1981).

One might expect that as sex roles change and a more egalitarian perspective takes hold, there will be less violence between husbands and wives. However, Whitehurst (1970) suggests that, at least in the short run, the opposite may be true. Changes that bring about greater sexual equality—such as changes in women's legal rights and employment status—will lead to strain and frustration for men attempting to retain their superior position. In some families, the result may be violence.

Sexuality in Marriage

According to Andrew Ward (1980: 75–76), even if two people have enjoyed sex before marriage, they should remember that it is going to change "because somewhere along the line one of you is going to realize that where once you were having a wholesome sexual relationship . . . , all of a sudden you're sleeping with a relative." This amusing statement points to a more serious reality: marriage can change sex. Sex can increase delight in marriage, or the enchantment of the earlier relationship can fizzle in the midst of the tensions of day-to-day married life. (For a more detailed discussion of sexuality and its physiological aspects, see Chapter 5).

Robert and Margaret Blood (1978), a husband-wife research team, point out that there is a reciprocal relationship between sex and other aspects of married life. Most couples are either satisfied with both the sexual and nonsexual aspects of their relationship or dissatisfied with both. Indeed, Morton Hunt (1974) found that almost no one in his sample of married couples found sex unpleasant when their marriages were going well. At the same time, hardly anyone found sex very pleasurable when their marriages were going badly.

Just as effort and communication are vital to other areas of marriage, time and talk are two major factors in creating the close-knit marital harmony that culminates in fulfilling sex (Saline, 1980). While sharing time alone can create a context for intimacy, open, honest conversation about thoughts and feelings can bind couples together. Indeed, communication between partners is essential (see Chapter 9). Levin and Levin (1975), in their survey of 100,000 women, found that the less frequently wives can discuss their sexual feelings and desires with their husbands, the less likely they are to report that their sexual lives are "good" or "very good."

One sexual problem almost every married couple faces at one time or another is boredom. How can couples keep sex interesting and exciting after years of lovemaking? Sex therapist Dr. Ruth Westheimer (1983) has some ideas for keeping monogamy from becoming monotonous. Basically, in her view, couples must find ways to avoid predictable behavior and the feeling that sex is an obligation. They should not be afraid to keep alive the playful side of sex: flirtation, experimentation, even silliness.

William Masters and Virginia Johnson (1970) have estimated that about half of all marriages in the United States have a sexual dysfunction or problem in sexual adjustment. In the view of Evelyn Duvall (1977), many difficulties stem from couples' inaccurate knowledge of sex, which leads to unrealistic expectations and disappointment. She adds that individual needs due to varying hereditary makeup, previous experiences, and differing ideas about the purposes of sex create barriers to sexual satisfaction. Duvall (1977: 198) observes that "guilt, shame, indecision and many times, deep and abiding hostility can become ingrained in the very fabric of sex and marriage."

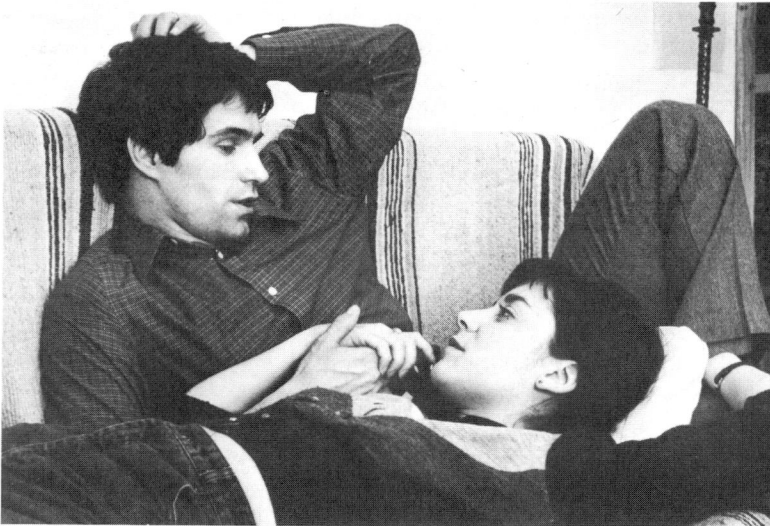

Time alone to share thoughts and feelings openly helps create the close-knit marital relationship that culminates in fulfilling sex.

Extramarital sex is far from rare in American society. Some studies have suggested that over one-quarter of the marriages surveyed were affected by at least one instance of extramarital sex. However, the authors are quick to caution that these were limited samples (in one case, professional married women; in the other, middle-class, middle-aged couples). Therefore, one should not casually generalize about the general population's sexual behavior based on these studies (Bell, Turner, and Rosen, 1975; Johnson, 1977).

Bell, Turner, and Rosen (1975) found that age was a significant factor in the likelihood of involvement in extramarital sex—primarily because younger age was related to a more liberal value system and lifestyle. Reiss, Anderson, and Sponaugle (1980) have suggested that the educational level of the individual might be an important factor. Other research indicates that the rates of extramarital sex vary among different cultural groups (Neubeck, 1969). All studies agree that rates of extramarital sex among husbands are higher than those of wives, but that rates among females are increasing (Bell, Turner, and Rosen, 1975).

Far from being acceptable to many married couples, most extramarital experiences were and are carried out secretly. Yet, with the advent of "open marriages," in which partners maintain a primary relationship but give one another permission to have other sexual relationships, there has been a marked change in sexual mores (O'Neill and O'Neill, 1972). Some couples are engaging in what has been termed co-marital or **consensual sex**—that is, extramarital sex with the knowledge and permission of one's mate. Like group marriages (see Chapter 2), these compromises with traditional marriage are attempts to overcome what some feel is the restrictive sexual exclusivity of monogamy.

Strengths in Marriage

What does it mean to describe a marriage as a "good" or "strong" marriage? According to Bennis, et al. (1968), a "good" relationship is one that serves the functions for which it was formed. Thus, if two persons marry in order to increase their joint income and they receive little emotional satisfaction, the marriage will nevertheless be considered a "good" one by this standard.

Since over 60 percent of all couples report that they are happily married, the nature of a strong marriage is clearly not limited to any one formula. Sociologists have attempted to define marital strengths in terms of good "adjustment" to the challenges of marriage. Adjustment is usually viewed in terms of husband-wife agreement, sharing of common interests, showing affection, having few complaints, confiding in one another, and not feeling lonely (Burgess and Cottrell, 1939). But others have criticized this notion of adjustment as too limiting. They challenge the ideal of a conflict-free marriage where the couple conforms to the status quo, and they suggest that a strong marriage is one in which partners help each other and push one another to achieve other goals (Spanier, 1976).

For most, a strong marriage means a "loving" marriage, a marriage in which both partners respect, admire, and trust each other and share understanding and affection. Being sensitive and continuing to do little things for one's partner are indications of a caring relationship. Other marital strengths include expressing a wide range of emotions, feelings, and ideas; enjoying each other's company whether at work or play; and providing encouragement, support, and acceptance. A study of support within marriage by Ronald Burke and Tamara Weir (1975) showed that, out of all their possible social contacts, both men and women se-

Enjoying each other's company is important in an intrinsic marriage where the marital relationship is the chief concern and source of pleasure.

lected their spouses as the people they would be most likely to turn to with their problems and anxieties.

In their 1966 study of 400 upper-middle-class married couples, Cuber and Harroff identified two desirable types of marriages: intrinsic and utilitarian marriages. For those involved in an **intrinsic marriage**, the marital relationship is the chief concern and source of pleasure. While partners may have other concerns, such as careers, friends, and family, the marriage comes first. There is great commitment to the spouse; partners expect that the relationship will satisfy their needs for physical, emotional, and even spiritual closeness.

In contrast, the **utilitarian marriage** is not established in order to express a highly intimate relationship. There is a relative absence of deep feeling; instead, the atmosphere is one of limited companionship. Some couples structure their lives around careers or social commitments, while others concentrate on the parental role. Cuber and Harroff found that this type of marriage seemed most functional or appropriate for the majority of their sample of upper-class couples. Yet it is hardly what most of us think of when we imagine a ''strong marriage.''

The demands that married couples face vary throughout the course of the life cycle, as does marital satisfaction. Figure 8–1 shows that both wives and husbands tend to be most happy in the beginning and end of the life cycle, and are least happy when they are the parents of schoolage children and adolescents.

A recent study of more than 1000 couples with and without children examined what they saw as the main demands facing them and the resources they had to deal with these demands (Olson, et al., 1983). The demands included illness strains (caused by sickness or injury to a family member), financial strains (too many expenses and not enough money to meet them), intrafamily strains (conflict or tension within the family), and work-family strains (changes in work responsibility, getting a new job, or getting laid off). Resources included the ability to manage money, to communicate well, to agree on goals and ideals, to share leisure activities, and to maintain good health habits.

In Chapter 17, we describe stress as an imbalance between demands and resources. Marital strength may be viewed as a balance of marital resources and demands. Therefore, a couple with a healthy balance of resources and demands would probably be happy and able to solve their problems in a harmonious and effective manner.

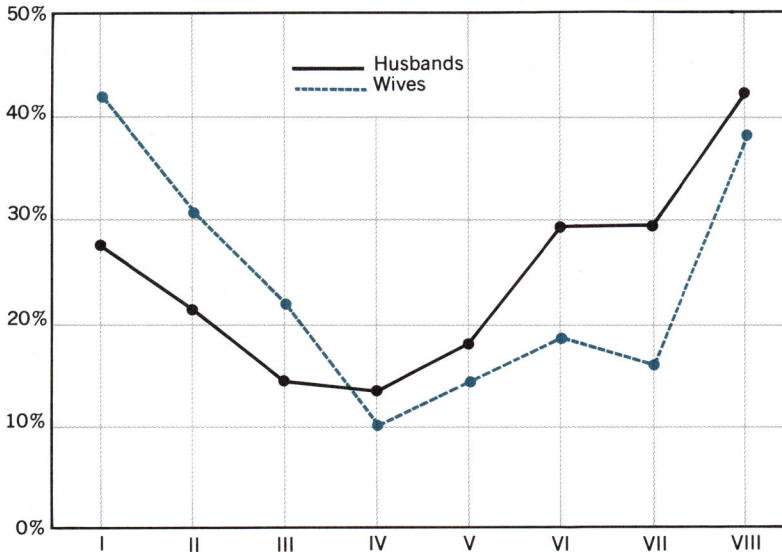

Percentage of individuals at each stage of the family life cycle reporting their marriage was going well "all the time." (Stage I, beginning families; Stage II, childbearing families; Stage III, families with preschool children; Stage IV, families with schoolage children; Stage V, families with teenagers; Stage VI, families as launching center; Stage VII, families in the middle years; Stage VIII, aging families.)

Figure 8–1 Marital satisfaction over the life cycle. (*Source*: Rollins and Feldman, February 1970, p. 25.)

Summary

Marriage has been described as the "axis" around which family life revolves. It brings new developmental tasks and challenges for the couple and for each partner as an individual. Erik Erikson sees marriage as a sign of personal growth, of preparing for a mature and productive adult life. It is not only a relationship between two persons, but also a formal arrangement between the couple and the larger social world.

Sociologist Jessie Bernard has pointed out that husbands and wives often experience marriage very differently. This is partly because of traditional sex roles: wives are socialized to meet the emotional needs of their husbands rather than focusing on their own needs. Traditional couples are more likely to assign certain marital roles to one spouse or the other; egalitarian couples often favor sharing all important roles.

Younger couples have been influenced by the current trend toward egalitarian values within marriage. However, in contrast to a philosophy advocating total equality within marriage, Rhona and Robert Rapoport have proposed a concept of equity that allows for variation in roles and responsibilities within a general framework of fairness.

Definitions of sex roles affect people's satisfaction within marriage. Traditional sex roles can become confining to one or both partners, but confusion about changing roles also leads to problems and even conflict. As roles have changed, marriage has become less of an economic exchange. Personal fulfillment and emotional satisfaction have become much more important in marriage.

The balance of power has been of particular interest to researchers since a 1960 study of decision-making in Detroit marriages conducted by Blood and Wolfe. Safilios-Rothschild has identified eight types of power that can be exercised within a marriage. Recent research suggests that money plays a central role in marital power. It establishes the balance of power not only in marriages, but also for heterosexual couples living together and for gay male couples.

Violence has long been a part of married life. Spouse abuse affects perhaps 25 to 30 percent of all marriages to some extent. It is found in every social class and ethnic group. By far the greatest amount of violence is committed by men against their wives. Men's wife-beating is often an expression of power, frustration, and desire for control. As is true of rape, female victims of spouse abuse are often unfairly blamed for the behavior of their violent husbands.

Marriage can change a couple's sexual relationship. Most couples are either satisfied with both the sexual and nonsexual aspects of their relationship or dissatisfied with both. Communication between partners is essential for a satisfying sex life. Masters and Johnson estimate that about half of all marriages in the United States have a sexual dysfunction or problem in sexual adjustment.

Sociologists have attempted to define marital strengths in terms of good "adjustment" to the challenges of marriage. For most, a strong marriage means a "loving" marriage, a marriage in which both partners respect, admire, and trust each other and share understanding and affection. Cuber and Harroff have identified two desirable types of marriages. In an intrinsic marriage, the marriage comes first, above all other concerns. There is great commitment to the spouse. By contrast, there is a relative absence of deep feeling in a utilitarian marriage. Couples may structure their lives around their careers, social commitments, or the parental role.

Developmental Task   A Marriage Checkup

Consider each statement carefully; then check the column that best expresses how satisfied you are with each area of your marriage.

	Almost Always	Some of the Time	Hardly Ever
1. I am satisfied with the help I receive from my partner when something is troubling me.	☐	☐	☐
2. I am satisfied with the way my partner discusses items of common interest and shares problem-solving with me.	☐	☐	☐
3. I find that my partner accepts my wishes to take on new activities or make changes in my lifestyle.	☐	☐	☐
4. I am satisfied with the way my partner expresses affection and responds to my feelings such as anger, sorrow, and love.	☐	☐	☐
5. I am satisfied with the way my partner and I share time together.	☐	☐	☐

Score two points for each time you checked ''almost always,'' one point for ''some of the time,'' and no points for ''hardly ever.'' Add up the points.

If your score ranges from seven to ten, it suggests that your relationship is meeting all, or almost all, your emotional needs. If your score ranges from four to six, it suggests you are only moderately satisfied. If your score is zero to three, it suggests that there are deep problems in the relationship.

Source: *Redbook*, January 1980.

Discussion Questions

1. In your view, what qualities are needed for a ''strong'' marriage?

2. Do you think that being married while a college student presents any specific adjustment problems? Discuss.

3. Which marital relationship do you find most desirable: husband-dominant, wife-dominant, or egalitarian? Why?

4. If you are married, would you describe your marriage as traditional or egalitarian? Explain. If you are not presently married, which type of marriage would you be most likely to choose? Why?

5. Which of the following marital roles do you think is most important: the therapeutic role, the child socialization role, the child-care role, the recreational role, or the sexual role? Why?

Key Words

Consensual Sex	**Intrinsic Marriage**	**Traditional Marriage**
Egalitarian Marriage	**Marital Power**	**Utilitarian Marriage**
Equity	**Marital Roles**	

Suggested Readings

Galvin, Kathleen M., and Brommel, Bernard J. *Family Communication: Cohesion and Change.* Glenview, Ill.: Scott, Foresman and Co., 1982. Through an application of family theories to marital and family interaction introduces the serious student to sociological frameworks.

Rubin, Lillian. *Worlds of Pain.* New York: Harper and Row, 1976. Documents, through in-depth interviews with blue-collar families, the difficulty in bridging the gap between masculine and feminine worlds to find intimacy in marriages.

Satir, Virginia. *Peoplemaking.* Palo Alto, Calif.: Science and Behavior Books, 1972. A down-to-earth classic on interpersonal communication written for the non-professional reader.

Scanzoni, John, and Szinovacz, Maximiliane. *Family Decision-Making: Sex Roles and Change Over the Life Cycle*, Beverly Hills, Calif.: Sage Publications, 1980. Questions of power, conflict, negotiation, and change applied to marriages and families through the life cycle.

Schram, Rosalyn W. ''Marital satisfaction over the life cycle: a critique and a proposal.'' *Journal of Marriage and the Family*, 1979, *41*, 7–14. Criticizes the way research has been done in studying marital satisfaction and suggests some alternatives. Useful to develop students' sophistication in reading research.

CHAPTER NINE

Communication and Conflict in Relationships

KEY TOPICS

—the process of communication—
—self-esteem and self-disclosure—
—sex roles and communication—
—ingredients of effective communication—
—conflict in relationships—
—types of conflict—
—managing conflict productively—
—marriage counseling and marital enrichment programs—

"You're late."

"Yeah, I guess."

"You couldn't have called, could you."

"I tried. The line was busy . . . as usual."

(Silence.)

"You could at least say you're sorry."

"Okay, okay, I'm sorry. So are you happy now?"

Sylvia and Al have just set the stage for a "pleasant" evening together. Dinner will be eaten in stony silence. Then the television will go on, and they will spend the rest of the evening totally avoiding conversation. At bedtime, perhaps Sylvia will murmur, ''I'm sorry I jumped on you earlier.'' And he may respond, ''That's all right. I should have made more of an effort to be on time.''

When two persons live together, own a house, share meals, make love, raise children, and hold a joint bank account, the quality of their lives is largely determined by how well they communicate and manage conflict. In this chapter, we will examine how couples communicate—what they do right, what they do wrong. We will show that the day-to-day conflicts of married life can actually lead to growth in the relationship and bring partners closer together.

Communication in Relationships

Communication refers to the process of exchanging desires, needs, and feelings as well as facts and opinions. There are four essential elements in any act of communication: the sender of the message, the receiver, the form of the message, and the content. It is important to understand the role of these four elements of communication in the exchange of messages within a marriage or intimate relationship.

For our purposes, the sender and the receiver are partners in such a relationship. A communication cannot take place unless one sends the message and the other receives it. **Interpersonal communication** is affected by the psychological condition and relationship of these two communicators. Their personalities, their feelings of self-esteem, their attitudes toward one another, their memories of past conversations or quarrels, their ''unwritten rules'' about communication, and the current state of their relationship all influence the nature of their communications.

The purpose of communication between partners is to increase understanding in the relationship and to elicit some response from the listener. However, researchers tell us that 85 percent of all messages sent in families are misunderstood (Watzlawick, et al., 1967). Clearly, communication is an uncertain and sometimes perilous process!

A message can be conveyed in words or in silence, through shouts or tears, in a chuckle or a caress. A rigid posture can send a message; so can a smile, a grimace, a yawn, and a pat on the head. Sometimes, of course, a message is communicated in writing—in a scrawled note on the kitchen bulletin board or a long, flowery love letter.

We learn to interpret any message both through the content of the words, the tone in which they are spoken, and the physical context in which the words are uttered. For example, Anne comes home and cheerily says, ''Hi, how was your day?'' Her husband Jim, sitting on the couch absorbed in a pile of books, says, ''Fine, honey,'' in a flat manner without even looking up. Anne concludes from his intent posture that he is worried about his upcoming exams and does not want to be disturbed. He conveyed his message not through his words, but through his body language.

The same words can change their meaning dramatically depending on one's tone of voice. If Larry asks calmly, ''Where is the toothpaste?'', Fran will assume he is merely asking for information. But if he shouts angrily, ''Where's the toothpaste?'', he may be saying, ''You idiot! You forgot to buy the toothpaste again, didn't you?''

A **mixed message** occurs when the words one speaks are contradicted by one's body language. A wife who says, ''No, of course I'm not mad,'' but then sits in rigid, icy silence is sending a mixed message. She is not admitting her anger, but is communicating it nevertheless. When a man tells his lover that he wants to hear all about her business trip to Paris—but sits intently watching a baseball game on television while she is speaking—he, too, is sending a mixed message. Often, as is true in these examples, we use words to try to cover up our real feelings, but they are expressed in our body language. This is especially true when the emotion is a negative one: anger, resentment, or boredom.

The content of a message can be of four types:

- A message can provide information ("Your mother called this afternoon." "The newspaper is in the living room.")

- A message can convey an emotion (anger, fear, love, contempt, concern, and so forth).

- A message can convey a sense of power or authority. It may be aimed at control of the partner, as is true of "you should" messages or commands ("Answer the phone, would you!" "No wife of mine will be seen in an outfit like that!")

- A message can convey an individual's values, beliefs, or dreams. Some writers call these "meaning messages" (Kantor and Lehr, 1975; Orthner, 1981).

Exchanging "meaning messages" about the crucial issues in their lives can bring a couple closer together. For example, one evening Sarah comes home late, stomps around the house, shouts at her children, and makes sarcastic remarks about her husband, Peter. Instead of reacting angrily to her rotten mood, Peter slips his arm around her shoulder and gently asks what's bothering her. Sarah eventually reveals that she's had a bad day at work and is afraid that her boss doesn't trust her. She shares her frustration about not having more responsibility on her job. In the next few minutes, Sarah talks with Peter about her career ambitions and goals, and admits both fears and hopes that she's never told him before. In this case, the exchange of a meaning message averted a potential quarrel and brought the couple to a new level of sharing and understanding.

Self-Esteem and Self-Disclosure

Groucho Marx once said that he would refuse to join any club that would accept him as a member. Many people seem to feel that way about their marriages; their low self-esteem makes them feel unworthy of their partners and fearful of open communication.

We have noted in other chapters that one's self-image influences both whom one chooses to marry and what one wants out of married life. Self-image also determines what one feels comfortable communicating in marriage. For example, low self-esteem might lead a person to fear rejection from a partner. The individual might feel, consciously or unconsciously: "Since I am a terrible person, my partner must somehow have been deceived or tricked into this marriage. No one could actually love me. It would be awful if he/she found out what I'm *really* like; that would be the end for sure. So I won't risk sharing my stupid thoughts and feelings; I'll just try to keep it all to myself and avoid arguments. That way maybe he/she won't leave me right away."

Therapist Lyman Wynne, et al. (1978) found that many couples reason in this manner. They spent a lot of time and energy "getting along," avoiding conflict, burying disagreement. In Wynne's view, these couples have "pseudomutual marriages." Both partners pretend to enjoy a harmonious and satisfying marriage, while in truth they are quite isolated from one another. Each is fearful of disclosing private concerns and hopes and, consequently, has a constricted and blocked-off emotional life. Their low self-esteem dramatically limits the communication and sharing in their marriage.

Virginia Satir (1972), a respected family therapist, argues that self-esteem is the basis for open and honest self-disclosure, or what she calls **leveling**. Satir pinpoints some of the common tactics for avoiding leveling in marriage: distracting, computing, placating, and blaming.

A "distractor" responds to a message by ignoring it or by engaging in some activity that shows the lack of importance he or she gives to the message. For example, when Sheila said, "Bob, I need to talk with you about our trip to see my sister," Bob replied, "Sure, go ahead," then picked up the newspaper and began to read. Other distraction techniques include whistling, humming, or turning on a noisy dishwasher or vacuum cleaner.

A "computing" response is one in which the receiver acts like a computer—cool, correct, rational, factual. Any emotional elements in the sender's message are disallowed and dismissed; only logical, reasonable statements are admitted to the discussion. Suppose that Sheila tells Bob: "It really hurts me that whenever I want to talk with you about something important, you hide behind the newspaper." Bob responds coldly: "Human beings have five senses, dear. I can use my sense of sight to read and my sense of hearing to listen to you at the same time. It's a scientific fact." He has moved from his original technique of distraction to a computing response.

A "blaming" response introduces faultfinding and personal attack into a discussion. When Sheila hears Bob's statement about reading and listening at the same time, she yells: "That's nonsense! If you cared about me and my feelings, you'd give me your *full* attention. You'd put down that newspaper!" Bob counterattacks: "You're

just like your mother! You have to be the total center of attention all the time."

A "placating" response is the opposite of a "blaming" response; yet both are ways of avoiding meaningful communication. As the argument continues, Bob finally says, "Well, Sheila, I guess you're right. I'll try to remember this for next time." But here the tone of his remarks is crucial. Rather than being a deeply felt admission and commitment to change, Bob's "placating" apology is instead a kind of "buy-off," a way of ending the argument by *appearing* to admit he is wrong. Bob's tone is flat and hostile; the next night, he will probably pick up the newspaper again when Sheila wants to talk with him.

According to Virginia Satir, only the leveler is a true communicator who feels self-confident enough to risk meaningful interaction. People with high self-esteem are more likely to be levelers. They believe in the rewards of **self-disclosure**—the intimate revelation of private thoughts, feelings, hopes, and frustrations. Self-disclosure means letting another person see you as you see yourself (Jourard, 1971). Self-disclosure involves risks: one might be laughed at, rejected, or ignored. But it also brings rewards: greater intimacy with a partner and more emotional support. Only self-disclosing partners can genuinely offer and receive support. One small business owner reports: "Ever since I was a little girl, I wanted to own a bakery. I told Fred about this dream of mine soon after we met; I was afraid he would laugh. But he always encouraged me, praising my brownies and pies, but also my ability to organize. After we were married, he helped me find the money to get started."

Confirming the Self-Image

Perhaps the most important function of a couple's communication is to validate and confirm each partner's sense of self (Fisher and Sprenkle, 1978; Watzlawick, et al., 1967). We noted in Chapter 4 that attraction between people is based partly on a sense that the other values and respects one's self-image. In a marriage, one continues to look for a "confirmation response" through which the spouse communicates: "I fundamentally accept you and what you want in our relationship." Thus, a wife who feels proud of her knowledge of art will feel validated if her husband asks her questions and listens to her respectfully while visiting art museums.

This can work both ways, of course: a spouse is in good position to know one's failings. One wife used to regale dinner guests with funny stories about her husband's unsuccessful attempts to fix the plumbing. The effect of the stories, however, was not humorous: he was made to look foolish and incompetent. This is a "rejecting response" in which the partner's self-esteem is undercut, not strengthened.

The process of confirmation is at the basis of intimacy and effective communication. It may be subject to the peculiar "rules" operating in a marriage or intimate relationship. Playwright Edward Albee dissects the marriage of a couple, George and Martha, in his play, *Who's Afraid of Virginia Woolf?* These two do nothing but fight—constantly, bitterly, destructively. But Albee penetrates beneath this surface of quarrelling to reveal how their shared illusions provide a basis for trust in their marriage. Here Martha reflects on how George confirms and supports her:

. . . George who is out somewhere there in the dark . . . George who is good to me and when I revile; . . . who can make me laugh, and I choke it back in my throat; who can hold me, at night, so that it's warm and whom I will bite so there's blood; who keeps learning the games we play as quickly as I can change the rules; who can make

me happy and I do not wish to be happy and yes I do wish to be happy. George and Martha: sad, sad, sad (Albee, 1964: 190–191).

Outwardly, George and Martha do not love and support one another. But, in reality, they have developed a complex (if painful) way of confirming each other's realities. This support sustains them and enhances the couple's self-esteem.

Limits to Total Honesty

Is there a point at which a relationship can drown in too much self-disclosure? Or is it best to be completely honest about everything? Marriage researchers suggest that partners who are less afraid to discuss their feelings achieve higher levels of satisfaction (Powers and Hutchinson, 1976). However, many satisfied couples report that they do not tell one another everything, mostly because they fear it would jeopardize the relationship (Dies and Cohen, 1973). One man commented: "I don't tell Sandy that I think this or that woman is gorgeous. I don't tell her that I think her cousin is not nearly as bright as she thinks he is. I don't show any enthusiasm for her lime jello dessert, but I've never told her outright that I don't really care for it. All these things are small to me, but they would really hurt her feelings. It's just not worth it."

Protecting the partner's feelings is one motive for holding back. Other motives might include fear of damaging or destroying the relationship. Some may choose not to tell a spouse about a casual love affair, or about something else that might threaten the marriage. Therefore, for couples who place high value on the stability of a long-term relationship, there are limits to the amount of self-disclosure.

Family researcher Shirley Gilbert (1976) has proposed that a very high degree of self-disclosure would benefit couples who have a

"Remember, total honesty between us was your idea. I hate it."

Drawing by Wm. Hamilton; © 1982 The New Yorker
Magazine, Inc.

strong commitment to each other and are willing to take risks. Their intimacy would be strengthened, not weakened, by intimate revelations (see Figure 9–1). There is, then, no one simple answer to the question of "how much self-disclosure is enough?" Each couple must decide for themselves on the basis of their own values, ideals, and expectations about marriage.

Communication Style: Defining the Relationship

The term **communication style** refers to the larger pattern of interaction in relationships. It describes the unwritten rules by which couples regulate their lives together. These rules may be acquired from the families we grow up in, and can carry over into our later relationships and marriages. Such rules are also influenced by level of education and social status; persons with less formal education are likely to talk together less and to share fewer interests (Komarovsky, 1976).

Marital therapist James Hawkins and his colleagues (1980) have classified couple communication styles into four broad categories: conventional, controlling, speculative, and contactful. "Conventional communicators" are likely to spend little time discussing emotional issues or personal values. They maintain a certain distance in relationships, sharing small-talk and everyday concerns but remaining ignorant of their partners' deeper feelings.

While conventional communicators often

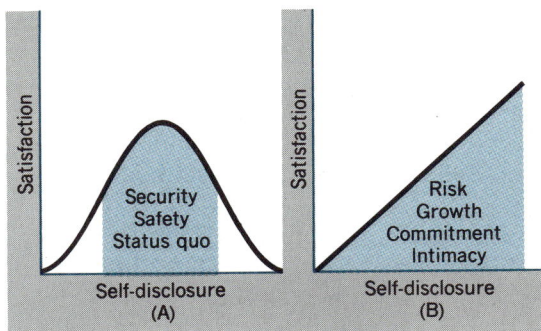

Figure 9–1 Two models of self-disclosure in marriage. (*Source*: Gilbert, July 1976, p. 221–229.)

act as if nothing is ever wrong, "controlling communicators" are happy to show their spouses that they are upset, but refuse to discuss the problem. Hawkins cites the example of a husband who stomps around the house when he's angry, but sharply denies that anything is wrong when his wife questions him. It is clear that *something* is wrong, but it is difficult, if not impossible, to find out what it is.

A "speculative communicator" is just the opposite. He or she will happily discuss a problem in abstract, reasonable terms, but will not share any of the feelings or emotions experienced. For example, when Leslie was passed over for a promotion, she told her husband Paul very calmly. She pointed out the excellent qualifications of the person who got the job and described all the pressures that the job entailed. Leslie added that other opportunities at her company would be opening up in the next few months. She did everything but share her disappointment and anger: she never cried, yelled, or called her boss names. For Leslie and other speculative communicators, the problem itself may be open to discussion with a spouse, but the personal, emotional side is definitely "off limits."

The "contactful communicator" talks about both a problem and his or her feelings. The spouse, therefore, is permitted to share fully in an important communication. Hawkins notes that while most couples claim that the contactful style is ideal, very few have actually attained it. Apparently, most American marriages are suffering from an absence of emotional expression between partners (Hawkins, et al., 1980).

Each communication style describes a dif-

"Controlling communicators" are happy to let their spouses know they are upset, but refuse to discuss the problem.

ferent type of marriage. A couple who view marriage as a total commitment involving every facet of their lives—what we described as an intrinsic marriage in Chapter 8— would probably be contactful communicators (or at least attempt to be). By contrast, a couple comfortable in a utilitarian marriage—where friends, family members, and outside interests retain a high degree of importance—might be satisfied with a conventional or speculative style of communication. Thus, communication style reflects and reinforces marital style; it tells us a great deal about what is going on in a relationship.

Sex Roles and Communication

Marie talks with frustration about her husband Hank: "I stopped by his office and his secretary knew that our older daughter had made the sweater he was wearing and that he loved it. The secretary knew I'd made a very special dinner the other night and he had loved that, too. So I said to him: 'Why didn't you tell Terry you liked the sweater?' He said: 'She knows.' I said: 'Why didn't you tell me the dinner was terrific?' He got all flustered and said, 'Well, after all, I ate it, didn't I?'" (DeWolf, 1983: 46, 50).

Like many wives, Marie complains that her husband doesn't talk to her enough. Hank, like many husbands, may counter that Marie talks too much about trivial or uninteresting things. In recent years, communication researchers have studied these complaints to see what effects sex-role socialization has on how couples communicate.

Sex-role socialization, as we discussed in Chapter 3, is the process of learning how to act in ways recognized as appropriate for one's sex; it is the development of behavior seen as "masculine" or "feminine." Men, for example, are taught that expressing strong emotions other than anger is "unmasculine." Truly masculine men, they may have learned, act like John Wayne,

who was usually awkward in his movie roles when trying to express tenderness or love to a woman. Or men might emulate the "Playboy ideal," look down on emotional attachments, and insist that sex is their only interest (Balswick and Peek, 1971; Gilbert, 1976).

The "strong, silent type" has been a traditional masculine image in the United States. In certain communications, silence by the receiver can be a sign of respect, a commitment to hear the sender's message without interruption. However, as Gloria Steinem (1983: 179) points out, "male silence (or silence from a member of any dominant group) is not necessarily the same as listening. It might mean a rejection of the speaker, a refusal to become vulnerable through self-revelation, or a decision that this conversation is not worthwhile."

In contrast to male socialization, women have been taught that the expression of positive emotions such as love is important and necessary, especially in family relationships. They have also been taught that it is "unladylike" to become angry and shout. Women may expect their husbands to be intensely interested in their every word, as was true of Ashley Wilkes in *Gone with the Wind*. Without question, women have been socialized to value interpersonal communication much more than men do.

What impact does this differential socialization have on married life? Men's communication role both reflects and reveals their power within marriage (see Chapter 8): men tend to dominate conversations, talk more frequently, and interrupt more than women do. Women, by contrast, are more likely to ask questions, apologize, or elaborate in order to "help along" the conversation. Men speak with greater certainty and intensity than women. Women's voices have more variable intonation—sometimes making them sound whiny or helpless, but also giving them a much greater range of tones

BOX 9–1

One Couple's Lack of Communication

Lillian Breslow Rubin, in her book *Worlds of Pain*, describes the meaningless, humorless, rather silent home life of a working-class couple who have been married for seven years:

Wife: Frank comes home from work; now it's about five because he's been working overtime every night. We eat right away, right after he comes home. Then I don't know. The kids play a while before bed, watch TV, you know, stuff like that. Then, I don't know; we don't do anything except maybe watch more TV or something like that. I don't know what else— nothing, I guess. We just sit, that's all.

Rubin: That's it? Nothing else?

Wife: Yeah, that's right, that's all. [A short silence, then angrily.] Oh, yeah, I forgot. Sometimes he's got one of those projects he works on. Like now, he's putting that new door in the kitchen. It's still nothing. When he finishes doing it, we just sit.

The husband has his own view of the family's home life:

Husband: Life is very predictable. Nothing much happens; we don't do much. Everyone sits in the same place all the time and does the same thing every night. It's satisfying to me, but not to her. I don't know. Maybe she wants me to go to a show or something once in a while. I don't know. She doesn't tell me.

Rubin: Don't you ask her?

Husband: No, I suppose I should, but it's really

hard to think about getting out. We'd need someone to stay with the kids and all that. Besides, I'm tired. I've been out all day, seeing different people and stuff. I don't feel like going out after supper again.

The wife adds: "He doesn't ever think there's anything to talk about. I'm the one who has to nag him to talk always, and then I get disgusted. . . . I just wish I could talk to him about things and he could understand. If he had more feelings himself, maybe he'd understand more. Don't you think so?"

Ironically, he is essentially in agreement with her: I'm pretty tight-lipped about most things most of the time, especially personal things. I don't express what I think or feel. She keeps trying to get me to, but it's hard. . . . Sometimes she gets to nagging me about what I'm thinking or feeling and I tell her, 'Nothing,' and she gets mad. But I swear, it's true, I'm not thinking about anything."

"Yakketty-yakkers, that's what girls are," he concludes. "Well, I don't know, guys talk, too. But, you know, there's a difference, isn't there? Guys talk about things and girls talk about feelings."

Lillian Breslow Rubin repeats this final statement for emphasis: "Guys talk about things and girls talk about feelings." For Rubin, this husband has concisely summarized the critical communication barrier that plagues marriage partners.

Source: Rubin, 1976:123–125.

for emotional expression (Henly and Thorn, 1977).

Not surprisingly, men tend to be much more satisfied with the level of marital communications than women. With regard to our earlier discussion of communication styles, women tend to feel that their husbands are not "contactful" enough; for many, this is a source of deep dissatisfaction in their marriages (see Box 9–1). Some men counter that their wives are too emotional— and not sufficiently analytic or rational—in marital discussions (Hawkins, et al., 1980). Indeed, one analysis of couples' arguments found that men consistently suggested compromises or solutions to the problem at hand, whereas women were so intent on expressing their feelings that they actually blocked resolution of conflicts (Feldman, 1980).

But traditional standards of sex-typed behavior are changing. New masculine role models have emerged, such as Alan Alda and Phil Donohue, who are interested in women's thoughts and feelings and supportive of feminism. At the same time, women are becoming more oriented to the corporate world with its emphasis on rational, unemotional analysis. These new cultural patterns may ultimately reshape marital communication styles.

Marriage, too, is changing. As noted in Chapter 8, couples are increasingly concerned about achieving emotional fulfillment in married life. They want their spouses to be companions and friends with whom they can talk, laugh, gossip, confide, argue, and share. If more couples continue to favor egalitarian marriages, it will certainly lead to changes in communication styles.

Of course, egalitarian marriage also puts added pressure on a couple's communication skills. When traditional sex roles are abandoned, virtually everything needs discussion and negotiation. Who will pay the bills? Who will do the laundry? Who has the right to initiate sex? Any of these subjects can lead to a useful, even intimate conversation—or to a colossal battle—depending on a couple's ability to communicate.

Ingredients of Effective Communication

If there is one word that holds the key to improved communication, that word is awareness. By learning more about yourself, your partner, and the process of sharing intimate feelings, you can promote better communication. The three crucial ingredients for the "aware communicator" are self-awareness, active listening, and empathy for one's partner.

Self-Awareness and Self-Esteem

The degree of one's self-awareness affects one's ability to communicate, especially in intimate relationships. For example, the wife who attacked her husband for coming home late was aware of and expressed her anger. But she may actually have been feeling a tangled web of emotions: loneliness, fear, jealousy, and so on. Often people speak before they have a clear idea of what their true feelings are. This can easily lead to poor communication: the husband who came home late cannot appreciate his wife's loneliness or fear if all he hears is her anger.

Some researchers have learned that couples often rely on expected or stock responses to situations. A wife may feel that she must always show her husband that she enjoys sex, when in fact it is true most of the time but not every time. A husband may believe that he ought to be angry when his wife goes out of town on a business trip, while actually he enjoys having a few days on his own. These stock images of how marriage partners should act inhibit couples from discovering and revealing their true feelings and unique responses to situations (Parlee, 1979).

Sherod Miller, Elam Nunnally, and Daniel Wackman (1975) of the University of Minnesota have taught many couples to improve their communication skills through greater self-awareness. They advise paying close attention to the information we take in with our five senses; to the thoughts or interpretations we have concerning this sensory material; to emotions, intentions (wishes, wants, desires), and actions. These researchers suggest trying to separate out these elements of consciousness from one another;

that is, trying to distinguish what one sees happening from what one interprets to be happening. For example, a man may see his wife talking excitedly to another man at a party; this is sensory material open to various interpretations. One is that his wife is flirting; another is simply that she is enjoying a stimulating conversation. The important point is that he must separate his perception of the incident from his interpretation. Miller and his colleagues believe that the more aware couples are of these dimensions, the better they can clarify their messages to each other.

Self-awareness, then, is the first element of effective communication. Self-awareness and self-esteem are often interrelated. Carol was talking with a friend about her interest in weaving and showed real enthusiasm when she described her loom, her projects, and an interesting yarn supplier in New England. Her friend replied, "I bet your husband's also interested in weaving." Carol was surprised: "Oh, Doug's much too busy at the bank to pay attention to the silly stuff that I do. He hardly knows about it."

Carol had defined her passion for weaving as "silly stuff," unworthy of her husband's interest. In fact, Doug might have become very interested and supportive if given the chance. Carol's poor sense of self-respect made that impossible. As the example illustrates, self-esteem is often necessary for effective communication. Carol must value herself and her work enough to believe that others, including her husband, would feel the same way. In general, when we feel comfortable about ourselves, we tend to be more skillful at listening, more sensitive to others, and better at sharing our ideas than when we feel inadequate, embarrassed, or unimportant (Burr, 1976).

Active Listening

"If a tree falls in the forest and there is no one present to hear it, has there been any sound?" This old puzzle highlights the critical role of listening in communication. The sender of a message must express feelings and concerns, but the receiver must listen attentively. Unless a message is received or heard, communication has not taken place. **Active listening** means devoting attention to the entire message of the sender—the words, the emotional cues contained in tone of voice or body language, anything that communicates meaning. Careful listening is a sign of respect—a respect sometimes given more easily to strangers than to our spouses or children. Often when one is "listening," he or she is mentally formulating a quick response, or thinking about the coming meal, or worrying about a troublesome problem at work. By contrast, genuine listening demands our full attention. When Bob began reading his newspaper while Sheila was speaking to him, he was hardly engaged in serious listening.

Effective listening is an active process. Therapists have recommended two useful techniques to help people improve their listening skills: role reversal and reflecting. In **role reversal**, individuals agree to change places temporarily to better understand each other. For example, Chet wanted to buy new furniture for the living room while his wife Arlene preferred to purchase a home computer. In practicing role reversal, Chet recited all the good reasons for buying the computer rather than the furniture; Arlene did the opposite. "It didn't lead to an instant solution," said Chet after their experiment, "but I really understood her position more clearly. I guess I hadn't listened carefully; I was so intent on convincing her I was right."

In **reflecting**—or what Thomas Gordon (1975) calls "active listening"—one person repeats ideas or feelings that the partner has just expressed. For example, a wife mentions to her husband that she feels she never has time for herself because of career and family responsibilities. The husband tries to reflect on the meaning of her remarks, possibly with a comment like, "You need some time when you can do what you want to do, not what you have to do."

Robert Harper (1958) has suggested that marital communication would be better if more couples were able to ask for and receive verbal feedback. It is frequently assumed that each understands the other's meaning, and yet this is often untrue. The techniques of active listening can minimize misunderstanding and miscommunication and lead to greater satisfaction and understanding.

Empathy and Respect

Empathy within marriage means caring for your partner; literally, it is "feeling another's feelings in yourself." Empathy seems to help married couples solve problems more effectively. Those couples who claim to be happiest are better able to predict how their partner would respond to a situation than those who are not as happy (Scheff, 1967; Schulman, 1974). The empathetic spouse takes into consideration the feelings and self-esteem of the partner when talking or listening. In some cases, this means not launching into a discussion of a sensitive issue when your partner has just returned after a stressful day at work. Social scientists have observed that the most difficult time of day for people to function as pleasant communicators is just before the evening meal (Bossard and Boll, 1956). Thus, it would appear risky to schedule a major talk the minute your spouse walks in the door.

Empathy in marriage may also require an understanding that your partner has a need for privacy (Pollak and Wise, 1979). Steve wanted his wife Elizabeth to give him a detailed accounting of her daily activities every night. Whenever she saw a friend, he expected to know everything that was said, especially if it concerned their marriage. Ulti-

mately, Elizabeth felt so invaded by his endless questions and demands that she left him. Steve proved unable to empathize; he never realized how his behavior made Elizabeth feel.

We spoke earlier of the importance of a partner in confirming and validating one's self-image. Awareness of his or her sensitivities and respectful treatment of these feelings is an essential ingredient of effective communication. "Jack is 6'7" and is very touchy about being so tall," revealed his wife, Sandra. "I have to watch myself when I feel like teasing him about it. He'll laugh and joke, but I know it hurts him more than he lets on. So I try to respect his feelings and avoid any teasing about his height."

Conflict in Relationships

When his love he saw at last
Arms about her he did cast
Then Aucassin wedded her,
Made her lady of Biaucaire.

Many years abode they there,
Many years in shade or sun,
In great gladness and delight.

Ne'er hath Aucassin regret
Nor his lady Nicolete. *

Once upon a time, the happily married couple was thought to live a conflict-free life. Like Aucassin and Nicolete, they never exchanged a harsh word, never felt angry about their partner's behavior, and worked out problems in a spirit of loving cooperation. Of course, like so many stories that begin "once upon a time," this one is more fantasy than fact. Marriage inevitably means conflict and disagreement. The ten-

*"Aucassin and Nicolete" in R. Sherman Loomis and Laura Hibbard Loomis (eds.), *Medieval Romances* (translated by Andrew Lang) New York: Modern Library, 1957, p. 283.

sion between meeting individual needs (for love, relaxation, privacy, and so forth) and the needs of the partnership (doing household tasks, earning money, raising children, getting along with in-laws) always leads to at least some difficult moments.

Marriage counselors have recently begun to emphasize that conflict can be productive for an intimate relationship. In contrast to the stereotype of bitter words, ruthless insults, and thrown plates, couples can learn to fight constructively. The latter option, many counselors argue, is preferable to repressing feelings of anger and resentment in order to avoid conflict. It is only through conflict that a dissatisfying relationship can be resolved and made more interesting (Scanzoni, 1979). In the words of the early Greek philosopher Heraclitus, "strife is the father of all."

Consequences of Avoiding Conflict

Harold Ruesch and his colleagues (1974) conducted an experiment with recently married couples to examine expression and avoidance of anger. The couples were asked to take part in role-playing scenes designed to bring them to a confrontation over an issue, such as the husband's desire to spend time alone. Over 15 percent of couples managed to avoid the suggestion of conflict: an even higher percentage of husbands avoided confronting their wives. Instead of taking responsibility for their desire to spend time alone, 25 percent of husbands blamed their jobs for their need to be away from their wives.

Ruesch believes that these "avoiders" wanted to escape the anxiety they felt about confronting their wives. "Never fighting" has its risks, however. In Ruesch's view, the negative feelings that are buried do not evaporate; they can instead "poison a relationship." Such avoidance may lead to what therapists call a "devitalized marriage" in which partners feel emotionally detached and indifferent to one another:

She: How was your day?

He: Fine. How was yours?

She: OK, you know, the usual.

He: Anything you want to do after dinner?

She: Oh, whatever you want, dear. . . .

The bland "devitalized" dialogue between these two, which eventually trails off into silence, is as meaningful as their conversations get. (Refer back to Box 9–1 for another marriage that can be viewed as devitalized.) George Bach and Peter Wyden (1969) would say that such couples have had an "emotional divorce." While burying all their anger, they have simultaneously lost their love and interest in one another.

Another possible substitute for openly expressed anger is what therapists call "passive-aggressive behavior," or indirect expression of negative feelings. Constant nagging, sarcastic remarks, and teasing are all forms of passive-aggressive behavior. One husband, resentful of his wife's career success, sabotaged an important evening with her boss by first acting bored and then starting an argument about who would win the upcoming presidential election.

Displacement is another form of passive-aggressive behavior. The individual is angry about one thing but expresses the anger over another subject (usually something petty). For example, one woman was annoyed about her husband's decision to quit his job and return to school for an M.B.A. Instead of telling him how she felt, she began complaining about the "clutter" of his books and papers within their small apartment (Lamanna and Reidman, 1981).

Not only can a relationship be "poisoned" by burying feelings of anger; the individual's physical and emotional well-being can also be affected. Illness, overeating, alcoholism, and depression are sometimes the result of holding everything inside rather than sharing emotions with one's partner.

Sources of Conflict

Often a marital conflict will begin with a minor incident, such as a pile of dirty underwear left on the bathroom floor. However, the potential for a serious explosion is always there, especially since each partner is generally well aware of the other's sensitivities. In the midst of a quarrel with emotions running high, a spouse may say, ''You're a complete failure in your profession'' or ''I'm ashamed to be seen with you since you got so fat.'' Such attacks can quickly destroy the trust upon which a relationship is built. Once certain things are said, neither partner can go on preserving little fictions that confirm the other's self-image (Waller and Hill, 1951).

Marital counselors report that couples seem to visit them most often with problems involving children, sex, money, use of leisure time, relatives, and infidelity. In short, any important issue in a couple's shared emotional, sexual, and financial partnership can be a source of difficulty (Beck and Jones, 1973). It is important to note that key areas of disagreement change during a family's life cycle. For example, constructive communication becomes somewhat more difficult during a couple's childbearing years (Orthner, 1976). Box 9–2 offers a further look at parental battles about their children.

Types of Conflict

The most basic distinction in analyzing conflict involves overt and covert conflict. **Overt conflict** is conflict that is open and can be directly observed. By contrast, **covert conflict** is hidden and cannot be directly observed. Covert conflict is essentially the same as the passive-aggressive behavior described earlier.

Overt conflict can take three forms: acute, progressive, or habituated. **Acute conflict**, most prevalent early in a marriage, is an argument about some specific event. It may involve intense outbursts of hostility in which each spouse attempts to inflict damage on the other. Acute conflict usually reflects the many undefined situations faced in the initial stage of marriage, such as determining who does what in the household. If new and undefined situations occur in later years—a move to a new city, the birth of a first child, the need for an in-law to move in with the couple—acute conflict may result. Unless couples can resolve an acute conflict, there is a high probability that it will become *progressive*. Each argument will build on the previous one, leaving more and more bitter feelings. The tendency for acute conflicts to become progressive may explain why so many couples separate during the first year of marriage. In some marriages, certain areas of conflict flare up periodically because a stable accommodation is never reached. Shelley immediately disliked Ron, her husband's older brother. Whenever it was time for his annual visit from the East Coast, she and her husband Sam would have a battle. This **habituated conflict** is unlike acute conflict in that there is less emotional investment and it tends not to get worse over time.

Covert conflict, by its very nature, is difficult to measure. There is widespread agreement, however, that many types of ''emotional withholding'' are common in marriage; the most widely recognized is withholding of sex. Frigidity, impotence, or just ''being too tired'' can be a way of expressing hostility and hurting your spouse. In the same way, almost any unexplained physical disorder—a headache, an ulcer, obesity—may reflect marital conflict. Many professionals see covert conflict as potentially more damaging to intimate relationships than open fighting. If conflict becomes overt, the individuals become well aware

B O X 9 - 2

When Parents Fight Over Kids

"Whenever Brian Garson corrects ten-year-old Melanie, his wife Cynthia becomes furious. Hearing even the nicest reprimand, she flashes back to her own mother's harshness. Brian, in contrast, blames his own younger sister's immaturity on his parents' leniency. He's determined not to repeat what he sees as their grave mistake" (Olds, 1981: 52).

Many American couples fight more frequently over their children than any other subject. In the view of Harold Feldman, professor of human development and family studies at Cornell University: "Differences in child rearing may be more central than anything else in a marriage. These issues go right to what the parent thinks life is all about and it's hard to compromise on that" (Olds, 1981: 52).

Feldman explored the subject of parental arguments over children by posing a series of childrearing dilemmas to 35 married couples. For example, he asked: "Every time you put your six-month-old down for a nap he howls the minute you leave the room. Would you pick him up? Would your spouse agree with your decision?" Another question was: "Your high school sophomore has been smoking marijuana with his friends. Would you forbid him to see these friends? Would your spouse?"

In Feldman's original test sample, no husband and wife were in full agreement. Even the most compatible couples disagreed on almost one-third of the test items. The majority of couples disagreed much more often.

Some children blame themselves for parental arguments that they overhear. Many family therapists believe that witnessing an occasional battle will not lead to long-term damage as long as parents make it clear that the child is not the cause of the problem. Moreover, there is a possible benefit: the child will see that parents can become angry with each other, express their feelings, and eventually resolve their difficulties. Learning that love and conflict can coexist may be a most valuable lesson.

Source: Olds, 1981: 52-55.

that there is a problem and may attempt to find a solution.

Managing Conflict Productively

Conflict is one of many ways that couples communicate. Yet, clearly, not all fights are constructive; the emotional damage that couples can inflict on one another is staggering. Moreover, emotional conflict may lead to physical outbursts, including violence against one's spouse. As noted in Chapter 8, spouse abuse is too common an occurrence in American society.

Constructive conflict is neither brutally honest nor aggressive. It involves giving gentle feedback to one's partner about the issue under discussion. While how marital couples resolve conflict can vary from couple to couple (see Box 9–3), therapists have offered certain guidelines for couples who wish to avoid destructive clashes and instead use conflict as a form of productive communication:

1. *Try not to engage in "kitchen-sink fighting."* One triggering incident may begin an argument, but soon issue after issue may be thrown into it, including the proverbial "kitchen sink." This obviously makes conflict resolution difficult, if not impossible. Even professional arbitrators or negotiators at the State Department could not function with that type of agenda!

2. *Talk in terms of issues, not personalities.* Mary Alice calls Alfredo "insensitive";

B O X 9 – 3

Research Brief:
How Do Married Couples Resolve Conflicts?

In a study by Bell, Chafetz, and Horn (1982), 30 middle-class married couples were interviewed about the marital conflicts they had experienced, how they attempted to resolve the conflicts, and who won. Four basic strategies were employed to resolve conflicts:

- *Authority*. One spouse attempts to make decisions (and win conflicts) believing he or she has the legitimate right to decide. This spouse will be successful if the partner agrees to his or her right to decide.
- *Control*. One spouse attempts to get the other to do what she or he wants—regardless of the desires of the other—through use of a bribe or threat.
- *Influence*. One spouse attempts to use information or persuasion to get the other to change his or her mind.
- *Manipulation*. One spouse attempts to gain compliance from the other by using subtle, covert behaviors such as crying, pouting, or guilt.

Among the researchers' findings were the following:

- Husbands use influence most frequently, followed by manipulation.
- Wives use influence most often, followed by control.
- Contrary to popular stereotypes, husbands use manipulation more often than wives do.
- In general, husbands win significantly more conflicts than wives, regardless of the strategies employed by either.
- In marriages in which both partners work outside the home, women win 62 percent of all conflicts. By contrast, wives who are full-time homemakers win only 25 percent of the time.
- The more educated the husband is, the more likely the marriage will be egalitarian in terms of conflict resolution.

Source: Bell, Chafetz, and Horn, 1982: 111–132.

he counters that she is "lazy" and "a chronic complainer." Such insults only make these partners feel more isolated and defensive. One way to avoid this trap is to use "I-statements." For example, a wife who was constantly angry about her husband's sloppy habits customarily began her tirades against him with "you pig!" When she changed her opening to "I feel sick when I see your clothes all over the bedroom," he was not as defensive and a dialogue began.

3. *Be an active listener*. Anger can make us deaf to everything but our own resentment and indignation. Although we may believe we know what our partner is saying, often we do not. The techniques of role reversal and reflecting—repeating or summarizing what you understood your partner to say—can improve communication and open the way to compromise.

It is also important to hear a partner's anger. Marriage researchers and therapists Robert and Margaret Blood cite anthropologist Ashley Montagu's idea that aggressive anger is a deformed aspect of love, an attempt to complete love when the individual feels unloved. "Anger," write the Bloods, "is pain crying for release. When listened to, it shows the way to needed change" (Blood and Blood, 1978: 360).

4. *Recognize that your mate's unhappiness is not always your responsibility*. Your partner's

irritation may have little to do with you, and more to do with a boss, a best friend, or an impending case of the flu. No spouse is totally responsible for all of the other's problems. It is best to allow your partner to have irrational moments and fits of temper, even if he or she occasionally blames you improperly.

5. *Do not threaten divorce unless you mean it.* Some individuals threaten divorce, separation, or "breaking up" in the midst of an argument as a shock tactic. The threat is not sincere; the real goal is to force the partner to pay more attention to their grievances. But, as Alan Loy McGinnis (1982:135) warns, "once two people begin discussing divorce it is surprising how quickly they can be living in separate apartments."

6. *Find a way for both sides to win.* In discussing the various strategies for reaching agreement in international diplomacy, professional negotiators Roger Fisher and William Ury (1982) suggest that both sides must search for a mutually agreeable solution. That way, neither loses or feels defeated, and a settlement is possible.

The same principle is valid in marital negotiating. Alex and Marie were battling about where to go on their summer vacation. He wanted to lie on an ocean beach; she preferred to "see the sights" in a major city. They came close to taking separate vacations but finally agreed on a compromise. They asked a travel agent for a list of cities with nearby beach areas and finally settled on Los Angeles.

Marriage Counseling

In the view of Tom Clark, president of the American Association for Marriage and Family Therapy: "Marriage is the single most complex entity short of nuclear fusion—and nuclear fusion may be less complicated" (Sanoff, 1983: 44). In struggling through the complexities of marriage—and the inevitable conflicts that result—many couples seek some form of assistance.

Marital therapy has become a popular approach in the last decade. A marriage therapist can sometimes help couples to clarify their difficulties and communicate with one another more effectively. Specific techniques

By repeating or summarizing what you understood your partner to say, you can improve communication and open the door for compromise.

used will vary depending on the therapist; however, most encourage couples to look at the patterns and unconscious rules of their relationship. One study of over 1500 couples in marital therapy found that over 60 percent had improved their relationships. When both partners went to therapy sessions, the improvement rate reached 70 percent (Gurman and Kniskern, 1978).

While accepting the value of marriage therapy, some counselors have become increasingly aware that this approach has a serious limitation: only those couples whose marriages are already in trouble are likely to undertake therapy. Consequently, an alternative approach known as "marital enrichment" was developed to assist a wider range of couples. In a sense, marital enrichment is a kind of preventive medicine that helps couples develop skills for dealing constructively with intimacy and conflict. In the opinion of David R. Mace, one of the pioneers in the field: "We must teach these skills if we are to prevent marriages from failing in disturbing numbers" (Collins, 1983: B9).

There are three basic models of marital enrichment programs: the "marriage encounter," which includes supervised intensive husband-wife interactions but normally has no group interactions; the "marriage communication lab," which usually offers a structured program with a planned content; and the largely unstructured "enrichment retreat" which develops entirely out of the needs of a group of married couples. In general, marital enrichment groups either meet for a continuous and intensive period (usually over a weekend) or for a series of evening meetings once a week.

"Marriage Encounter" is an international movement whose local affiliates, often church-based groups, offer weekend programs. The twin bases for marriage encounter are faith, which has a theological derivation, and dialogue, which has a psy-

chological foundation (Genovese, 1975). Although the activities are confined to direct husband-wife confrontations—stimulated by testimonies from leader couples under the direction of a religious leader—the social and religious support provided by the group nevertheless plays an important role in the experience. This approach has become so popular that in New York marriage encounter weekends are booked as much as two years in advance.

The marriage communication lab makes extensive use of exercises geared to improve intracouple and intercouple interactions. For example, the Minnesota Couples Communication Program (MCCP) focuses on teaching communication skills (Nunnally, et al., 1975). Partners carry on dialogues about such sensitive issues as sex and money in front of a larger group. Other participants offer feedback on how effectively the couple has communicated and identify areas of weakness. Practice assignments are also provided so that each couple can continue working on these skills between group sessions.

Enrichment retreats take shape around the expressed needs of a particular group of couples. It is understood that there will be no exchange of opinions. Instead, the retreat is viewed as an exchange of experiences which group members will attempt to understand. One couple may begin by discussing a specific problem they are having; other couples will provide feedback and support.

Marriage enrichment groups are not therapy groups; the participation of couples with serious emotional difficulties is discouraged. They are unlike encounter groups in that confrontation tactics are not employed. In general, marital enrichment groups are problem-oriented and emphasize development of more rewarding behavior patterns. The best facilitators are often married couples who participate as members of a group rather than assuming a separate, authoritative role.

In struggling through the inevitable conflicts in marriage, couples often seek assistance in the form of marital therapy.

Marriage counselor and researcher David Mace suggests that many couples are unable to deal effectively with disagreement and conflict. "The basic task that most couples need to do," he argues, "is to build an in-depth relationship by learning to use their anger positively" (Collins, 1983: B9). As Mace (1975) points out, however, there are three "roadblocks" or cultural pressures that keep couples from seeking marital assistance through counseling or enrichment groups:

- The "myth of naturalism," or the idea that anyone can make marriage work just by following their instincts.
- "Privatism," or the notion that marriage is a very personal and private matter that should not be discussed openly with outsiders.
- "Cynicism," which encourages the view that only fools need to learn how to be married. Couples who are cynical about the value of marital assistance will never ask for help until the situation becomes desperate.

In some marriages, separation is the only mutually satisfactory solution to conflict.

Over 25 percent of all couples who file for divorce reach an agreement and reconcile before the divorce is granted. But, for many others, separation is an answer to painful problems. In Blood's (1974: 312) words, "Peaceful loneliness is an improvement over perpetual conflict." We will examine separation and divorce more fully in Chapter 14.

Summary

Communication is the process of exchanging desires, needs, and feelings as well as facts and opinions. There are four essential elements in any act of communication: the sender of the message, the receiver, the form, and the content. A communication cannot take place unless someone sends the message and someone else receives it.

A message can be conveyed in words or in silence, through shouts or tears, in a chuckle or a caress. We learn to interpret any message through the content of the words, the tone in which they are spoken, and the physical context in which the words are uttered. The same words can change their meaning dramatically depending on one's tone of voice.

Many couples avoid conflict and bury disagreements. Distracting, computing, placating, and blaming are common tactics for avoiding open and honest self-disclosure, or what Virginia Satir calls leveling. People with high self-esteem are more likely to be levelers; they are willing to risk self-disclosure for the intimacy and emotional support it can bring. The process of confirming another's self-image is at the basis of intimacy and effective communication.

The term "communication style" is used to describe the unwritten rules by which couples regulate their lives together. James Hawkins and his colleagues have classified couples into four broad categories of communicators: conventional, controlling, speculative, and contactful. Only the contactful talk openly about a problem and their feelings.

Sex-role socialization has encouraged many men to hide or hold in all strong emotions other than anger. By contrast, women have been encouraged to express positive emotions such as love while refraining from expressions of anger. Men tend to dominate conversations, talk more frequently, and interrupt more than women do. Many women feel that men are not "contactful enough" and find this a source of deep dissatisfaction in their marriages. However, new cultural patterns and the trend toward egalitarian relationships may reshape marital communication styles.

Self-awareness is the first element of effective communication. Active listening is also important. Therapists have recommended two useful techniques to help people improve their listening skills: role reversal and reflecting. Empathy and respect for one's spouse are also necessary for productive communication.

Marriage counselors have begun to challenge the romantic ideal of a conflict-free marriage; they note that conflict can be useful in an intimate relationship if couples learn to fight constructively. Those who avoid conflict entirely may end up with meaningless "devitalized marriages" or may engage in manipulative passive-aggressive behavior.

Overt conflict is conflict that is open and can be directly observed. It can take three forms: acute, progressive, or habituated. By contrast, covert conflict is hidden and cannot be directly observed.

Therapists have offered certain guidelines for couples who wish to manage conflict productively. They must avoid "kitchen-sink fighting," talk in terms of issues rather than personalities, engage in active listening, and find a way for both sides to win during a disagreement. It is important not to threaten divorce unless you really mean it.

Many couples have turned to marriage counselors or marital enrichment programs in recent years. One study of marital therapy found that over 60 percent of couples had improved their relationships. There are three basic models of marital enrichment programs: the "marriage encounter," the "marriage communication lab," and the largely unstructured "enrichment retreat."

Discussion Questions

1. Why do you think that people who have a high self-esteem are more open about communication than those with low self-esteem?

2. Do you agree that men are really less communicative about feelings and emotions than women? Are women less rational than men? Why?

3. If you were told that someone had a *controlling* style of communication, what would you infer about that person's attitude and expectations of his or her partner? What does this communication style say about the relationship? Do the same for conventional, speculative, and contactful styles.

4. Ellen and Tom's son Fred has the flu and has to stay home from school for a few days. Ellen tells Tom she cannot stay home because she has a report to submit to her boss; Tom says he has a presentation and a crucial appointment he cannot miss or postpone. Soon the two are in the midst of a major battle: "You always think your job is so important. Well, it isn't, at least not when it comes time to paying the bills every month! If it wasn't for my job, we'd starve!" "Some father you are! Don't you care about your son? Only last month you were too busy to make it to the school open house! Now you're too busy to care for him when he's ill!"

Suppose you are a marriage counselor called in to help them with this problem. How could you advise them to negotiate the solution in a more constructive manner?

Key Words

Active Listening	**Empathy**	**Mixed Message**
Acute Conflict	**Habituated Conflict**	**Overt Conflict**
Communication	**Interpersonal Communication**	**Reflecting**
Communication Style		**Role Reversal**
Covert Conflict	**Leveling**	**Self-Disclosure**

Suggested Readings

Derlega, Valerian, and Chaikin, Alan. *Sharing Intimacy: What We Reveal to Others and Why*. Englewood Cliffs, N. J.: Prentice-Hall, 1975. Examines the process of self-disclosure in forming friendships, marriages, and other relationships.

Fisher, Roger and Ury, William. *Getting to Yes*. New York: Penguin Books, 1982. A comprehensive guide for developing successful negotiation skills.

Mace, David. *Prevention in Family Services: Approaches to Family Wellness*. Beverly Hills, Calif.: Sage Publications, 1983. Emphasizes the importance of marriage enrichment programs to foster rewarding and high-quality marriage relationships.

Miller, Sherod, Nunnally, Elam, and Wackman, Daniel. *Alive and Aware: Improving Communication in Relationships*. Minneapolis: Interpersonal Communication Program, 1975. Focuses on helping individuals develop effective communication skills in intimate relationships.

Scoresby, Lynn. *The Marriage Dialogue*. Reading, Mass.: Addison-Wesley, 1977. Discusses the importance of communication in marriage and the roles it plays in love, intimacy, sexual expression, decision-making, negotiation, and conflict management.

CHAPTER TEN

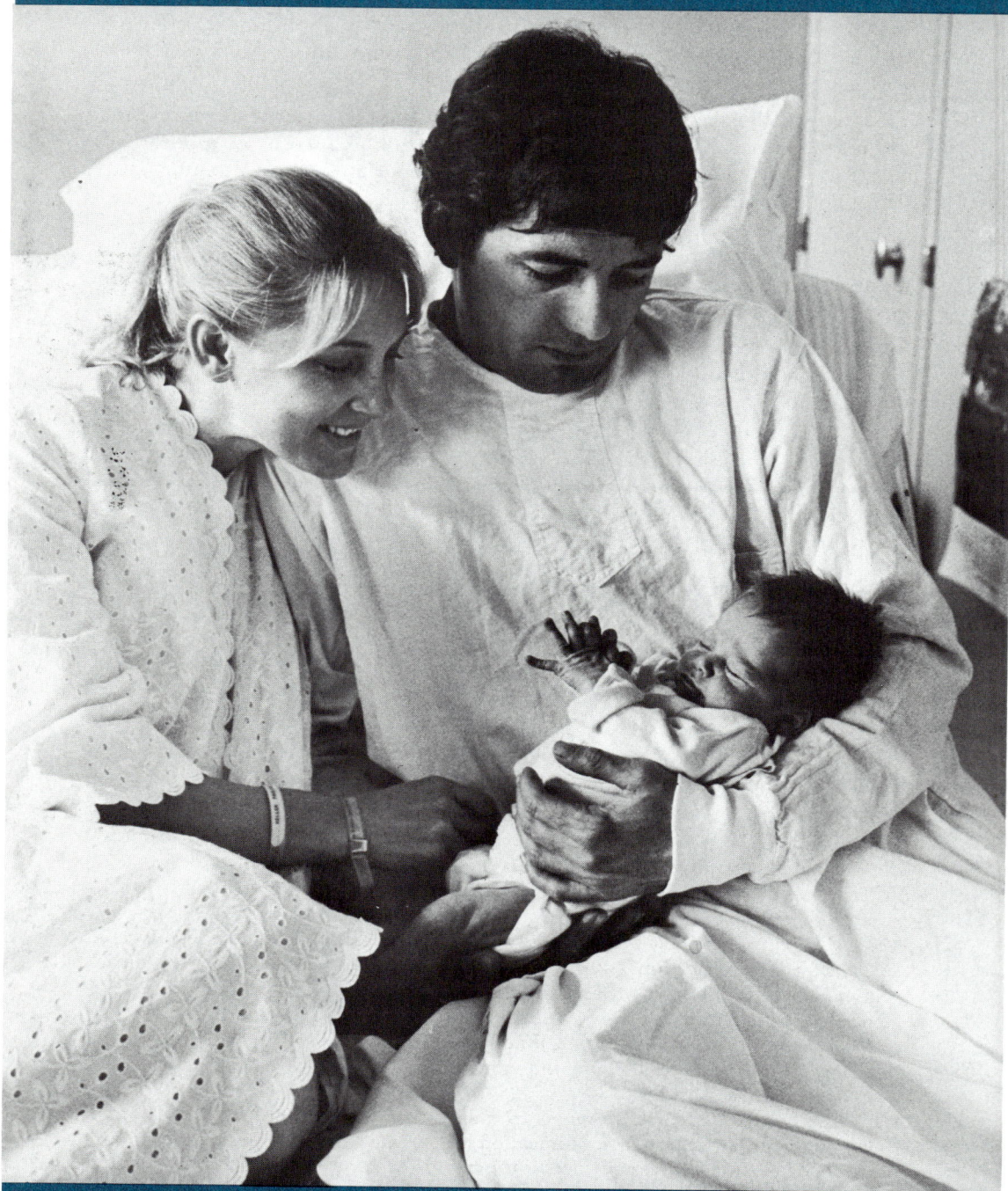

Pregnancy and Childbirth: The Decision Making Process

Paul and Joan, both 22, were married last summer and hope to have children as soon as possible. Although they initially discussed waiting for a year until they could save money, they later decided not to delay parenthood. They firmly believe that having children will be an important part of their lives and their marriage. ''We talk about it all the time,'' says Joan. ''Sure, we may have some financial problems, but so did our parents. Things will work out; our kids will have wonderful lives.''

Luis and Mercedes are about the same age as Paul and Joan, but are not as certain about having children. ''We know we don't want children right now,'' say Mercedes. ''Our jobs are not that secure, and we have a large mortgage to pay off. There are too many financial pressures. Still, when I see my friend Linda with her baby, I know I want a child someday.'' Luis, however, has other concerns: ''A baby would really change our lives. It's not just the money; kids take a lot of your time and energy. And our marriage would be totally different, maybe less satisfying.''

Choosing whether or not to be a parent is really a twentieth-century option. The advent of reliable birth control methods (see Chapter 5) has allowed couples to have a sexual relationship without necessarily becoming parents. In this chapter, we will focus on the decisions that married couples face regarding pregnancy and childbrith. Particular attention will be given to decisions regarding readiness for parenthood, prenatal care, forms of childbirth, and adoption. We will also examine the transition to parenthood as a crisis, and the impact having children has on a couple's relationship.

Choosing or Rejecting Parenthood

Animals reproduce because of an instinct; by contrast, human beings must be socialized into a desire to become parents. There are many personal and social goals involved in the decision to have children. Some couples have children because they believe that reproduction is the reason for human existence and they want to extend their family line. Others need to express affection and

concern through the parental role. Still others seem to choose parenthood because they feel it will reflect on their goodness and serve as a visible, concrete statement of maturity and confidence.

These are not the only reasons for becoming parents. Some individuals hope that their offspring will fulfill their own unattained ambitions. They may want a child to become President of the United States, an opera singer, or a professional basketball star. Others have children in order to force a marriage, repair a faltering relationship, or please their own parents. Needless to say, it can be dangerous to use childbearing as an answer for basic marital problems.

Children have been viewed as economically valuable in many periods of history (and still are today in less developed societies). A family running a farm, for example, can certainly use as many helping hands as possible. But for most American families living in urban or suburban areas, children are a serious expense rather than a financial advantage. The cost of childrearing is generally divided into two components: direct maintenance costs, which include actual expenses for food, clothing, education, and health care; and opportunity costs, or the income that parents forego when raising children (as when one parent stays home to take care of the children and remains outside of the paid labor force).

Estimates of the total economic cost of raising a child in the United States from birth to college age range from $85,000 to $247,000 in 1982 dollars. The figure jumps to $323,000 for high-income families who wish to send a son or daughter to a private college or university for four years. It is interesting to note that black families spend a larger proportion of their income on children than do white families. The same is true of younger and well-educated parents in contrast to older and less-educated parents (Olson, 1983). The time dimension of parenting is also formidable; parents who raise two children to age 18 spend about 13,000 hours in childrearing time, over and above routine housework.

Of course, the role of parent also has noneconomic costs that cannot be quantified. No one will deny that raising children is a difficult and often frustrating responsibility. The role of mother or father demands long hours and intense involvement. The child may be viewed as an infringement on a couple's established patterns of affection and intimacy, or on an individual's career ambitions. For women, the childrearing role mandated by traditional sex roles has often meant sacrificing independence, self-esteem, and careers outside the home. Limpus (1970), for example, argues that it is a woman's relationship to her children (rather than to her husband) which prevents serious commitment to a career.

For some American couples, the economic and noneconomic costs of having children outweigh the benefits. Consequently, about 5 percent of Americans have declared their intention not to have children. Leni and her husband Stan are afraid that a child would strain their eight-year-old marriage and have decided to remain childfree. Linda, who is 45 and married, feels a woman's intelligence is better served "if she's not constantly driving the kids to ballet, gymnastics and piano lessons" (Francke, et al., 1980: 96).

The reasons why people reject parenthood are as personal and varied as the reasons why others want to have children. In one study of 55 couples who voluntarily chose not be become parents, the wives cited as their most important reasons the desire for more personal freedom, the desire for greater time and intimacy with their husbands, and career demands. For husbands, the most important reasons for remaining childfree included the desire for more personal freedom, disinterest in being a parent,

and the desire to restrict family responsibilities. Other reasons mentioned by these couples were financial concerns, feelings about overpopulation, and dislike of children (Cooper, et al., 1978). It should also be noted that some individuals avoid childbearing because they know they are carriers of hereditary diseases such as Tay-Sachs disease or Sickle cell anemia.

Some of these reasons for remaining childfree are reactive (or responses to the disadvantages of having children), while others are attractive (or responses to the advantages of an adult-centered lifestyle). As is true of other important family decisions, the choice to become (or not become) a parent is a response to various pushes and pulls. Interestingly, however, about two-thirds of childfree couples were not always clear about avoidance of parenthood. Instead, they made a series of decisions to postpone having children until a future time that never arrived. Jean Veevers (1973, 1980), a family researcher who has studied childless couples, suggests that they move through four distinct stages: an initial delay for a definite period of time, a postponement for an indefinite period, an open acknowledgment that they may never want children, and, finally, a conclusion that childlessness is a permanent rather than transitory state.

Married couples who choose to remain childfree have often been victims of negative stereotyping. In a society that has traditionally regarded parenting as an expected part of marriage, such couples have been labeled as immature, unstable, unnatural, irresponsible, selfish, and sexually inadequate. For this reason, childfree couples may minimize social contacts with disapproving parents and friends. Some join organizations such as the National Alliance for Optional Parenthood or the National Organization for Nonparents which provide support and encouragement for those who reject parenthood (Ory, 1976).

The incidence of remaining childfree appears to be higher in urban than rural settings, among couples who fall into higher socioeconomic and educational categories, and among those who are religious (Bram, 1974; Gustavus and Henley, 1971; Veevers, 1973). The apparent rise in the number of childless American couples may result in part from the fact that members of the "baby boom" generation have reached their twenties and thirties. Demographers speculate that, while this group may delay having children, the incidence of voluntary childlessness will be much lower than was anticipated in the 1970s.

Readiness for Parenthood

Once couples have decided they want children, the next question is: "When should we have a child?" Since a baby leads to major changes in married life and to serious financial and emotional responsibilities, careful planning for the future is ideal. The timing, spacing, and number of children are important considerations in planning for parenthood.

Timing

Many sensitive issues must be faced by a married couple as they discuss the timing of their childrearing. How long should they be married before they undertake parenthood? Are they too young or too old to become parents? Is it the "wrong time" because of their careers?

Length of Marriage

Most experts in the field of family planning advise young couples to wait before having a first child so that they have time to adjust to marriage. They can enjoy one another's attention and become more secure financially before facing the additional demands of parenthood. By contrast, a couple that rushes too quickly into having children may subsequently experience divorce and a custody battle.

Age

The likelihood of birth defects, prematurity, stillbirths, and what doctors generally call "the poor outcome of pregnancy" increases dramatically if parents are either too young or too old. Even taking into consideration such important factors as living conditions, education, and socioeconomic background, the age of parents nevertheless affects the well-being of children.

Medical research suggests that the preferred time for a woman to conceive is between the ages of 20 and 35. If she is younger or older, there are increased risks both for her and for the baby. Mothers 17 years old or younger are more likely to have babies with birth defects or babies born prematurely. The chances of giving birth to an infant with **Down's Syndrome** (a genetic mutation that causes mental retardation) increase from one in 1500 for women under 30 to one in 130 for women ages 40 to 45 (Nye, 1976; Whelan, 1976).

While most of us are aware that the mother's age is an important consideration in planning the timing of children, the father's age can also be important. The ability of a man to impregnate a woman declines after the age of 40 (Menning, 1977). Moreover, several types of birth defects, including Down's Syndrome, can result more frequently when fathers are of increasing age.

Recent studies have revealed a decided rise in the number of women who have chosen to begin parenthood in their thirties or early forties. For many, career decisions or infertility made an earlier pregnancy undesirable or impossible. They may feel they have established themselves at their jobs, have built secure marital relationships, and are now ready for parenthood. Modern

B O X 1 0 – 1

Research Brief:
The Increased Costs of Teenage Childbearing

Denise Dillard and Louis Pol have attempted to calculate the hidden economic costs of raising children for mothers who begin parenthood as teenagers. The researchers identified three factors contributing to the increased costs for teenage mothers:

- *Education.* Women who have their first child while in their teens average two fewer years of education than those who delay childbearing until their twenties.
- *Labor force participation.* Having a first child as a teen is associated with lower rates of employment and lower wages when employed. Teenage mothers tend to have less educational attainment, less work experience, and higher subsequent fertility than other working mothers.
- *Subsequent fertility.* Becoming a parent during teen years is strongly associated with having a large family in later life. Teen mothers have fewer opportunities in the job market and may center their lives on childbearing rather than low-paying work.

These factors translate into higher direct costs for childbearing for teenage mothers. On the average, such women have three more children than mothers who delay childbearing until their twenties. Even more important are the increased opportunity costs experienced by teenage mothers. They will spend fewer hours in the paid labor force and receive a lower hourly wage because of their comparatively limited education. Moreover, the opportunity costs continue even after active parenting has ended because these women may still be relegated to low-paying jobs.

Source: K. D. Dillard and L. G. Pol, "The Individual Economic Costs of Teenage Childbearing." *Family Relations,* April 1982, 249–259.

methods of detecting prenatal abnormalities have allowed women to be less concerned over medical risks than were previous generations of women.

Costs of Prenatal Care and Birth

As noted earlier, having children is expensive. The average cost of a normal hospital delivery with no complications in the early 1980s exceeded $1000 in Minneapolis-St. Paul and Salt Lake City and was over $1600 in Baltimore (Council of Community Hospitals, 1983). Cribs, blankets, and diapers also cost money. Child-care costs can become a major item in a family's budget if both mother and father continue to work outside the home. Moreover, as Box 10–1 illustrates, the costs of childbearing can be even higher for teenage mothers.

Career Commitment

American society accepts the fact that some women must work for economic reasons; however, more and more women regard working outside the home as desirable for its own sake (General Mills American Family Report, 1981). As we will explore more fully in Chapter 15, it is not easy to combine a full-time career and parenting responsibilities. Since women still shoulder the larger share of parenting duties, those women committed to full-time careers are more likely to postpone having children than are women less involved in work outside the home.

Number and Spacing

Like the decision as to whether to have children, the decision as to how many to have reflects inner feelings about how we want to live our lives, what we expect for ourselves, and what practical steps we will take to arrange our future in a particular way (Figley, 1973). Currently, most married couples report that they would prefer a two-child family. Some believe that an only child will be lonely, spoiled, or selfish—although there is no research evidence to support this view. The two-child ideal is favored by many couples who wish to have both a son and a daughter.

The proper spacing of children depends on the particular needs and circumstances of each family. However, certain insights offered by researchers may be useful in planning a family. For example, the longer the time period parents take to complete the family, the better their financial position is likely to be (Reimer and Maiolo, 1977). Parents who spread out having three children over 12 years will experience less financial stress than parents who have three children within four or five years (Oppenheimer, 1976). Researchers have also found that the shorter the time period between pregnancies, the greater the likelihood of birth defects and difficulties at birth. Moreover, in the long-term Collaborative Prenatal Project of the National Institutes of Health—which involved nearly 60,000 women and their children—it was noted that children born only a short interval after the birth of a previous baby had significantly lower intelligence than other children when tested at age four.

Certain studies have indicated a definite relationship between children's intelligence and their birth order, with first-borns scoring higher than second-borns and so forth (Belmont and Marolla, 1973). Zajonc (1976), however, suggests that it is the family configuration—how many brothers and sisters and how close in age they are—rather than the birth order per se that influences intellectual development. According to his theory, the negative effects of late birth order can be reduced if there is a large gap between a child and the next older sibling. The crucial factor, then, may be the amount of time that parents have available for each individual child.

In addition to the possible effects on intelligence, birth order and spacing can have an impact on children's emotional development. For example, a child may feel trapped because of her or his position in the family group (Jenkins, 1971). Stephanie, the oldest of four children, resented the responsibility thrown on her for the care of her younger siblings. Ralph, the younger of two brothers, had an unhappy adolescence because his

The two-child family is currently the preferred family size in America.

B O X   1 0 – 2

Research Brief:
Being a Middle Child

Jeannie Kidwell of the University of Tennessee was interested in examining the effects of being a middle child on one's self-esteem. She did secondary analysis (that is, she used data already collected by other researchers for a different study) of a national sample of more than 2200 adolescent males that included personal interviews and group-administered questionnaires. Kidwell divided her sample into firstborn children (27 percent), lastborns (24 percent), and middleborns (42 percent). "Only children" (7 percent) were not included in her analysis.

Kidwell reported the following findings:

- Middleborns have significantly lower self-esteem than either firstborns or lastborns.
- The lowest level of self-esteem for middle children occurs when adjacent siblings are roughly two years older or younger.

- The self-esteem of middleborn males was enhanced if all siblings were female, making each the only boy in his family.

Kidwell explained her findings by use of a "uniqueness theory." According to this approach, firstborns and lastborns have a special status within the family. They receive more recognition than middle children—except when the middleborn is the only male child in the family. This status, through its uniqueness, is associated with higher self-esteem and offsets being a middle child.

Source: Jeannie Kidwell, "The Neglected Birth Order: Middleborns." *Journal of Marriage and the Family,* February 1982, 223–235.

older brother always had greater freedom and privileges. In most families, there are definite roles and consequences associated with being an oldest child, a middle child, or a youngest child (see Box 10–2).

Genetic Counseling

Each year more than 250,000 American infants are born with physical or mental defects that may lead to early death or lifelong illness. Fortunately, it is now possible to predict and prevent many of these occurrences through **genetic counseling**. This service combines knowledge of heredity and laboratory testing to provide prospective parents with the statistical odds of their children inheriting certain diseases or defects. Patterns of inheritance are currently known for several hundred specific birth defects, including Tay-Sachs disease (found in about 100

births per year, mainly among Jews whose ancestors came from Central and Eastern Europe), Sickle cell anemia (affecting one out of every 400 to 600 black children), and phenylketonuria (PKU) (characterized primarily by mental retardation).

The first step for a family in getting genetic counseling is to recognize the need. This may result from personal concern about possible recurrence of a condition that affected other members of the family, or it may be suggested by a physician. Genetic counseling is provided by several types of doctors, among them family doctors, but more specialized testing is performed at genetic counseling centers found across the country.

For example, when Will and Joan were deciding whether to have a child, they were worried that they might pass on Sickle cell anemia. The disease had affected Joan's uncle and Will's second cousin. "If both of us were carriers, we knew there was a good chance our child could get the disease," noted Will. "The people at the clinic asked a lot of questions about both families, took blood tests, examined us thoroughly, and then told us the results. It turned out there was only a small risk in our case, but they really saved us from a lot of needless worry."

By obtaining a complete family medical history and conducting thorough physical examinations, the counselor will be able to tell a couple whether genetic problems are present. If so, the counselor will be able to offer a rather accurate probability forecast concerning the odds that any individual child of the couple will inherit the birth defect. In some cases, the counselor can do little more than offer a general statement of odds. In many instances, however, the forecast can be combined with information about ways of preventing the disorder and medical treatments that can lessen its impact on the child and the family.

Even if a woman is already pregnant, genetic counseling can still be valuable when a birth defect is suspected. Prenatal diagnosis is conducted to detect certain types of birth defects before the child is born. It is made possible by a procedure known as **amniocentesis** early in the woman's pregnancy (between the fourteenth and sixteenth weeks). Amniocentesis entails insertion of a thin, hollow needle into the uterus and withdrawal of a small sample of amniotic fluid that surrounds the developing fetus. Since the fluid contains fetal cells, it can yield useful information for genetic analysis. If there is evidence that the fetus has a serious, perhaps fatal, disorder for which there is no known treatment, parents have an opportunity to decide if they wish to discontinue the pregnancy.

Although amniocentesis has added a new dimension to genetic counseling, it has notable limitations. A "normal" result does not guarantee a healthy baby since many birth defects cannot be detected through prenatal screening. As a result, amniocentesis is recommended only if a woman has an increased risk of those defects that can be measured by this method. Indications of risk include the mother being above the age of 35; having had a child with a chromosomal abnormality (e.g., mongolism) or neural tube defects (e.g., spina bifida); or both parents being known carriers of a gene that causes an inherited metabolic disorder (e.g, Tay-Sachs disease).

Infertility

All of us have heard dire warnings about the problem of overpopulation. Yet, ironically, many couples in the United States and other nations face quite a different problem: they are unable to conceive children. **Infertility**, which is usually defined as the inability to conceive or give birth to a live baby after about one year of effort, affects about one couple in six in this country (Mazor, 1979). Recent data indicate that 15 to 20 percent of these couples will eventually conceive and become parents.

Causes of Infertility

Infertility is generally caused by some physical condition affecting one or both parents. It is estimated that in about 40 percent of infertile couples, the man is infertile (Speroff, et al., 1973). The most common causes of infertility among men are (1) low sperm count, (2) low motility of the sperm, which means that they do not move with sufficient vigor into the uterus after ejaculation, and (3) sperm that are somehow deficient. These conditions, in turn, can be caused by infectious diseases such as mumps or venereal disease, by the failure of the testes to descend into the scrotum, or by the presence of a varicocele (varicose condition of the veins of the spermatic cord). Recently, it has been suggested that exposure to toxic substances such as industrial chemicals may lead to low sperm counts. Certain drugs, among them those used in cancer treatment, have also been found to reduce fertility. Even a high fever from a minor cold can reduce fertility for the 72-day sperm production cycle. Infertility can also occur if the seminal fluid (the whitish, sticky material ejaculated at orgasm) is not secreted in the proper amount, or if an obstruction exists in the seminal passage from the testicle to the end of the penis. **Impotence**, or the inability to achieve or maintain an erection for the length of intercourse, precludes conception. While impotence is often psychological in nature, fundamentally caused by fear, it can also result from sexual inexperience (as with adolescents), use of alcohol or other drugs, fatigue, or debilitating disease (Masters and Johnson, 1970).

The most common causes of infertility in women are (1) failure to ovulate, (2) blockage of the fallopian tubes, and (3) cervical mucus, often called ''hostile mucus,'' that does not permit the passage of sperm. Although a woman may have regular menstrual periods, ovulation may nevertheless fail to occur because of inadequate secretions of certain hormones, a cyst on her ovaries, or a condition known as **endometriosis** (a thickening of the mucous membrane lining the uterus). Of course, if the fallopian tubes are blocked as the result of some type of obstruction, the egg cannot move through them to meet the sperm and conception is impossible. Infertility can also result if a woman's uterus is ''retroverted''—that is, positioned so that it is difficult for sperm to enter (Brecher and Brecher, 1966).

In some situations, a combination of factors in both partners may lead to infertility. For example, a woman may have an allergic response to a man's sperm, causing her to produce antibodies that destroy the sperm. A couple may also be lacking in knowledge and may not realize the importance of timing intercourse to coincide with the woman's ovulation.

Scientific Advances

Medical researchers have made important advances in the treatment of infertility. Many physicians, hospital clinics, and research facilities now specialize in dealing with infertility problems. Indeed, the last decade has seen the use and growing acceptance of such controversial techniques as fertility drugs, sex therapy, artificial insemination, and implantation within a woman's uterus of a human egg fertilized outside her body (the ''test tube baby'').

Fertility drugs are used to overcome infertility caused by a woman's inability to ovulate. However, these drugs have stirred serious debate because, while they stimulate ovulation, they often have an overstimulating effect and cause multiple births. Giving birth to three, four, or more babies at one time is often dangerous both for the mother and the infants; the physical, psychological, and economic stress placed on the family unit can be overwhelming.

Sex therapy has been used very effectively to assist couples who have nonphysical problems that affect their ability to conceive. Difficulties with premature ejaculation, impotence, or a woman's inability to become sexually aroused may lead to avoidance of intercourse. The counseling and support of a sex therapist can encourage better communication between partners; the therapist can also pass along useful information that may counteract people's fears and mistaken ideas about sexuality.

Artificial insemination can be used when the husband, or wife, or both is the cause of infertility. Sperm are taken from the husband or an anonymous donor and are injected into the wife's vagina during her fertile period. If infertility has resulted from the male's low sperm count, this method allows collection of his ejaculate over a period of time. The increased concentration of sperm brings it within the normal range needed for fertilization.

Through artificial insemination, a woman is now able to conceive and carry a child for another couple. This **surrogate mother**, as she is generally called, is paid a fee and agrees to be artificially inseminated with the sperm of a man whose wife is unable to conceive. According to their agreement, the surrogate mother carries the baby to term and gives up the infant upon delivery. Obviously, this technique can lead to many problems, even when used in connection with a reputable fertility clinic. For example, in an increasing number of cases the surrogate mother ultimately decides to keep the child. It is not clear whether she can be legally forced to give up the baby—even if she has signed a written contract with the infertile couple.

The technique of "in vitro" or "test tube fertilization" begins with surgical removal of an egg from a woman's body. The egg is united with a sperm in a glass dish and then reinserted inside the woman. While this method has received widespread media attention, it has serious medical limitations. Some women cannot tolerate the surgery; others lack functioning ovaries or cannot produce healthy eggs. Overall, test tube fertilization has only a 25 percent rate of success (Slade and Biddle, 1983).

In July, 1983, a team of California doctors reported a new advance in reproductive physiology. Two pregnancies were achieved through a technique known as "in vivo fertilization" or "adoptive pregnancy" in which an embryo is transferred from one woman's body to another. Sperm from a prospective father is first placed in the uterus of a healthy female donor. Within the first week of pregnancy, the resulting embryo (a tiny clump of about 100 cells) is moved from her womb to the womb of a second woman. She carries it to term and becomes known as the baby's mother. This technique may be preferable to the "test tube" method since it does not require surgery for the woman who carries the baby to term (Lyons, 1983).

Coping with Infertility

Cara, 34, has been hoping to get pregnant for over two years. She and her husband Don finally decided to go to a specialist to narrow down the cause of the problem. But, before that, it had been hard for either to admit that something might be physically wrong, and the tension between them grew. "We began to fight a lot," reveals Cara, "and not just about this. Once he implied I wasn't a complete woman if I couldn't conceive. That really hurt me, so I got back at him with a crack about his masculinity."

It is important to recognize the psychological stress that an infertile couple may experience, especially when each partner blames the other. Resentment, anger, and the feeling of being cheated tie into feelings of incompetence and self-doubt. Historically, most societies have encouraged fertility and have placed great pressure on infertile couples. Even today, infertility often represents a tragedy—and even a source of guilt and shame—for many couples hoping to raise children.

Pregnancy

The mother provides the total prenatal environment for an unborn baby during the first and most critical year of its existence. Consequently, her health and well-being are inextricably linked with that of the baby.

There is much that a woman can do—not only during these nine crucial months, but even before—to make this environment healthy, nourishing, and free of hazards that may lead to malformations.

Prenatal Care

Every pregnant woman requires good prenatal care supervised by a physician well aware of current medical research. Regular checkups are essential during pregnancy, even if they seem routine and unnecessary. Through knowledge of the mother's health status and medical history, the physician can quickly recognize any needs for special care that the mother or child may have after birth.

In order to encourage prenatal care, many obstetricians and family physicians charge prospective parents a package fee for prenatal supervision, delivery, hospital visits, and postnatal checkups. The fee remains the same even if there is a complication during pregnancy or childbirth. Because good prenatal care is so important for both mothers and unborn children, efforts are underway to make it more available without charge for women who cannot afford the expense.

Nutrition

Most doctors recommend that expectant mothers maintain a nourishing diet (see Table 10–1) rich in protein, minerals, vitamins, carbohydrates, and fats. The mother also needs enough calories to maintain her own good health and deliver a healthy infant.

Although the food supply of the growing fetus comes ultimately from the mother's bloodstream via the semipermeable membrane of the placenta and the umbilical cord, the role of nutrition in the course and outcome of pregnancy remains unclear. Some studies show that when a pregnant woman has an adequate diet, her child will benefit; when her diet is inadequate, the child will suffer (Read, et al., 1973). However, other research suggests that what the expectant mother eats has little effect on her child (Stein, et al., 1972). There is also disagreement about which time period during pregnancy is most important in terms of fetal nourishment. The findings alternately point to early pregnancy (Vore, 1971), the middle three months (Stein and Susser, 1976), and the last three months (Naeye, et al., 1973) as the critical period.

Smoking

As she sits down to relax and enjoy a cigarette, a pregnant woman probably will not realize that she may be hurting the well-being of her unborn baby. Indeed, more and more evidence is available to indicate that nicotine has a harmful effect on the fetus. On the average, the smoker is twice as likely to deliver a low-birthweight baby as the nonsmoker (U.S. Department of Health, Education and Welfare, 1973). *The 1980 Surgeon General's Annual Report* warned that women who smoke "have more premature or underweight infants, suffer more complications during pregnancy, and have more stillbirths. Their babies also are more likely to suffer the sudden-infant-death syndrome, or crib death" (*Newsweek*, January 28, 1980: 83).

Alcohol

The **fetal alcohol syndrome** affects children born to women who drink excessively during pregnancy (Christoffel and Salafsy, 1975; Jones, et al., 1973; Palmer, et al., 1974). It can lead to retardation in growth, motor development, and intelligence. For example, Ruth, always a heavy drinker, became pregnant with Jason only thirty days after giving birth to her first child, Tanya. Overwhelmed by the combination of a new baby and another pregnancy, Ruth frequently became intoxicated. When especially depressed, she

Table 10–1   The ideal prenatal diet

Nutritional element	Food source	Function
Protein	Meat, fish, eggs, cheese, milk, poultry	Vital for growth of the baby. Keeps mother's body in good repair. Greater protein intake needed during pregnancy.
Vitamins	Fresh fruit, vegetables, whole grain cereals, bread	Generally promote good health. Help protect against infection and diseases. Regulate body processes. Needed in greater supply during pregnancy.
☐Vitamin A	Carrots, spinach, lettuce, beets, squash, peaches	Insures proper development of baby's eyes.
☐Vitamin B	Whole grain cereals and breads	Releases energy in food.
☐Vitamin C	Oranges, grapefruit and other citrus fruits, tomatoes	Helps build healthy gums and teeth.
☐Vitamin D	Milk	Develops strong bones and teeth.
Minerals	Milk, nuts, meat, fruits, vegetables, whole grain cereals	Needed for sturdy bones and teeth, healthy blood, and proper regulation of elimination.
☐Iron	Liver, meats, raisins, leafy vegetables, prunes	Prevents maternal anemia and helps fetus develop its own blood supply.
☐Calcium and phosphorus	Milk, cheese, cabbage, nuts, wheat germ	Helps build baby's bones and teeth.
Fats and carbohydrates	Vegetable oils, butter, potatoes, corn, sugars, starches, breads	Needed for heat and energy.

combined her drinking with tranquilizers or "uppers." At birth, Jason's head was extremely small and he cried almost all the time. He even had a seizure while in the hospital. As he grew older, he became extremely restless and had difficulty focusing his attention. Doctors decided the boy was probably a victim of fetal alcohol syndrome.

The degree of damage experienced by the child corresponds to the degree of alcohol in the mother. Currently, there is no meaningful postnatal treatment to counteract fetal alcohol syndrome. By the time the symptoms are apparent in the child, it is already too late. Researchers are not certain exactly how the alcoholism causes the birth defects; it may be that alcohol poisons the fetus. It is clear that heavy drinkers who become pregnant should give up liquor if they wish to have healthy babies.

What about the "moderate" drinker, the "social drinker"? Is it necessary to totally avoid alcohol during pregnancy in order to "be on the safe side"? At this point, there is no clear answer as to how much alcohol is too much. The National Institute on Alcohol Abuse and Alcoholism recommends that pregnant women not have more than two drinks per day. Gynecologist and obstetrician Dr. Neils Lauersen, author of *Childbirth with Love*, recommends that:

- women who are attempting to conceive, or who are in the first trimester (first three months) of pregnancy, should either not drink or drink only occasionally;
- women in the last six months of pregnancy should not exceed a limit of two mixed drinks, or two 5-ounce glasses of wine, or two 12-ounce cans of beer, per day;
- pregnant women should not "save up" their daily quota of alcohol and then engage in "binge drinking." Such "binge drinking" is more harmful than consistent drinking of small amounts (Stephen, 1983).

Drugs

There have been many dramatic cases of damage to the fetus as a result of women's drug use during pregnancy. The most horrifying involved British children born with missing arms and legs whose mothers had taken the painkiller thalidomide during the 1960s. Use of tranquilizers, especially during the first six weeks of pregnancy, has been associated with infants' mental retardation, deafness, and defects of the heart, joints, and limbs (Milkovich and Van Denberg, 1974).

Some doctors advise pregnant women to refrain from taking any medicine—even such over-the-counter remedies as aspirin, cold medicines, caffeine, and vitamins—unless it is absolutely necessary in managing a serious condition such as diabetes or high blood pressure. In 1982, the U.S. Food and Drug Administration required that every over-the-counter drug feature a warning on its package concerning potential effects on the fetus.

When even aspirin and vitamins are suspect, there can be little doubt about the potential dangers of taking such drugs as LSD (Lysergic Acid Diethylamide), morphine, or heroin during pregnancy. Although it has been widely publicized that LSD may damage the chromosomes of the mother or father (Berlin, 1969; Jacobson and Berlin, 1972), the full meaning of LSD studies is not yet clear. Most physicians advise that neither men nor women who plan to have children should take LSD, as there may be later chromosomal damage.

Like LSD, morphine and heroin should be avoided by pregnant women. A mother who is addicted to morphine or heroin at the time of delivery usually passes on her addiction to the baby. These addicted infants must go through a period of withdrawal immediately after birth. This can be quite dangerous; severe withdrawal may end in death (Henly and Fitch, 1966).

Pregnancy and the Couple's Relationship

Without question, pregnancy leads to dramatic changes in a couple's relationship. For some couples, the effect is positive and enriching: the excitement of the coming birth brings a deeper love and tenderness. For others, pregnancy inaugurates a distressing and tense period in the relationship, dominated by anxieties about money, the mother's health, and the heavy responsibilities of parenthood. Most couples experience a little of both—the joy and the pressure.

Role Changes

It is inevitable that parenthood will lead to some degree of role change in the relationship between a husband and a wife. Each couple must make decisions about how they will divide the responsibilities of child care; ideally, child-care planning will begin with serious discussions during the period of pregnancy. Many considerations must be weighed, including each partner's talents and goals and the family's financial needs.

Some husbands take on increased household responsibilities—especially ''heavy work''—when their wives are pregnant (Feldman, 1971). ''I found myself taking on more of my share of vacuuming, carrying groceries, and hauling loads of laundry up and down stairs,'' said one man. ''I believe in an equal-responsibilities relationship, but I really wanted to do what I could to help her through the pregnancy.'' One of the most satisfying aspects of expectant fatherhood is being supportive and nurturant toward one's wife; some researchers call this ''empathetic responding'' (Barnhill, et al., 1979).

Sexual Activity

For many couples, pregnancy begins a time of increased sexual activity. The fears and difficulties of birth control are not an issue, thereby allowing a ''vacation'' from worry and responsibility. Since the procreative aspects of sexuality are temporarily set aside, lovemaking can be experienced solely as an act of affection, enjoyment, and communication.

Some women feel particularly feminine and loving while pregnant, and find they have a heightened interest in sexual activity. Others feel awkward, unattractive, and decidedly ''unsexy.'' The hormonal changes that take place during pregnancy may be responsible for diminished (as well as increased) sexual desire among women.

Men's sexual responses during this period also vary. Some men find their wives' physical appearance unattractive. Others feel protective and reluctant to make sexual overtures; they are fearful of harming the fetus or inciting early labor (Masters and Johnson, 1966). By contrast, still other men experience the period of pregnancy as one of closeness. Intense feelings of affection and tenderness are inspired by the creation of a new life; these feelings are expressed through lovemaking as well as in other ways.

Physicians no longer counsel against sexual activity during the early months of pregnancy, except in rare cases where miscarriage or early labor is likely. However, many doctors insist that sexual activity is not advisable during the last few weeks before the expected delivery date.

Childbirth

''How do you plan to have your baby?'' Only a few years ago, this question would have brought looks of surprise; today it has become a common query. Parents can choose among various options regarding where the baby is to be delivered, who will assume responsibility for the delivery, and certain specific procedures relating to childbirth and delivery.

The Process and Forms of Childbirth

The process of childbirth is divided into three stages: (1) the gradual dilation or opening of the cervix; (2) the delivery of the baby; and (3) the expulsion of the placenta, known as the afterbirth. The length of each stage varies from woman to woman. Generally, the first stage will last about 15 hours for first-time mothers and half that for others. The second stage is shorter than the first, while the third may last from a few minutes to an hour (see Table 10–2 and Figure 10–1).

There are two main forms of childbirth: participating and nonparticipating. In nonparticipating childbirth—the procedure commonly used since Queen Victoria popularized chloroform anesthetic delivery—a woman is sedated during labor and does not necessarily help to push out her baby. The mother's muscles are not relaxed, and she does not stay in control of contractions.

According to Tanzer and Block, most women today give birth by the nonparticipating method. Here is one woman's description of her experience: "On a Tuesday at about 6 A.M. I felt some pressure pains. In midafternoon I called my doctor and at 7:15 went to the hospital. He found me already in labor. About ten he gave me a shot that put me to sleep and I had Tommy at around midnight. The first thing I remember is Henry telling me I'd had a boy. Later I found out that the doctor had told me about the baby in the delivery room and had even shown him to me. But that hadn't registered at all . . ." (Tanzer and Block, 1972: 226–227).

Figure 10–1 The process of childbirth. (*Source*: Haeberle, 1982, p. 91.)

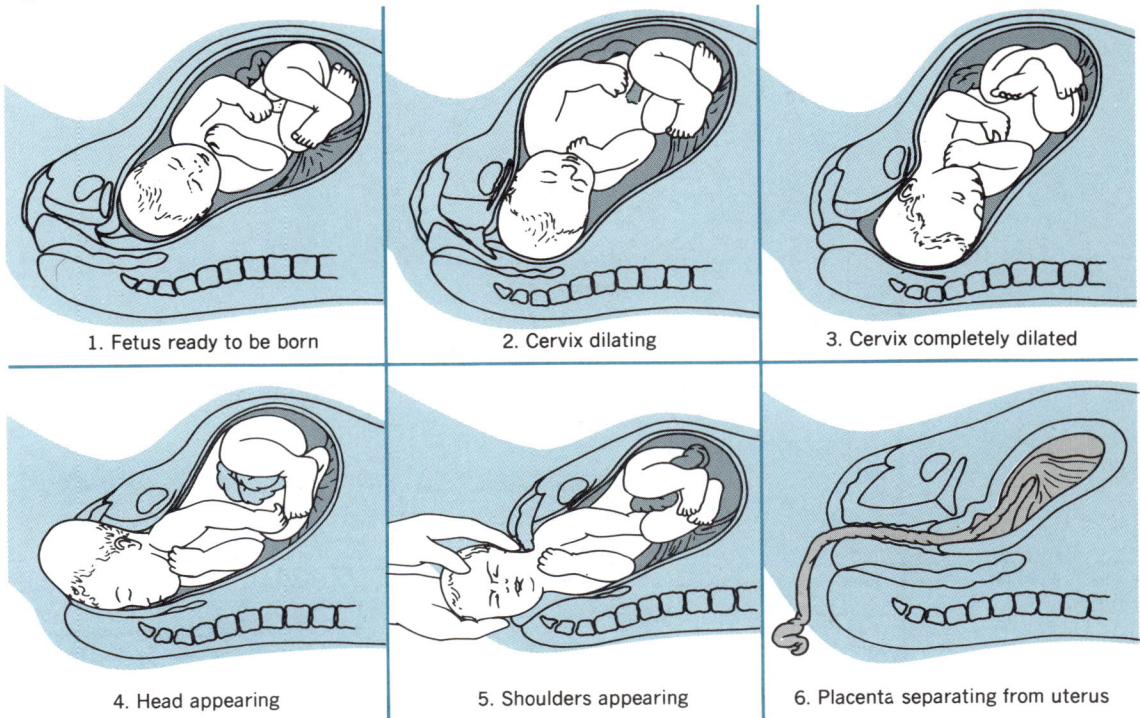

1. Fetus ready to be born

2. Cervix dilating

3. Cervix completely dilated

4. Head appearing

5. Shoulders appearing

6. Placenta separating from uterus

Table 10–2 The stages of labor

Stage	Development
First	As a result of uterine contractions ("labor pains"), cervix becomes effaced (thinned out and flattened). It finally dilates (opens) to about 4 inches [10 centimeters] in diameter so that the baby can pass into the vagina.
☐(1) Early phase	Initial contractions not painful, coming 15 to 20 or more minutes apart and lasting 45 to 60 seconds.
☐(2) Late phase	Reached when cervical opening stretches to 5–8 centimeters. Shorter and more intense than early phase.
☐(3)Transition phase	Final stretching of the cervix from 8 to 10 centimeters. Shortest, most intense, most painful phase of the three.
Second	Begins when cervix is fully dilated to 10 centimeters and fetus has moved into vagina. Ends with birth of the baby. Mother assists in birth by contracting her abdominal muscles and bearing down during contractions. With baby's head out of mother's body, mucus removed from nose and mouth.
Third	Begins with birth of the baby and ends with expulsion of placenta, the organ that nourishes the baby in utero. Umbilical cord clamped and cut. Placenta separates from uterine wall and is expelled along with fetal membrane. Uterus begins to contract and shrink back to normal size.

In "prepared" childbirth, both parents become educated in the childbearing process. Together they attend classes, lectures and demonstrations.

A growing number of women are choosing participating methods, which allow them to be fully awake and involved during childbirth. In "natural" childbirth, women are not sedated. This used to be the only way women had babies, and it is still the only way in some cultures. Under this method, nature simply takes its course: the woman relaxes and allows the uterus to contract effectively.

"Prepared" childbirth differs from natural childbirth in that both parents educate themselves in the childbearing process, generally by attending classes, lectures, and demonstrations together. Special relaxation techniques and breathing exercises are taught to accommodate women during different stages of labor. The mother, therefore, is prepared to give birth without anesthesia but with the assistance of the doctor, the nurses, and her husband. Currently, about 40 percent of all newborns are delivered by the prepared method.

The most popular method of prepared childbirth is the Lamaze Method, introduced in the 1950s by the French obstetrician, Fernand Lamaze. Clarice, 24, describes how her first child was delivered using this method: "When I got into bed in the hospital, Steve was annoyed at me because I couldn't relax. 'Stop fooling around, be yourself! Relax!' Steve kept telling me. After a while I listened to him. He was always there. It was such a comfort to have

BOX 10-3

Research Brief:
Father-Infant Bonding

While there has always been considerable concern about mother-infant bonding as a prerequisite for healthy infant and child development, Brent Miller and Sheila Bowen focused instead on fathers and experiences that might influence father-infant attachment. The authors recorded observations of father-infant interactions in a hospital room 24 hours after delivery. In addition, they collected information on fathers' attendance at preparenthood classes and whether the fathers were present for delivery.

Among the researchers' findings were the following:

- Fathers present at their infants' delivery showed more attachment behaviors (inspection, smiling, talking to the baby) than fathers who were not present at the deliveries.
- There were no differences in the level of attachment behavior exhibited by fathers who had attended preparenthood classes as compared with fathers who had not.
- Even when infants were sleeping during observed interactions, fathers still exhibited certain attachment behaviors, such as holding and smiling.
- Fathers who came from smaller families exhibited more attachment behaviors with their infants than fathers from larger families.

The authors caution that the presence of fathers at delivery may not actually cause more attachment behaviors, but may simply reflect a greater interest in parenting in general.

Source: B. C. Miller and S. L. Bowen, "Father-to-Newborn Attachment Behavior in Relation to Prenatal Classes and Presence at Delivery." *Family Relations*, January 1982, 71–78.

him there. First they took me to a non-Lamaze labor room where my husband couldn't go. I would have been shattered, but he got them to move me into a Lamaze room. It took a lot of concentration to keep up with the contractions and they were getting pretty bad. . . . I was thinking of asking to be put out when my own doctor arrived, all smiles. I had a new spurt of energy, I felt that bearing-down feeling with the contractions and at about the fourth one I had it down to a science and felt complete relief. The delivery itself was nothing. I never felt so happy in my life. I can't tell you the wonderful feeling I had inside me" (Tanzer and Block, 1972: 231–233).

While prepared childbirth classes have focused primarily on the expectant mother, there is recent and increasing interest in the father's role (see Box 10-3). Some researchers believe that the husband's presence contributes to the mother's well-being by providing what Maslow calls a "peak experience," a feeling of extraordinary elation (Tanzer and Block, 1972). Others argue that the husband has his own "rights"—the right to coach the mother in her labor and delivery and the right to take part in the experience of childbirth (Gold and Gold, 1977). Certainly, the idea that the husband's presence is important is not new. As early as 1947, Dr. Robert Bradley advocated "husband coaching" as a calming and soothing influence for women in the midst of delivery.

The prepared method of childbirth is not for everyone. Some women have no interest in delivering their babies in this manner. In addition, certain labors are simply longer, harder, and more frustrating than others. While there appears to be a consensus among physicians that the least medication during childbirth is preferable, childbirth should not become an endurance test for the mother. Many options are now available. Some, in the form of local anesthesia, reduce pain but still allow mothers to actively participate in the delivery of their children.

Complications of Childbirth

Birth is the most hazardous time of life. Some 3.5 percent of American babies do not survive the period spanning the last four weeks of pregnancy, the process of birth itself, and the four weeks immediately after birth. Many of these infants die primarily because of abnormalities arising during the prenatal period which make it impossible for them to sustain life outside the womb. Events occurring at the time of birth also cause a wide range of damage to infants— from death to injuries so minor that they may only show up years later as small difficulties in learning.

While there are many potential dangers in the process of birth, most birth injuries that result in death or long-term difficulties involve the infant brain, which seems especially vulnerable during birth. The two major injuries involve a breaking of the blood vessels of the brain (called hemorrhaging) caused by strong pressures on the head of the fetus, and lack of sufficient oxygen (known as anoxia) caused by the infant's failure to begin to breathe after separation from the maternal source of oxygen. Parents often feel guilty, angry, and victimized when a child suffers such an injury during birth.

In the last few years, medical researchers have made substantial progress in the avoidance of serious birth trauma. A new device called a fetal heart monitor can be placed externally on the mother's abdomen or can be internally attached to the head of the fetus during labor. This device aids in early detection of fetal distress by monitoring the fetal heartbeat. As a result, many babies who might have experienced severe distress are now brought into the world by a surgical procedure, **Caesarean delivery**, in order to prevent prolonged exposure to adverse conditions.

Premature birth can also lead to health-related complications. It is estimated that 7.6 percent of hospital births in the United States are categorized as premature or small-for-date. Because the sight of a premature

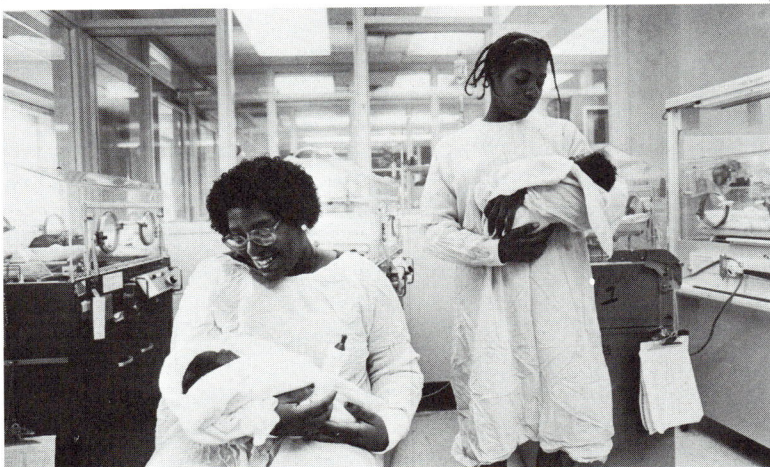

Because premature babies appear to thrive when given attention, parents of these infants are encouraged to visit them frequently in intensive care nurseries, taking time to talk, hold, dress, and help with the infant's feeding.

infant isolated in a hospital is often intimidating to parents, some avoid contact with their children. It is generally accepted, however, that prenatal attention is helpful for the development of such infants. Indeed, premature babies appear to thrive better when given attention than when left alone in incubators. Parents are therefore encouraged to visit such babies, hold them, talk to them, dress them, and help with their feeding (Scarr-Salapatek and Williams, 1973).

The outlook for premature babies is generally better than ever before. A few years ago, miniature babies weighing less than 2 pounds had virtually no chance of survival. Today, through advances in modern neonatal care, such babies are occasionally nursed into normal existence. Moreover, obstetricians are experimenting with new drugs known as beta-adrenergics which can stop and prevent labor contractions that begin as early as the sixth month of pregnancy. Even if it is too late to completely stop the contractions, delivery can at least be delayed for a day. This allows enough time for the injection of steroids, powerful hormonal drugs that speed the development of a baby's lungs.

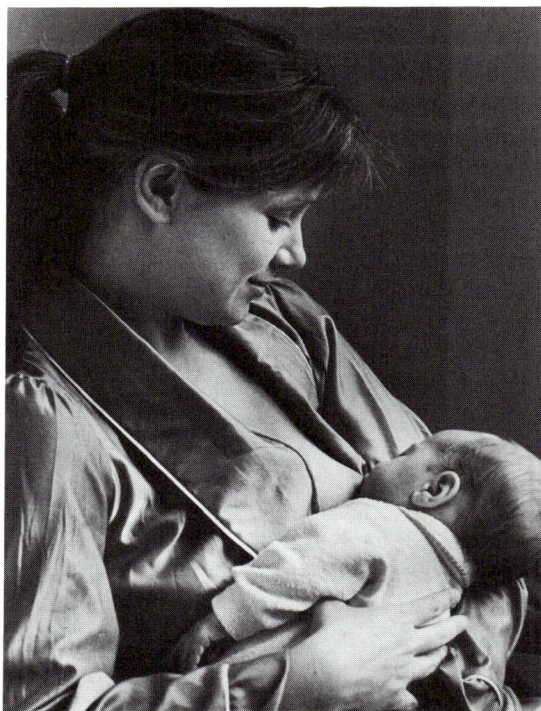

Stressing the importance of the close psychological bond established between mother and child, physicians and women are increasingly recommending breast-feeding as a rewarding and enjoyable experience for the mother.

Family-Centered Maternity Care

The increasing interest of both women and men in becoming more actively involved in childbirth has led to refinements in maternity care known as **family-centered maternity care**. This approach generally involves the presence of the husband during labor and delivery and the conscious participation of the mother in childbirth. It includes prior education of the couple concerning pregnancy, childbirth, and breastfeeding. The entire family unit may become involved, including a couple's other children. Birth may take place in a hospital, a home, or a child-bearing center. The critical consideration is that care is patient-centered, with all members of the immediate family viewed as patients.

Breastfeeding

Breastfeeding is often encouraged by advocates of family-centered maternity care. While babies thrive in our society whether breastfed or bottle-fed, both women and physicians are increasingly recommending breastfeeding as a satisfying and enjoyable experience for mothers. Advocates stress the importance of the close psychological bond established between mother and child. In addition, there are certain health-related advantages to breastfeeding. Breast milk is more easily digested by babies than bottle milk. Breastfed babies are more resistant to disease during infancy and may even have a lower rate of crib death.

Midwives

Throughout most of human history, attending to childbirth has been viewed as "women's work." Even as late as 1910, 50 percent of American babies were born at home, often with the assistance of the **midwife**. Currently, 90 percent of babies are delivered in hospitals, generally by physicians. Yet, with the new emphasis on birth as a family-centered event, there has been a rebirth in the art of midwifery. Nurse-midwives have been accepted in many parts of the nation; some hospitals have such professionals on their staff. Under the "team" approach to obstetrics, a nurse-midwife provides prenatal care and manages the bulk of uncomplicated deliveries. A physician provides backup support and takes over when operative procedures are required.

Alternative Birth Centers

Prospective mothers who want medically safe, family-oriented maternity care can have the best of both worlds at alternative birth centers. These small, private institutions are completely dedicated to the principles of family care; their emergence reflects the growing desire for warm, supportive childbearing environments. As another reflection of this trend, certain large hospitals have established multipurpose labor/delivery/recovery rooms known as "birthing suites." An entire childbirth experience can take place in these suites, which combine the comfortable furnishings of a home with sophisticated medical equipment. If there are complications, mother or child can quickly be moved to other units of the hospital for testing or even surgery.

Home Births

Some couples feel that their own homes are the most natural settings for childbirth. In the years 1972 to 1975, while the total number of births in the United States declined, the number of home births rose by 60 percent (Gold and Gold, 1977). This increase in childbirth at home was, in part, an expression of protest over skyrocketing prices for obstetrical care and impersonal hospital procedures.

Advocates of home birth emphasize such benefits as better treatment of the mother, intimate involvement of the husband, and the immediate, close parental-infant attachment. Home birth also allows other children in a family an opportunity to witness and become involved in a sibling's birth. However, there is a two to five times higher risk of infant loss associated with out-of-hospital delivery. In 1977, in the state of California alone, 79 home-delivered babies died who would have lived if born in hospitals. California also reported 25 stillbirths per 1000 out-of-hospital deliveries, as compared with 9.9 stillbirths per 1000 hospital births (American College of Obstetrics and Gynecology, 1978).

Adoption

Adoption is an alternative way of becoming a parent for those who cannot conceive children; it "involves becoming a parent through a legal and social process rather than a biological process" (Kadushin, 1980: 465). While most adoptive parents select this option because of infertility problems, this is not always the case. Parents with their own biological offspring may decide to adopt as well, sometimes choosing a child from a different race or a child with a physical handicap. Adoptions by fertile applicants who wish to enlarge their families are known as preferential adoptions (Feigelman and Silverman, 1979).

While biological parents require no intermediary in achieving parenthood and need not pass a test of adequacy, adoptive parents depend on agencies and must satisfy their requirements. Once the adoptive process is complete, such parents face all the problems of adjustment and change in accepting a child into the family that other parents face with the birth of a new child. Yet they may feel a greater sense of accountability for their performance as parents and may be concerned with the problem of whether they really feel the child "belongs" to them. Kadushin (1980: 487) suggests that adoptive parents harbor "residual feelings about the unknown hereditary elements behind the child's behavior."

The most difficult and unique problem faced by adoptive parents is often telling the child that he or she is adopted and helping the child to understand and accept this fact. It is generally agreed that it is desirable for the parent to tell the child rather than keeping the information secret forever. The child may discover the truth from other sources, which could endanger his or her trust in the adoptive parents. In addition, their silence could ultimately suggest that there is something "bad" about adoption. While there is disagreement about when adoptive children should be told, most agencies recommend that parents begin gradually introducing children to the idea of adoption at a fairly early age through use of such books as *Why Was I Adopted?* (Livingston, 1978).

The concern with telling is related to another aspect of adoption—increasingly, adoptive children are demanding more detailed information about their roots and possible contact with their biological parents. For some time, Great Britain, Finland, and Israel have permitted adoptees to gain access to their birth records. In the United States, the desire to learn about one's natural parents is most common among adolescents seeking to resolve identity problems (Triseliotis, 1973). However, there is also pressure for information from adults who were adopted as children. As a result, more and more states are permitting access to adoption records if there is a petition to the courts for "good cause." The main problem is that "good cause" has not been clearly defined. On the whole, there is growing support for the view that neither the biological parents nor the adoptee should have an absolute right to confidentiality or disclosure, and that freer access to nonidentifying background information should be granted.

Adoptive parents are not always married couples. In a few cases (especially involving older children), single persons may be accepted as adoptive parents. In general, however, the agencies with the power to determine who "deserves" a child rely on standards reflecting dominant societal norms. Consequently, those who live in communes, who are homosexual or lesbian, or who otherwise violate traditional standards will find it difficult to adopt children.

Adoption procedures can be tedious, time-consuming, and emotionally draining. The anxiety is often severe as you wait to learn if you have been "accepted" as suitable adoptive parents, and if there is a child available for you. Many have found it helpful to talk about these pressures with their spouse, with friends, with a social worker, or in a postadoptive group provided by an agency (Chappelear and Fried, 1967; Pettigrew, 1969; Schwartz, 1968).

The Impact of Having Children

Unlike any other adult role, parenthood is irrevocable; "there are ex-spouses and exjobs, but not ex-children'' (Rossi, 1968: 32). The parenting role is also unique in that there is no gradual shift into the roles and duties of parenthood. One night a husband and wife are alone; the next there is a totally dependent infant sharing their home. Can we say, then, that the transition to parenthood is actually a ''crisis'' event, as has been suggested by some researchers (Dyer, 1963; Hobbs, 1965; Le Masters, 1957)?

Transition to Parenthood as a Crisis

E. E. LeMasters (1957) argued that our culture supports a romanticized view of parenthood which creates unrealistic expectations. Because of his belief that parents feel disenchanted after having their first child, he investigated the effects of a first baby on the marital relationship. In his interviews with 46 middle-class couples, 83 percent reported an extensive or severe crisis in adjusting to the baby's presence.

In this context, the term ''crisis'' is used to illustrate how disorganized or disrupted a family feels (Burr, 1973). In the LeMasters study, mothers reported that after the birth of their first child they lost sleep, experienced chronic fatigue, became worried about housekeeping or their appearance, or gave up social contacts. Fathers reported similar feelings and also indicated that there had been a decline in their wives' sexual responsiveness. Everett Dyer (1963) concluded that the severity of this postbirth ''crisis'' was dependent on (1) the degree of marital and family organization at the time of the baby's birth; (2) the degree of the couple's preparation for parenthood; (3) the degree of adjustment in the marital relationship after birth; and (4) such variables as whether the child had been planned and the number of years married before the birth.

Most couples who reported severe crisis in Dyer's study were able to recover and reorganize their relationships several months after the birth of a first child. Daniel Hobbs (1965) found that 86 percent of the couples he interviewed reported only slight ''crisis'' reactions. The ease or difficulty of making the transition to parenthood may be associated with the parents' perceptions regarding change. Transition to parenthood was found to be less stressful for both men and women when the child was planned and had not been conceived before marriage.

Other factors can also ease this transition. The longer women have been married, the better their health, and the easier their pregnancies, the less likely they are to experience severe crisis after birth. Men are less likely to report disturbing after-effects if they are older and if they view the role of father as important in comparison to other roles. The final key variable is the baby. The child's temperament helps to shape the challenge of parenthood; women with quiet, healthy babies who eat and sleep well experienced less than average difficulty in adjusting to parenting (Russell, 1974).

Both personal and marital stress seem to increase, especially for mothers, after a first baby is born (Miller and Sollie, 1980). The new mother and father are concerned about how they will relate to the child as individuals and how it will relate to each of them. In learning to care for their baby, parents receive input from many sources, including their own parents, friends, neighbors, professionals, and the media. Some of these inputs can be helpful in adjusting to new roles and responsibilities. But, ultimately, the outcome depends on the personal resources of each individual and the couple as a unit.

Whether it is termed a crisis or a normal developmental event, becoming a parent involves many profound changes in behavior. If a couple is unprepared, unable, or unwilling to make the required changes, a great deal of stress will result.

Constraints on the Couple Relationship

The physical demands placed on a couple after the arrival of a new baby are often overwhelming. Sleepless nights, additional housework, and seemingly endless piles of dirty diapers can put great strain on even the most even-tempered parents. Moreover, most new parents are somewhat intimidated by newborn babies and feel unsure of themselves. Their insecurity leads to worry that they will not live up to unrealistic standards regarding being a "good parent."

The availability of effective contraceptive methods (see Chapter 5) has made it easier to reestablish sexual relations after childbirth. Married couples do not have to worry about having an unplanned pregnancy too soon after the arrival of a baby (Aldous, 1978). Nevertheless, many couples find it difficult to quickly and smoothly resume their previous pattern of sexual intimacy after the birth of a first child. The mother may feel disinterested in sex because of hormonal changes in her body, fear of pain or discomfort, or simple fatigue from the strains of motherhood. In addition, she may have negative feelings about herself because of the weight gain inherent in pregnancy. For a man, this can be an especially tense time. A husband and father may feel that he is competing with his child for his wife's attention. This was certainly true for Ted, who had been married to Lisa for five years before Justin was born. About a month after the birth, Ted realized he was feeling jealous of his infant son, who seemed to have become the total center of Lisa's world. "We never have time to play tennis, to make love, even to have a decent conversation," complained Ted. "She's always fussing over the kid. I know he's just a baby, but what about *me*? I need her, too."

As this example illustrates, parenthood can bring role strains to the established husband-wife relationship. In particular, the roles of parent and spouse often come into conflict; the exclusive couple relationship developed during dating and early marriage is disrupted by the needs of the baby (Simmel, 1950). As Figure 10-2 illustrates, the two-way interactional pattern of husband and wife suddenly becomes a complex, six-way pattern when they have a child.

Women are especially anxious about the potential competition between marital and maternal roles, and the danger that their husbands will feel "discounted." New mothers reported higher stress in their marriages after a baby had been born rather than before, and even higher marital stress by the time the baby was eight months old (Barnhill, et al., 1979; Dyer, 1963; Miller and Sollie, 1980; Russell, 1974). As noted earlier, husbands are often eager to assist their wives with physical tasks during pregnancy. Yet, once the children are born, women assume the overwhelming responsibility for home and child care—even when they also work outside the home. In a study by Walker (1971) of 1300 families from var-

Figure 10–2 Effect of a child on family interactional patterns. (*Source*: Adapted from Bigner, 1979, p. 103.)

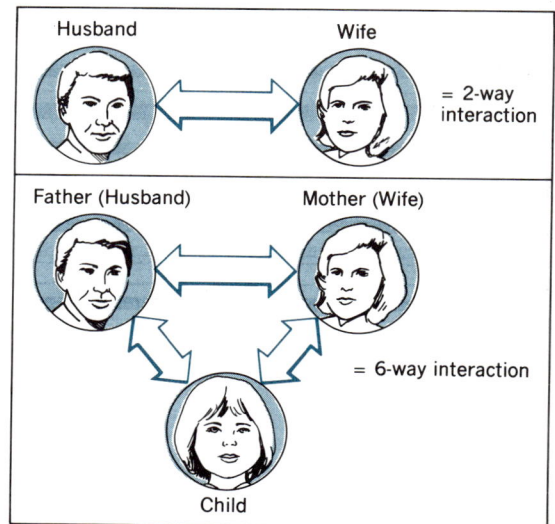

ied socioeconomic backgrounds in which the youngest child was no more than one year old, the disparity in women's and men's household labor clearly emerged. Nonemployed wives devoted 3.8 hours per day to physical and other care of family members; their husbands spent 0.7 hours per day in these activities. Employed women still devoted 2.7 hours per day to these home responsibilities; their husbands' contribution was 1.1 hours per day.

For women who give up outside employment to care for a new baby, there is a dramatic shift in roles. The husband becomes the sole breadwinner and the wife becomes dependent on him financially. The marital power balance (see Chapter 8) is changed (Blood and Wolfe, 1960). Childrearing duties may also force such mothers to withdraw from other roles, such as being a political volunteer. Even friendships may suffer if the mother no longer has the time and energy for socializing (Aldous, 1978).

Summary

Many personal and social goals are involved in the decision to have children. Some couples need to express affection and concern through the parental role; others hope that their offspring will fulfill their own unattained ambitions. It can be dangerous to use childbearing as an answer for other marital problems.

For some American couples, the economic and noneconomic costs of having children outweigh the benefits. Consequently, about 5 percent of Americans have declared their intention not to have children. Their reasons include the desire for more personal freedom, the desire for greater time and intimacy with a spouse, and disinterest in being a parent. Married couples who choose to remain childfree have often been victims of negative stereotyping.

The timing, spacing, and number of children are important considerations in planning for parenthood. Most experts advise young couples to wait before having a first child so that they have time to adjust to marriage. Medical research suggests that the preferred time for a woman to conceive is between the ages of 20 and 35. Most couples report that they would prefer a two-child family. The longer the time period parents take to complete the family, the better their financial position is likely to be.

Infertility, usually defined as the inability to conceive or give birth to a live baby after about one year of effort, affects about one American couple in six. In about 40 percent of infertile couples, the man is infertile. Medical researchers have made important advances in the treatment of infertility through the use of artificial insemination, fertility drugs, sex therapy, and implantation of fertilized eggs within the uterus (the "test tube baby"). Still, an infertile couple experiences psychological stress; in some instances, each partner blames the other.

Every pregnant woman requires good prenatal care supervised by a physician well aware of current medical research. Most doctors recommend that expectant mothers maintain a nourishing diet rich in protein, minerals, vitamins, carbohydrates, and fats. There is increasing evidence to indicate that nicotine has a harmful effect on the fetus. A pregnant mother's alcoholism or drug abuse can also be dangerous for her children.

Without question, pregnancy leads to dramatic changes in a couple's relationship. Some husbands take on increased household responsibilities while their wives are pregnant. Men's and women's sexual responses during the period of pregnancy vary.

There are two main forms of childbirth: participating and nonparticipating. Most women today give birth by the nonparticipating method. However, a growing number of women are choosing to use participating methods which allow them to be fully awake and involved during childbirth. The most popular method of prepared childbirth is the Lamaze Method, introduced in the 1950s by the French obstetrician, Fernand Lamaze.

Birth is the most hazardous time of life. Some 3.5 percent of American babies do not survive the period spanning the last four weeks of pregnancy, the process of birth itself, and the four weeks immediately after birth. Most birth injuries that result in death or long-term difficulties involve the infant brain. Premature birth can also lead to health-related complications, but the outlook for premature babies is better than ever before due to medical advances.

Adoption involves becoming a parent through a legal and social process rather than a biological process. Adoptions by fertile applicants who wish to enlarge their families are known as preferential adoptions. Probably the most difficult and unique problem faced by adoptive parents is telling the child that he or she is adopted and helping the child to understand and accept this fact.

Developmental Task   *Coping with the Role Transition to Parent*

Instructions: Read through the list of Parenthood Preparation Tasks. IF YOU HAVE NOT YET BECOME A PARENT, check YES or NO indicating whether or not you are likely to do the tasks. IF YOU ARE ALREADY A PARENT, check YES or NO indicating whether or not you did the task before your child was born.

Please be honest with yourself.

"Parenthood Preparation" Tasks	Would you or did you do the task listed?	
	YES	NO
I. LEARN ABOUT THE PARENT ROLE BY:		
Taking classes?	——	——
Practice caring for an infant?	——	——
Reading literature on infant care and parenthood?	——	——
Talking to new parents?	——	——
Talking to your own parents, in-laws, friends who are parents?	——	——
II. PLANNING AND PREPARING FOR NEW FAMILY NEEDS BY:		
Preparing baby's room and clothing well in advance of arrival?	——	——

Finding good day care if you need it   ____   ____

Finding good medical care for mother and child   ____   ____

Learning about and following through with good nutrition and exercise   ____   ____

III.   **COME TO AN AGREEMENT ON WHAT YOU AND YOUR PARTNER SHOULD DO OR NOT DO IN YOUR ROLE AS PARENTS BY:**

Discussing who will be responsible for child care and other family tasks   ____   ____

Resolving conflict about expectations or finding ways to minimize the disruptive effects of such conflict   ____   ____

Deciding who will take time off work to meet child-care needs   ____   ____

IV.   **CLARIFY VALUES AND GOALS SO THEY FIT A PARENTING LIFESTYLE BY:**

Timing the arrival of children so they will not be born at times when there are important competing goals (e.g., job promotion requiring more time at work)   ____   ____

Deciding how to allocate personal and couple time to fit new parenting lifestyle   ____   ____

Redefining the couple relationship so both marital and parenting needs are met   ____   ____

Putting personal ambitions in perspective with family needs   ____   ____

Incorporating childrearing goals into a new family lifestyle   ____   ____

EXAMINE AND DISCUSS YOUR RESULTS

Add all the "yes" answers and rank your family:

	"yes" points
Well prepared	12–17
Moderately prepared	6–11
Minimally prepared	0–5

Source: Adapted from Burr, 1976.

Discussion Questions

1. In the 1970s, a popular advice columnist printed a letter from a disgruntled mother who said she wished she had never had children. Reader response to this letter was overwhelming, and the columnist subsequently conducted a survey to discover how common this feeling was. The vast majority of respondents agreed with the letter-writer; they, too, wished they had remained childfree. Why do you think this feeling has become so common? Is it more difficult to raise children than it was in the past? Or is it simply that there is greater freedom for parents to express such views?

2. In your view, when is the ideal time to have children?

3. What is the ideal number of children for a family? Which factors are responsible for your decision: population factors, economic factors, views of personal freedom?

4. If you are a parent:

  a. What surprised you most (pleasantly or unpleasantly) about parenthood?

  b. In what ways were you well-prepared? In what ways were you poorly prepared?

  c. Who has been the most help to you in coping with parenthood?

  d. What do you wish you had done differently?

  e. Which of your decisions and actions are you happiest with?

5. How do you feel about the various forms of childbirth available to today's parents?

6. How would you feel if a spouse told you that he/she cannot have children? Would it threaten your feelings of self-worth? How would you handle the situation?

Key Words

Adoption

Amniocentesis

Artificial
  Insemination

Caesarean Delivery

Down's Syndrome

Endometriosis

Family-Centered
  Maternity Care

Fetal Alcohol
  Syndrome

Genetic Counseling

Impotence

Infertility

Midwife

Surrogate Mother

Suggested Readings

Claus, Marshall H., and Kenell, John H. *Parent-Infant Bonding.* 2d edition. St. Louis, Mo.: C. V. Mosby, 1982. Offers important information on the psychological significance of the circumstances of childbirth.

Fox, Green Litton (ed.). *The Childbearing Decision: Fertility Attitudes and Behavior.* Beverly Hills, Calif.: Sage Publications, 1982. Explores our choices about how, when, and whether to have children.

La Rossa, Ralph, and La Rossa, Maureen Mulligan. *Transition to Parenthood: How Infants Change Families.* Beverly Hills, Calif.: Sage Publications, 1981. A theoretical discussion of entry into parenthood based on case histories of 20 couples.

Leifer, Myra. *The Psychological Effects of Motherhood: A Study of First Pregnancy.* New York: Praeger, 1982. Explores the effects of a birth on the couple relationship, the development of maternal feelings, and the clash of expectations versus reality.

Nilsson, Lennart, Ingelman-Sundberg, Alex, and Wirsen, Claes. *A Child Is Born.* New York: Dell, 1966. A practical guide to pregnancy and childbirth with photographs of fetal development.

Pederson, Frank (ed.). *The Father-Infant Relationship: Observational Studies in a Family Setting.* New York: Praeger, 1980. Five research studies focusing on the father and his contribution to child development

Mothers, Fathers, and Children

KEY TOPICS

—the parent-child relationship—
—styles of discipline—
—the parental roles of the mother and the father—
—parenting the infant, the preschool child, and the schoolage child—
—parenting a child with special needs—
—child abuse—
—incest—

Who of us is mature enough for offspring before the offspring themselves arrive? The value of marriage is not that adults produce children but that children produce adults.

—Peter De Vries

Having a family is like having a bowling alley installed in your brain.

—Martin Mull

Raising young children is far from glamorous. It means endless tying of shoelaces, visits to the pediatrician, and quests for bathrooms in shopping areas. Parents must adapt to the sleeping schedules of their children, arbitrate sibling rivalries, and cope with intrusive childrearing ''advice'' from in-laws. Ultimately, parenting means being responsible for the needs of children even when you feel tired, worried, depressed, and quite needy yourself. The never-ending role of the parent is certainly as difficult as any challenge faced during adult life. Yet, as mothers and fathers commonly report, it brings incomparable rewards. If the strains of parenting are much more intense than many couples anticipate, so too are the thrills and joys.

As we will see throughout this chapter and Chapter 12, raising children can be a stressful experience. In a 1977 survey commissioned by the General Mills Corporation, a nationwide sample of 1230 parents reported that they worried about the job they were doing (Yankelovich, et al., 1977). Indeed, we are living in an age of "self-conscious parenthood" in which mothers and fathers look to experts for guidance in childrearing. Every year there are even more books, magazine articles, and television programs aimed at helping the perplexed and anxious parent.

The prevalence of child abuse and neglect dramatically reflects poor adaptation to the stresses and demands of parenting. In responding to these demands, parents employ three basic coping techniques: (1) reliance on support systems and helping networks, such as day care or assistance from friends and family; (2) balancing multiple role responsibilities by combining parenting with work outside the home and other interests; and (3) seeking assistance from professional sources (such as parent education courses), from parent support groups, or from the media and literature (Miller and Myers-Walls, 1982).

In using a life cycle approach to parenting, we will focus on raising young children in Chapter 11 and on raising adolescents in Chapter 12. In this chapter, we will discuss the use of discipline in the parent-child relationship; differences in parenting styles

based on social class, race, and ethnicity; and the specific roles of the mother and the father. The particular challenges of dealing with infants and toddlers, preschool children, schoolage children, and children with special needs will be analyzed. Finally, we will look at two distressing social problems related to parenting: child abuse and incest.

The Parent-Child Relationship

An old Jewish proverb says that "more than the calf wishes to suck, the cow wishes to give suckle." This underscores the fact that the parent-child relationship represents an exchange: the parent provides love and material support while the child responds with affection and obedience. Ideally, both parent and child gain satisfaction from the relationship.

Sociologists John and Letha Scanzoni (1981) point out that children learn at an early age how to please parents by complying with their rules and commands: "Jeremy, come pick up your toys for Mom!" "Anna, please, it's time for your bath." As children come to understand, compliance provides the basic "exchange"

of the parent-child relationship. For most parents, the goal of this exchange process is to help the child grow to become a healthy adult.

Discipline and Self-Esteem

Discipline is an essential part of raising children. Ideally, parents should assist children in learning to control their own behavior, develop self-discipline, accept responsibility for their own actions, and become sensitive to the needs and feelings of others.

There is no one "best method" of discipline since, in most cases, discipline should be suited to the individual child and the specific situation. Like Dr. Benjamin Spock—whose volumes on *Baby and Child Care* (1945 and 1974) have been the dominant guidebooks for two generations of American parents—Great Britain's Dr. Hugh Jolly (1975) notes that moderate methods of discipline may be most desirable. By contrast, the extremes of too much or too little discipline can produce children who are frightened to move out of fear that they will be punished—or who vandalize the home in the name of free expression.

The terms **permissiveness**, **authoritarianism**, and **authoritativeness** are often used to classify parental styles of discipline, and to define the type and degree of control exercised by parents (Baumrind, 1978). The permissive parent attempts to be accepting and nonpunitive in dealing with the child's impulses, desires, and actions. The authoritarian parent values obedience; he or she favors forceful punitive measures to keep children in their place. Finally, the authoritative parent attempts to direct the child's activities in a rational, issue-oriented manner. He or she encourages a verbal "give and take," talks openly with the child about reasons for parenting decisions, and solicits the child's reactions and objections. Baumrind advocates authoritative control and suggests it

can achieve reasonable conformity to group standards without a loss of individual autonomy or self-assertiveness.

There is general agreement among experts that inconsistent parental behavior is bad for children. This is certainly true in terms of discipline. Studies of delinquency have repeatedly shown that a higher incidence of inconsistent or erratic discipline by one parent or between parents contributes to antisocial behavior, including aggression (Andry, 1960; Bandura and Walters, 1959).

Frightened by the often unfounded or oversimplified reports of how parental mistakes have caused emotional disturbances in children, many parents have turned to the increasingly abundant "how to" literature on the market. They search, sometimes desperately, for the right "technique" that will turn them into perfect parents. However, there is no mystery about the most important factors for promoting children's intellectual, emotional, and social development. Children need parental support, warmth, and acceptance (Walters and Stinnett, 1971), or, in the words of educator A. S. Neill, "love and approval."

Specific childrearing techniques appear to be much less important. If children receive genuine affection from their parents and are confident of being loved and accepted, they are likely to view themselves as persons of worth. They tend to be emotionally stable, happy, cooperative, and friendly; they are also better able to love and accept others (Williams and Stith, 1974).

Consistent, just, and supportive treatment from parents helps children to view the world as a safe, reliable place where they can trust others. If children receive respectful treatment at home, they are better able to develop a sense of **self-esteem**. For example, Herb used to pick up his daughter Laura after nursery school with a grimace: "Not another painting! It's just more stuff for the trash." By contrast, Ned, a friend of

A child who receives genuine affection from his parents and is confident of being loved and accepted, is likely to view himself as a worthwhile person.

Herb's, would talk with his son Paul about each painting and post many of them on the walls of his home and office. Herb made his daughter feel unimportant and stupid; Ned helped his son to feel talented and appreciated.

While in the early 1970s parents were often instructed in specific childrearing techniques, more recent researchers have emphasized general parenting goals. Paramount among these goals is providing the warmth and acceptance that children find so important. Ideally, a reasonable degree of freedom should be combined with firm guidance. Many current books on child care borrow from the best of earlier efforts—for example, from the transactional analysis approach of Eric Berne (1964) or the Parent Effectiveness Training (PET) of Thomas Gordon (1975). The primary emphasis of these approaches was on opening lines of communication between parents and children. Children were encouraged to express their feelings within a supportive home environment.

What about children's rights? Until the nineteenth century, the law regarded children solely as the property of their parents. More recently, children's rights have been widely recognized by American courts. Child abuse is no longer considered acceptable, and there is increasing recognition of children's rights to be free of harassment and harsh punishment at school. In many states, children are entitled to the protection of a lawyer if they have committed a delinquent act that requires a court appearance. Even the great deference once accorded to parents in their choice of medical treatment for offspring is being contested as judges consider whether such decisions are, indeed, in the child's "best interests."

Parenting Differences: Class, Race, and Ethnicity

Studies have indicated that parenting styles differ along class lines. Working-class parents stress obedience to parental commands and adherence to proper rules; middle-class parents are more concerned with the child's ability to make his or her own decisions (Erlanger, 1974). Generally, middle-class parents are more likely to use reasoning, isolation, disappointment, and guilt in disciplining children. Working-class parents rely instead on ridicule, shouting, and physical punishment.

In an interesting study of parental discipline in public places, Brown (1979) found no significant differences along social class lines. Both middle- and working-class parents preferred more restrictive techniques when there children misbehaved in public. Brown suggests that many parents feel they themselves are being judged based on their children's behavior in public places. Such parents may view public misconduct as an "emergency situation" and respond with techniques of discipline that they believe will produce the quickest results—such as hitting or yelling.

The parenting styles of black Americans can only be understood in light of the legacy of slavery. As James Comer (1980: 49) observes:

For three quarters of a century after slavery, many black families . . . prepared their children to accept a degraded position in the society. Parents crushed aggression in children, especially boys. A black father in Texas scolded his teenage son who was beaten for entering a bus before whites: "You know you ain't got no business gittin on the bus before the white folks."

Comer adds that the harsh discipline sometimes evident in contemporary black families is directly related to the black parents' need to " 'beat the badness out of the boy' . . . lest it cause him to forget his place with the white policeman." While such suppression of children was necessary for black survival, it was harmful to the youths' self-esteem and ultimately to their social development.

Mexican-American parents have faced the special challenge of preparing children to survive and cope in a society that is primarily non-Hispanic. Throughout American history, many immigrant groups have been expected to abandon their distinctive cultural identities as the price of acceptance. As T. C. Wheeler (1971: 10) writes:

The sole sacrifice which America has asked of its immigrant sons [and daughters] has been denial of origin, and the consequences of that denial, though often invisible, are real. Changed names, altered faces, dropped religions are but the conspicuous signs of the identity crisis in America.

Some Hispanic parents, concerned about prejudice and discrimination, have encouraged their children to assimilate into the majority culture. They may even discourage the children from speaking Spanish "so you won't suffer like we did," "so you won't be held back in school," and "because you'll never get a good job if you speak English with an accent." However, Mexican-American and other Hispanic parents are increasingly stating a preference that their children maintain their ability to speak Spanish, learn about and become proud of their ethnic heritage, and actively participate in both the minority culture and the dominant Anglo culture (Ramirez and Cox, 1980).

The Role of the Mother

"Suddenly, I had to devote myself to the child totally. I was under the illusion that the baby was going to fit into my life, and I found that I had to switch my life and my schedule to fit *him*. You think, 'I'm in love, I'll get married, and we'll have a baby.' First there's two, then three, it's simple and romantic. You don't even think about the work."

"I hate ironing their pants and doing their underwear, and they never put their clothes in the laundry basket. . . . The worst time of day is 4 p.m., when you have to get dinner started, the kids are tired, hungry, and crabby—everybody wants to talk to you about *their day* . . . your day is only half over."

"I had anticipated that the baby would sleep and eat, sleep and eat. Instead, the experience was overwhelming. . . . I want to do *other* things, like to become involved in things that are worthwhile—but I don't have the physical energy to go out in the evenings. I feel like I'm missing something . . . the experience of being somewhere with people and having them talking about something—something that's going on in the world" (Rollin, 1970: 15–17).

The comments of these three mothers, quoted in a 1970 magazine article entitled, "Motherhood: Who Needs It?", typified the unprecedented questioning of traditional norms about motherhood during the 1960s and early 1970s. Beginning with the widespread attention given to two outspoken books—Simone de Beauvoir's *The Second Sex* and Betty Friedan's *The Feminine Mystique* (see Box 11-1)—an increasing number of women began to wonder about the assumption that women's "nature" dictated that they confine themselves to the roles of wife, mother, and homemaker. Sociologist Alice Rossi (1968), instead of staying with the typical research question of the time, "What is the effect of mothers on their children?", chose to ask, "What is the effect of children on their mothers?"

What is the traditional mother role which feminists challenged in the 1960s and 1970s? Historically, the mother had been viewed as the primary agent carrying out what Parsons and Bales (1955) call the **expressive role** in family socialization. She was expected to remain at home, create an affectionate retreat for her hardworking husband, and offer un-conditional love to her children. The mother was allowed hobbies, volunteer efforts in her community, and sometimes even a paying job. Yet her critical task—dwarfing all others in importance—was to be a good mother to the children and a good companion for her husband. It was her responsibility to build the family into a harmonious and smooth-functioning unit within society (Duvall, 1946).

Has this traditional role changed in recent decades? Only to an extent. Among middle-class families, a good mother is still evaluated in terms of her functions in the home. She is the parent who cooks food, helps little babies, takes care of children, gives kisses, keeps children from doing what they should not do, and yet does not spank. She is nurturing, supportive, an "enabler" who assists other family members to achieve their full potentials (Schvaneveldt, et al., 1970).

Ironically, the changes in family relationships spurred by contemporary feminism—most notably the increase in the number of wives and mothers who work outside the home—has made motherhood even more difficult. E. E. LeMasters (1970), a well-known specialist on parenting, suggests that too much is expected of American mothers not only by society, but also by their families and the mothers themselves. As we will explore more fully in Chapter 15, the American mother now has to be "Super-Mom." Even when she has a demanding career outside the home, she still is responsible for the vast majority of child-care and housekeeping duties.

"Men speak so casually of the magic of being a mother," says Christine sarcastically. "Well, let me tell you about that magic. I work 30 hours a week as a bookkeeper. When I leave work, I'm already tired. But I have to tear off in the car to pick up my son at his day care center and my daughter at elementary school. After we get home, I have to keep an eye on the kids

B O X   1 1 – 1

Betty Friedan on the Feminine Mystique

In 1963, in her pioneering work, *The Feminine Mystique*, feminist author Betty Friedan directly challenged the traditional view that women were happiest when functioning as full-time wives and mothers. Friedan wrote movingly of the dissatisfaction of suburban wives, referring to their anguish as ''the problem that has no name'':

Gradually, without seeing it clearly for quite a while, I came to realize that something is very wrong with the way American women are trying to live their lives today. I sensed it first as a question mark in my own life, as a wife and mother of three small children, half-guiltily, and therefore half-heartedly, almost in spite of myself, using my abilities and education in work that took me away from home. . . .

The problem lay buried, unspoken, for many years in the minds of American women. It was a strange stirring, a sense of dissatisfaction, a yearning that women suffered in the middle of the twentieth century in the United States. Each suburban wife struggled with it alone. As she made the beds, shopped for groceries, matched slipcover material, ate peanut butter sandwiches with her children, chauffeured Cub Scouts and Brownies, lay beside her husband at night—she was afraid to ask even of herself the silent question—''Is this all?''

For over fifteen years there was no word of this yearning in the millions of words written about women, for women, in all the columns, books, and articles by experts telling women their role was to seek fulfillment as wives and mothers. Over and over women heard in voices of tradition and of Freudian sophistication that they could desire no greater destiny than to glory in their own femininity. . . . All they had to do was devote their lives from earliest girlhood to finding a husband and bearing children. . . .

In the fifteen years after World War II, this mystique of feminine fulfillment became the cherished and self-perpetuating core of contemporary American culture. Millions of women lived their lives in the image of those pretty pictures of the American suburban housewife. . . . They gloried in their role as women and wrote proudly on the census blank: ''Occupation: housewife.'' . . .

But on an April morning in 1959, I heard a mother of four, having coffee with four other mothers in a surburban development fifteen miles from New York, say in a tone of quiet desperation, ''the problem.'' And the others knew, without words, that she was not talking about a problem with her husband, or her children, or her home. Suddenly they realized they all shared the same problem, the problem that has no name. They began, hesitantly, to talk about it. Later, after they had picked up their children at nursery school and taken them home to nap, two of the women cried, in sheer relief, just to know they were not alone.

Source: Friedan, 1974.

while somehow making dinner for four. If my husband's in a generous mood, he'll clear the table. He *never* does the dishes. On Saturday, I have to do all the shopping for the week. And then my husband complains because I don't have the energy to go out and party on Saturday night! Party? I just want to sleep.''

The Role of the Father

''I'll never forget what happened when I was ten years old. My mother had just died and my sister and I were standing beside the casket bawling,'' says a 70-year-old San Francisco man. ''When my father saw my tears, he grabbed me by the shoulders and said, 'We're *men*; we're not going to cry. We're going to be strong.' I've swallowed my tears for sixty years and all I've got to show for it is a lifelong lump in my throat and mean memories of my father'' (Pogrebin, 1982: 43).

Traditionally in American society, the role of the father has been that of provider and head of the family unit. As such, he was viewed as having the **instrumental role** in the family (Parsons and Bales, 1955). The father's responsibilities for childrearing were deemphasized; fathers were seen more as a source of discipline than of affection and nurturance. As the example above illustrates, those fathers who valued the traditional masculine attributes of toughness and dominance often fell far short as warm, loving parents.

Today, an increasing minority of fathers are taking an active role in childrearing from the delivery room onward. ''Fathering classes'' sponsored by hospitals and child-care clinics are jammed with men who want to learn how to handle and diaper their infants. Most men now agree that when both parents work outside the home, mothers and fathers should play an equal role in caring for their children (General Mills American Family Report, 1981). Yet, egalitarian rhetoric aside, very few fathers actually play a major role in day-to-day child care.

In past decades, social science research on fathering focused on the father as a role model or on the impact of the fathers' absence as a result of military duty, divorce, or death. More recently, researchers have learned that fathers are important in the first years of a child's life and throughout his or her development (Biller, 1974). In the view of Dr. T. Berry Brazelton, a leading specialist in infant and child care, ''there's no question that a father is essential to children's development'' (Collins, 1979). It has also been shown that mothers can perform better in their parenting functions when fathers provide emotional support (Pedersen, 1976).

There are few significant differences in the way infants attach to fathers and mothers. Fathers can be as protective, giving, and stimulating as mothers; men have the potential to be as effective in childrearing as women. Interplay between father and infant may be distinctive from that of mother and infant (Kotelchuck, 1973; Parke, et al., 1972; Parke and O'Leary, 1975; Parke and Swain, 1976). For example, mothers often socialize with their babies by playing games like ''pat-a-cake'' and playing with toys. By contrast, fathers engage the baby in vigorous, physically stimulating games (Lamb and Lamb, 1976). Mothers more frequently hold the baby as a means of controlling the child; fathers more typically hold the baby in order to play.

Despite differeing styles, mothers and fathers can be equally effective as parents. Dr. Brazelton notes that fathers do not offer ''some qualitatively better kind of stimulation; it's just different.'' In his view, the

Fathers can be equally as effective as parents as mothers.

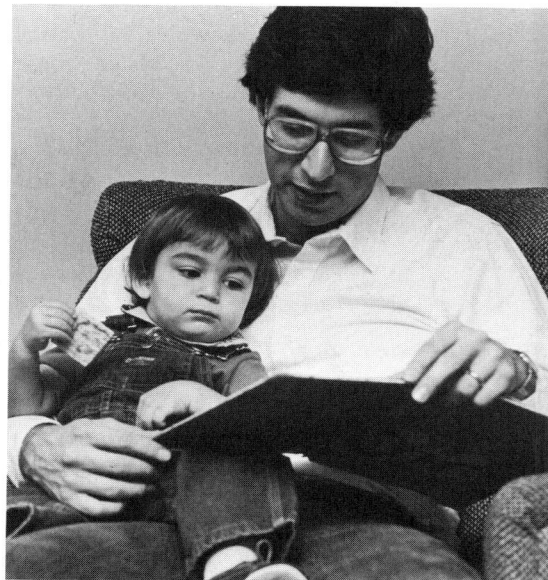

B O X   1 1 - 2

An Anecdote About Fathers and Child Care

Feminist author Letty Cottin Pogrebin, an expert on non-sexist childrearing, reports an instructive anecdote about fathers, mothers, feminism, and child care:

> While a faculty member was introducing me to a college lecture audience, the hushed auditorium was pierced by a tiny child's high voice imitating a fire-engine siren. There was much rustling as heads turned toward the back where a man was trying to silence a baby of 18 months or so. The baby responded with "wrroooeeeee," just as the introducer spoke my name. I sensed the collective embarrassment, watched the father hustle toward the exit, child in arms, nervously patting the child to keep it still.
>
> From the podium, I called after him: "To the father in the back row, please remain with us. If your baby begins squealing during my speech, I will make an extra effort to be heard and the audience will listen a little harder. Although you happen to be a man, you are in the position of millions of women who, because of their sole responsibility for their children, exempt themselves from public events,

or are excluded from places of education or entertainment."

> "When we assume some of that responsibility," I continued, "we help parents remain in our midst. If we have learned to work, think, speak, and listen to one another over the sounds of male technology—over the air conditioners, phones, jet planes, stock market tickers, photocopiers, wire service machines, and computers—we can make an accommodation for the human sound of one baby in a college auditorium."
>
> The audience roared their approval. The father stayed in his seat. I delivered my speech and eventually the baby fell asleep.
>
> A few days later, my husband and I attended a concert in Manhattan. When a baby started mewing in the balcony, its father stayed, but its mother carried it from the concert hall.
>
> Perhaps when more fathers are caretakers of children and more mothers are in control of the podium, family needs will be accommodated in public life.

Source: Pogrebin, 1982: 44.

baby is looking for emotional richness from "at least two different interactants to learn about the world" (Collins, 1979: 181–182). Viewing mothers and fathers as equally capable in parenting could lead to an increase in what John DeFrain and others call "androgynous" or "shared" parenting. In his study of androgynous parents who shared child care responsibilities relatively equally (with neither partner taking more than 60 percent of child-care duties), DeFrain (1979) discovered that these parents enthusiastically endorsed this style of parenting. They reported greater personal happiness as well as better relationships with their children and their marital partners.

Still, the 50-50 family is far from typical (see Box 11-2). Letty Cottin Pogrebin (1982: 46) notes that "in terms of *time* alone, the typical American father has a long way to go to achieve parity parenthood." She notes that in one survey of children's feelings about their fathers:

- Half the preschool children questioned preferred television to their fathers.
- Half the children surveyed wished that their fathers would spend more time with them.
- Only one-third of children of divorced parents said they see their fathers regularly.

But the time dimension of fathering, while significant (especially to overburdened ''Super-Moms''), may not be the central issue. In the view of James Levine, an influential researcher on the subject of fatherhood: ''Where we really miss the boat is when we say the male role is changing, and cite as evidence the fact that men are changing diapers, bottle feeding, etcetera.'' Levine feels the heart of the question is whether the father develops a sense of emotional responsibility for his children: ''It's not just the taking *care* of kids, but it's who carries around that inner *sense* of caring, that extra dimension of emotional connection'' (Collins, 1979: 184).

Parenting Over the Life Cycle

As a child grows up, the demands on his or her parents change dramatically. It is quite different to parent an infant, a preschool child, and a schoolage child. Each stage of child development involves specific parenting tasks that must be integrated into the parent's own developmental challenges. Consequently, both the developmental cycles of the child and the parent influence the changing parent-child relationship.

Parenting the Infant and Toddler

Erik Erikson (1950) calls infancy the period of learning to trust. Parents must help a child trust them by understanding the infant's needs and responding to them adequately. When the baby cries, mother or father will come and comfort it; when the baby is hungry, parents will feed it. If the parents leave the room and both are out of the baby's sight, it must come to know that they will return. This pattern of constant care allows the baby to learn to trust others. As a result, early parental behavior has a crucial impact on a child's future emotional health.

As the child moves into the toddler stage, parents must begin to accept her or his growing independence. This stage of development, which Erikson calls the period of seeking autonomy, builds on the trust learned earlier. The child starts crawling and walking without assistance. Speech also emerges, and not always the words parents want to hear. ''She can't say much yet,'' says one weary mother, ''but she sure can say, 'No!' '' Such defiance of parental authority is possible only because of the child's already-established trust and dependence on the parent.

There are seven basic elements in fostering the physical, emotional, cognitive, and social development of children (see Table 11–1). In addition, parents must attempt to protect the life and health of infants and toddlers. More babies die of preventable accidents during their first year of life than in any single year of the preschool and schoolage period. They may choke on food or other objects, suffocate, fall, or drown. Consequently, it has become common practice to ''childproof'' the home and yard. Medicine cabinets and closets containing drugs or poisonous cleaning substances are locked or closed with special latches. Fences and gates are erected to keep infants and toddlers out of streets and swimming pools. The ''childproof caps'' placed on medicine by pharmacies save the lives of many children. Finally, parents insure that their children are immunized against such diseases as smallpox, diptheria, tetanus, polio, and measles.

While fulfilling these important child-rearing tasks, parents face their own developmental challenges. In the view of developmental theorist Evelyn Duvall (1977), both parents must:

1. *Reconcile conflicting conceptions of roles.* More than one young mother has had to realize that having a child means fewer nights

Table 11-1   Stimulating optimum infant development

Seven basic elements

Provide adequate nutrition—proteins, vitamins, minerals, and other necessary nutrients.

Deal with a baby in distress—with colic, diarrhea, infection, and so forth.

Stimulate in accordance with an infant's needs, tolerance level, and capacity for enjoyment.

Communicate, especially through tactile and conversational contacts.

Provide opportunities for the exercise of emerging sensory-motor functions: feeling, touching, banging, throwing, and combining things, as well as relating supportively with other children and adults.

Encourage the infant's efforts to develop new skills; to cope with problems; and to amuse, comfort, feed, and progressively care for itself.

Continue warm relationships with the mother, the father, siblings, and other relatives and friends.

Source: Lois Barclay Murphy, "Children Under Three: Finding Ways to Stimulate Development." *Children*, 1969, *16*(2): 48–49.

out with friends. A new father must accept the fact that his wife can no longer give him her full attention in the evening. Each parent must reevaluate his or her own role and that of the spouse. Parents must also develop a workable conception of what they expect from the child.

2. *Accepting and adjusting to the strains and pressures of parenthood.* This means learning to care for the infant competently while providing full opportunities for the child's development. For example, a parent must accept that he or she will often have to put the child's needs ahead of the par-

"Childproofing" your home is critical during the years when you have a toddler.

ent's. The child may need to be cuddled or read to at a time in which the parent is tired and needs to be alone.

3. *Maintaining the couple relationship.* The new parents must maintain a satisfying relationship, share the responsibilities of parenthood, and keep alive some sense of personal autonomy. Some couples, for example, set aside regular times for each to be alone and for both parents to be together and away from childrearing duties.

4. *Exploring and developing a sense of being a family.* Parents must find satisfaction in whole-family activities, such as trips to parks or museums, which can be enjoyed by all family members. Some can be shared with other families with young children.

Parenting the Preschool Child

Today the term ''preschooler,'' generally used to refer to a child between the ages of two and one-half and five, almost seems a misnomer. With more and more mothers entering the paid labor force, many children of preschool age spend part or all of the day in school settings—whether they be day care facilities or preschool classrooms. Thus, the issue of separation and autonomy is now considered of major importance in the development of the preschool-age child (Erikson, 1963).

Management of separations is an essential aspect of parenting the preschool child (Rapoport, et al., 1977). In the past—because of the emphasis placed on the value of a child's attachment to a single figure, ordinarily the mother—many parents felt anxious about leaving their young children in the care of anyone else. ''I remember how tense my mother was about leaving me with a sitter,'' says Janet, now 28 and a mother herself. ''It went on till I was at least six or seven. If my parents went out to a movie, my mother would call just before the film started and just after it ended. Sometimes she'd even call in the middle of the film!''

Currently, there is a growing feeling that young children can benefit from many relationships, including those with both parents, siblings, peers, and other adults. Consequently, parents are letting go earlier and are becoming more open to day care and other alternatives. ''My son began day care a little before he was three, and he loved it right away,'' notes Janet. ''I think it's healthy for him to spend time with other kids, even with other adults. He shouldn't be around me all the time; it's not ideal for either of us.''

Another sensitive issue for parents of preschoolers is how to respond to a child's aggressive behavior. Traditionally, young children's aggressiveness was considered naughty or selfish. Parents were expected to punish the ''snatch and grab'' behavior of the typical two-year-old and the quarrelsome, boasting tendencies of the typical four-year-old. For a time, there was a shift toward more permissive treatment of preschool-age children. However, there is presently a shift toward greater firmness in responding to a child's aggressive conduct. Even Dr. Benjamin Spock (1974), author of the classic *Baby and Child Care* and a longtime advocate of permissiveness, now calls for firmer parental guidance.

A final issue of great concern to parents of preschoolers is the child's developing gender identity (see Chapter 3). In the preschool period, boys are more active, aggressive, and interested in objects; girls, by contrast, are more compliant, emotionally expressive, and interested in people. The debate continues about whether these differences reflect biological inheritance, socialization into traditional sex roles, or both (Maccoby and Jacklin, 1974).

Parenting the Schoolage Child

In this chapter, the "schoolage child" will be viewed as the child ranging from age five or six to age 11 or 12. Parenting a child during this period requires accepting his or her increasing independence without deserting the child. As children move toward peer groups and away from reliance on the family unit, support from parents is important. Erikson calls this a time of industry as the child learns to win recognition by performing tasks set by teachers or peers.

For the parent as well as the child, school entry brings with it a new set of experiences. Schoolchildren take their parents with them into the larger community and its interests. "When Sally began first grade, I was basically a full-time homemaker with few interests besides my family and cooking," says June, a black mother aged 35. "Within three months, I found myself chairing a committee for the P.T.A. A year later, I got involved in a city council race because one of the candidates endorsed huge cuts in the school budget. Now, ten years after Sally entered elementary school, I'm on the county board of supervisors. In a real way, it all began when I went to my first P.T.A. meeting."

Although the school environment becomes important in shaping the child's behavior during this period, parents remain the key figures in teaching the child how to live (Mussen, et al., 1969). Parents do, however, face the new challenge of accepting the influence of others, including peers and teachers, on their children. This can be especially sensitive since the schoolage child becomes increasingly aware of social and moral issues (Kohlberg, 1964, 1968; Piaget, 1932, 1948; Wilson, et al., 1967).

Parents of schoolage children have another serious concern: what if Johnny or Janey does not do well in school? The two factors crucial to developing achievement motivation are the child's desire to please his or her parents and the child's identification with parents who serve as effective models of intellectual mastery. If a parent is interested in books or computers or carpentry, children may emulate this example and take an interest in this activity.

Schools can help to overcome the impact of sexism and racism as barriers to accomplishment. Although there is considerable evidence that sex-typed attitudes and behaviors are firmly implanted by age five, both parents and schools can encourage nontraditional options for boys and girls. For example, if a school sponsors a girls' soccer team and gives this project serious backing, girls may learn to enjoy competitive sports and accept athletics as "natural" for women.

Evelyn Duvall (1977) lists the developmental tasks of the parents of schoolage children as enjoying life with their children, encouraging children's growth, and providing for their special growth needs. While parents play an important role in this stage of child development, this period is usually less hectic than earlier stages since household routines have been established and children are not growing as rapidly. By and large, schoolage children are satisfied with their family relationships and enjoy involvement in family activities.

Parenting Children with Special Needs

Webster's Third New International Dictionary (1971: 1027) defines the term "handicap" as "a disadvantage that makes achievement unusually difficult, especially a physical disability that limits the capacity to work." As Newson and Hipgrave (1982: 4) note: "In ordinary language when we say someone is handicapped, all we really mean is that they are weak in a particular area—they may or may not be strong in other areas.'' More than 35 million Americans are disabled or ''differently-abled''—terms preferred to the sometimes derogatory label ''handicapped.''

Parents of a disabled child face a great deal of hard work and stress. The individual child's handicaps, the slow pace of his or her development, the special educational arrangements needed, and the required physical care and companionship combine to create pressures on the parents. In addition, the parent-child relationship may be intensified by the child's dependence, isolation from peers, and, in the case of retarded children, prolonged immaturity.

In some cases, a disabled child will remain economically and emotionally dependent on the family throughout his or her lifetime. Neither parent may be able to look forward to a time at which parental responsibilities have been fulfilled. While the families of disabled children must deal with many differing problems, depending on the type and severity of the child's handicap, all must accept the fact that their children have special needs, recognize the child's strengths and limitations, and go on from there.

Recognizing and Accepting the Problem

Parents who have no handicaps are almost always shocked by the fact that they have given birth to a disabled child. Their own sense of adequacy shaken, many experience a grief reaction and become preoccupied with their own sorrow. Often there is a denial that the child is as handicapped as the doctors insist, followed by a stage of feeling that they may have the ''miracle child'' who will defy all statistics and predictions.

Many parents of disabled children erroneously blame themselves for the disability and take on a heavy burden of responsibility and guilt (Robinson and Robinson, 1965). It is true that certain handicaps may be avoided: those that result from the mother taking a harmful drug during pregnancy (see Chapter 10), from an injury during the birth process, or from a childhood accident or illness. Most parents, however, find some degree of relief when they learn that many factors can interfere with fetal development and that their child was probably damaged before birth by something over which they had no control.

The presence of a disabled child often causes a crisis in a family of nonhandicapped persons (Farber, 1959, 1960). The child is sometimes viewed as an intruder; his or her relationship with the family may be filled with fear, anger, frustration, and guilt. Clinical research has repeatedly shown that the greatest influence on the family's acceptance or rejection of the child is the mother's attitude. If she deals with the situation with reasonable acceptance and assurance, the rest of the family will generally follow her example.

Another important factor in the child's acceptance is the initial explanation given to other siblings, grandparents, and the rest of the family (Buscaglia, 1975). Parents who wish to avoid an unpleasant responsibility will often rationalize that other children are ''too young to understand'' and thereby fail to give them vital information about their disabled brother or sister. Unfortunately, there can be an emotional cost to this avoidance. In one family of a child with Down's Syndrome, the parents decided not to discuss the problem with the two older children before bringing the baby home from the hospital. Subsequently, their four-year-old, greatly disturbed by the baby's appearance, shouted in tears: ''Take it back; it's not pretty. I hate it'' (Buscaglia, 1975: 76).

While many factors influence parents' ability to raise a disabled child, the most im-

If a mother's attitude towards her disabled child is one of acceptance and assurance, other family members will usually follow her example.

portant appear to be their strength, their satisfactions in other areas of life, their economic circumstances, and the specific needs of the child. Studies have revealed that the parents' level of intelligence is an especially significant factor if the child is retarded (Michaels and Schucman, 1962). Thus, in families that highly value intellectual achievement, the mentally disabled child may fall far short of their ideal. By contrast, families that value physical fitness and athletic ability more highly may have greater difficulty accepting a physically handicapped child than one who is retarded. It must be noted, how-

ever, that what is viewed as a curse by some parents may be accepted as a challenge by many others (see Box 11–3).

Effects on the Family

A number of practical problems make living with a disabled child especially demanding. The family budget may be strained to provide special medical care, therapy, or schooling for the child. One parent may have to stay with the child at all times, thus depriving the family of a potential income. Baby-sitters may be necessary for the disabled

BOX 11-3

Facing Cerebral Palsy

Curtis Funk watched as his eight-year-old son Jeremy walk in his distinctive style. He continued watching as a four-year-old said to Jeremy, "Boy, you walk funny." The father felt a flash of anger, but let the remark pass. He decided that, as a victim of cerebral palsy, Jeremy would have to hear many similar remarks in the future. In Curtis Funk's words, "He's going to have to face it."

In medical terms, cerebral palsy means altered muscle tone. When Jeremy was diagnosed at age 18 months, there was no way of knowing exactly what effects the disease would have on him when he was four or ten or twenty. Now, at the age of eight, Jeremy's gait, muscle coordination, ability to use his hands, eyesight, and hearing have all been affected by cerebral palsy.

The Funks, knowing early on that Jeremy's future was uncertain, decided that they wanted his life to be as full as possible. Since he didn't enjoy physical activity, they concentrated on developing his mind. Their effort paid off: Jeremy

is considered a gifted second-grader at the school for orthopedically handicapped children that he attends. He is active in the stamp club and on the school newspaper; he enjoys educational television, Beethoven, and Bach. Only his impaired vision and hearing have kept him from joining a regular class. His teacher believes he will be able to make that switch within a year or two; in her view, "Jeremy will be one of our success stories."

Jeremy's parents take things one day at a time. They wonder whether Jeremy will ever be able to live on his own, but focus on the immediate future rather than long-range doubts. "I don't think too much about it because I don't know," says Jeremy's mother Lois. "Hopefully what we can do is look at him, find his strong points, emphasize them, and not think what he'll do with them. I just want to develop what he's got."

Source: Hoagland, 1982: D1.

child even at an age at which most children can be left alone.

The family's social life is also affected by the presence of a child with handicaps. It may be difficult to visit friends, attend social events, or entertain at home. Even going to church or to a restaurant may present problems since many Americans feel uncomfortable with those who are "different." Strained relationships with friends, neighbors, and relatives sometimes result.

The day-to-day care of the child may require great control, patience, and sometimes the sacrifice of parental goals. Many parents attempt to deny their irritation with children who have seriously disrupted their lives. Some feel guilt because they are more drawn to their nonhandicapped children, and overcompensate with almost royal treatment of

the disabled child. When this occurs, siblings usually feel neglected and resentful. The physical exhaustion and emotional strain of caring for a disabled child can lead to parental irritability, frequent tears, or unreasonable outbursts of temper.

Still, many families cope successfully with raising a child with special needs (refer back to Box 11–3). It is essential that they receive accurate medical and educational counseling; for example, many parents are unaware that almost all states have mandated programs for the education of exceptional children. Conversations with other parents of disabled children are both informative and reassuring since parents are reminded that their problems are not unique. Parents who cope well maintain a positive attitude, make special efforts to plan family outings, and also take time out for themselves to pursue their own interests. They must realize that they do not need to be on call every minute for the disabled child (McCubbin, et al., 1982).

Many families report special benefits because of the presence of disabled children. One father of a boy with cerebral palsy notes: ''Having Jimmy opened my eyes to differences in people. He's so happy, he tries so hard, and he's just as valuable as any other human being. I know I've changed my judgmental attitude toward others; Jimmy taught me to change.'' The elder sister of a retarded child recalls: ''Our family really pulled together because of her. Maria loves music and we began to sing together a lot because it was something we *all* could enjoy. I never felt deprived because of my sister; she's just a special member of the family.''

Child Abuse and Neglect

Stuart looks pale as he recalls his childhood. ''My father began beating me when I was five,'' he says with a shaking voice. ''It went on till I ran away from home at 15. When he had a bad day at work, he'd beat me. When he lost money gambling at the track, he'd beat me. When his back was bothering him, he'd beat me. If my mother tried to stop him, he'd beat her, too. A few times, he hurt me enough that I had to see the doctor. But the terror was the worst part, even more than the pain. All I remember is being afraid. And ashamed, like somehow it was my fault.''

The abuse of children, most often by their own parents, is a major social problem in the United States. Indeed, it may be one of the leading causes of death in young children. The National Center for Child Abuse and Neglect has estimated that there are approximately one million abused and neglected children in this country, and that 365 to 700 children die each year from **child abuse**. However, researchers agree that such estimates are far from precise because of varying legal definitions of child abuse and failure to report cases (Millor, 1981).

Historically, society has not been troubled by the mistreatment of children. Many societies sanctioned practices that we now view as abusive. For example, fathers in ancient Rome were permitted to kill their unwanted children. In nineteenth century London, 80 percent of illegitimate babies who were put out to nurse died; unscrupulous nurses collected the fee and then did away with the infants. **Infanticide**, the killing of babies, has been accepted in many cultures as a means of controlling population size and eliminating children with birth defects.

It is only within the last two decades that significant attention has been focused on child abuse as a social problem. Researchers have revealed that horrifying practices still exist—from babies being dumped in boiling water and burned by cigarettes to children being beaten with baseball bats and electrical cords. Four categories are commonly used to classify the behavior of abusive parents:

- Physical violence, which indicates physically harmful action against a child, such as inflicting burns, bruises, and fractures.
- Physical and emotional neglect, or the failure of the parent to properly safeguard the health, safety, and well-being of the child. Physical neglect may involve the failure to properly feed or clothe a child; emotional neglect, which usually accompanies physical abuse, may take the form of locking children in closets or attics for days at a time.
- Emotional abuse, which occurs when a child is continually ignored, rejected, berated, abandoned, or terrorized.
- Sexual abuse, or the exploitation of young

children through such actions as incest, molestation, or rape.

Contrary to stereotypes, most abusive parents are not incurably abnormal, psychotic, or criminal. Researchers have found that these adults are unable to cope with the stresses of day-to-day life in any other way (see Chapter 17). Their anxieties and frustrations are vented on those who are typically smaller, weaker, and dependent: their children.

An American physician, C. Henry Kempe, coined the term "battered child syndrome." Kempe and his associates at the National Center for the Prevention and Treatment of Child Abuse and Neglect—associated with the University of Colorado's School of Medicine in Denver—have over 20 years' experience working with families in which a child has been battered, seriously neglected, or sexually exploited. They suggest that child abuse occurs in the presence of four factors:

1. The parents have a background of emotional or physical deprivation. Often they themselves were victims of abuse or neglect.
2. The child is viewed as disappointing or unlovable (e.g., the child is disabled or viewed as badly behaved).
3. The family faces a crisis, financial or otherwise.
4. The family has no effective source of aid or communication at the time of crisis, no trusted source to whom they can turn for help.

The first factor identified by Kempe—past history as a victim of abuse—is most often linked to later abusive behavior as a parent. This repetition of abuse from one generation to the next is known as the "cycle of abuse." Yet other factors should not be overlooked. For example, if the child is the result of one parent's former marriage and is resented by the new spouse—or if the child is the "wrong" sex or resembles a disliked relative—he or she may be abused. In some instances, the parent is threatened by the child, who is viewed as a rival, and retaliates with abuse or neglect.

While child abuse cuts across educational, social class, racial, and ethnic boundaries, a profile of the potentially abusive parent has emerged. He or she is usually immature, feels isolated and distrustful, and often lacks self-control. Like their children, abusive parents have negative self-images; they were brought up to see themselves as bad, worthless, and unlovable.

Kempe and Kempe (1978) have observed that infants are typically abused during moments of crisis, often trivial incidences as when an infant's continual crying at night wakes up a parent. The most frequent irritants appear to be messy feeding, toilet training accidents, and crying. Some abusive parents become enraged at such moments, as if the infants' behavior is a rejection of parental love. While clearly not a rational act, abuse is frequently followed by strong feelings of grief and guilt.

Young abused children are said to have a "frozen watchfulness," their eyes scanning the environment for danger while their faces remain immobile. It is as if they can take nothing for granted and must always be on the lookout to please adults and avoid trouble. Of course, not all abused children fit this picture; some are negative, aggressive, and hyperactive. They do not listen to directions, they hit out at other children, and they seem unmoved by disapproval (Kempe and Kempe, 1978).

Most media coverage of child abuse focuses on the victimization of younger children. Clearly, the very young child is more vulnerable since he or she cannot easily run away or seek help. However, it must be re-

B O X 1 1 – 4

A Letter from an Incest Victim

The following letter was sent by a teenager to a researcher writing a book about incest:

To Whom It May Concern:

I am a seventeen-year-old girl with several painful memories of a near-incestuous relationship with my father. (I am not sure if it was total incest in that I never had intercourse with him, although that's what he wanted—it was mainly molestation.)

I have been considering writing a book on my life myself, though I'm not sure how to go about it.

Therefore, I am more than willing to help you, for I feel I have a lot to tell.

The reasons I wanted to write the book are that I want to bring this awful thing to the public's attention so that we can *do something about it. It must stop!*

I would never wish on *any* child what I've gone through.

I know it will be painful for me, but it's worth every painful memory if it will somehow contribute to the termination of incest.

Wendy

Source: Armstrong, 1978: 75–76.

---

membered that older, schoolage children are also abused and neglected. These cases are less frequently diagnosed by authorities, partly because older children are more inclined to cover up parental abuse as a shameful secret. In addition, older abused children may show evidence of behavior difficulties such as hyperactivity, stealing, and school failure, which leads to acceptance of parents' explanations that they were merely ''punishing'' their children. In a study of 100 runaway or delinquent adolescents, 84 had been neglected or abused before age six; 92 had been mistreated or sexually abused in the previous 18 months (Steele, 1976).

Incest and Other Forms of Sexual Abuse

Professionals and the general public often shy away from discussion of the sexual abuse of children and underestimate its severity and extent. Nevertheless, such abuse occurs frequently in our society, especially against young girls. Sexual abuse can take different forms, such as incest (which involves sexual relations between family members), **pedophilia** (which involves an unrelated adult's nonviolent sexual contact with a child, e.g., genital fondling), and rape or violent molestation.

As we noted in Chapter 5, underreporting of incest is considered to be massive. Most experts agree that incest occurs in as many as one in ten families, typically involving fathers and daughters (Fulman, 1984). Many incestuous relationships begin when children are between the ages of eight and twelve; some last over a period of years.

It would be difficult to overstate the emotional damage suffered by the typical incest victim (see Box 11–4). Susan Forward and Craig Buck (1978: 19) note that:

Incest is almost always a devastating experience for the victim. Its emotional and psychological impact is destructive for several reasons—partly because of our cultural reactions to incest, to a greater degree because the child is thrust into an adult role for which he or she is unprepared, and, most tragically, because of the aggressor's betrayal of the child's trust and dependence. . . .

The people they have learned to depend on, trust, and love suddenly turn on them in a bewildering, terrifying, often physically painful fashion.

Forward and Buck add that the devastation caused by incest is especially severe because it occurs within the family environment: "There is no stranger to run from, no home to run to. The child cannot feel safe in his or her own bed. . . . The aggressor is always there."

According to psychologist Rashmi Skadegaard, most fathers involved in incestuous relationships have poor relationships with other adults, including their wives. Such men may be socially isolated, but they are controlling personalities (Fulman, 1984). Ironically, many are devoted churchgoers whose religious beliefs seem to contribute to their incestuous behavior in a surprising way: they feel it is wrong to go outside the family to meet unfulfilled sexual needs. One religiously committed aggressor, when asked by police why he had turned to incest with his daughter rather than an affair or encounters with prostitutes, replied with shock: "What? And cheat on my wife?" (Forward and Buck, 1978: 32).

Pedophilia typically involves children between the ages of two and adolescence, whereas incestuous relationships may begin in toddlerhood and continue into adult life. Incest that continues into adolescence is often particularly damaging to victims because of the adolescent's heightened awareness and involvement in identity formation and peer group standards. The most hopeful note concerning this disturbing social problem is that the long taboo prohibiting open discussion of incest and other forms of sexual abuse of children seems to be dissolving. Programs for the treatment and prevention of child abuse have become more common across the United States.

Summary

The parent-child relationship represents an exchange: the parent provides love and material support while the child responds with affection and obedience. There is no one "best method" of discipline since, in most cases, discipline should be suited to the individual child and the specific situation. There is general agreement among experts that inconsistent parental behavior is bad for children. If children receive respectful treatment at home, they are better able to develop a sense of self-esteem.

Generally, middle-class parents are more likely to use reasoning, isolation, disappointment, and guilt in disciplining children; working-class parents, by contrast, rely on ridicule, shouting, and physical punishment. The harsh discipline sometimes evident in contemporary black families must be understood in light of the legacy of slavery and fear of police. Mexican-American parents have faced the special challenge of preparing children to survive and cope in a society that is primarily non-Hispanic.

Traditionally, mothers have been expected to carry out the expressive role in the family. E. E. LeMasters, a well-known specialist on parenting, suggests that too much is expected of American mothers not only by society, but also by their families and the mothers themselves. The father has traditionally been viewed as the instrumental leader of the family as well as the provider. Recent research suggests that fathers are important in the first years of a child's life and throughout his or her development.

Erik Erikson calls infancy the period of learning to trust. Parents must help a child trust them by understanding the infant's needs and responding to them adequately. As the child moves into the toddler stage, parents must begin to accept his or her growing independence. Erikson calls this the period of seeking autonomy. Management of separations is an essential aspect of parenting the preschool child. Currently, there is an increasing feeling that young children can benefit from many relationships with peers and adults.

The schoolage period is called the stage of industry by Erikson; the child learns to win recognition by performing tasks set by teachers and peers. Although the school environment becomes important in shaping the child's behavior during this period, parents remain the key figures in teaching the child how to live.

More than 35 million Americans are disabled or "differently abled." Parents of disabled children may initially deny the problem or unfairly blame themselves. The greatest influence on the family's acceptance or rejection of a disabled child is the mother's attitude. Living with such a child can be especially demanding for parents and other siblings, yet many families cope successfully with raising a child with special needs.

The abuse of children is a major social problem in the United States. Historically, many societies have not been troubled by the abuse of children. It is only in the last two decades that significant attention has been focused on child abuse as a social problem. The four principal categories of abusive behavior are physical violence, physical and emotional neglect, emotional abuse, and sexual abuse. Abusive parents are unable to cope with the stresses of day-to-day life and vent their anxieties and frustrations on their children. Past history as a victim of abuse is often linked to later abusive behavior as a parent.

Sexual abuse of children occurs frequently in the United States, especially against young girls. It can take the forms of incest, pedophilia, and rape or violent molestation. Most experts agree that incest occurs in as many as one in ten families, typically involving fathers and daughters. Incest is almost always a devastating experience for the victim.

Discussion Questions

1. What do you consider to be the most important element of successful parenting?

2. Do you consider the current expanded role of the mother to be a positive or negative change for most women? Discuss.

3. Are fathers taking an active enough interest in childrearing? What role should fathers take?

4. Would you describe your parents as authoritarian, permissive, or authoritative? Discuss.

5. As a parent, which type of discipline do you (or would you) practice: authoritarian, permissive, or authoritative?

6. Which stage of child development do you think is most difficult for parents: infancy, preschool, or schoolage? Why?

7. What would you find most difficult in parenting a disabled child?

8. Which form of child abuse do you see as most destructive: physical violence, physical or emotional neglect, emotional abuse, or sexual abuse? Why?

Key Words

Authoritarianism

Authoritativeness

Child Abuse

Discipline

Expressive Role

Infanticide

Instrumental Role

Pedophilia

Permissiveness

Self-Esteem

Suggested Readings

Boston Women's Health Collective. *Ourselves and Our Children.* New York: Random House, 1978. Parents' feelings, thoughts, and experiences about the process of parenting.

Brooks, Jane B. *The Process of Parenting.* Palo Alto, Calif.: Mayfield Publishing Co., 1981. Designed for parents and containing practical information of child development combined with a range of strategies for coping with the complexities of parenting.

Harmen, David, and Brin, Orville G. *Learning to Be Parents: Principles, Progress, and Methods.* Beverly Hills, Calif.: Sage Publications, 1980. Presents a complete picture of the current state of affairs in the area of teaching parents how to raise children.

Martin, Harold P. (ed.). *The Abused Child: A Multidisciplinary Approach to Developmental Issues and Treatment.* Cambridge, Mass.: Ballinger Publishing Co., 1976. The consequences of child abuse and how to meet the abused child's cognitive, emotional, and social needs.

Meiselman, Karin C. *Incest: A Psychological Study of Causes and Effects with Treatment Recommendations.* San Francisco, Calif.: Jossey-Bass, 1978. A thorough and readable review of the circumstances of incest and effects on personality development, including material from the author's research.

Napier, Augustus, with Whitaker, Carl. *The Family Crucible.* New York: Harper and Row, 1978. A powerful explanation for the lay reader of the process and theory of family therapy, using a case study of a family progressing through the therapeutic process.

Young, Virginia. "*Family and childhood in a southern black community.*" *American Anthropologist*, 1970, *72*:1, 269–288. A classic study of childrearing among young families in an American black subculture.

CHAPTER TWELVE

Family Transitions in the Middle Years

KEY TOPICS

—how adolescent and adult developmental changes affect family life—
—parents and peers as competing influences on teenagers—
—adolescent sexuality and teen pregnancy—
—drug and alcohol use among adolescents—
—teen runaways and suicides—
—how children leaving home affects the couple relationship—
—the returning young adult—

When I was a boy of fourteen, my father was so ignorant I could hardly stand to have the old man around. But when I got to be twenty-one, I was astonished at how much he had learned in seven years.

—Mark Twain

The newspapers abound with horror stories involving teenagers. Sandra, 14, ran away from her home in the Midwest and was later arrested for prostitution in Philadelphia. Jack, 17, stabbed his father during a bitter quarrel over use of the family car. Leah, 15, became pregnant, had an abortion, and soon became pregnant again. Stan, 16, overdosed on heroin and had to be hospitalized. He barely survived the experience.

With such reports filling the media, it is not surprising that adolescence is largely viewed as a period of turbulence. Yet mounting evidence suggests that these disturbing accounts are far from typical (Douvan and Adelson, 1966; Offer and Offer, 1969, 1972). The process of the teenager's conflict with and detachment from his or her parents actually seems less traumatic than tradition and theory hold.

Of course, the extreme disturbances of behavior described in much of the literature on adolescence do exist. But such disturbances appear to occur mainly in families in which both parents and children expect a sharp discontinuity between the child and adolescent roles, as well as in families in which there is a disdain for parental values. The latter situation is especially common in lower class "disadvantaged" families and in the upper middle class and intellectual group (Hamburg, 1974).

According to popular opinion, the parent-adolescent relationship is much more troubled and explosive than ever before in American history. However, by comparing the characteristics of family life described by high school students in 1924 and 1977, Bahr (1980) found little support for this view. There was no evidence that parent-child conflict occurred more often in 1977 than it had in 1924. One of the two most frequent sources of disagreement in both years was the hour at which students got home at night. But there have been changes since the 1920s: today's parents are much more concerned with improving their emotional relationships with adolescent children, spending time with them, and valuing their opinions and growing independence.

This chapter will begin with a discussion of adolescent physical and emotional development, with special focus on identity formation. Developmental challenges during this period, such as the competing influences of parents and peer groups, will be analyzed. We will examine sexual activity among teenagers and adolescent pregnancy. Social problems affecting adolescents, including drug and alcohol abuse, anorexia, and running away, will be studied. Finally, we will look at how family life is affected when children leave home—and when they continue to live with their parents well into adulthood.

Adolescent Challenges

Adolescence as we know it is a relatively recent phenomenon. Before the twentieth century, children went through puberty and immediately entered some type of apprenticeship in the adult world (see Box 12–1). For example, at one time in the nineteenth century, 40 percent of the factory workers in New England were children. Young girls would work from 4:30 in the morning until 7:00 at night, with only short breaks for breakfast and lunch. They lived in rooming houses, often six to a room (Atwater, 1973).

The best known early advocate of a protected period of adolescence was psychologist G. Stanley Hall. Writing in 1904, Hall argued that adolescence was a delicate and difficult transitional period in which the individual is torn by conflict. In his view, the adolescent must be shielded from the complex pressures of adulthood in order to ensure safe passage into it (Goleman, 1980).

In contemporary Western society, adolescence lasts much longer than was true in the nineteenth or early twentieth century. It begins earlier in good part because puberty emerges some four months sooner each decade (Blos, 1971). Adolescence also continues longer because our sophisticated technological society requires much more extensive schooling. This prolongs an adolescent's financial dependence on his or her parents.

Physical Changes

During early adolescence, concern over one's body image and physical attractiveness is pervasive. Tanner (1971: 907) suggests that:

For the majority of young persons, the years from 12 to 16 are the most eventful ones of their lives so far as their growth and development is concerned. Admittedly, during fetal life and the first year or two after birth, developments occurred still faster . . . but the subject . . . was not the fascinated, charmed, or horrified spectator that watches the developments, or lack of developments, of adolescence.

By experiencing rapid growth and devel-

B O X   1 2 - 1

Before There Was Adolescence

Two generations ago in Kentucky, a wedding took place. The bride was almost 15 years old and the groom was not yet 16. They were given a tract of bottom land by their parents and were helped with the building of their small farmhouse. The whole town turned out for the roof-raising and its accompanying festivities. Merely by getting married, this boy and girl made the transition from childhood to adulthood . . . and found themselves a part of the adult community in which they had both grown up. . . .

Two generations ago in New York City, a nine-year-old girl landed at Ellis Island. Both her parents and all her grandparents had died in Eastern Poland, and she was grudgingly welcomed to the New World by her only surviving relative, an aunt. Pinning up her hair and putting on a long dress, the little immigrant got herself a job in a factory. She enrolled in a night school, first to learn English and later to earn her citizenship and a high school diploma. At 18 she was admitted to a school of nursing, where, on her very first day as a student nurse, she met and fell in love with an intern. Not until they had both completed their training and had been earning a living for a few years did they feel secure enough to invest in an apartment, an office, and the hope of success. They finally set their wedding date when the bride was 24 and the groom was 28 years old.

In the period before and during World War I, neither of these two couples had anything like what social scientists today would call an adolescence. Their grandchildren more readily fit our image of typical American teenagers. . . .

Source: McCandless and Coop, 1979:2.

opment over a relatively short period of time, adolescents are forced to see a redefinition of their body image. There is extensive research showing that the type of body image held by adolescents influences their self-concepts. For example, Gunderson (1965) reported that males of adolescent age expressed a desire to be six feet tall and weigh 170 to 180 pounds. As their own height and weight deviated from these ideals, there was an accompanying dissatisfaction with their own bodies.

The changes that occur during puberty not only affect body size and proportions, but also the maturation of sex organs. While the range of ages at which puberty takes place is very wide for both males and females, puberty typically begins about two years earlier for girls than for boys. The timing of puberty has significant (and differing) behavioral consequences for members of each sex. In general, findings reveal that early maturing boys and, to a somewhat lesser extent, late maturing girls share an advantage (Jones, 1965; Jones and Mussen, 1958; Mussen and Jones, 1957). Early maturing boys appear to be more accepted by their peers. They are perceived as more attractive by both peers and adults, excel in athletic ability, and enjoy leadership roles and enhanced heterosexual status. By contrast, boys who are late maturers may suffer socially because they cannot (or are not allowed to) participate in athletic activities. Their appearance and behavior may bring rejection or isolation from the peer group. When studied at age 17, late-maturing males showed a negative self-concept, prolonged dependency needs, and a rebellious attitude toward parents (Mussen and Jones, 1957).

The case of Shawn, a high school sophomore, is illustrative. The smallest boy in the school, Shawn is still physically quite immature, essentially having the body of a twelve-year-old. He feels "weird." He has adjusted to the constant teasing of his peers, but he is resentful of the impact of his appearance on his social status: "The girls think of me as a cute younger brother. They have no interest in going out with me. Would I be such a better person if I were six inches taller?"

For girls, early maturation leads to problems, especially in relations with male peers. They may be teased about their breasts, and they sometimes develop an exaggerated image of their appearance because of people's reactions. At the same time, if boys show an interest in them and they are responsive, they may face disapproval from parents and teachers who feel it is too soon. While the late maturing female may experience a more negative body image than the early maturer, she often appears outgoing and assured and displays leadership abilities (Jones and Mussen, 1958).

Establishing Identity and Independence

The primary developmental task of adolescence is establishing a sense of **identity** separate from one's parents. According to Erik Erikson (1968: 19), identity provides a "subjective sense of invigorating sameness and continuity" for the adolescent. It means learning "who I am" and "what place I want to have in the world." The adolescent begins to adopt a personal value system, establish short-range and long-range goals, and learn how to deal maturely with authority. As is well known, teenagers increasingly question parental standards and turn to their peers for standards of dress, taste in music, and choice of activities (Stinnett and Walters, 1967).

The task of establishing a sense of identity is approached by adolescents in several different content areas, among them career

choice, political beliefs, religious and philosophical beliefs, sex roles and sexual identity, and interpersonal relationships. It is not unusual for different areas of identity to occupy the youth's attention at different points in time (Abend, 1974; Coleman, 1978). There is often constant exploration: the teenager tries on potential roles, tests them out with peers and parents, assesses reactions to "the new me," and decides whether or not to incorporate the role as part of his or her identity. While peer group pressures are unquestionably important, parents can have great impact in assisting (or hindering) their children's experiments during this critical period of transition.

Reuben Hill (1980) has argued that identity formation is facilitated by parents who direct their children by reasoning, who encourage verbal give-and-take with adolescents, and who value and support their children's growing independence. Such parents provide the security of a home base as the teenager builds stronger ties with peer groups and explores his or her identity. Studies have shown that adolescents tend to identify with the same-sex parent (Lueptow, 1980; Stinnett, et al., 1974).

The development of one's sexual identity is obviously an especially sensitive aspect of adolescence. Janet Chafetz (1974) points out that there is intense pressure on adolescent females to conform to stereotypical notions of femininity. Many teenage girls are encouraged to view the quest for identity as nothing more than the search for a mate; consequently, they may be pressured into sexual relationships in order to attract or "hold" boyfriends. Teen pregnancies, premature marriages, and emotional problems may result.

Kathy, a shy, studious girl, went through a dramatic change when she turned fifteen. In earlier years, she had not been judged as especially attractive either by her peers or by herself. However, on her fifteenth birthday,

Kathy decided that she would become "a real knockout." She slimmed down to a size seven, changed her hair color, began wearing makeup, and bought flashy clothes. Soon she was asked out by a high school senior with a rather wild reputation.

Kathy spent most of her sophomore year partying with her boyfriend's older, more sophisticated crowd. Her grades plummeted and her classmates began avoiding her. A long-time best friend stopped speaking to Kathy, feeling that Kathy had become too slick and superficial. When her boyfriend, a marijuana user, began pressuring her to take hard drugs with him, she abruptly ended the relationship. She then felt totally alone—scorned by both the clique she had joined and her former friends.

Chafetz (1974) adds that the struggle for sexual identity is also difficult for adolescent males. Not only are these youths expected to demonstrate their physical prowess and bravery; they are simultaneously pressured to prove their masculinity through sexual exploits. Chafetz suggests that such pressures often produce a vicious cycle of anxiety and lies about sexual conquests, and contribute to sexual exploitation of teenage girls.

Evelyn Duvall (1977) points out that the racial, ethnic, and social class backgrounds of adolescents influence both the priorities they place on developmental tasks confronting them and their success in achieving these goals. For example, lower middle-class and lower-class adolescents striving for upward mobility may focus on getting good grades in high school so that they can win scholarships to college. By contrast, middle- and upper-class youths may approach high school academics much less seriously, believing they will go to college no matter what because of their families' affluence.

Many adolescents, of course, never even finish high school, much less college. Inner-city teenagers are more sexually active in early adolescence than more affluent peers.

As one result, a significant number of adolescent females become pregnant, cutting short their education and possibilities for upward mobility. Males from inner-city backgrounds who drop out of high school find it hard to obtain employment, and even harder to obtain jobs with decent wages and some hope of advancement. For these adolescents, the struggle to develop a sense of identity clearly takes on a different character than it does for the privileged youth of white suburbs.

Adolescents and Parents

"I can't stand living with them," says Joanne, 14. "They don't understand me, they don't understand what it's like to be young. They won't let me play the stereo; they won't even let me put up a poster of Michael Jackson in my room. 'It's our house, it's our house,' that's all my mother ever says. Don't I have *any* rights?"

"She's telling the truth; it *is* our house," replies her mother, Sarah. "She wants to run her own life; well, she's not ready to. Listen, if I had spoken to my parents the way she speaks to us, I'd have been slapped around till I was blue. When she can support herself, when she's of legal age, then let her do what she wants. But, for now, if she won't respect our feelings, she'll at least obey our decisions. That's the bottom line."

Deliberate baiting and temperamental outbursts by adolescents can tax even the most tolerant and patient of parents. To make matters worse, many adults have little or no recollection of their own behavior as teenagers and are likely to be shocked, angered, or hurt by their children's explosions or what they view as their children's disregard for adult attitudes and values (see Box 12–2). This reaction may be compounded by guilt among parents who feel they ought to be more competent (Lauton and Freese, 1981).

B O X 1 2 – 2

Research Brief:
The Generation Gap: Fact or Fiction?

Many parents of adolescents lament that youth are going astray, abandoning the values and attitudes that parents cherish. But is there actually a "generation gap" separating parents and their children? In a study by A. C. Acock and V. L. Bengston (1980), 466 father-mother-youth triads were asked to state their opinions on nine political and religious questions. In addition, the youths were asked to predict the responses of their parents.

Among the researchers' findings were the following:

- Youths were frequently incorrect in their predictions regarding parents' opinions. Specifically, they perceived their parents to be much more conservative than they actually were.

- Youths predicted that their parents were highly similar in their attitudes; the survey data, however, revealed that mothers and fathers often differed.

- Mothers' responses were found to be more predictive of their children's attitudes than fathers' responses—leading the researchers to question the common view that the father plays the dominant role in attitude socialization within the family.

Source: A. C. Acock and V. L. Bengston, "Socialization and Attribution Processes: Actual Versus Perceived Similarity Among Parents and Youth." *Journal of Marriage and the Family*, August, 1980, 500–515.

But what is a "competent" parent of adolescents? Most experts on adolescent development stress the importance of being loving, compassionate, and understanding. While a teenager's behavior may seem outrageous, it is nevertheless true that repeated assurances of parental love are essential for an adolescent's sense of security and self-esteem. As Evelyn Dùvall (1977: 306) states: "A young person is more likely to accept himself or herself when there is a climate of acceptance within the family."

It is important for parents to keep communications open with teenagers by showing a willingness to talk and listen carefully. Such behavior can serve as an effective antidote to the adolescent's tendency to become isolated. On the other hand, insistence on intimate conversation may be viewed as an intrusion. Teenagers need privacy; most want their own possessions and their own private thoughts and space.

It is sometimes suggested that adolescents cannot and do not want to communicate with their parents. However, in their extensive work with adolescents, Jane Norman and Myron Harris (1981) found that more than eight out of ten could talk to their parents—at least some of the time. Most do, in fact, want to share more of their lives and feelings with their parents. When these teenagers were asked what advice they would offer to parents who wanted to improve their relationships with adolescent children, they replied:

- Listen and understand.
- Be up-front and honest.
- Trust us, and let us learn from our mistakes.
- Do not live in the past.
- Discipline, but do not dominate.
- Compromise.

- Show that you love, care, and will be there.

Every child needs and deserves parental control. By setting limits on behavior, parents help the teenager to know exactly what they expect—whether in terms of household chores or curfews. Yet parental standards must be reasonable and must change as the adolescent matures. As the youth becomes more self-directed and responsible, parents often must work at the task of trusting and believing in her or him.

Robert E. Grinder (1973) has identified two reasons why parents may have difficulty in recognizing an adolescent's need to be viewed as a maturing, responsible individual: the parents' cultural impoverishment and personality constrictions. "Cultural impoverishment," according to Grinder, refers to the problem of anticipating events that the youth will confront in his or her future. This, in turn, leads to fear that recognized values and institutions may not persist, and results in more authoritarian controls intended to enforce conformity. "Personality constrictions" are parents' internal conflicts over the fact that their children are becoming increasingly autonomous and are thereby thwarting the parents' "need to be needed."

Parents of teenagers must walk a difficult tightrope. They must gradually give adolescents more of a voice in family decision-making while at the same time standing firm against unreasonable testing of limits. In the view of Evelyn Duvall (1977), parents of adolescents find this stage of life most satisfying when they do not expect too much from themselves or their children, and are instead content simply to enjoy each other and family life.

The Influence of the Peer Group

In the 1980s, parents often think of themselves as competing with adolescent peer groups in their attempt to socialize and control their children. But are peers as influential as parents sometimes fear? Research supports the view that peer influences peak during the early junior high school years (Costanzo and Shaw, 1970). However, the impact of parental opinions also decreases throughout junior high and high school years. Apparently, then, as teenagers grow older they rely less on their parents' views, but there is no accompanying shift to friends as a source of values, standards, or ideas (Curtis, 1975).

An adolescent's first steps toward independence are explored through the peer group. Indeed, the adolescent peer group serves as a training ground for the development of various skills and social roles. However, there is substantial variation in the effect of a peer group depending on such factors as gender and socioeconomic status.

Janet Chafetz (1974) suggests that middle-class male peer groups expect members to be good (but not too good) in academics, involved in extracurricular activities, competent in athletics, and fairly independent of their families. By contrast, working-class and lower class peer groups denigrate school success and instead value independence, physical courage, and adventuresome qualities. Within female peer groups, there are no comparable differences based on social class. Internal prestige structures are based on each member's ability to attract desirable males as dates or "steadies."

Children who are susceptible to peer influence tend to come from homes in which one or both parents are frequently absent, or from homes in which parents are viewed as less affectionate and less firm in discipline. In the view of Urie Bronfenbrenner (1975: 32) of Cornell University: "Attachment to age mates appears to be influenced more by a lack of attention and concern at home than by any positive attraction of the peer group itself."

Teen Sexuality and Adolescent Pregnancy

As is well known, sexual activity among today's teenagers is widespread (Jones and Placek, 1978; Zelnik and Kantner, 1977). While social surveys continue to suggest strong parental interest in sex education for their teenage children (Roberts and Gagnon, 1978; Scales and Everly, 1977)— and teenagers generally wish they could talk more freely with their parents about sexual behavior (General Mills American Family Report, 1979)—parents nevertheless do not give much formal sex education to their adolescent offspring (Fox, 1978).

To the extent that it does occur, mothers are the primary source of sexual information (Elias, 1978; Fox and Inazu, 1978). Fathers are most notable for their lack of participation in the sexual socialization of their children. Because of the predominant role of the mother, daughters tend to fare better than sons in receiving sexual instruction within the family (Fox, 1978).

Most social science research on the sexuality of young people has focused on daughters and on the importance of the mother-daughter relationship in determining a girl's sexual behavior. Evidence from several studies suggests that non-virgins are more likely to have poor communication with their mothers (Chilman, 1974; Fox and Inazu, 1979; Kanter and Zelnik, 1972). In a recent study involving 449 girls between the ages of 14 and 16, Inazu and Fox (1980) found that a girl's report of her relationship with her mother was by far the strongest predictor of sexual experience. The more favorable the mother-daughter relationship, the less likely the daughter was to have had sex.

What about the influence of peers on an adolescent's sexual behavior? In general, adolescents are more influenced by peers than

Within the family, mothers are the primary source of sexual information; not surprisingly, daughters tend to receive more such information from their families than sons.

An adolescent's sexual behavior is more influenced by peers than by parents.

by parents; not surprisingly, peers tend to be much more permissive in their attitudes (Kaats and Davis, 1970). Peers also appear to be a more frequent source of birth control information than parents. In fact, the attitudes of friends toward use of contraception are related to actual use by a teenager (Thompson and Spanier, 1978).

One study of 15-to-19-year-old women showed that those whose views on premarital sex resembled those of their friends (as opposed to their parents) had more premarital sexual experience. Yet, while a majority used contraceptives, their usage was inconsistent. Consequently, this group was more likely to become pregnant than those teenagers more influenced by their parents (Shah and Zelnik, 1981).

As we noted in Chapter 5, teen pregnancy has become a major social problem in the United States. In the last decade, out-of-wedlock births by adolescents have increased by 75 percent. More than one-tenth of females age 15 to 19 become pregnant; so, too, do approximately 30,000 girls under the age of 15 each year. Moreover, among those who experience teen pregnancy, repeat pregnancies are quite common (Zelnik and Kantner, 1977).

Why has adolescent pregnancy reached such startling proportions? As has been extensively documented, teenagers experience greater pressure to experiment sexually—both from peers and the media—than was true for earlier generations. In addition, many adolescent girls are still pitifully unaware of when and how they can become pregnant. They may actually believe that they will not get pregnant because they have not made a conscious decision to have a child (Kantner and Zelnik, 1972; Shouse, 1975).

Some researchers studying the rise in teenage pregnancy have pointed to such physiological causes as early menarche, the prolonged period of adolescence, and improved overall health among young people (Cutright, 1972; Meyerowitz and Malev, 1973; Rauh, et al., 1973). Others stress psychological factors such as the adolescent's sense of self-worth and family relationships (Abernethy and Abernethy, 1974). In addition, research indicates that lower socioeconomic status is related to increased incidence of adolescent pregnancy. Obviously, many factors influence a teenager's sexual behavior and likelihood of becoming pregnant (Kane, et al., 1974).

Teen pregnancy has many negative consequences for the mother. She is likely to experience school disruption, and her problems multiply if she leaves school too soon. It will be difficult to find a job; this, in turn, will lead to long-term financial problems. In addition, the young mother must bypass many of the challenges and activities of adolescence as she adapts to parenthood. If she decides to keep the child, she will certainly have little time for school activities or socializing with friends. Should she marry the father, marital instability often results (Furstenberg, 1976a, 1976b).

Even pregnancy itself is a special burden for the adolescent mother. Teenagers often ignore critical elements of prenatal care: they may fail to eat properly, may drink too much, or may take drugs. Pregnancy is frequently denied in its earliest stages, which can initiate a vicious cycle placing both mother and child in long-range physical and emotional risk.

Yet not all adolescent mothers are relegated to lives of poverty and disappointment. Some are able to reorganize their lives and to make substantial progress toward realizing personal goals. One key predictor of future success is continuing one's education. Although teenage parents are more likely to drop out of school than their classmates (Card and Wise, 1978), not every adolescent who becomes pregnant terminates her education. In 1976, a federal program gave the well-motivated and achievement-oriented mother an opportunity to continue her education both during pregnancy and after delivery. (See Title IX, Educational Amendments of 1972, 86 Stat. 373; 20 U.S.C. 1681.)

The parents of the pregnant teenager usually respond to the news by getting angry, although this feeling is often accompanied by a strong sense of shame and guilt. Family members may view the pregnancy as a symbol of failed aspirations for the entire family. They may subsequently move toward greater acceptance as the pregnancy continues (Osofsky, 1968).

In determining how to handle an unwanted or unplanned pregnancy, many adolescent females wish to consult their parents. Legalization of abortion laws in the last decade allows teenagers to terminate their pregnancies without their parents' knowledge. Nevertheless, most girls turn to their mothers for assistance in reaching a decision about what to do (Rosen, 1980). Moreover, as growing numbers of unwed and pregnant adolescents choose not to give up their babies, many decide to remain living at home with their parents.

Furstenberg (1980b) discovered that the quality of the relationship between a teen mother and her parents during the pregnancy foreshadowed her subsequent choice of where to live. In households where the parent-child bond was close, the unwed mother was less likely to marry. If she decided to remain single, she usually continued living with her parents for at least several years after giving birth.

Teen mothers were much more likely to remain in two-parent households than in mother-headed households. This may be because more space and greater economic resources were available in the two-parent household. The teen's mother would often be able to stay home and care for the baby, allowing her daughter to resume her education or accept a job. Indeed, the parents of such young mothers often assume a strong role in childrearing. Their support can be crucial in helping their daughters to cope successfully with the stress of early parenthood (Furstenberg, 1980b; Kellam, et al., 1977; Presser, 1980).

What about the adolescent father? While in some cases he chooses to stay away from the mother and child, in other instances he is prevented from seeing them by his own parents, the parents of the mother, or the mother herself. While an increasing number of teen fathers who do not marry the mother are assuming a childrearing role after the birth, this is still the exception. Most adolescent mothers receive little emotional or financial support from their children's fathers (Furstenberg, 1976a, 1976b; Parke, et al., 1980).

Social Problems of Adolescents

The skyrocketing rate of teen pregnancy is merely one of many social problems associated with adolescence in the 1980s. Others include drug and alcohol usage, anorexia nervosa, teenage runaways, and adolescent suicide. In the view of psychologist Elaine Moor, who has worked with teenagers for 15 years, there has been a shocking increase in depression and apathy among adolescents during the last five years. Moor adds that contemporary American society is producing "a huge group of adolescents who are unequipped to make the transition from late childhood to self-sufficient young adulthood" (Peterson, 1983: 4D).

Drug and Alcohol Use

Use of illegal drugs has become a common phenomenon in our society and reached record proportions by the late 1970s. In a 1978 nationwide study of high school seniors, 10.7

percent reported daily use of marijuana and 5.7 percent stated they drank alcohol daily. Weekly or occasional use was, of course, much higher. Moreover, drug use was not limited to marijuana and alcohol. Some 13 percent of the seniors had experimented with inhalants such as glue sniffing; 15 percent had used hallucinogens like LSD; 14 percent had tried cocaine. Other figures were 24 percent for stimulants like speed, 17 percent for sedatives, 18 percent for tranquilizers, and 14 percent for heroin and other opiates (Johnston, et al., 1978).

While American youths may still have a higher level of drug use than adolescents in any other industrialized nation, there has been a noticeable decline in the last few years. While in 1978 one in nine adolescents reported smoking marijuana daily, the proportion had dropped to one in fourteen by 1981 (Johnston, et al., 1982). Surveys first began detecting a trend toward caution and disapproval of drug use in 1980. By 1981, nearly 60 percent of students questioned said that marijuana users face a "great risk" of harming themselves—up from only 35 percent in 1978.

Those who had quit using marijuana reported that they had done so for both health and psychological reasons; 52 percent were concerned about a loss of energy or ambition resulting from marijuana. In addition, students who were users had experienced mounting disapproval from their friends. By contrast, there was no reported decline in alcohol use; 41 percent of survey respondents said they had consumed five or more drinks in a row at least once during the two-week period preceding the interview.

Statistics on alcohol usage by young Americans are most disturbing. In a study of Iowa school children, one-third of the sixth graders questioned reported that they were drinking by the age of nine. By high school, 50 percent of teenagers are regular drinkers;

32 percent drink heavily at least once a week. The consequences can range from serious alcoholism to fatal traffic accidents (see Box 12–3). A December, 1983 report concluded: "While not as publicized as the more exotic drugs young people experiment with, alcohol is still the most misused drug of all by American youth" (Konigsberg, et al., 1983: 80).

Which adolescents are at greatest risk? Studies have suggested that greater involvement in marijuana and alcohol usage is associated with the following factors:

- Greater valuing of independence than of academic achievement.
- Lesser religious commitment.
- Greater tolerance of deviance.
- Incompatibility between parents and friends.
- Greater influence of friends relative to parents.
- Involvement in other problem behaviors.
- Lesser involvement in conventional behaviors (Donovan and Jessor, 1978; Jessor, et al., 1980).

It is often argued that drug abuse is a product of family stress. In a study by Duncan (1977), drug-dependent adolescents were found to experience more life stress than a standard population of adolescents. Barbara Hyde Messer, coordinator of a drug abuse prevention program, notes that adolescence is a period of change filled with anxiety: "There are so many things converging on kids at once. Their bodies are changing, they're exploring relationships, trying to succeed in school, thinking about their futures, trying to figure out exactly who they are. If a lot of adults use alcohol to cope, imagine how easily kids slip into that syndrome, too" (Konigsberg, et al., 1983: 86).

Family therapist Nicholes Weingarten

Studies indicate that by high school as many as 50 percent of adolescents are regular drinkers.

B O X   1 2 – 3

A Drunk Driving Tragedy

The photographs of the five teenage girls spread across the front page of a Boston newspaper looked like an excerpt from a high school yearbook. The young faces shone with hope and promise. But for four of these girls, the future held no promise at all, for they were the victims of a grisly automobile accident . . . and all four were legally drunk at the time of their deaths.

It began innocently enough. They had told their parents they were going to a movie. As their Volkswagen rounded a curve on the highway, rock music blasting from the tape deck, it suddenly swerved across the double line and plowed into an Oldsmobile. When rescuers were finally able to pry the wreckage apart, only one of the girls could be saved.

Soon afterward, investigators revealed what they had found: bottles of vodka, brandy and beer amid shards of glass and twisted steel at the accident site; the driver's license of one girl's 21-year-old sister, which had been used as identification to buy liquor; and enough alcohol in the blood of the dead girls to classify them all as legally drunk. Indeed, the blood alcohol content of the girl who was driving was a staggering .47 percent, a level the medical examiner likened to surgical anesthesia. (You are considered legally drunk when your blood alcohol level is .10 percent, and .40 percent is enough to kill you.)

Their community's shock at this quadruple tragedy soon turned to disbelief. None of these girls were troublemakers; all were, according to their local high school principal, "nice kids."

Source: Konigsberg, Weinhouse, and Wechsler, 1983:80.

(1980) argues that drug abuse in adolescence always reflects some type of family dysfunction. The troubled teenager serves as a "symptom carrier," allowing parents and siblings to avoid their own problems and conflicts by focusing on the "bad child." In some cases, the youth's drug or alcohol problem may actually keep the parents together. Weingarten suggests that effective treatment therefore requires a family-oriented approach in which the adolescent abuser is viewed as trying to help the family in some way through his or her behavior.

Anorexia

"I was dying. I was starving to death. I could not walk because there was no fat in my feet. I could not sit for more than ten minutes because my bones would hurt—I had nothing to sit on. I had acute chest pains. You could see all the veins in my body." These are the words of Ellen, a young woman from a privileged background who became a victim at age 15 of the disorder **anorexia nervosa**. By her third year of college, five-foot-tall Ellen had starved herself down to 70 pounds (*U.S. News and World Report*, August, 1982: 47).

Anorexia was first observed in 1689 when an English physician began treating a woman he described as "a skeleton only clad with skin." Currently, the disorder is found in at least 1 percent of American women aged 12 to 25. Some observers believe that the true number of anorexics could exceed 500,000, some 95 percent of whom are female. The typical victim of the disorder is a young woman from a middle- or upper-class home who was always considered the perfect child—intelligent, attractive, well-behaved, successful in school.

A related eating disorder, bulimia, involves gorging on food followed by self-induced vomiting. One victim, Barbara, reports: "I used to eat incredible amounts of food and even take food from garbage cans. . . . I was vomiting 10 to 12 times a day, so much that the acid was eating away my teeth. It is a disease as real as leprosy" (*U.S. News and World Report*, August 30, 1982: 48).

Why do young women turn to anorexia and bulimia? One view is that they have found it difficult to establish independent identities within their families, and are desperately trying to assert power by controlling their diets and bodies. It must also be noted that the ideal female form in the United States is quite thin, an image perpetuated by fashion magazines appealing to women. Julie, a recovered anorexic, admits: "I thought I could be more popular with my friends and like myself better if I was as thin as those models" (*U.S. News and World Report*, August 30, 1982: 48).

Teen Runaways

The General Accounting Office of the federal government has estimated that at least one million American children are absent from their homes each year. Roughly half are runaways who voluntarily leave at an average age of 15; the rest are "push outs" who are forced to leave by their parents. The vast majority of teen runaways return home within two days, but thousands stay away for weeks, months, or even years and are classified as "missing persons" (Mann, 1983).

The 1974 passage of a federal law, the Runaway Youth Act, was a dramatic sign of nationwide concern about this growing social problem. The act provides funds for shelters and for counseling of runaway teenagers. It also finances a toll-free telephone number that adolescents can call for assistance if they are considering running away from home or already have.

Running away may be an attempt to communicate frustration, a demand for independence, or an escape from an intolerable home environment. While girls run away almost as frequently as boys, they tend to have different reasons for doing so. Boys often are reacting to the absence of sufficient control, whereas girls may be repelled by too much control in the home (Wolk and Brandon, 1977). Dr. Martin H. Stein, medical director of a Virginia treatment center, observes: "The problem in getting through to runaways is that, on the surface at least, most have what look like perfectly good reasons for leaving." Many come from homes destroyed by alcoholism, beatings, or sexual abuse (Mann, 1983: 64).

Homeless juveniles often travel to large cities or beach towns. Their lives are typically characterized by hitchhiking, shoplifting, searching for odd jobs, panhandling, use of drugs, and work as prostitutes. Robbie Callaway, executive director of the National Youth Work Alliance, reports that "the incidence of criminal activity rises sharply with the length of time a kid is away from home." Almost all youths on the road for more than two weeks become either the perpetrator or the victim of a crime (Mann, 1983: 64).

Suicide

Alicia was an outstanding 18-year-old, a high school cheerleader, president of her school's honor society chapter, and generally popular with peers and adults. An outgoing young woman, Alicia had been despondent over the death of her cousin and best friend, Amy, in an auto accident. She began spending a great deal of time alone in her room. One night, after a serious quarrel with her boyfriend over their respective college plans, Alicia went into her closet and hung herself.

Statistics indicate that at least 7,000 American teenagers kill themselves annually, while as many as 400,000 attempt suicide. While the highest rate of suicide in this country is among persons 80 years old and over, the second highest group is aged 15 to 19. In fact, suicide for persons 24 years and under has increased by 250 percent in the last two decades. Among adolescents, the 18-year-old leaving home for the first semester of college shows the highest rate of suicide. The separation anxiety is clearly much more troubling than many youths anticipate (Comer, 1982; Giffen and Felsenthal, 1983; Thornton, 1983).

Suicide attempts are obviously the most drastic and desperate actions that teenagers can take to show their frustration or independence. Adolescents attempt or commit suicide for the same reasons that adults do: the end of an intimate relationship, the death of a friend, a self-image as a failure, a feeling of helplessness. Stressful relationships with parents or a history of child abuse can also be contributing factors to adolescent suicide. Psychologist Michael Peck, an expert on the problem, suggests that we are witnessing an epidemic of suicidal communication among the young: "It is a way of saying: 'Someone help me.' Youths are desperate, unhappy, confused and compulsive. They can't think of any other way out" (Thornton, 1983: 66).

Adolescence and Family Transitions

As children approach late adolescence, a family faces important transitions. The teenager may leave home, thereby leaving parents with a childless "empty nest." Or the adolescent may continue living at home as a younger adult, sometimes for an indefinite period. In either case, parents are not merely reacting to the child's presence or absence; they are simultaneously experiencing other transitions and changes as they reach middle age.

Launching

Lydia, 18, had a bitter argument with her parents about how late she could stay out. The next day, she left their home in the suburbs of Toronto and moved into an apartment in the city with three friends. She knows her parents are upset about her departure and concerned about how she will support herself. In candid moments, Lydia admits that she, too, is frightened about her future. But she adds: "I want people to see I'm not a child anymore. I felt confined at home, overprotected. You can't be a human being if you can't live your own life" (Goleman, 1980: 53).

The stage of the family life cycle known as **launching** occurs when the children leave their parental home. It begins when the first child departs and ends when all children are gone (the **empty nest**). The launching stage may be brief in a one-child family; it may last for many years if there are five or six children or if one continues to live at home as a young adult.

Evelyn Duvall (1977: 322) suggests that "the major family goal" of the period of launching "is the reorganization of the family into a continuing unity while releasing matured and maturing young people into lives of their own." This is complicated, however, by the fact that our society has no fixed time at which children are expected to move out. The timing of any child's launching is flexible, depending on various social and economic factors. While some young adults leave home at the completion of high school in order to live in a college dormitory or to share an apartment with a friend, others prefer to wait until they have married and are ready to begin their own families.

According to current family research, the

meaning of a child's leaving home needs to be understood in terms of its impact on the family as a whole. Just as this passage has great psychological significance for the child, it has major consequences for the parents' sense of purpose. As Goleman (1980: 61) points out, parental worries about a child's departure may actually "reveal more self-doubt than realistic concern." For example, a parent who says a 20-year-old daughter is too immature to live on her own may actually be afraid that life without the child at home will be meaningless.

For the young person being launched, this is a highly stressful period. Psychologist Joseph Adelson, director of a clinic at the University of Michigan, notes that "leaving home can be catastrophic. It's an underrecognized problem. . . . When students . . . leave home for college, they often regress, become anxious. They sometimes come unraveled" (Goleman, 1980: 53). Havighurst (1972: 83) adds that "early adulthood is the most individualistic period of life, and the loneliest one." The young adult must begin to tackle the most important tasks of life, often with a minimum of assistance.

This stress can take its toll. We noted earlier that 18-year-olds in their first semester of college have a disturbing rate of suicide. Other newly launched adolescents may attempt to escape the decision-making of early adulthood by use of alcohol or drugs. Still, most are able to cope with this demanding transition period. They get an education and choose a vocation; they find a mate or establish autonomy as single persons.

Parents at Midlife

Midlife is a time of uncertainty for many American men and women. The pervasive emphasis on youth in our society can be difficult for those in their forties and fifties who are trying to maintain a positive self-image. Midlife is stressful not only because children are departing the nest (or remaining too long); there is also the growing recognition that one is aging and life is not forever. Illnesses increase, friends and acquaintances die, and the middle-aged man or woman realizes that there is only a limited time left to fulfill unattained goals (Zacks, 1980).

Reevaluation of one's past accomplishments and failures is common during the midlife period. If the individual decides that her or his life has had little significance, the result may be immediate and dramatic changes. These may be constructive (beginning a new career) or destructive (excessive use of alcohol and drugs). Some adults initiate extramarital affairs in midlife; there is a very high divorce rate at this time.

Zacks (1980) has identified three typical individuals who experience midlife transition problems:

- The married man. Having worked hard for decades to establish himself in his career and support his family, he is suddenly filled with doubts about his past decisions.

- The married woman. Having devoted herself to home and family, she becomes restless and unhappy as her children no longer seem to need her. She is often driven by an urgent desire to do something before it is too late.

- The career woman. Having focused on professional advancement, she may suddenly miss the family she never had.

There is serious debate, however, about whether the midlife stage should properly be viewed as a period of crisis. While both popular and academic writers accept this judgment about midlife (Feldman and Feldman, 1975; LeShan, 1974; Levinson, et al., 1978; Sheehy, 1974), others challenge the validity of their arguments (Brim, 1976). Bernice Neugarten (1976), for example, emphasizes that the events that typically occur in midlife—including aging and launching—

Midlife transitions can be difficult for the married woman who, having devoted herself to home and family, suddenly becomes restless as her children no longer need her.

the future with great enthusiasm'' (Baruch, et al., 1980: 196–201).

Neugarten's view of midlife explains the severe problems experienced by the growing number of **"displaced homemakers"** who find themselves divorced or widowed in their middle years. Most married with the expectation that they would stay married throughout their lives; many depended on their husbands for financial support. Suddenly, in midlife, they are faced with the unexpected challenge of becoming emotionally and economically self-sufficient. While this is difficult enough for a "launched" adolescent, it is often even more difficult for a middle-aged woman unaccustomed to being on her own (Targ, 1979).

An Empty Nest

The empty nest—the stage at which children have departed from the family home—has often been considered a time of stress for parents, especially older parents (Harkins, 1978). Generally, it has been viewed as more stressful for the mother, particularly when she has devoted most of her adult years exclusively to childrearing (Bart, 1975; Lowenthal and Chiriboga, 1972; Perrucci and Barg, 1974). However, other research suggests that this stage brings positive changes for many couples. As one parent said, "The nest may be empty but it sure is comfortable" (Miller and Myers-Walls, 1983).

Helen and Frank, for example, found that when their youngest daughter moved out to go to college, "it was strange at first, so quiet. We could suddenly be free to spend time by ourselves without worrying about the kids." Helen decided to go back to school and ultimately began a new career in social work. Frank cut down on his working hours and devoted more attention than ever before to his long-time hobby, portrait painting.

For women in particular, the empty nest

do not constitute a crisis because they are expected and gradual.

In line with this approach, research has revealed that many women report a marked increase in self-esteem during their midlife years. Judy, 41, says, "I spent my life from 30 to 40 watching a group of children go from birth to being fairly independent. Now I will have increasing time and my activities are going to be very interesting." Carolyn, the coordinator of a women's studies program, reports: "It is marvelous to be 53. It represents everything I've been through. I have no desire to be 30 again, or 40. I look to may finally allow an opportunity to pursue long-delayed ambitions and interests. Many women apparently feel a sense of relief when their children leave home (Rubin, 1978). National surveys reveal that women who have launched all their children experience greater enjoyment of life than women at a similar age with one or more children still living at home (Glenn, 1975). While children continue to be a source of pride and interest, mothers no longer face the daily burden of child care and discipline (Lowenthal and Chiriboga, 1972). Our society is providing increased opportunities for middle-aged women who wish to return to school or the paid labor force; this has been an important factor in making the empty nest period a satisfying time for women (Bird, 1979).

What about the father whose children have left home? Those who were constantly preoccupied with career and financial pressures may look back with regret on their lack of involvement in family life. Others may be eager to enjoy the freedom and financial security that sometimes accompany the emptying of the nest.

Lewis (1979) and his colleagues found that the empty nest period was particularly difficult for fathers who were older, had fewer children, had less satisfying marriages, or had been very close to their children. For example, George had been so involved with his two sons that he virtually ignored his deteriorating relationship with his wife. When both sons decided to go to college a few hundred miles away, George went into a serious depression. He realized he no longer had much in common with his wife, and he felt terribly alone.

The "Returning" Young Adult

When Jeanie graduated from college at age 23, she left her parents' home and got her own apartment. Four years later, she lost her job at a bank and moved back in with her parents. "It used to bother me that I was back home," she recalls, "but not anymore. I know more and more young people who are being forced into the same situation. My mother knows I'm not trying to be a leech; she knows it's only temporary" (Lindsey, 1984: 18).

Like Jeanie, more and more young adults are continuing to live at home well into their twenties. Thus, the "empty nest" syndrome is giving way to quite a different phenomenon: the "full nest." Such factors as the high rate of unemployment, the skyrocketing costs of education and housing, the trend toward later first marriages, and the high divorce rate have all contributed to this change in family living patterns.

For some young adults, living at home is an unbeatable bargain. Tom, a recent college graduate, notes: "My room is comfortably furnished. I have my folks' two color TVs, a video recorder, and an elaborate stereo system at my disposal. My mom's cooking is great—what a deal! I couldn't possibly afford this type of luxury in my own apartment." But, for others, living at home is a source of frustration rather than luxury. Elena, a 32-year-old secretary, moved into her mother's home with her two children after separating from her husband. She complains that "Mom tries to make every decision for me, which undermines my authority with my children" (*U.S. News and World Report*, October 25, 1982: 71).

From the perspective of the young adult's parents, the child living at home may be a mixed blessing. Some parents look forward to middle age, hoping that they will be able to pursue long-deferred goals after their children are grown and independent. One Florida mother of five, whose children periodically move back when they are having financial difficulties, explains: "Kids today don't realize that we have our parental dreams just like they have their dream. Our dream has been to travel. But how can we do that when there is always somebody moving back in?'' (Lindsey, 1984: 18).

Parents of returning young adults sometimes complain that their offspring wish to be babied and take no responsibility for cooking and household duties. Another frequent source of conflict in such homes is parents' attempt to assert authority. A 55-year-old Denver mother, whose 24-year-old daughter moved back home to save money for future schooling, admits: ''When the kid moves back home, the parents still treat her as a child. I do that, and she resents it and I see why. But if we're supporting her, she should be answerable for her actions. It has caused some disharmony'' (*U.S. News and World Report*, October 25, 1982: 70).

The Couple Relationship

The period of a couple's middle years often lasts longer than any other stage of the family life cycle. In many instances, a married couple has 16 to 18 years between the departure of their last child and the death of the first spouse (Duvall, 1977).

Studies have shown that the marriage relationship in the middle years is important for personal life satisfaction. Marital happiness seems to increase after a couple's children leave home; this period is second only to the honeymoon stage in reported overall happiness. For many middle-aged wives and husbands, companionship is the most rewarding aspect of marriage (Glenn, 1975; Hayes and Stinnett, 1971; Rollins and Feldman, 1970).

Postparental couples commonly turn to one another and reestablish their relationship once children are no longer living at home (Petranek, 1970, 1971). Some studies suggest that marital role tension is reduced after the children leave (Rollins and Cannon, 1974; Spanier, et al., 1975). Couples make fewer complaints about each other; they have essentially made peace with the

Marital happiness often seems to increase during the ''empty nest'' stage of the life cycle.

spouse's habits and foibles. "Oh, he still asks the same dumb questions," says Ruthann, "but I'm used to them now." Both empathy and communication contribute to marital success in the middle years—especially when the partners have satisfying communications and do not judge each other negatively (Johnson, 1968; Lowenthal and Chiriboga, 1972; Saunders, 1969).

As in all age groups, middle-aged adults have differing levels of sexual interest and activity. Those who enjoyed sex during early adulthood usually continue to be sexually active in middle age—although physical health becomes an increasingly important factor affecting sex drive after age 40. Research suggests that regular sexual expression is also important in maintaining effective sexuality; in other words, there is some truth to the phrase, "use it or lose it." This is particularly true for the aging male, who is most vulnerable to lack of stimulation.

There appears to be a sharp upturn in sexual inadequacy in men after age 50; some have labeled this time the "male menopause." Sex researchers William Masters and Virginia Johnson (1966) report that men who experience a lack of responsiveness are typically affected by one or more of the following: boredom with the regular sex partner, preoccupation with work, mental or physical fatigue, overindulgence in food or drink, illness or spouse's illness, and fear of failure.

Many middle-aged men express a fear of impotence. Some avoid sex because of their fear of failure, while others turn to sexual relations with someone other than their wife to prove they do not have a problem. Thus, men in the middle years appear to be more vulnerable to extramarital affairs because of waning physiological capacities and a need for sexual reassurance (Johnson, 1968).

There is little evidence that age affects the sexual capacity of women in a physiological sense. The **menopause**, or cessation of menstruation, which usually occurs in the late forties or early fifties is probably the most significant physiosexual change experienced by the middle-aged woman. Many myths surround this change: that menopause decreases a woman's sex drive, or conversely that she becomes sexually insatiable. Contrary to popular belief, few women experience difficulties associated with menopause.

While menopause signals the end of a woman's reproductive years, it does not mean that her sexual enjoyment is over. A woman's reaction to menopause depends largely on her feelings about herself. For those whose youth and physical attractiveness have been a primary source of self-esteem, or for those who equate femininity with childbearing, menopause can be traumatic. Many women, however, find that their sexual lives can be more rewarding and free of anxiety when family demands are reduced and there is no possibility of becoming pregnant (Masters and Johnson, 1966; Neugarten, 1970).

Our society has perpetuated a cruel stereotype of women over 45 as overweight battleaxes, unable to please their husbands. Despite this image, which some women internalize, there is frequently a burst of energy at the time of menopause—far from the old mythic idea that you can drift into some kind of haze (Henig, 1982). "I can do twice as much as I used to," reports a radiant 52-year-old woman who manages a large department store. "It's wonderful!"

In terms of sex roles, **role reversal** (less differentiation among marital roles) appears common among middle-aged married couples (Lowenthal and Chiriboga, 1972; Neugarten, 1968a). This may result from a wife's entry or reentry into the paid labor force (Targ, 1979). At present, more than half of the nation's middle-aged women are employed outside the home. The chances of a wife's holding a job are greater during this period than at any other point in the family life cycle (Eshleman, 1974). Some women wish to build up family financial resources depleted during the childrearing years; others want to feel competent and productive outside the home.

Summary

In an historical sense, adolescence is a relatively recent phenomenon. During early adolescence, concern over one's body image and physical attractiveness is pervasive. The primary developmental task of adolescence is to establish a sense of identity separate from one's parents. The development of one's sexual identity is obviously an especially sensitive aspect of adolescence.

Most experts on adolescent development stress that parents should be loving, compassionate, and understanding. They should keep communications open with teenagers by showing a willingness to talk and listen carefully. By setting a limit on behavior, parents help teenagers to know exactly what to expect—whether in terms of household chores or curfews.

Research supports the view that peer group influence peaks during the early junior high school years. An adolescent's first steps toward independence are explored through the peer group. There is substantial variation in the effect of a peer group depending on such factors as gender and socioeconomic status.

Parents do not give much formal sex education to their adolescent offspring. To the extent that it does occur, mothers are the primary source of sexual information. The more favorable the mother-daughter relationship, the less likely the daughter is to have sex. Teen pregnancy has become a major social problem in the United States. Many adolescent girls are still pitifully unaware of when and how they can become pregnant. Teen pregnancy has many negative consequences for the mother.

Social problems associated with adolescence include drug and alcohol use, anorexia nervosa, teenage runaways, and adolescent suicide. There has been a noticeable decline in drug use among American teenagers in recent years, but no reported decline in alcohol use. The typical victim of anorexia is a young woman from a middle- or upper-class home who was always considered the perfect child. Of the roughly one million American children absent from home each year, roughly half are runaways, while the rest are "push outs" forced to leave by their parents. Suicide for persons 24 years of age and under has increased by 250 percent in the last two decades.

The stage of the family life cycle known as launching occurs when the children leave their parental home. It begins when the first child departs and ends when all children are gone (the empty nest). Launching has great psychological significance both for the child and for the parents' sense of purpose. Midlife is a time of uncertainty for many American men and women, not only because children are departing the nest, but also because the signs of aging cannot be avoided. Reevaluation of one's past is common during the midlife period. There is serious debate among researchers as to whether the midlife stage should properly be viewed as a crisis.

The empty nest period has often been viewed as a time of stress for parents, especially for mothers. However, some women find that it allows them an opportunity to pursue long-delayed ambitions and interests. In many families, children in their twenties are living at home as young adults, thereby establishing a "full nest." Such factors as the high rate of unemployment, the skyrocketing costs of education and housing, the trend toward later first marriages, and the high divorce rate have contributed to this phenomenon.

The period of a couple's middle years often lasts longer than any other stage of the family life cycle. Marital happiness is said to increase after a couple's children leave home. As in all age groups, middle-aged adults have differing levels of sexual interest and activity. In terms of sex roles, role reversal appears common among middle-aged couples.

Discussion Questions

1. Which adolescent task did you find most difficult: establishing identity, establishing independence, or adjusting to physical changes? Why?

2. What do you find (or would you find) most difficult about being the parent of an adolescent?

3. Were you a late or early maturer? How did this affect your relationship with peers and adults?

4. Were your parents a primary source of your current knowledge about sex? Do you consider this to be an important parenting task? Why?

5. What do you see as the major difficulties of being a pregnant adolescent? How would you act as a parent if your teenage child became pregnant?

6. In your family, was "launching" more difficult for you or for your parents?

7. Has midlife been a time of crisis for your parents? How do you think you will respond to this time of life?

8. If you are presently living at home with your parents or planning to return to the "nest" after college, what do you see as the drawbacks and benefits? If you did not choose this option, what were your reasons for not doing so?

Key Words

Adolescence	Empty Nest	Menopause
Anorexia Nervosa	Identity	Role Reversal
Displaced Homemaker	Launching	

Suggested Readings

Giffen, Mary, and Felsenthal, Carol. *A Cry for Help*. New York: Doubleday, 1983. Offers enlightening insights on adolescent suicide.

Haley, Jay. *Leaving Home: The Therapy of Disturbed Young People*. Hightstown, N.J.: McGraw-Hill, 1980. Focuses in a practical way on the transitional stage of adolescence and the problems that can develop.

Levinson, Daniel, et al. *The Seasons of a Man's Life*. New York: Ballantine, 1978. Uses interview data to discuss American men's stages of adult development and the implications for family life.

Rossi, Alice. "Life-span theories and women's lives." *Signs* 6(1), Fall, 1980: 4–32. A review and synthesis of the sociological theories of adult women's development.

Rubin, Lillian. *Women of a Certain Age: The Midlife Search for Self*. New York: Harper and Row, 1979. Presents women's self-perceptions as they sort out their lives and examine their priorities.

CHAPTER THIRTEEN

Families in the Later Years

KEY TOPICS

—attitudes toward the elderly—
—the diversity of the elderly—
—the husband/wife relationship in later years—
—parents and their older children—
—the role of the grandparent—
—facing retirement and widowhood—

Not by physical force, not by bodily swiftness and agility, are great things accomplished, but by deliberation, authority, and judgment; qualities with which old age is abundantly provided.

—Cicero

For the young man is handsome, but the old superb. Fire is seen in the eyes of the young, but it is light that we see in the old man's eyes.

—Victor Hugo

Everyone is too old for something, but no one is too old for everything.

—Anonymous

''Ruth Stauffer is 69. She is a retired professor of English, never married, an unabashed smoker who wears a turquoise ring and no other jewelry, . . . well-worn twill pants and a smile that transforms a room. She paints her own Christmas cards, despite failing eyesight; enjoys her martinis, even when exercising; and explains, 'I retired early, while I could still ride a bicycle.' She saw a friend of hers retire just in time to die. 'I didn't want that to happen to me. I love to travel. I love people. I love politics.' She indulges freely in all three. She returned to her native Colorado, designed her A-frame house, planted it on 60 acres, and between trips to Europe, she lives there in Devil's Gulch where she is a Democratic committee-woman, teaches poetry and Shakespeare, writes for the local historical society and is director and tour guide for the local museum'' (Barbour, 1982: G6).

Is an active woman like Ruth Stauffer ''old''? In American society, an individual is usually thought to be old at age 65 because that is the age at which people become eligible for full social security benefits. Moreover, many business firms consider an employee ready for retirement at 65. Yet aging is a process, not a state; one doesn't wake up one day and discover that one is old. In many important ways, a person can be "old" at 50 or "young" at 80.

Education has been found to be an essential factor in determining how "old" people become as they age chronologically. The more educated they are, the more resources they have and the less likely they are to show mental impairment. In the late 1970s, the average elderly American had merely completed elementary school; by the year 2000, most will have graduated from high school. This should open greater options for senior citizens, allowing them to work and be productive for a much longer period of time (Maas and Kuypers, 1974).

Whereas in 1900 there were only three million Americans over the age of 65, by 1980 there were more than 24 million. According to projections, there will be about 31 million Americans over age 65 by the year 2000. At that point, 16 percent of the nation's population will be 65 or older, compared with 10.5 percent in 1975 (U.S. Bureau of the Census, 1980).

On July 1, 1983, the United States reached a milestone. For the first time in the nation's history, there were more persons over 65 (27.4 million) than teenagers (26.5 million). This was a dramatic indication that, as the media has often proclaimed, the "graying of America" is upon us. According to the Bureau of the Census, Americans over the age of 65 are probably the fastest growing age cohort in the country (Moore, 1983).

In particular, there has been a substantial rise in the number of persons 75 and older. Bernice Neugarten (1974) has broken down the general category of the elderly into two

groups: the "young old" and the "old old." The first group, aged 55 to 75, includes those who have retired from full-time work, and yet remain vigorous and active. But it is the "old old"—those over 75, the senior citizens most likely to experience serious illness—whose numbers have swelled by 37 percent in the last decade alone (Moore, 1983).

This chapter deals with families in the later stages of the life cycle. We will begin by discussing the diversity of the elderly population of the United States and American attitudes toward older citizens. The husband-wife relationship during later years will be given special attention, as will the relationships between parents and their older children. Finally, we will examine three critical developmental challenges often experienced by the elderly: grandparenthood, retirement, and widowhood.

The Diversity of the Elderly

For the most part, Americans have a rather negative attitude toward old age. Stereotypes of the elderly abound: they are allegedly sick, tired, uninterested in sex, mentally slow, forgetful, less able to learn things, grouchy, withdrawn, self-pitying, isolated, unproductive, and defensive (McTavish, 1971). Ethel Shanas (1980: 9), a sociologist who has done important research on the lives of older persons, observes:

Our society is oriented toward youth. We deprive older people of work, their major source of income, and thus make it impossible for them to compete for goods and services in the market-place. For older persons who prefer not to work forever, and they are the majority, we downgrade their leisure-time activities and view these as trivial. We accept in the young modes of behavior we condemn or at least frown upon among those in the middle or later years.

While there have been certain improvements in the mass media treatment of the elderly in recent years, research continues to indicate that the young, the middle-aged, and the elderly all consider being old as less desirable than being young. As Kalish (1975: 14) points out:

No wonder many people resent growing old. Not only do the elderly frequently suffer significant losses in psychomotor skills, in visual and auditory sensitivity, in income and in work opportunities, but they must deal with the essentially negative and often patronizing attitudes of younger people.

The elderly apparently receive the greatest respect in societies that permit them to retain the greatest degree of economic and political power (Simmons, 1945). However, American culture increasingly seems to value youth and change rather than maturity and stability.

It must be stressed that—contrary to all stereotypes—the elderly population of the United States is a diverse group. For example, while many of the nation's poor are over 65, 70 percent of the elderly own their own homes and 84 percent of these homeowners have no mortgage (Moore, 1983). While the elderly account for one-quarter of the total national health care bill, only 5 percent of those over 65 live in institutions. Only one in five senior citizens will ever have to live in a nursing home (Langway, et al., 1982). In short, a substantial proportion of older persons are "doing quite well, thank you." They enjoy more than adequate incomes, reasonably good health, and active social lives; they also make important social and economic contributions to the nation.

As is well known, Ronald Reagan became President of the United States when he was 70 years old. The British Columbian Indian chief Dan George began a new career as a film actor when he was well past 80. Many less famous persons pursue new activities or hobbies when they retire. "I had always wanted to do oil painting," notes one woman. "When we retired and moved to San Diego, I began to paint the ocean. After a few years, I got a show in a local gallery and even sold a few of my paintings. I didn't make a fortune, but the thrill—well, it was almost beyond words. To know that someone else wanted my work to hang in their home!"

Jerry, a retired accountant, had always wanted to work with people rather than numbers. After sitting around bored for a year, he decided to begin a new part-time career. He went to a nearby hospital, got information about training programs, and began studying to become an emergency room aide. "I spent most of my life helping people to find tax shelters. Now, in a small way, maybe I can help the doctors and nurses to save someone's life. Even when I'm just talking to a patient or family member, and I can see them relax a bit, I feel like I've done something. I want my last years to be special."

The elderly of the United States are diverse not only in terms of income and health, but also in terms of their racial and ethnic backgrounds. In general, older members of minority groups face a double burden of prejudice and discrimination based on race or ethnicity and age. Those who have immigrated from Latin America, Asia, or Eastern Europe, for example, may experience serious language problems. Finally, elderly blacks and Hispanics may cling to traditional values and find it difficult to relate to the political militancy of their children and grandchildren (Kalish, 1975).

Politics represents a final area in which the diversity of American senior citizens is quite evident. While some older persons assume a low profile and essentially withdraw from social and political involvements, an increasing number have come together to fight for the rights of the elderly and "Gray Power." Groups such as the Gray Panthers,

BOX 13–1

Tish Sommers and the Older Women's League

At age 67, fighting not only ageism and sexism, but also a slow-growing cancer, long-time political organizer Tish Sommers is attempting to build the Older Women's League (OWL) into a formidable national membership organization. Sommers, who created the National Organization for Women's Task Force on Older Women and was a key figure in starting a movement of displaced homemakers, relishes this latest challenge.

Sommers hopes that OWL, launched in 1981, will ultimately become a critical link between the feminist movement and activist elderly groups. Initially, OWL has focused on such bread-and-butter issues as social security benefits, access to health care insurance, and pension reform. Its message can be blunt; one organizing manual states: "If we are older women, we had better face it. Euphemisms don't change reality."

Sommers calls herself a "free-lance agitator"; her theme, from her earliest political days, has been: "Organize—don't agonize." She admits that "I'll probably die in harness; I doubt that I can hold back the monster within me." But, she adds, "my immortality would be a viable, living organization helping to overcome fear and dread of aging among women—and a society turning the corner in human rights."

Source: Sweet, 1982: 61, 80.

led by Maggie Kuhn, and the Older Women's League (OWL), led by Tish Sommers (see Box 13–1), have strongly challenged the ageism (or age prejudice) in our society and have lobbied in government circles for programs that will benefit senior citizens.

Many observers believe that age is regaining respect in the United States. A new generation of older people—better educated, more affluent, healthier, and more active than previous elderly generations—is redefining the notion of being "old." In the view of Bernice Neugarten, a specialist on aging, we are moving toward an "age-irrelevant society" in which people will remain active and competent much longer than in the past. This will enhance both society's image of the elderly and their own self-images (*The New York Times*, 1982).

Relationships During Later Years

During the later years, the family is adjusting to the changing statuses and roles of every member. Parents are getting older and must adjust to retirement, to increased leisure time, to possible declining health, and to the deaths of friends, family, and even a spouse. Children, too, are coping with developmental transitions; they are raising their own families and becoming more involved in caring for their parents (Carter and McGoldrich, 1982).

An early and continuing theme underlying theory and research on old age in the past two decades is the progressive **disengagement** or withdrawal of aging persons from activities in the surrounding world. Advocates of the disengagement perspective argue that this tendency to withdraw is natural, because of factors such as retirement, the deaths of friends and relatives, and the realization of one's own mortality. However, critics of disengagement theory insist that the elderly do not wish to withdraw and that such withdrawal is harmful for both the elderly and the larger society.

One finding pertinent to disengagement theory is clear: the family remains the focus of the aging person's social interactions and the main provider of social support. As their world becomes more constricted, older persons find that their relationships with their spouses, children, grandchildren, and siblings become more important. Table 13–1 shows that the majority of older Americans have living relatives and are in contact with them frequently.

The Husband-Wife Relationship

Laura and Sidney, both in their mid seventies, have been married for 46 years. "We've had our ups and downs," admits Sidney, "but all in all it's been a wonderful life. I've never been bored; she's always fascinating." Laura agrees: "I hate it when we're apart. No matter how other things are going, I always feel better when he's around."

Elderly married persons are happier and live longer than those who are single, widowed, or divorced. It appears that marriage solves most of the needs for love and companionship felt by the aging couple. According to research, marriage contributes to morale and continued activity during the later years. Many older couples see their marital relationships as just as satisfying—if not bet-

Table 13–1   Contact with family

Family with whom contact is maintained	Percentage of population having family	When last seen (Percentage)				
		Within last day or so (including live with)	Within last week or two	A month ago	Two to three months	Longer ago than 3 months
Children						
Persons 18 to 64 years old	73	87	8	2	1	2
Persons 65 years old and over	81	55	26	8	3	8
Brothers & sisters						
Persons 18 to 64 years old	91	31	31	12	6	20
Persons 65 years old and over	79	22	22	15	10	31
Parents						
Persons 18 to 64 years old	70	48	24	9	5	14
Persons 65 years old and over	4	32	23	8	11	26
Grandchildren						
Persons 65 years old and over	75	46	28	10	5	11
Grandparents						
Persons 18 to 64 years old	30	24	20	18	8	30

Source: Harris and Associates, 1975.

For many elderly couples intimacy continues to be an important aspect of their relationship.

ter—than in earlier phases of the life cycle (Lasswell, 1973; Rollins and Feldman, 1970).

In their study of 408 older husbands and wives, Stinnett, Carter, and Montgomery (1972) found that companionship and the ability to express true feelings to each other were viewed as the two most rewarding aspects of marriage in the later years. Respect, love, and sharing of common interests were also rated as important elements of a successful marriage. Frequently mentioned problems included housing, poor health, and financial difficulties.

Traditionally, American society has decreed that sex, love, and romance are primarily for the young, and that it is "not quite nice" or is even "abnormal" for older persons to have sexual yearnings (McCary, 1978). As one example, a woman in her late forties was helping her mother pack for a trip to Israel. The mother, in her late seventies, was complaining about packing and unpacking for her husband, a lecturer and constant traveler. As a result, the daughter suggested that her mother might want to stay home and let a valet accompany her husband on his latest trip. Astonished by her daughter's naivete, the older woman indignantly responded: "There are some things a man servant cannot do!"

A nationwide sex survey of the elderly by Bernard Starr and Marcella Bakur Weiner revealed that 97 percent reported a continuing strong interest in sex. A 79-year-old woman said that sex "gives me a zest for life"; an 84-year-old man called it "one of the supreme pleasures of living." The frequency of lovemaking among elderly couples questioned averages 1.4 times a week, comparable to Alfred Kinsey's data on 40-year-olds (Phillips, 1981: 1).

Other studies suggest that not only do many of those in their seventies and eighties continue to enjoy sex, but also that sexual activity is highly beneficial to health. Although there is a slowing down in sexual capacity among both men and women, their sexual pleasure continues and may even increase. Higher levels of education and socioeconomic background are associated with a positive interest in sex at advanced ages (Feigenbaum, et al., 1966; Lobsenz, 1975; Martin, 1974).

If sex is beneficial and pleasurable for the elderly, why do so many older persons shrink from it? James McCary (1978) notes that, for some, the aging process serves as a comfortable excuse for giving up an activity that has always been filled with anxiety. For many others, however, societal disapproval and ridicule over the sexuality of the elderly are more important. These negative attitudes are accepted and internalized by senior citizens, who feel guilty about their sexual feelings and needs. McCary (1978: 229) concludes that "once society's attitude has changed, older people will enjoy a fuller, healthier sex life than has been observed in the past."

While divorce is infrequent among the elderly, it is increasing. As with younger couples, more flexible divorce laws and greater social tolerance have permitted older couples to end marriages that have lasted decades. Of course, the increase in divorce among the aged may simply be a function of people living longer. In the past, few couples lived long enough to spend many decades together; thus, few marriages were put to this test.

Remarriage is quite common in this age group both among widowed and divorced persons. The most important basis for remarriage late in life is companionship (Vinick, 1978). In the words of one widower: "My first wife died about the time I retired; life seemed pretty empty for a while. But then I met Sandra and found an incredible burst of energy. I had never been out of the country before, but through her prodding we went to Japan. I loved being in a foreign culture, and now we go on a long trip to a different part of the world each year. My goal is to see as much as I can before I die." As is true earlier in the life cycle, meaning and purpose in later years can be enhanced by a positive marital relationship.

Sibling Relationships

Among older Americans, about 80 percent have at least one brother or sister living. In general, most elderly persons have about twice as much contact with children and parents as with siblings. However, some women are on the phone with their siblings almost daily and may have as much contact with them as with their children (Harris, 1975; Parson, 1978; Shanas, 1973).

Researchers disagree as to whether elderly siblings are more likely to become close as they get older (Adams, 1968a; Shanas, et al., 1968). Certainly a good number seek to restore family loyalties and to renew ties with their brothers and sisters. In some cases, elderly siblings decide to live together after leading totally separate lives for decades. This is often true among widows and widowers, among never-married senior citizens, and among those without children. Indeed, siblings are especially important in the lives of older persons who never marry (Shanas, et al., 1968).

According to Joan Aldous (1978), sibling relationships that have remained close over the years provide an additional source of companionship in later stages of life. Sister-sister ties have been observed to be stronger than sister-brother ties, with brother-brother ties weakest of all (Adams, 1968a). The death of a sibling, especially if the relationship was close, may shock a person more than the death of any other family member. Troll (et al., 1979: 123) observes: "Since they are of the same family and same generation, their death brings home one's mortality with great immediacy.''

Parents and Their Older Children

There is a widespread belief in our society that aging individuals can no longer rely on their families for assistance and support. Current research on the family, however, lends little credence to the stereotype of lonely, isolated older persons abandoned by their families (Shanas, 1979a, 1979b; Shanas and Sussman, 1979). Indeed, recent studies suggest that intergenerational relations a century or more ago were not as harmonious, nor was contact as frequent, as nostalgia has made them appear (Anderson, 1977). Currently, there is a great deal of contact, mutual aid, and affection shared between older family members and their kin (Bengston and Treas, 1980; Shanas, 1979a, 1979b).

Interaction

Contrary to stereotypes, there is considerable contact between aging parents and their adult children (see Table 13–1). Often visits with parents are a kind of ''monitoring'' or checking to see that all is well. These visits may be combined with other activities such as shopping, recreation, or attendance at religious services.

This ''visiting linkage'' is generally strongest between mothers and daughters (Troll, et al., 1979). In fact, husbands are more likely to stay in touch with their wives' parents than their own unless the wife makes the effort to remain in contact with the husbands' parents (Adams, 1968a, 1968b).

Living Arrangements

As noted in Chapter 2, the impression that the American family of earlier generations consisted of three generations living harmoniously under one roof is somewhat of a myth. Prior to the twentieth century, life expectancy often prevented the overlap of three generations. Even when they survived, most of the elderly did not live with their children (Laslett, 1976). Consequently, the three-generation family has always comprised less than 10 percent of all families in those societies we know about.

Currently in the United States, both older persons and their adult children place great value on independent living; few wish to share the same household (Hess and Markson, 1980; Streib and Hilker, 1980). An example is Paula, 86, who lives in a senior-citizen residence in New York City. Although her only daughter lives in Michigan, Paula does not wish to move to the Midwest. ''Of course it's nice to be with your children,'' Paula says. ''But they have to work, and I'd just sit there alone in their big house. My home is here, and my friends are here—it's more important to be near my friends'' (Moore, 1983: 34).

Most persons 60 years and older live alone or with a spouse (Atchley, 1977). In 1975, only 18 percent of the elderly lived in a household with one of their children (Shanas, 1979a). Thus, in terms of preference, the intergenerational household with an adult child and an elderly parent is an ''alternate lifestyle'' for the aged (Brubaker and Brubaker, 1981). When the elderly do live with a child, it is usually a daughter (Lopata, 1973; Shanas, et al., 1968).

One of the most interesting findings of family studies in Western societies is that older persons want ''intimacy at a distance'' (Rosenmayr and Kockeis, 1963). Again and again in surveys, case studies, and clinical observations, it is clear that the elderly wish to live close enough to regularly see children and grandchildren, but want to remain in their own households for as long as possible.

In the United States, 34 percent of all persons over 65 with children live within ten minutes' distance of at least one child. As illustrated in Table 13–1, frequent contacts with children and grandchildren are common. Yet, as Shanas (1979b) points out, these data do not tell us if such contacts are brief or lengthy, friendly or hostile.

Similarly, we know little about the quality of interchange in households shared by older people and their adult children. Studies document that stress can arise as a result of divergent views of childrearing, dependency of family members on one another, and lack of adequate understanding of aging (Robinson and Thurnher, 1979). Helena Lopata (1973) indicates that when families share living quarters, this may reflect a crisis situation rather than a preferred choice. In her study, the reasons commonly given for such living arrangements were lack of sufficient funds for an older person to live alone, poor health, and death of a spouse.

Moreover, the sharing of living quarters by older parents and adult children was seen as a temporary arrangement. Carter and Glick (1976) indicate that co-residence is more likely to occur when the household head is very young or very old, when the family income level is low, and when the older family member is nonwhite. Indeed, more older black and other minority persons

While the elderly want to live close enough to regularly see children and grandchildren, they usually want to remain on their own for as long as possible.

B O X 1 3 – 2

Day Care for the Elderly

A year ago, 73-year-old Charles Crandall, suffering serious heart problems, seemed headed for a nursing home. He suspects that had this occurred, "I don't think I would be living now." Instead, with the assistance of social service agencies in California, he remains in his San Francisco apartment. But, three times a week, Crandall spends five hours at a day care center for adults, where he meets his friends and works with a nurse, a physical therapist, and a nutritionist. Crandall believes that his experience at the center has given him "the incentive to live."

American adult day care centers, modeled after British "day hospitals," offer part-time supervision and nursing care for the elderly. They are an especially welcome alternative for those who need more care than neighborhood senior citizen centers provide, but are not so ill that they require institutionalization. These day care centers are also of great assistance to families of the infirm elderly. One Dallas woman reports that she has been able to keep her nursing job because her 80-year-old father spends time at a center. She adds that, while he was depressed and hopeless when he arrived, he is now directing dances at the center, a transformation she views as "a miracle."

At present, there are some 800 centers across the United States, which can be divided into two types. Adult day "health" centers focus on providing medical services such as physical therapy, whereas "social" day care centers emphasize social and recreational activities. Unfortunately, many centers face funding difficulties. Few private medical insurance companies provide such coverage, and federal support has been cut back by nearly 25 percent under the Reagan administration.

Source: Wallis, Dolan, and Foote, 1982: 60; Langway, et al., 1982: 60–62, 65; and Moore, 1983: 30–37.

---

live with their children than do whites of similar ages (Bengston, et al., 1977). Gelfand and Fandetti (1980) report that white middle-class families, by contrast, are more likely to purchase care for dependent elderly parents by putting them in nursing homes or hiring a live-in companion. Day care for elderly parents is increasingly becoming an option in many American cities (see Box 13–2).

Dr. Robert N. Butler, a specialist in geriatric medicine, notes that "the single greatest fear we have in this country is the fear of growing old, losing our mind and being put away in a nursing home. It overshoots cancer as a national phobia. And its impact on the family is enormous" (Moore, 1983: 30). Yet, contrary to popular fears, adult children do not commonly or quickly dump their elderly parents in institutions. Cur-

rently, only about 5 percent of older persons live in institutions. Almost half have organic brain disease; the average age at admission is 80. The point at which an older person's failing health requires consideration of institutionalization or a nursing home placement is a time of crisis for a family (Butler, 1975; Kramer and Kramer, 1976).

Old age homes and nursing homes are, by and large, found unsatisfactory by both the elderly and their children. They are regarded simply as a last resort when other alternatives are no longer feasible. In the view of Pollak and Wise (1979: 127), placing a senior citizen in such an institution "symbolizes the last step before death, it diminishes the old person socially and psychologically, it fills the children with guilt about not having taken the parent into their own homes, and it is expensive."

While households comprised of unrelated elderly persons are becoming more common, at present only a fraction of the elderly live in such communal arrangements as "Share-a-Home." At this created family unit, which is neither a boarding house nor nursing home, members have assumed legal authority over their own lives. They hire and fire staff, plan menus, pay for room and board, and have the services of a car and driver to take them shopping, to church, or to the doctor (Streib and Hilker, 1980).

Mutual Aid

Older parents and their adult children not only maintain frequent contact, but also provide mutual assistance. Research indicates that the American family persists as a major source of aid to the elderly; elderly parents continue to turn first to their children for care and services even when outside agencies are available to fulfill these functions (Shanas, 1979a; Worach-Kardas, 1979). In the view of Dr. Robert Butler, "It's time to get away from the rhetoric about how awful we are to our elderly. The family is the No. 1 caretaker, and it's very responsible" (Langway, et al., 1982: 60).

Contrary to the often-held notion of a one-way flow of aid to the elderly, actual patterns of assistance between older parents and their adult children are two-way. In 1975, seven out of every ten persons age 65 and over with children reported that they gave help to their children; the same proportion reported that they received help from their children (Shanas, 1980). There appear to be class differences in assistance patterns; middle-class parents more often provide financial aid while working-class parents more often help through child-care or household management services (Adams, 1964; Aldous, 1967).

While many Americans are under the impression that older parents are usually a financial drain on their adult children, routinely requiring monetary aid, this again appears to be a myth. Only 4 percent of older persons in the United States reported receiving regular financial aid from their children (Streib and Schneider, 1971). Moreover, in their study of mutual aid patterns in 100 three-generation families in Minneapolis, Reuben Hill and his associates (1970) found the least differences between help given and received in the area of money. The oldest generation gave almost as much money to children and grandchildren as it received. By contrast, grandparents received much more than they gave in the areas of emotional gratification, household management, and protection during illness.

As a general rule, it seems that aging parents continue to assist their children in one area or another for as long as they are able. Consequently, a shift from aid-giving may coincide with a deterioration in parents' health or financial resources (Troll, et al., 1979). When elderly parents and adult children live in the same household, it is often assumed that the children are providing care and shelter for the parents. Quite the opposite is sometimes true: older persons may be offering shelter and care to divorced or widowed children.

Ethel Shanas (1980) points out that as adult children have children of their own, they reach a better understanding with their parents, or what Blenkner (1965) calls **filial maturity**. As a result, turning to parents for aid seems to become easier, with old quarrels resolved or forgotten. A key factor, of course, is that adult children become more aware of their parents' struggles as they experience parenting themselves.

As families of four living generations have become commonplace, some members of the grandparent generation have found themselves in the middle. They are not only experiencing their own aging, retirement, and perhaps health and financial problems, but are also expected to be the major social support for their own parents. Some may feel torn between the needs of their quite elderly parents and those of their children and grandchildren. Just as members of the great-grandparent generation may never have expected to live so long, many in this second generation never expected to be looking after their parents so late in life (Shanas, 1980).

The issue of dependency in parent-child relations becomes increasingly important as aging parents experience a decline in their capacities or fear that decline is imminent. Such emotional dependence is related to the personality types of older persons; it is not an inevitable characteristic of old age (Goldfarb, 1969; Rosow, 1967). In fact, many senior citizens resent being dependent and would much rather maintain control over their own environment than call on others for help. Ironically, this resentment can sometimes cause them to complain, worry, and become even more dependent.

According to Walsh (1980), the resolution of dependency issues requires that the older person accept his or her strengths and limitations and become dependent when necessary. The adult child must not only take responsibility for what he or she can appropriately do for the aging parent, but must also recognize what he or she cannot and should not do. If an aging parent becomes overly dependent on adult children and the children encourage this dependence, a vicious circle may result. The more the child takes on, the more helpless the parent becomes, and so forth.

Along with good health, the elderly's financial independence is instrumental in having both generations feel good about each other (Johnson and Bursk, 1977). Despite the common pattern of mutual aid discussed earlier, a good relationship between these two generations generally depends on the aged parents' ability to cope independently of their adult children.

Critical Challenges of Later Years

Erik Erikson (1963) used the phrase "integrity versus despair" to refer to the developmental crisis of old age. By integrity, he meant a coming to terms with one's life accomplishments, satisfactions, and difficulties; an acceptance of the new status one has reached; and an ability to deal with past failures and the reality of aging.

In a study of adjustment to aging among elderly men, Reichard, Livson, and Petersen (1962) identified three personality types who adjusted well to aging and two who adjusted poorly. The largest group of those who adjusted well was the "mature" group; these men moved easily into old age and accepted themselves realistically. They were able to find genuine satisfaction in day-to-day activities and personal relationships. Since they felt their lives had been rewarding and purposeful, they were able to grow old without regret. A second group of "rocking chair men" was generally passive, welcoming the opportunity to be free of responsibility during old age. Finally, a third group of men, called "armored" by researchers, was unable to face passivity or helplessness. These men warded off their dread of physical decline by remaining active.

Among those who adjusted poorly to aging—"despairing" in Erikson's terms—the largest group was "angry men" bitter over failure to achieve their life goals. These men were unable to reconcile themselves to growing old, and they often blamed others for past disappointments. A second group of "self-haters" looked back on the past with a sense of failure but turned their resentment inward. Increasing signs of aging only underscored their feelings of inadequacy.

In the following sections, we will discuss three major transitions faced by many elderly persons: grandparenthood, retirement, and widowhood.

Facing Grandparenthood

While grandparenthood is often associated with old age, many current grandparents are in their forties or early fifties; some are still caring for their own aging parents. Young children now see grandparents as an older but active generation; today's grandmothers and grandfathers tend to be employed rather than retired. Thus, while we have chosen to discuss grandparenthood in our chapter on families in the later years, it could also have been included in Chapter 12, where we examined families in the middle years.

At present, about three-fourths of older Americans have living grandchildren. While few grandparents live in the same homes as their grandchildren, about 70 percent live within an hour's drive and see them at least every week or two. Nearly half see a grandchild every day or two (Harris and Associates, 1975). In a study of 300 younger children, Kornhaber and Woodward (1981) found disappointment and bitterness among children who perceived their grandparents as remote or uncaring. The "valued grandparent" appears to be an earned and acquired status, involving the personal qualities of the individual and not automatically ascribed to one's position in the family (Troll, et at., 1979).

How do grandparents feel about their role? Some do not feel close to their grandchildren and do not enjoy coping with the noise, the energy, the slamming doors, and the spilled milk. "When he cries or needs a diaper change, I just hand him back to my son," admits one grandmother. "I raised five children and it wasn't fun. Now I want some peace and quiet. My grandson has his

parents and his sister; he doesn't need me around, too." Others find grandparenthood difficult because it brings them into conflict with their children. "I hate the way my son and daughter-in-law spoil the kids," says one grandfather. "They won't listen to me, and we battle whenever I'm over there. It's a real problem."

But, for still others, grandparenthood is a thrill and a joy. "I live for the time when I see little Keith," reports Lurlene, a 60-year-old first-time grandmother. "My husband would live in Florida year-round if I'd go along, but I absolutely refuse. It's difficult enough being there for four months during the winter and not seeing the baby. I'm the total doting grandmother who thinks her grandson is perfect. And I'm lucky because my daughter-in-law is so open to my relationship with little Keith."

The prime significance of grandparenthood involves biological renewal and continuity: the aging adult sees himself or herself extended into the future. Moreover, for some, grandparenthood offers an opportunity to succeed in a new emotional role—even to be better as a grandparent than he or she was as a parent. "I wasn't close enough with my sons," says one elderly man with obvious regret. "I was too busy, I was too focused on business success. I missed their growing up. I'm not going to make the same mistake with my grandchildren."

The sex and sex-role attitudes of a grandparent tend to influence the closeness of the grandparenting bond. Grandfathers are generally more remote from grandchildren than grandmothers, and are less comfortable with the grandparenting role (Atchley, 1977; Clark and Anderson, 1967; Neugarten and Weinstein, 1964). Part of the problem may be that older men view grandparenting as similar to the childrearing role traditionally seen as "women's work." As younger fathers become more involved in child care,

For many older adults the grandparenting role offers them the chance to succeed in a new emotional role, and perhaps be better as grandparents than they were as parents.

they may find the transition to grandparenthood easier than their own fathers did.

The relationship between grandparents and grandchildren is also shaped by the grandparents' relationships with their own children. The middle generation often decides how much interaction will be permitted, thereby either promoting or hindering the development of emotional bonds between grandparents and grandchildren (Hill, et al., 1970; Robertson, 1975, 1976). One grandmother who lives near her children bitterly reports that they say they will visit and bring the grandchildren, but they never do. "I've lost the grandchildren and they've lost me," she concludes (Footlick and Salholz, 1981: 76).

A third influence on the relationship between grandparents and grandchildren is the age of the grandchildren. As both generations grow older, they appear to enjoy each other less (Aldous, 1978). For example, while eight- and nine-year-olds from white, middle-class families prefer to play with their grandparents, eleven- and twelve-year-olds are more interested in being indulged by grandparents than in playing with them (Kahana and Kahana, 1971). On their part, grandparents often feel that older grandchildren do not want to bother with them, and so they turn their attention to younger grandchildren.

When grandparents live nearby, are interested in their children and grandchildren, and spend time with them, all three generations are more likely to enjoy the grandparent-grandchildren relationship (Boyd, 1969; Robertson, 1977; Wood and Robertson, 1976). Arthur Kornhaber and Kenneth L. Woodward note that this relationship not only provides children with love and affection, but also enables grandparents to feel cared for and needed at a time at which society may be telling them they are unimportant. ''Grandparents and grandchildren do not have to do anything to make each other happy,'' argue Kornhaber and Woodward. ''Their happiness comes from being together'' (Footlick and Salholz, 1981: 76).

While about 40 percent of the older persons in the United States are great-grandparents, little attention has been given to the great-grandparenting role. Those among the ''old old,'' or what Shanas (1980) calls ''the new pioneers,'' have few valued role models as great-grandparents. While this role may bring joy and a sense of fulfillment, it can also be a source of bewilderment as the lifestyles of the young become increasingly different from those of the oldest generation.

Coping with Retirement

''Funny things happen,'' observes Hank, a retired graphic artist who continues to do free-lance consulting for his long-time employer. ''You reach for something you've been reaching for for years, and you miss by about a quarter of an inch. Getting up some mornings, the whole thing seems like a fight against gravity—your stomach sags, your eyes sag, your feet sag. . . . But I guess I'd drop dead if I stopped working'' (Gelman, 1982: 56).

While more than 1.5 million Americans are entering **retirement** each year, an increasing number are having second thoughts about this decision. Some do not want to settle for retirement income; others wish to stay

Retirement can provide time to engage in lifelong interests.

B O X 1 3 – 3

Research Brief:
How Satisfied Are Wives When Their Husbands Retire?

In a study by Hill and Dorfman, 36 women who had not been in the paid labor force for at least 10 years were interviewed about their reactions to their husbands' recent retirement. Through content analysis of these interviews, the researchers found:

- The most consistent factor associated with four measures of satisfaction among wives was their husbands' participation in household tasks.
- The couples usually made joint decisions about trips and entertainment, but not about finances. Joint decision-making about entertainment was associated with wives' satisfaction.
- Other important factors associated with wives' satisfaction were health of the husband, adequate finances, shared leisure-time activities, and voluntary retirement of the husband.

- Early retirement by younger husbands and poor health as a reason for retirement were associated with lower life satisfaction among wives.

Wives reported enjoying the companionship and flexible schedules afforded by retirement, but they were sometimes dissatisfied if the husband did not have enough to do and the couple was together too much. When asked to make suggestions for new retirees, the wives felt that women should continue their preretirement activities while retired husbands should try to stay busy.

Source: E. A. Hill and K. T. Dorfman, ''Reaction of Housewives to the Retirement of their Husbands.'' *Family Relations*, April 1982: 195–200.

---

active, at least in part-time work. Indeed, occupational retirement is one of the most significant transitions of later life and can lead to a major adaptive challenge for older family members.

For the individual who retires—particularly for men but increasingly for women as well—there is a loss of meaningful employment roles, a sense of productivity, and work relationships that have been central throughout adult life. The retired person is suddenly denied a major source of self-esteem (Sheldon, McEwan, and Ryser, 1975). While working women may experience less difficulty with their own retirement if they continue their role as homemakers, they often have greater difficulty with their husband's retirement, which may bring loss of social status and friends (Heyman, 1970). Until recently, discussions of retirement

were based solely on the experiences and problems of men, but today both sexes are being studied by researchers (see Box 13–3).

Retirement can represent a significant adjustment for the married couple as the husband and wife are now free to spend most of their waking and sleeping hours together (Medley, 1977). This may be experienced either as a blessing or a curse, depending on how each chooses to deal with leisure-time options. Clara, for example, found the constant presence of her husband Phil to be unsettling. ''He sits around the house all day doing nothing,'' she complained. ''He expects me to wait on him 24 hours a day. He doesn't want to go out and do things with me, yet he resents it if I make plans to play cards or see a movie with my girlfriends. It's been awful.''

Nevertheless, research has revealed that

most individuals report positive attitudes toward retirement (Kell and Patton, 1978; Streib and Schneider, 1971). Juan and Luisa, a retired couple in their mid-sixties, have become a whirlwind of activity since they retired. "We're having a ball," laughs Luisa. "We travel around the country seeing our children and grandchildren. We've taken up new hobbies and become active in the church's senior citizens group. Now Juan's talking about how we should take a ballroom dancing class. He says, 'If we've got to go some day, we might as well go out dancing.'"

While we might expect that those persons most satisfied with and committed to their jobs would have the most negative attitudes toward retirement, the actual evidence does not support this assumption. Seltzer and Atchley (1971: 16) conclude that "it is apparently possible for people to be highly committed to their profession and at the same time have other things that they might like to do as well." Since the vast majority of retired persons voluntarily relinquish their work roles, and numerous older workers opt for early retirement, it appears that retirement is not typically perceived as a dreaded crisis (George, 1980).

Of course, some Americans may have a rosy view of retirement beforehand but find the reality of retired life to be quite disappointing. Money is certainly a key factor in such instances; sharp curtailment of family income is one of the immediate retirement adjustments for most families. Indeed, when levels of adjustment (life satisfaction) are reported to be lower among retirees than older workers, much of the difference is directly attributed to levels of income (Fox, 1977).

Recent government estimates indicate that fewer than half of American workers are covered by a pension plan. Consequently, the financial worries of the elderly have intensified recently as the stability of the social security system has come into question. As the "graying of America" continues, the number of persons reaching retirement age increases while the proportion of workers paying into the social security fund decreases. When the "baby boom" generation born in the 1940s and 1950s gets older, this problem will become even more severe. Some fear that social security payroll taxes could double; others worry that the entire system could collapse. Such a collapse would be a disaster for many elderly persons and families who rely on social security benefits as their primary source of income (Anderson and Hager, 1981).

In general, successful coping with retirement depends significantly on whether a person's postretirement activities develop out of lifelong needs and interests. A study by the National Institute of Mental Health (Sheldon, McEwan, and Ryser, 1975) identifies four common patterns that people follow in retirement:

- Maintenance, which occurs when the retiree tries to satisfy the same needs in the same way as before by making extraordinary efforts to continue working.

- Withdrawal, which occurs if the individual views retirement as a time to relax and gives up former interests without adopting new ones.

- Changing activities, which means that the individual engages in a new set of activities in order to satisfy the same needs.

- Satisfying a new and different set of needs, which is the strategy of those retirees who see these years as a time to accomplish long-deferred ambitions and goals.

Of these patterns, maintenance and withdrawal apparently are most typically chosen by retired persons.

The Strain of Widowhood

The death of a spouse ranks highest among the possible stressors of old age. In fact, it is not uncommon for the surviving partner to be so upset that he or she soon "dies from grief." In practical terms, **widowhood** (a term we will use to refer to both men and women who have lost a spouse through death) involves many losses for the survivor. He or she loses a familiar companion with whom a lifetime of experiences had been shared, a partner in parenting, and even a source of income or pension payments.

For the elderly in particular, the loss of a mate through death can be a devastating blow (Cohen and Gans, 1978). The older person quite naturally views death differently from a younger adult. Not only is the loss of the spouse traumatic in itself; it is also a vivid reminder that the survivor's own time may be running out (Cummings and Henry, 1961).

Difficulties of Widowhood

Widowhood has long been recognized as an important and common role change that occurs primarily in later life (Atchley, 1972). While greater attention has been paid to the problems of widows than those of widowers, various studies suggest that most individuals are able to cope with the adjustments that widowhood requires. At the same time, however, grief, unhappiness, and lower morale are all more common among widows and widowers than among others of the same age (Riley and Foner, 1968). Indeed, the widowed are more likely to see themselves as old and lonely than are married persons of similar ages (Atchley, 1975).

Because women live longer than men, and because men in our society marry women younger than themselves, there are five times as many widows as widowers in the United States (Miller, 1978; Neugarten, 1968a, 1968b). While fewer than 5 percent of widows remarry, most widowers under the age of 70 marry again (Cleveland and Gianturco, 1976). There is disagreement among researchers as to whether widowhood is more difficult for older women than for older men (Bell, 1971; Berardo, 1968, 1970; Lopata, 1973). It is clear that older widows are worse off than older widowers in terms of both finances and prospects for remarriage (Troll, et al., 1979). However, widowers are more likely to die than widows within a few years after the death of a spouse (Helsing, et al., 1981). Box 13–4 looks at the particular difficulties faced by older men who experience widowhood.

Widowhood usually begins with a period of mourning or **bereavement**. The extent of grief that the surviving spouse feels, as well as the way he or she copes with that grief, will vary from individual to individual. Some may go through an intense period of depression and withdrawal, and then gradually recover within the next year. Others may need much more time, while some may never accept the death of the beloved spouse. In a survey of Chicago widows conducted by Helena Lopata (1973), a specialist on widowhood, 48 percent said they were over their husbands' death within a year, while 20 percent indicated they had never gotten over the loss and probably never would.

Numerous studies have found that men and women react somewhat differently to bereavement. Women tend to cry and self-mutilate more; men cry less and are generally less expressive of emotion, but direct anger and aggression away from themselves. Men experiencing widowhood in our society often feel that they have lost a part of themselves—certainly reflecting the traditional view of women as helpmates for men—whereas women feel deserted or abandoned (Glick, et al., 1974; Rosenblatt, et al., 1976).

B O X 1 3 – 4

The Pain of Widowers

Menachem Begin and his wife Aliza were married for 43 years. When she died after a long illness, there was a visible decline in Begin's health and spirits. Her death was ultimately viewed as a major factor in her husband's decision to resign as Prime Minister of Israel.

"She was his emotional reference point," observes Anne Rosberger, executive director of the Bereavement and Loss Center of New York. "Now there is no one with whom he can share confidences, no one to whom he can show physical or emotional frailties. We see this very often in high-ranking executives who have lost wives after long marriages—the loneliness of command, the increasing isolation, the ill health, self-doubt" (Dullea, 1983: B12).

Whether or not a man is a political leader or a powerful business executive, he is likely to suffer greatly from the death of his wife. In fact, according to a study by three researchers from the Johns Hopkins University School of Medicine—Knud J. Helsing, Moyses Szklo, and George W. Comstock—widowhood dramatically increases the likelihood of death for male survivors but not for women. The overall mortality rate was 26 percent higher for widowers than for married men, and 61 percent higher for widowers aged 55 to 64 than for married men in the same age group.

Why are widowers more likely than widows to die within a few years after the death of a spouse? A number of theories have been proposed to explain this difference:

- Researcher Knud J. Helsing suggests that "women may be more adaptable. They may have more of a sense of survivability." They may also feel more at ease living alone than men do.
- Traditional sex roles contribute to men's denial of feelings of grief, fear, and loneliness. It may be damaging to hide such feelings; an intense period of bereavement may be important in recovering from the loss of a spouse.
- Because of patterns of longevity, men do not expect to outlive their wives. Consequently, they may not be emotionally prepared to cope with widowhood.

Source: Dullea, 1983:B12; Helsing, et al., 1981:45.

As if the death of a cherished spouse were not enough for an elderly person to handle, many must face conflicts over the inheritance of the deceased. When there is no will, the laws of the 50 states vary as to how much of the estate will automatically be awarded to the surviving spouse. Therefore, a widow or widower may be thrown into a dispute with his or her children, with siblings of the deceased, or with other relatives over money and property. The widow or widower often bears the brunt of the animosity generated in such battles, especially if the marriage had been a remarriage for the deceased (Titus, et al., 1979).

Adjustment to Widowhood

When death ends a marriage of many decades, it can be difficult to rebuild one's life without the lost spouse. Autonomy of personality, close continuing friendships, a realistic philosophy of life, economic security, and meaningful personal interests all facilitate a healthy adjustment to widowhood. Atchley (1975) has attached a great deal of importance to income adequacy in determining how individuals adjust to widowhood. He contends that insufficient income not only increases anxiety during widowhood, but also reduces social participation, thereby leading to loneliness.

By contrast, Lopata (1973) asserts that participation and adjustment following widowhood are primarily influenced by personality, attitudinal, and ethnic factors. She found that widows cope with losing their previous identities as wives in different ways. Role-oriented women turn to new roles by beginning a new job, increasing involvement in a job they already hold, or becoming more active in social and civic organizations. Those who need confirmation of their personal qualities may become more involved with friends and family.

Widowhood has its most immediate impact on family roles. Patterns of mutual aid are commonly altered: contacts with in-laws are often lost, whereas closer associations with siblings may be resumed (Shanas, et al., 1968). Older widows usually grow closer to their daughters and more distant from their sons (Adams, 1968a, 1968b). In part, this reflects the caretaking role traditionally expected of women in American society (see Chapter 3). Daughters, much more than sons, are expected to offer emotional support to their widowed parents.

Findings indicate that friendship relationships, rather than extended family ties, lead to less loneliness and worry and to a feeling of usefulness and individual respect within the community (Arling, 1976). However, the impact of friendships on widowhood often depends on the proportion of friends who are also widows or widowers. If the individual is one of the first among his or her peer group to become widowed, support and concern may be somewhat lacking. Friends may feel awkward about grief and death, and may wish to avoid thinking about how they themselves may soon die or experience widowhood. On the other hand, if the widowed individual has many friends who have previously experienced the death of a spouse, he or she may receive great comfort from those quite familiar with the problem.

It is this desire to be with people who have shared the same struggles that has led to the popularity of self-help groups such as the Widow-to-Widow program. Joan, whose husband died when she was 58, found that her married friends began to avoid her. "I wasn't part of a couple anymore, and they didn't know how to deal with me," she recalls. "A few kept trying to fix me up, long before I was ready to date again, just so they wouldn't have an odd person at a dinner party."

Joan found the emotional support she needed in a widows' self-help group at a local community center. "The first meeting I went to just blew me away. Those women immediately understood how I felt about my husband's death, my financial problems, my friends' discomfort, everything. Some had many more difficulties than I did; they were older and really frightened about the future. But they weren't hung up on their own troubles; they were really open to hearing about me as well."

Remarriage is becoming an option for many elderly widows and widowers, especially for men who find many more women available (Cleveland and Gianturco, 1976). While adult children may frown on elderly widowed parents who seek companionship with the opposite sex, such relationships can be important in adjusting to widowhood. For widowers, remarriage has another benefit: it dramatically lowers their rate of mortality. For men under 55 who remarry, the death rate is at least 70 percent lower than for those who do not; for men aged 55-64, it is 50 percent lower (Helsing, et al., 1981).

It is sometimes assumed that all widows and widowers wish to remarry; this is not necessarily the case (Cohen and Gans, 1978). For some, no one can replace the deceased spouse; others wish to avoid conflict with children who would see such a remarriage as an act of disloyalty. In addition, economic and legal constraints have contributed to a recent trend of cohabitation among the elderly (see Chapter 2). Some elderly couples are choosing to live together without marriage, despite the social stigma this entails for their traditional-minded generation (Bernikow, 1982).

Summary

As the media has often proclaimed, the "graying of America" is upon us. According to the Bureau of the Census, Americans over the age of 65 are probably the fastest growing age cohort in the nation. In particular, there has been a substantial rise in the number of persons 75 and older, sometimes called the "old old."

For the most part, Americans have a rather negative attitude toward old age. Negative stereotypes concerning the elderly abound. American culture increasingly seems to value youth and change rather than maturity and stability. Contrary to all stereotypes, the elderly population of the United States is a diverse group. While some are poor and/or confined to nursing homes, many enjoy more than adequate incomes, reasonably good health, and active social lives. In general, older members of minority groups face a double burden of prejudice and discrimination.

Elderly married persons are happier and live longer than those who are single, widowed, or divorced. It appears that marriage solves most of the needs for love and companionship felt by an aging couple. In contrast to stereotypes, many of those in their seventies and eighties continue to enjoy sex. However, societal disapproval and ridicule of the sexuality of the elderly continues. While divorce is infrequent among the elderly, it is increasing.

About 80 percent of older Americans have a sister or brother living. Most maintain much closer contact with children than with siblings, but siblings are especially important in the lives of older persons who never marry. The death of a sibling may shock a person more than the death of any other family member since it brings home one's own mortality.

There is a great deal of contact, mutual aid, and affection shared between older family members and their kin in American society. Eighty-one percent of the elderly have seen their children within the last week or two. However, most do not live with their children, but instead live alone or with a spouse. Older persons generally prefer "intimacy at a distance." Only about 4 to 5 percent of older persons live in institutions. Old age homes and nursing homes are, by and large, found unsatisfactory by both the elderly and their children.

Contrary to the often-held notion of a one-way flow of aid to the elderly, actual patterns of assistance between older persons and their adult children are two-way. For example, the oldest generation gives almost as much money to children and grandchildren as it receives. As a general rule, aging parents continue to assist their children in one area or another for as long as they are able.

At present, about three-forths of older Americans have living grandchildren. The "valued grandparent" appears to be an earned and acquired status, involving the personal qualities of the individual. Grandfathers are generally more remote from grandchildren than are grandmothers. The middle generation often plays a decisive role in promoting or hindering the emotional bonds between grandparents and grandchildren.

More than 1.5 million Americans are retiring each year. For the individual who retires, there is a loss of meaningful employment roles, a sense of productivity, and work relationships that have been central throughout adult life. Nevertheless, most individuals report positive attitudes toward retirement. Money is a key factor in satisfaction with retirement; sharp curtailment of family income can be a serious problem.

The death of a spouse ranks highest among the possible stressors of old age. Loss of a mate is not only traumatic in itself for the elderly, but is also a vivid reminder that one's own time may be running out. Because women live longer than men, and because men in our society marry younger women, there are five times as many widows as widowers. It is clear that older widows are worse off than older widowers in terms of both finances and prospects for remarriage.

Discussion Questions

1. What is your image of an ''old person''? How have your formed this image?

2. What are your attitudes toward aging? Are you fearful of growing old, or are you looking forward to old age? Why?

3. Do you think you will adjust well to occupational retirement? Why?

4. How do you think you will cope with widowhood? Why?

5. How would you describe your relationship with your grandparents? Was it, or is it, a close and important relationship?

6. How do you think you would react to the grandparenting role? Why?

7. As a married adult with your own family, how would you feel about aging parents living in the same household?

Key Words

Bereavement   **Filial Maturity**   **Widowhood**

Disengagement   **Retirement**

Suggested Readings

Martin, Elmer P., and Martin, Joanne M. *The Black Extended Family*. Chicago: University of Chicago Press, 1980. Focuses on the position of the elderly in Southern Black families.

Ragan, Pauline K. (ed.) *Aging Parents*. Los Angeles, Calif.: University of Southern California Press, 1979. A multidisciplinary look at older parents and their adult children designed for college students or those with a personal interest in the topic.

Sena-Rivera, Jaime. ''La Familia Chicano.'' In Rosenfeld, Jeffrey P. (ed.), *Relationships: The Marriage and Family Reader*. Glenview, Ill.: Scott, Foresman, and Co., 1982. Shows the integration of the elderly into the family among Chicanos.

CHAPTER FOURTEEN

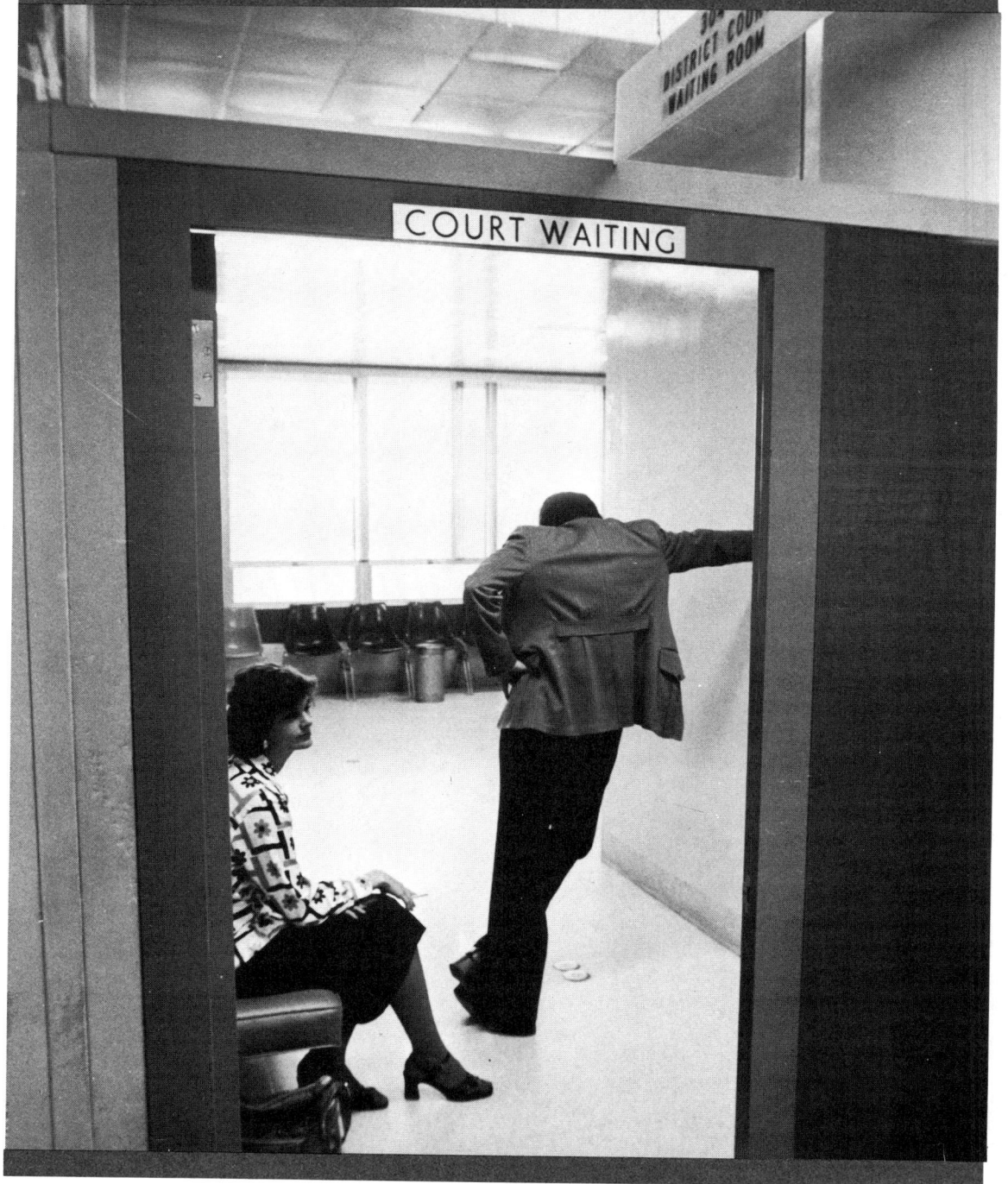

Divorce, the Solo Parent, and Remarriage

KEY TOPICS

—explanations for the high divorce rate—
—the process of divorce—
—the impact of divorce on spouses and children—
—legal issues concerning divorce—
—child custody—
—the economic and role strain of single parenthood—
—children's adjustment to single-parent families—
—the transition to remarriage—
—challenges for the parent, stepparent, and children in a remarriage—

Divorce is undoubtedly one of the greatest stresses a human being can experience. It is second only to the distress suffered from the loss of a loved one. . . . Anyone approaching divorce with calm and composure is probably not facing the situation realistically.

—Dr. Lee Salk

Mrs. C. described her predicament a few months after she and her husband of eight years sepa-

rated: ''I feel like I'm treading water in a tidal wave.''

—Reported by J. Wallerstein and J. Kelly

A 1983 *Newsweek* report on divorce in the United States began: ''Is there anyone in the land who has not heard a friend or a child or a parent describe the agony of divorce?'' (Press, et al., 1983: 42). Sadly, the answer is probably "no." **Divorce**, the act of legally dissolving a marriage, has become commonplace in our society.

In 1982, the year in which the number of divorces among American couples dropped for the first time in 20 years, there were roughly one million divorces in this nation. In the past 100 years, the rate of divorce has risen from approximately 1 per 1000 marriages to more than 20 per 1000 marriages. It is expected that as many as half of all marriages in the 1980s will end in divorce (see Figure 14–1 and Box 14–1). Consequently, the United States has the highest rate of divorce among the world's industrialized nations (Glick and Norton, 1977).

Within the United States, divorce rates vary by region; they are lowest in the Northeast and generally increase as one moves westward. While there is no single explantion for these variations, population differences in values and attitudes, age, and religious affiliation may be relevant. For example, a greater percentage of the population of the West is younger and more divorce prone. By contrast, a large proportion of people in the Northeast are Roman Catholic, a religion that forbids divorce.

While blacks and other nonwhite races are more likely to get divorced than are whites, divorce among Mexican Americans is less common. Traditionally, those Americans with higher incomes and educational levels have tended to have lower rates of divorce. More recently, however, the middle class has begun to "catch up" with the comparatively higher rate of divorce among the working class. The probability of divorce is high for those who marry while young, as well as for those who marry when the woman is pregnant. Moreover, the earlier in a marriage a child is born, the greater the likelihood of marital separation (Falicov and Karrer, 1980; Furstenberg, 1976; Hillman, 1962; Shoen, 1975; Yorburg, 1978).

These divorce statistics underscore the fact that divorce does not occur randomly throughout the life span of American families. Instead, it is most prevalent in the early stages of family life. Most divorces occur before the sixth year of marriage; the average age of first divorce is 29 for men and 27 for women (Westoff, 1977).

This chapter will begin by examining the painful reality of divorce in the United States. We will focus on the causes of di-

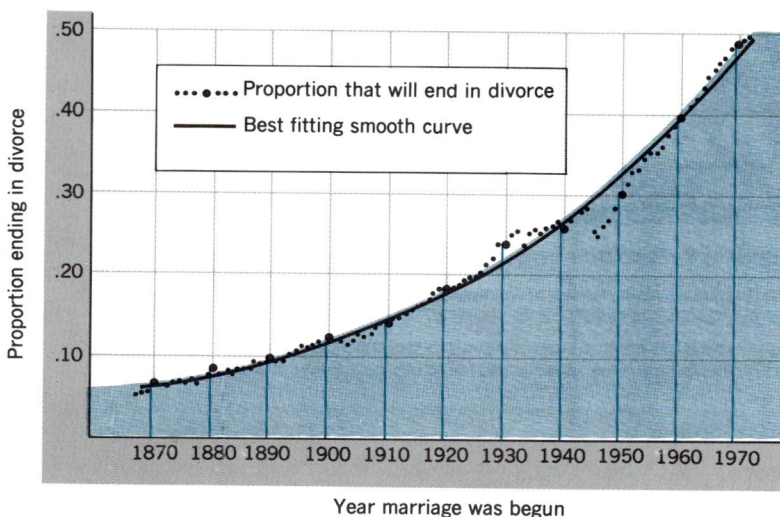

Figure 14–1 Proportion of marriages begun in each year that will end in divorce, 1867–1973. (*Source*: Cherlin, 1981, p. 23.)

BOX 14-1

Research Brief:
Probability of Staying Married

The research staff of *Good Housekeeping* reported that for every 100 couples married in 1983, half will eventually divorce. According to the U.S. Bureau of the Census, of every 100 couples married in 1983:

- 19 will divorce before their fifth anniversary.
- 14 more will before their tenth anniversary.
- 7 more will before their 15th anniversary.
- 7 more will before their 25th anniversary.
- 3 more will before their 50th anniversary.

In the 20-year period from 1960 to 1980, the number of divorced men and women in the United States more than tripled. However, this does not mean that Americans have given up on marriage. Census data also indicate that three out of four divorced women and five out of six divorced men eventually remarry, many within three years of their divorce.

Source: "Marriage in America: From Roosevelt to Reagan." *Good Housekeeping*, Vol. 186, January, 1983: 182–183.

vorce, the impact on marital partners and their children, divorce counseling and mediation, and legal battles over child custody and property settlements. Then we will turn to the growing number of single-parent families in the nation, many of which result from divorce. Particular attention will be given to the economic strain, role strain, and social isolation experienced by single parents. Finally, we will analyze the complexities of remarriage, including the shifting relationships among biological parents, stepparents, biological children, and stepchildren.

Divorce

In November, 1980, the American public overwhelmingly chose Ronald Reagan, a man who had divorced and remarried, as President of the United States. The election of a divorced candidate now seems hardly worthy of comment; yet in earlier generations divorce was virtually an automatic end to one's political career. Thus, Reagan's victory reflected the changing attitude toward divorce in our society. Most Americans, whatever their moral and religious feelings about divorce, have recognized that high divorce rates are a fact of life.

Causes of Divorce

Why has the divorce rate in the United States reached such high proportions? Some argue that the traditional vow of "till death us do part"—symbolic of the institution of marriage—is simply obsolete, no longer meeting the needs of Americans late in the twentieth century. Others insist that the rising divorce rate is part of a general decline in morality and family values. While both arguments may have a bearing on the problem, let us consider some explanations which sociologists use to interpret these statistics.

First, the idea that most couples traditionally stayed married for decades has little basis in fact. The 40- or 50-year marriage was never common. In the past, marriages rarely lasted more than 20 years because people died at younger ages. Lawrence Stone (1977), a British historian who has studied family life, notes that most marriages today last longer than in any previous period of history, precisely because of the declining mortality rates for young adults. Stone argues that contemporary divorce may be a "functional substitute" for death as a way of escaping from an unhappy marriage.

Second, our definition of a "normal" family—a happily married couple, with two well-adjusted children, a dog, and a beautiful suburban home—is based on the ideal family of the 1950s. Some have suggested that the family of the 1950s was not "normal" or typical at all. Indeed, Figure 14–1 shows that those who married in the late 1940s and early 1950s had lower rates of divorce than would be expected from the long-term trend. Note that in the figure the actual divorce rates fall well below the "trend" line.

Some have speculated that these Americans—who grew up in the 1930s during the hardships of the Depression and came of age during World War II—may have put an especially high value on stability and family life. Consequently, it is suggested, they divorced less frequently than might have been expected (Cherlin, 1981; Elder, 1974). Whatever the reason, the decline in long-lasting marriages during the 1960s and 1970s should be seen in the context of a long-term, 100-year trend, rather than solely in sharp contrast to the families of the 1950s.

The long-term rise in the number of women working outside the home has also affected the nation's divorce rate. In the past, men needed women to perform the time-consuming work involved in preparing food, making clothing, and raising children; women needed men for financial support. Technological and social changes have made these economic motives for partnership much less important than they were in the nineteenth century. Women who work outside the home no longer need to be financially dependent on their husbands.

There is little doubt that the entry of increasing numbers of women into the paid labor force has altered the expectations, roles, and balance of power in many marriages (see Chapter 8). In certain cases, there is a resulting strain in the relationship. Jó Ellen, for example, had always been frightened of her domineering husband, Richard. At times she considered leaving him but was held back by fears that she would not be able to support herself. After she began working as an administrative assistant in an advertising agency, she realized she could support herself in the business world. Within a year, Richard demanded that Jo Ellen quit her job and have a baby. Instead, she moved out and filed for divorce.

Since the mid-1960s, many states have reformed divorce laws to make it much easier to end marriages. In the past, the courts required specific reasons or grounds for granting a divorce, such as adultery or desertion. However, 48 of the 50 states now have "no-fault" divorce laws. Typically, the only grounds for divorce is irretrievable breakdown of the marriage—no questions asked, no blame assigned to either party. As a result, the legal process is much less of an ordeal for the couple and their children.

The rise of singlehood as an acceptable lifestyle (see Chapter 6) may also contribute to the current high rates of divorce. It is difficult to leave a marriage if you have no sense that a better life is possible away from your spouse. As singlehood becomes a more desirable alternative, those who are unhappily married may feel an additional "pull" to opt for divorce.

These are all "macro" explanations, which focus on the broad reasons for the rise in divorce. But what about the "micro" view? How can devoted married couples end up as bitter enemies within a few years? How can couples married for 20 years drift apart to the point that they become virtual strangers?

BOX 14-2

A Matrimonial Lawyer Talks About Divorce

The following are excerpts from a 1981 interview with Chicago attorney Herbert A. Glieberman, who has specialized in divorce and family law for 28 years:

Q. What is the single biggest reason couples split up?

A. No. 1 is the inability to talk honestly with each other, bare their souls and treat each other as their best friend. In my practice, . . . I see people who played games with one another when they were dating in that they always put their best foot forward. They talked mostly about superficial things in order to impress one another.

But after the wedding was over, those couples found it hard to talk, to lay out a week's plan—let alone a life's plan. They failed to anticipate that they were going to change with age and that their interests and ideas would change.

I find that too many people talk right through each other rather than to each other—especially when it comes to anything that's important. The lack of communication brings on drinking, infidelity or physical or mental abuse.

Q. How could couples be better prepared for marriage?

A. I've been a very strong advocate that schools, from the kindergarten grades up, ought to spoon-feed students as to what family structure is all about. If they do miss such training in their own family, as so many unfortunately do, they will at least know that there's a role model that they can emulate. One school system I know of actually had a project in which high-school students had mock marriages and had to plan family finances and talk about other problems couples face.

Ideally, every state ought to have, for anybody who wants to marry, a compulsory program of at least six months' duration that would deal with marriage and its obligations, responsibilities, and joys—with input from clergy, home economists, lawyers, psychiatrists, and psychologists.

For some, such a program would indicate that they are not marriage material. Others might realize that they are still too young or are not really prepared emotionally or financially to enter into marriage. A third group would marry right away and have a better overall view of the step they're taking and may gain insights that will improve their marriage.

Source: U.S. News and World Report, July 20, 1981: 53–55.

Clearly, the answer is probably different for each married couple (see Box 14–2). In their book, *Divorce: How and When to Let Go,* John and Nancy Adam (1979) list some of the more common reasons why marriages fall apart. These include:

- Destructive or irritating habits.
- Lack of interest in or concern for the partner.
- Violence or psychological abuse in the relationship.
- Violence or psychological abuse against children.
- Lack of common interests.
- Jealousy about an extramarital affair.
- Obstruction of needs and desires (as when one partner refuses to have sex with the other).
- Conflicts over sex-role divisions.
- Unforeseen changes in the relationship, as when one partner becomes mentally ill, physically disabled, or is sent to prison.

The Process of Divorce

Under Islamic law, a husband may divorce his wife by simply repeating three times in public that he wants a divorce. In Hindustan, a man can dissolve a marriage by calling his wife "mother." By contrast, in our society divorce is much more complicated and generally occurs in stages. Let us consider a case example to illustrate the process of divorce in the United States.

Martine and John, the parents of a son named Christopher, were married for four years. They met and fell in love while college students. Shortly after John began graduate school in psychology, Martine became pregnant. They decided to marry immediately, both feeling certain of their love and wanting to be parents.

When Chris was six months old, Martine took a job selling high-quality cosmetic products in a department store. She began meeting representatives of cosmetics firms and became interested in the industry. About a year later, she was hired by a major cosmetics firm as a district sales manager. Her new job required her to travel regularly and meet with buyers from retail outlets. Martine was immediately successful in sales, earning many bonuses and eventually a promotion.

John's graduate school schedule allowed him to spend many hours caring for Chris. But he showed little interest in Martine's work, viewing her job as merely a temporary measure until he finished his Ph.D. John was absorbed in his research projects and believed his academic work was far more important than her sales efforts. In the midst of one especially tense conversation, John remarked in an offhand manner that she was "selling a lot of useless junk to a lot of ignorant housewives."

The couple's friends were amazed at how different the two were. Every day, she went to work in her linen suit, fashionably done hair, and impeccable makeup; he went off to school in jeans and a sport shirt. Martine loved ballet and opera, but John spent hours watching football and basketball on television. John constantly complained that the family didn't travel to exciting places, but Martine, who was on the road more than she liked, much preferred to spend free moments at home with her son.

Just after Christopher's third birthday, Martine began feeling very depressed. Her job was going well, but she felt like she had no energy. When she visited her doctor, he asked her questions about her work, about her son, and about her marriage. "Everything's fine," she snapped back angrily. "Why are you asking about that?" But, after she left the office, she began to think about why she had been so defensive. Slowly, she admitted to herself that she was receiving little satisfaction from her relationship with John.

A few weeks later, Martine went to New York for a sales meeting. After a long day in meetings, she went out to dinner with a company marketing manager to whom she was very attracted. Martine enjoyed being with a man who respected her work, and she was well aware of the contrast between this man and John.

A few days after she got back from her trip, Martine told John that she was unhappy with the marriage. She insisted that they go together to a marriage counselor. At first, John was stunned; then he became angry: "I'm the one who sacrifices to take care of Chris, and you're the one who's unhappy. That's absurd!"

John reluctantly agreed to go to counseling sessions, and the couple saw a counselor for almost a year. At first, their relationship improved; they found they could talk more easily. However, counseling began to bring out how different they were, how they lived in two different worlds. In heated sessions, it became obvious that neither John nor Martine really respected the work the other did.

After a bitter quarrel about money, Martine decided she wanted a trial separation. She moved into an apartment near their home, but was lonely and missed Chris terribly. Within a month, she had moved back. But their disagreements quickly resumed, and the tension between them was greatly intensified because of the separation. Finally, they agreed that a formal separation followed by a divorce was the only solution.

Martine and John began telling their families and friends about the separation, and started meeting with their lawyers about terms for divorce. They had no problem dividing their assets, but they went through long and unpleasant negotiations concerning child custody. At first, John insisted on sole custody, arguing that he had spent much more time taking care of Chris. In the end, both partners agreed to a joint-custody arrangement. Chris would live with John during the week and spend weekends with Martine. Neither could move out of town without forfeiting primary custody to the other. Almost a year after the agreement, John and Martine were officially divorced.

The day of the decree was a bitter one for Martine. "I had bottled up a lot of feelings, and they all came out that day. I tore up a whole bunch of pictures of us when we were first in love. Maybe someday I'll want those pictures back, I don't know. But it sure felt good to tear them up." For John, the experience was numbing. "When I got my copy of the divorce decree, I just felt dead. I couldn't cry, I couldn't scream, I couldn't feel anything. I drank half a bottle of wine alone that night and went to bed."

During the early part of their separation, each of them found it difficult to adjust to being single again. Both felt like failures; neither was interested in a new romance. Their loneliness was compounded by the embarrassment of friends, who suddenly stopped inviting one (or often both) to social events.

It took about two years for John and Martine to recover from the worst of their pain. Martine got a job with a different cosmetics firm, which gave her a surge of confidence. She began dating a writer who admired her success and shared many of her interests. John finished his doctorate and became a school psychologist. He remarried about 1½ years after the divorce became final. John and Martine maintain a cordial but essentially distant relationship. They confer frequently about Chris, but avoid almost any other topic of conversation.

For some, the divorce process may be characterized by an initial period of denial, in which one or both partners refuse to face the possibility that the marriage may be dying. Martine's initial reaction was to strongly deny that her marriage had anything to do with her feeling of depression. Such denial is often followed by a period of depression and disorientation, in which there is a general withdrawal from social contacts. While in their year of counseling, John and Martine cut back sharply on dealings with their respective families. As John remembers, "We couldn't stand having to play the happy couple, and we knew none of them wanted to hear the truth."

Next comes a period of heightened feelings of betrayal, leading to anger first at one's spouse and possibly at members of the opposite sex in general. After Martine's initial separation, John's trust in her was totally shattered. In the midst of any fight, he would throw the accusation at her: "I'll bet you're going to move out again, aren't you?" Finally, there is a gradual period of readjustment, in which each partner realizes that the marriage is over, gains insight into the self, and plans for the future (Weinglass, et al., 1978).

This process can take years, as partners separate, reconcile, and separate again. Many bonds created during marriage must be broken. Anthropologist Paul Bohannon (1970) has suggested that divorce is a com-

The process of divorce may be characterized by an initial period of denial when one or both individuals refuse to accept the fact that their marriage is ending.

plex personal event involving at least six different experiences (or ''stations'') of divorce:

- The legal divorce, which formalizes the arrangement and allows the opportunity for remarriage.
- The emotional divorce, which results from the loss of a love object.
- The economic divorce, or division of property.
- The co-parental divorce, which involves child custody arrangements.
- The community divorce, which requires reexamining relationships with families, ex-in-laws, and friends.
- The psychic divorce, or the adjustment to singlehood.

It should be stressed that many feelings brought out in a divorce—anger at the former spouse, guilt over one's behavior, sadness about the loss of closeness—can continue long after the legal divorce has been completed (Fisher, 1974).

In addition, a family must redefine itself as part of the overall process of divorce. It may subsequently be viewed as a single-parent family, or alternately as a family with two households. Divorce researcher Constance Ahrons (1983) has introduced the term **binuclear family** not only to describe the post-divorce, two-household family, but also to avoid stigmatizing family members. The traditional phrase, ''broken home,'' implies that a one-parent household is unhealthy, abnormal, and perhaps even immoral. Because of rising divorce, most researchers agree that it is important to eliminate loaded terminology that casts a negative light on alternatives to the nuclear family.

The Impact of Divorce

We are rapidly moving toward a time when having a direct experience with divorce—in the marriage of one's parents, in one's own marriage, or in the marriage of a child—will be the norm. If present rates hold, by the time they are sixteen, about one-third of all white children and three-fifths of all black children born between 1970 and 1973 will experience disruption in their families (Cherlin, 1981: 26). Thus, an ever-increasing number of individuals must deal with the need to reestablish order and continuity in their family lives.

Of course, while divorce is increasing in frequency, it will never become matter-of-fact. Even when love has long vanished, the termination of a marriage can cause long hours—or years—of heartache and difficulty for one or both partners, and certainly for their children.

Impact on Spouses

The breakup of a marriage is likely to cause both pain and stress. Studies of newly divorced couples indicate that they usually suffer at least some degree of loneliness, unhappiness, personal disorganization, and anxiety. Their work efficiency is diminished, and they may turn to such problem behaviors as drinking (Goode, 1956; Rose and Price-Bonham, 1973; Weiss, 1976). The strain of divorce involves not only anger at the former spouse, but also genuine conflicts of interest over property division, support payments, child custody, and visitation rights.

Undergoing divorce can shatter one's personal life. Intimate bonds with a trusted lover are broken, and relationships with children are changed. Old friends may feel uncomfortable about the divorce and become distant. At least one spouse must make new living arrangements and perhaps find a different job in a different community.

In a study of the reactions of 500 men and women to the divorce experience, Albrecht (1980) found that almost one-fourth of these individuals characterized their divorce experience as traumatic. An additional 40 percent stated that the experience had been stressful (see Table 14–1). Divorce was perceived as more traumatic by women than by men. Moreover, studies of admission rates

for psychiatric care indicate that these rates are substantially higher for divorced persons than for those married and living with their spouses (Bloom, 1975). Among white females and both white and nonwhite males, the suicide rate is higher among the divorced than among persons of any other marital status (National Center for Health Statistics, 1970).

Divorced persons—especially divorced women—often have financial problems as they adjust to living on reduced incomes. If the husband was the primary or sole breadwinner in the family and subsequently remarries, he may find it difficult to support two households. Or he may not wish to; Atkin and Ruben (1976: 101) describe a "not uncommon story":

Ethel R. remarries and takes the two children to live with her new husband halfway across the continent. Norman R. is angry at his ex-wife for taking the children so far away that he can scarcely afford to visit them once a year. (He may also be unconsciously angry at her for finding a new mate, for being happy while he's still miserable.) For a while he continues to send money for child support regularly. Eventually he remarries. Money gets tight. Guiltily he cuts the allowance. One child, two children arrive. Money gets tighter. More guiltily, he misses payments. His second wife resents having to pinch and scrape so that he can send money to kids he hardly ever hears from. Resentments pile up. . . . Finally letters stop altogether. So do his checks.

Only one-third of divorced mothers receive child support payments; a 1983 *Newsweek* article called this "an epidemic of lawlessness that is rivaled, perhaps, only by income-tax cheating." Given the uncertainties of alimony and child support payments, and the continuing economic discrimination against women in the paid labor force, divorced women with children have become "the nation's new poor." Sociologist Lenore Weitzman points out that their in-

Table 14–1 Reactions and adjustments to the divorce experience (percentage distribution)

	Combined sample	Female	Male
Characterization of divorce experience			
Traumatic, a nightmare	23	27	16
Stressful, but bearable	40	40	40
Unsettling, but easier than expected	20	19	24
Relatively painless	17	13	20
Most difficult period			
Before decision to divorce	55	58	50
After decision, but before final decree	22	20	25
Just after the divorce	21	19	23
Now	3	3	3
Best time for self and children			
Before decision to divorce	13	8	22
After decision, but before final decree	6	6	5
Just after the divorce	14	15	12
Now	67	71	62
Situation now compared with pre-divorce period			
Better	93	93	91
Same	5	4	7
Worse	2	3	2
Situation now compared with immediate post-divorce period			
Better	91	92	90
Same	7	5	9
Worse	2	3	1

come declines by 73 percent in the first year after divorce, whereas the income of a divorced man increases by 42 percent (Press, et al., 1983: 42).

The financial problems of divorced persons can lead to ripple effects: taking a second or new job, poorer health care, and fewer opportunities for rest and relaxation (Albrecht, 1980; Brandwein, et al., 1974; Stein, 1970). In addition to monetary ills, numerous other factors contribute to the trauma associated with divorce. Among these are the legal process itself—the unpleasant task of dealing with lawyers and judges—as well as the pain felt by children as the reality of divorce sinks in.

In the Albrecht (1980) survey mentioned earlier, the most common reason identified as a cause of stress and trauma was the feeling of personal failure. Like Martine and John, the couple described in our case example, many experience divorce as a blow to their self-esteem. Nevertheless, 93 percent of survey respondents reported that their situation was better after the divorce.

Men and women exhibit distinct differences in their adjustment to divorce (Hetherington, 1977). While both spouses experience changes in self-concept, men tend to undergo more changes initially because they generally move out of the home and familiar surroundings. As a result,

Table 14–1   (continued)

	Combined sample	Female	Male
Property settlement made			
None	33	39	23
Most to respondent	8	11	4
50-50 split	40	40	41
Most to spouse	11	7	17
All to spouse	8	4	15
Feelings about property settlement			
Good or very good	70	73	68
Frustrated, unhappy	26	22	32
Just glad to get out	4	6	1
Change in participation in clubs and organizations			
More participation	37	39	35
No change	44	39	50
Less participation	19	22	15
Change in contact with relatives			
More contact	32	37	25
No change	55	52	60
Less contact	12	10	15
Post-divorce income compared with friends after divorce			
Much lower	31	48	7
Somewhat lower	16	18	12
About the same	39	27	57
Somewhat higher	11	6	17
Much higher	3	1	7

Source: Albrecht, 1980: 61 and 63.

many feel a lack of identity and rootlessness, and complain of a lack of structure in their lives. Divorced women report that they feel unattractive and helpless, and may find it difficult to be without the identity of married woman.

Hetherington found that, for both spouses, the period of one year after divorce was the worst time of all. At this stage of adjustment, 75 percent of women and 50 percent of men believe that their divorce was a mistake. The ex-husband feels like a failure as a spouse, parent, worker, and social being; the ex-wife regrets that she has less and less in common with her still-married friends. While shortly after divorce the wife who left her husband is adjusting better than the wife who was left, one year later this is no longer a factor in her success at adjusting to divorce.

In this first year on their own, both divorced women and men are likely to live rather frenetically. They sign up for self-improvement courses, exercise programs, and night classes in an attempt to improve their self-concepts and meet new people. Ron, divorced five years ago, remembers his first year alone as a blur of activity: "I intentionally worked long, long hours. Whenever I left work, I had plans. I dated a lot, I went to every party in sight, I went on skiing weekends, I played tennis, I took Spanish lessons.

I did everything I could to make sure I was never home alone. Because whenever I was, I'd think about Carol and the kids, and I couldn't handle it. It was best to just stay on the move and never stop.''

Two years after divorce, life for both sexes has improved. Yet differences remain: the ex-husband is likely to be in better shape psychologically than his ex-wife and is more likely to have remarried. For both, the most important factor in regaining a positive self-image is the establishment of a satisfying intimate relationship. In addition, with some of the trauma of divorce over, many men and women find that they value their new-found independence, privacy, and freedom (Bradley, et al., 1977).

Impact on Children

''Ann, who was not quite ten, tearfully told us a year after her parents separated, 'I worry about my Mom. I love her very much, but I have feelings. I'm afraid when Mom takes a long time to come home. She once tried to commit suicide . . . because of my Dad. . . . It wasn't until long after the divorce that she stopped crying. I think of her jumping off the Golden Gate Bridge. Mom thinks no one worries about her—but I do!' '' (Wallerstein and Kelly, 1980: 4).

Most children do not want their parents to divorce—even if the marriage is obviously in crisis—yet divorce is increasing nevertheless. One out of three American children growing up in the 1980s will see his or her parents' marriage dissolve; the Census Bureau currently reports that a similar proportion of children live in homes without at least one of their biological parents. Moreover, according to a study by Frank Furstenberg, half of the children of divorced families have not seen their fathers in at least a year (Bane, 1979; Press, et al., 1983).

Although there has been substantial research on the impact of divorce on children, the findings are varied and often contradictory. While some researchers suggest that the scars of divorce never truly heal, others suggest that children eventually bounce back after the initial period of disruption and distress. In her review of recent research, Cynthia Longfellow (1979) argues that rather than trying to discover the effects of divorce itself, it is more useful to examine divorce in the context of the overall changes in family life it brings about.

In over 90 percent of divorced families, the father leaves while the mother remains with the children. Longfellow suggests that his absence from the household may have great impact—both directly and indirectly—on family members. This is not because a father is essential for "normal development," but rather because, in his absence, the family income is generally reduced, its social position is changed, and the mother faces a stressful existence. For example, the strain of living under economic hardship, as most families headed by single mothers do, may take a psychological toll on both mothers and children (Bane, 1979). E. E. LeMasters (1970: 405) points out that "being the head of a household is, for most women, an 18-hour day, seven days a week, and 365 days a year job."

The findings of numerous studies strongly suggest that marital conflict has a negative impact on children's adjustment (Nye, 1957; Rutter, 1971; Zill, 1978). However, it is unclear if separation of the warring parents immediately ends the stress associated with conflict, or if the effects of such conflict on children are more long-lasting.

As part of the "children of divorce project"—which involved intensive interviews with 60 California families at the time of divorce, 18 months later, and five years later—researchers Judith Wallerstein and Joan Kelly (1980) found that the degree of parental conflict prior to divorce was not re-

Research Brief:
Daughters' Suffering from Divorce

It has been widely believed that sons are more affected by divorce than daughters. However, according to two separate studies, daughters of divorced parents may suffer more lasting emotional harm.

In a study of 500 outpatients of the Psychiatric Youth Service of the University of Michigan, psychologist Neil Kalter found that:

- nearly two-thirds of adolescent females whose parents had divorced had problems with alcohol, drugs, or promiscuous sexual activity;
- more than half had histories of intense conflict with their mothers; and
- most had severe problems in terms of self-esteem.

Similarly, in a study of 131 children of divorce in Northern California, psychologist Judith Wallerstein found that divorce had particular impact on daughters. She observed that, in a number of the young women, "we see a vulnerability . . . we don't find in the young men."

Source: Norma Peterson, "Daughters suffer most after divorce," *USA Today*, December 5, 1983: 4D.

lated to the post-divorce adjustment of their sample of middle-class preschool children. If the parents continued to fight even after the divorce, however, there was a negative impact on children's adjustment. Moreover, in a study of college students—all of whom had experienced divorce before they were 16— half reported that it was the pre-divorce conflict that had produced most of their stress (Leupnitz, 1979). Apparently, then, many psychological problems experienced by children which are commonly linked to separation and divorce may stem mainly from the conflict between the parents, rather than the termination of the marriage per se.

A paramount factor in how well children adjust to divorce is the ability of the custodial parent (almost always the mother) to recover her stride as a parent. If she is able to create an ordered and secure home with a clear routine, children clearly benefit. Yet the role of the father after divorce is also extremely important. Children who adjust most effectively have regular—even if relatively infrequent—contact with their fathers (Wallerstein and Kelly, 1980).

It is important to stress that children's reactions to divorce vary depending on their sex (see Box 14–3) and age (see Table 14–2). For example, one of the most characteristic reactions of preschool children is self-blame. By contrast, children aged seven to ten do not blame themselves for the divorce, but feel rejected and abandoned by the departing parent. Adolescents are painfully aware of their anger, sadness, and feelings of loss. Moreover, they often worry that in their own adult lives they will be unable to maintain enduring intimate relationships (Wallerstein and Kelly, 1980).

Recently, Judith Wallerstein (1983) has begun reporting on the preliminary findings of a 10-year followup of the "children of divorce project." She suggests that the long-term strain of divorce still affects many children and adolescents, who mourn the loss of a stable family life. On a more positive note, while many youths resented their parents'

Table 14–2   Children's reactions to divorce

Age	Characteristic reactions to divorce
Preschool (2½ to 6 years)	Preschool children were frightened and confused and blamed themselves. There was a great need for physical contact with adults. Children expressed fear of being sent away or being replaced. Only 5- and 6-year-olds were able to express feelings and to understand some of the divorce-related changes.
Early latency (7-8 years)	Children expressed feelings of sadness and loss, fear, and insecurity. They felt abandoned and rejected, although they did not blame themselves. They had difficulty in expressing their anger toward their fathers. They felt angry at their mothers for sending the fathers away but were afraid of incurring their mothers' wrath. They held an intense desire for the reconciliation of their parents, believing that the family was "necessary for their safety and continued growth."
Later latency (9-10 years)	Later latency children had a more realistic understanding of divorce and were better able to express their feelings of intense anger. They did not feel responsible for the divorce but were ashamed and morally outraged by their parents' behavior. Their loyalties were divided between the parents, and they frequently felt lonely and rejected.
Adolescence (15-18 years)	Adolescents were the most openly upset by the divorce. They expressed strong feelings of anger, sadness, shame, and embarrassment. Divorce forced the adolescents to see their parents as individuals and to reassess their relationships with each parent. They also reexamined their own values and concepts about what is a good marital relationship. Most were able to disengage themselves from their parents' conflict by a year following the divorce.

Adapted from J. Wallerstein and J. Kelly, "The Effects of Parental Divorce: Experiences of the Child in Later Latency," *American Journal of Orthopsychiatry*, 46, 1976, pp. 256–269. Reprinted, with permission, from the American Journal of Orthopsychiatry. Copyright 1976 by the American Orthopsychiatric Association, Inc.

breakup at the time of the five-year followup and continued to fantasize that the family would reunite, they now have forgiven their parents for divorcing.

Joanne, 18, was hurt and angry at the time of her parents' divorce. "I sat on top of my dresser and cried and refused to leave my dad's house. I thought it was wrong of my mother to move. Even worse, she had lied to me. She had *promised* me she wouldn't get a divorce." Subsequently, she shifted her resentment to her father: "He started dating too soon. I thought it wasn't fair because my mom was sitting home depressed. I felt her pain. That was the hardest part for me." Today, Joanne says she understands why they ended their marriage: "My par-

ents grew in such separate ways that I can hardly imagine them ever having been married" (Peterson, 1983: 4D).

Wallerstein (1983) has suggested that children of divorce must master six interrelated coping tasks in order to make a successful adjustment:

1. *Facing the reality of the divorce.* "My daddy sleeps in my bed every night," claimed one smiling child who, in truth, had not seen his father for weeks. "He will come back to us when *he* grows up," said another (Wallerstein, 1983: 234). Many children fantasize for years about how the family will reunite, often through their

own heroic efforts to mend the rift. Most children, even young children, give up such fantasies and acknowledge the painful reality of divorce by the end of the first year of separation.

2. *Keeping a distance from the conflict.* Gwen, age 10, complained to the researchers that she had lost interest in her school, her friends, and her piano lessons, "in everything since Dad left." She constantly thought about how he was "making out" with his girlfriend, and also about her mother's relationship with her new boyfriend. "How can I concentrate at school," Gwen asked, "thinking about Mom and Dad kissing and making love with other people?" (Wallerstein, 1983: 236).

Clearly, it is important that children return to their customary activities and relationships. This allows them some degree of distance, some world of their own, separate from their troubled parents. In Wallerstein's (1983: 235) words, "the child needs to take appropriate steps to safeguard his or her individual identity and separate life course." While most children are able to accomplish this task within a year to a year and a half after the separation, a significant number, especially at adolescence, are not.

3. *Resolving the loss.* Wallerstein views this task as the single most difficult one resulting from divorce. The child feels deeply rejected, unloved, and powerless because of the divorce and one parent's departure. Yet he or she must nevertheless find the strength to come to terms with the loss of a parent from the household, familiar daily routines, the stability of the intact family, and sometimes even a longtime home and neighborhood. Many children are not able to negotiate this task; those who do often benefit from a regular visiting relationship with the absent parent.

4. *Resolving anger and self-blame.* Wallerstein points out that children and adolescents do not accept the concept of "no-fault divorce." They may blame one parent, both parents, or themselves. Intense anger may be maintained for many years and can alienate children from both parents. However, as noted earlier, reconciliation is often evident at the ten-year mark.

5. *Accepting the permanence of the divorce.* Even when children face the reality of divorce, they may continue to harbor fantasies about restoring their parents' marriage. Sometimes, of course, one parent may also cling to such hopes, which only encourages the child. Most strikingly, the remarriage of both parents does not necessarily drive away the child's fantasies about the family reuniting at some later date.

6. *Building realistic hopes for the future.* At the ten-year followup, Pamela, age 24, said: "I'm afraid to use the world 'love.' I tell my boyfriend that I love him, but I can't really think about it without fear" (Wallerstein, 1983: 241). Like Pamela, most children of divorce are terrified of repeating their parents' mistakes. It is difficult to trust someone else and believe in the reliability of intimate relationships. To do so, the child of divorce will have to accomplish the five tasks above and come to feel that he or she *is*, in fact, lovable and worthy of caring.

Legal Issues

Because marriage is a legal agreement in which the state is involved as a third party, a couple wanting to dissolve their marriage must go through a legal process to obtain the state's permission. Until the 1970s, the divorce laws of the United States were based on the principle of fault; the guilty spouse was to be punished for his or her misconduct. State laws specified the conditions under which divorce could be granted and judged each marriage accordingly. While grounds for divorce differed from state to state, the most common were cruelty, desertion, and nonsupport.

With the introduction of ''no-fault'' divorce laws—beginning with the passage of the California Family Law Act in 1970—courts began granting divorce upon proof that the marital relationship had irretrievably broken down. In fact, the term ''divorce'' was replaced by ''dissolution of the marriage.'' In the last decade, the nation's divorce laws have been virtually revolutionized (see Table 14–3). Concepts such as joint

Table 14–3   The ''Revolution'' in Divorce Laws

Concept	As interpreted by various states
No-fault divorce	Forty-eight of the nation's 50 states now employ some type of ''no-fault'' divorce grounds, such as mutual consent, incompatibility, or living apart for a specified period of time.
Child support	Child support is no longer automatically seen as the primary obligation of the father. In most states, it is now viewed as the responsibility of both parents, depending on their respective ability to pay. In some states, child support and visitation rights may be linked.
Support enforcement	Many states have adopted stronger measures aimed at parents who fail to pay court-ordered child support. In some cases, the offending parent's wages may be garnisheed; in others, he or she may be subject to contempt proceedings and imprisonment. Some states have an arrangement with the computerized Federal Parent Locator, permitting them to trace delinquent parents and enforce support judgments across state lines.
Child custody	The traditional presumption favoring mothers has eroded to some extent. In 28 states, joint custody is either permitted or given priority when it is deemed to be in the best interests of the child.
Custody enforcement	Many states have enacted stronger legislation against ''child snatching'' by parents. The Uniform Child Custody Jurisdiction Act, intended to discourage parents from moving children to a new state in the hopes of winning a more favorable custody ruling, has been accepted in 48 states.
Grandparents' rights	A total of 42 states now allow grandparents to seek visitation rights if visitation is denied by the custodial parent. Some states are moving to extend this right to siblings, uncles, and aunts.
Spousal support	Formerly known as alimony, spousal support or maintenance is generally awarded for a limited time to assist the spouse to become self-supporting. It may be awarded to either a husband or a wife.
Property division	Most states have developed guidelines to promote a fair division of a couple's wealth. Four ''community property'' states have mandated an equal division of property.
Homemaker's contribution	In 31 states, judges are required to view the work of a homemaker as a marital asset in distributing the couple's property.

Source: ''For Divorce, a 'Revolution' in the Courtroom,'' *The New York Times*, February 7, 1983: A14.

custody and visiting rights for grandparents, which were unheard of in the 1970s, have become commonplace today.

Child Custody

Child custody arrangements determine which parent will live with and take primary responsibility for the child. Until the 1840s, women had few legal rights. Children were essentially viewed as the property of their fathers, who automatically were granted custody if a marriage ended. By the twentieth century, custody of children was commonly given to mothers. Because of traditional sex-role attitudes, it was assumed that women would be better parents than men. More recently, fathers have increasingly been viewed as competent parents. Many have been given custody of their children by judges—even when mothers have petitioned for custody themselves.

A number of factors have contributed to the changing perspective on child custody arrangements (Weiss, 1979a). There is growing skepticism about women's "natural superiority" as parents. In the case example we presented earlier, John took primary responsibility for his son's care while Martine worked at a full-time job. Obviously, John invested more hours in caretaking than Martine did; there was no reason to assume that she was inherently a better parent. Proponents of "father's rights" also argue that when both divorced parents will be working full-time, the father can hire a babysitter just as well as the mother (Gersick, 1979).

Joanne Shulman of the National Center on Women and Family Law points out that mothers continue to receive custody in 90 percent of divorce cases, primarily because fathers do not want the children. When fathers do launch court battles, however, they stand nearly a 50 percent chance of gaining custody. Some feminists have charged that men use custody fights to gain revenge on women who left them; other fathers may

have a different incentive. "I've seen lots of fathers come on like they're some kind of caring parent when all they want is a bigger share of the pie," reports Los Angeles lawyer John Bernbrock. "The mother wants the kids and she doesn't have anything else to trade" (Press, et al., 1983: 44).

An increasing number of divorcing parents are adopting **joint custody**—a legal agreement to share, often equally, the rights and responsibilities of childrearing following divorce. Advocates of this "co-parenting" arrangement stress that all parties will benefit since the child maintains a close relationship with both parents. Parental conflict may be reduced since a custody battle is avoided and the parents will need to cooperate with each other in sharing childrearing. In addition, neither parent must face the difficult burden of being a full-time single parent (Noble and Noble, 1975).

Law professor David Chambers suggests that joint custody has become the "pet idea" of the decade. Indeed, a majority of states now have some type of joint-custody law, and others are considering such proposals. Nevertheless, joint custody has its critics. New York City psychiatrist Richard Gardner charges that it has become a kind of "judicial cop-out," adding that "it certainly is easier for a judge to award joint custody than to deliberate about all the mind-boggling facts involved in a custody conflict" (Press, et al., 1983: 44).

Perhaps the key drawback of joint custody is that the child must become accustomed to two separate authority figures whose exact roles and powers are often unclear. Many practical problems may arise as the child constantly moves from one home to another. In addition, it may be unrealistic to assume that two adults who could not get along during their marriage will later be able to harmoniously share childrearing and decision-making (Abrabanel, 1979; Dullea, 1976; Goldstein, et al., 1973; Nehls and

Morganbesser, 1980). Finally, as Robert Weiss (1979a) observes, joint custody may have been effective thus far primarily because it has been adopted by enthusiasts determined to make this new idea work.

Custody issues are further complicated when there are many children. Should the family be split up, with older children going to live with the father and younger ones with the mother? Should he be granted the boys while she gets the girls? And what about the rights of grandparents and other relatives? Most states now permit grandparents to go to court to demand visitation rights (see Box 14–4).

One of the drawbacks in a joint custody arrangement can be the child's feeling as though he or she is being shuffled from one home to another.

Support and Property Settlements

Dividing up possessions and property can be one of the most emotional aspects of divorce. "We built that house together, literally," says Susan, a middle-aged architect. "We had contractors do some of the work, but we did a lot of it ourselves. There was no problem dividing our money or other possessions, but that house, well, we each would have killed for it. Finally, after months of negotiations, we agreed that he'd have it for the summer and I'd have it for the rest of the year. It didn't work; we kept fighting about the agreement after it was signed. The only choice left was to sell the house and split the profits. So we did, and now neither of us lives in the house we built. Can you believe that?"

Things can get equally tense when a family owns a business or a farm. The divorce not only throws turmoil into their personal lives, but also threatens their livelihood. One couple, for example, had a small graphic arts agency. They had to agree on how to divide their equipment, their files, even their list of clients. One of their largest clients, a staunchly religious person opposed to divorce, refused to hire either of them again.

Alimony—support payments given to a spouse who has been dependent on his or her partner—is awarded by judges after considering such factors as the duration of the marriage, the needs of each partner, and the ability of the supported spouse to earn his or her own living. Traditionally, men were the sole breadwinners of families, and alimony was awarded to women. However, with the increase in the number of women working in the paid labor force, judges have cut back dramatically on alimony awards.

According to sociologist Lenore Weitzman, only 13 percent of California mothers with custody of preschool children receive alimony. Noting that many of these women have difficulty finding jobs and receive in-

B O X   1 4 – 4

Visiting Rights for Grandparents

Donna Sullivan and her husband Jerrell lost their 24-year-old son Rick and two grandchildren in a tragic 1979 automobile accident. Subsequently, their daughter-in-law Bonnie moved into her own parents' home and refused to allow the Sullivans to visit or even speak with their two remaining grandchildren.

When the Sullivans went to court in Illinois, they found that state law had no provisions for visiting rights for grandparents. Donna Sullivan decided it was time for the law to change. She became the leader of a dedicated lobbying effort that has had at least some success. Currently in Illinois, if there is a divorce or one parent dies, any grandparent has the right to see a judge and request visiting privileges. The judge determines whether such contacts are in the best interests of the child; grandparents are merely guaranteed a hearing at which they can state their case.

Five years ago, the concept of grandparents' visiting rights was virtually unknown. Yet today, as in Illinois, 42 states allow grandparents to go to court and request visitation. The battle to protect grandparents' rights is expected to continue; Colorado lawyer Roger Stevens has proposed a model law that would guarantee visiting rights to grandparents except in cases where a judge determines there will be danger to a grandchild's health or emotional development.

Source: Press, et al., January 10, 1983: 47–48.

adequate child support payments, she charges that "divorce is a financial catastrophe for women" (Press, et al., 1983: 46–47). As one response to this growing problem, Congress recently passed a law allowing many former spouses to obtain a share of military pension benefits. While most states already have provisions that alimony terminate on remarriage, some states are allowing termination of alimony when the recipient is living with someone else.

Child support, like alimony, was long viewed solely as the responsibility of the husband. However, the pattern is again changing. In Maryland, for example, courts ruled that the state Equal Rights Amendment made child support an obligation shared equally by both parents. It added that courts should not consider the sex of the parent in making child support awards. Thus, in a family in which the husband wins sole custody of the children but has substantially less income than the wife, she may be ordered to pay him child support.

Child support has been called a "public-policy nightmare" simply because many fathers fail to pay. According to a study by the Census Bureau, judges order fathers to make support payments in only 60 percent of divorce cases; moreover, only half of those ordered to pay actually make full payments. The judicial system has traditionally been lenient or even lax in dealing with such fathers. As attorney Marsha Elser observes, "Judges don't yet think of not paying child support as a crime." One consequence is that many mothers cannot make ends meet and are forced to turn to welfare (Press, et al., 1983: 47).

Divorce Counseling

Like marriage counseling, **divorce counseling** is a therapeutic process, but its aim is the dissolution rather than the rehabilitation of a marriage. At first, some may find the idea of divorce counseling rather bizarre: "Why counsel people on how to get divorced?" In fact, such counseling can help divorcing and divorced persons to gain a better understanding of their personal and marital conflicts. This is no small benefit; those who understand what went wrong in their first marriage probably have a better chance of avoiding a repetition of the pattern. In addition, divorce counseling can be important in helping people to cope with the difficult adjustment to divorce.

A major characteristic of divorce counseling is that the focus is not on blaming either spouse or on their flaws of character. Instead, the counselor emphasizes that the overall situation is unsatisfactory. Ending the marriage, while obviously painful, must be seen as an opportunity for growth rather than despair (Froiland and Hozman, 1975; Krantzler, 1974). Time is an important factor in such counseling, as it is in the process of divorce itself. Generally, there are three periods of counseling: pre-divorce (which is concerned with whether or not to divorce), counseling during the divorce, and post-divorce. The particular stage that a couple is in will greatly influence their counseling needs (Fisher, 1974).

Tim and Cindy began counseling just before filing for their divorce. "Within three sessions, it was clear that the marriage was over," admits Cindy. "We came there hoping that Ruth, our counselor, would have some magical way of saving the marriage. Once we realized that she didn't, that no one can give a couple any magic answer, we knew it was over."

They stopped seeing Ruth while the divorce was moving through the courts. Six months after the decree became final, however, they began seeing Ruth again. "We have joint custody of our kids and it was getting pretty sticky," remembers Tim. "It was hard to separate our real issues about the kids from our old resentments. We tried, but it just wasn't working. Finally, one day, after a bad fight on the phone, Cindy called

back and said, 'Why don't we go talk to Ruth?' We saw her for another six months, and it really helped."

Initially, divorce counseling often focuses on legal issues, especially child custody arrangements and the feelings they set off. In terms of the parent-child relationships, counseling can assist parents in maintaining supportive and consistent behavior. Within the economic domain, divorce counseling often focuses on the many demanding roles of the custodial single parent. Finally, counseling can be useful for parents as they attempt to reestablish social relationships after a divorce.

Some family therapists have advocated use of **mediation** (sometimes also referred to as conciliation) methods of settling the disagreements of a divorcing couple without the trauma of an actual court trial. Unlike general divorce counseling sessions, mediation focuses primarily on structuring a divorce settlement. "I don't want to know about their bad marriage," says one New York mediator. "That's irrelevant" (Press, et al., 1983: 45).

Since many of the critical issues in a divorce are emotional in nature, therapists may in some respects be better qualified than lawyers to produce equitable, lasting, and satisfying settlements. Mediation can be especially useful in determining custody and visitation arrangements, which can be explosive when contested in court (Nichols and Troester, 1979). At present, 23 states use mediators as part of the judicial process.

Some observers have recommended that divorce clinics closely associated with the legal system be established to meet the needs of families (Peterson and Cleminshaw, 1980). In addition to sponsoring counseling, these clinics would run classes and small-group sessions to provide information about the experience of divorce and emotional support. Unlike counseling sessions—which deal with couples one at a time—such clinics could efficiently offer services to a wide range of couples.

Issues Facing the Solo Parent

The high divorce rate of the United States has made the solo- or single-parent family the nation's fastest growing family form. At present, about one million families per year are experiencing divorce. Consequently, in 1980, 20 percent of American children were living in homes where there was only one parent; of these children, 70 percent were the offspring of divorced or separated parents (Bureau of the Census, 1980). Most of these solo parents are women, but recent trends in child custody suggest that an increasing number of men will be in this position by the mid-1980s.

Economic Strain

"Sarah . . . was working 80 hours a week as a process server to support herself and her son and avoid the welfare rolls. After almost a year of this existence, she decided to go back to school, hoping that a degree would allow her to find more meaningful work and give her more time with her son. She reduced her working time to 40 hours a week, obtained a bank loan, and enrolled for 15 units of undergraduate study. In two weeks of trying to live up to this schedule, she had a breakdown. Friends recall her sitting in the corner and crying. She does not remember.

She was hospitalized for a short time and then went home to live with her family. While her mother took care of her son, she was able to rest. Eventually, she got back on her feet and returned to school—only to discover as she neared graduation with an "A" average, that graduate schools weren't interested in giving her a scholarship. Her male friends, many with poorer academic records,

fared better. She quit school in despair and is once again living on welfare" (Griffin, 1973: 44).

Sarah's story is certainly more dramatic than most, but divorce and separation bring serious consequences for many American families. A two-income family may become a one-income plus child support payments family; a one-income family may have to stretch a single salary over two households. As a result, families headed by single women form a substantial proportion of America's poor.

Mary Jo Bane (1979), a sociologist who specializes in family policy issues, has noted that the expenses of raising small children often exceed what a single woman is likely to earn or receive from her ex-husband. Studies of single-parent families receiving **Aid to Families with Dependent Children (AFDC)**, most of which are headed by women, reveal that they face a major financial crisis at least once a month. Often they must borrow money from family or friends in order to get by (LeMasters, 1970).

Finding a job is difficult enough for anyone in a society with serious unemployment, but it can be especially difficult for single parents. Some companies are not eager to hire single parents with young children, fearing that they will not be able to fulfill work responsibilities. The single parent may have to take time off to care for a sick child, or may have to leave work early to pick up children after school or day care. Maria recalls that her boss refused to let her work overtime on a Tuesday so that she could leave early on Wednesday and see her son in the school play. "He said I was being irresponsible and unprofessional. I had arranged coverage with a co-worker and everything; it was no big deal. Imagine being one of his kids!"

Even if she finds a job, the single mother, like other working women, can expect to earn a salary far lower than that of men.

BOX 14–5

A Feminist Speaks of Single Motherhood

In a 1973 article entitled ''Confessions of a Single Mother,'' feminist poet and author Susan Griffin wrote the following:

What exactly does a mother do when she has a broken foot? What does a mother do when she has to go to work and her child is sick? I remember the day my daughter woke up with a stomach ache and I took her to the doctor for a urine sample. I had cancelled a morning hour of teaching, thus forgoing my salary. (Like many single mothers, I work part-time and haven't the luxury of sick leave.)

When we got to the doctor's office, however, my daughter could produce no urine. We agonized for an hour and a half. ''You'll have to come back later in the day,'' the receptionist told me. But, by this time, my daughter's stomach ache had vanished, and I had hoped to take her to day care so that I could return to work.

''Can't I get the sample at home?'' I asked. ''I can't come back today, I have to work.'' The receptionist picked up a buzzing phone before she darted righteously at me, ''Your daughter's health should come first.'' ''She has to eat, too,'' I mumbled as we hurried out the door.

If we go to work, there are always guardians of the public morality to make us feel guilty for not being at home with our children. If we live on welfare, we are the object of political pogroms, of the unending curiosity of social workers, of the Kafkaesque bureaucracy. In any case, we are likely to be poor; likely to be tired; and, despite all our efforts, likely to be witnesses to the suffering of our children.

Source: Griffin, 1973: 41–42, 44.

Moreover, as noted earlier, child support payments ordered by the courts are an unreliable source of income; many divorced fathers are behind on their payments. Single fathers raising their children may also experience added financial pressures. Middle-class men report the need to purchase services such as house cleaning which they never had to use before (George and Wilding, 1972; Katz, 1979).

Sylvia, age 34, sums it up: ''I've really had to change my standard of living since the divorce. The savings that David and I had are gone. The kids complain that they don't have lots of things that their friends do, and it's true. But how do you explain to a seven-year-old and a five-year-old why you can't buy them what their friends have?''

Role Strain

The single parent's role is one of double duty. In addition to making ends meet financially and running a household, the single parent often must be both mother and father to the children. Not surprisingly, most find single parenting to be an overwhelming series of responsibilities (see Box 14–5). Since there is no socially defined blueprint regarding the proper role of a single parent, such mothers and fathers feel uncertain and anxious (Mendes, 1976).

Dating presents new problems for the single parent; taking on the role of boyfriend, girlfriend, or lover may be particularly demanding in view of the many other responsibilities already present. Moreover, since many single parents eventually marry or remarry, further adjustments become necessary. Rhona found these role shifts particularly troublesome. "I had been the classic dependent wife, and when Felix left me, I was a wreck. But I pulled myself together; I had to for my daughter's sake. After a while, I got high on being the solo parent. I had the power for once, and I didn't have to answer to anyone. When I started getting close to Alex, the man who's now my husband, I realized I wasn't so crazy about sharing my daughter—or my parental authority—with him. But, in the end, when I saw how much she adored him, and how understanding and supportive he was with her, I let it happen."

Divorced parents often return to live with their own parents in order to obtain emotional support and financial assistance (see Chapter 13). This can generate conflict if the parent must function as a parent with his or her children while being treated like a child by his or her parents. Betty, a divorced mother of two boys, lived in her mother's house for six months but finally moved out: "My mother treated me, a 32-year-old woman, with less respect than I treat my four-year-old son. And her sniping at me really upset my older son. I couldn't stay there."

Loneliness and Social Isolation

While not all solo-parent families deal with financial crisis, all single parents must face life alone (Stinnett and Birdsong, 1978). The children are a comfort as well as a responsibility, but there is generally no other adult in the home offering companionship, understanding, and affection. Furthermore, because of the many demands associated with single parenting, it is often difficult for the single mother or father to meet new people, attend social functions, and become active in community life. Relatives and friends may gear their socializing to two-parent families, thus further isolating the single parent.

Single fathers have reported that their most intensely felt emotion upon assuming this role was loneliness. They experienced a radical change in lifestyle which included a loss of adult companionship, new working patterns, and new leisure activities (George and Wilding, 1972; Katz, 1979). Many complain of the never-ending responsibilities they face both on the job and at home. "When does it stop?" asks Ken with an almost helpless expression on his face. "I've got a tough job to occupy the day, and then I come home and have to take care of two kids. I'm always tired, I never get enough sleep, I have no social life. I haven't read a book for six months."

Research in England and the United States has suggested that the first few years of single parenthood—the "transition period"—are usually the most difficult socially and emotionally (Gingerbread, 1973; Weiss, 1973). While isolation is most evident in this period, the single parent usually has a gradual recovery. Many find that old friendships are disrupted, but also that a new friendship network (sometimes with other single parents) emerges.

Social support is crucial in one's adjustment to single parenthood. One researcher found that those who had remained heads of single-parent families for an extended time generally were lacking in support (Smith, 1980). Certainly it would be helpful if social service agencies offered more extensive family counseling, financial counseling, and psychiatric care to single-parent families in all socioeconomic groups, and if day care were much more commonly available (Stinnett and Birdsong, 1978).

The international organization "Parents Without Partners" aims to lessen the isolation and alienation of single parenthood and to educate single parents as to more effective childrearing. However, "Parents Without Partners" is by design an advisory, educational, and therapeutic organization, not a social club. Thus, many single parents may decide to join singles' groups run by community centers or religious organizations in order to reestablish social relationships, find social support, and perhaps meet a new partner.

While much of the research on single parenthood has concentrated on the strains and stressors of this role, it must be noted that single parenthood has its benefits as well. "It's been the greatest time of my life," declares Lucinda enthusiastically. "I've not only become a better parent, but I've faced up to the need to be practical about a career. When I was married, I pursued lots of possibilities, but always with the fall-back position that my husband would take care of me. Now I feel I've grown-up; I know I have to do it myself."

Single parents have the freedom (as well as the burden) of making independent decisions. They can assume a variety of new roles and learn many new skills. For example, a woman who never balanced a checkbook before her divorce will soon learn to do so as a solo parent. This role leads to a more flexible attitude toward sex-typed work; single fathers mend their children's clothing while single mothers fix the car and shovel the snow.

Some psychologists have suggested that performing multiple roles at the same time can be fulfilling and that those persons with the most responsibilities are the happiest, least depressed members of our society (Gove, 1972; Spreitzer, et al., 1979). Consequently, single parenthood should not be viewed solely in negative terms; it may be a time of personal growth, gains in self-esteem, and new beginnings in one's work life.

The Parent-Child Relationship

Many solo parents feel guilty and frustrated about their role as parents. The single parent is often so busy combining work and domestic duties that he or she feels constantly tired, impatient, and irritable when with the children. "I feel like I yell at my daughter all the time, like I'm a terrible mother," says one woman. "She needs a lot from me, and she deserves a lot, but by the end of the day I just don't have it to give."

Solo parents must explain the divorce to the children and help them cope with the stigma of being "different." The emotional upheaval of marital dissolution can leave children suffering from low self-esteem and guilt; many feel responsible for the breakdown. These feelings can lead to rebellious or problem behavior.

The strains of divorce may result in a complicated and sometimes unhealthy three-way relationship between the custodial parent, the absent parent, and the child. In some cases, children play off one parent against the other; in others, parents compete for the affection or approval of the child. Even more seriously, children may be bombarded with lectures about the other parent's faults and misdeeds, or may be pressured into spying on one parent by the other. One jealous man, for example, would grill his nine-year-old son about his ex-wife's boyfriend.

Children's roles within the household also change in a single-parent family. In general, they have to accept more responsibility for looking after themselves and assisting the single parent in running the home. Older siblings may be expected to serve as quasi-parents for younger siblings (Gardner, 1976; George and Wilding, 1972). Weiss (1979b: 101) notes that "often they are asked, in a way, to assume some of the concerns of management, to move from the role of subordi-

In the single-parent household, children must accept more responsibility in looking after the home and themselves.

nate member of the household to that of the junior partner.''

In addition, children in a one-parent home may become somewhat like friends and confidants for the solo parent, thereby leading to greater closeness than before. ''It's wonderful and bizarre at the same time,'' says Elena, 39, about her relationship with her daughter Marcia, 16. ''We're both dating! I mean, I'm supposed to be her mother, but in some ways it's like we're sisters. She gives me advice on what to wear. To be honest, she's had more recent dating experience than I have.''

An often-overlooked aspect of the single parenthood situation is the effect on the absent parent. ''The first year after the divorce, I missed my kids terribly,'' says one father. ''I was afraid that they wouldn't remember me, that my ex-wife would find someone else who would quickly replace me with my kids. I saw them on weekends, but it wasn't enough.'' Such fears, in the view of sociologists Frank Furstenberg and Graham Spanier (1982), often lead absent parents to work harder at parenting when they are with their children and to make dedicated efforts to maintain civil relationships with the custodial parents.

But other parents are less devoted to their children's welfare and are content to see them on a part-time, occasional basis. ''I love being with my daughter,'' says Ron, 42, an electrical engineer, ''but Sundays and three weeks in the summer is plenty for me. Lucy always said I wasn't cut out to be a father; I guess she was right. If I saw my daughter a lot more than I do, I wouldn't handle it well.''

Adjustment of Children

The effects of parental absence on children have been a matter of debate for years, but at present there are no definitive conclusions. One reason is that numerous studies, among them the research by Victor George and Paul Wilding (1972) on the effects of motherlessness on children, rely on the perceptions of the single parent in attempting to understand the impact on the child. But, clearly, the parent's perspective may be quite different from the child's actual feelings about being in a single-parent home.

Past research has tended to view single-parent families in a negative light and to focus on their problems. Studies often explored whether juvenile delinquency, emotional instability, and mental retardation were more prevalent among children from single-parent homes. Although most children from such households are quite normal, delinquent and maladjusted youths often have grown up in families that experienced a breakup (Rutter, 1971). But it is unclear whether this is because of the effects of living in an unhappy home, of parental divorce, or of subsequent time spent in a single-parent environment.

There is evidence to show that children from one-parent families do not perform as well in school as those from two-parent homes. The former show substantially more absenteeism, truancy, discipline problems, suspensions, expulsions, and dropouts, and have more difficulty in reading (Kettering Foundation, 1980; Pringle, et al., 1967). Nevertheless, some researchers have suggested that the single-parent family may not be as negative an influence on children's development as has been commonly assumed. For example, Burchinal (1964), in his research on children of divorce, found no differences in the personal and social adjustment of adolescents from two-parent families, single-parent homes, and families in which remarriage had occurred.

It has been noted that children in single-parent homes are generally better adjusted than those living in unhappy, two-parent homes (Burgess, 1970). Since children living with solo parents are often given greater responsibility than those in two-parent homes, the single-parent experience may actually be beneficial. In Weiss's (1979b: 110) view, "the demands made on them for autonomy and responsibility may lead to growth. . ., to self-esteem, independence, and a genuine sense of confidence." Such children may regret never having had an idealized carefree youth, but may gain pride from contributing so much to their family's well-being.

LeMasters (1970: 410) may well be correct when he contends that "one *good* parent is enough to rear children adequately or better in our society." With the increasing focus on the rise of the single-parent family, it seems certain that more and more researchers will be attempting to clarify how this environment influences the emotional, intellectual, and social development of children and adolescents.

Remarriage

Samuel Johnson once defined remarriage as "the triumph of hope over experience." Apparently, hope is dominant in the United States today since one out of every three marriages is a remarriage. Yet this hope seems justified; most remarried persons report that they are much happier in their second marriages than they were in their first (Cherlin, 1981). While certain remarriages result after widowhood, we will focus in this section on those couples who remarry after divorce.

Four out of five divorced persons eventually remarry, and two-thirds remarry within five years after their divorce. This includes five out of every six men and three out of every four women. The typical age of remarriage is 25 to 34 for men and 20 to 29 for women (Bureau of the Census, 1980; Westoff, 1977).

According to the National Center for Health Statistics (1980), the likelihood of remarriage during the first five years after divorce is greater for white women than for black women, greater for those divorced before the age of 25 than for those who divorce at a later age, and greater for those with less than a high school education than for those with one or more years of college. In general, divorced persons are more likely to marry others who have divorced than they are to marry widowed or single persons. Remarriage is twice as likely, age for age, among divorced women than widowed women. Divorced men are three times more likely to remarry than never-married men are to marry a first time (Glick and Norton, 1973, 1977).

The remarriage rate after age 30 is substantially lower for women than for men. This is partly because many divorced women have responsibility for children from a previous marriage. Potential mates may view their families as an emotional as well as financial liability. As a result, while 80 percent of women who are under 30 and childless remarry, this is true for only 66 percent of all women (Glick and Norton, 1977).

An estimated one million American children under the age of 18 become stepchildren each year. Earlier divorce and remarriage increases the probability not only that children from a first marriage will be affected, but also that spouses in a remarriage will have their own children. Remarried families now comprise 13 percent of all families in the United States (Furstenberg, 1979; Visher and Visher, 1979).

While the remarried family form may continue to remain in the minority, it—along with the single-parent family—may eventually outnumber the surviving first marriage that has traditionally represented the ideal American family form. As this becomes more likely, researchers are concluding that the high divorce rate implies disillusionment with specific marital partners rather than with the institution of marriage (Larsen, 1980).

The Transition to Remarriage

During the transition period from newly acquired singlehood to remarriage, an individual must work through his or her feelings regarding the first marriage and reestablish a sense of personal identity. A key initial adjustment is getting used to dating again. "I felt terrified at first," remembers one divorced man. "I didn't know how to make that kind of nervous small talk. I certainly didn't want to go to singles' bars. But dating helped me to stop feeling married."

Many relationships leading to remarriage may proceed with caution since the individuals are wary of repeating previous marital mistakes (Krantzler, 1974). On the other hand, such relationships may develop more rapidly since both individuals may view themselves as mature adults who have learned from experience (Hunt, 1966). Psychotherapist Laura Singer observes: "There is a more deliberate choice of a partner. Now you know what you're looking for, so there's a great deal more selectivity. There tend to be fewer idealistic distortions" (Clark, 1983: 42).

While homogamy is an important factor influencing first marriage choices (see Chapter 7), men and women in their late twenties, their thirties, or older tend to meet people from diverse backgrounds at work or in interest groups. As a result, remarriage is often less homogamous than first marriage; remarried partners vary more in age as well as in educational and religious background. For example, both Paul and his first wife were 24 at the time of their marriage. They were trained as teachers at the same college, were Jewish, and were active in local Democratic politics. Paul became divorced at age 28 and remarried at 37. His second wife was ten years younger, was raised as a Presbyterian, worked as a lab assistant, and was more interested in the arts than politics. While younger adults like Paul are likely to marry less homogamously the second time around, the reverse is often true of older adults. Widows and widowers, in particular, are likely to marry someone who reminds them of their first spouse or whom they have known for years (Troll, et al., 1979).

While society can exert strong pressures on divorced persons to remarry, some do not wish to marry again. They may have established an alternative to marriage, such as cohabitation, or may simply prefer living as singles (Furstenberg, 1980a; Ross and Saw-hill, 1975). In the words of one divorced woman, "I'm sure that marriage is a failing institution. It's just too restrictive. I've lived with Mike for five years without a marriage contract and it's been the best five years of my life."

Many reasons lead people to remarriage. Some cannot survive on one income and need financial support; others desire the intimacy and love that a healthy marriage can provide. Still others find it difficult to live as single persons; they feel awkward, lonely, cut off from married friends, and somewhat alienated from society. Occasionally, people remarry for inadequate or destructive reasons—to prove that they can succeed in marriage or to punish a former spouse, for example.

Complexities of Remarriage

Divorce and remarriage have often served to replace poor marriages with good ones. Judith Wallerstein and Joan Kelly (1980) report that most of the remarriages they studied were more gratifying both emotionally and sexually than earlier marriages had been. They add that remarriage appears to spur on or accompany significant improvements in attitude and mental health. Of course, remarriages can also bring their own difficulties. Couples come to them with "excess baggage" from their first marriage—either ingrained ways of doing things or fear of making the same mistakes. Ideally, a couple establishing a remarriage household must understand how previous marital experiences influence them and must avoid trying to recreate the mold of a previous marriage (Waller and Messinger, 1979).

Role Changes and Role Ambiguity
Husbands, wives, and children, and even grandparents must work through a series of role changes resulting from remarriage. For example, roles that were appropriate in a single-parent family may have to be redefined for a remarriage. A teenage son who viewed himself as "the man of the house" suddenly finds that an adult man is about to move in as his stepfather. Sex-role arrangements may also be different after remarriage; childrearing is less strictly viewed as women's work, and many women expect more participation in household tasks from their new husbands than they did in their first marriages (Fishman and Hamel, 1981).

There are no clearly defined role expectations in American society concerning the relationships between a stepmother or stepfather and stepchildren. Indeed, the role of stepparent seems to be approached with anxiety (Duberman, 1975). The classic images of the "wicked stepmother" and "harsh stepfather" may induce fears about this new relationship among both children and adults.

In many cases, stepparents expect to feel "instant love" for the new child, even though they know it takes time to develop such feelings. Children may resent their stepparents and be jealous of their intimacy with the natural parent. Another common fear is that the stepparent will replace the natural parent and the child will never see the latter again. Remarriage finalizes the parents' divorce, thus ending many children's hopes that their parents will get back together.

Challenges for the Parent and Stepparent
A stepfamily is a union of two households, and this can bring special problems. The stepparent must deal with a child who has been raised by someone else, with different family values and traditions (Kompara, 1980). Whether it be an argument over the "right" way to make pizza or rules for video game and television privileges, everything may require negotiation. Three problem areas most often mentioned by parents in a re-

marriage are disciplining the children, adjusting to the habits and personalities of the children, and gaining their acceptance (Schlesinger, 1975). Stepfamily integration is made more difficult by continued ties with previous family members which keep memories of the past alive (Messinger, 1976). The newly married couple may, therefore, find it difficult to create a ''circle of privacy'' that excludes children and ex-spouses (Fishman and Hamel, 1981).

Most researchers view adjustment to stepparenthood as being most demanding for the stepmother. In good part, this is because women still take prime responsibility for childrearing in the vast majority of families. The stepmother must establish close relationships with the children of her new husband, and she may also have to deal with the anxieties of her own children in living with a new stepfather and stepsiblings (Wallerstein and Kelly, 1980). Interestingly, 70 percent

of younger stepmothers in one study had excellent relationships with their stepchildren, compared to only 52 percent of those over 40 years of age (Duberman, 1973).

Competition and jealousy are sensitive issues in stepfamilies—although, of course, they are far from absent in other types of families. ''Johnny is the image of her first husband,'' complained one stepfather about his stepson. ''Whenever I see the kid, I think of his father. My wife tries to reassure me, but I guess I'm still a bit scared that she'll go back to her first husband. The worst part is that sometimes I take it all out on the kid, and it isn't his fault.''

Arguments over children represent the main source of conflict within stepfamilies. Some parents and stepparents feel caught in complex tests of loyalty involving the new spouse, their biological children, and their stepchildren. Ruth, 36, has two children from her first marriage and is also raising

Because a stepfamily is a union of two different households, time and patience are necessary for the members to adjust to one another.

her new husband's young daughter. "It gets crazy," she laughs. "Everybody wants to be number one with everyone else. My husband and I try to reassure the kids—and each other—as much as we can."

Recent "how to" books emphasize that great patience and time are needed for stepparents and stepchildren to develop warm and trusting relationships (Berman, 1980; Maddox, 1975; Visher and Visher, 1979). Ruth strongly concurs: "The first year was awful; our marriage almost went under. But, in time, the kids realized that no one was trying to *replace* anyone else, that they could have the natural parents and stepparents as well. I'm not quite sure how or why, but it does seem to be working."

Challenges for the Children

Challenges for children of remarriage include maintaining relationships with their biological parents—one of whom is absent— as well as building a new relationship with a stepparent. Children often resist the new stepfamily relationships as an expression of loyalty to their biological parents and the former marriage (Visher and Visher, 1979). Some children feel that a stepparent interferes with the closeness they shared with the natural parent; this is often no more than simple jealousy. If remarriage follows a significant single-parent period, the child may have been accustomed to spending a great deal of time alone with the custodial parent—time that must now be shared with a stepparent and perhaps with stepchildren.

Wallerstein and Kelly (1980) found that remarriage enhanced the lives of many children, especially those in elementary school or younger. Children fared best, however, when they could continue a relationship with both biological parents and were not pulled by adults in two opposing directions. Rosanna, now an adult, says of her teenage years: "I was always caught in the middle. My father couldn't handle the fact that my mother had remarried, and bugged me about it whenever I saw him. My mother and my stepfather, with whom I lived, hated my father and pressured me about not seeing him. None of them really thought about me and what I needed."

Some children benefit from being part of two households (Visher and Visher, 1983). One adult reflects: "I learned to appreciate different things from my two families. My Mom and stepfather loved the outdoors and camping, and would take me on a long trip every summer. My father preferred museums and the theatre, and dragged me along whenever he went. So I was exposed to a lot of different worlds." On the other hand, about 25 percent of the children in the Wallerstein and Kelly study, mostly those aged ten or older at the time of remarriage, reported that their emotional needs were not met by their remarried families. In some cases, the newly married couples may have been so focused on their own needs and happiness that they neglected the children's problems.

Expanding Network of Kin

For both children and adults, a remarriage leads to a changing network of kin relationships. While the first marriage may be over, "many of the relationships linger on, for better or worse" (Berman, 1980: 46). Of course, the new network of relatives that a spouse brings must be established as part of the new remarried family.

Paul Bohannon (1970) refers to these linkages of family and former family members as a "divorce chain"—a new version of the extended family. A child may suddenly have eight grandparents (four of whom are actually stepgrandparents), stepsiblings living with him or her, and stepsiblings living apart from him or her, as well as numerous aunts and uncles. Figure 14–2 shows the relationship network of a remarried couple with no children; Figure 14–3 presents the

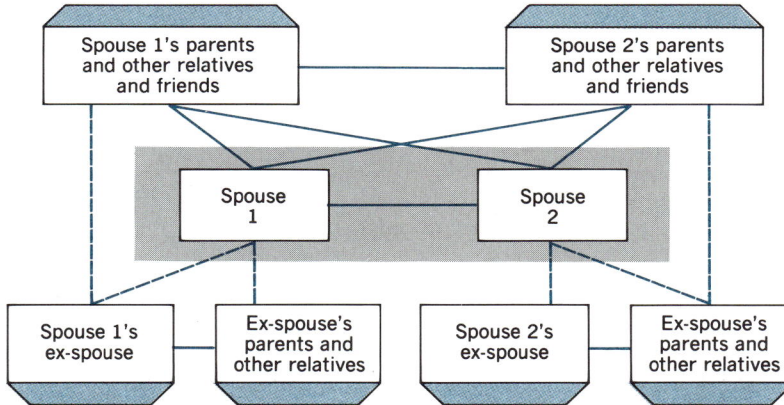

Figure 14–2 Relationship network for a remarried couple with no children. (*Source*: From *Marriage and Family Life* by James G. Larsen, Ph.D., LaCrescenta, Ca, 1981. Used by permission.

even more complicated network of a remarried couple that has children at the time of remarriage.

The issue of who is included or excluded from the new family network can become quite sensitive. While some welcome the opportunity to gain new kin, others prefer to maintain previous ties and remain distant from new step-relatives. For many adults and children, there are serious losses after a remarriage as valued relatives become estranged. Chuck, an only child now in his second marriage, notes sadly: ''I was very close to my first wife's brother. It was wonderful because I had always wanted a brother. From the day she left my house, he's never spoken to me. Not once. I've never really gotten over it.''

In response to the increase in divorce and remarriage, some social service agencies, community centers, and religious organizations have begun to offer stepfamily self-help

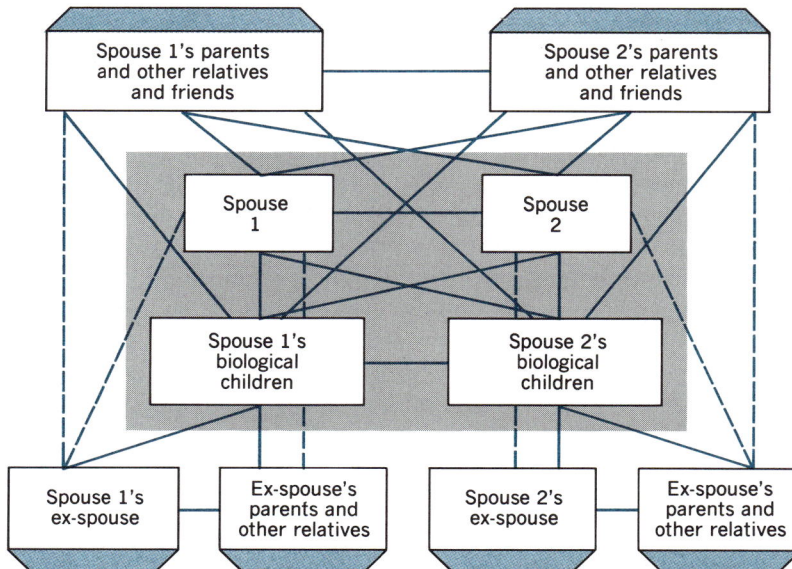

Figure 14–3 Relationship network for a remarried couple with children at the time of the remarriage. (*Source*: From *Marriage and Family Life* by James G. Larsen, Ph.D., LaCrescenta, Ca, 1981. Used by permission.

groups. At such sessions, members of a step-family can discuss their problems and share experiences with others. This sharing of information, frustration, and joy can assist parents and children in adjusting to this complex form of family life.

Summary

Divorce, the act of legally dissolving a marriage, has become commonplace in our society. There were roughly one million divorces in the United States in 1982. It is expected that as many as half of all marriages in the 1980s will end in divorce. Most divorces occur before the sixth year of marriage.

Many factors have contributed to the rising rate of divorce. Women who work outside the home no longer need to be financially dependent on their husbands. Since the mid-1960s, many states have reformed divorce laws to make it much easier to end marriages. Singlehood has also become a more acceptable lifestyle.

The breakup of a marriage is likely to cause both pain and stress. In one study, almost one-fourth of divorced men and women characterized the divorce experience as traumatic. Because of the uncertainties of alimony and child support payments, and the continuing economic discrimination against women in the paid labor force, divorced women with children have become "the nation's new poor." For both spouses, the period one year after divorce is the worst time of all.

While some researchers suggest that the scars of divorce never truly heal for children, others counter that children eventually bounce back after the initial period of disruption and distress. In over 90 percent of divorced families, the father leaves while the mother remains with the children. His absence from the household has great impact on family members in terms of reduced income and stress.

Judith Wallerstein has suggested that children of divorce must master six interrelated coping tasks in order to make a successful adjustment: (1) facing the reality of divorce; (2) keeping a distance from the conflict; (3) resolving the loss; (4) resolving anger and self-blame; (5) accepting the permanence of the divorce; and (6) building realistic hopes for the future.

In the last decade, the nation's divorce laws have been virtually revolutionized. Fathers have been increasingly viewed as competent parents, although most do not contest child custody. Many parents are agreeing to share their children through joint-custody arrangements. A total of 42 states now allow grandparents to go to court and request visiting rights. With the increase in the number of women in the paid labor force, judges have cut back sharply on alimony awards.

A major characteristic of divorce counseling is that the focus is not on blaming either spouse. Generally, there are three periods of counseling: pre-divorce, during the divorce, and post-divorce. Some family therapists have advocated the use of mediation in order to settle the disagreements of a divorcing couple.

In 1980, 20 percent of American children were living in homes in which there was only one parent. Families headed by single women form a substantial proportion of America's poor. Both mothers and fathers find single parenting to be an overwhelming series of responsibilities. Because of these many demands, it is often difficult for the single parent to meet new people, attend social functions, and become active in community life. However, single parenthood also has its benefits, including the freedom to make independent decisions and assume a variety of new roles.

At present, there are no definitive conclusions regarding the effects of parental absence on children. There is evidence to show that children from one-parent homes do not perform as well in school as those from two-parent homes. However, LeMasters argues that ''one *good* parent is enough to rear children adequately or better in our society.''

Currently, one out of every three American marriages is a remarriage. Four out of five divorced persons eventually remarry; two-thirds remarry within five years after their divorce. The typical age of remarriage is 25 to 34 for men and 20 to 29 for women.

The remarriage rate after age 30 is substantially lower for women than for men.

Husbands, wives, children, and even grandparents must work through a series of role changes resulting from remarriage. There are no clearly defined role expectations concerning the relationships between a stepmother or stepfather and stepchildren. A stepfamily is a union of two households, and this can bring special problems. Most researchers view adjustment to stepparenting as being most demanding for the stepmother.

Discussion Questions

1. Do you view the rise in divorce statistics over the past two decades as a positive or negative occurrence in American family life? Why?

2. At what stage in the family life cycle do you think you would find adjustment to divorce most difficult? Why?

3. Do you think divorce counseling can be helpful? When and how?

4. What do you consider the single most difficult issue facing a single parent? Why?

5. What do you see as the benefits and drawbacks of growing up as a child in a single-parent home?

6. It has been suggested that growing up in a single-parent home fosters early maturity. If so, do you think this is desirable or undesirable for the child?

7. What do you think would be most challenging about the role of stepparent?

Key Words

Aid to Families with Dependent Children (AFDC)

Alimony

Binuclear Family

Child Support

Divorce

Divorce Counseling

Joint Custody

Mediation

Suggested Readings

Adam, John H. and Nancy. *Divorce: How and When to Let Go.* Englewood Cliffs, N.J.: Prentice-Hall, 1979. A guide to the separation process and the difficulties of letting go of a spouse.

Berman, Claire. *Making It as a Step-parent: New Roles/New Rules.* Garden City, N.Y.: Doubleday, 1980. Deals with practical aspects of stepparenting such as discipline, money, living arrangements, when to seek professional help, and how to set up support groups.

Block, Joel D. *To Marry Again.* New York: Grosset and Dunlap, 1979. Offers guidance for the new marital relationship and successful stepparenting.

Fisher, Esther Oshiver (ed.). *Impact of Divorce on the Extended Family.* New York: Haworth, 1981. Effects of divorce on family members viewed from the perspective of psychologists, sociologists, economists, and legal experts.

Gardner, Richard A. *The Boys and Girls Book About One-Parent Families.* New York: G. P. Putnam's, 1978. Written to be used by children, but is also helpful for adults; deals with issues and adjustments of single-parent family life.

Ramos, Suzanne. *The Complete Book of Child Custody.* New York: G. P. Putnam's, 1979. Written for parents; explains the legal and psychological aspects of various child custody alternatives.

CHAPTER FIFTEEN

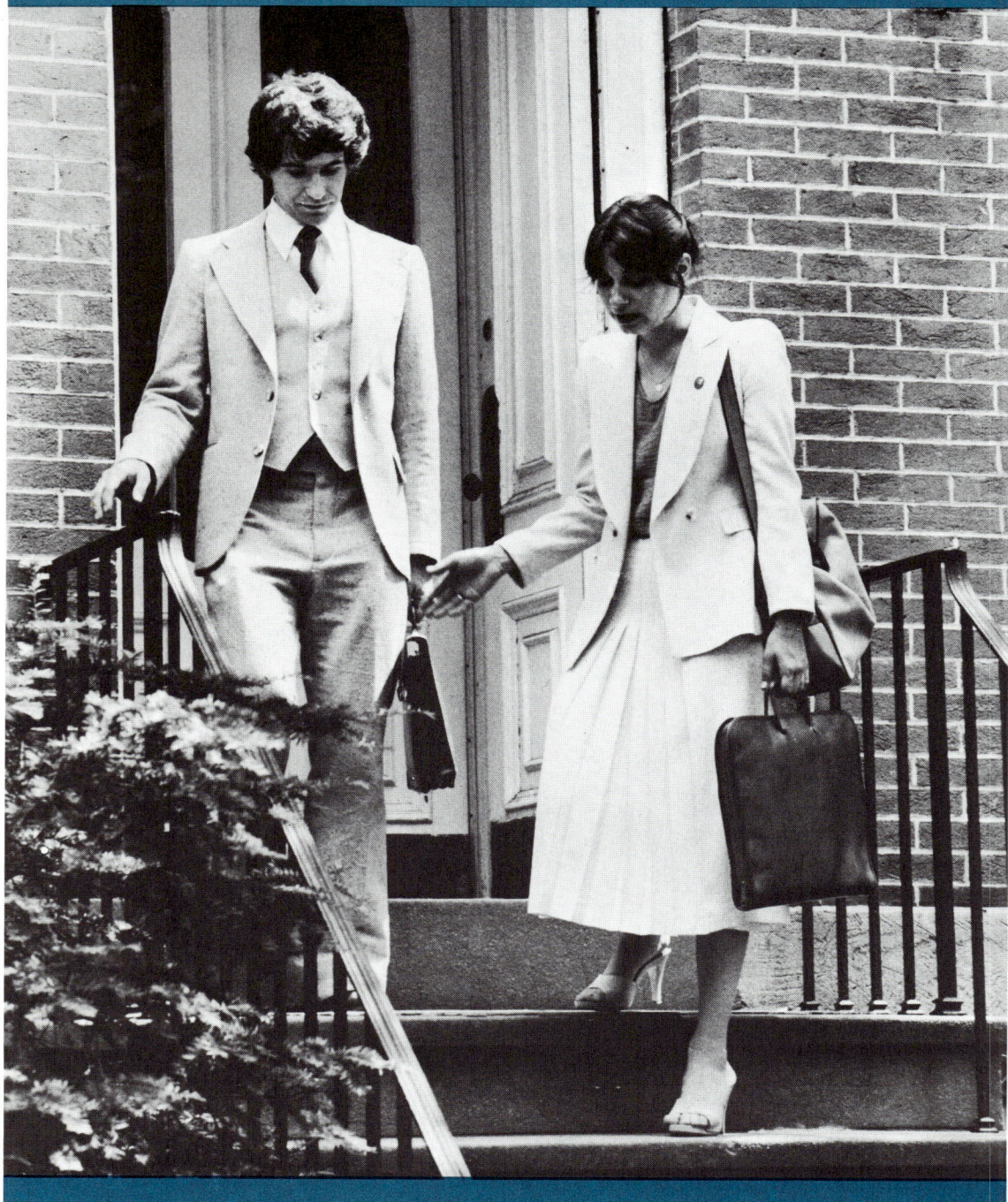

Balancing Relationships: Work, Self, and Family

Prizewinning newspaper columnist Ellen Goodman (1979: 54) describes the ''Superwoman'' syndrome:

Super Woman gets up in the morning and wakes her 2.6 children. She then goes downstairs and feeds them a Grade A nutritional breakfast and then goes upstairs, gets dressed in her Anne Klein suit, and goes off to her $35,000 a year job doing work which is creative and socially useful. Then she comes home from work and spends a meaningful hour with her children because, after all, it's not the quantity of time—it's the quality of time.

Following that, she goes into the kitchen and creates a Julia Child 60-minute gourmet recipe for dinner which the family eats while having a wonderful discussion about the checks and balances of the U.S. government system. The children go upstairs to bed and she and her husband spend another hour in their own meaningful relationship at which point they go upstairs and she is multiorgasmic until midnight.

Attempting to seek a balance between work and family can be difficult if one is anything less than a Superwoman or Superman. It is especially difficult when adults do not set priorities for themselves, but instead expect that they will perform all of their multiple roles to perfection (Gilbert, et al., 1981). In the words of one working mother:

I went back to work full-time after three and one-half months of maternity leave when Jeffrey was born. I didn't want to let my superiors down, and I was afraid they'd discover I could be replaced. But I was overwhelmed. I was miserable. All I ever did was work and do errands. I wasn't allowed to experience either Jeffrey or my career fully. But I didn't want to give up either one of them (Shreve, 1982: 42).

As we have indicated throughout this textbook, family relationships do not exist in a vacuum; families change in response to the changing demands of the larger society. In Chapter 15, we will focus on the trend toward families in which both husband and wife work outside the home, and the difficulty of balancing work and family responsibilities. We will examine the strains experienced by the working family, and how the couple relationship and management of children are affected by dual careers. Particular attention will be given to the strategies of family members in coping with multiple roles and of certain employers in attempting to assist families in this effort.

Women in the Workforce

The number of women in the paid labor force of the United States has almost doubled since the early 1960s. Currently, about 60 percent of adult women are in the workforce, including 58 percent of all mothers. Whereas women represented only one-third of the labor force in 1960, this proportion will rise to one-half by 1990. In another important change, American women are now working during their peak childbearing years. Many continue to work while they are pregnant; one-third return to their jobs before their babies are one year old (Kamerman, 1982).

Clearly, there has been a dramatic change in American family and work patterns over the last few decades. The model of the traditional nuclear family—with a mother stay-

Many American women are choosing to work while they are pregnant and return to their jobs soon after giving birth.

ing home to run the house and care for the children while a father goes off to work—is no longer dominant. Instead, many contemporary families have two parents who both work outside the home and share (not necessarily equally) responsibility for childrearing and housekeeping.

Why has this change occurred? For most families, there is a simple incentive: money. The inflation of the 1970s cut sharply into the spending power of many Americans. It became almost impossible, for example, for a family with only one average-sized income to buy a house. Thus, the benefits of the wife working outside the home became apparent. "My husband never wanted me to work," reports Wanda, a beautician. "But, after we had our second child, it was obvious we needed more money. There was no other way." Families without a working wife lag appreciably behind others in terms of income and standard of living. In particular, black and Hispanic families without a second wage-earner are extremely deprived when compared with the average income of white families (Nye, 1974b).

Technological changes have also had a notable influence on women's greater participation in the workforce. The improvement in reliable methods of birth control has allowed families to plan when they want to have children, which is important in balancing parenting and careers. In addition, the availability of home appliances such as the dishwasher, vacuum cleaner, and microwave oven has reduced the need for a full-time homemaker.

While financial need and technological change have affected the increase in the number of women who work outside the home, the desire for achievement and satisfaction has certainly been another key factor. Women today have more education than their mothers and grandmothers. They view their jobs and careers not only as a source of income, but also a source of pride

(General Mills American Family Report, 1981). Women who hold jobs as steelworkers, stockbrockers, lawyers, or nuclear physicists receive praise for showing strength and independence in a "man's world." Many have found that their work enhances their self-respect and well-being (see Box 15–1)—just as is the case for men.

It is important to stress that poor women have always worked to enhance their families' incomes. Their efforts have not always appeared in statistics compiled by the Department of Labor because many worked in their homes. They took in laundry, did sewing, sold magazine subscriptions, or did piecework for factories. In the past, black women often found it easier to find paying work than their husbands did due to discrimination against black men. Consequently, the recent increase in the dual-worker family has attracted attention not because this arrangement is new, but rather because it has become more popular among the white middle class.

As noted above, the most common pattern of American family life today is the **dual-employed family** in which both parents work outside the home. An example is the family of Wanda, the beautician quoted earlier, and her husband Frank, a shipping clerk for a large manufacturing firm. A subgroup is the **dual-career family** in which both husband and wife have demanding jobs, often with high pay and high status, to which they are both strongly committed. Stan, a film director, and Rachel, an entertainment lawyer, are an example of a dual-career family.

Some dual-career families have "commuter marriages"; they live at least part of each week in different cities where each holds a valued job. For example, Joseph Duffy, 50, and Anne Wexler, 53, were married for eight years when Duffy became chancellor of the University of Massachusetts in Amherst. Wexler had already estab-

B O X   1 5 – 1

Research Brief:
Enhancing the Well-being of Women

Grace Baruch, Rosalind Barnett, and Caryl Rivers of the Wellesley College Center for Research on Women have conducted in-depth interviews with over 300 women in an effort to identify the primary components of women's well-being. The women interviewed were between 35 and 55 years of age; there was a diverse range of job-family situations in the sample.

Among the important findings of this study were the following:

- There are two dimensions to women's well-being: mastery and pleasure. Mastery includes self-esteem, a sense of control over one's life, and low levels of depression. It is achieved largely through work—the "doing" side of life. Pleasure is tied to the "feeling" aspect of life; it consists of happiness, satisfaction, and optimism derived primarily from fulfilling interpersonal relationships.

- The myth that people must choose between work and family has never been true for men. Apparently, for women as well, well-being is highest when they take on multiple roles.

- Role strain at midlife is more of a problem for full-time homemakers than for women in the paid labor force. This is probably because the latter learn to cope with stress in response to multiple demands from diverse roles.

- The centrality of work for women's well-being has evolved out of changing social conditions such as the rise of the women's movement, the need for more skilled workers, and the economic necessity for two-paycheck families.

- Women in high-prestige occupations report higher well-being than those in low-prestige occupations.

The authors conclude that women should be encouraged to think broadly about the possibilities open to them. They should reject the notion that "anatomy is destiny," and instead, like their male contemporaries, they should claim an equal share of the ambitions as well as the frustrations of life.

Source: Grace Baruch, Rosalind Barnett, and Caryl Rivers. *Lifeprints: New Patterns of Love and Work for Today's Women.* New York: McGraw-Hill, 1980.

---

lished herself in Washington, D.C., as head of a political consulting firm. They decided to remain married while living apart during the week. On weekends, Wexler generally flies to Massachusetts to spend time with her husband. She admits: "We don't view this as the ideal way to live, but we have to if we want to pursue our careers" (Sanoff, 1983: 45).

About 33 percent of American families still hold to the traditional pattern of one wage-earner and one parent serving as full-time homemaker (Hayghe, 1981). As we learned in Chapter 14, the **solo wage-earner–solo parent family** form has become more common. In this type of family, one parent must juggle all wage-earning and childrearing responsibilities. Donna, a 28-year-old divorced architect with a four-year-old daughter, has lived the demanding existence of a single mother for the last two years.

In certain occupations, the spouse of an employee—usually the wife but sometimes the husband—becomes almost a second worker. For example, the wife of a corporate executive must entertain her husband's business associates; the husband of a politician may make speeches and campaign along with her. The term **two-person single**

career has been introduced to describe this family pattern and to underscore the important contribution made by the often-overlooked spouse (Portner, 1983).

These various family forms have become an important part of American life. In the remainder of this chapter, we will focus on the most common form: the family with two working parents.

The Working Family: Strains and Stressors

''She's an economist at a large metropolitan bank; he's an attorney specializing in real estate. Both Ellen and Richard have Ivy League diplomas and impressive professional credentials. Calm, conscientious, and exceptionally good-natured, they've been quietly successful with business dealings and friends. But Ellen became pregnant shortly after a big promotion.

'' 'We've always wanted children,' says Richard, 'but I can't give up my job—I'm a partner in my firm. And Ellen shouldn't have to give up hers, either. It's just that we've read and heard so much about young babies needing their parents. The bank says Ellen can take about four months off and still keep her position and I can help with the shopping and cleaning. Still, we'll have to hire a housekeeper when Ellen returns to work. Will the baby suffer if we leave him with someone else all day? Money's not the problem, but we want to do what's good for the baby, too'' (Price, 1979: 74).

When both parents work outside the home, the family must deal with particular strains and stressors. Many are different from the strains and stressors that confront the traditional family with a homemaker mother and a wage-earner father. The balance of marital power is affected by the fact that each spouse works. In addition, children must be cared for by someone other than their parents for at least part of the day.

Role Changes

The problem of **role overload** has been shown to be a common and serious source of strain for working parents, particularly for working mothers (see Box 15–2). Despite a hectic day in the factory, at the office, or in the classroom, a working parent must come home to function as cook, nurse, disciplinarian, housekeeper, counselor, shopper, chauffeur, listener, and so forth. Not surprisingly, working parents complain about being tired and never having enough time to fulfill all their duties.

In the past, role overload was less of a problem since mothers and fathers had separate and clearly defined roles. Each parent could concentrate fully on his or her assigned responsibilities. Yet there were costs to this "orderly" division of labor for both mothers and fathers. Women lost the opportunity to function productively in the workforce, which provides a feeling of competence and self-esteem (see Box 15–1). At the same time, men missed out on the joys of childrearing and became emotionally distant from their own children.

Many couples in dual-employed families profess an egalitarian philosophy, arguing that husbands and wives have equal rights and responsibilities within the family. Yet this philosophy is not always translated into action: equal sharing of family and household tasks remains rare. Women still bear most of the responsibility for looking after their homes and children (Keith and Brubaker, 1979).

In one study, husbands in two-career families were found to do about 13 hours of family work per week, compared with 28 hours per week for wives (Piotrowski, 1979). A major survey of two-career couples by the New York-based research organization,

B O X   1 5 – 2

The Lopsided Lives of Modern Women

In a 1980 column in *Newsweek*, Ann Berk, station manager of a Washington, D.C., television station and mother of Melinda, wrote the following:

Most working women in their 30s and 40s are physically exhausted and emotionally drained, hysteria nibbling around the edges of their lives. They're the ones who still believed in having babies, who were taught to please men and sometimes even enjoyed it. And while they no longer worry about floors you can eat off, they find it hard to shelve their children's needs and the desires, however quaint in the 1980s, of their men. Those in their 20s who think they have a lock on sanity because they've decided against having children and permanent attachments may wake up when they're 50, if they haven't succumbed to a heart attack or lung cancer, to find themselves curiously empty.

However women play it, there are hard choices to be made that all entail loss—and while the career clock is ticking away, so is the lifeline to the rest of the territory that remains steadfastly theirs. For babies still turn to their mothers, women still usually keep the children after a divorce, do the cooking, the cleaning, and the laundry and decorate the house and call the plumber. There are still ballet lessons and piano and softball practice, dental appointments and teacher conferences, and no one has yet found a way to eliminate adoles-

cence. The beat goes on—it's merely in double time now.

. . . The trouble is that we continue to have unrealistic expectations of ourselves. We want to have it all, and for many women—whether because of something within themselves that defies logic but is deeply ingrained, or because no one else will help—that means *doing* it all. And of course, when we fall short, as we inevitably must, we feel guilty. . . .

Men have always known that work is draining. They took the heat for coming home and collapsing, ignoring the kids and only half-attending their wives—but in the end their responsibilities were clear: bring home the bacon and take out the garbage. For women there is no such delineation—neither our society nor our inner selves have kept pace with equal employment opportunity. Nourishment and local environmental protection are still the province of women, and however one may intellectualize the phenomenon, it will still be so. Maybe we can't help it.

For those of us who have taken a bite of the other guy's pie, there is an extraordinary, exhilarating, and gratifying taste sensation that is instantly addictive. There is also permanent indigestion. As the male sibling I rivaled used to say whenever we flipped for first—heads I win, tails you lose.

Source: Berk, September 29, 1980: 17.

Catalyst (1981), revealed that wives were generally responsible for laundry, cooking, shopping, and housecleaning, while husbands were responsible for car and home maintenance, yardwork, and gardening. Child care was more equally shared than other tasks, although wives assumed slightly more responsibility than their husbands (Rapoport and Rapoport, 1978a).

These findings clearly indicate that tradi-

tional sex roles are still alive in two-career couples. Why is it that American families have been so slow to change the division of household and childrearing duties—even when the wife has assumed a demanding job outside the home? While many women have come to think differently about work and family, fewer men have changed their views. Many continue to feel that housework and child care are ''women's work,'' that they must be more successful than their wives, and that their careers are more important.

But it is not only men who resist equalizing family roles and responsibilities. The traditional sex roles of American society (see Chapter 3) continue to influence women as well. For example, some women have been socialized to feel that holding a job is "unfeminine," and they are reluctant to abandon their role as homemakers. Matina Horner (1977), a researcher and President of Radcliffe College, has written extensively on women's "fear of success." She contends that women actually fear that achieving success and recognition in their work will make them less attractive as women. This could lead a woman to turn down a promotion or to hide her ideas and skills.

Women who cling to family and home responsibility may be exhibiting another side of this fear. A wife may feel guilty if her husband helps out around the house, as if his efforts mean that she is inadequate as a spouse. Others may prefer to perform household tasks because this area provides their family power base (Pleck, 1981). British researchers Rhona and Robert Rapoport (1978b), well known for their studies of family life, suggest that it may be difficult for some women to relinquish traditional roles and accept the new demands on them in egalitarian relationships.

The resentments that accompany role shifting—or lack of shifting—can be a strain for couples and families. "Al does more around the house than most men," remarks his wife Ann. "He takes turns getting dinner, and does the vacuuming on Saturdays. But if one of the kids gets sick or has a dentist appointment, there's no question that I'm the one who stays home. There's still a double standard." Al counters: "I'm expected to do my share of the housework and not complain. But when it comes to fixing the car or paying the bills, she becomes a helpless woman again."

At present, there is a lack of available role models for wives and husbands who are struggling to break away from traditional patterns. At a time of rapid social change, couples cannot turn to a widely accepted "blueprint" for how they should divide roles and responsibilities. One husband is proud of the fact that he does all the cooking for his family; his neighbor and best friend refuses even to try. This ambiguity itself can be a barrier for couples attempting to resolve conflicts over family roles (McCubbin, 1979).

Effects on the Couple Relationship

"Greg and Karen . . . , both in their late 20s, have taken turns accommodating each other's interests from the time they met as college undergraduates. . . . They moved to Chicago when Greg was accepted for law school there, costing Karen a chance for a full-time reporting job in Miami. Then, at the cost of Greg's position in a law firm, they moved to New York when Karen was offered a spot in the main office of *Business Week* magazine. They see their flexibility as a matter of 'maximizing' the happiness of the household. They also divide housework on the basis on who is more competent or available to do what" (*Newsweek*, January 16, 1978, p. 55).

Just as balancing work and household responsibilities affects family roles, it also has direct effects on a couple's relationship. Marital satisfaction and marital power will be affected by the occupational choices and division of family responsibilities of the husband and wife.

Marital Satisfaction and Adjustment

According to Carl Ridley (1973), overinvolvement in one's career can lead to marital strain. If either spouse is so highly involved in work that family obligations are excluded, there may be strain in the marriage. Ridley concluded that marital adjustment was highest when the husband was rated "medium" and the wife "low" in terms of job involvement (Hill, 1978).

Orden and Bradburn (1969) found that both partners are happier when the wife is working out of choice rather than economic necessity. If she does not wish to work outside the home but must do so in order to help make ends meet, she may feel resentful and transfer this resentment to her husband. However, other researchers suggest that marital adjustment and satisfaction are improved when both partners work since each may feel economically self-sufficient and personally productive (Rapoport and Rapoport, 1975; Safilios-Rothschild, 1976).

Despite the fact that female professionals have a higher divorce rate than women in general (Rosow and Rose, 1972), most dual-career couples nevertheless report a high degree of marital satisfaction. The benefits of dual-career life apparently more than compensate for such disadvantages as exhaustion and reduced time for social activities (Rice, 1979; St. John-Parsons, 1978).

Marital Power and Conflict

The distribution of power in the marital relationship marks another important difference between traditional couples and dual-employed couples. When neither partner is dependent on the other for financial support, each is freer to exercise power in the relationship and ultimately to leave if not satisfied.

Studies in the United States (Bahr, 1972; Blood, 1963), as well as cross-cultural research (Blood, 1976; Kandel and Lesser, 1972; Safilios-Rothschild, 1976), suggest that wives who work outside the home tend to have greater marital power than nonemployed wives. The former have greater influence in family decisions about finances and about having and raising children. Working-class wives apparently gain more marital power through employment than do middle-class wives (Bahr, 1972).

It should be noted that career competition can lead to marital strain. For example, Michelle and Charlie are both lawyers in private practice. Michelle is envious of Charlie's much higher salary and his job with a prestigious law firm. However, Charlie was jealous when Michelle was named chair of an important bar association committee. Both lawyers need to be competitive to succeed in their work; yet this competitiveness carried over into their marriage and created strain.

Management of Children

No matter how a working couple divides household duties while childless, having children introduces definite pressures toward a return to traditional sex roles (Rice, 1979). Even if the father helps with childrearing, the major responsibility still falls on the mother, thereby leading to some degree of role overload for women (Bryson and Bryson, 1978; Holahan and Gilbert, 1979; Johnson, 1977).

The conflict between professional and maternal roles is especially difficult for dual-career women who report a high commitment to both work and family (Gilbert, et al., 1981). Even couples who attempt "shared childrearing" (each works half-time and stays home half-time) find that social pressures and expectations can undermine what they have tried. In the area of childrearing, perhaps more than any other, societal norms seem to work against dual-employed parents. Thus, it is not surprising that such couples tend to have fewer children than those with only one spouse working outside the home (Holmstrom, 1972).

Studies of dual-career families point to an emphasis on enhancing the resourcefulness, responsibility, and independence of the child (Johnson, 1977; Rapoport and Rapoport,

1971; St. John-Parsons, 1978). While parents often worry that the mother's employment will adversely affect children's psychological and social development, it appears that, for the female child, maternal employment in a satisfying and rewarding job is related to positive patterns of development. For the male child, few positive or negative effects are consistently evident (Burr, 1973; Etaugh, 1974; Hoffman and Nye, 1974).

Mothers who are satisfied with their employment serve as important role models for their daughters, who often show high achievement needs and career aspirations (Etaugh, 1974; Hoffman, 1974). For example, Alina, 17, wants to follow in the footsteps of her mother and become a physician. While her mother is a pediatrician, Alina hopes to become a medical researcher. She explains: "Of course I want to have a career. I've seen how important it is to my mother, how much she loves her work, how much she gives her patients. If I can get half that much satisfaction from studying the causes of disease and finding new treatments, it would be really exciting."

Children of working mothers have been found to perceive smaller differences between masculine and feminine roles than do children whose mothers are full-time homemakers (Etaugh, 1974). The key factor in this type of socialization is the attitude of the parents. If they feel guilty or unhappy about the mother working outside the home, the children may come to share their ambivalence. But if the parents feel positive about the mother's holding a job, the children will accept this arrangement (Hoffman, 1974; Portner, 1983).

Another source of worry for the dual-employed family is finding quality child care. Researchers Rhona and Robert Rapoport (1978) found that parents resort to a wide variety of child-care arrangements because high-quality day care is often expensive and difficult to find, and because there is considerable variation in what families consider desirable. Moreover, a 1981 study by the U.S. Civil Rights Commission found that the absence of a "cohesive or well-articulated" child-care policy in the nation has limited women's job opportunities. The Commission suggested that many women are unable to take full-time jobs because they cannot find satisfactory child care (Norgren and Cole, 1982).

Deciding whom to trust as a "substitute parent" is a sensitive family issue. Many dual-employed families must combine a series of alternatives—taking different shifts so that one parent will always be at home, hiring babysitters, exchanging child care informally with neighbors and friends, getting assistance from relatives, or using informal day care or nursery programs.

In a survey of five European countries (Hungary, France, Sweden, East Germany, and West Germany) and the United States, Sheila Kamerman (1980) found that families in all six nations needed all-day, out-of-home services for children aged six months to six years. Before- and after-school care for preschool and primary schoolage children is a universal need; yet none of these nations provides adequate coverage or even systematic data on such care. France has certain schools that provide supervised care before and after school hours and on holidays; Sweden is encouraging the establishment of separate after-school programs known as "leisure-time centers." On the whole, however, such services are scarce, especially in the United States.

Even when child care is accessible, many parents remain reluctant to send their preschool children to day care centers, fearing emotional harm. The research of child psychologist Jerome Kagan and his associates at Harvard University has helped to alleviate such fears. Kagan's studies indicate that, provided that the centers are well staffed and well equipped, no significant differences are found in intellectual growth, social development, and ability to achieve a close relationship with the mother between children cared for at day care centers and those raised at home by their mothers (Shreve, 1982). Day care researchers admit, however, that there are still many unanswered questions about the impact of day care, including the effects on infants and the possible harm caused by poor-quality care.

With most dual-employed parents functioning on extremely tight schedules, many observers, including Jane Price (1979), have talked about the importance of "quality time" with children. This is defined as fun,

loving, caring moments when parents give children their exclusive attention. Price points out that there is no single formula for the desirable amount of time to spend with a child and no single prescription as to how such time should be spent. Both of these factors will vary from child to child and according to his or her temperament and age.

Other Work-Family Strains

Job burnout occurs when one puts a great deal of energy into a job without receiving the anticipated satisfactions. Fatigue, apathy, frustration, and even depression are common symptoms of job burnout. Those with emotionally demanding positions, such as teachers and nurses, are especially susceptible to job burnout.

When a person gets all of his or her self-esteem from success on the job, is unable to say "no" to demands from employers or bosses, and does not have anything else that provides pleasure or satisfaction, burnout is a predictable result. For example, Frank, a teacher in a "tough" junior high school, did spectacularly well in his first ten years. But, over time, he began to wear down a bit. Each year, he faced a new set of students with the same overwhelming problems. He helped some—more than most teachers could—but was unable to reach many. One spring, after putting in especially long hours, Frank asked his principal for a leave of absence beginning at the end of the school year. His short-term goal: a job using a computer or doing bookkeeping, in which the emotional demands on him would be limited.

Like Frank, many victims of burnout initially take on more and more work in an attempt to meet the demands of the job. This increased workload severely strains the individual's marriage and family life, thereby undermining his or her main source of non-work-related emotional support (Walker, 1973). Family members may feel ignored by the burnout victim; as they become more resentful, they will be increasingly unsympathetic to his or her feelings and needs. To break this dangerous pattern, the burnout victim must find other, nonwork sources of pleasure, achievement, and satisfaction. Greater involvement in family life—even a special family vacation—can be helpful in overcoming this problem.

Families of military personnel face special work demands. The military member must have a unique devotion to his or her job; the family, to some extent, must share that devotion. It may need to adjust to the military person's long absences on tours of duty. In addition, the military family may have to move around the country—and even from country to country—every few years. This limits the career options for the military spouse and forces the children to change friends and schools regularly. Finally, there is an ever-present danger of injury or death on the job.

Police officers and firefighters, like military personnel, risk their lives in performing their duties. Their families, too, must be accepting of the special dedication that is required in these careers. "I left my husband because I just couldn't stand being married to a firefighter," says Bobbi with sadness. "I really loved him, too. It wasn't the crazy hours; it was the fear. I barely got through the first year. Then, after one of his buddies got killed when a roof fell in, I went into a panic. I couldn't handle my own terror, and it wasn't fair to him to have to deal with it constantly. We tried to work it out, but we just couldn't. I really hope he'll find someone who can deal with the situation better."

The loss of income and economic uncertainty resulting from unemployment can obviously lead to severe strain in a family. The degree of hardship experienced depends on whether or not the person is eligible for unemployment insurance, whether the layoff is short-term or permanent, whether the individual continues to receive health insurance from the company or union, and whether or not the family has another wage-earner (Voydanoff, 1983).

In certain cases, family members reluctantly must redefine their roles and responsibilities. If a husband loses his job, the wife may have to relinquish her homemaking duties and seek employment; the husband may have to assume childrearing tasks; teenage children may have to get jobs to help support the family. The unemployed family member may become discouraged; and his or her loss of self-esteem may lead to worry and concern among other family members. Not surprisingly, alcohol abuse and family violence increase when a family experiences unemployment (Elder, 1974; Root, 1977; Voydanoff, 1983).

Coping with Work-Family Demands

The key word in coping with work-family demands is "balance." While the "Superwoman" attempts to be perfect in all roles, the balancer sets priorities and makes compromises. Both husbands and wives must engage in such balancing if a dual-employed family is to satisfy all members. The proper balance for each spouse must be one of "me" (time for self), "we" (time for spouse and family), and "they" (time for one's job and for community groups). One of the key challenges of the 1980s is finding innovative ways to change family and work arrangements so that such a balance can be realized.

Strategies of Family Members

Just as working families vary as to the type and degree of strain they experience, they also vary in their strategies for dealing with strain. Obviously, those who hope to be "super-achievers," succeeding splendidly in all roles, may be setting up unrealistic expectations for themselves. One cannot cope with the demands of work, marriage, and children to perfection; there are simply too many competing pressures.

An important way of developing realistic expectations is to accept the need for balancing priorities and making compromises. The house does not need to be vacuumed once a day; some work-related travel can be refused. A dual-employed couple may compromise by deciding that each will work part-time and share child-care responsibilities. Others may decide that one spouse will quit his or her job for a few years while the children are small and accept the cost to his or her career and the family budget.

Under the concept of **role-cycling**, parents plan their careers and families so that the demands of these roles do not peak at the same time. Thus, a young doctor might choose not to have children until after she has established herself in private practice; an attorney might decide that he will have more time for fatherhood and childrearing after he has made partner in a law firm.

Many dual-employed families accept the fact that they must rely on outside support for assistance with family tasks, particularly child care. In the words of one salesman: "My wife and I love our son and want to spend as much time as possible with him. But we don't have to be there every minute. He has contact with many adults—his day-care teachers, his babysitters, his grandparents. We don't have to be the only people who love him and care for him; we're happy just being 'support players'" (Shreve, 1982: 46).

Successful functioning in a dual-employed family is likely to require careful planning and organization by all family members (Rice, 1979). In fact, scheduling and list-making are considered essential by many couples who are coping successfully with work and family demands. Steve, a biology professor at a state university, is married to Christine, an administrator for a federal agency. He reports: "Chris calls me every day around 3:00 P.M. We decide when

we're each going to get home, who'll do the grocery shopping, and who will cook dinner. We only talk for a few minutes, but we make sure what each of us will do."

Planning time to be alone, out with one's friends, and together as a couple away from the children is important in maintaining sanity and avoiding burnout. Christine says that she and Steve have one weeknight every week in which they are totally "off." In addition, they hire a babysitter one night each weekend so that they can get out of the house. During the basketball season, they see a college game each Saturday night. "It's a great escape," Christine laughs. "It's our time when we can go be kids ourselves. We bring tons of popcorn, stuff ourselves with hot dogs, and root like crazy. What a change from being responsible all the time!"

Like Christine and Steve, many dual-employed couples "buy" time by paying others to help them. They may hire babysitters or send their children to day care centers. More affluent dual-career couples employ housekeepers, cleaning services, and gardeners. Steve notes: "I'd really like to do all the gardening myself, but there just isn't time. After two years of doing it and making myself exhausted, I decided I had to cut back on at least some time-consuming tasks. The garden was one of them."

Traditionally, a full-time wife and mother was expected to cook a wonderful dinner every night for her returning husband and the children. But when both spouses are returning from work every night already tired, cooking becomes a problem. Consequently, many working families eat at restaurants or fast-food outlets frequently. Christine admits, "Sometimes I feel guilty about it, but it's the only practical option when our schedules are jammed. On the average, I cook twice a week, Steve cooks three times, and we eat out twice. But if we're both under a lot of work pressure one week, we might eat out or bring home take-out food almost every night. It's a compromise; what can I say?''

In order to cope with life as a dual-employed family, it is important to focus on the positive aspects of this stressful option. There are many concrete benefits, including the additional income, the social contacts from work, and the increased autonomy and self-esteem of both spouses. Families who view their situation as rewarding—despite all the sacrifices and frustrations—cope more successfully than those who see it as impossibly difficult and destructive (Paloma, 1972; Skinner, 1983).

This is certainly the case for Steve and Christine. Steve says, ''We gripe about it all the time. But the truth is that we love being busy, we love having lots of different things to do. We couldn't live any other way.'' Christine concurs emphatically: ''Remember, this is my second marriage. My first husband insisted that I stay home and play the good little wife. I was bored stiff. Now I may be tired a lot, and I don't have as much time to play tennis and go sailing as I'd like. But I love my work, I love my husband, I love my kids, and I wouldn't give any of it up.''

Strategies in the Workplace

It is clear that parents in dual-employed families must make certain adjustments and compromises in order to balance their work and home responsibilities. However, a survey of ''androgynous parents''—defined as parents who share child care relatively equally, with neither spouse responsible for more than 60 percent of the total family time allocated to child care—reveals that job demands are the most serious problem cited by such parents. For example, 44 percent of mothers and 38 percent of fathers cite the difficulty of matching their work schedules. Almost two-thirds of androgynous parents (66 percent of mothers and 64 percent of fathers) believe that society could better assist

couples who wish to share childrearing and other family duties by providing for more flexible work schedules (DeFrain, 1979).

With the dramatic increase in the number of women, including working mothers, in the paid labor force, employers cannot pretend that families are the same as they traditionally were. Consequently, many employers have begun to introduce special policies to help families deal with the pressures on their time. Large organizations such as corporations and government agencies have become more flexible partly because they have realized that a worker's worries about his or her children and home responsibilities can limit productivity. The Department of Defense, for example, has recognized that it may lose qualified professionals because of family needs and pressures. A motto currently used by the Army—''We recruit soldiers, but we retain families''—reflects the growing tendency to view family issues and concerns as part of an employer's social responsibility.

Perhaps the best known policy alternative resulting from this new employer awareness is **flextime**, which allows employees to determine when to begin and end the workday within certain general guidelines. For example, Jerry works as a researcher in a state welfare office. He has the option of beginning work at any time from 6:30 A.M. to 9:30 A.M. and working for eight hours (with a one-hour lunch break). Jerry has opted for a shift beginning at 6:30 A.M. and ending at 3:30 P.M. This allows him to be home when his children return from school in the afternoon. His wife, who works a more traditional 9:00 to 5:00 day, cares for the children in the early morning and helps them get off to school.

Flextime is a great help for Jerry and his wife in sharing child-care and household responsibilities. Indeed, as Rosabeth Moss Kanter (1978: 14) observes: ''For working women in traditional kinds of families, single parents with sole responsibility for children, or men who expect to share family tasks, flextime seems to permit a more comfortable synchrony of work and family responsibilities." A related but more unusual option, **flexiplace**, allows workers to perform their duties at home while maintaining their connection to an office through computer terminals (Kamerman, 1982).

Employers can also assist dual-employed families by offering more part-time jobs with benefits. One method of doing so, **job sharing**, involves dividing one full-time position into two half-time jobs. Martha and Elise share a job in the marketing department of a large food manufacturing company. "We each work on separate aspects of the projects we are assigned," says Elise, "But we keep each other well informed about our progress. It's good for us since we both have young kids. And it's good for the company; they get two creative geniuses for the price of one!" Some firms are offering part-time jobs to older workers as a means of gradually easing them into retirement (Sands, 1982).

Child care at the workplace is obviously beneficial for many working parents. Some medical centers, universities, and industries are offering day care centers on the job so that parents can be close to their children during the workday. Most of these centers are subsidized by the employer. Other firms, which offer no on-site child care, have chosen instead to contribute to the day care expenses of their employees.

While presently only a limited number of businesses are offering flexiplace options, this practice may become more commonplace as computers enable employees to work at home while maintaining their connection to an office.

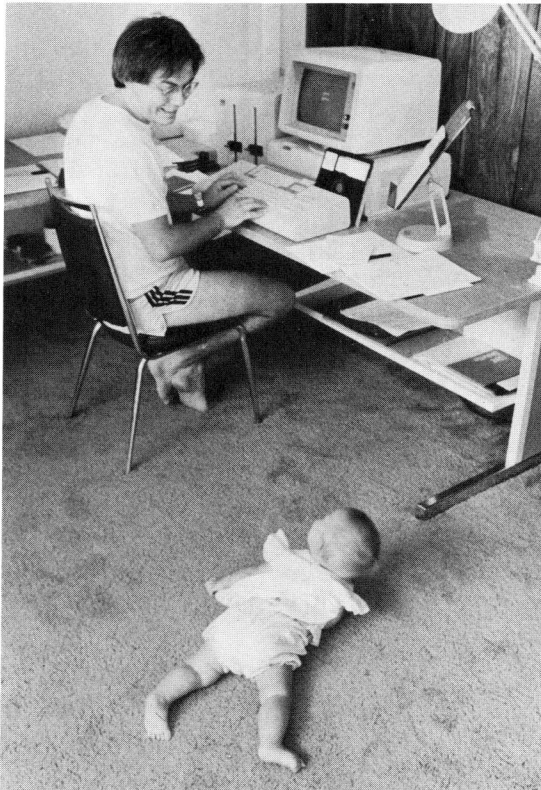

Emerging "cafeteria-style" benefit plans allow an employee to select the benefit package most appropriate for his or her needs. For example, Joan's husband had an excellent medical plan through his company which covered the entire family. As a result, she did not need medical coverage through her firm and decided to trade the medical plan for a child-care plan. Other employees may find it attractive to receive more vacation days or a company-sponsored annuity. As long as the total cost is the same for each employee, each can design a package best suited to personal or family requirements.

There are still other ways that employers can help families to adjust to job-related stressors. Early notice concerning pending layoffs or plant closings is clearly valuable. A tolerant and understanding company will accept an employee's refusal to move to a new city because of family demands. Many firms assist transferred employees in selling their homes and buying new ones. In addition, a firm may attempt to help spouses of transferred employees who are seeking jobs in their new communities (Brooks, 1981).

There is little doubt that there has been progress in terms of employers' responses to the needs of working parents. Nevertheless, the situation remains far from ideal. The Catalyst (1981: 4) survey of 374 American corporations concluded that "the discrepancy between the number of corporate respondents who favored innovative practices and the number of companies which actually had them was great, particularly for cafeteria approach to benefits, financial support of community-based childcare facilities, flexible work hours, and flexible work places."

Summary

The number of women in the paid labor force of the United States has almost doubled since the early 1960s. As a result, many contemporary families have two parents who work outside the home and share responsibility for childrearing and housekeeping. The need for greater family income, technological changes in birth control and home appliances, and women's desire for achievement and satisfaction have all contributed to the increase in the number of women in the workforce. The dual-employed family, in which both parents work outside the home, is now the most common pattern of American family life.

In the dual-career family, both spouses have demanding jobs, often with high pay and high status. About 33 percent of American families hold to the traditional model with one wage-earner and one full-time homemaker. In addition, the solo wage-earner-solo parent family has become more common.

When both parents work outside the home, the family must deal with particular strains and stressors. Role overload is a serious source of strain; many working parents complain about being tired and never having enough time to fulfill all their duties. Equal sharing of family and household tasks remains rare; women still bear most of the responsibility for looking after their homes and raising children. Thus, traditional sex roles are still alive in two-career couples.

Balancing work and household responsibilities affects a couple's relationship. Both partners are happier when the wife is working by choice rather than because of economic necessity. Most dual-career couples report a high degree of marital satisfaction. Wives who work outside the home tend to have greater marital power than nonemployed wives.

The conflict between professional and maternal roles is especially difficult for dual-career women who report a high commitment to both work and family. Mothers who are satisfied with their employment serve as important role models for their daughters, who often show high achievement needs and career aspirations.

Both husbands and wives must balance demands if a dual-employed family is to satisfy all members. A dual-employed couple may compromise by deciding that each will work part-time and share child-care responsibilities. Under the concept of role cycling, parents plan their careers and families so that the demands of these roles do not peak at the same time. Successful functioning in a dual-employed family is likely to require careful planning and organization by all family members.

Androgynous parents cite job demands as their most serious problem and believe that employers should provide for more flexible work schedules. Such innovations as flextime, flexiplace, job sharing, child care at the workplace, and "cafeteria-style" benefit plans are designed to ease the strain on working parents. However, there remains a gap between corporate statements and actual policies on such issues.

Developmental Task   Family Index of Balance

2 - FALSE   3 - MOSTLY FALSE   4 - MOSTLY TRUE   5 - TRUE

Answer each of the questions carefully by deciding whether it is false, mostly false, mostly true, or true for you. Put the corresponding number in the box to the right of the question.

1. I give up personal time for myself so that our family can do things together . . . .

2. I invest time and energy in doing things which are good for me personally and which develop my sense of competence . . . .

3. I believe that to be successful a person's primary commitments should be to work and/or community activities which may mean personal or family sacrifice . .

4. It is important to me to follow a family routine and maintain our traditions and special times together . . . . . .

5. I encourage and allow time for individual family members to do what each member wants even though it may create a hardship for the family as a unit . . . .

6. I put a major share of my time and energy in work, community, and social activities which occur away from the home and family . . . .

7. I insist that family members give first priority to family activities over that of individual, work, or community activities . . . .

8. The demands I feel from work and/or community involvement are so great that I have little or no time for the family or personal activities . . . .

9. I feel that personal growth and development can be achieved best by giving all family members the independence they want . . . .

10. I believe that the best thing for both individuals and society is when one's primary investments of time and energy are to maintain a strong, stable family unit . . . . . .

11. I believe that the family and community will be better off in the long run if each family member is free to make his/her primary investment in oneself . . . .

12. I want and encourage my family members to be very active and involved in work, community, and social activities separate from home . . . .

Add up the numbers in each column and enter
the TOTALS here →

M W T

The totals for *M*, the "Me" Balance, *W*, the "We" Balance, and I, the "They" Balance can be interpreted by referring to the triangle below. Where are you in this triangle?

THE FAMILY BALANCE TRIANGLE

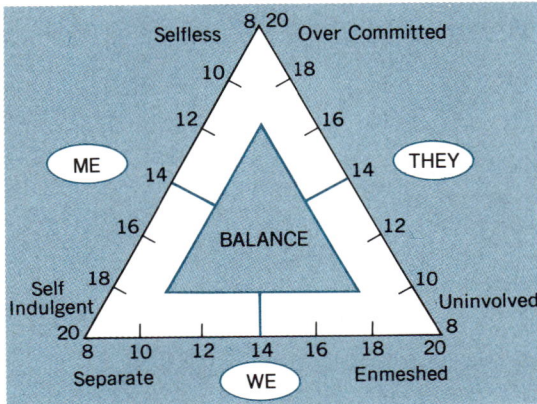

How well are you balancing ME—WE—THEY in your life? Mark an "X" on each side of the Family Balance Triangle by the number which indicates your score for ME, WE and THEY.

Discussion Questions

1. If you are presently involved in a marriage in which both spouses work outside the home—or if you plan to do so—what are your reasons for this choice?

2. Do you think that employers will become more sensitive to the needs of families raising children? Which innovations do you think will be most important in assisting such parents?

3. In your family, has employment of both spouses enhanced or hindered marital adjustment? Do you think it would in the future? Why?

4. If you are or were part of a dual-worker family—either as a child, spouse, or parent—has time management been a problem? What efforts have family members made to ease this problem?

5. If you are (or become) a parent in a dual-employed family, how would you define "quality time" with your child?

6. Do you think too many American women are trying to be Superwoman? If so, why? What pressures exist to make women attempt to prove they can be perfect in all roles at once?

Key Words

Dual-Career Family

Dual-Employed Family

Flexiplace

Flextime

Job Burnout

Job Sharing

Role Cycling

Role Overload

Solo Wage-Earner— Solo Parent Family

Two-Person Single Career

Suggested Readings

Aldous, Joan (ed.). *Two Paychecks: Life in Dual-Earner Families.* Beverly Hills, Calif.: Sage Publications, 1983. Provides fresh views and data on conflicts between home and office, distribution of household labor, family stress due to time constraints, and effects on family relationships.

Berk, Sarah Fenstermaker (ed.). *Women and Household Labor.* Beverly Hills, Calif.: Sage Publications, 1980. Examines household labor in relation to women's status by classifying the issues and discussing methods for study.

Feinstein, Karen Wolk. *Working Women and Families.* Beverly Hills, Calif.: Sage Publications, 1979. An excellent introduction to the issues, as well as summaries of current thought.

Hall, Francine, and Douglas Hall. *The Two-Career Couple.* Reading, Mass.: Addison-Wesley, 1979. A look at the major issues of concern to dual-career families.

Pepitone-Rockwell, Fran. *Dual-Career Couples.* Beverly Hills, Calif.: Sage Publications, 1980. A useful book for students or counselors. Integrates current thinking and research in two-career marriages.

Stewart, Phyllis L., and Muriel G. Cantor (eds.). *Varieties of Work.* Beverly Hills, Calif.: Sage Publications, 1982. A collection of articles showing how autonomy, control, and status help to determine occupational status, and focusing on the participation of women in the paid labor force.

CHAPTER SIXTEEN

Money, Finances, and the Family Budget

KEY TOPICS

—how family financial needs change during the life cycle—
—sources of income for American families—
—credit, insurance, housing, and other family expenses—
—savings and investments—
—financial decision-making—
—common financial problems—
—financial planning—

Lack of money is the root of all evil.
—George Bernard Shaw,

Mr. J. idled by a lengthy factory strike, and despondent over his inability to find more than an occasional short-time job, accused his wife of being wasteful, buying unnecessary ''frills'' for the two young children, and squandering their small savings by running up grocery and other bills. . . . She reacted by ''going home'' to her mother, with the children. Two weeks later, Mr. J. attempted suicide, leaving a note that he was a ''failure'' and Mrs. J. could manage better without him ''in the way.'' To the mental health counselor he later explained that the family would at least have received social security benefits—more money than he was earning or had re-ceived in the form of unemployment insurance benefits.

When the Js reviewed with the counselor their income and financial needs, the husband was able to see that he had been expecting Mrs. J. to manage the household on irregular income supplemented by the credit to which he had objected. He had been unwilling to acknowledge their financial need, refusing to discuss with his wife ''*her* budget,'' and becoming increasingly angry about the mounting bills (Atkin and Rubin, 1976: 357).

From earliest childhood, when we are told we cannot have a certain toy because it costs too much, we learn that money is a very important part of daily living. We quickly become aware of its significance not only as a means of exchange, but as a symbol of status, influence, authority, power, and security. In our society, success is often equated with financial achievement; consequently, money or its absence strongly affects our feelings of self-worth (Feldman, 1976). Edith Atkin and Estelle Ruben (1976: 93) point out that:

For some people money represents love. Or it serves as a substitute for love. For others it means security—not just economic security but emotional security. To pathological hoarders, hanging on to money or possessions is like hanging on to life itself.

The presence or absence of financial resources influences both the physical well-being of family members and the quality of their personal relationships. In the United States, the struggle to pay bills and live within a family's means is the chief source of family quarrels and marital conflict (Feldman, 1976; Landis and Landis, 1968). There are five reasons why this is the case:

1. Families depend on money to obtain the products and services they use.
2. The partner who earns most of the family's money is often not the one who spends most of it.
3. American marriages are generally egalitarian enough (see Chapter 8) for each partner to feel that he or she deserves some voice in decision-making.
4. Unlike certain family problems, financial problems are spread over the entire life cycle.
5. Financial problems are more tangible than most other problems (Blood and Blood, 1978).

In this chapter, we will examine financial issues that affect American families. We will begin by looking at the way in which a family's economic needs and resources change during the life cycle. Wages, income, government assistance, and other sources of income will be discussed, as will such expenses as food, housing, taxes, credit payments, and insurance. The important task of budgeting will be studied, and we will analyze family decision-making styles.

Children learn early the importance of money when they count their savings to buy a desired toy.

Family Finances and the Life Cycle

It is commonly acknowledged that monetary needs and expenditures vary with changing family circumstances. The type of lifestyle that a couple desires may vary during the life cycle, as does the cost of setting up and maintaining a household. There are three major periods of financial ''squeeze'' that a family typically faces.

The cost of keeping teenagers clothed makes this stage of the family life cycle financially demanding.

The first occurs with the birth of a couple's first child. When Cecile and Marvin had their first child, Cecile quit her job to stay home with her baby. Therefore, just at the time when the family's expenses rose significantly, there was a decrease in family income. Researchers have found that family financial disagreements reach a maximum level in response to this "squeeze" (Lansing and Morgan, 1955).

The second squeeze is evident when a family's children reach adolescence. George, 42, talks about the way in which his two teenage children affect the family budget: "The car insurance rate soared when our oldest started driving. Our fourteen-year-old daughter feels she'll be a social outcast if she doesn't have designer sweat pants and contact lenses. While we're fortunate to have a respectable income, it's sure easy to spend it on the kids."

A child between 12 and 17 years old costs about three times as much as one aged five or younger. Indeed, having children is an expensive proposition in the United States.

During the childrearing years, expenses for food, housing, transportation, education, recreation, insurance, and medical care all increase greatly. It is estimated that it costs at least $85,000 (in 1980 dollars) to raise a child from conception to age 18. Many families also must add an additional $25,000 to $40,000 for college expenses (Blood and Blood, 1978; Espenshade, 1980).

The final period of financial squeeze is associated with retirement; a couple's income can decline as much as 50 percent during this time (Gordon and Lee, 1977). The percentage of households below the poverty line is almost twice as high for those over 65 as for those aged 22 to 64 (Troll, et al., 1979). At present, one out of four retired persons has no resources beyond his or her monthly social security check, which was originally intended only as a form of supplemental government assistance (*Newsweek*, 1981).

Ella, 74, a retired garment worker living alone, is typical of the aged poor. She rents a tiny apartment, buys food only when it is on sale in her local supermarket, and rarely leaves her home. Her social security benefits barely cover her food and housing costs, and leave her virtually no money for anything else. ''I saved some money from my job, but it's almost all gone now. When I hear talk of them cutting social security, I get scared. How am I going to get by?''

Still other factors influence the life cycle financial demands on families. Social class differences lead to certain different expectations and economic aspirations. For example, while lower-class teenagers often share the middle-class desire to wear current fashions, drive a new sportscar, or receive a college education, they are well aware that their parents cannot easily provide these things. As a result, such teenagers may have to take part-time jobs in order to earn their own spending money and save for college tuition.

The general health of the economy, of course, can have dramatic effects on a family's financial situation at any point during the life cycle. Rampant **inflation** (a sharp and continuing rise in price levels) or unemployment can be especially damaging. The closing of a steel plant, for example, can lead to unemployment for thousands of workers in a city. Those who have spent decades working at the plant may find it difficult to begin new careers when already middle-aged.

In 1981, the median or midpoint of incomes for an American family of four was $22,390. About 2 percent of all families had incomes over $75,000; however, 7.4 percent had incomes below the poverty level of $9,287. The percentage of families living in poverty is much higher for blacks (34 percent) and Hispanics (more than 26 percent). In addition, families headed by women are also much more likely to be poor (U.S. Bureau of Labor Statistics, 1982). Obviously, a family's nutrition, housing, health care, and education will be adversely affected if it has limited financial resources. As these data in-

dicate, American society is far from achieving sexual and racial equality.

The Family Budget

A **budget** is a plan to adjust expenses to income in order to assist in meeting financial goals. In this section, we will examine sources of income and major expenses for American families, as well as how a family can develop a workable budget.

Sources of Income

Most married couples receive income from wages and salaries. When a couple has insufficient funds to meet their needs, they often solve this problem by having both spouses work, by ''moonlighting'' (having one or both partners hold two jobs at once), or by lowering expenses. Producing needed goods within the household can also serve as a source of income. For example, a home garden measuring one-sixth of an acre can produce $561.25 worth of fresh vegetables annually (Hughes, 1977).

As noted in Chapter 15, the dual-employed family—with two parents working outside the home—has become much more common. In 1979, the median income of families with only one wage-earner was $19,947. By contrast, in families with two or more wage-earners, the median income was $28,179 (U.S. Census of Population and Housing, 1980). Having a second wage-earner, therefore, can significantly improve a family's financial status.

Government assistance programs are designed to aid low-income families. For example, the Aid to Families with Dependent Children (AFDC) program is funded by both federal and state governments. It provides cash payments to poor families that meet eligibility requirements. Medicaid and Medicare programs provide medical care, respectively, for those with low incomes and for the elderly. Unemployment insurance is paid to workers who have been laid off their jobs; it provides a percentage of their wages and helps during financial emergencies. In the late 1970s, about 34 percent of American families were eligible for some type of government assistance program (Projector and Roer, 1982).

Social security is a federal income insurance program. Wage-earners pay a percentage of their income into a fund administered by the federal government. When they reach 65, or if they become disabled, they can collect monthly payments from this same fund. In addition, dependent family members of contributors who have died may be eligible for social security benefits. As noted in Chapter 13, the financial health of the social security system is far from good; monthly payments to recipients currently exceed the amount of money paid by contributors. The demise of social security would have a devastating financial impact on older citizens and families; efforts to reform the system are underway.

Investment income is money paid as interest on family savings in bank accounts, money market funds, stocks or bonds, and trust funds. For a few wealthy American families, this is their primary source of income. For most others, however, investment income merely supplements wages and salaries.

The Economic Value of a Homemaker

One important but often overlooked source of family income or net worth is the contribution made by a full-time homemaker. Since homemakers do not receive paychecks, the value of their work is not as simple to quantify as it is for many wage-earn-

ers. Moreover, because our society tends to respect work based on the amount of money it brings, many sneer at "women's work" as being without much worth. They ignore the effects of the homemaker's labor and energy in enriching the quality of family life.

Take the case of Ellen Hoffman, 39, who decided she wanted to work outside the home after 18 years as a full-time mother and homemaker. What skills did she have? How could she transfer these skills to the paid labor force? When first preparing her resume, Ellen did not feel very confident. She could only think of the drudgery of her role—of the hours spent doing the laundry, changing diapers, driving the children to appointments, and cleaning the stove.

As Ellen Hoffman thought further about her "job" over the last 18 years, however, she realized it was far more than drudgery. She had prepared and supervised the family budget, designed and made Halloween costumes for the children, organized family outings and a 40-person family reunion, and scheduled meals and transportation for a busy household. In short, she had functioned as the manager of a complex operation, serving as part-time teacher, coordinator, purchasing agent, artist, and counselor.

How might one place a monetary value on Ellen's contribution to her family's quality of life? Economists view this problem in different ways. Some focus on the **replacement cost**—how much would it cost Ellen's family if they had to pay for all the services she provided? While certain estimates fall at about $10,000 per year—emphasizing the comparatively low pay scale for housekeepers and child-care workers—others attach more weight to the managerial and creative skills involved in the homemaker role. Consequently, they have estimated the worth of a full-time homemaker at more than $40,000 per year (Kandel, 1981).

Economists also estimate the worth of the

Although unpaid, the work of the full-time homemaker has real economic value.

homemaker by examining the **opportunity cost** of her not working outside the home. In other words, how much could the homemaker earn if she held a paying job in the workforce? By this reasoning, a woman trained as an accountant but working as a full-time homemaker would be ''worth'' more than a homemaker with no special skills that are valued in the job market.

Whatever the system of evaluation used, it is important to understand that the homemaker contributes substantially to a family's well-being. Although unpaid, the work of the homemaker has real economic value. The exact worth of the homemaker's labor has become a major issue in divorce cases, where the court must determine how family assets should be divided.

Expenses

Table 16–1 illustrates how American families at high-, moderate-, and low-income levels spent their resources in 1981. Not surprisingly, the most expensive items for families at all levels were food, housing, transportation, and income taxes. Note, however, that the proportion or percentage of total family income spent on these necessary items differs for the three income levels. For example, while the higher income family spends only 20 percent of its total income on food, the lower income family spends 30 percent.

Families at different stages of the life cycle, as discussed earlier, will have different expenses. Thus, a young family with small children will have greater child-care expenses than a family with ''launched'' children. The place where a family lives will also affect its expenses; residents of New York City will probably pay more for housing than those living in Helena, Montana.

The percentage of a family's income paid in taxes will serve as a reminder that Uncle Sam always takes his share. Certain expenses, however, may be deducted from the tax bill, thereby reducing a family's tax burden. Each family member (including dependent children) is allowed a personal deduction. Interest payments on home mortgages and other purchases are deductible, as are certain medical expenses and other items.

It is important to realize that Congress and state legislatures can exert influence on family life and financial decision-making through changes in the tax system. For example, many young families might not have purchased a home in the late 1970s because of soaring interest rates. Some did so, despite these interest costs, because tax deductions were allowed for such payments.

Every expense in a family's budget should be considered carefully. Three of the most complex and sensitive issues for each family devising a budget are housing, insurance, and credit.

Housing

Like other aspects of family life, housing requirements vary over the life cycle. As newlyweds, a couple eager to save money may choose to live with the wife's or husband's parents, or to rent a small apartment. When children arrive, however, the family generally feels a need for more space and will typically rent a larger apartment or buy a house. When children leave home, many couples move to smaller quarters that require less time and money. Finally, older retired persons with a diminished income may decide on more modest surroundings.

Unlike citizens of other nations—such as China, where even educated members of the upper class live in high rise "communities" with four or more persons sharing two or three rooms—many Americans expect that they will live in spacious, comfortable surroundings. Indeed, buying a single-family home remains an essential element in the "American dream" and serves as an important source of self-esteem (Chilman, 1978).

Unfortunately, with housing costs and interest rates becoming prohibitive, the goal of

Table 16-1   Annual budget for a family of four at different income levels

Item	Income levels (1981 dollars)					
	Lower income		Middle income		Higher income	
	Dols.	Pct.	Dols.	Pct.	Dols.	Pct.
Food	4545	(30)	5843	(23)	7366	(19)
Housing	2817	(18)	5546	(21)	8423	(22)
Transportation	1311	(9)	2372	(9)	3075	(8)
Clothing	937	(6)	1333	(5)	1947	(5)
Personal care	379	(2)	508	(2)	719	(2)
Medical care	1436	(9)	1443	(6)	1505	(4)
Other costs (life insurance, charitable contributions, leisure)	1265	(8)	2217	(9)	3690	(10)
Social security	1036	(7)	1703	(7)	1993	(5)
Personal income tax	1596	(10)	4473	(18)	9340	(25)
Total budget expenses	15,322	(99)	25,438	(100)	38,058	(100)

Source: U.S. Bureau of Labor Statistics, 1982.

owning a home has become an ''impossible dream'' for many American families. The average cost of a new house has exceeded $100,000 and is much higher in some areas. Fewer and fewer families are able to produce a substantial down payment, and monthly mortgage payments are commonly far in excess of the ''rule of thumb'' advocated by most economists: 20 to 30 percent of the family's take-home income. While home ownership was viewed as an excellent investment in the 1970s, current housing values are barely keeping up with inflation.

Renting is the obvious alternative to buy-

While buying a house remains an essential part of the ''American Dream,'' home ownership is available to fewer and fewer families in the 1980s.

ing a home since it provides greater financial flexibility. If you lose your job or are transferred to another city, your monetary commitment lasts only as long as your lease. Unlike home owners, a renter is not responsible for paying taxes and insurance or for making major repairs (Porter, 1976). However, fewer rental apartments are available in many cities because of rising fuel, operating, and construction costs and an explosion in conversion of rental apartments into condominiums.

As we move into the twenty-first century, the trend may be toward smaller homes, prefabricated homes (mobile homes), and more multifamily housing (e.g., duplexes and townhouses). Builders may use higher **density** to keep prices within the reach of a wider range of families. House sharing may become more common as young families and single-parent families move in with relatives to reduce their expenses.

Insurance

Insurance is a legal contract whereby an insurer offers cash assistance after unexpected catastrophes such as death, illness, fire, or theft. In order to receive insurance benefits, the insured person agrees to make regular payments to the insurance company. Essentially, insurance serves as a form of protection for families who could be severely damaged by an unexpected and substantial financial burden.

Many couples with children or elderly dependents find that life insurance is desirable. If the wage-earner (or wage-earners) dies, life insurance payments provide income for surviving family members. Many types of life insurance are available; it can be confusing to determine which best meets the needs of a family.

While the death of a family's sole wage-earner can be devastating, the same can be true if he or she is disabled. Disability insurance allows the wage-earner to provide a family with up to $3500 per month—or two-thirds of his or her salary—whichever is the lesser amount. Since rates are lower for younger persons, it is wise to purchase life and disability insurance as soon as you have family members dependent upon your income.

Insurance may also be needed for any property, home, furniture, automobile, or other personal belongings whose loss would require a heavy replacement cost. Liability insurance for your car—required by law in many states—protects you from paying huge amounts of damages if an accident involving your car causes death, injury, or extensive property destruction. Such insurance protects the victim of an accident as well by guaranteeing him or her adequate financial compensation. It can be useful for a home or apartment since costly injuries and accidents may occur to those who visit or work in your home.

The skyrocketing cost of medical care—which has risen much faster than the overall cost of living—has made it virtually a necessity to have some type of health insurance. For those families who do not have health insurance, a serious illness can threaten financial disaster, especially if long-term hospitalization is required. Proposals for a system of national health insurance have been endorsed by prominent legislators, but none has ever been passed by Congress.

A family's insurance needs will change as it moves from one stage of the life cycle to the next. Therefore, it may be necessary to periodically review and update your family's insurance program. Many families buy more insurance coverage after an important change in lifestyle, such as the birth of another child or the purchase of a new home.

Credit Cards and Installment Payments

Credit is the arrangement that allows a person to purchase a product or service without paying for it at the time. It is a way of bor-

rowing money and, when properly used, can be a tool for budgeting. For most Americans, the use of "plastic money" has increasingly become a way of life. Unlike the generation of our grandparents, when few, if any, purchases were made using credit, many individuals today think little of charging household appliances, hospital costs, vacations, clothing, gasoline, food, and even haircuts.

In addition to the use of credit cards, the use of installment credit—making a down payment and signing a contract to pay the rest of the money in monthly installments—has also become common. Installment credit is used by those who wish to make purchases that they cannot immediately afford, yet are unwilling to defer ownership until cash payment is possible. This alternative to full and immediate payment can be costly since the seller always adds a finance charge, sometimes as high as 4 percent per month on the unpaid balance. Thus, if you buy a product on installment, there is a chance you could be paying a true annual interest rate of 48 percent.

In general, the use of charge accounts can be beneficial since the buyer postpones payment and thus can use his or her cash for a longer period of time. The key factor, as in installment buying, is whether you can pay your bill before finance charges begin. For example, the cost of credit from major credit cards can range as high as 22 percent per year. The longer the repayment period and the lower the monthly payment, the greater the total interest or finance charge becomes, and therefore the greater the cost of buying on credit.

Credit misuse is common in the United States. For example, Joanna and Henry each earned modest incomes from their work in a bookstore. But Henry felt he had to have all the latest in stereo, television, and video equipment. He constantly bought new equipment on credit, using two credit cards

"Can I put my credit card payments on my credit card?"

GUINDON by Guindon © 1982 Los Angeles Times Syndicate. Courtesy of News America Syndicate.

in his name and one in Joanna's. Before long, the couple was in deep financial trouble, all three credit cards had been suspended, and the resulting conflict and tension had become a major threat to their marriage.

For every 20 American families that take out a loan to purchase a new car or use a credit card to buy a major appliance, one will wind up in financial difficulty (Rankin, 1979). Most financial counselors recommend limiting credit payments (excluding mortgage payments) to no more than 15 to 20 percent of take-home income. Families ideally should be certain that they are borrowing for real needs such as a home, a car, or educational expenses, or for emergencies such as an illness. It is not advisable to use credit extensively in order to boost one's morale, to increase status, or to buy on impulse (Porter, 1976).

Job-hunters in a new field find that they face a double-bind: you cannot get your first job if you do not have relevant experience. There is a similar double-bind in terms of credit. Establishing credit is based on your ability to repay the money you will borrow. Yet your ability to pay is generally based on your past experience in paying bills on time. Other considerations are the amount of money you earn and save, the length of time you have held your present job, and your sense of responsibility and trustworthiness.

While some Americans turn to relatives for loans, most rely on public lending institutions such as commercial and savings banks, credit unions, and finance companies. Until 1971, when the Federal Fair Credit Reporting Act was passed, you had no recourse if you were refused credit or a loan. Now, through this legislation, you may review all records to see if the information obtained was accurate. If it cannot be verified, the credit agency must delete it from your file. Any disputed information must be rechecked for accuracy. Even if adverse material is correct, it can only remain in your credit records for seven years. Any information pertaining to bankruptcy can be deleted after 14 years.

Until recently, it was impossible for a married woman to obtain credit in her own name. Garrison (1976) has stressed the importance of married women establishing their own "creditability" since many will later become separated, divorced, or widowed. If the woman has not built a credit history in her own name while married, it will be much more difficult to obtain credit when she is no longer married.

The 1975 Equal Credit Opportunity Act has been called "an enormous boon to married women who want to develop an individual credit history" (Rankin, 1983: 119). The Act's major provisions are as follows:

• Married women can have credit cards in

their own names, make direct loans, and purchase homes.

- No one can be refused credit simply because she is a woman, or on the basis of marital status alone.
- Creditors cannot ask applicants about their childbearing plans or their use of contraceptive methods.
- Alimony and child support must be considered as part of one's income for credit purposes.
- In assessing a woman's credit history, lenders must weigh her participation with her husband in joint credit accounts.

Controlling the Budget

For most Americans, the term "budget" has a negative connotation, symbolizing the unpleasant need to tighten the family purse-strings and accept a lifestyle ruled by thrift and denial. As a result, many· families hate the idea of a budget and refuse to keep one. But a budget is not an enemy; it is merely a plan for managing financial resources and restricting unnecessary or unwise purchases.

As Blood and Blood (1978: 529) point out, a budget is not a cure-all: "even for disciplined persons, it is never more than a prediction of how money will be spent." Still, such a prediction can be welcome and useful. Many weary Americans constantly complain, "I just don't know where all our money goes." An accurate budget will tell them where it goes: how much is spent on housing, food, transportation, and so forth.

While many young couples begin married life without a fixed budget or money management system, most quickly learn that they must develop some type of financial plan. This is certainly true for those who find they are soon out of money after cashing their paychecks, who cannot pay existing bills, or who wish to save money but seem unable to do so. Whether one member of a couple handles all family finances or each takes an active role, preparing a budget encourages both individuals to cooperate and negotiate about spending and saving.

Reuben Hill's (1963) research indicates that the more a family plans its financial decisions, the more efficient their behavior is. Moreover, families that take time to plan their expenditures are less likely to regret their purchases. While parents are often reluctant to involve children in family financial discussions and planning, most financial advisors encourage children's participation as early and as fully as their understanding and maturity permit. Feldman (1976: 389) argues that "the benefit to the children of learning financial responsibility and management through participation cannot be overestimated."

Three basic steps are involved in setting up a budget (see Table 16–2). First, you must calculate your family's monthly take-home income, including each spouse's monthly paycheck (minus social security payments and federal, state, and local income taxes) and any interest or dividend income from checking or savings accounts, stocks, or bonds. The sum of these assets represents the amount of money your family has available for spending each month.

Second, you must calculate your fixed or nondiscretionary monthly expenses, such as your rent or mortgage payment, utility and telephone bills, child-care expenses, insurance premiums, transportation costs, and medical and dental bills. If you add these fixed monthly expenses and subtract the total from your monthly take-home income, you can see how much money is left over for other necessities, that is, discretionary expenses, which vary from month to month.

These discretionary expenses include such items as food, clothing, entertainment, charitable contributions, personal care, and household supplies, as well as savings. The final step in the budget process is taking

Table 16–2   Developing a monthly budget for a four-person family

Sources of income		
Husband's take-home pay		_____
Wife's take-home pay		_____
Income from husband's second job		_____
Interest earned on bank accounts		_____
Other (interest and dividends from stocks, money market funds, certificates of deposit)		_____
	Total	_____
Nondiscretionary or fixed expenses		
Mortgage and home maintenance		_____
Utilities		_____
Telephone		_____
Child care		_____
Insurance (medical, car, life, household)		_____
Transportation (car payments, gasoline, upkeep)		_____
Medical and dental		_____
Taxes (income, property)		_____
	Total	_____
Discretionary or variable expenses		
Food		_____
Clothing		_____
Personal care		_____
Household supplies		_____
Entertainment		_____
Contributions		_____
Gifts		_____
Miscellaneous		_____
Savings		_____
	Total	_____

these discretionary expenses into account. If you wish to live within your means, your total monthly discretionary expenses must be the same as or less than the difference between your income and your nondiscretionary expenses.

For example, imagine that the Carson family has a total monthly income of $2000—$800 in wages earned by Mr. Carson, $1100 in wages earned by Mrs. Carson, and $100 in interest income from government savings bonds. The family's nondiscretionary expenses—including a substantial mortgage payment on their home and property taxes—come to $1200 per month. If the Carsons wish to *save* money, their discretionary expenses must be kept below $800 per month.

Savings

If your discretionary expenses are substantially less than the monthly difference between annual income and nondiscretionary expenses, you may wish to increase your savings. While some individuals view saving money as an act of self-denial, it is often essential in order to meet long-term financial goals (such as sending a child to college or retirement) as well as short-term goals (such as a family vacation).

Savings allow a family to buy desired items in the future without paying costly interest charges or going into debt. They also provide peace of mind; the family has a fund available in case of emergency. While most financial experts counsel individuals to save a minimum of 10 percent of their spendable income, this is most often easier said than done.

Investments

The basic principle of investing is that you use money in order to make even more money. Bank savings accounts are relatively risk-free but offer a limited return on your investment. By contrast, investing in stocks and bonds carries greater risk—if the value of the stock declines significantly, you may *lose* money—yet has the promise of a greater profit.

In addition to the return on your money and the risk of a loss, other important investment considerations are liquidity and time. **Liquidity** refers to the ease with which your investment can be converted into cash if you should need it. A family that has invested heavily in real estate may be in trouble if there is a sudden and unexpected need for cash. In thinking about the time factor, you must weigh how long your money will be tied up (a disadvantage, for example, of a 10-year bank certificate of deposit offering high interest) and also the amount of time required for an investment to yield its return.

Taxes are a final consideration for investors. It is essential to study how much income tax will have to be paid on an investment. Regardless of how much profit you initially make on your investment, the critical question is how much you will actually get to keep.

You must review your family budget periodically since your projected spending plan can be thrown off by changes in family makeup, unusual expenses, and fluctuations in prices. Should the cost of living rise, you will need greater income simply to maintain the same purchasing level.

Financial Decision Making

''I just wish things at home could be a little more like they are at the office. I'm used to a place where you decide what to do when you need to, and then you get things done. But he's so indecisive. He can't make up his mind about anything. It's always, 'Well, I don't know what to do' . . . or 'What will so and so think. . . .' I liked the fact that he'd spend a lot on me when we were going together, but . . . we're not a couple of kids anymore. We have responsibilities, and he needs to carry his share of the load more'' (Burr, 1976: 140).

''She usually gets her way more than I do, but when something is really important to me and I let her know it, she lets me have my way. One thing we have always been able to do is talk about our problems long enough that both of us usually feel good about what we decide to do'' (Burr, 1976: 139).

One couple has effective and satisfying decision making; the other does not. A married couple faces many important decisions throughout the family life cycle: where to live, whether and when to have children, how to divide childrearing and household responsibilities, and so forth. One complex area of decision making—as noted earlier, the chief source of family conflict—involves the family's budget and finances.

Financial Management

How much money should we spend on a new home? On a new car? How should we decide about our financial priorities? These questions plague many American couples. Our values and previous experiences with money not only shape the major financial decisions we make (such as whether a wife and mother should retain her full-time job or stay home with the children), but also the small daily decisions that establish a family's financial patterns. While we may have questioned our own parents' extravagance or frugality, we often repeat their spending habits as we reach adulthood.

Decision making is concerned with integrating values, goals, standards, and resources in a way that leads to action. It is the first important skill needed for effective financial management (Bratton, 1971). Effective decision making involves learning about and selecting among alternatives, or else finding a satisfying compromise. It is useful to be knowledgeable about the subject of a decision (e.g., the advantages and drawbacks of various home computers on the market), to have a clear understanding of your purposes (e.g., knowing exactly how you plan to use your home computer), and to be sensitive to the feelings of those affected by the decision (e.g., realizing that your wife is afraid you will become addicted to the computer and will ignore her and your children).

Indeed, when groups of people have been asked to assess decisions, they have generally rated as satisfactory those that took into account the feelings of the person involved (Bratton, 1971). Since discrepancies can exist between individual needs and desires and family interests, the question of self-interest versus the overall family welfare can be central (Paolucci, et al., 1977).

For example, the Marks family of Baltimore had to decide about a summer vacation. Dad preferred to go to a warm climate and lie in the sun for two weeks, but Mom was keen on seeing historic sites in New England. The eight-year-old twin boys were determined to get to an amusement park with a "scary" roller coaster. In the end, the family researched various alternatives and devised a compromise that satisfied all members. They would travel to the Boston area and spend the first few days of the vacation visiting amusement parks. Next they would spend a few days touring Boston and nearby towns, with special emphasis on historic sites. Finally, they would go to Cape Cod for a few days of sun, swimming, and sailing.

An important decision seldom stands alone and is often influenced by other decisions. For example, a family's decision to purchase a house may require that the wife return to outside employment, the husband take a part-time job on weekends, and the couple borrow money from their in-laws. The major or "central" decision influences other "satellite" decisions. A key element of financial management is learning to foresee which satellite decisions may be needed as a consequence of a central decision (Bratton, 1971).

Who makes the central and satellite decisions for a family? This is not always a question of who is "boss" (see Chapter 8), but of who knows most about the subject of a decision, who is most affected by it, and who must take responsibility for it. In our earlier example of the purchase of a home computer, if it is to be used primarily by the father and teenage daughter, they may take the dominant role in deciding which computer to buy.

Generally, joint financial decision making

is characteristic of young, middle-class families; wife-dominated decision making, of lower-income and older families; husband-dominated decision making, of higher-income families (Ferber, 1973). Couples interviewed every six months since 1968 on their patterns of bill payment and financial decision making have reported a predominant shift from joint action to dominance by the wives (Ferber and Lee, 1974). Interestingly, the number of major financial decisions decreases over the years of a marriage (Fitzsimmons, et al., 1971).

Deacon and Firebaugh (1975) suggest that, on the whole, patterns of decision making employed by marital partners are remarkably similar in different countries and under different circumstances. Major financial decisions are made jointly or by the husband; day-to-day household decisions are made by the wife. Similarly, in a number of cross-cultural studies, Blood and Hill (1970) found that life insurance and other questions of high finance were largely viewed as the husband's domain. Wives generally decided about food budgets, clothing expenses, and children's allowances. Important decisions affecting both partners, such as those involving the family home or the choice of a vacation, were essentially made jointly.

Types of Financial Problems

Individuals and families vary greatly in their ability to plan their lives, manage their economic affairs, and set realistic goals regarding income and expenditures. Affluent families may require assistance from bankers, investment counselors, and stockbrokers who will suggest ways to invest money in order to increase its earning power. They may also turn to tax accountants in order to boost their deductions and reduce their taxable income. By contrast, poor families may be struggling with unemployment and may

need advice from a social worker as to how to deal with being in debt.

In general, the financial problems brought to social service agencies fall into four categories:

- Insufficient income, or unexpected reduction in income, due to unemployment, economic recession, or inflationary impact on fixed income.
- Lack of skill in making money management choices.
- Impact of emotional difficulties, such as debts accumulated because of neurotic needs or disturbed family relations.
- Effects of a crisis, such as the death, long-term illness, or disability of the family breadwinner.

Often a family's financial and emotional problems are interrelated. Thus, a skillful financial counselor will have to understand many of the psychological issues generally treated by other types of counselors (Feldman, 1976).

Many families that need financial advice never request such help. Jim, an unemployed factory worker, admits: "I absolutely refused to go to a stranger and talk about our finances. I already felt like a failure; I assumed other people would see me that way, too." In recent years, however, there has been greater acceptance of such counseling. Like Jim, who finally did meet with a financial counselor, many Americans have become willing to talk frankly with a professional about intimate aspects of family life.

Types of Financial Counseling

Financial counseling may take the form of advice-giving—what is generally termed "deliberation together"—or other techniques aimed at enabling the family to function more effectively. The particular techniques chosen by the counselor will depend on his or her evaluation of the feelings, capabilities, and needs of the family members involved. Inherent in the process of "deliberation together" is the recognition that individuals and families seeking financial counseling should accept maximum responsibility for solving their own problems. Thus, instead of "taking over" and providing the family with a detailed blueprint for their financial future, the counselor will encourage family members themselves to do most of the needed thinking and planning. Long-term counseling goals are usually aimed at improving the family's stability and financial self-sufficiency (Feldman, 1976).

For families with limited incomes, short-term goals may focus on maintaining a satisfactory quality of basic goods and services. The long-term goal will often be to help the family increase its income—whether by increasing the number of wage-earners or helping a primary breadwinner to obtain training and ultimately a better job. Jim, the unemployed factory worker quoted above, worked with his counselor on changing his occupation. Since he already felt like a failure, the idea of entering a new and unfamiliar field was quite threatening. But, with the assistance of the counselor and support from his family, Jim began a training program for computer programmers.

Debt counseling may be required if a family needs help in working out a plan with creditors (people or agencies to whom money is owed). If there are several creditors, the family may be encouraged to consolidate its debts by obtaining a single manageable loan or a "prorating plan" in which a certain portion of available income is paid to each creditor monthly. Should the family's indebtedness require more drastic action, a court-supervised plan for paying off debts, known as a **wage-earner plan**, may be enacted. Declaring **bankruptcy** is the only legal means by which debts can be canceled without payment.

Planning for Retirement and Death

Although the social security system is designed to provide income and insurance for older Americans, and many have pension plans through their jobs, it has become increasingly common for people to develop a savings plan for retirement. Individual Retirement Accounts (IRAs) allow individuals and families to plan for retirement by protecting part of their annual income from income taxes. Banks, stockbrokers, attorneys, and investment companies can all be helpful in developing a family retirement plan.

Estate planning refers to the process of making a will, deciding how you want your property distributed after death, determining who should care for your children (if they are minors), and so forth. Seventy percent of Americans die **intestate**, that is, without a will. While most of us probably wish to avoid thinking about our own death, making a will is nevertheless a valuable idea. Estate planning eliminates legal problems, may reduce inheritance taxes, and can minimize family conflict and financial distress.

Effective financial counseling requires a sensitivity not only to the economic meaning of money, but also to its emotional and social meanings. As Feldman (1976) indicates, financial counseling can be an extremely influential means of helping families to resolve basic relationship problems. It can open a couple's communication and give them a greater awareness of their patterns of interaction.

Summary

In our society, money or its absence strongly affects our feelings of self-worth. The struggle to pay bills and live within a family's means is the chief source of family quarrels and marital conflict.

A family typically faces three major periods of financial "squeeze" during the life cycle. The first occurs with the birth of a couple's first child. The second is evident when children reach adolescence. The final period of squeeze is associated with retirement. The general health of the economy can have dramatic effects on a family's financial situation at any point during the life cycle.

A budget is a plan to adjust expenses to income in order to assist in meeting financial goals. Most married couples receive income from wages and salaries. Government assistance programs, social security, and investments are also sources of income. An important but often overlooked source of family income is the contribution made by a full-time homemaker.

The most expensive items for American families are food, housing, transportation, and income taxes. With housing costs and interest rates becoming prohibitive, the goal of owning a home has become an "impossible dream" for many American families. Insurance serves as a form of protection for families who could be severely damaged by an unexpected and substantial financial burden.

Credit is a way of borrowing money; when properly used, it can be a tool for budgeting. However, credit misuse is common in the United States. Establishing credit is based on your ability to repay the money you borrow. Until recently, it was impossible for a married woman to obtain credit in her own name.

The more a family plans its financial decisions, the more efficient its behavior is. There are three basic steps in setting up a budget: calculating monthly take-home income, calculating fixed or nondiscretionary expenses, and taking discretionary expenses into account.

Savings can be essential in meeting long-term financial goals; they also provide financial security in case of emergency. The basic principle of investing is that you use money in order to make even more money.

Financial decision-making often involves balancing individual interests against the overall family welfare. On the whole, major financial decisions are made jointly or by husbands; day-to-day household decisions are made by the wife.

Financial counseling—or "deliberation together"—is aimed at enabling the family to function more effectively. Instead of "taking over" and providing the family with a detailed blueprint for its financial future, the counselor will encourage family members themselves to do most of the needed thinking and planning.

Discussion Questions

1. At what stage of your own family's development would you say money was the greatest source of conflict? Why do you think your family had the most financial problems at this stage?

2. Do you or your parents "keep a budget"? If so, has it been effective? If not, why not?

3. Do you consider owning your own home to be part of the "American dream"? Discuss.

4. Should consumer protection agencies discourage Americans from buying on credit? Why or why not?

5. Why do you think patterns of financial decision-making among spouses are so similar cross-culturally? Do you think there will be major changes in these patterns as more women enter the paid labor force?

6. If you were in financial difficulty, would you agree to see a financial counselor? How would you feel about receiving this type of aid?

Key Words

Bankruptcy	**Inflation**	**Liquidity**
Budget	**Insurance**	**Opportunity Cost**
Credit	**Intestate**	**Replacement Cost**
Density	**Investment Income**	**Wage-Earner Plan**
Estate Planning		

Suggested Readings

Davis, Ken, and Taylor, Tom. *Kids and Cash: Solving a Parent's Dilemma*. La Jolla, Calif.: Oak Tree Publications, 1979. Provides the economic facts-of-life material which parents need to help children become economically competent.

Feldman, Frances L. *The Family in Today's Money World*. New York: Family Service Association of America, 1976. Focuses on the meaning of money to individuals and families and the way they use it within the society's economic climate.

CHAPTER SEVENTEEN

Coping with Change and Stress

Throughout this textbook, we have examined problems experienced by American families during the life cycle. Poverty, divorce, child abuse, teenage alcoholism, "launching"—these are but a few of the stressful challenges that place pressure on family units. The earliest family stress research included studies of how families endured the social and political turmoil of the Depression and World War II. More recent interest in stress has grown out of the work of Dr. Hans Selye (1974) and other physicians who found a definite relationship between general health or disease and the life events an individual had experienced.

This chapter will focus on how families behave when under stress. We will begin by examining predictable and unexpected stressor events that originate inside or outside the family. Special stressors, such as intercultural or interracial marriage and racism, will be analyzed. Two models devised to understand family stress will be introduced. Finally, we will study the coping strategies used by individuals and families in reacting to stress.

Family Stress: Some Basic Concepts

Before we can understand the nature of stress within the family, we must define a few basic concepts used by researchers. **Stressors** are those life events or changes that are so serious or drastic that they require changes in the family system. For example, the death of a parent is a stressor because other family members must redefine roles and learn to survive without the missing adult. On the other hand, the birth of a child is also a stressor because it requires important changes in family routines. A stressor event, therefore, is not necessarily bad or unpleasant; it can be a joyous event that nevertheless dictates adjustments by family members.

Stress is not part of the event itself, but rather is part of the family's response to the stressor. When a family's resources are inadequate in light of the demands on it, the resulting tension or imbalance constitutes **stress**. In order to adapt to stress, the family must correct this imbalance. Family **distress** occurs when members face extreme psychological pressure and there is a great deal of conflict in the family. **Eustress** is a term used to refer to a positive type of stress that takes place when families benefit from or enjoy facing the challenges of life (Selye, 1974). For example, a family may pull together and feel much closer to one another after surviving a natural disaster such as a hurricane or flood.

Stressors on the Family

Table 17–1 offers one method for classifying the changes that affect family life. Stressor events may originate inside or outside the family. Many are **normative stressors**, that is, predictable or expected changes that all or most families experience. The adjustments required when a couple has its first child would fall into this category. By contrast, some unexpected or unusual changes affect only certain families and are classified as nonnormative. An automobile accident leaving a teenage daughter or son a paraplegic would clearly be a nonnormative stressor.

Normative Changes Inside the Family

As we have emphasized throughout this book, families change throughout the life cycle in response to normal human growth and development (Aldous, 1978). Each of us grows, ages, and ultimately dies. In earlier chapters, we discussed the impact of such developmental events as the birth of a child or a parent's midlife transition, which force family members to shift their perspectives and roles (Miller and Sollie, 1980; Rubin, 1978).

For example, when Melanie was 14, she began to feel less comfortable at home and more resentful of her parents' rules. She had always had a close relationship with her younger brother but suddenly didn't want to spend time with him anymore. Melanie be-

Table 17–1   Typology of stressors

	Inside the family	Outside the family
Normative	Birth of a child Death of a family member Other developmental transitions	Work/family strains Economic depression
Nonnormative	Serious or chronic illness in family Divorce, remarriage Alcoholism of family member Intercultural marriages	Unemployment War, revolution Natural disasters Racism and prejudice

gan arguing frequently with her mother and had confrontations with her father over his rules about her socializing.

After about six months of conflict, Melanie's parents realized that they had to adopt new methods of discipline to deal with their teenager. Instead of simply ''laying down the law,'' they became more tolerant of her desire to spend time with her friends and stay out later in the evening. ''It was almost like learning to be a parent again,'' recalls her mother wearily. ''But it is satisfying to see her growing up and becoming more mature.''

For Melanie's family, her transition to adolescence meant a change in routines, rules, and methods of decision-making. ''We couldn't just tell Melanie what to do anymore,'' says her father. ''We had to discuss things with her, give her reasons for our rules, and stay open to compromise.'' All family members were adapting to a stressor of normative developmental change. Table 17-2 provides an overview of the major developmental issues for children and adults during the life cycle.

It is important to remember that the interplay of developing individuals in a family affects the level of stress. Each is simultaneously growing and changing, meeting challenges of his or her own personal development, while adapting to changes in others. For example, a baby's developing sense of trust is influenced by his mother's and father's developmental growth. A 35-year-old working parent deals with the demands of a new baby much differently than does a 17-year-old parent still struggling to establish identity and independence.

The death of a family member is another obvious example of a normative change that leads to stress. Grieving family members experience a period of emotional turmoil and often must make dramatic changes in the

The death of a family member can result in a period of emotional turmoil and can often make dramatic changes.

way they function. The most significant factors that shape the degree of disruption caused by the death of a family member are: (1) the timing of the death in the life cycle (i.e., whether the family member is a child or a grandparent); (2) the nature of the death (whether sudden or due to a long illness); (3) the openness or expressiveness of the family about the death; and (4) the functional and emotional role of the deceased within the family (Herz, 1980).

Table 17-2 Developmental changes and demands

Family life cycle stages	Child members		Adult members	
	Individual developmental age—specific tasks and needs	Expected transitional events and typical problems	Individual developmental age—specific tasks and needs	Expected transitional events and typical problems
I. Establishment				
II. Childbearing	Infancy, 0–3 yrs. Tasks: Basic trust vs. mistrust, Autonomy vs. shame and doubt Needs: Mothering, care, learning, verbal and conceptual skills	Role transition for parents, working mothers, absent fathers. *Typical Problems:* Inadequate parenting, unwanted children, neglect and abuse, marital conflict, physical handicaps, mental retardation		
III. Families with preschool children	Preschool, 3–6 yrs. Tasks: Initiative vs. guilt Needs: Learning, socialization, play	Child's separation from home Changing tasks of childrearing *Typical problems:* Inadequate socialization, lack of supervision, behavioral reactions		
IV. Families with schoolchildren	Grade school, 6–13 yrs. Tasks: Industry vs. inferiority Needs: Intellectual and social stimulation	Expanding world and increasing stimuli to be coped with *Typical problems:* Social and learning failures	Mature adult, 21–65 Tasks: Generativity vs. stagnation Needs: Expanding opportunities for self-development in life roles	Household management and care *Typical problems:* Family breakdown, divorce; financial needs or mismanagement; parent-child conflict; work, career failure; disability, personality disorganization; death of family and friends

Stage	Developmental Characteristics	Description and Problems
V. Families with adolescents	High school, 13–18 yrs. Tasks: Identity vs. role confusion. Needs: Achievement, partial separation from parents	The time for decisions about sexual identity, work, and the future. *Typical problems:* Identity crises, alienation, addictions, delinquency, school maladjustment
VI. Families launching children	Young adult, 18–21. Tasks: Intimacy vs. isolation. Needs: Opportunities for self-fulfillment in adult roles	Leaving home, marriage, working. *Typical problems:* Unwed parenthood, school/work maladaptation, marital conflict, addictions, crime
VII. Families in postparental years VIII. Aging Families	Aged adult, 65 and over. Tasks: Integrity vs. despair. Needs: Living arrangements, physical care, continuing opportunities for self-development in role of aged	Physical and mental depletion. Loss of friends and separation from family, retirement. *Typical problems:* Sickness, loneliness, social isolation, economic deprivation

If a parent dies, there is generally a serious financial impact on surviving family members. However, even seemingly "small," day-to-day changes can have important symbolic meaning. A basic shift in who sits where at the dinner table may serve as a painful reminder that a loved one is missing and will not return. Leading family scholar Reuben Hill (1958) has called death a "crisis of dismemberment" for the family; he pictures the family as a body that has lost an arm or a leg and must adjust to functioning in quite a different way.

Normative Changes from Outside the Family

In addition to responding to the developmental needs of family members, families must also adapt to daily demands from outside the family. The best example is the pressure placed on parents because of their jobs (General Mills American Family Report, 1981; Skinner, 1980). Long or irregular work hours, frequent or extended travel, forced geographical moves, and, perhaps above all, the daily frustrations of a job affect both the individual and the family.

Routine absence resulting from long hours and travel may make it difficult for a mother or father to fulfill certain family roles, including companionship with children and the spouse, attendance at family and school functions, and participation in household duties (Kanter, 1977; Renshaw, 1976). Work-related stress associated with time pressure and separations can leave little time for home and family. Forced relocation is not only expensive—the family may have to sell its home and buy a new one on short notice—but also carries noticeable social-psychological costs associated with a nomadic lifestyle. The frequently transferred family, in particular, can experience emotional and interpersonal strain when it is isolated from such traditional supports as an extended family, close friends, and stable community relationships. Moreover, relocation often poses problems for the spouse who has serious educational or career ambitions.

Economic events such as prolonged inflation or recession are also classified as normative changes because they affect almost all families to some extent. Widespread economic decline in one region of the nation, such as the automobile industry in Michigan, leads to lower tax revenues and cutbacks in social services. Many families cite the rising cost of living brought on by inflation as the major reason that both parents have entered the paid labor force (General Mills American Family Report, 1981).

Nonnormative Changes Inside the Family

Nonnormative conditions or events affecting family members can vary widely. For example, if a parent or child is born with or contracts a serious illness (see Box 17–1), the family will have to change its routine to care for the sick person and deal with the resulting emotional stress (McCubbin, et al., 1983). The afflicted member may face separation from family and friends due to extended hospitalization; loss of work or family roles; changes in appearance or body functions; and feelings of anger and helplessness over the illness.

Major adaptive tasks for both the patient and his or her family include dealing with pain and incapacity; dealing with the hospital staff and day-to-day procedures; preserving a reasonable emotional balance; maintaining relationships with family and friends; and preparing for what may be an uncertain future (Moos and Tsu, 1976). It should be noted that the effects of a child's death on parents are profound: separation and divorce occur in an estimated 70 to 90 percent of such cases (Schiff, 1977; Tietz, et al., 1977).

Alcoholism, another example of a non-

B O X   1 7 - 1

A Family Deals with a Child's Illness

John D. was the eldest of seven children, an active 12-year-old boy involved in many activities. The family was close, and Mr. D's job provided them with a reasonably good financial situation. The parents were understandably shocked when told that John had leukemia. Their initial reactions were typical of those of other parents, but they expressed their shock and grief openly and together. . . .

From the start, Mr. and Mrs. D. knew they must talk to their son about the diagnosis. They told him he had a serious illness that most children did not survive and encouraged him to trust the physicians, who would do everything within their power to keep him as well as possible for as long as they could. John and his parents were able to cry together over the implications of the illness. Mr. and Mrs. D. also talked with John's 10-year-old sister about the situation, since the two children were especially close.

The parents clearly wanted to be as honest as possible with John. The limited time remaining was doubly precious and was not to be wasted playing games or jeopardizing relationships. The pain of accepting their child's impending death would be even more unbearable if he turned away from them and no longer trusted them. They had never lied to him and were sure their frankness allowed them to trust, respect, and love each other.

At times, the family had to express feelings of sadness by crying and mourning and no one tried to inhibit this. Mr. and Mrs. D. allowed John time to himself, but he was always free to go back to one or both of them with questions that were bothering him. He was a remarkable child whom everyone enjoyed. He was a bright sensitive boy who wrote a science paper on leukemia for which he received an "A."

Source: Kaplan, et al., 1973: 64.

---

normative stressor, may be viewed as an illness that carries an accompanying social stigma. Many Americans assume that alcoholism does not happen in healthy families. Consequently, nonalcoholic family members feel guilty and ashamed because someone in the family is suffering from alcoholism.

Financial, sexual, and communication problems generated from an alcoholic's behavior only worsen as the condition deteriorates. After an initial period of denial of the problem—often followed by frantic efforts to quickly cure it—the alcoholic family eventually reorganizes itself, and members change their customary roles (Jackson, 1962). For example, the wife of an alcoholic husband may assume responsibility for paying bills and managing family finances. Such efforts at family adjustment may have a short-term value since the family's stability is maintained. But, in the long run, such sacrifices can be harmful to family members. In certain cases, they may unintentionally encourage the alcoholic, who may decide that the family is functioning quite well despite his or her drinking.

Other examples of nonnormative stressor events that have been discussed in greater detail earlier in this book include family violence (see Chapter 8), which generates fear, shame, and anger; and separation and divorce (see Chapter 14), which require complete reorganization of family roles.

Nonnormative Changes from Outside the Family

Rare or unexpected pressures on a family from the surrounding environment would be considered nonnormative changes from outside. A natural disaster, such as a flood or tornado, could destroy a family's home, farm, or business. Deaths, injuries, and loss of property are familiar results of such events with which families must cope. If family leaders become overwhelmed in the aftermath of such disasters, leadership will shift to other family members. Such a shift in roles may be accepted during the emergency but may lead to tensions much later (Hill and Hansen, 1962).

A community's response to a disaster will influence how much families suffer. The Red Cross may provide much-needed temporary assistance; the federal government may offer low-interest loans to disaster areas that can relieve immediate financial distress. Environmental problems—such as the discovery of chemical pollution near the Love Canal in New York, or the nuclear accident at Three Mile Island in Pennsylvania—can also be extremely stressful for American families.

Political events, such as wars and revolutions, can separate families, kill or injure family members, and destroy property and communities. If one lives in an extremely unstable political environment—for example, the city of Beirut, Lebanon, in the late 1970s and early 1980s—there can be an almost-constant tension and fear (Freud and Burlingham, 1943; Milgram and Milgram, 1975).

The Pile-up of Stressor Events

Change does not always come in the form of an isolated event, nor does it necessarily happen at a convenient time. Every stressor event brings with it related **hardships**. For example, when Elliot was laid off from his job, his family was not financially prepared and had to make new arrangements. Elliot took over much of the child care and housework so that his wife, Carol, could put in more hours in her job as a waitress. This was a hardship since neither wanted this drastic change in family roles.

After four months under the new division of responsibility, Elliot and Carol realized they could no longer afford the rent on their apartment and would have to find a smaller place. In their new, cramped quarters, the children had to double up on bedrooms and had little room to play. Moreover, the neighborhood was crime-ridden; Carol had her purse stolen one night outside the building and became afraid to work late.

Why are some families able to cope with an unexpected disaster such as a tornado and others never seem to adjust?

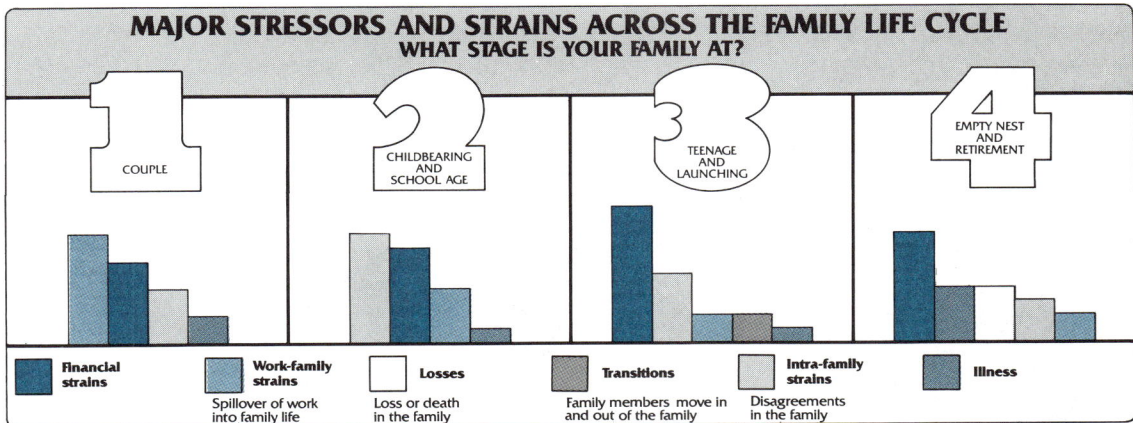

MAJOR STRESSORS AND STRAINS ACROSS THE FAMILY LIFE CYCLE
WHAT STAGE IS YOUR FAMILY AT?

1 COUPLE

2 CHILDBEARING AND SCHOOL AGE

3 TEENAGE AND LAUNCHING

4 EMPTY NEST AND RETIREMENT

Financial strains

Work-family strains
Spillover of work into family life

Losses
Loss or death in the family

Transitions
Family members move in and out of the family

Intra-family strains
Disagreements in the family

Illness

Figure 17–1 Stressors and strains across the family life cycle. (*Source*: McCubbin, 1983, pp. 4–5.)

As Elliot became more discouraged about finding another job, his drinking increased, as did the frequency of arguments with Carol. Consequently, one initial stressor event—the primary breadwinner's loss of a job—had led to an entire cluster of hardships. At the same time, the family was dealing with the normative developmental changes in the children that would take place no matter what: the two-year-old's tantrums, an older child's fear about beginning junior high school, and so forth.

When a family must cope with a cluster of events, changes, and hardships all at once, sociologists say it is experiencing a **pile-up** of stressors (McCubbin and Patterson, 1982). The more problems the family must face, the more strained are its finances, emotions, energy, and other resources. When demands begin to far outweigh resources, there is a danger of crisis.

As families develop and change over time, they discover that some stages of family life are more stressful than others. In their national survey of 1000 families, David Olson and his colleagues at the University of Minnesota, learned that families are under stress most of the time (Olson et al., 1983). Figure 17–1 indicates the most frequent stressors and strains in family life.

Special Stressors

Some stressors fit into more than one category of the typology described above. For example, death happens to everyone, so it must be considered normative. But what about the sudden death of a young child in a car accident? Such a violent, traumatizing, unexpected event would probably be classified as nonnormative. What about divorce? Family scholar Constance Ahrons (1983) argues that since nearly half of all new marriages will end in divorce, it is time to view divorce as a normative experience.

There are certain stressors, however, which, although a part of everyday life for some Americans, are so extreme and atypical of most people's lives that they are categorized as nonnormative. Marriage between persons of different races or cultural backgrounds is an example of a nonnormative stressor that arises inside the family or relationship. By contrast, the stress on minority

Racism and prejudice can be an ever-present source of stress for many minority groups.

families from racism comes from the larger society and is outside the family.

Racism and Prejudice

Racism and prejudice lead to serious and long-term stress for blacks, Native Americans, Hispanics, Asians, and other racial and ethnic minority groups. Unemployment rates are much higher for nonwhites than for whites; poverty is much more common for nonwhites. While discrimination in employment and housing may be illegal, it nevertheless persists as a feature of American society.

According to Harriette McAdoo of Howard University (1982), the most oppressive source of stress for blacks continues to be the interplay of racism, discrimination, and economic isolation. In a study of stress among middle-class black families, she found that they felt that insidious, and sometimes overt, discrimination at work interfered with their career development. Peters and Massey (1983: 196) argue that blacks are faced with "the constant threat and actual periodic occurrences of intimidation, discrimination, or denial because of race."

Cultural differences between minority groups and the dominant society can also lead to stress. In the Chicano (or Mexican American) culture, the nuclear family is typically embedded within an extended family network. Control of social behavior is exercised mainly through the family rather than other social institutions (Falicov and Karrer, 1980). While many Chicanos rely on the extended family for mutual financial support, child care, and emotional support, dependence on this network may simultaneously interfere with the process of integrating into "American ways."

There is frequently a "lack of fit" between the dominant society and the immigrant family. This is true today for Mexican, Cuban, Vietnamese, and Chinese immigrants, but it was also true in earlier times for Irish, Italian, Jewish, and Polish immigrants. Patterns that may have been appropriate for a family in a rural village in Europe, Asia, or Latin America may not be functional in a large, impersonal American city. Thus, the norms, values, and role behaviors learned in one's home country become a source of stress in the new land and add to the normal developmental stresses faced by all families, immigrant or not.

Migration for current nonwhite immigrants brings with it an additional problem: the family is thrown into a disadvantaged position as part of a racial, ethnic, or socio-economic minority. Studies on the accultur-ation of immigrant groups suggest that the integration of native and traditional values with those of the dominant American culture is a conflictual process that takes at least three generations (Schulz, 1974). In certain cases, children adapt more quickly to the re-quirements of their new homeland, learning English and accepting American customs. But this, too, can cause family stress: par-ents may be upset if their children casually discard the values of the native culture.

Intercultural or Interracial Marriage

"We're just another couple," insist Ger-maine and Walter. Initially, they report that they have "no special problems." But fam-ily members on both sides have been far less than enthusiastic about their interracial marriage. When Germaine's parents heard that she was dating a black man, they wrote her a blistering letter, calling her "a slut." Walter's mother, who had warned him never to bring home a white woman, was also antagonistic.

Walter admits it is a struggle for him to reconcile his marriage to Germaine with his awareness as a black man. "At times, I feel like a cop-out. . . . I wonder what I'm doing in this situation. Not very often . . . some-times . . . in the middle of the night. Being married to Germaine will make things harder—above all for the children we hope to have. But Germaine understands me, I've never been able to talk as openly to anyone. After a while, marriage was the only thing that made any sense. I'll be stuck with her the rest of my life, but that's okay. I love her" (Downs, 1971: 64).

Although intercultural and interracial marriages are probably more common and accepted today than they were 20 years ago,

they can be quite stressful. By definition, these families are formed through a union involving persons from two different ways of life. Each group, to some extent, has its own model of what marriage and family life should be like. Extended family members of each spouse—parents, grandparents, and so forth—may emphasize their native culture's distinctive view of proper sexual relation-ships, childrearing, and family roles. Lan-guage can be another barrier; isolation, frus-tration, and hostility can result from communications problems (Ratliff, et al., 1978). Finally, in addition to these internal family strains, the larger American society remains suspicious of—if not openly hostile to—intercultural and interracial marriages.

Certain combinations of spouses may be more compatible than others. For example, a Chinese American man marrying a Ha-waiian woman may find that their concepts of marriage fit well together since both cul-tures highly value childbearing and close ties to the extended family. By contrast, Filipino culture is much more tolerant of infidelity than is American culture; an American wife might find it difficult to accept behavior that her Filipino immigrant husband considers "normal" (Markoff, 1977).

There is little doubt that a racial inter-marriage, such as the marriage of Walter and Germaine, is subject to especially in-tense pressures in the United States. Race remains an explosive issue in our society, with the bitter legacy of slavery hardly for-gotten. An interracial couple sometimes finds little support from either spouse's fam-ily and faces the sensitive task of raising chil-dren of mixed heritage in a nation that is far from achieving racial equality.

Managing Stress

Why is it that some families adjust to stress-ful life events with comparative ease—and actually appear to search for challenging new experiences—while others suffer and deteriorate when confronted with even minor stressors? Within the field of family studies, family scholars have attempted to identify which families, under what conditions, and using which resources and coping behaviors, are best able to make positive adaptations to stressful situations. The earliest theoretical framework devised to address these questions was the ABCX family crisis model advanced by Reuben Hill (1949, 1958), who initially studied the stressors of family separation and reunion during World War II. The key concepts in this model are the stressor event and the amount of change it causes (''a'' factor), the family's resources for dealing with the event (''b'' factor), the family's definition of the event (''c'' factor), and **crisis** (''x'' factor). The first three factors all influence **family vulnerability**, that is, the family's ability to prevent a stressor event from creating a crisis (Hansen, 1965). Crisis must be understood as a relative concept; it can mean a small amount of disorganization, such as a single-parent family being unable to find satisfactory child-care arrangements, or more serious turmoil and conflict, such as occurs when there is a divorce.

The Double ABCX model, advanced by Hamilton McCubbin and Joan Patterson (1982, 1983) builds on Hill's model but extends it in order to describe how families adapt to crises over time. Drawing from studies of families of prisoners of war, families coping with the care of chronically ill children, families coping with normal transitions, and military families located in war zones, McCubbin, Patterson, and other family social scientists of the Minnesota Family Stress, Coping and Health Project have discovered that four important factors appear to determine which families will adapt to stressful life circumstances. First, is the pile-up of stressful events; that is, how

well a family adapts is partly determined by how many stressful life events are occurring at about the same time. Second, family adaptation to stress is determined by the family's strengths and **resources**. Families with open and supportive communication among members appear to do better. Families that are flexible, that can change how they behave, are better able to endure the hardships of married life and raising children. Third, families with good **coping** skills are likely to endure even the most difficult of family stressors. Coping is defined as the family's efforts to work together to reduce the demands and tensions created by the stressor. Fourth, the family's appraisal of and the meaning they attach to the stressful situation is vitally important. A family who can define a problem as something manageable is also likely to be able to handle the problem.

Family efforts to manage stress may be viewed as a balancing act. As we see in Figure 17–2, for example, the pile-up of stressors facing a newly divorced mother and her children may greatly outweigh the family's existing resources.

The Coping Family

As mentioned in the previous section, family scholars use the term ''coping'' to refer to a family's efforts to adapt to stress. Coping involves two distinct but related tasks. A family must respond to the immediate and practical requirements of its external situation. For example, if it loses its home through a fire or flood, the family must find a new place in which to live. However, members must also deal with the emotions generated by the stressor event. In the aftermath of losing a long-time home, the family may feel angry, frightened, depressed, or helpless (Moos and Tsu, 1976). These important tasks are not necessarily dealt with at the

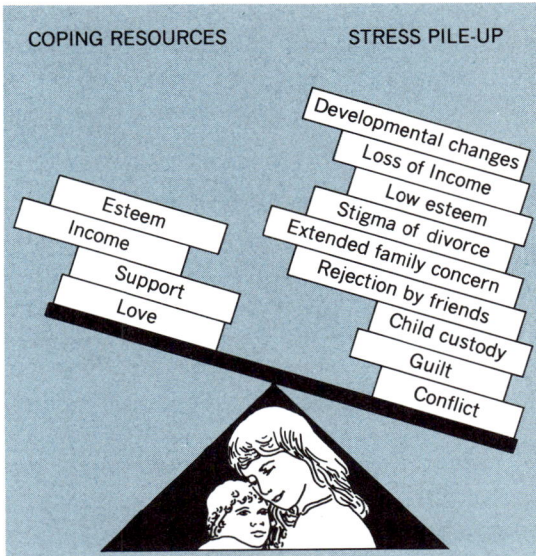

Figure 17-2 The pileup of stressors facing a divorced mother and her children outweighs the resources. Family stress is a relationship between the pileup of demands on one side and the available family resources to cope on the other. The key is to maintain a balance between the two.

same time. The immediate need to locate new housing may take precedence over working through a sense of loss.

Generally, coping occurs in two phases: an acute phase in which energy is directed toward minimizing the impact of the stress, and a reorganization phase in which the new reality is faced and accepted. Psychiatrist Gerald Caplan (1964) has identified seven characteristics of effective coping behavior that are appropriate in reacting to many of life's stressor events:

1. Active exploration of the problem.
2. Open and free expression of both positive and negative feelings.
3. Actively seeking help from others, including friends, relatives, and community services.
4. Breaking down a problem into manage-

able aspects and working them through one at a time. For example, in dealing with a rebellious teenager, parents might choose to focus on major issues such as drug usage and schoolwork rather than minor problems such as his or her untidy room.

5. Maintaining an awareness of fatigue, emotional strain, and the need to pace one's efforts. A family with a severely retarded child might accept the fact that it needs ''break time'' away from the child's demands.
6. Remaining flexible and willing to change one's behavior and family roles.
7. Preserving a basic trust in oneself and in family members, and maintaining a sense of optimism about overcoming setbacks and crises.

Coping as a Source of Stress

Certain coping strategies are less effective than others because they do little to solve long-range problems. At their worst, these strategies themselves become additional sources of stress. For example, when Ron's father was diagnosed as having cancer, Ron insisted on denying the problem and convincing his parents that the doctors must be wrong. Getting a second opinion was a reasonable precaution, but when the second doctor offered the same report as the first, Ron took his father to a third doctor and then a fourth. This not only allowed the disease to progress for months without treatment, but also forced the entire family to bury fears that ultimately had to be faced.

Family violence, such as spouse or child abuse, can be understood as both a source of stress and a way of coping with problems. Researchers suggest that such violence is usually a learned response to stress. A man who feels ''pushed around'' at his job may have learned, through his own father's similar behavior, that he can use violence against his wife or child to demonstrate that he is still "in charge" at home. This repetition of violent behavior from generation to generation is known as the "cycle of abuse."

Many researchers have found that people are more violent when experiencing such stresses as unemployment, unhappiness at work, or pregnancy (Eisenberg and Micklow, 1977; Gelles, 1974; Gil, 1970; Prescott and Letko, 1977; Steinmetz, 1978). According to this analysis, violent behavior represents an attempt to relieve tension and reassert control in response to stress. In this sense, it is a personal coping strategy.

Unfortunately, this misguided effort becomes a major source of stress for the family as whole. The victim of violence may be seriously injured; the entire household becomes terrified by the atmosphere of fear created. Children are typically ashamed and confused by a parent's violence, and often blame themselves for the problem (Cottle, 1980). When coping strategies generate this type of stress, they are regarded as "dysfunctional" by researchers (McCubbin and Figley, 1983).

Functional Coping Strategies

Functional coping strategies can be defined as those actions or attitudes that lead to improvement in the family situation. While each specific stressor requires that particular actions be taken, certain types of behavior are successful to some degree in handling many kinds of stressor events (McCubbin, 1979; McCubbin and Figley, 1983; McCubbin and Patterson, 1983).

Among the more positive coping strategies (McCubbin, 1979) are the following:

1. Maintaining family togetherness—taking time to do things with the children and plan family outings.
2. Developing self-reliance and self-es-teem—learning new skills to help deal with the problem.
3. Developing social support—spending time with friends and family, accepting their assistance, participating in clubs and community organizations.
4. Developing a positive outlook—remaining optimistic, even in the face of serious problems.
5. Learning about the problem—reading books, attending classes, seeking out medical and other professional advice.
6. Reducing tension—whether by getting exercise, watching television, maintaining interest in hobbies, talking things out, or crying.
7. Balancing coping efforts—using many coping strategies in a balanced manner as one attempts to look after oneself and other family members.

Social Support

Recently, researchers studying family stress have discovered a strong relationship between the role of the community as a source of social support and the ability of the family to cope with stress and change (McCubbin and Patterson, 1982). As noted in earlier chapters, social support is simply help given by one person to another. It may serve to comfort or strengthen a family member, or it may provide specific and useful information.

According to physician Sidney Cobb (1979), social support, sometimes known as "communicative caring," has three basic components:

- Emotional support, leading the recipient to believe he or she is cared for and loved.
- Esteem support, leading him or her to feel respected and valued.
- Network support, leading the recipient to feel he or she has a defined position in a network of communication and mutual obligation.

B O X   1 7 – 2

Research Brief:
The Family's Impact on Health

Lois Pratt of Jersey City State College was interested in how family structure and interaction might affect the level of health and health behaviors of family members. She conducted detailed interviews with a representative sample of 273 families drawn from a New Jersey city of about 150,000. Each family had a husband, a wife, and at least one child aged nine to thirteen. Members were interviewed separately using structured questions and response categories.

Pratt found that five components of family structure and interaction are associated with more effective personal health practices and higher levels of health:

1. *Freedom and Responsiveness to Individual Members.* Personal autonomy is encouraged; conformity is not required. There is tolerance for a certain level of deviance and disagreement. The family is responsive to the particular interests and needs of each member.

2. *Regular and Varied Interaction among Family Members.* All family members regularly participate in family tasks, in leisure, in physical activity, and in verbal and nonverbal communication. Involvement of the father in these shared activities has an important impact on positive health practices.

3. *Regular Links with the Broader Community.* Family members participate in external groups and activities and have positive relationships with others in the community. Through these associations, family members are enriched and supported. They gain new information and establish a connection to a larger social reality. Mother and child links to the community are strongly associated with positive health practices.

4. *Flexible and Egalitarian Structuring of Relationships.* Power is shared equally among spouses and, where appropriate, among children. Tasks are divided among members in a flexible way based on individual interests and abilities rather than age and sex norms.

5. *Active Coping Effort.* There is an active attempt to deal with life's problems and challenges by seeking out new information, opportunities, and resources. Family members are willing to experiment with new strategies and believe in the family's ability to master its life situation.

Pratt has used the term "the energized family" to characterize a family that exhibits these five qualities. In her view, these principles should be emphasized in family life education and health education.

Source: L. Pratt. *Family Structure and Effective Health Behavior: The Energized Family.* Boston: Houghton Mifflin, 1976.

Cobb argues that social support plays a vital role in maintaining good health (see Box 17-2). Support may come from a variety of sources, including friends, neighbors, relatives, and self-help groups (Litwak and Szelenyi, 1969; Martinez, 1977; Zunin, 1974).

Many studies indicate that social support makes individuals and families less vulnerable when they experience such stressor events as losing a job or participating in a difficult line of work (Cobb, 1982; Gore, 1978; Maynard, et al., 1980); raising a chronically ill child (de Araujo, et al., 1973; Nevin, et al., 1979); recovering from a natural disaster (Erickson, 1976); or adjusting to war-induced separations (McCubbin, et al., 1976). Peter Stein (1981) suggests that single people may become hospitalized more often than married people because of an absence of social support. When seriously ill, they

may not have anyone to care for them at home and therefore may be more likely to go to a hospital.

Summary

Stressors are those life events or changes that are so serious or drastic that they require changes in the family system. Stressor events may originate inside or outside the family; they may be normative (predictable or expected changes experienced by most or all families) or nonnormative.

Each stressor event brings with it related hardships. When a family must cope with a cluster of events, changes, and hardships all at once, sociologists say it is experiencing a pile-up of stressors.

Certain stressors are so extreme and atypical of most people's lives that they are categorized as nonnormative—even though they are a part of everyday life for some Americans. Racism and prejudice, as well as intercultural or interracial marriage, fall into this category.

The earliest theoretical framework devised to explain the differing adjustments of families to stressful life events was Reuben Hill's ABCX family crisis model. The key concepts in this model are stressors (the "a" factor), resources (the "b" factor), the definition of the event (the "c" factor), and crisis (the "x" factor). The first three factors all influence a family's vulnerability, that is, its ability to prevent a stressor event from creating a crisis. The Double ABCX model advanced by Hamilton McCubbin and Joan Patterson builds on Hill's model, but extends it in order to describe how families adapt to crises over time.

Family scholars use the term "coping" to refer to a family's efforts to adapt to stress. Coping involves two distinct but related tasks: responding to the immediate and practical requirements of a situation and dealing with the emotions generated by a stressor event. Certain coping strategies can themselves become additional sources of stress. Functional coping strategies can be defined as those actions or attitudes that lead to improvement in the family situation. Researchers have found that there is a strong relationship between the role of the community as a source of social support and the ability of the family to cope with stress and change.

Developmental Task   Family Inventory of Life Events and Changes

The *Family Inventory of Life Events and Changes* (FILE) is a family life change inventory. It can help you determine how much stress your family is under now.

Since family members are connected to each other, a life change for any one member affects the whole family in some way. A family is a group of two or more persons related by blood, marriage, or adoption.

Instructions:
- Read each statement in FILE and decide whether it happened to you or any member of your family during the past year. Check YES or NO.

FAMILY LIFE CHANGES	Experienced During Past Year		YOUR SCORE
	YES	NO	
1. Increase of husband/father's time away from family	☐	☐ 46	☐
2. Increase of wife/mother's time away from family	☐	☐ 51	☐
3. A member appears to have emotional problems	☐	☐ 58	☐
4. A member appears to depend on alcohol or drugs	☐	☐ 66	☐
5. Increase in conflict between husband and wife	☐	☐ 53	☐
6. Increase in arguments between parent(s) and child(ren)	☐	☐ 45	☐
7. Increase in conflict among children in the family	☐	☐ 48	☐
8. Increased difficulty in managing teenage child(ren)	☐	☐ 55	☐
9. Increased difficulty managing schoolage children (6–12 yrs)	☐	☐ 39	☐
10. Increased difficulty managing preschool children (2–6 yrs)	☐	☐ 36	☐
11. Increased difficulty managing toddler(s) (1–2 yrs)	☐	☐ 36	☐
12. Increased difficulty managing infant(s) (0–1 yr)	☐	☐ 35	☐
13. Increase in the amount of "outside activities" which the child(ren) are involved in	☐	☐ 25	☐

FAMILY LIFE CHANGES	Experienced During Past Year YES	NO		YOUR SCORE
14. Increased disagreement about a member's friends or activities	☐	☐	35	☐
15. Increase in the number of problems or issues which don't get resolved	☐	☐	43	☐
16. Increase in the number of tasks or chores which don't get done	☐	☐	35	☐
17. Increased conflict with in-laws or relatives	☐	☐	40	☐
18. Spouse/parent was separated or divorced	☐	☐	79	☐
19. Spouse/parent has an ''affair''	☐	☐	68	☐
20. Increased difficulty in resolving issues with a former or separated spouse	☐	☐	47	☐
21. Increased difficulty with sexual relationship between husband and wife	☐	☐	58	☐
22. Spouse had unwanted or difficult pregnancy	☐	☐	45	☐
23. An unmarried member became pregnant	☐	☐	65	☐
24. A member had an abortion	☐	☐	50	☐
25. A member gave birth to or adopted a child	☐	☐	50	☐
26. Took out a loan or refinanced a loan to cover increased expenses	☐	☐	29	☐
27. Went on welfare	☐	☐	55	☐
28. Change in conditions (economic, political, weather) which hurts the family business	☐	☐	41	☐
29. Change in agriculture market, stock market, or land values which hurts family investments and/or income	☐	☐	43	☐
30. A member started a new business	☐	☐	50	☐
31. Purchased or built a home	☐	☐	41	☐
32. A member purchased a car or other major item	☐	☐	19	☐
33. Increasing financial debts due to overuse of credit cards	☐	☐	31	☐
34. Increased strain on family ''money'' for medical/dental expenses	☐	☐	23	☐
35. Increased strain on family ''money'' for food, clothing, energy, home care	☐	☐	21	☐

FAMILY LIFE CHANGES	Experienced During Past Year		YOUR SCORE
	YES	NO	
36. Increased strain on family "money" for child(ren)'s education	☐	☐ 22	☐
37. Delay in receiving child support or alimony payments	☐	☐ 41	☐
38. A member changed to a new job/career	☐	☐ 40	☐
39. A member lost or quit a job	☐	☐ 55	☐
40. A member retired from work	☐	☐ 48	☐
41. A member started or returned to work	☐	☐ 41	☐
42. A member stopped working for extended period (e.g., laid off, leave of absence, strike)	☐	☐ 51	☐
43. Decrease in satisfaction with job/career	☐	☐ 45	☐
44. A member had increased difficulty with people at work	☐	☐ 32	☐
45. A member was promoted at work or given more responsibilities	☐	☐ 40	☐
46. Family moved to a new home or apartment	☐	☐ 43	☐
47. A child/adolescent member changed to a new school	☐	☐ 24	☐
48. Parent/spouse became seriously ill or injured	☐	☐ 44	☐
49. Child became seriously ill or injured	☐	☐ 35	☐
50. Close relative or friend of the family became seriously ill	☐	☐ 44	☐
51. A member became physically disabled or chronically ill	☐	☐ 73	☐
52. Increased difficulty managing a chronically ill or disabled member	☐	☐ 58	☐
53. Member or close relative was committed to an institution or nursing home	☐	☐ 44	☐
54. Increased responsibility to provide direct care or financial help to husband's and/or wife's parent(s)	☐	☐ 47	☐
55. Experienced difficulty in arranging for satisfactory child care	☐	☐ 40	☐
56. A parent/spouse died	☐	☐ 98	☐
57. A child member died	☐	☐ 99	☐
58. Death of husband's or wife's parent or close relative	☐	☐ 48	☐

FAMILY LIFE CHANGES	Experienced During Past Year		YOUR SCORE
	YES	NO	
59. Close friend of the family died	☐	☐ 47	☐
60. Married son or daughter was separated or divorced	☐	☐ 58	☐
61. A member "broke up" a relationship with a close friend	☐	☐ 35	☐
62. A member was married	☐	☐ 42	☐
63. Young adult member left home	☐	☐ 43	☐
64. A young adult member began college (or post-high school training)	☐	☐ 28	☐
65. A member moved back home or a new person moved into the household	☐	☐ 42	☐
66. A parent/spouse started school (or training program) after being away from school for a long time	☐	☐ 38	☐
67. A member went to jail or juvenile detention	☐	☐ 68	☐
68. A member was picked up by police or arrested	☐	☐ 57	☐
69. Physical or sexual abuse or violence in the home	☐	☐ 75	☐
70. A member ran away from home	☐	☐ 61	☐
71. A member dropped out of school or was suspended from school	☐	☐ 38	☐
FAMILY LIFE CHANGE SCORE			☐

How to Determine Your Family Life Change Score

- You can see numbers written beside the boxes. These numbers, called *stress scores*, represent the average amount of adjustment most people think this event would require when experienced by a family.

For every statement you checked 'YES' write the *stress score* in the box in the column titled 'YOUR SCORE.'

For example	YES	NO		YOUR SCORE
59. Close friend of the family died	✓	☐	47	47

Remember, record your scores only for those events your family or you experienced.

- You are now ready to calculate your score. Add up the scores in the boxes.

Write this number in the box marked "FAMILY LIFE CHANGE SCORE."

• Compare your family's score with the ranges of scores in the chart below. These ranges of scores will tell you where your score falls in relation to the scores of the rest of the population.

For example, if your score was 540, your family falls in the moderate risk category.

WHAT YOUR SCORE MEANS:

750 + High risk—Check with a counselor. Take special care of yourself and your family.

501—749 Moderate risk—Be careful. Be aware of the pressures on yourself and your family.

0—100 Low risk—Relax a little; this looks okay for yourself and your family.

Discussion Questions

1. In your opinion, what are the specific stressors that you are facing at this time in your life? List them and decide how many are due to the stage of development you are in.

2. Choose one of the following events that may have happened to you or your family. Consider the specific problems and tasks it raises for families. List the pile-up of stressors, normative and nonnormative, that may accompany these stressor events:

    a. Geographical move.
    b. Chronic illness of a family member.
    c. Death of a family member.
    d. Unplanned pregnancy.
    e. Natural disaster.
    f. Loss of a job by a family member.
    g. Intercultural or interracial marriage.

3. Are you presently, or have you ever been, a member of an ethnic or racial minority family, or of an intercultural family? If so, what are some of the specific stressors you have had to face because of this identity? If not, what do you imagine the specific stressors might be for a racial minority family?

4. Think of the most recent situation in which you were faced with a specific stressor event. What was the event? How were you able to cope with the stress? What might you do differently if it happened again, or if you had an opportunity to change your past behavior?

5. What sources of social support have you sought in dealing with family stressors and crisis? How did these individuals or organizations assist you?

Key Words

Coping	**Family Vulnerability**	**Resources**
Crisis	**Hardships**	**Stress**
Distress	**Normative Stressors**	**Stressors**
Eustress	**Pile-Up**	

Suggested Readings

Erikson, Kai T. ''Everything in its path: The Buffalo Creek flood and family trauma in Appalachia.'' In Albin, M. and Carollo, D. (eds.), *Family Life in America, 1620–2000*. St. James, N.Y.: Revisionary Press, 1981. Describes a flood in a West Virginia community and traces subsequent events and their impact on family relationships.

Finkelhor, David, and Gelles, Richard J. (eds.). *The Dark Side of Families: Current Family Violence Research*. Beverly Hills, Calif.: Sage Publications, 1983. An overview of current research and major controversies in the study of family violence.

Massie, Robert, and Massie, Susan. *Journey*. New York: Knopf, 1975. An account by parents of the experience of caring for a hemophiliac child.

Stack, Carol B. *All Our Kin: Strategies for Survival in a Black Community*. New York: Harper and Row, 1975. A participant-observer study of a coping style to manage long-term distress among poor blacks.

Unger, Steven (ed.). *The Destruction of American Indian Families*. New York: Association on American Indian Affairs, 1977. Describes the stress and change experienced by Native American families in the last century.

Abarbanel, A., 1979. *Shared Parenting After Separation and Divorce: A Study of Joint Custody.* American Journal of Orthopsychiatry 49:320–329.

Abend, S., 1974. *Problems of Identity: Theoretical and Clinical Application.* Psychoanalytic Quarterly 43:606–637.

Abernethy, V., and G. Abernethy, 1974. *Risk for Unwanted Pregnancy Among Mentally Ill Adolescent Girls.* American Journal of Orthopsychiatry 44:442–450.

Adams, B., 1964. *Structural Factors Affecting Parental Aid to Married Children.* Journal of Marriage and the Family 26:327–331.

———, 1968a. *Kinship in an Urban Setting.* Chicago: Markham.

———, 1968b. *The Middle-class Adult and His Widowed or Still Married Mother.* Social Problems 16:51–59.

———, 1973. *Can the Family Survive Alternative Lifestyles?* Forum (November):4–8.

Ahrons, C., 1983. *Divorce.* In H. McCubbin and C. Figley (eds.), *Stress and the Family.* Vol. 1: *Coping with Normative Transitions.* New York: Brunner Mazel.

Albee E., 1964. *Who's Afraid of Virginia Woolf?* New York: Pocket Books.

Albrecht, S., 1980. *Reactions and Adjustments to Divorce: Differences in the Experiences of Males and Females.* Family Relations 29 (January):59–68.

Aldous, J., 1967. *Intergenerational Visiting Patterns: Variation in Boundary Maintenance as an Explanation.* Family Process 6:235–251.

———, 1978. *Family Careers: Developmental Change in Families.* New York: John Wiley and Sons.

Anderson, H. and M. Hager, 1981. *The Crisis in Social Security.* Newsweek (June):25–27.

Anderson, M., 1977. *The Impact on the Family Relationships of the Elderly of Change Since Victorian Times in Governmental Income-Maintenance Provision.* In E. Shanas and M. Sussman (eds.), *Family, Bureaucracy, and the Elderly.* Durham: Duke University.

Andry, R., 1960. *Delinquency and Parental Pathology.* London: Methuen.

Anthony, E., and C. Chiland, 1978. *The Child in His Family.* Vol. 5: *Children and Their Parents in a Changing World.* New York: John Wiley and Sons.

Arling, G., 1976. *The Elderly Widow and Her Family, Neighbors, and Friends.* Journal of Marriage and the Family 38(3):757–768.

Armstrong, L., 1978. *Kiss Daddy Goodnight.* New York: Pocket Books.

Atchley, R., 1971. *Retirement and Work Orientation.* Gerontologist 11:29–32.

———, 1972. *The Social Forces in Later Life.* Belmont, Calif.: Wadsworth.

———, 1975. *Dimensions of Widowhood in Later Life.* Gerontologist 15:176–178.

———, 1977. *The Social Forces in Later Life.* 2d ed. Belmont, Calif.: Wadsworth.

Atkin, E., and E. Rubin, 1976. *Part-time Father.* New York: Vanguard.

Atwater, E., 1973. *Adolescence.* Englewood Cliffs, N. J.: Prentice-Hall.

Babikian, H., and A. Goldman, 1971. *A Study of Teenage Pregnancy.* American Journal of Psychiatry (128):755–760.

Bach, G., and P. Wyden, 1968. *The Intimate Enemy.* New York: William Morrow and Co.

Bahr, H., 1980. *Changes in Family Life in Middletown, 1924–77.* Public Opinion Quarterly 35–52.

Bahr, S., 1972. *A Methodological Study of Conjugal Power. A replication and extension of Blood and Wolfe.* Unpublished doctoral dissertation. Washington State University.

Balswick, J., and C. Peck, 1971. *The Inexpressive Male: A Tragedy of American Society.* Family Coordinator 20:363–368.

Banaszynski, K., 1983. *Victims Describe Fear and Isolation.* Minneapolis Tribune (July 3): 1A, 4A.

Bandura, A., and R. Walters, 1959. *Adolescent Aggression.* New York: Ronald.

Bane, M., 1976. *Here to Stay: American Families in the Twentieth Century.* New York: Basic Books.

———, 1979. *Marital Disruption and the Lives of*

Children. Journal of Social Issues 32:103–117.

Barbour, J., 1982. *The Gray Wave*. Fresno Bee (March14):G1,G6.

Bardis, P., 1964. *Family Forms and Variations Historically Considered*. Pp. 403–461 in H. T. Christensen (ed.), *Handbook of Marriage and the Family*. Chicago: Rand McNally.

Barnard, J., and M. Fain, 1980. *Five Make-or-Break Marriage Challenges*. Redbook (April):173–178.

Barnhill, L., G. Rubenstein, and N. Rocklin, 1979. *From Generation to Generation: Father-to-Be in Transition*. Family Coordinator (April):229–235.

Barrett, K., 1982. *Date Rape: A Campus Epidemic?* MS., (September):48–51, 130.

Bart, P., 1975. *The Loneliness of the Long-Distance Mother*. In J. Freeman (ed.), *Women: A Feminist Perspective*. Palo Alto, Calif.: Mayfield.

Baruch, E., 1980. *The Politics of Courtship*. Dissent (Winter)27:56–63.

Baruch, G., R. Barnett, and C. Rivers, 1980. *A New Start for Women at Midlife*. New York Times Magazine (December 7):196–201.

Bates, F., 1956. Position, role, and status. Social Forces (34):313–321.

Baumrind, D., 1978. *Parental Disciplinary Patterns and Social Competence in Children*. Youth and Society 9:239–276.

———, 1980. *New Directions in Socialization Research*. American Psychologist 35 (July):639–652.

Beauchamp, W., 1983. *A 2nd AIDS Epidemic*. New York Times (August 7): E21.

Beck, D., and M. Jones, 1973. *Progress on Family Problems*. New York: Family Service Association of America.

Belkin, G., and N. Goodman, 1980. *Marriage, Family and Intimate Relationships*. Chicago: Rand McNally.

Bell, A., and M. Weinberg, 1978. *Homosexualities: Study of Diversity Among Men and Women*. New York: Simon and Schuster.

Bell, D., J. Chafetz, and L. Horn, 1982. *Marital Conflict Resolution: A Study of Strategies and Outcomes*. Journal of Family Issues (March):111–113.

Bell, R., 1971. *Marriage and Family Interaction*. 3d ed. Homewood, Ill.: Dorsey Press.

Bell, R., S. Turner, and L. Rosen, 1975. *A Multivariate Analysis of Female Extramarital Coitus*. Journal of Marriage and the Family (37):375–384.

Belmont, L., and A. Marolla, 1973. *Birth Order, Family Size and Intelligence*. Science 182:1096–1101.

Bem, S., 1975. *The Measurement of Psychological Androgyny*. Journal of Consulting and Clinical Psychology 42:155–162.

Bengtson, V., P. Kasschau, and P. Ragan, 1977. *The Impact of Social Structure on the Aging Individual*. In J. Birren and K. Schaie (eds.), *Handbook of the Psychology of Aging*. New York: Van Nostrand Reinhold Co.

Bengtson, V., and J. Treas, 1980. *Intergenerational Relations and Mental Health*. In R. Sloan and J. Birren (eds.), *Handbook of Mental Health and Aging*. New York: Prentice-Hall.

Bennis, W., E. Schein, F. Steele, and D. Berlen, 1968. *Interpersonal Dynamics*. Homewood, Ill.: Dorsey Press.

Berardo, F., 1968. *Widowhood Status in the U.S.: Perspectives on a Neglected Aspect of the Family Life Cycle*. Family Coordinator 17:191–203.

———, 1970. *Survivorship and Social Isolation: The Case of the Aged Widower*. Family Coordinator 19(1):11–25.

Berger, B., B. Hackett, S. Cavan, G. Zickler, M. Millar, M. Noble, S. Thieman, R. Farrell, and B. Rosenbluth, 1972. *Child Rearing Practices of the Communal Family*. In A. Skolnick and J. Skolnick (eds.), *Family in Transition*. Boston: Little, Brown.

Berger, M., 1971. *Trial Marriage: Harnessing the Trend Constructively*. Family Coordinator 20 (January):38–43.

Berk, A., 1980. *Modern Woman's Double Life*. Newsweek (September 29):17.

Berlin, C., 1969. *Effects of LSD Taken by Pregnant Women on Chromosomal Abnormalities of Offspring*. Pedriatric Herald, January/February.

Berman, C., 1980. *Making It as a Stepparent: New Roles/New Rules*. Garden City, New York: Doubleday.

Bernard, J., 1972. *The Future of Marriage*. New York: Bantam.

———, 1975. *Women, Wives, Mothers: Values and Options*. Chicago: Aldine Publishing Co.

Berne, E., 1964. *Games People Play: The Psychology of Human Relationships*. Secaucus, N.J.: Castle Books.

Bernikow, L., 1982. *Alone: Yearning for Companionship in America*. New York Times Magazine (August 15):24–34.

Bigner, J., 1979. *Parent-Child Relations*. New York: Macmillan Publishing Co.

Biller, H., 1974. *Paternal Deprivation*. Lexington, Mass.: D. C. Heath.

Bird, C., 1979. *The Best Years of a Woman's Life*. Psychology Today 13 (June):20–26.

Blenkner, M., 1965. *Social Work and Family Relationships in Later Life with Some Thoughts on Filial Maturity*. Pp. 46–59 in E. Shanas and G. Streib (eds.), *Social Structure and the Family*. Englewood Cliffs, N.J.: Prentice-Hall.

Blood, R., 1963. *The Husband-Wife Relationship*. In F. Nye and L. Hoffman (eds.), *The Employed Mother in America*. Chicago: Rand McNally.

———, 1969. *Kinship Interaction and Marital Solidarity*. Merrill-Palmer Quarterly 15:171–183.

———, 1974. *Resolving Family Conflicts*. In R. Cavan (ed.). *Marriage and the Family in the Modern World*. New York: Thomas Y. Crowell.

———, 1976. *Love Match and Arranged Marriage*. New York: The Free Press.

Blood, R., and M. Blood, 1978. *Marriage*. 3d ed. New York: The Free Press.

Blood, R., and R. Hill, 1970. *Comparative Analysis of Family Power Structure: Problems of Measurement and Interpretation*. In R. Hill and R. Konig (eds.), *Families in East and West*. The Hague: Mouton and Co.

Blood, R., and D. Wolfe, 1960. *Husband and Wives: The Dynamics of Married Living*. Glencoe, Ill.: The Free Press.

Bloom, B., 1975. *Changing Patterns of Psychiatric Care*. New York: Behavioral Publications.

Blos, P., 1971. *The Child Analyst Looks at the Young Adolescent*. Daedelus 10:4(Fall):961–978.

Blumberg, P., and P. Paul, 1975. *Continuities and Discontinuities in Upper-Class Marriages*. Journal of Marriage and the Family 37(February):63–77.

Blumstein, P., and P. Schwartz, 1983. *American Couples*. New York: William Morrow.

Bohannon, P., 1970. *Divorce Chains, Households of Remarriage and Multiple Divorces*. In P. Bohannon (ed.), *Divorce and After*. Garden City, New York: Anchor.

Bossard, J., and E. Boll, 1966. *The Sociology of Child Development*. New York: Harper and Row.

Bowman, H., and G. Spanier, 1978. *Modern Marriage*. 8th ed. New York: McGraw-Hill.

Boyd, R., 1969. *The Valued Grandparent: A Changing Social Role*. Pp. 70–102 in *Living in the Multigeneration Family*. Institute of Gerontology, No. 3 (January).

Bradley, B., J. Berman, M. Suid, and R. Suid, 1977. *Single: Living Your Own Way*. Reading, Mass.: Addison-Wesley.

Bram, S., 1974. *To Have or Have Not: A Social Psychological Study of Voluntary Childless Couples, Parents-to-Be and Parents*. Unpublished doctoral dissertation, University of Michigan at Ann Arbor.

Brandwein, R., C. Brown, and E. Fox, 1974. *Women and Children Last: The Social Situation of Divorced Mothers and Their Families*. Journal of Marriage and the Family 36:498–514.

Bratton, E., 1971. *Home Management Is . . .* Boston: Ginn and Co.

Brecher R., and E. Brecher (eds.), 1966. *An Analysis of Human Sexual Response*. New York: Signet Books.

Brecher, J., and M. Lau, 1980. *Comrade Lonely Hearts*. Newsweek (December 29):27.

Brim, O., 1976. *Theories of the Male Mid-Life Crisis*. Counseling Psychologist 6:2–9.

Broderick, C., 1966. *Sexual Behavior Among Pre-Adolescents*. Journal of Social Issues 22 (April):6–21.

———, 1971. *Beyond the Five Conceptual Frameworks: A Decade of Development in Family Theory*. Journal of Marriage and the Family (33):139–159.

Broderick, C., and H. Pulliam-Krager, 1979. *Family Process and Child Outcomes*. Pp. 604–614 in W. Burr, R. Hill, F. Nye, and I. Reiss (eds.), *Contemporary Theories About the Family*. Vol. 1. New York: Macmillan.

Brooks, T., and E. Marsh, 1979. *The Complete Directory to Prime Time Network TV Shows: 1946 to Present*. New York: Ballantine.

Bronfenbrenner, U., 1975. *The Challenge of Social*

Change to Public Policy and Developmental Research. Paper presented at the meeting of the Society for Research in Child Development.

————, 1977. *The Calamitous Decline of the American Family*. Washington Post (January 2).

————, 1979. *The Ecology of Human Development*. Cambridge, Mass.: Cambridge University Press.

Brooks, A., 1981. *Job Help for Wives*. New York Times 3(August 30):8.

Brown, B., 1979. *Parents' Discipline of Children in Public Places*. Family Coordinator (January):67–71.

Brownmiller, S., 1975. *Against Our Will: Men, Women and Rape*. New York: Simon and Schuster.

Brubaker, T., and E. Brubaker, 1981. *Adult Child and Elderly Parent Household*. Alternative Lifestyles 4(May):242–256.

Bryson, J., and R. Bryson, 1978. *Dual-Career Couples*. Psychology of Women Quarterly 3(1):whole issue.

Burchinal, L., 1964. *Characteristics of Adolescents from Unbroken, Broken, and Reconstituted Families*. Journal of Marriage and the Family 26:44–51.

Burgess, E., 1926. *The Family as a Unity of Interacting Personalities*. The Family (March):3–9.

Burgess, E., and L. Cottrell, 1939. *Predicting Success or Failure in Marriage*. Englewood Cliffs, N.J.: Prentice-Hall.

Burgess, E., and P. Wallin, 1943. *Homogamy in Social Characteristics*. American Journal of Sociology (49):109–124.

————, 1953. *Engagement and Marriage*. Chicago: J. B. Lippincott.

Burgess, E., H. Locke, and M. Thomas, 1963. *The Family*. 3d ed. New York: American.

Burgess, J., 1970. *The Single Parent Family: A Social and Sociological Problem*. Family Coordinator 19:142.

Burke, R., and T. Weir, 1975. *Giving and Receiving Help with Work and Non-Work Related Problems*, Journal of Business Administration (6):59–78.

Burr, W., 1972. *Role Transitions: A Reformulation of Theory*. Journal of Marriage and the Family 34 (August):407–416.

————, 1976. *Successful Marriage: A Principles Approach*. Homewood, Ill.: Dorsey Press.

Burr, W., R. Hill, F. Nye, and I. Reiss (eds.), 1979. *Contemporary Theories About the Family*. New York: The Free Press.

Buscaglia, L., 1975. *The Disabled and Their Parents: A Counseling Challenge*. Thorofare, N.J.: Charles B. Slaok.

————, 1982. *Living, Loving, and Learning*. New York: Fawcett Columbine.

Butler, R., 1975. *Psychiatry and the Elderly: An Overview*. American Journal of Psychiatry 132:893–900.

Cadwallader, M., 1966. *Marriage as a Wretched Institution*. Atlantic Monthly 218 (November):62–66.

Calderone, M., (ed.), 1964. *Manual of Contraceptive Practice*. Baltimore: Williams and Wilkins.

Cale, R., J. Henton, J. Koval, F. Christopher, and S. Lloyd, 1982. *Premarital Abuse—a Social Psychological Perspective*. Journal of Family Issues 3:79–80.

Caplan, G., 1964. *Principles of Preventive Psychiatry*. New York: Basic Books.

Cargan, L., and M. Melko, 1982. *Singles: Myths and Realities*. Beverly Hills, Calif.: Sage Publications.

Card, J., and L. Wise, 1978. *Teenage Mothers and Teenage Fathers: The Impact of Early Childbearing on the Parents' Personal and Professional Lives*. Family Planning Perspectives 10:199–205.

Carter, E., and M. McGoldrich, 1982. *The Family Life Cycle*. In F. Walsh (ed.), *Normal Family Processes*. New York: Guilford Press.

Carter, H., and P. Glick, 1976. *Marriage and Divorce: A Social and Economic Study*. Cambridge, Mass.: Harvard University Press.

Catalyst, 1981. *Corporations and Two-Career Families: Directions for the Future*. New York: Catalyst Career and Family Center.

Cattell, R., and J. Nesselroade, 1967. *"Likeness" and "Completeness" Theories Examined by 16 Personality Factor Measures on Stably and Unstably Married Couples*. Laboratory of Personality and Group Analysis, University of Illinois.

Cazenave, N., 1979. *Middle Income Black Fathers: An Analysis of the Provider's Role*. Family Coordinator 28:583–593.

Chafetz, J., 1974. *Masculine/Feminine or Human? An Overview of the Sociology of Sex Roles*. Itasca, Ill.: F. E. Peacock Publishers.

Chappelear, E., and J. Fried, 1967. *Helping*

Adopting Couples Come to Grips with Their New Parental Roles. Children 14(6) (November-December):223–226.

Char, W., 1977. *Motivation for Intercultural Marriage.* Pp. 33–40 in W. Tseng, J. McDermott, Jr., and T. Maretzki (eds.), *Adjustment in Intercultural Marriage.* Honolulu: University Press of Hawaii.

Charney, I., 1975. *Marital Love and Hate.* Pp. 303–313 in K. Kammeyer (ed.), *Confronting the Issues.* Boston: Allyn and Bacon.

Cherlin, A. J., 1981. *Marriage, Divorce, Remarriage.* Cambridge, Mass.: Harvard University Press.

Chilman, C., 1974. *Some Psychosocial Aspects of Female Sexuality.* Family Coordinator 23 (April):123–131.

———, 1978. *Habitat and American Families: A Social-Psychological Overview.* Family Coordinator 27(April):105–111.

Christoffel, K., and I. Salafsy, 1975. *Fetal Alcohol Syndrome in Dizygotic Twins.* Journal of Pediatrics 87(6):963–967.

Clark, M., and B. Anderson, 1967. *Culture and Aging.* Springfield, Ill.: Charles C. Thomas.

Clark, N., 1983. *Divorce and Remarriage: For Better or Worse the Second Time Around.* Harper's Bazaar (July):42,48,52.

Clatworthy, N., and L. Schied, 1977. *A Comparison of Married Couples: Premarital Cohabitants and Non-Premarital Cohabitants.* Unpublished manuscript. Ohio State University.

Clavan, S., and E. Vatter, 1972. *The Affiliated Family: A Device for Integrating Old and Young.* Gerontologist 12:407–412.

Cleveland, W., and D. Gianturco, 1976. *Remarriage Probability After Widowhood: A Retrospective Method.* Journal of Gerontology 31(1):99–103.

Collins, G., 1979. *A New Look at Life with Father.* New York Times Magazine (June 17):B4.

———, 1983. *Fifty Years of Keeping Couples Together.* New York Times (November 14):B9.

Collins, J., 1974. *Adolescent Dating Intimacy: Norms and Peer Expectations.* Journal of Youth and Adolescence (4):317–328.

Comer, J., 1980. *The Black Family: An Adaptive Perspective.* Pp. 43–53 in M. Fantini and R. Cárdenas (eds.), *Parenting for a Multicultural Society.* New York: Longman.

Constantine, L., and J. Constantine, 1972. *The Group Marriage.* In M. Gordon (ed.), *The Nuclear Family in Crisis: The Search for an Alternative.* New York: Harper and Row.

———, 1973. *Group Marriage: A Study of Contemporary Multilateral Marriage.* New York: Macmillan.

Coombs, R., 1966. *Value Consensus and Partner Satisfaction Among Dating Couples.* Journal of Marriage and the Family 28:167–173.

Cooper, P., B. Cumber, and R. Hartner, 1978. *Decision-Making Patterns and Post-Decision Adjustment of Child-Free Husbands and Wives.* Alternate Lifestyles (February):71–94.

Coopersmith, S. 1967. *The Antecedents of Self-Esteem.* San Francisco: Freedman.

Copelon, R., 1981. *Danger—A Human Life Amendment is on the Way.* Ms. Magazine (February):46–74.

Coppinger, R., and P. Rosenblatt, 1968. *Romantic Love and Subsistence Dependence of Spouses.* Southwestern Journal of Anthropology 24 (Autumn):310–319.

Corrales, R., 1975. *Power and Satisfaction in Early Marriage.* Pp. 197–216 in R. Cromwell and D. Olson (eds.), *Power in Families.* New York: John Wiley and Sons.

Coser R., and L. Coser, 1974. *The Principle of Legitimacy and its Patterned Infringement in Social Revolution.* Pp. 94–106 in R. Coser (ed.) *The Family, Its Structure and Function*, 2nd ed. New York: St. Martin's Press.

Costanzo, P., and M. Shaw, 1970. *Conformity as a Function of Age Level.* Child Development 37(December):967–975.

Cottle, T., 1980. *Children's Secrets.* New York: Doubleday and Co.

Council of Community Hospitals, 1983. *Twin Cities Hospital Prices.* Minneapolis: Hospital Education and Research Foundation.

Cretser, G., and J. Leon, 1979. *Intermarriage in the U.S.: The Last 50 Years.* Paper presented at the Pacific Sociological Association, Anaheim, California, April.

Crist, T., 1971. *Contraceptive Practices Among College Women.* Medical Aspects of Human Sexuality 5(11):168–176.

Cuber, J., and P. Haroff, 1966. *The Significant Americans: A Study of Sexual Behavior Among the Affluent.* New York: Appleton-Century-Crofts.

Cummings, E., and W. Henry, 1961. *Growing Old*. New York: Basic Books.

Current Population Reports, 1980. *Household and Family Characteristics*. (Series P-20, No. 366, March).

Curtis, R., 1975. *Adolescent Orientations Toward Parents and Peers: Variations by Sex, Age, and Socioeconomic Status*. Adolescence 10:483–494.

Cutright, P., 1972. *The Teenage Sexual Revolution and the Myth of an Abstinent Past*. Family Planning Perspectives. 4:24.

Dalton, R., 1980. *Reassessing Parental Socialization: Indicator Unreliability Versus Generational Transfer*. The American Political Science Review 74:421–431.

Daly, M., 1979. *Gyn-Ecology: The Metaethics of Radical Feminism*. Boston: Beacon Press.

David, D., 1978. *The Commune Movement in the Middle 1970s*. In B. Murstein (ed.), *Exploring Intimate Lifestyles*. New York: Springer.

Davis, M., 1973. *Intimate Relations*. New York: The Free Press.

Deacon, R., and F. Firebaugh, 1975. *Home Management: Context and Concepts*. Boston: Houghton Mifflin.

deAraujo, G., P. Van Arsdel, T. Holmes, and D. Dudley, 1973. *Life Change, Coping Ability and Chronic Intrinsic Asthma*. Journal of Psychosomatic Research 17(December):359–363.

DeBurger, J., 1961. *Selected Factors in Premarital Experience Related to Marital Adjustment*. Unpublished master's thesis, Indiana University.

DeFrain, J., 1979. *Androgynous Parents Tell Who They Are and What They Need*. Family Coordinator 28(2):237–243.

DeLora, J., and C. Warren, 1977. *Understanding Sexual Interaction*. Boston: Houghton Mifflin.

DeLora J., C. Warren, and C. Ellison 1980. *Understanding Human Sexuality*. Boston: Houghton Mifflin.

Deutsch, C., 1981. *Love and Marriage*. Parents Magazine 56:3 (March):20–22.

Deutscher, I., 1959. *Married Life in the Middle Years*. Kansas City, Missouri: Community Studies.

DeWolf, R., 1983. *Speak to Me, Baby*. Ladies Home Journal 9(September):46,50–51,138.

Dies, D., and L. Cohen, 1973. *Content Consideration in Group Therapist Self-Disclosure*. Paper presented at the American Psychological Association Convention.

Donovan, J., and R. Jessor, 1978. *Adolescent Problem Drinking: Psychosocial Correlates in a National Sample Study*. Journal of Studies on Alcohol 39:1506–1524.

Dore, R., 1958. *City Life in Japan*. Berkeley, Calif.: University of California Press.

Doudna, C., 1983. *American Couples: Surprising New Findings About Sex, Money and Work*. Ms. Magazine (November):116,119.

Douvan, E., and J. Adelson, 1966. *The Adolescent Experience*. New York: John Wiley and Sons.

Dowd, M., 1983. *For Victims of AIDS, Support in a Lonely Siege*. New York Times (December 5): B1, B6.

Downs, J., 1971. *Black/White Dating*. Life 70:20 (May):56–61.

Drabeck, T., W. Key, P. Erickson, and J. Crowe, 1975. *The Impact of Disaster on Kin Relationships*. The Journal of Marriage and the Family 37:481–494.

Duberman, L., 1973. *Step-Kin Relationships*. Journal of Marriage and the Family (35):283–292.

———, 1975. *The Reconstituted Family: A Study of Remarried Couples and Their Children*. Chicago: Nelson-Hall.

———, 1977. *Marriage and Other Alternatives*. New York: Praeger.

Dullea, G., 1976. *Joint Custody—Is Sharing the Child a Dangerous Idea?* New York Times (May 24):24.

———, 1983. *Widowers and Their Grieving*. New York Times (September 21):B12.

Duncan, D., 1977. *Life Stress as a Precursor to Adolescent Drug Dependence*. International Journal of the Addictions 12(8):1047–1056.

Durden-Smith, J., 1980. *Male and Female—Why?* Quest/80 4(8):15–19, 93–97, 99.

Dutton, L., 1923. *Going Together*. Indianapolis: Bobbs-Merrill.

Duvall, E., 1946. *Conceptions of Parenthood*. American Journal of Sociology 52(3):193–203.

———, 1971. *Marriage and Family Development*, 5th ed. Philadelphia: J. B. Lippincott.

———, 1977. *Marriage and Family Development*, 6th ed. Philadelphia: J. B. Lippincott.

Duvall, E., and R. Hill, 1948. *Report of the Com-*

mittee for the Dynamics of Family Interaction. Prepared at the request of the National Council on Family Life.

———, 1960. *Being Married.* New York: Association Press.

Dyer, E., 1963. *Parenthood as Crisis: A Re-Study.* Marriage and Family Living 25:196–201.

———, 1979. *The American Family: Variety and Change.* New York: McGraw-Hill.

Eckland, B., 1980. *Theories of Mate Selection.* Pp. 132–140 in J. Henslin (ed.), Marriage and Family in a Changing Society. New York: The Free Press.

Eisenberg, S., and P. Micklow, 1977. *The Assaulted Wife: ''Catch 22'' Revisited.* Women's Rights Law Reporter 3–4 (Spring-Summer):138–161.

Elder, G., Jr., 1974. *Children of the Great Depression.* Chicago: University of Chicago Press.

———, 1975. *Age Differentiation and the Life Course.* Pp. 165–190 in A. Inkeles, J. Coleman and N. Smelser (eds.), Annual Review of Sociology (1).

Elias, J., 1978. *Adolescents and Sex.* Humanist (March/April):29–31.

Ellis, A., and A. Abarbanel, 1961. *The Encyclopedia of Sexual Behavior.* New York: Hawthorn Books.

Erickson, K., 1976. *Everything in Its Path: Destruction of the Community in the Buffalo Creek Flood.* New York: Simon and Schuster.

Erikson, E., 1963. *Childhood and Society.* New York: W. W. Norton.

———, 1968. *Identity: Youth and Crisis.* New York: W. W. Norton.

Erlanger, H., 1974. *Social Class Differences in Parents' Use of Physical Punishment.* In S. Steinmetz and M. Straus (eds.), *Violence in the Family.* New York: Dodd, Mead.

Eshleman, J., 1974. *The Family: An Introduction.* Boston: Allyn and Bacon.

Espenshade, T., 1980. *Raising a Child Can Now Cost $85,000.* Washington, D.C.: Population Reference Bureau.

Etaugh, C., 1974. *Effects of Maternal Employment on Children: A Review of Current Research.* Merrill-Palmer Quarterly 20(2):71–98.

Etzioni, A., 1977. *The Family: Is It Obsolete?* Journal of Current Social Issues 14:1.

Evans, R., 1964. *Conversations with Carl Jung.* Princeton, N.J.: Van Nostrand.

Falicov, C., and B. Karrer, 1980. *Cultural Variations in the Family Life Cycle: The Mexican-American Family.* Pp. 383–425 in E. Carter and M. Goldrick (eds.) *The Family Life Cycle: A Framework for Family Therapy.* New York: Gardner Press.

Farber, B., 1959. *Effects of a Severely Mentally Retarded Child on Family Integration.* Monograph of Social Research Child Development 24(71).

———, 1960. *Family Organization and Crisis: Maintenance of Integration in Families With a Severely Mentally Retarded Child.* Monograph of Social Research Child Development 25(75).

———, 1966. *Kinship Laterality and the Emotionally Disturbed Child.* In B. Farber (ed.), *Kinship and Family Organization.* New York: John Wiley and Sons.

Feigelman, W., and A. Silverman, 1979. *Preferential Adoption: A New Mode of Family Formation.* Social Casework: The Journal of Contemporary Social Work 60 (May):296–305.

Feigenbaum, E., M. Lowenthal, and M. Trier, 1966. *Sexual Attitudes in the Elderly.* Paper presented at the Gerontological Society, New York.

Feldman, F., 1976. *The Family in Today's Money World.* New York: Family Service Association of America.

Feldman, H., 1971. *The Effect of Children on the Family.* In A. Michel (ed.), *Family Issues of Employed Women in Europe and America.* Leiden: E. G. Brill.

Feldman, H., and M. Feldman, 1975. *The Family Life Cycle: Some Suggestions for Recycling.* Journal of Marriage and the Family 37:277–284.

Feldman, L., 1980. *Husband-Wife Differences in Marital Problem Identification.* Unpublished data.

Ferber, R., 1973. *Family Decision Making and Economic Behavior.* In E. Sheldon (ed.), *Family Economic Behavior: Problems and Prospects.* Philadelphia: J. B. Lippincott.

Ferber, R., and L. Lee, 1974. *Husband-Wife Influence in Family Purchasing Behavior.* Journal of Consumer Research 1(June):43–45.

Figley, C., 1973. *Child Density and the Marital Re-*

lationship. Journal of Marriage and the Family 35:272–282.

Finkelhor, D., 1979. *Sexually Victimized Children.* New York: The Free Press.

Fisher, B., and D. Sprenkle, 1975. *Therapist's Perceptions of Healthy Family Functioning.* International Journal of Family Counseling 6: 9–17.

Fisher, E., 1974. *Divorce: The New Freedom.* New York: Harper and Row.

Fisher, R., and W. Ury, 1982. *Getting to Yes.* New York: Penguin Books.

Fishman, B., and B. Hamel, 1981. *From Nuclear to Stepfamily Ideology.* Alternative Lifestyles 4(2):181–204.

Fitzsimmons, C., D. Lanery, and E. Metzen, 1971. *Major Financial Decisions and Crisis in the Family Life Span.* North Central Regional Research Publication No. 208. Lafayette, Ind.: Purdue University Agricultural Experiment Station.

Footlick, J., and E. Salholz, 1981. *Bringing Back Grandma.* Newsweek (May 11): 76.

Forward, S., and C. Buck, 1978. *Beytrayal of Innocence.* New York: Penguin.

Fox, G., 1978. *The Family's Role in Adolescent Sexual Behavior.* In *Teenage Pregnancy and Family Impact: New Perspectives on Policy.* Washington, D.C.: George Washington University.

Fox, G., and J. Inazu, 1978. *Talking About Sex: Patterns of Mother-Daughter Communication.* Paper presented at the annual meetings of the Michigan Sociological Association, Detroit.

———, 1979. *The Effect of Mother-Daughter Communication on Daughters' Sexual and Contraceptive Knowledge and Behavior.* Presented at the annual meetings of the Population Association of America, Philadelphia.

———, 1980. *Patterns and Outcomes of Mother-Daughter Communication About Sexuality.* Journal of Social Issues 36(1):7–29.

Fox, J., 1977. *Effects of Retirement and Former Work Life on Women's Adaptation in Old Age.* Journal of Gerontology 32:196–202.

Francke, C., P. Abramson, and T. Maitland, 1980. *Childless By Choice.* Newsweek (January 14):96.

Frazier, F., 1939. *The Negro Family in the United States.* Chicago: University of Chicago Press.

Freud, A., and D. Burlingham, 1943. *War and Children.* New York: International University Press.

Friday, N., 1973. *My Secret Garden.* New York: Trident Press.

———, 1979. *Men in Love.* New York: Delacorte.

Friedan, B., 1963. *The Feminine Mystique.* New York: Dell.

Froiland, T., and T. Hozman, 1975. *A Proposed Model for Divorce Counseling.* Paper presented at the meeting of the American Personnel and Guidance Association, New York, March.

Fromm, E., 1956. *The Art of Loving.* New York: Harper and Row.

Fullerton, G., 1977. *Survival in Marriage,* 2nd ed. New York: Holt, Rinehart and Winston.

Fulman, R., 1984. *Incest: Airing an Ancient Taboo.* New York Daily News (January 9):25.

Furstenberg, F., 1976a. *Unplanned Parenthood: The Social Consequences of Teenage Child-Rearing.* New York: The Free Press.

———, 1976b. *The Social Consequences of Teenage Pregnancy.* Family Planning Perspectives 8(4): 148–164.

———, 1979. *Recycling the Family: Perspectives for a Neglected Family Form.* Marriage and Family Review 2(3):1–21.

———, 1980a. *Remarriage: Introduction to Journal of Social Issues.* Journal of Social Issues 1 (December): 443–454.

———, 1980b. *Burdens and Benefits: The Impact of Early Childbearing on the Family.* Journal of Social Issues 36(1):64–87.

Furstenberg, F., and G. Spanier, 1982. *Remarriage After Divorce: A Longitudinal Analysis of Well-Being.* Journal of Marriage and the Family (August):709–720.

Gallup, G., 1982. *Jobs Up as Part of Women's Ideal.* Minneapolis Tribune (August 8): 12A.

Gardner, R., 1976. *Psychotherapy with Children of Divorce.* New York: Aronson.

Garrison, M., 1976. *Credit-Ability for Women.* Family Coordinator 25(3):241–248.

Gebhard, P., 1977. *The Acquisition of Basic Sex Information.* Journal of Sex Research 13 (August):148–169.

Gelfand, D., and D. Fandetti, 1980. *Suburban and Urban White Ethnics: Attitudes Toward Care of the Aged.* Gerontologist 20:588–594.

Gelles, R., 1974. *The Violent Home.* Beverly Hills, Calif.: Sage Publications.

Gelman, D., 1982. *Growing Old, Feeling Young.* Newsweek (November 1):56–60.

General Mills American Family Report, 1979. *Family Health in an Era of Stress.* Minneapolis: General Mills.

———, 1981. *Families at Work: Strengths and Strains.* Minneapolis, General Mills.

Genovese, R., 1975. *Marriage Encounter.* Pp. 47–58 in S. Miller (ed.), *Marriages and Families: Enrichment Through Communication.* Beverly Hills, Calif.: Sage Publications.

George, L., 1980. *Role Transitions in Later Life.* Monterey, Calif.: Brooks/Cole.

George, V., and P. Wilding, 1972. *Motherless Families.* London: Routledge and Kegan Paul.

Gersick, K., 1979. *Fathers by Choice: Divorced Men Who Receive Custody of Their Children.* Pp. 307–323 in G. Levinger and O. Moles (eds.), *Divorce and Separation.* New York: Basic Books.

Giffen, M., and C. Felsenthal 1983. *A Cry for Help.* New York: Doubleday.

Gil, D. 1970. *Violence Against Children: Physical Child Abuse in the United States.* Cambridge, Mass.: Harvard University Press.

Gilbert, L., C. Holohan, and L. Manning, 1981. *Coping with Conflict Between Professional and Maternal Roles.* Family Relations 30(July): 419–426.

Gilbert, S., 1976. *Self-Disclosure, Intimacy, and Communication in Families.* Family Coordinator 25(3):221–232.

Gingerbread, The Association of One Parent Families, 1973. *One Parent Families—A Finer Future.* London, England.

Glenn, N., 1975. *Psychological Well-Being in the Postparental Stage: Some Evidence from National Surveys.* Journal of Marriage and the Family 37:105–110.

Glenn, N., and C. Weaver, 1977. *The Marital Happiness of Remarried Divorced Persons.* Journal of Marriage and the Family (May):331–337.

Glick, I., R. Weiss, and C. Parkes, 1974. *The First Year of Bereavement.* New York: John Wiley and Sons.

Glick, P., 1975. *A Demographer Looks at American Families.* Journal of Marriage and the Family 37:15–26.

———, 1977. *Updating the Life Cycle of the Family.* Journal of Marriage and the Family 39 (February): 5–13.

———, 1979. *Future American Families.* COFO Newsletter (Summer):2–5.

———, 1980. *Remarriage: Some Recent Changes and Variations.* Journal of Social Issues 1 (December):344–378.

Glick, P., and A. Norton, 1973. *Perspectives on the Recent Upturn in Divorce and Remarriage.* Demography 10(August):301–314.

———, 1977. *Marrying, Divorcing, and Living Together in the U.S. Today.* Population Bulletin 32(5). Washington, D.C.: Population Reference Bureau.

Glick, P., and G. Spanier, 1981. *Cohabitation in the U.S.* In P. Stein (ed.)., *Single Life: Unmarried Adults in Social Context.* New York: St. Martin's Press.

Gold, E., and C. Gold, 1977. *Joyous Childbirth, Manual for Conscious Natural Childbirth.* Berkeley, Calif.: And/Or Press.

Goldfarb, A., 1969. *The Psychodynamics of Dependency and the Search for Aid.* In R. Kalish (ed.), *The Dependencies of Old People.* Ann Arbor: Institute of Gerontology, University of Michigan.

Goldstein, B., 1976. *Human Sexuality.* New York: McGraw-Hill.

Goldstein, J., A. Freud, and A. Solnit, 1973. *Beyond the Best Interests of the Child.* New York: The Free Press.

Goleman, D., 1980. *Leaving Home: Is There a Right Time to Go?* Psychology Today (August):52–61.

Good Housekeeping, 1982. *Rape: The Likeliest Time, Place, and Victim* (July):195.

———, 1983. *Marriage in America: From Roosevelt to Reagan* 186(January):182–183.

Goode, W., 1956. *After Divorce.* Glencoe, Ill.: The Free Press.

———, 1963. *World Revolution and Family Patterns.* Glencoe, Ill.: The Free Press.

———, 1964. *The Family.* Englewood Cliffs, N.J.: Prentice-Hall.

Goodman, E., 1979. *The New Ideal American Woman.* In L. Van Gelder, *Ellen Goodman: A Columnist You Can Trust.* Ms Magazine (March).

Gordon, L., and S. Lee, 1977. *Economics for Consumers.* New York: Van Nostrand.

Gordon, M., 1964. *Assimilation in American Life: The Role of Race, Religion and National Origins.*

New York: Oxford.

Gordon, T., 1975. *Parent Effectiveness Training.* New York: New American Library.

———, 1980. *Significant Sociocultural Factors in Effective Parenting.* Pp. 3–16 in M. Fantini and R. Cardenas (eds.), *Parenting in a Multicultural Society.* New York: Longman.

Gore, S., 1978. *The Effect of Social Support in Moderating the Health Consequences of Unemployment.* Journal of Health and Social Behavior 19 (June):157–165.

Gove, W., 1972. *Sex, Marital Status and Suicide.* Journal of Health and Social Behavior 13:204–213.

Greenhouse, L., 1983. *Court Reaffirms Right to Abortion and Bars Variety Local Curbs.* New York Times (June 16):A1,B11.

Griffin, S., 1973. *Confessions of a Single Mother.* Ramparts (April):41–42,44.

Grinder, R., 1973. *Adolescence.* New York: John Wiley and Sons.

Gubrium, J., 1975. *Being Single in Old Age.* International Journal of Aging and Human Development 6 (1):29–41.

Gunderson, E., 1965. *Body Size, Self-Evaluation and Military Effectiveness.* Journal of Personality and Social Psychology 2(6):902–906.

Gurman, A., and D. Kniskern, 1978. *Deterioration in Marital and Family Therapy: Empirical, Clinical and Conceptual Issues.* Family Process 17:3–20.

Gustavus, S., and J. Henley, 1971. *Correlates of Voluntary Childlessness in a Select Population.* Social Biology 18:227–284.

Gutman, H., 1976. *The Black Family in Slavery and Freedom.* New York: Random House.

Haeberle, E., 1982. *The Sex Atlas.* New York: Continuum.

Halpern, H., 1982. *How to Break Your Addiction to a Person.* New York: McGraw-Hill.

Hamachek, D., 1971. *Encounters with the Self.* New York: Holt, Rinehart and Winston.

Hamburg, B., 1974. *Early Adolescence: A Specific and Stressful Stage of the Life Cycle.* Pp. 101–124 in G. Coelho, D. Hamburg and J. Adams (eds.), *Coping and Adaptation.* New York: Basic Books.

Hansen, D., 1965. *Personal and Positional Influence in Formal Groups: Compositions and Theory for Research on Family Vulnerability to Stress.* Social Forces 44(December):202–210.

Harkins, E., 1978. *Effects of Empty Nest Transition on Self-Report of Psychological and Physical Well-Being.* Journal of Marriage and the Family 40(August):549–556.

Harlow, H., and M. Harlow, 1962. *The Effect of Rearing Conditions on Behavior.* Bulletin of the Meninger Clinic 26:213–224.

Harper, R., 1958. *Communication Problems in Marriage and Marriage Counseling.* Marriage and Family Living 20 (May):107–112.

Harris, L., and Associates, 1975. *The Myth and Reality of Aging in America.* Washington, D.C.: National Council on Aging.

Harry, J., 1983. *Gay Male and Lesbian Relationships.* Pp. 216–234 in E. Macklin and R. Rubin, *Contemporary Families and Alternative Lifestyles: Handbook on Research and Theory.* Beverly Hills, Calif.: Sage Publications.

Havighurst, R., 1972. *Developmental Tasks and Education,* 3d ed. New York: David McKay Co.

Havighurst, R., and B. Neugarten, 1962. *Society and Education.* Boston: Allyn and Bacon.

Hawkes, G., and M. Taylor, 1975. *Power Structure in Mexican and Mexican-American Farm Labor Families.* Journal of Marriage and the Family (November):807–811.

Hawkins, J., C. Weisberg, and D. Ray, 1980. *Spouse Differences in Communication Style: Preference, Perception, Behavior.* Journal of Marriage and the Family 42:585–593.

Hayes, M., and N. Stinnett, 1971. *Life Satisfaction of Middle-Aged Husbands and Wives.* Journal of Home Economics 63:9 (December):669–674.

Hayghe, H., 1981. *Husbands and Wives as Earners: An Analysis of Family Data.* Monthly Labor Review (February).

Heer, D., 1966. *Negro-White Marriage in the United States.* Journal of Marriage and the Family. 27 (August):262–273.

Heider, F., 1946. *Attitudes and Cognitive Organization.* Journal of Psychology (21):107–112.

Helsing, K., M. Szklo, and G. Comstock, 1981. *Not so Merry Widowers.* Time (August 10):45.

Henig, R., 1982. *Dispelling Menstrual Myths.* New York Times (March 7):64–65.

Henley, N., and B. Thorne, 1977. *Womanspeak and Manspeak: Sex Differences and Sexism in Com-*

munication. In A. Sargent (ed.), *Beyond Sex Roles.* St. Paul, Minn.: West Publishing Co.

Henly, W., and B. Fitch, 1966. *Newborn Narcotic Withdrawal Associated with Regional Enteritis in Pregnancy.* New York Journal of Medicine (66):2565–2567.

Henslin, J., 1980. *Cohabitation: Its Context and Meaning.* Pp. 101–115 in J. Henslin (ed.), *Marriage and Family in a Changing Society.* New York: The Free Press.

Herz, F., 1980. *The Impact of Death and Serious Illness on the Family Life Cycle.* Pp. 223–240 in E. Carter and M. McGoldrick (eds.), *The Family Life Cycle: A Framework for Family Therapy.* New York: Gardner Press.

Hess, B., and E. Markson, 1980. *Aging and Old Age.* New York: Macmillan.

Hetherington, E., M. Cox, and R. Cox, 1977. *Beyond Father Absence: Conceptualization of Effects of Divorce.* In M. Hetherington (ed.), *Contemporary Readings in Child Psychology.* New York: McGraw-Hill.

Heyman, D., 1970. *Does a Wife Retire?* Gerontologist 10:54–56.

Hill, C., Z. Rubin, and L. Peplau, 1976. *Breakups Before Marriage: The End of 103 Affairs.* Journal of Social Issues 32:147–168.

Hill, R., 1949. *Families Under Stress.* New York: Harper and Row.

———, 1958. *Generic Features of Families Under Stress.* Social Casework 39:139–150.

———, 1963. *Judgment and Consumership in the Management of Family Resources.* Sociology and Social Research 47:446–460.

———, 1971. *Modern Systems Theory and the Family: A Confrontation.* Social Science Information 10 (October):7–26.

———, 1978. *The Family and Work: Rivals or Partners?* Family Perspective (Spring):57–64.

———, 1980. *The Early Adolescent and the Family.* The 79th Yearbook of the National Society for the Study of Education. Chicago: University of Chicago Press.

Hill, R., and D. Hansen, 1960. *The Identification of Conceptual Frameworks Utilized in Family Study.* Marriage and Family Living 22(4) November:299–311.

———, 1962. *The Family in Disaster.* In G. Baker and D. Chapman (eds.), *Man and Society in Disaster.* New York: Basic Books.

Hill, R., and C. Joy, 1980. *Operationalizing the Concept of Critical Transition to Generate Phases of Family Development.* Paper prepared for discussion meetings with Japanese Scholars in Kyoto and Tokyo, Japan.

Hill, R., and R. Rodgers, 1964. *The Developmental Approach.* Pp. 171–211 in H. Christensen (ed.), *Handbook of Marriage and the Family.* Chicago: Rand.

Hill, R., N. Foote, J. Aldous, R. Carlson, and R. MacDonald, 1970. *Family Development in Three Generations.* Cambridge, Mass.: Schenkman.

Hillman, K., 1962. *Marital Instability and Its Relation to Education, Income and Occupation: An Analysis Based on Census Data.* Pp. 603–608 in R. Winch, R. McGinnis, and H. Barringer (eds.), *Selected Studies on Marriage and the Family.* New York: Holt, Rinehart, Winston.

Hirsh, B., 1976. *Living Together: Guide to the Law for Unmarried Couples.* Boston: Houghton Mifflin.

Hite, S., 1977. *The Hite Report.* New York: Dell.

Hoagland, D., 1982. *A Son with Palsy: He's Going to Have to Face It.* Fresno Bee (March 10).

Hobbs, D., 1965. *Parenthood as Crisis: A Third Study.* Journal of Marriage and the Family 27(3):367–372.

Hoffman, L., 1974. *Psychological Factors.* Pp. 32–62 in L. Hoffman, and F. Nye (eds.), *Working Mothers: An Evaluative Review of the Consequences for Wife, Husband and Child.* San Francisco: Jossey-Boss.

Hoffman, L., and F. Nye (eds.) 1974. *Working Mothers: An Evaluative Review of the Consequences for Wife, Husband and Child.* San Francisco: Jossey-Boss.

Holahan, C., and L. Gilbert, 1979. *Conflict Between Major Life Roles: The Women and Men in Dual-Career Couples.* Human Relations 32:451–467.

Holmstrom, L., 1972. *The Two Career Family.* Cambridge, Mass.: Schenkman.

Hoover, H., and K. Hoover, 1979. *Concepts and Methodologies in the Family, an Instructor's Resource Handbook.* Boston: Allyn and Bacon.

Horner, M., 1977. *The Motive to Avoid Success and Changing Aspirations of College Women.* In J. Bardwick (ed.), Readings on the Psychology of Women. New York: Harper and Row.

Hoult, T., L. Henze, and J. Hudson, 1978. *Courtship and Marriage in America*. Boston: Little, Brown.

Howell, M. C., 1973. *Employed Mothers and Their Families*. Pediatrics 52:252–263.

Hughes, G., 1977. *How Much is a Garden Worth?* FCX Vegetable Garden Guide. Raleigh, N.C.: Farmers' Cooperative Exchange.

Hughes, H. (ed.), 1971. *Life in Families*. Boston: Holbrook Press.

Hunt, M., 1966. *The World of the Formerly Married*. New York: McGraw-Hill.

_____, 1972. *The Future of Marriage*. Pp. 399–412 in J. Delora and J. DeLora (eds.), *Intimate Lifestyles: Marriage and Its Alternatives*. Pacific Palisades, Calif.: Goodyear Publishing Co.

_____, 1974. *Sexual Behavior in the 1970s*. Chicago: Playboy Press.

Hyde, J. 1979. *Understanding Human Sexuality*. New York: McGraw-Hill.

Inazu, J., and G. Fox, 1980. *Maternal Influence on the Sexual Behavior of Teenage Daughters*. Journal of Family Issues 1(March):81–102.

Isaacson, W., 1983. *Hunting for the Hidden Killers*. Time 122:1(July 4):50–55.

Jackson, J., 1962. *Alcoholism and the Family*. In D. Pittman and C. Snyder (eds.), *Society, Culture and Drinking Patterns*. New York: John Wiley and Sons.

Jacobson, B., 1977. *Battered Women*. Civil Rights Digest 9(Summer):3–11.

Jacobson, C., and C. Berlin, 1972. *Possible Reproductive Detriment in LSD Users*. Journal of the American Medical Association 222(11):1367–1373.

Jacoby, S., 1974. *49 Million Singles Can't All Be Right*. New York Times Magazine (February 17):41–49.

Janeway, E., 1981. *Incest: A Rational Look at the Taboo*. Ms. Magazines (November):61–64,78, 81,109.

Jedlicka, D., 1981. *Automated Go-Betweens? Mate Selection of Tomorrow*. Family Relations 30(July):373–376.

Jenkins, G., 1971. *Helping Children Reach Their Potential*. Chicago: Scott, Foresman and Co.

Jessor, R., J. Chase, and J. Donovan, 1980. *Psychosocial Correlates of Marijuana Use and Problem Drinking in a National Sample of Adolescents*. AJPH 70:6(June):604–613.

Johnson, E., and B. Bursk, 1977. *Relationships Between the Elderly and Their Adult Children*. Gerontologist 17 (February):90–96.

Johnson, R., 1968. *Marital Patterns During the Middle Years*. Unpublished Doctoral Dissertation, Minneapolis: University of Minnesota.

_____, 1970. *Some Correlates of Extramarital Coitus*. Journal of Marriage and the Family (32):449–455.

Johnson, W., 1977. *Establishing a National Center for the Study of Divorce*. Family Coordinator 26: 263–268.

Johnston, L., G. Bachman, and P. O'Malley, 1978. *Drug Use Among American High School Students 1975–1977*. DHEW Pub. No. (ADM) 78–619. National Institute on Drug Abuse, Washington, D.C.: Superintendent of Documents, U.S. Government Printing Office.

_____, 1982. *Drug Use Among American High School Students 1978–1981*. DHEW National Institute on Drug Abuse, Washington, D.C.: Superintendent of Documents, U.S. Government Printing Office.

Jolly, H., 1975. *Book of Child Care*. London: Allen and Unwin.

Jones, A., and P. Placek, 1978. *Teenage Women in the USA: Sex, Contraception, Pregnancy, Fertility and Maternal and Infant Health*. In *Teenage Pregnancy and Family Impact: New Perspectives on Policy*. Washington, D.C.: George Washington University.

Jones, K., D. Smith, C. Ulleland, and A. Streissguth, 1973. *Pattern of Malformation in Offspring of Chronic Alcoholic Mothers*. Lancet 1:1267.

Jones, M., 1965. *Psychological Correlates of Somatic Development*. Child Development 36:899–911.

Jones, M., and P. Mussen, 1958. *Self-Conceptions, Motivations, and Interpersonal Attitudes of Early and Late Maturing Girls*. Child Development 29:491–501.

Jourard, S., 1971. *The Transparent Self*. New York: Van Nostrand.

Kaats, G., and K. Davis, 1970. *The Dynamics of Sexual Behavior of College Students*. Journal of Marriage and the Family 32(August):390–399.

Kadushin, A., 1980. *Child Welfare Services*. New York: Macmillan.

Kahana, E., and B. Kahana, 1971. *Theoretical and*

Research Perspectives on Grandparenthood. Aging and Human Development 2:(4):261–268.

———, 1980. *Statistical Abstract of the United States*. U.S. Bureau of the Census.

Kalish, R., 1975. *Late Adulthood: Perspectives on Human Development*. Monterey, Calif.: Brooks/Cole.

Kamerman, S., 1980. *Childcare and Family Benefits: Policies of Six Industrialized Countries*. Monthly Labor Review (November):23–28.

———, 1982. *Work and Family: Conflict or Consonance*. In H. McCubbin, R. Pitzer, J. Comeau, and C. Davidson (eds.), *Stress and Work: Addressing the Needs of Children, Youth and Parents*. St. Paul, Minn.: Family Social Science.

Kandel, D., and G. Lesser, 1972. *Marital Decision Making in American and Danish Urban Families: A Research Note*. Journal of Marriage and the Family 34:134–138.

Kandel, M., 1981. *What Woman Earn*. New York: Linden Press.

Kando, T., 1978. *Sexual Behavior and Family Life in Transition*. New York: Elsevier.

Kane, F., C. Moan, and B. Bolling, 1974. *Motivational Factors in Pregnant Adolescents*. Diseases of the Nervous System 35(3):131–134.

Kanin, E., K. Davidson, and L. Scheck, 1970. *A Research Note on Male-Female Differentials in the Experience of Heterosexual Love*. Journal of Sex Research 6:64–72.

Kanter, R., 1977. *Work and Family in the United States: A Critical Review and Agenda for Research and Policy*. New York: Sage Publications.

———, 1978. *Jobs and Families: Impact of Working Roles on Family Life*. Children Today (March/April):11–15,45.

Kanter, R., D. Jaffe, and D. Weisberg, 1975. *Coupling, Parenting and the Presence of Others: Intimate Relationships in Communal Households*. Family Coordinator 24:(4):433–452.

Kantner, J., and M. Zelnik, 1972. *Sexual Experience of Young Unmarried Women in the United States*. Family Planning Perspectives 4:9–18.

Kantor, D., and W. Lehr, 1975. *Inside the Family: Toward a Theory of Family Process*. San Francisco: Jossey-Bass.

Kaplan, D., A. Smith, R. Grobstein, and S. Fischman, 1973. *Family Mediation of Stress*. Social Work 18(July):60–69.

Kaplan, H., and C. Sager, 1971. *Sexual Patterns at Different Ages*. Medical Aspects of Human Sexuality (June):10–23.

Kash, S., 1984. *Birth-Control Survey: Sterilization Tops List in U.S.* Ms. Magazine (January):17.

Katchadourian, H. and D. Lunde, 1972. *Fundamentals of Human Sexuality*. New York: Holt, Rinehart and Winston.

Katz, A., 1979. *Lone Fathers: Perspectives and Implications for Family Policy*. Family Coordinator (October):521–528.

Keith, P., and T. Brubaker, 1979. *Male Household Roles in Later Life: A Look at Masculinity and Marital Relationships*. Family Coordinator 28:497–502.

Kell, D., and C. Patton, 1978. *Reaction to Induced Early Retirement*. Gerontologist 18:173–180.

Kellam, S., M. Ensminger, and J. Turner, 1977. *Family Structure and the Mental Health of Children*. Archives of General Psychiatry 34:1012–1022.

Kempe, R., and C. Kempe, 1978. *Child Abuse*. Cambridge, Mass.: Harvard University Press.

Kempler, H., 1976. *Extended Kinship Ties and Some Modern Alternatives*. Family Coordinator (April):143–148.

Kephart, W., 1954. *Some Variables in Cases of Reported Sexual Maladjustment*. Marriage and Family Living 16:241–243.

Kerckhoff, A., and K. Davis, 1962. *Value Consensus and Need Complementarity in Mate Selection*. American Sociological Review 27:295–303.

Kestenberg, J., 1968. *Phases of Adolescence: With Suggestions for Correlations of Psychic and Hormonal Organizations. III. Puberty, Growth, Differentiation and Consolidation*. Journal of American Academy of Child Psychiatry 7:108–151.

Kettering Foundation of National Association of Elementary School Principals, 1980. *Woe Is One*. Time 116(10):56.

Kilgo, R., 1972. *Can Group Marriage Work?* Sexual Behavior 2 (March):14.

———, 1982. *Gay Ghettoes*. Journal of Homosexuality 4 (Summer):363–379.

Kinsey, A., W. Pomeroy, and C. Martin, 1948. *Sexual Behavior in the Human Male*. Philadelphia: W. B. Saunders.

Kinsey, A., W. Pomeroy, and C. Martin, 1953. *Sexual Behavior in the Human Female*. Philadelphia: W. B. Saunders.

Klein, J., G. Calvert, N. Garland, and M. Polomo, 1969. *Pilgrim's Progress I: Recent Developments in Family Theory*. Journal of Marriage and the Family (31):677–687.

Knox, D., 1970. *Conceptions of Love at Three Developmental Levels*. Family Coordinator (April): 151–157.

Knox, D., and K. Wilson, 1981. *Dating Behaviors of University Students*. Family Relations (April):255–258.

Kohlberg, L., 1964. *Development of Moral Character and Moral Ideology*. Pp. 383–436 in L. Hoffman and M. Hoffman (eds.), *Review of Child Development Research*. New York: Russell Sage Foundation.

———, 1968. *Moral Development*. International Encyclopedia of the Social Sciences. New York: Macmillan and the Free Press.

Kolodny, R., 1980. *Adolescent Sexuality*. Presented at the Michigan Personnel and Guidance Association Annual Convention. Detroit (November).

Komarovsky, M., 1967. *Blue-Collar Marriage*. New York: Vintage Books.

———, 1976. *Dilemma of Masculinity*. New York: W. W. Norton.

Kompara, D., 1980. *Difficulties in the Socialization Process of Stepparenting*. Family Relations 29:69–73.

Konigsberg, D., B. Weinhouse, and J. Wechsler, 1983. *Teenagers and Alcohol: Holiday Hazard, Year-Round Tragedy*. Ladies Home Journal 100 (December):78,80,86–87,141.

Kornhaber, A., and K. Woodward, 1981. *Grandparents/Grandchildren, The Vital Connection*. New York: Anchor Press.

Kotelchuck, M., 1973. *The Nature of the Infant's Tie to His Father*. Paper presented at the meeting of the Society for Research in Child Development, Philadelphia, March 29—April 1.

Kramer, C., and J. Kramer, 1976. *Basic Principles of Long-Term Patient Care*. Springfield, Ill.: Charles C. Thomas.

Krantzler, M., 1974. *Creative Divorce*. New York: M. Evans.

Kreps, J., and R. Leaper, 1976. *Home Work, Market Work, and the Allocation of Time*. Pp. 61–81 in J. Kreps (ed.), *Women and the American Economy: A Look to the 1980's*. Englewood Cliffs, N.J.: Prentice-Hall.

Laker, R., 1982. *Gilded Splendour*. New York: New American Library.

Lamanna, M., and A. Reidman, 1981. *Marriages and Families: Making Choices Throughout the Life Cycle*. Belmont, Calif.: Wadsworth.

Lamb, M., 1977a. *Father-Infant and Mother-Infant Interaction in the First Year of Life*. Child Development 54:167–181.

———, 1977b. *The Development of Mother-Infant and Father-Infant Attachments in the Second Year of Life*. Developmental Psychology 13(6):637–648.

Lamb, M., and J. Lamb, 1976. *The Nature and Importance of the Father-Infant Relationship*. Family Coordinator 25(October):379–385.

Lamouse, A., 1969. *Family Roles of Women: A German Example*. Journal of Marriage and the Family 31:145–152.

Landis, J., and M. Landis, 1968. *Building a Successful Marriage*. 5th ed. Englewood Cliffs, N.J.: Prentice-Hall.

Langley, R., and R. Levy, 1977. *Wife Beating: The Silent Crisis*. New York: E. P. Dutton.

Langway, L., M. Zabarsky, M. Hager, S. Russell, L. Donosky, and L. Prout, 1982. *How America Treats Its Elderly*. Newsweek (November 1):60–62,65.

Lansing, J., and J. Morgan, 1955. *Consumer Finances over the Life Cycle*. In L. Clark (ed.), *Consumer Behavior*. Vol. 2. New York: New York University Press.

Larson, J., 1980. *Remarriage: Myths, Realities and Complexities*. Family Life (November and December):1–16.

Laslett, P., 1972. *Household and Family in Past Time*. Cambridge, England: University Press.

———, 1976. *Societal Development and Aging*. In R. Binstock and E. Shanas (eds.), Handbook of Aging and the Social Sciences. New York: Van Nostrand Reinhold Co.

Lasswell, M., 1973. *Looking Ahead in Aging: Love After Fifty*. Pp. 518–524 in M. Lasswell and T. Lasswell (eds.), *Love, Marriage, Family: A Developmental Approach*. Glenview, Ill.: Scott, Foresman and Co.

Lasswell, M., and T. Lasswell, 1982. *Marriage*

and the Family. Lexington: D.C. Heath and Company.

Lauton, B., and A. Freese, 1981. *The Healthy Adolescent: A Parent's Manual*. New York: Scribner's.

Lee, J., 1973. *The Colours of Love*. Toronto: New Press.

LeMasters, E., 1957. *Parenthood as Crisis*. Marriage and Family Living 19:352–355.

_____, 1970. *Parents Without Partners*. Pp. 157–174 in *Parents in Modern America*. Homewood, Ill.: Dorsey.

Leo, J., 1982. *Herpes: The New Scarlet Letter*. Time, (August 2):62–66.

LeShan, E., 1974. *The Wonderful Crisis of Middle Age*. New York: Warner.

Leslie, G., and E. Leslie, 1977. *Marriage in a Changing World*. New York: New American Library.

Leupnitz, D., 1979. *Which Aspects of Divorce Affect the Children?* Family Coordinator (January): 79–85.

Leuptow, L., 1980. *Social Structure, Social Change and Parental Influence in Adolescent Sex-Role Socialization: 1964–1975*. Journal of Marriage and the Family (February):93–103.

Levin, R., and A. Levin, 1975. *Sexual Pleasure: The Surprising Preferences of 100,000 Women*. Redbook (September):5.

Levinger, G., 1966. *Sources of Marital Dissatisfaction Among Applicants for Divorce*. American Journal of Orthopsychiatry 36(5):803–807.

Levinson, D., C. Darrow, E. Klein, M. Levinson, and B. McKee, 1978. *The Seasons of a Man's Life*. New York: Alfred A. Knopf.

Lewis, R., P. Freneau, and C. Roberts, 1979. *Fathers and the Postparental Transition*. Family Coordinator 28(October):514–520.

Limpus, L., 1970. *The Liberation of Women: Sexual Repression and the Family*. In H. Gadlin and B. Garskof (eds.), *The Uptight Society*. Belmont, Calif.: Brooks/Cole.

Lindsey, B., 1929. *The Companionate Marriage*. New York: Garden City Publishers.

Lindsey, R. 1984. *A New Generation Finds It Hard to Leave the Nest*. New York Times (January 15):18.

Lipman-Blumen, J., 1975. *The Implications for Family Structure of Changing Sex Roles*. Social Casework (February):67–79.

Litwak, E., 1960. *Geographic Mobility and Extended Family Cohesion*. American Sociological Review 25:385–394.

_____, 1965. *Extended Kin Relations in an Industrial Democratic Society*. In E. Shanas and G. Streib (eds.), *Social Structure and the Family: Generational Relations*. Englewood Cliffs, N.J.: Prentice-Hall.

Litwak, E., and I. Szelenyi, 1969. *Primary Group Structures and Their Functions: Kin, Neighbors, and Friends*. American Sociological Review 34 (August):465–481.

Livingston, C., 1978. *Why Was I Adopted?* Secaucus, N.J.: Lyle Stuart.

Lobsenz, N., 1975. *Sex After Sixty-Five*. Public Affairs Pamphlet No. 519. New York: Public Affairs Committee.

Locke, H., 1951. *Predicting Adjustment in Marriage: A Comparison*. New York: Henry Holt and Co.

Longfellow, C., 1979. *Divorce in Context: Its Impact on Children*. Pp. 288–306 in G. Levinger and O. Moles (eds.), *Divorce and Separation*. New York: Basic Books.

Loomis, R., and L. Loomis (eds.) 1957. *Medieval Romances*. New York: Modern Library.

Lopata, H., 1973. *Widowhood in an American City*. Cambridge, Mass.: Schenkman Publishing Co.

Lowenthal, M., and D. Chiriboga, 1972. *Transition to the Empty Nest*. Archives of General Psychiatry 26:8–14.

Lowenthal, M., M. Thurnher, and D. Chiriboga 1975. *Four Stages of Life*. San Francisco: Jossey-Bass.

Lowy, L., 1979. *Social Work with the Aging*. New York: Harper and Row.

Luckey, E., 1960. *Marital Satisfaction and Its Association with Congruence of Perception*. Marriage and Family Living (22):49–54.

_____, 1966. *Number of Years Married as Related to Personality Perception and Marital Satisfaction*. Journal of Marriage and the Family 28 (February):44–48.

Lynch, J., 1977. *The Broken Heart: The Medical Consequences of Loneliness in America*. New York: Basic Books.

Lyons, R., 1983. *2 Donated Human Embryos Said to Impregnate 2 Women.* New York Times (July 22):1, 6.

Maas, H., and J. Kuypers, 1974. *From Thirty to Seventy: A Forty Year Longitudinal Study of Adult Life Style and Personality.* San Francisco: Jossey-Bass.

Maccoby, E., and C. Jacklin, 1974. *The Psychology of Sex Differences.* Stanford: Stanford University Press.

Mace, D., 1975. *We Call It ACME.* Pp. 33–46 in S. Miller (ed.), *Marriages and Families: Enrichment Through Communication.* Beverly Hills, Calif.: Sage Publications.

Macklin, E., 1972. *Heterosexual Cohabitation Among Unmarried College Students.* Family Coordinator 21:463–472.

———, 1974. *Going Very Steady: Cohabitation in College.* Psychology Today (November): 53–59.

Maddox, B., 1975. *The Half Parent.* New York: New American Library.

———, 1982. *Homosexual Parents.* Psychology Today 62(February):66–69.

Malinowski, B., 1974. *The Principle of Legitimacy.* Pp. 51–63 in R. Coser (ed.), *The Family, Its Structure and Function.* 2d ed. New York: St. Martin's Press.

Mann, J., 1983. *An Endless Parade of Runaway Kids.* U.S. News and World Report 94(January 17):64.

Manuchin, S., 1974. *Families and Family Therapy.* Cambridge, Mass.: Harvard University Press.

Marciano, T., 1975. *Variant Family Forms in a World Perspective.* Family Coordinator 24(October):407–420.

Maretzki, T., 1977. *Intercultural Marriage: An Introduction.* Pp. 1–11 in W. Tseng, J. McDermott, T. Maretzki, and G. Jones (eds.), *Adjustment in Intercultural Marriage.* Honolulu: University Press of Hawaii.

Markoff, R., 1977. *Intercultural Marriage: Problem Areas.* Pp. 51–61 in W. Tseng, J. McDermott, T. Maretzki, and G. Jones (eds.), Adjustment in Intercultural Marriage. Honolulu: University Press of Hawaii.

Marsden, D., 1969. *Mothers Alone: Poverty and the Fatherless Family.* London: Allen Lane.

Martin, C., 1974. *Aging and Society Study.* Reported by Jack Gourlay in Sarasota Herald-Tribune (March 1): 10A.

Martinez, T., 1977. *Alternative Mental Health Resources for the Spanish-Speaking: Latins Helping Networks.* Paper presented at a meeting of the American Psychological Association, San Francisco (August).

Masnick, G., and M. Bane, 1980. *The Nation's Families: 1960–1990.* Boston: Auburn House.

Masters, W., and V. Johnson, 1966. *Human Sexual Response.* Boston: Little, Brown.

———, 1968. *Playboy Interview: Masters and Johnson.* Playboy (May):67–82 and 194–202.

———, 1970. *Human Sexual Inadequacy.* Boston: Little, Brown.

———, 1979. *Homosexuality in Perspective.* Boston: Little, Brown.

Masters, W., V. Johnson, and R. Kolodny, 1982. *Human Sexuality.* Boston: Little, Brown.

Maynard, P., N. Maynard, H. McCubbin, and D. Shao, 1980. *Family Life and the Police Profession: Coping Patterns Wives Employ in Managing Job Stress and the Family Environment.* Family Relations 29(October):495–501.

Mazor, M., 1979. *Barren Couples.* Psychology Today 12(May):101–108.

McAdoo, H., 1982. *Levels of Stress and Family Support in Black Families.* In H. McCubbin, A. Cauble, and J. Patterson (eds.), *Family Stress, Coping and Social Support.* Springfield, Ill.: Charles C. Thomas.

McBroom, W., 1981. *Parental Relationships, Socioeconomic Status, and Sex-Role Expectations.* Sex Roles 7(10):1027–1033.

McCandless, B., and R. Coop, 1979. *Adolescents: Behavior and Development*, 2d ed. New York: Holt, Rinehart, and Winston.

McCary, J., 1978. *Human Sexuality*, 3d ed. New York: Van Nostrand Reinhold Co.

McCubbin, H. 1983. *Family Stress and Family Coping.* Appleton, Wisc.: AAL Well To Do Series.

McCubbin, H., and C. Figley (eds.), 1983. *Stress and the Family: Coping with Normative Transitions.* New York: Brunner Mazel.

McCubbin, H., and J. Patterson, 1982. *Family Adaptation to Crises.* In H. McCubbin, A. Cauble, and J. Patterson (eds.), *Family Stress, Cop-*

ing and Social Support. Springfield, Ill.: Charles C Thomas.

_____, 1983. *The Family Stress Process*. In H. McCubbin, M. Sussman, and J. Patterson (eds.), *Social Stress and the Family*. New York: Haworth.

McCubbin, H., J. Patterson, M. McCubbin, L. Wilson, and W. Warwick, 1983. *Parental Coping and Family Environments: Critical Factors in the Home Management and Health Status of Children with Cystic Fibrosis*. In D. Bagarozzi, T. Jurich, and R. Jackson (eds.), *New Perspectives in Marriage and Family Therapy: Issues in Theory Research and Practice*. Palo Alto: Human Science Press.

McCullers, C., 1977. *The Ballad of the Sad Cafe and Other Stories*. New York: Bantam.

McDaniel, C., Jr., 1969. *Dating Roles and Reasons for Dating*. Journal of Marriage and the Family 31(February):97–107.

McDowell, B., and H. Umlaus (eds.)., 1977. *Women's Almanac*. New York: Newspaper Enterprise Association, Inc.

McGinniss, A., 1982. *The Romance Factor*. New York: Harper and Row.

McKenry, P., L. Walters, and C. Johnson, 1979. *Adolescent Pregnancy: A Review of the Literature*. Family Coordinator (January): 17–28.

McTavish, D., 1971. *Perceptions of Old Age: A Review of Research Methodologies and Findings*. Gerontologist 11(4):90–102.

Mead, G., 1934. *Mind, Self and Society*. Chicago: University of Chicago Press.

Mead, M., 1933. *Sex and Temperament in Three Primitive Societies*. New York: Morrow.

_____, 1966. *Marriage in Two Steps*. Redbook 127(July):48–49, 84–86.

Medley, M., 1977. *Marital Adjustment in the Post-Retirement Years*. Family Coordinator 26:5–11.

Mendes, H., 1976. *Single Fathers*. Family Coordinator 25:439–444.

Menning, B., 1977. *Infertility: A Guide for the Childless Couple*. Englewood Cliffs, N.J.: Prentice-Hall.

Messinger, L., 1976. *Remarriage Between Divorced People with Children from Previous Marriages: A Proposal for Preparation for Remarriage*. Journal of Marriage and Family Counselors 2:193–200.

Meyerowitz, J., and J. Malev, 1973. *Pubescent Attitudinal Correlates Antecedent to Adolescent Illegitimate Pregnancy*. Journal of Youth and Adolescence 2:251–258.

Michaels, J., and H. Schucman, 1962. *Observations on the Psychodynamics of Parents of Retarded Children*. American Journal of Mental Deficiencies 66:568–573.

Michel, A., 1967. *Comparative Data Concerning the Interaction in French and American Families*. Journal of Marriage and the Family 29:337.

Milano, E., and S. Hall, 1978. *Sex-Roles in Dating: Paying vs. Putting Out*. In S. Hall and E. Milano (eds.), *Interpersonal Relationships in Marriage and the Family*. Appalachian State University.

Milgram R., and N. Milgram, 1975. *The Effects of the Yom-Kippur War On Anxiety Level and Israeli Children*. Paper presented at the International Conference on Psychological Stress and Adjustment in Time of War and Peace, Tel Aviv, Israel (January).

Milkovich, L., and B. Van Denberg, 1974. *Effects of Prenatal Meprobamate and Chlordiazpoxide Hydrochloride on Human Embryonic and Fetal Development*. New England Journal of Medicine 291(December 12):1268–1271.

Miller, B., and D. Sollie, 1980. *Normal Stresses During the Transition to Parenthood*. Family Relations 29(October)429–465.

Miller, B., and J. Myers-Wall, 1982. *Stresses of Parenting*. In H. McCubbin and C. Figley (eds.), *Stress and the Family*. New York: Brunner Mazel.

_____, 1983. *Parenthood: Transitions In and Out*. In H. McCubbin and C. Figley (eds.), *Stress and the Family*. Vol. 3 *Coping with Normative Crises*. New York: Brunner Mazel.

Miller, S., 1978. *Will the Real "Older Woman" Please Stand Up?* In M. Seltzer, S. Corbett, and R. Atchley (eds.), *Social Problems of the Aging: Readings*. Belmont, Calif.: Wadsworth.

Miller, S., E. Nunnally, and D. Wackman, 1975. *Alive and Aware: Improving Communication in Relationships*. Minneapolis: Interpersonal Communication Program.

Millor, G., 1981. *A Theoretical Framework for Nursing Research in Child Abuse and Neglect*. Nursing Research 30(March/April):78–83.

Minnesota Department of Corrections, 1981. *Report to the Legislature on Program for Battered Women*. St. Paul.

Monahan, T., 1971. *Interracial Marriage and Divorce in Kansas and the Question of Unstability of Mixed Marriages*. Journal of Comparative Family Studies (Spring):107–120.

———, 1976. *The Occupational Class of Couples Entering into Interracial Marriages*. Journal of Comparative Family Studies 7:2(Summer):175–192.

Money, J., 1980. *Love and Love Sickness*. Baltimore: Johns Hopkins University Press.

Money, J., and A. Ehrhardt, 1972. *Man and Woman, Boy and Girl*. Baltimore: Johns Hopkins University Press.

Montagu, A., 1971. *Touching: The Human Significance of the Skin*. New York: Harper and Row.

Moore, D., 1983. *America's Neglected Elderly*. New York Times Magazine (January 30):30–37.

Moos, R., and V. Tsu, 1976. *Human Competence and Coping*. Pp. 3–16 in R. Moos (ed.), *Human Adaptation: Coping with Life Crises*. Lexington, Mass.: D. C. Heath and Co.

———, 1977. *The Crisis of Physical Illness*. Pp. 3–21 in R. Moos (ed.) Coping with Physical Illness. New York: Plenum Medical Book Co.

Murdock, G., 1949. *Social Structure*. New York: Macmillan.

Mursheim, B., 1980. *Mate Selection in the Seventies*. Journal of Marriage and the Family 42(4)(November):777–792.

Murstein, B., 1971. *Stimulus—Value—Role: A Theory of Marital Choice*. Journal of Marriage and the Family 32(3):465–481.

Mussen, P., and M. Jones, 1957. *Self-Conceptions, Motivations and Interpersonal Attitudes of Late- and Early-Maturing Boys*. Child Development 28:243–256.

Mussen, P., J. Conger, and J. Kagan, 1969. *Child Development and Personality*. New York: Harper and Row.

Naeye, R., W. Blanc, and C. Paul, 1973. *Effects of Maternal Nutrition on the Human Fetus*. Pediatrics 52(4):494–503.

National Center for Health Statistics, 1970. *Mortality from Selected Causes By Marital Status*. Series 20:8A and 8B. Washington, D.C.: U.S. Government Printing Office.

———, 1980. *Advance Data*. No. 58, Washington, D.C.: U.S. Government Printing Office (February 14).

National Council on Family Relations, 1982. *Report*. Vol. 27, No. 4(December).

Nehls, N., and M. Morgenbesser, 1980. *Joint Custody: An Exploration of the Issues*. Family Process 19(2):117–125.

Neubeck, G. (ed.), 1969. *Extramarital Relationships*. Englewood Cliffs, N.J.: Prentice-Hall.

Neugarten, B., 1968a. *Middle Age and Aging*. Chicago: University of Chicago Press.

———, 1968b. *Adult Personality: Toward a Psychology of the Life Cycle*. In B. Neugarten (ed.), *Middle Age and Aging*. Chicago: University of Chicago Press.

———, 1970. *Dynamics of Transition of Middle Age to Old Age*. Journal of Geriatric Psychology 4:71–87.

———, 1974. *Age Groups in American Society and the Rise of the Young-Old*. Annals of the American Academy 415(September):187–198.

———, 1976. *Adaptation and the Life Cycle*. Counseling Psychologist 6:16–20.

Neugarten, B., and K. Weinstein, 1964. *The Changing American Grandparent*. Journal of Marriage and the Family 26(2):199–204.

Newson, E., and T. Hipgrave, 1982. *Getting Through to Your Handicapped Child*. Cambridge, England: Cambridge University Press.

Newsweek, 1978. *How Men are Changing*. 91(January 16):52–56.

———, 1980. *Bad News for Women Smokers*. (January 28):83.

New York Post, 1981. *Incest Said to Be Near Epidemic Proportions*. (November 23):43.

New York Times, 1979. *Incest* (December 3):9.

———, 1982. *Births to Single Women in 1980 Found at Record* (December 5):A35.

———, 1982. *Skinner Tells Colleagues His Personal Strategies for Managing Old Age* (August 24):19.

Newcomb, T., 1953. *An Approach to the Study of Communicative Acts*. Psychological Review (60):393–404.

Nichols, R., and J. Troester, 1979. *Custody Evaluations: An Alternative?* Family Coordinator (July):399–407.

Noble, J., and W. Noble, 1975. *The Custody Trap*. New York: Hawthorn Books.

Nock, S., 1979. *The Family Life Cycle: Empirical or Conceptual Tool?* Journal of Marriage and the

Family (February):15–26.

Norgren, J., and S. Cole, 1982. *Heaven Help the Working Mother*. The Nation (January 23): 77–80.

Norman, J., and M. Harris, 1981. *The Private Life of the American Teenager*. Rawson, Wade.

Norman, M., 1980. *The New Extended Family*. New York Times (November 23):26, 44, 46, 53, 54, 147, 162, 166, 173.

———, 1983. *Homosexuals Confronting a Time of Change*. New York Times (June 16):1,13.

Nunnally, E., S. Miller, and D. Wackman, 1975. *The Minnesota Couple Communication Program*. Pp. 59–73 in S. Miller (ed.), *Marriages and Families: Enrichment Through Communication*. Beverly Hills, Calif.: Sage Publications.

Nye, F., 1957. *Child Adjustment in Broken and in Unhappy Unbroken Homes*. Marriage and Family Living 19:356–361.

———, 1974a. *Emerging and Declining Family Roles*. Journal of Marriage and the Family (May):238–245.

———, 1974b. *Sociocultural Context*. Pp. 1–31 in L. Hoffman and F. Nye (eds.), *Working Mothers: An Evaluative Review of the Consequences for Wife, Husband and Child*. San Francisco: Jossey Boss.

Nye, F., and F. Berardo, 1966. *Emerging Conceptual Frameworks in Family Analysis*. New York: Macmillan.

Nye, F., and S. McLaughlin, 1976. *Role Competence and Marital Satisfaction*. Pp. 191–205 in F. Nye (ed.), *Role Structure and Analysis of the Family*. Beverly Hills, Calif.: Sage Publications.

Nye, F., 1976. *Role Structure and Analysis of the Family*. Beverly Hills, Calif.: Sage Publications.

Offer, D., 1969. *The Psychological World of the Teenager: A Study of Normal Adolescent Boys*. New York: Basic Books.

———, 1972. *Attitudes Toward Sexuality in a Group of 1500 Middle-Class Teenagers*. Journal of Youth and Adolescence 1:81–90.

Olds, S., 1981. *Danger Zone: When Parents Fight Over Kids*. Ladies Home Journal (May): 52–55.

Olson, D., 1972. *Marriage of the Future: Revolutionary or Evolutionary Change*. Family Coordinator 21(October):383–393.

———, 1977. *Communication and Intimacy*. Un-published manuscript, University of Minnesota.

———, 1983. *How Effective is Marriage Preparation?* In D. Mace (ed.), *Prevention in Family Services*. Beverly Hills, Calif.: Sage Publications.

Olson, D., and R. Cromwell (eds.), 1975. *Power in Families*. New York: John Wiley and Sons.

Olson, D., H. McCubbin, H. Barnes, A. Larsen, M. Muxen, and M. Wilson, 1983. *Families: What Makes Them Work*. Beverly Hills, Calif.: Sage Publications.

Olson, L., 1983. *Costs of Children*. Lexington, Mass.: Lexington Books.

O'Neill, N., and G. O'Neill, 1972. *Open Marriage*. New York: Avon Books.

Oppenheimer, V., 1976. *The Easterlin Hypothesis: Another Aspect of the Echo to Consider*. Population and Development Review 2:433–437.

Oppong, C., 1970. *Conjugal Power and Resources: An Urban African Example*. Journal of Marriage and the Family 32:676–680.

Orden, S., and N. Bradburn, 1968. *Dimensions of Marriage Happiness*. American Journal of Sociology 73 (May):715–731.

———, 1969. *Working Wives and Marriage Happiness*. American Journal of Sociology 74:392–407.

Orlofsky, J., and M. Windle, 1978. *Sex-Role Orientation, Behavioral Adaptability, and Personal Adjustment*. Sex Roles 4:801–811.

Orthner, D., 1976. *Patterns of Leisure and Marital Interaction*. Journal of Leisure Research 8:39–111.

———, 1981. *Intimate Relationships: An Introduction to Marriage and Family*. Reading, Mass.: Addison-Wesley.

Ory, H., A. Rosenfield and L. Landman, 1980. *The Pill at 20: An Assessment*. Family Planning Perspectives 12:6 (November/December): 278–283.

Ory, M., 1976. *The Decision to Parent or Not: Normative and Structural Components*. Paper presented at the annual meeting of the National Council on Family Relations, New York City.

Osofsky, H., 1968. *The Pregnant Teenager*. Springfield, Ill.: C.C. Thomas.

Pagelow, M., 1976. *Preliminary Report on Married Women*. Paper presented at the Second International Symposium on Victimology, Boston (September).

Palmer, R., M. Ouellette, L. Warner, and R. Leichtman, 1974. *Congenital Malformations in Offspring of Chronic Alcoholic Mothers.* Pediatrics 53(4):490–494.

Paloma, M., 1972. *Role Conflict and the Married Professional Woman.* In C. Safilios-Rothschild (ed.), *Toward a Sociology of Women.* Lexington, Mass.: Xerox College Publishing.

Paolucci, B., O. Hall, and N. Axinn, 1977. *Family Decision Making: An Ecosystem Approach.* New York: John Wiley and Sons.

Papalia, D., and S. Olds, 1979. *Human Development.* New York: McGraw-Hill.

Parke, R., and S. O'Leary, 1975. *Father-Mother-Infant Interaction in the Newborn Period: Some Findings, Some Observations, and Some Unresolvable Issues.* In K. Reigel and J. Meacham (eds.), *The Developing Individual in a Changing World.* Vol. II. *Social Environmental Issues.* The Hague: Mouton.

Parke, R., S. O'Leary, and S. West, 1972. *Mother-Father-Newborn Interaction: Effects of Maternal Medication, Labor, and Sex of Infant.* Proceedings of the 80th Annual Convention of the American Psychological Association, 85–86.

Parke, R., T. Power, and T. Fisher, 1980. *The Adolescent Father's Impact on the Mother and Child.* Journal of Social Issues 36(1):88–106.

Parke, R., and D. Swain, 1976. *The Father's Role in Infancy: A Re-Evaluation.* Family Coordinator 25(October):365–371.

Parlee, M., 1979. *Conversational Politics.* Psychology Today (May):48–54.

Parson, E., 1978. *The Capacity for Empathy: An Investigation of the Relationship Between Interpersonal Sensitivity Patterning of Psychological Type as a Function of Race, Sex, Birth Order and Other Variables.* Dissertation Abstracts International (August):39:1052.

Parsons, T., 1953. *A Revised Analytical Approach to the Theory of Social Stratification.* Pp. 92–128 in R. Bendix and S. Lipset (eds.), *Class, Status and Power.* Glencoe, Ill.: The Free Press.

———, 1965. *The Normal American Family.* Pp. 31–50 in S. Farber, P. Mustacchi, and R. Wilson (eds.), *Man and Civilization: The Family's Search for Survival.* New York: McGraw-Hill.

Parsons, T., and R. Bales, 1955. *Family, Socialization and Interaction Process.* Glencoe, Ill.: The Free Press.

Pasnau, R., 1972. *Psychiatric Complications of Therapeutic Abortion.* Obstetrics and Gynecology 40(2):252–256.

Patterson, J., and H. McCubbin, 1984. *Gender Roles and Coping.* Journal of Marriage and the Family (46)1:95–104.

Pederson, F., 1976. *Does Research on Children Reared in Father Absent Families Yield Information on Father Influences?* Family Coordinator 25(4):459–464.

Peplau, L., 1981. *What Homosexuals Want in Relationships.* Psychology Today (March):28–34.

Perrucci, C., and D. Barg (eds.), 1974. *Marriage and the Family: A Critical Analysis and Proposals for Change.* New York: McKay.

Peters, M., and G. Massey, 1983. *Mundane Extreme Environmental Stress in Family Stress Theories: The Case of the Black Family in White America.* Pp. 193–218 in H. McCubbin, M. Sussman and J. Patterson (eds.) *Social Stress and the Family: Advances and Developments in Family Stress Theory and Research.* New York: The Haworth Press.

Peterson, C., and W. Gove, 1980. *An Update on the Literature on Marital Adjustment: The Effect of Children and the Employment of Wives.* Unpublished paper, Vanderbilt University.

Peterson, G., and H. Cleminshaw, 1980. *The Strength of Single-Parent Families During Divorce Crisis: An Integrative Review with Clinical Implications.* Pp. 435–443 in N. Stinneff, B. Chesser, J. DeFrain, and P. Knaub (eds.), *Family Strengths: Positive Models for Family Life.* Lincoln, Nebr.: University of Nebraska.

Peterson, N., 1983a. *Teen-Age Apathy, Epidemic of the '80's.* USA Today (November 8):4D.

———, 1983b. *Daughters Suffer Most After Divorce.* USA Today (December 5):4D.

Petranek, C., 1970. *Postparental Spouses' Perception of Their Dyadic Interaction as Related to Their Life Satisfaction.* Tallahassee, Fla.: Department of Sociology, Florida State University.

———, 1971. *The Forgotten Phase of Life—The Postparental Period of Marriage.* Unpublished manuscript.

Pettigrew, B., 1969. *Group Discussions with Adoptive Parents.* Child Adoption 1:39–42.

Phillips, R., 1981. *Sex After 60: Snow on the Roof Only Masks a Roaring Blaze.* Chicago Tribune (August 9):XII 1.

Piaget, J., 1932/1948. *The Moral Judgment of the*

Child. Chicago: The Free Press.

Pietropinto, A., and J. Simenauer, 1979. *Husbands and Wives*. New York: Times Books.

Piotrowski, C., 1979. *Work and the Family System*. New York: The Free Press.

Pleck, J., 1981. *Husbands' Paid Work and Family Roles: Current Research Issues*. In H. Lopata (ed.), *Research on the Interweave of Social Roles: Women and Men*. Vol. 3. Greenwich: Jai.

Pogrebin, L., 1980. *Growing Up Free: Raising Your Child in the '80's*. New York: McGraw-Hill.

_____, 1982. *Are Men Discovering the Joys of Fatherhood? Big Changes in Parenting*. Ms. Magazine (February):41–46.

Polk, B., 1974. *Male Power and the Women's Movement*. Journal of Applied Behavioral Science 10(3):415–431.

Pollak, O., and E. Wise, 1979. *Invitation to a Dialogue*. New York: S P Medical and Scientific Books.

Pollock, D., 1981. *The Stepfamily: How to Put Your Best Foot Forward*. Fresno Bee (April 5):B1,B4.

Porter, S., 1976. *Money Book*. New York: Avon.

Portner, J., 1983. *Work and Family: Achieving a Balance*. In H. McCubbin and C. Figley (eds.), *Stress and the Family*. Vol. 1: *Coping with Normative Transitions*. New York: Brunner Mazel.

Powers, W., and K. Hutchinson, 1979. *The Measurement of Communication Apprehension in the Marriage Relationship*. Journal of Marriage and the Family 41:39–95.

Prescott, S., and C. Letko, 1977a. *Spouse Violence: Factors Affecting Women, Children, and Marriage*. Paper presented at the meeting of the Western Social Science Association, Denver (April).

_____, 1977b. *Battered Women: A Social Psychological Perspective*. Pp. 72–96 in M. Roy (ed.), *Battered Women: A Psychosociological Study of Domestic Violence*. New York: Van Nostrand Reinhold.

Press, A., P. Clausen, W. Burger, P. Abramson, J. McCormick, and S. Cavazos, 1983. *Divorce American Style*. Newsweek (January 10):42–48.

Presser, H., 1980. *Sally's Corner: Coping with Unmarried Motherhood*. Journal of Social Issues 36(1):107–129.

Prial, F., 1982. *More Women Work at Traditional Male Jobs*. New York Times (November 15): 1, 22.

Price, J., 1979. *How to Have a Child and Keep Your Job*. New York: St. Martin's Press.

Pringle, M., et al., 1967. *11,000 Seven-Year-Olds*. Longmans.

Projector, D., and M. Roer, 1982. *Studies in Income Distribution, Family Demography and Transfer Payments During the 1970s*. Washington, D.C.: U.S. Department of Health and Human Services, SSA Publication 13–11776(September).

Rallings, E., 1976. *The Special Role of Stepfather*. Family Coordinator 25:445–449.

Ramey, E., 1973. *Sex Hormones and Executive Ability*. Annals of the New York Academy of Sciences 208 (March):237–245.

Ramey, J., 1972. *Emerging Patterns of Innovative Behavior in Marriage*. Family Coordinator 21:435–456.

Ramirez M. III, and B. Cox, 1980. *Parenting for Multiculturalism*. Pp. 54–62 in M. Fantini and R. Cárdenas (eds.), *Parenting in a Multicultural Society*. New York: Longman.

Rankin, D., 1979. *How Not to Get Too Deep in Debt*. Redbook (November):98–103.

_____, 1983. *What Women Need to Know About Money*. Ladies Home Journal (April):119.

Rapoport, R., 1963. *Normal Crises, Family Structure and Mental Health*. Family Process 2:68–80.

Rapoport, R., and R. Rapoport, 1971. *Early and Late Experiences and Adult Behavior*. British Journal of Sociology 22(1):16.

_____, 1975. *Men, Women and Equity*. Family Coordinator 24(October):421–432.

_____, 1978a. *Dual-Career Families: Progress and Prospects*. Marriage and Family Review 1 (September-October):3–12.

_____, 1978b. *Working Couples*. London: Routledge and Kegan Paul.

Rapoport, R., R. Rapoport, and Z. Strelitz, 1977. *Fathers, Mothers and Society, Perspectives on Parenting*. New York: Vintage Books.

Rathus, S., 1983. *Human Sexuality*. New York: Holt, Rinehart and Winston.

Ratliff, B., H. Moon, and G. Bonacci, 1978. *Intercultural Marriage: The Korean-American Experience*. Social Casework (April):221–226.

Rauh, J., L. Johnson, and R. Burket, 1973. *The Reproductive Adolescent*. Pediatric Clinics of North America 20:1005–1020.

Read, M., J. Habicht, A. Lechtig, and R. Klein, 1973. *Maternal Malnutrition, Birth Weight, and Child Development*. Paper presented before the International Symposium on Nutrition, Growth and Development, Valencia, Spain.

Reichard, S., F. Livson, and P. Petersen, 1962. *Aging and Personality*. New York: John Wiley and Sons.

Reimer, R., and J. Maiolo, 1977. *Family Growth and Socioeconomic Status Among Poor Blacks*. Unpublished manuscript.

Reiss, I., 1960. *Premarital Sexual Standards in America*. New York: The Free Press.

_____, 1972. *Toward a Sociology of the Heterosexual Love Relationship*. In I. Reiss (ed.), *Readings on the Family System*. New York: Holt, Rinehart and Winston.

_____, 1976. *Family Systems in America*, 2nd ed. New York: Holt, Rinehart, and Winston.

_____, 1980. *Family Systems in America*, 3d ed. Hinsdale, Ill.: Dryden Press.

Reiss, I., R. Anderson, and G. Sponaugle, 1980. *A Multivariate Model of the Determinants of Extramarital Sexual Permissiveness*. Journal of Marriage and the Family (May):395–411.

Renshaw, J., 1976. *An Exploration of the Dynamics of the Overlapping Worlds of Work and Family*. Family Process 15:143–165.

Rice D., 1979. *Dual-Career Marriage: Conflict and Treatment*. New York: The Free Press.

Ridley, C., 1973. *Exploring the Impact of Work Satisfaction and Involvement on Marital Interaction When Both Partners are Employed*. Journal of Marriage and the Family 35:229–237.

Riley, M., and A. Foner, 1968. *Aging Society*. Vol. I: *An Inventory of Research Findings*. New York: Russell Sage Foundation.

Rimmer, R., 1966. *The Harrad Experiment*. Los Angeles: Sherburn Press.

Ritchie, O., and M. Koller, 1964. *Sociology of Childhood*. New York: Appleton-Century-Crofts.

Roberts, E., and J. Gagnon, 1978. *Family Life and Sexual Learning*. Vol. 1: *Summary Report*. Cambridge, Mass.: Population Education.

Robertson, J., 1975. *Interaction in Three Generation Families, Parents as Mediators: Toward a Theoretical Perspective*. International Journal of Aging and Human Development 6(2):103–110.

_____, 1976. *Significance of Grandparents: Perceptions of Young Adult Grandchildren*. Gerontologist 16:137–140.

_____, 1977. *Grandmotherhood: A Study of Role Conceptions*. Journal of Marriage and the Family (February):165–173.

Robinson, B., and M. Thurnher, 1979. *Taking Care of Aged Parents: A Family Cycle Transition*. Gerontologist 19:586–593.

Robinson, H., and N. Robinson, 1965. *The Mentally Retarded Child: A Psychological Approach*. New York: McGraw-Hill.

Robinson, I., and D. Jedlicka, 1982. *Change in Sexual Attitudes and Behavior of College Students from 1965 to 1980*. Journal of Marriage and the Family (February):237–240.

Rodgers, R., 1973. *Family Interaction and Transcription: The Developmental Approach*. Englewood Cliffs, N.J.: Prentice-Hall.

Rollin, B., 1970. *Motherhood: Who Needs It?* Look Magazine 34(September 22):15–17.

Rollins, B., and K. Cannon, 1974. *Marital Satisfaction over the Family Life Cycle: A Reevaluation*. Journal of Marriage and the Family 36:271–282.

Rollins, B., and H. Feldman, 1970. *Marital Satisfaction over the Life Cycle*. Journal of Marriage and the Family 32(February):20–28.

Root, K., 1977. *Workers and Their Families in a Plant Shutdown*. Paper presented at the Annual Meeting of the American Sociological Association, August.

Rosaldo, M., and L. Lamphere, 1974. *Woman, Culture, and Society*. Stanford, Calif.: Standford University Press.

Rose, R., T. Gordon, and I. Bernstein, 1972. *Plasma Testosterone Levels in the Male Rhesus: Influences of Sexual and Social Stimuli*. Science 178(4061):643–638.

Rose, V., and S. Price-Bonham, 1973. *Divorce Adjustment: A Woman's Problem?* Family Coordinator 22:291–297.

Rosen, L., and R. Bell, 1966. *Mate Selection in the Upper Class*. Sociological Quarterly 7:157–166.

Rosen, R., 1980. *Adolescent Pregnancy Decision Making: Are Parents Important?* Adolescence 15 (57)(Spring):43–54.

Rosenblatt, P., and P. Cozby, 1972. *Courtship Patterns Associated with Freedom of Choice of Spouse*. Journal of Marriage and the Family 34(November):689–695.

Rosenblatt, P., R. Walsh, and D. Jackson, 1976.

Grief and Mourning in Cross-Cultural Perspective. New Haven: HRAF Press.

Rosenmayr, L., and E. Köckeis, 1963. *Propositions for a Sociological Theory of Aging and the Family.* International Social Science Journal 15:410–426.

Rosenthal, E., 1970. *Divorce and Religious Intermarriage: The Effect of Previous Marital Status upon Subsequent Marital Behavior.* Journal of Marriage and the Family (August):435–440.

Rosow, I., 1967. *Social Integration of the Aged.* New York: The Free Press.

Rosow, I., and K. Rose, 1972. *Divorce Among Doctors.* Journal of Marriage and the Family 34:587–598.

Ross, H., and I. Sawhill, 1975. *Time of Transition: The Growth of Families Headed by Women.* Washington, D.C.: Urban Institute.

Rossi, A., 1968. *Transition of Parenthood.* Journal of Marriage and the Family (February):26–39.

Rubenstein, C., 1983. *The Modern Art of Courtly Love.* Psychology Today (July):40,43–49.

Rubin, L., 1976. *Worlds of Pain.* New York: Basic Books.

———, 1978. *Women of a Certain Age: The Midlife Search for Self.* New York: Harper and Row.

Ruesch, H., W. Barry, R. Hertel and M. Swain, 1974. *Communication, Conflict, and Marriage.* San Francisco: Jossey-Bass.

Russell, C., 1974. *Transition to Parenthood: Problems and Gratifications.* Journal of Marriage and the Family 36:294–301.

Rutter, M., 1971. *Parent-Child Separation: Psychological Effects on the Children.* Journal of Child Psychology and Psychiatry 12:233–260.

Safilios-Rothschild, C., 1967. *A Comparison of Power Structure and Marital Satisfaction in Urban Greek and French Families.* Journal of Marriage and the Family 29:345.

———, 1976. *The Dimensions of Power Distribution in the Family.* In H. Grunebaum and J. Christ (eds.), *Contemporary Marriage: Structure, Dynamics, and Therapy.* Boston: Little, Brown.

SAG's Nolan Blasts T.V. Portrayal of Women, 1978. Broadcasting (June 5):55.

Sager, C., 1976. *Marriage Contracts and Couple Therapy: Hidden Forces in Intimate Relationships.* New York: Brunner Mazel.

Saline, C., 1980. *Feeling Close.* McCall's Magazine 108(October):34–36.

Sanday, P., 1973. *Toward a Theory of the Status of Women.* American Anthropologist 75:1682–1700.

Sands, S., 1982. *Implementing Corporate Solutions to Work/Family Stresses.* In H. McCubbin, R. Pitzer, J. Comeau, and C. Davidson (eds.), *Stress and Work: Addressing the Needs of Children, Youth, and Parents.* St. Paul, Minn.: Family Social Science.

Sanguilano, I., 1978. *In Her Time.* New York: William Morrow.

Sanoff, A., 1983a. *19 Million Singles: Their Joys and Frustrations.* U.S. News and World Report (February):53–56.

———, 1983b. *Marriage: It's Back in Style!* U.S. News and World Report (June 20):44–47, 50.

Sarbin, T., and V. Allen, 1968. *Role Theory.* In G. Lindsey and E. Aronson (eds.), *The Handbook of Social Psychology*, 2d ed. Vol. I. Reading, Mass.: Addison-Wesley.

Sarr-Salapatek, S., and M. Williams, 1973. *The Effects of Early Stimulation on Low-Birth-Weight Infants.* Child Development (44):94–1001.

Satir, V., 1964. *Conjoint Family Therapy.* Palo Alto, Calif.: Science and Behavior Books.

———, 1967. *I John, Take Thee Mary—For the Next Five Years.* Christian Century 84(September):1182.

———, 1972. *Peoplemaking.* Palo Alto, Calif.: Science and Behavior Books.

Saunders, L., 1969. *Social Class and Postparental Perspective.* Ph. D. Dissertation, University of Minnesota.

Sawyer, S., 1980. *Lifting the Veil on the Last Taboo.* Family Health. 12(June):43.

Scales, P., and K. Everly, 1977. *A Community Sex Education Program for Parents.* Family Coordinator 1:37–45.

Scanzoni, J., 1975. *Sex Roles, Life-Styles, and Childrearing: Changing Patterns in Marriage and the Family.* New York: The Free Press.

———, 1979. *Social Processes and Power in Families.* In W. Burr, R. Hill, R. Nye and I. Reiss (eds.), Contemporary Theories About the Family: Research Based Theories. Vol. 1. New York: The Free Press.

Scanzoni, J., and G. Fox, 1980. *Sex Roles, Family and Society: The Seventies and Beyond.* Journal of Marriage and the Family 42(4):743–756.

Scanzoni, L., and J. Scanzoni, 1981. *Men, Women and Change: A Sociology of Marriage and Family*. 2d ed. New York: McGraw-Hill.

Scheff, T., 1967. *Toward a Sociological Model of Consensus*. American Sociological Review. 32:32–46.

Schiff, H., 1977. *The Bereaved Parent*. New York: Crown Publishers.

Schlesinger, B., 1975. *The One-Parent Family*. Toronto: University of Toronto.

Schulman, M., 1974. *Idealization in Engaged Couples*. Journal of Marriage and the Family 36:139–147.

Schulz, D., 1974. *The Changing Family: Its Function and Future*, 2d ed. Englewood Cliffs, N.J.: Prentice-Hall.

Schvaneveldt, J., M. Fryer, and R. Ostler, 1970. *Concepts of "Badness" and "Goodness" of Parents as Perceived by Nursery School Children*. Family Coordinator 19:98–103.

Schwartz, G., and D. Merten, 1980. *Love and Commitment*. Beverly Hills, Calif.: Sage Publications.

Schwartz, W., 1968. *Group Work in Public Welfare*. Public Welfare 26(October):348–356.

Science Digest, 1983. *New Data on Reproductive Deaths*. 91(March):91.

Seligson, M., 1973. *The Eternal Bliss Machine: America's Way of Wedding*. New York: William Morrow and Co.

Seltzer, M., and R. Atchley, 1971. *The Impact of Structural Integration into the Profession on Work Commitment, Potential for Disengagement, and Leisure Preferences Among Social Workers*. Sociological Focus 5:9–17.

Selye, H., 1974. *Stress Without Distress*. New York: Lippincott and Co.

Seward, R., 1973. *The Colonial Family in America: Toward a Socio-Historical Restoration of Its Structure*. Journal of Marriage and the Family (February):58–70.

Shah, F., and M. Zelnik, 1981. *Parent and Peer Influence on Sexual Behavior, Contraceptive Use, and Pregnancy Experience of Young Women*. Journal of Marriage and the Family (May):339–348.

Shah, F., M. Zelnik, and J. Kanter, 1975. *Unprotected Intercourse Among Unwed Teenagers*. Family Planning Perspectives 7:39–43.

Shanas, E., 1973. *Family-Kin Network and Aging in Cross-Cultural Perspective*. Journal of Marriage and the Family 35(August):505–511.

———, 1978. *A National Survey of the Aged*. Final report to the Administration on Aging. Washington, D.C.: U.S. Department of Health, Education and Welfare.

———, 1979a. *The Family as a Social Support System in Old Age*. Gerontologist 19(2):169–174.

———, 1979b. *Social Myth as Hypothesis: The Case of the Family Relations of Old People*. Gerontologist 19(1):3–9.

———, 1980. *Older People and Their Families: The New Pioneers*. Journal of Marriage and the Family (February):9–15.

Shanas, E., and M. Sussman, 1979. *The Family in Later Life: Social Structure and Social Policy*. Paper prepared for a meeting on Stability and Change in the Family, Committee on Aging, National Research Council, Annapolis, Maryland (March 22–24).

Shanas, E., P. Towsend, D. Wedderburn, H. Friis, P. Milhhoj, and J. Stehouwer, 1968. *Older People in Three Industrial Societies*. New York: Atherton Press.

Shapiro, S., D. Slone, L. Rosenberg, D. Kaufman, P. Stolley, and O. Miettinen, 1979. *Oral Contraceptive Use in Relation to Myocardial Infarction*. The Lancet 1:743.

Sheehy, G., 1974. *Passages: Predictable Crises of Adult Life*. New York: E. P. Dutton.

Sheldon, A., P. McEwan, and C. Ryser, 1975. *Retirement Patterns and Predictions*. Washington, D.C.: U.S. Superintendent of Documents.

Shoen, R., 1975. *California Divorce Rates by Age at First Marriage and Duration of First Marriage*. Journal of Marriage and the Family 37:548–555.

Shonick, H., 1975. *Pre-Marital Counseling: Three Years' Experience of a Unique Service*. Family Coordinator (July):321–324.

Shouse, J., 1975. *Psychological and Emotional Problems of Pregnancy in Adolescence*. In J. Zackler (ed.), *The Teenage Pregnant Girl*. Springfield, Ill.: C. C. Thomas.

Shreve, A., 1982. *Careers and the Lure of Motherhood*. New York Times Magazine (November 21):38–56.

Shribman, D., 1983. *Foes of Abortion Beaten in Senate on Amendment Bid*. New York Times (June 29):A1,A16.

Silverstein, C., 1979. *A Family Matter*. New

York: McGraw-Hill.

_____, 1981. *Man to Man*. New York: William Morrow.

Simmel, G., 1950. *The Sociology of Georg Simmel*. New York: The Free Press.

Simmons, L., 1945. *The Role of the Aged in Primitive Society*. New Haven, Conn: Yale University Press.

Simpson, I., K. Back, and J. McKinney, 1966. *Attributes of Work, Involvement in Society, and Self-Evaluation in Retirement*. In I. Simpson and J. McKinney (eds.), Social Aspects of Aging. Durham, N.C.: Duke University Press.

Sirjamaki, J., 1964. *The Institutional Approach*. Pp. 33–50 in H. Christensen (ed.), *Handbook of Marriage and the Family*. Chicago: Rand McNally.

Skinner, D., 1980. *Dual-Career Family Stress and Coping: A Literature Review*. Family Relations 29(4):October.

_____, 1983. *Dual-Career Families: Strains of Sharing*. In H. McCubbin and C. Figley (eds.), Stress and the Family. Vol. 1: Coping with Normative Transitions. New York: Brunner Mazel.

Skolnick, A., 1978. *The Intimate Environment*. Boston: Little, Brown.

Slade, M., and W. Biddle, 1983. *A New Option for the Infertile*. New York Times (July 24):22E.

Slater, E., and M. Woodside, 1951. *Patterns of Marriage: A Study of Marriage Relationships in the Urban Working Class*. London: Cassell.

Slob, K., 1982. *Female Genital Mutilation in Egypt*. Paper presented at International Conference on Family Sexuality, Minneapolis.

Smart, W., 1983. *Unwed Father Wins Battle for Daughter*. Minneapolis Tribune, January 16.

Smith, M., 1980. *The Social Consequences of Single Parenthood: A Longitudinal Perspective*. Family Relations 29(January):75–81.

Spanier, G., 1976. *Measuring Dyadic Adjustment: New Scales for Assessing the Quality of Marriage and Similar Dyads*. Journal of Marriage and the Family 38(February):15–28.

Spanier, G., R. Lewis, and C. Cole, 1975. *Marital Adjustment over the Family Life Cycle: The issue of curvilinearity*. Journal of Marriage and the Family 37:263–275.

Speroff, L., R. Glass, and N. Kese, 1973. *Clinical Gynecologic Endocrinology and Infertility*. Baltimore: Williams and Wilkins.

Spock, B., 1945. *The Common Sense Book of Baby and Child Care*, New York: Duell, Sloan and Pearce.

_____, 1974. *Baby and Child Care*, 3d ed. New York: Pocket Books.

Spreitzer, E., E. Synder, and D. Larson, 1979. *Multiple Roles and Psychological Well-Being*. Sociological Focus 12:141–148.

St. John-Parsons, D., 1978. *Continuous Dual-Career Families: A Case Study*. In J. Bryson and R. Bryson (eds.), *Dual-Career Couples*. New York: Human Sciences.

Stack, C., 1974. *All Our Kin*. New York: Harper and Row.

Stafford, R., E. Backman, and P. diBona, 1977. *The Division of Labor Among Cohabiting and Married Couples*. Journal of Marriage and the Family 39(February):43–57.

Starr, B., and M. Weiner, 1981. *Sex and Sexuality Among the Mature Years*. New York: Stein and Day.

Starr, P., and N. Alamuddin, 1981. *Marriage-Lebanese Style*. Natural History (April)90:8–10.

Steele, B., 1976. *Violence Within the Family*. In R. Helfer and C. Kempe (eds.), *Child Abuse and Neglect: The Family and the Community*. Cambridge: Ballinger.

Stein, H., 1981. *Feelings Will Out*. Esquire (October):26–29.

Stein, P., 1978. *The Lifestyles and Life Chances of the Never-Married*. Marriage and Family Review 4(July/August):1–11.

_____, 1981. *Singlehood: An Underdeveloped Area of Family Relationships*. Paper presented at National Council on Family Relations Annual Meeting, Milwaukee, Wisconsin, October.

Stein, R., 1970. *The Economic Status of Families Headed by Women*. Monthly Labor Review 93(December):3–10.

Stein, Z., and M. Susser, 1976. *Maternal Nutrition and Mental Competence*. In J. Lloyd-Still (ed.), *Malnutrition and Intellectual Development*. Littleton, Mass.: Publishing Sciences Group.

Stein, Z., M. Susser, G. Jaenger, and F. Manolla, 1972. *Nutrition and Mental Performance*. Science 173:40–43.

Steinem, G., 1981. *The Ultimate Invasion of Privacy*. Ms. Magazine (February):43–44.

_____, 1983. *Outrageous Acts and Everyday Rebel-*

lions. New York: Holt, Rinehart, and Winston.

Steiner, G., 1981. *The Futility of Family Policy*. Washington, D.C.: Brookings Institution.

Steinmetz, S., 1977a. *The Cycle of Violence: Assertive, Aggressive and Abusive Family Interaction*. New York: Praeger.

————, 1977b. *Wife Beating, Husband Beating: A Comparison of the Use of Physical Violence Between Spouses to Resolve Marital Fights*. In M. Roy (ed.), *Battered Women: A Psychosociological Study of Domestic Violence*. New York: Van Nostrand Reinhold Co.

————, 1978. *Violence Between Family Members*. Marriage and Family Review 1:3 (May/June):2–15.

Stephen, B., 1983. *Pregnancy and Childbirth—Attitudes Are Changing*. New York Daily News (December 29):38.

Stephens, W., 1963. *The Family in Cross-Cultural Perspective*. New York: Holt, Rinehart, and Winston.

Stinnett, N. 1975. *Child-Rearing Goals*. Unpublished study.

Stinnett, N., and C. Birdsong, 1978. *The Family and Alternate Life Styles*. Chicago: Nelson-Hall.

Stinnett, N., L. Carter, and J. Montgomery, 1972. *Older Persons Perceptions of Their Marriages*. Journal of Marriage and the Family (November):665–670.

Stinnett, N., J. Collins, and J. Montgomery, 1970. *Marital Need Satisfaction of Older Husbands and Wives*. Journal of Marriage and the Family 32:428–434.

Stinnett, N., J. Farris, and J. Walters, 1974. *Parent-Child Relationships of Male and Female High School Students*. Journal of Genetic Psychology 125:99–106.

Stinnett, N., and C. Kreps, 1972. *Values Relating to the Development of Character*. Journal of Home Economics 64:53–57.

Stinnett, N., and J. Walters, 1967. *Parent-Peer Orientation of Adolescents from Low-Income Families*. Journal of Home Economics 59(1):37–40.

Stolte-Heiskanen, V., 1974. *Social Indicators for Analysis of Family Needs Related to the Life Cycle*. Journal of Marriage and the Family (August):592–599.

Stone, L., 1977. *The Family, Sex and Marriage in England, 1500–1800*. New York: Penguin Books.

Straus, M., 1974. *Leveling, Civility and Violence in the Family*. Journal of Marriage and the Family 36:13–19.

Streib, G., 1958. *Family Patterns in Retirement*. Journal of Social Issues 14:46–60.

Streib, G., and M. Hilker, 1980. *The Cooperative Family: An Alternative Lifestyle for the Elderly*. Alternative Lifestyles 3:167–184.

Streib, G., and C. Schneider, 1971. *Retirement in American Society*. Ithaca, N.Y.: Cornell University Press.

Stryker, S., 1964. *The Interactional and Situational Approaches*. Pp. 125–170 in H. T. Christensen (ed.), *Handbook of Marriage and the Family*. Chicago: Rand McNally.

Sussman, M., 1953. *The Help Pattern in the Middle-Class Family*. American Sociological Review 18:22–28.

————, 1971. *Changing Families in a Changing Society*. Forum 14 in Report to the President: White House Conference on Children. Washington, D.C.: U.S. Government Printing Office.

————, 1975. *The Four F's of Variant Family Forms and Marriage Styles*. Family Coordinator 12:563–576.

————, 1978. *The Family Today*. Children Today (March-April):32–45.

Sussman, M., and L. Burchinal, 1962. *Kin Family Network: Unheralded Structure in Current Conceptualizations of Family Functioning*. Marriage and Family Living 24:231–240.

Sussman, M., J. Cates, and D. Smith, 1974. *The Concept of Testamentary Freedom*. Pp. 377–383 in R. Coser (ed.), *The Family, Its Structure and Function*. 2nd ed. New York: St. Martin's Press.

Sweet, E., 1982. *Tish Sommers: Organize—Don't Agonize*. Ms. Magazine (January):61,80.

Tanner, D., 1978. *The Lesbian Couple*. Lexington, Mass.: Lexington Books.

Tanner, J., 1971. *Sequence, Tempo and Individual Variation in the Growth and Development of Boys and Girls Aged Twelve to Sixteen*. Daedalus (Fall):907–930.

Tanzer, D., and J. Block, 1972. *Why Natural Childbirth?* Garden City, N.J.: Doubleday.

Targ, D., 1979. *Toward a Reassessment of Women's Experience at Middle Age*. Family Coordinator (July):377–382.

Tavris, C., and S. Sadd, 1977. *Great News About*

Men and Sex. Redbook 149(October):124–125,184–188.

Terman, L., 1951. *Correlates of Orgasm Adequacy in a Group of 556 Wives*. Journal of Psychology 32:115–172.

Thompson, L., and G. Spanier, 1978. *Influence of Parents, Peers, and Partners on The Contraceptive Use of College Men and Women*. Journal of Marriage and the Family 40(August):481–492.

Thornton, J., 1983. *Behind a Surge in Suicides of Young People*. U.S. News and World Report 94(June 20):66.

Tietz, W., L. McSherry, and B. Britt, 1977. *Family Sequelae After a Child's Death Due to Cancer*. American Journal of Psychotherapy 31(3):417–425.

Tietze, C., 1981. *Induced Abortion: A World Review*. New York: Population Council.

Time, 1981. *Socko Performances on Campus*. (September 21):118:66–67.

Titus, S., P. Rosenblatt, and R. Anderson, 1979. *Family Conflict over Inheritance of Property*. Family Coordinator (July):337–346.

Train, J., 1980. *Better Crass Than Sorry*. Forbes (September 29):176.

Triseliotis, J., 1973. *In Search of Origins*. London: Routledge and Kegan Paul.

Troll, L., S. Miller, and R. Atchley, 1979. *Families in Later Life*. Belmont, Calif.: Wadsworth.

Tudiver, J., 1980. *Parents and the Sex-Role Development of the Pre-School Child*. Pp 33–49 in C. Stark Adamo (ed.), *Sex Roles: Origins, Influences and Implications for Women*. Montreal: Eden's Press Women's Publications.

Turchi, B., 1975. *The Demand for Children: The Economics of Fertility in the United States*. Cambridge, Mass.: Ballinger.

Udry, J., 1966. *The Social Context of Marriage*. Philadelphia: J. B. Lippincott.

———, 1974. *The Social Context of Marriage*. 3d ed. Philadelphia: J. B. Lippincott.

U.S. Bureau of Labor Statistics, 1982. *Autumn 1981 Urban Family Budgets*. Washington, D.C.: U.S. Department of Labor, April.

U.S. Bureau of the Census, 1980. *Statistical Abstract of the United States*. 101st ed. Washington, D.C.

U.S. Commission on Civil Rights, 1979. *Window Dressing on the Set: An Update*. Washington, D.C.: U.S. Government Printing Office.

U.S. Department of Health, Education and Welfare, 1970. *Monthly Vital Statistics Report*.

———, 1973. *The Health Consequences of Swallowing*. Washington, D.C.

U.S. News and World Report, 1981. *Why So Many Marriages Fail*. 91(July 20):53–55.

———, 1982. *Herpes: How Common? How Dangerous? Can it Be Cured?* 93(August 30):61.

———, 1982. *Anorexia: The "Starving Disease" Epidemic*. 93(August 30):47–48.

———, 1982. *When the "Empty Nest" Fills Up Again*. (October 25):70–71.

———, 1983. *One-Parent Family: The Troubles and the Joys*. (November 28):57–58,62.

Veevers, J., 1973. *Voluntary Childless Woman: An Exploratory Study*. Sociology and Social Research (57):356–366.

———, 1974. *The Lifestyle of Voluntarily Childless Couples*. In L. Larson (ed.), *The Canadian Family in Comparative Perspective*. Toronto: Prentice-Hall.

———, 1980. *Childless by Choice*. Toronto: Butterworth.

Vinick, B., 1978. *Remarriage in Old Age*. Family Coordinator 27:359–363.

Visher, E., and J. Visher, 1983. *Stepparenting: Blending Families*. In H. McCubbin and C. Figley (eds.), *Stress and the Family*. Vol. 1: *Coping with Normative Transitions*. New York: Brunner Mazel.

Visher, J., and E. Visher, 1979. *Stepfamilies: A Guide to Working with Stepparents and Stepchildren*. New York: Brunner Mazel.

Vital Statistics, 1976. *U.S. Department of Health, Education and Welfare*.

Vore, D. H., 1971. *Prenatal Nutrition and Postnatal Intellectual Development*. Paper presented at the annual meeting of the Society for Research in Child Development, Minneapolis.

Voydanoff, D., 1983a. *Unemployment*. In C. Figley and H. McCubbin (eds.), *Stress and the Family*. Vol. 2: *Coping with Catastrophes*. New York: Brunner Mazel.

———, 1983b. *Sudden Unemployment and the Family*. In C. Figley and H. McCubbin (eds.), *Stress and the Family*. Vol. 2: *Coping with Catastrophes*. New York: Brunner Mazel.

Walker, K., 1971. *ARS Summary Report of Time Used for Household Work*. Ithaca, N.Y.: Cornell University.

———, 1973. *Household Work Time: Its Implication for Family Decisions*. Journal of Home Economics 65(October):7–11.

Walker, K., and L. Messinger, 1979. *Remarriage After Divorce: Dissolution and Reconstruction of Family Boundaries.* Family Process 18(2):185–192.

Waller, W., and R. Hill, 1951. *The Family: A Dynamic Interpretation.* New York: Dryden Press.

Wallerstein, J., 1983. *Children of Divorce: The Psychological Tasks of the Child.* American Journal of Orthopsychiatry (April):230–243.

Wallerstein, J., and J. Kelly, 1980. *Surviving the Breakup: How Children and Parents Cope with Divorce.* New York: Basic Books.

Wallis, C., B. Dolan, and C. Foote, 1982. *Day Care Centers for the Old.* Time (January 18):60.

Walsh, F., 1980. *The Family in Later Life.* Pp. 197–220 in E. Carter and M. McGoldrick (eds.), *The Family Life Cycle: A Framework for Family Therapy.* New York: Gardner Press, Inc.

Walster, E., and G. Walster, 1978. *A New Look at Love.* Reading, Mass.: Addison-Wesley.

Walters, J., and N. Stinnett, 1971. *Parent-Child Relationships: A Decade Review of Research.* Journal of Marriage and the Family 33:70–111.

Ward, A., 1980. *Ward's Words of Wisdom for Husbands and Wives.* Atlantic Monthly Magazine 246:2 (August):75–77.

Washington, M., 1982. *Working at Single Bliss.* Ms. Magazine (October):55–59.

Watkins, C., 1983. *Victims, Aggressors and the Family Secret.* St. Paul, Minn.: Minnesota Department of Public Welfare.

Watzlawick, P., J. Lemick, and D. Jackson, 1967. *Pragmatics of Human Communication.* New York: W. W. Norton.

Webster's Third New International Dictionary, 1971. Chicago: G. and R. Merriam.

Weingarten, N., 1980. *Treating Adolescent Drug Abuse as a Symptom of Dysfunction in the Family.* Pp. 57–62 in B. Ellis (ed.), *Drug Abuse from the Family Perspective.* Rockville, Md.: U.S. Department of Health and Human Services.

Weinglass, J., K. Kressel, and M. Deutch, 1978. *The Role of Clergy in Divorce: An Exploratory Survey.* Journal of Divorce 2(1):57–82.

Weiss, R., 1973. *Loneliness.* Cambridge, Mass.: MIT Press.

———, 1976. *The Emotional Impact of Marital Separation.* Journal of Social Issues 32(1):135–145.

———, 1979a. *Issues in the Adjudication of Custody when Parents Separate.* Pp. 324–336 in G. Levinger and O. Moles (eds.), *Divorce and Separation.* New York: Basic Books.

———, 1979b. *Growing Up a Little Faster.* Journal of Social Issues 35(4):97–111.

Weitzman, L., 1975. *To Love, Honor, and Obey? Traditional Legal Marriage and Alternative Family Forms.* Family Coordinator 24(4):531–538.

Weitzmann, L., C. Dixon, J. Bird, N. McGinn, and D. Robertson, 1978. *Contracts for Intimate Relationships: Study of Contracts Before, Within, and in Lieu of Marriage.* Alternative Lifestyles 1 (August):303–378.

Weller, R., 1968. *The Employment of Wives, Dominance, and Fertility.* Journal of Marriage and the Family 30:437–442.

Westheimer, R., 1983. *Recipe for a Sexual Marriage.* Cosmopolitan (June):90–100.

Westoff, L., 1977. *The Second Time Around: Remarriage in America.* New York: Viking Press.

Wheeler, T., 1971. *The Immigrant Experience.* New York: Pelican.

Whelan, E., 1976. *A Baby. . .Maybe?* New York: Bobbs-Merrill.

Whitehurst, R., 1970. *Violence in Husband-Wife Interaction.* Paper presented at the National Council on Family Relations, Chicago.

Williams, J., and M. Stith, 1974. *Middle Childhood: Behavior and Development.* New York: Macmillan.

Wilson, J., N. Williams, and B. Sugarman, 1967. *Introduction to Moral Education.* Harmondsworth, Ind.: Penguin.

Winch, R., 1958. *Mate Selection.* New York: Harper and Row.

———, 1963. *The Modern Family.* Rev. ed. New York: Holt, Rinehart, and Winston.

Wolk, S., and J. Brandon, 1977. *Runaway Adolescents' Perceptions of Parents and Self.* Adolescence 12:175–187.

Wood, V., and J. Robertson, 1976. *The Significance of Grandparenthood.* In J. Gubrium (ed.), *Time, Roles, and Self in Old Age.* New York: Human Science Press.

Woods, L., and J. Corwin, 1977. *Letter to the Editor.* Village Voice (August 15):4.

Worach-Kardas, H., 1979. *Family and Neighbourly Relations—Their Role for the Elderly.* Pp. 39–47 in G. Dooghe and J. Helander (eds.), *Family*

Life in Old Age. The Hague: Martinus Nijhoff.

Wynne, L., R. Cromwell, and S. Matthysse, 1978. *The Nature of Schizophrenia: New Approaches to Research and Treatment.* New York: John Wiley and Sons.

Yankelovich, D., 1981. *New Rules: Searching for Self-Fulfillment in a World Turned Upside Down.* New York: Random House.

Yankelovich, Skelly and White, Inc., 1977. *Raising Children in a Changing Society.* General Mills American Family Report, Minneapolis.

Yllo, K., 1978. *Nonmarital Cohabitation: Beyond the College Campus.* Alternative Lifestyles 1(February):37–54.

Yorburg, B., 1978. *Recent Trends in American Family Life.* Intellect (March):348.

Zacks, H., 1980. *Self-Actualization: A Midlife Problem.* Journal of Contemporary Social Work (April):223–233.

Zajonc, R., 1976. *Family Configuration and Intelligence.* Science 197:227–236.

Zelnik, M., and J. Kantner, 1977. *Sexual and Contraceptive Experience of Young Unmarried Women in the U.S., 1976 and 1971.* Family Planning Perspectives 9:135–142.

———, 1980. *Sexual Activity, Contraceptive Use, and Pregnancy Among Metropolitan-Area Teenagers: 1971–1979.* Family Planning Perspectives 12:230–237.

Zerof, H., 1978. *Finding Intimacy: The Art of Happiness in Living Together.* New York: Random House.

Zill, N., 1978. *Divorce, Marital Happiness and the Mental Health of Children: Findings from the Foundation for Child Development National Survey of Children.* Paper prepared for National Institute of Mental Health Workshop on Divorce and Children. Bethesda, Md.

Zimmerman, S., 1978. *Reassessing the Effect of Public Policy on Family Functioning.* Social Casework 59(October):541–547.

Zuengler, K., and G. Neubeck, 1983. *Sexuality.* In H. McCubbin and C. Figley (eds.), Stress and the Family. Vol. 1: *Coping with Normative Transitions.* New York: Brunner Mazel.

Zunin, L., 1974. *A Program for the Vietnam Widow: Operation Second Life.* Pp. 218–224 in H. McCubbin, B. Dahl, P. Metres, Jr., E. Hunter, and J. Plag (eds.), *Family Separation and Reunion.* Washington, D.C.: U.S. Government Printing Office.

GLOSSARY

Abortion   The expulsion or removal of the fetus from a woman's body before it is viable.

Acquired Immune Deficiency Syndrome (AIDS)   A fatal disease, presumably caused by a virus, which attacks the body's immune system leaving the body defenseless to fight off infection. Homosexual men, particularly susceptible, comprise the highest risk category.

Active Listening   Listening that involves carefully devoting one's attention to the other's verbal and nonverbal messages in an attempt to understand the entirety of the message.

Acute Conflict   An argument, that usually involves intense emotional outbursts of hostility, which is about a specific event. This form of conflict is most prevalent in early marriage.

Adaptation   A slow, usually unconscious modification of an individual's behavior in order to adjust to his or her cultural surroundings.

Adolescence   The transitional stage in human development between puberty and adulthood. It extends through the teen years and terminates legally at the age of majority.

Adoption   Becoming a parent through a legal process.

Affiliated Family   A family where one or more older persons, recognized as part of the kin network and called by a kin term, share in the family's responsibilities and emotional burdens.

Aid to Families with Dependent Children (AFDC)   A governmental income maintenance program for children of mothers unable to provide adequately for their needs.

Alimony   Support payments made to a spouse who has been dependent on his or her partner.

Amniocentesis   A medical procedure that involves inserting a thin needle through the pregnant woman's abdominal wall into the uterus and withdrawing a small sample of amniotic fluid which surrounds the fetus. Genetic

analysis of the fetal cells contained in the fluid is then done.

Anorexia Nervosa   An hysterical aversion to food; most common among adolescent girls.

Androgynous   Being both male and female. Androgynous individuals are able to express either masculine or feminine behaviors.

Artificial Insemination   A medical procedure used to impregnate a woman which consists of taking sperm from her husband or from an anonymous donor and injecting it into her vagina during her fertile period.

Authoritarianism   A parental style of discipline that values obedience and favors punitive, forceful measures to control the child.

Authoritativeness   A parental style of discipline in which the parent attempts to direct the child's activities in a rational, issue-oriented manner and encourages communication of thoughts and feelings.

Autoeroticism   A general term describing one-person sex and including masturbation and fantasy.

Bankruptcy   A legal process whereby an individual cancels out his/her debts without payment.

Bereavement   Period of mourning following death of a loved one.

Binuclear Family   A family in which the parents are divorced and living in separate residences but are both still active in parenting.

Budget   A plan designed to coordinate income and anticipated expenses in order to help families in meeting financial goals.

Caesarean Delivery   A surgical procedure in which the baby is delivered through an incision in the mother's abdominal wall and uterus.

Cervical Cap   A large, rubber, thimblelike birth control device that fits tightly over the cervix and blocks the entrance to the vagina.

Child Abuse Extreme neglect or physical, emotional, or sexual harm inflicted on a child by the parents or parent surrogates.

Child Support Payments made by one ex-spouse to the other for the economic support of the children.

Chromosome The threadlike carriers of the genes found in the nucleus of each cell of a sexually reproducing animal. Human cells contain 23 pairs of chromosomes, each one of the pair contributed by one parent.

Circumcision Surgically removing the fore-skin of the penis.

Clitoris A small, erectile organ at the upper end of the vulva, homologous with the penis.

Cohabitation A man and a woman living to-gether in an intimate relationship without the legal sanction of marriage.

Cohort A group of individuals born in the same period whose timing of critical transition points in their family life cycle can often be de-termined through records such as U.S. Cen-sus data.

Coitus The penetration of the penis into the vagina.

Combination Birth Control Pill An oral con-traceptive that contains a combination of syn-thetic estrogen and synthetic progesterone.

Common Law Marriage A marriage that be-comes legally sanctioned after the couple has lived together as wife and husband for a cer-tain period of time. Common law marriages are considered valid in 15 states and the Dis-trict of Columbia.

Communication In marriage, the process of sharing thoughts, feelings, information, and impressions with one's spouse.

Communication Style The larger pattern of interaction in relationships that describes the unwritten rules by which couples regulate their lives together.

Compatibility Extent to which a couple's characteristics (e.g., temperaments, needs, and values) fit together.

Complementary Needs Needs of an individual that are gratified by his/her partner.

Concept A general idea of or notion about hu-man relationships.

Condom A form of birth control used by men and made of rubber or tissue that covers the penis and prevents the entry of sperm into the vagina.

Conjugal Love Marital love; love that is char-acterized by a more quiet feeling than the soaring intensity of romance.

Consensual Sex Extramarital sex with the knowledge and permission of one's mate.

Coping In family stress theory, refers to the ef-forts made by the family to adapt to stress.

Courtly Love A type of love characterized by chivalrous devotion to a lady.

Covert Conflict Conflict that is hidden and cannot be directly observed.

Coverture Feudal doctrine that stated that the status of a married woman was under the au-thority and protection of her husband. In es-sence, a woman's loss of legal rights after mar-riage.

Credit An arrangement that allows an individ-ual to buy goods or services without paying for them at the time of purchase.

Crisis A state in which the family is unable to restore stability and experiences continuous pressure to make changes in the family struc-ture and patterns of interaction.

Cunnilingus Stimulating a woman's genitals with the tongue.

Density In describing housing, the number of families living within a certain area.

Diaphragm A shallow, cuplike birth control device made of soft rubber with a springy outer edge, inserted in the vagina to cover the uterus and used with spermicidal jelly.

Differentiation The specialization of institu-tional functions that characterizes complex, urban American society.

Dilation and Curettage (D and C) A method of abortion in which the cervix is dilated and a spoonlike instrument called a curette is in-serted through the cervix to scrape the lining of the uterus, removing embryonic material.

Discipline   Process whereby children are taught to control their own behavior and conform to the standards and expectations of their parents and society.

Disengagement   Withdrawal of a person from activities in the world around him/her into the family.

Displaced Homemaker   Women who have maintained the homemaker role, but because of being widowed or divorced must find the means to be financially and emotionally self-supporting.

Distress   Stress that is defined by the family unit as unpleasant or undesirable.

Divorce   The act of legally dissolving a marriage.

Divorce Counseling   A therapeutic process that focuses on dissolution of a marriage.

Double Standard   The value that permitted men to be sexually active but required women to remain virgins until marriage.

Douching   A method of birth control in which the vagina is flushed out after coitus with a spermicidal solution.

Down's Syndrome   A form of mental retardation caused by a genetic mutation.

Dual-Employed Family   A family arrangement in which both parents work.

Dual-Career Family   A family arrangement in which both parents are engaged in demanding jobs to which they have a strong commitment.

Egalitarian Marriage   A marriage in which both spouses contribute to the financial support of the family and share equally in decision making and responsibilities of home management and childrearing.

Empathy   A means of caring for one's partner by feeling another's feelings in oneself.

Empty Nest   The stage in the family life cycle in which all the children have moved away from the family home.

Endogamy   Pressure to marry within a certain group, such as members of one's own race or religion.

Endometriosis   A condition that involves a thickening of the mucous membrane lining the uterus, one of the causes of infertility.

Engagement   The period of time beginning with when a couple announces their intention to marry and ending with their wedding.

Equity   The presence of equal opportunity in marriage plus the feeling of fairness if there is an inequality of conditions.

Erogenous Zones   Sexually sensitive parts of the body—the mouth, earlobes, neck, breasts, etc.

Estate Planning   A process of making a will; deciding how one's property will be distributed and minors cared for after death.

Eustress   A positive kind of stress whereby a family benefits from or enjoys the challenge of life's demands.

Exogamy   Pressure to marry outside a specified group, such as outside one's family or sex.

Exosystem   Social settings that affect what happens within an individual's immediate environment (e.g., the nation's economy).

Expressive Role   Behaviors directed at providing for the emotional needs of family members which were traditionally expected of the wife/mother.

Fallopian Tubes   Extremely narrow tubes connected to the uterus that serve as the pathway through which the egg leaves the ovaries and the sperm reaches the egg.

Family-Centered Maternity Care   A form of maternity care that involves the entire family in the childbirth process. It generally includes prenatal education of the couple about pregnancy, childbirth, breastfeeding, and infant care, and the husband is usually present for the labor and delivery. In some settings, the couple's other children may also be present for the labor and delivery.

Family Life Cycle   A model designed to explain the behavior patterns of a family from the time the family is formed until its dissolution.

Family Vulnerability   A family's ability to prevent a stressor event from creating a crisis.

Fellatio Stimulating the penis or scrotum with the tongue or mouth.

Foreplay Sexual activity that precedes intercourse.

Fetal Alcohol Syndrome A collection of symptoms including retardation in growth, intelligence, and motor development found in children born to women who drink excessively during pregnancy.

Filial Maturity An understanding achieved of one's own parents and what they did or tried to do, as a result of having children oneself.

Flextime An employment policy that allows employees to work a flexible eight-hour day.

Flexiplace An innovative employment option that allows employees to work at home with connection to the office through a computer terminal.

Gay A term used by the homosexual culture to label themselves. It implies an acceptance of and lack of shame about their sexuality and lifestyle.

Genetic Counseling A service that provides prospective parents with the statistical odds of their children inheriting certain diseases or defects. The odds are determined by laboratory tests and knowledge of heredity.

Gender Identity An awareness one has of being either male or female.

Genital Herpes A highly contagious venereal disease characterized by small, painful blisters on the genitalia.

Gonorrhea An infectious disease of the genitourinary tract, rectum, and cervix transmitted chiefly by sexual intercourse.

Group Marriage Three or more individuals who consider themselves married to one another and live together on a communal basis, sharing home, children, money, and sexual intimacy.

Habituated Conflict Conflict that builds up over a disagreement that is never directly resolved. This type of conflict often involves less emotional investment than acute conflict.

Hardships Demands placed on a family that are associated with a specific stressor event.

Hermaphrodite An individual who has a combination of male and female organs, or whose organs are not easily distinguishable as male or female.

Historical Time The social era in which a person is born and lives.

Homogamy Tendency to marry someone who is similar to oneself in several critical ways such as age, race, educational background and socioeconomic class.

Hormones Substances secreted by certain glands that stimulate activity in specific organs of the body.

Hysterotomy A method of abortion that involves surgically removing the fetus through the abdomen.

Identity An individual's sense of self as developed through experience and interpersonal relationships.

Impotence The inability of some men to achieve or maintain an erection of the penis for the length of intercourse.

Incest A form of coercive sex among family members.

Individual Time A person's own life span from birth to death.

Individualistic Theories Theories of mate selection that stress the importance of an individual's emotional experiences and subconscious needs and drives in selecting a potential partner.

Infanticide Killing of babies.

Infertility The physical inability to conceive or give birth to a live child.

Inflation In economics, a term indicating an abnormal increase in available currency and credit beyond the proportion of available goods, resulting in a sharp and continuing rise in price levels.

Instrumental Role Traditional role expected of the husband-father—that of economic provider for the family.

Insurance A legal contract by which an insurer will provide cash payments for unexpected catastrophes in exchange for regular payments from the insured person.

Intercourse See *coitus.*

Intermarriage Marriage between individuals with differing cultural, religious, or racial backgrounds.

Interpersonal Communication Communication that is affected by the psychological condition and relationship of the two communicators.

Intestate A term that refers to the death of an individual who has not made a will.

Intrauterine Device (IUD) A small, flexible piece of sterile plastic material with nylon strings, inserted into the uterine cavity and used as a method of birth control.

Intrinsic Marriage A marriage in which the husband and wife consider their relationship to be their chief concern and source of pleasure. All other concerns are considered subordinate to the relationship.

Investment Income Money paid as interest on family savings in bank accounts, money market funds, stock or bonds, and trust funds.

Job Burnout A condition resulting from an individual putting a great deal of energy into a job that does not yield expected benefits. Symptoms of burnout include fatigue, feelings of frustration, apathy, and depression.

Job Sharing An employment option in which two or more individuals share one full-time position.

Joint Custody A legal agreement between divorced parents to equally share the rights and responsibilities of childrearing.

Labia Majora Two rounded folds of tissue that form the external lateral boundaries of the vulva; also called the "outer lips."

Labia Minora Two narrow folds of tissue enclosed within the cleft of the labia majora; also called the "inner lips."

Laparoscopy A form of sterilization in which a small incision is made into the abdomen and the fallopian tubes are cauterized with a small instrument.

Launching A stage in the family life cycle when the children in the family are departing from their parents' home.

Leveling Honest and open self-disclosure that is based on high self-esteem.

Liquidity The ease with which an investment can be converted into cash for immediate use.

Love Readiness A state of being in which an individual is particularly receptive to and interested in finding love.

Macrosystem A social setting that includes a community's ideology and its organization of social institutions.

Marital Power The amount of control or authority each individual commands within the marital relationship.

Marital Roles The group of behaviors and attitudes, reflecting individual needs and cultural expectations, a husband and wife are expected to demonstrate in the marital relationship.

Marriage Squeeze Because women tend to marry men who are two or three years older than themselves, there was an excess of available women and a shortage of available men two years after the baby boom of World War II. This concept also implies that older men have a larger pool of women from which to choose.

Masturbation Some form of direct physical stimulation of oneself—one's genitals, breasts, or other body parts—in order to produce sexual excitement.

Mediation A method of settling the disagreements of a divorcing couple without a court trial.

Menopause Cessation of menstruation normally occurring in a woman's late forties or early fifties.

Mesosystem A social setting in which a person participates (e.g., the school or work setting).

Microsystem The immediate social setting in which an individual lives (e.g., the family unit).

Midwife A person, generally a woman, who is trained to assist in childbirth. Nurse-midwives in the United States provide prenatal care and manage uncomplicated births.

Mixed Message A communication that results when a verbal message is contradicted by ''body language'' or the physical message.

Mons Pubis Fatty pads of tissue that lie below the skin over the pubic bone.

Myotonia Contractions of muscles throughout the body during sexual response.

Normative Stressors Those events that are short term, are expectable and occur in most families, and involve entrances into and exits from a social role as a result of normal movement through the life cycle (e.g., transition to parenthood, children leaving home, retirement).

Norms Agreed upon standards of acceptable behavior.

Nuclear Family A household of husband, wife, and children living apart from the wife's and husband's parents with husband as breadwinner and wife as homemaker.

Opportunity Cost Used in estimating the monetary worth of a homemaker; involves looking at how much a woman could earn if she was employed outside the home.

Orgasm The height of sexual arousal which involves involuntary muscle contraction, release of sexual tension, and a heightened feeling of pleasure.

Ovaries The pair of female reproductive glands that produce ova.

Overt Conflict Conflict that is open and can be directly observed.

Ovulation Expulsion of an egg from the ovary, which occurs once a month from puberty to menopause.

Palimony A legal suit in which one cohabiting partner sues the other for financial support after the relationship has ended.

Parallel Needs Needs of an individual that are not gratified by his/her partner.

Pedophilia Sexual abuse involving an adult's nonviolent sexual practices with a child.

Penis The tubular-shaped male organ of copulation and urinary excretion.

Periodic Abstinence A birth control method involving the systematic avoidance of sexual intercourse during the woman's fertile period.

Permissiveness A parental style of discipline that is nonpunitive and accepting of children's impulses, feelings, and behavior.

Petting A term that includes physical contact, caressing, and fondling that stops short of intercourse.

Pile-Up The combination of events, hardships, and stressors experienced by a family at one time.

Platonic Relationship A close friendship that does not include sexual expression.

Position Consists of a certain location in social groups to which are assigned a collection of rights and duties. In the family, the positions consist of husband-father, wife-mother, son-brother, etc

Premarital Contracts Agreements written by couples about to be married that state each person's expectations, rights, and responsibilities within the marriage.

Primogeniture The right of the eldest child, especially the eldest son, to inherit the entire estate of one or both of his parents.

Prenatal The period occurring before birth.

Propinquity Tendency to marry those individuals with whom we come into close or regular contact.

Rape A form of sexual violence in which a woman is assaulted and there is penetration of the vagina, mouth, or anus by the penis without mutual consent.

Reflecting A technique used in communication in which one person repeats to another person what he/she hears that person saying or feeling.

Relationship The term presently used in our society to describe all types of coupling.

Replacement Cost A term used in estimating the monetary worth of a homemaker; involves focusing on how much it would cost a family if it had to pay for the services being provided by the homemaker.

Resources   In the context of family stress theory, psychological, social, interpersonal, and material characteristics of individual family members, the family unit, and the community. Resources can be used to meet the demands and needs of the family.

Retirement   A major transition in the life cycle whereby an individual withdraws from occupational activity.

Role   Consistent behavior appropriate to a particular situation that has developed through an individual's interactions with others and is influenced by sanctions and preexisting norms.

Role Cluster   The total number of roles (e.g. disciplinarian affection-giver) that make up a position (e.g. father-husband) at one particular time.

Role Cycling   Parental planning of roles so that the demands of the family and of their careers don't peak at the same time.

Role Overload   A condition that occurs when an individual is responsible for an excessive number of duties associated in a certain role, for example, the working mother or father. This is a common source of strain for working parents.

Role Reversal   A technique used in communication in which individuals agree to change places temporarily—the sender of the message becomes the receiver and vice-versa. In reference to marriage in the later years, less differentiation between marital roles.

Role Sequence   The behavioral changes in any one role over time.

Scientific Method   A systematic, organized series of steps that ensures maximun objectivity and consistency researching a problem.

Scrotum   The loose pouch of skin, located at the base of the penis, which holds the testes.

Self-Disclosure   The intimate revelation of private thoughts, feelings, hopes, and frustrations.

Self-Esteem   An individual's sense of being worthwhile or valued.

Sex Roles   Learned patterns of behaviors specifically associated with being male or female.

Sexually Transmitted Disease (STD)   An infectious disease that is transmitted primarily through sexual contact. Forms of STD include genital herpes, syphilis, and gonorrhea.

Singlehood   The state of being unmarried. This may be due to never having married, or to divorce or widowhood.

Social Learning Theory of Sexual Identity   A theory that contends that children learn behavior appropriate to their particular sex as a result of parental rewards for appropriate behavior and punishment of inappropriate behavior.

Social Support   The support individuals receive from each other in the form of affection, esteem, assistance, and information.

Social Time   A person's timetable as characterized by important social events and transitions such as marriage and retirement.

Socialization   The process of a person's learning—from parents, peers, social institutions, and other sources—the skills, knowledge, and roles necessary to become a competent and socially acceptable member of a society.

Socioculture Theories   Theories of mate selection that stress the importance of a variety of controls such as race, social class, and physical proximity in selecting a potential partner.

Solo Wage-Earner-Solo Parent Family   A family arrangement in which one parent is solely responsible for both wage-earning and parenting.

Spermicides   Vaginal foams, creams, jellies, and similar chemical contraceptives that work by killing sperm on contact and by blocking the entrance to the cervix.

Spontaneous Abortion   Another name for a miscarriage or expulsion of the fetus from the woman's body before it is viable.

Stage   Divisions within the family life cycle that are different enough from one another to constitute separate periods.

Stress   A part of a family's response to a stressor; the tension or imbalance caused when the family's resources are believed to be inadequate for the demands placed on it.

Stressors Life events or changes of such consequence that they produce or have the potential to produce change within the family (e.g., marriage, parenthood, death).

Surrogate Mother A woman who is paid a fee to be artificially inseminated with the sperm of a man whose wife is unable to conceive. The surrogate mother then carries the baby to term and surrenders it to the couple.

Syphilis An infectious disease transmitted chiefly by sexual intercourse and characterized by local formation of ulcerous skin eruptions and systemic infection leading to general paralysis.

Testamentary Freedom A principle of American law that states that an individual may select almost any person or institution to inherit his or her estate.

Testes Two oval-shaped organs that serve as male reproductive glands, producing sperm and the male sex hormone, testosterone.

Traditional Marriage A form of marriage in which the husband is expected to be sole provider for his wife and children, and the wife is expected to stay home to manage the house and care for the children. Until the 1970s this was the most common marital form.

Trial Marriage A man and woman living together with the expressed intent of getting married in the future.

Tubal Ligation A form of sterilization involving major surgery in which the fallopian tubes are cut, a small section is removed, and the ends are tied.

Two-Person Single Career A family arrangement whereby the spouse of the wage-earner becomes almost like a second worker, for example, politicians' wives who participate in campaigning.

Uterus or "Womb" The pear-shaped organ of gestation that receives and holds the fertilized egg during the development of the fetus and is the principal agent in its expulsion at birth.

Utilitarian Marriage A relationship that is established or maintained for purposes other than to be the couple's chief concern and source of pleasure.

Vacuum Aspiration A method of abortion that involves dilation of the cervix and the introduction of a small tube into the uterus to remove its contents by vacuum pressure.

Vagina The tubelike organ that serves as a passageway for menstrual flow and delivery of a baby, and is also the organ into which the penis is inserted during intercourse.

Variable Measurable trait or characteristic that is subject to change under different conditions.

Vasectomy A form of sterilization that involves making a small incision in the scrotum through which the vas deferens are cut, tied, and coagulated.

Vasocongestion Swelling of male and female sex organs as a result of an increased amount of blood flow in that region.

Vulva The external female sex organs including the clitoris, mons pubis, inner lips (labia minora), outer lips (labia majora), and the vaginal opening.

Wage-Earner Plan Court-supervised plan for paying off debts.

Widowhood Role change that involves loss of one's spouse through death.

Withdrawal A form of birth control in which the man withdraws his penis from the vagina before ejaculating.

Zygote The fertilized egg which develops into a human fetus.

PHOTO CREDITS

Chapter 10

Opener: Ed Lattau/Photo Researchers. Page 200: Michael Hayman/Click/Chicago. Page 211: Ken Karp. Page 213: Jim Anderson/Woodfin Camp. Page 214: Erika Stone/Photo Researchers.

Chapter 11

Opener: Michael Hayman/Photo Researchers. Page 288: Michael Kagan/Monkmeyer. Page 232: Marjorie Pickens. Page 235: Sybil Shelton/Monkmeyer. Page 238: David S. Strickler/Monkmeyer.

Chapter 12

Opener: Rocky Weldon/Leo de Wys. Page 256: Michael Heron/Woodfin Camp. Page 257: Olive R. Pierce/Stock Boston. Page 260: Joseph Szabo/Photo Researchers. Page 265: Burk Uzzle/Woodfin Camp. Page 267: Marjorie Pickens.

Chapter 13

Opener: Bettye Lane/Photo Researchers. Page 279: Meg Gerken/Click/Chicago. Page 281: Alice Kandell/Photo Researchers. Page 296: Linda Ferrer/Woodfin Camp. Page 287: Marjorie Pickens.

Chapter 14

Opener: Bruce Roberts/Photo Researchers. Page 305: Ken Karp. Page 314: Maureen Fennelli/Photo Researchers. Page 321: Jane Kramer/EKM-Nepenthe. Page 325: Christa Armstrong/Photo Researchers.

Chapter 15

Opener: Teri Leigh Stratford/Photo Researchers. Page 334: Teri Leigh Stratford/Photo Researchers. Page 347: Richard Laird/Leo de Wys.

Chapter 16

Opener: Ed Lettau/Photo Researchers. Page 354: Frank Siteman/The Picture Cube. Page 355: F.W. Binzen/Photo Researchers. Page 358: Burke Uzzle/Woodfin Camp. Page 360: Ken Karp.

Chapter 17

Opener: Susan Rosenberg/Photo Researchers. Page 375: David Strickler/Monkmeyer. Page 380: Mike Maple/Woodfin Camp. Page 382: David Budnik/Woodfin Camp.

SOURCE NOTES

Chapter 2:

Page 16 **Box 2–1:**   Reprinted with permission of The Free Press, a Division of Macmillan, Inc. from *Dual-Career Marriage: Conflict and Treatment* by David C. Rice. Copyright © 1979 by The Free Press.

Page 18 **Box 2–2:**   From *Living Together: A guide to the Law for Unmarried Couples* by Barbara Hirsch. Copyright © 1976 by Barbara B. Hirsch. Reprinted by permission of Houghton Mifflin Company.

Page 26 **Table 2–2:**   Table 7–3 from *Mariage and Family Development*, Fifth Edition, by Evelyn Millis Duvall (J.B. Lippincott Company). Copyright © 1957, 1962, 1967, 1971, 1977 by Harper & Row, Publishers, Inc. Reprinted by permission of the publisher.

Page 27 **Figure 2–1:**   Figure 7–2 from *Marriage and Family Development*, Fifth Edition, By Evelyn Millis Duvall (J.B. Lippincott Company). Copyright © 1957, 1962, 1967, 1971, 1977 by Harper & Row, Publishers, Inc. Reprinted by permission of the publisher.

Page 27 **Table 2–3:**   From Family Careers: Developmental Change in Families, J. Aldous, copyright © 1978 by Wiley, New York, p. 93. Reprinted by permission.

Chapter 3:

Page 41 **Box 3–2:**   From *Worlds of Pain* by Lillian Breslow Rubin. © 1976 by Lillian Breslow Rubin. Reprinted with permission of Basic Books, Inc., Publishers.

Page 44 **Figure 3–1:**   F.J. Prial in *The New York Times*, November 15, 1982. Copyright © 1982 by The New York Times Company. Reprinted by permission.

Chapter 4:

Page 56 **Table 4–1:**   From *Coping With Normative Transition, Vol. I*, H. McCubbin and C. Figley (eds.), copyright © 1983 by Brunner/Mazel, Inc., New York, p. xxii. Reprinted by permission.

Chapter 5:

Page 74 **Box 5–1:**   From I.E. Robinson and D. Jedlicka, ''Change in Sexual Attitudes and Behavior of College Students from 1965 to 1980,'' *Journal of Marriage and the Family*, 44, 1, pp. 237–240, 1982. Copyright © 1982 by the National Council on Family Relations, Minneapolis, MN 55414. Reprinted by permission.

Page 82 **Figure 5–3:**   From *Understanding Human Sexuality*, J.S. Hyde, copyright © 1979 by McGraw-Hill Book Company. Reprinted by permission.

Page 82   **Figure 5-4:**   From *Understanding Human Sexuality*, J.S. Hyde, copyright © 1979 by McGraw-Hill Book Company. Reprinted by permission.

Page 87   **Figure 5-5:**   From *The Sex Atlas: A New Illustrated Guide* by Erwin J. Haeberle. Copyright © 1981 by the author. Reprinted by permission of The Continuum Publishing Company.

Page 99   **Figure 5-7:**   *Time*, April 6, 1981, p. 27. Copyright 1981 Time Inc. All rights reserved. Repinted by permission from Time.

Chapter 6:

Page 111   **Figure 6-1:**   "Americans Living Alone . . . And Who They Are." Reprinted from *U.S. News & World Report*, Feb. 21, 1983, copyright, 1983, U.S. News & World Report, Inc. Reprinted by permission.

Page 112   **Table 6-1:**   Stein, P. "The Lifestyles and Life Chances of the Never Married." Used with permission of the Haworth Press, Inc., from *Marriage and Family Review*, Volume 1, Number 4, copyright 1978. All rights reserved.

Page 113   **Figure 6-2:**   From *Marriage, Divorce, Remarriage*, A. Cherlin, copyright © 1981 by Harvard University, Cambridge, MA. Reprinted by permission.

Page 115   **Table 6-2:**   Stein, P. "The Lifestyles and Life Chances of the Never Married." Used with permission of the Haworth Press, Inc., from *Marriage and Family Review*, Volume 1, Number 4, copyright 1978. All rights reserved.

Chapter 7:

Page 139   **Figure 7-1:**   From *Successful Marriage: A Principles Approach*, W. Burr, The Dorsey Press, Homewood, Illinois, p. 289, copyright © 1976 by Wesley Burr. Reprinted by permission.

Chapter 8:

Page 167   **Figure 8-1:**   From B.C. Rollins and H. Feldman, "Marital Satisfaction over the Family Life Cycle," *Journal of Marriage and the Family*, 32, 1, 1970. Copyright © 1970 by the National Council on Family Relations, Minneapolis, MN 55414. Reprinted by permission.

Chapter 9:

Page 179   **Figure 9-1:**   From S. Gilbert, "Self-disclosure, Intimacy, and Communication in Families," *Family Coordinator*, 25, 3, 1976, 221–229. Copyright © 1976 by the National Council on Family Relations, Minneapolis, MN 55414. Reprinted by permission.

Page 181   **Box 9-1:**   From *Worlds of Pain* by Lillian Breslow Rubin. © 1976 by Lillian Breslow Rubin. Reprinted by permission of Basic Books, Inc., Publishers.

Chapter 10:

Page 209   **Figure 10-1:**   From *The Sex Atlas: A New Illustrated Guide* by Erwin J. Haeberle. Copyright © 1981 by the author. Reprinted by permission of The Continuum Publishing Company.

Chapter 11:

Page 231   **Box 11–1:**   From *The Feminine Mystique* by Betty Friedan, by permission of W.W. Norton & Company, Inc., Copyright © 1974 by Betty Friedan.

Page 233   **Box 11–2:**   L.C. Pogrebin, ''Are Men Discovering the Joys of Fatherhood? Big Changes in Parenting,'' Reprinted from *Ms.* Magazine, February 1982; copyright © 1982 by *Ms.* Foundation for Education and Communication. Reprinted with permission.

Chapter 13:

Page 277   **Table 13–1:**   From *Myth and Reality of Aging in America*, 1977, published by the National Council on the Aging, Inc.

Chapter 14:

Page 298   **Figure 14–1:**   From *Marriage, Divorce, Remarriage*, A. Cherlin, copyright © 1981 by Harvard University Press, Cambridge, MA. Reprinted by permission.

Page 301   **Box 14–2:**   Excerpted from a copyrighted interview in *U.S. News & World Report* of July 20, 1981. Reprinted by permission.

Page 306–307   **Table 14–1:**   From S. Albrecht, ''Reactions and Adjustments to Divorce: Differences in the Experience of Males and Females,'' *Family Relations*, 29, 1, pp. 61, 63, 1980. Copyrighted 1980 by the National Council on Family Relations, Minneapolis, MN 55414. Reprinted by permission.

Page 312   **Table 14–3:**   From *The New York Times*, February 7, 1983, p. 14. Copyright © 1983 by The New York Times Company. Reprinted by permission.

Chapter 15:

Page 338   **Box 15–2:**   From A. Berk, ''Modern Woman's Double Life,'' *Newsweek*, copyright © 1980, by Newsweek, Inc. All rights reserved. Reprinted by permission.

INDEX